W9-CEJ-517

Flea Market Trader

Fourteenth
Edition

**THOUSANDS OF ITEMS WITH
CURRENT VALUES**

COLLECTOR BOOKS
A Division of Schroeder Publishing Co., Inc.

Editorial Staff Research and Editorial Assistants
Michael Drollinger, Donna Newnum, Loretta Suiters
Cover Design:
Beth Summers
Layout:
Holly C. Long & Kelly Dowdy

Collector Books
P.O. Box 3009
Paducah, KY 42002-3009

www.collectorbooks.com

The current values in this book should be used only as a guide. They are not intended to set prices, which vary from one section of the country to another. Auction prices as well as dealer prices vary greatly and are affected by condition and demand. Neither the editors nor the publisher assumes responsibility for any losses which might be incurred as a result of consulting this guide.

Searching For A Publisher?

We are always looking for people knowledgeable within their fields. If you feel there is a real need for a book on your collectible subject and have a large comprehensive collection, contact Collector Books.

INTRODUCTION

The *Flea Market Trader* is a unique price guide, geared specifically for the convenience of the flea market shopper. Several categories have been included that are not often found in general price guides, while others on antiques not usually seen at flea markets have been omitted. The new categories will serve to introduce you to collectibles that are currently coming on, the best and often the only source for which is the market place. As all of us who religiously pursue the circuits are aware, flea markets are the most exciting places in the world to shop; but unless you're well informed on current values those 'really great' buys remain on the table. Like most pursuits in life, preparation has its own rewards; and it is our intention to provide you with the basic tool of education and awareness toward that end. But please bear in mind that the prices in this guide are meant to indicate only general values. Many factors determine actual selling prices; values vary from one region to another, dealers pay various wholesale prices for their wares, and your bargaining skill is important too.

We have organized our listings into general categories for easy use; if you have trouble locating an item, refer to the index. The values we have suggested reflect prices of items in mint condition. NM stands for minimal damage, VG indicates that the items will bring 40% to 60% of its mint price, and EX should be somewhere between the two. Glassware is assumed clear unless a color is noted. Only generally accepted abbreviations have been used.

The Editors
Sharon and Bob Huxford

ABBREVIATIONS

dia — diameter
ea — each
EX — excellent
gal — gallon
lb — pound
lg — large
med — medium
M — mint
MIB — mint in box

NRFB — never removed from box
pc — piece
pr — pair
pt — pint
qt — quart
sm — small
sq — square
VG — very good
(+) — has been reproduced

Action Figures

The first line of action figures Hasbro developed in 1964 was GI Joe. It met with such huge success that Mego, Kenner, Mattel, and a host of other manufacturers soon began producing their own lines. Though GI Joe, Marx's Best of the West series, and several of Mego's figures were 12", others were 8" or 9" tall, and the most popular size in the last few years has been 3¾". Many lines came with accessory items such as vehicles, clothing, and guns. Original packaging (most now come on cards) is critical when it comes to evaluating your action figures, especially the more recent issues — they're seldom worth more than a few dollars if they've been played with. Values given MIB or MOC can be reduced by at least 60% when appraising a 'loose' figure in even the best condition. The market for action figures in general has become very soft over the past couple of years; there is very little interest in some of the lines that were once selling fairly well. We've tried to include those where trading is most active; some of these lines are beginning to show slight to moderate price increases.

Note: Some titles came in more than one size. MOC figures are the smaller standard size, while MIB figures are usually from 8" to 12" tall. Assume loose figures to be standard size unless noted otherwise. For more information refer to *Schroeder's Toys, Antique to Modern,* published by Collector Books.

See also GI Joe; Star Wars.

A-Team, accessory, Corvette (w/Face figure), Galoob, MIP **25.00**
A-Team, accessory, Headquarters Camp, Galoob, MIB **65.00**
A-Team, accessory, Off Road Attack Cycle, Galoob, MIB .**25.00**
A-Team, figure, Amy Allen, Galoob, 6½", MOC, from $30 to......................................**40.00**
A-Team, figure, BA, Face, Hannibal or Murdock, Galoob, 6½", MOC, ea..................**32.00**
A-Team, figure, BA Baracus, Face or Murdock, Galoob, 6½", MOC, ea........................**32.00**
Action Jackson, accessory, Campmobile, Mego, MIB **90.00**
Action Jackson, accessory, Scramble Cycle, Mego, MIB..............**45.00**
Action Jackson, figure, any color hair or beard, Mego, MIB.........**35.00**
Adventures of Indiana Jones, accessory, Arabian Horse, Kenner, M......................**65.00**
Adventures of Indiana Jones, figure, Indiana, Kenner, M........**120.00**
Adventures of Indiana Jones, figure, Indiana, Kenner, MOC, from $400 to **500.00**
Adventures of Indiana Jones, figure, Marion Ravenwood, Kenner, M......................**95.00**
Adventures of Indiana Jones, figure, Toht, Kenner, 3¾", MOC..**35.00**
Archies, figure, any, Marx, MOC .**75.00**
Batman (Dark Knight), accessory, Joker Cycle, Kenner, MIB ..**25.00**

4

Batman (Dark Knight), accessory Night Glider, Kenner, MOC **40.00**

Batman (Dark Knight), figure, Sky Escape Joker, Kenner, MOC **35.00**

Batman (Movie), figure, Batman (any except sq jaw), Toy Biz, MOC **10.00**

Batman (Movie), figure, Joker (hair curl), Toy Biz, MOC........**25.00**

Batman Returns, accessory, Batmissile Batmobile, Kenner, EX **40.00**

Battlestar Galactica, figure, Colonial Warrior, Mattel, 12", MIP **90.00**

Battlestar Galactica (1st Series), figure, any, Mattel, EX..**13.00**

Best of the West, accessory, Circle X Ranch, Marx, MIB, from $135 to..........................**200.00**

Best of the West, accessory, Jeep & Horse Trailer, Marx, MIB............................**150.00**

Best of the West, accessory, Travel Case, Marx, NM.............**30.00**

Best of the West, figure, Fighting Eagle, Marx, complete, MIB **175.00**

Best of the West, figure, Jamie West, complete, NM (EX box) **75.00**

Best of the West, figure, Janice West, complete, NM (EX box) **60.00**

Best of the West, figure, Jay West, complete, NMIB.............**95.00**

Best of the West, figure, Jed Gibson, complete, M **315.00**

Best of the West, figure, Johnny West, complete, EX........**50.00**

Best of the West, figure, Josie West, Marx, MIB **90.00**

Best of the West, figure, Princess Wildflower, Marx, complete, NM..................................**75.00**

Best of the West, figure, Sam Cobra, complete, M........**60.00**

Best of the West, figure, Sheriff Garrett, Marx, complete, NM (VG box)........................**135.00**

Best of the West, horse, Flame, Marx, palomino, complete, EX (EX box)........................**110.00**

Best of the West, horse, Thunderbolt, Marx, bay, no accessories, NM **50.00**

Big Jim accessory, Action Set #76505, 1960s, MIB, $55.00. (Photo courtesy Old Tyme Toy Store)

Big Jim, accessory, Jungle Truck, Mattel, MIB....................**35.00**

Big Jim, accessory, Motocross Honda, complete, NM....**15.00**

Big Jim, accessory, Rescue Rig, Mattel, complete, M.......**35.00**

Big Jim, accessory, Sky Commander Jet, Mattel, MIB **50.00**

Big Jim, figure, Baron Fangg, Mattel, MIB....................**55.00**

Big Jim, figure, Big Jeff, #7316, MIB................................**30.00**

Big Jim's PACK, figure, Big Jim, Mattel, MIB **100.00**

Big Jim's PACK, figure, Warpath or The Whip, Mattel, MIB, ea **85.00**

Bionic Woman, figure, Jaime Sommers (w/purse), Kenner, MIB **180.00**

Bionic Woman, outfit, Gold Evening Gown, MIB **15.00**

Black Hole, figure, Dan Holland, Mego, 12", MIB **80.00**

Bonanza, figure, any w/horse, American Character, MIB.**250.00**

Bonanza, horse, any, American Character, MIB, ea **80.00**

Buck Rogers, figure, Mego, 12", MIB, from $65.00 to $85.00. (Photo courtesy Old Tyme Toy Store)

Captain Action, accessory, Buck Rogers outfit, Ideal, complete, M....................................**100.00**

Captain Action, accessory case, 14x12", M, $300.00. (Photo courtesy Old Tyme Toy Store)

Captain Action, accessory, Lone Ranger outfit, Ideal, complete, EX **250.00**

Captain Action, accessory, Parachute Pack, Ideal, complete, NMIB **175.00**

Captain Action, accessory, Survival Kit, Ideal, 1966, MIB **250.00**

Captain Action, figure, Action Boy, Ideal, 12", complete, EX.**250.00**

Captain Action, figure, Captain Action, Ideal, MIB (w/parachute offer)...................**675.00**

Captain Action, outfit, Batman, Ideal, EX **175.00**

Captain Action, outfit, Flash Gordon, Ideal, MIB......**625.00**

Captain Action, outfit, Super Boy, Ideal, NMIB **750.00**

Charlie's Angels (Movie), figure, any, Jakks Pacific, MIB.............**40.00**

Charlie's Angels (TV Series), figure, any, Hasbro, MOC **80.00**

CHiPs, accessory, motorcycle, Mego, for 8" figures, MIB **80.00**

CHiPs, figure, Mego, sm, MOC, ea, from $22 to **32.00**

CHiPs, figure, Ponch, 8", M (EX card), from $75.00 to $100.00. (Photo courtesy Old Tyme Toy Store)

Clash of the Titans, figure, Pegasus, MOC...............**80.00**

Dukes of Hazzard, figure, Bo or Luke, Mego, 8", MOC, ea .**52.00**

Dukes of Hazzard, figure, Boss Hogg, Mego, sm, MOC ...**22.00**

James Bond, figure, Bond (Pierce Brosnan), Medicom, MOC .**85.00**

James Bond (Moonraker), figure, Bond, Mego, MIB **175.00**

Lone Ranger Rides Again, accessory, Prairie Wagon, Gabriel, MIB **40.00**

Lone Ranger Rides Again, accessory, Tribal Teepee, Gabriel, MIB **50.00**

Lone Ranger Rides Again, figure, any, Gabriel, MIB, from $65 to **85.00**

Lone Ranger Rides Again, horse, any, Gabriel, MIB, from $50 to **60.00**

M*A*S*H, accessory, Jeep w/Hawkeye, TriStar, 1981, MIB **30.00**

M*A*S*H, figure, BJ, Hawkeye or Hot Lips, Durham, 8", MOC, ea **75.00**

M*A*S*H, figure, Klinger (in dress), Tri-Star, MOC **35.00**

Major Matt Mason, accessory, Satellite Locker, Mattel, 1967, EX **30.00**

Major Matt Mason, accessory, Space Station, Mattel, 1966, MIB **250.00**

Major Matt Mason, figure, Doug Davis, Mattel, w/helmet, EX **60.00**

Major Matt Mason, figure, Jeff Long, Mattel, w/helmet, VG **75.00**

Man From UNCLE, figure, Illya Kuryakin, Gilbert, 12", NMIB **350.00**

Marvel Super Heroes, figure, Daredevil, Toy Biz, M **18.00**

Marvel Super Heroes, figure, Invisible Woman (vanishing), Toy Biz, MOC **125.00**

Marvel Super Heroes (Secret Wars), accessory, Doom Copter, Mattel, MIP **30.00**

Marvel Super Heroes (Secret Wars), figure, Captain America, Mattel, MOC **26.00**

Masters of the Universe, accessory, Fright Zone, Mattel, MIB **130.00**

Masters of the Universe, accessory, Monstroid, Mattel, MIB..**50.00**

Masters of the Universe, figure, Beast Man or Blade, Mattel, NM, ea **22.00**

Masters of the Universe, figure, Extender, Mattel, MOC.**35.00**

Masters of the Universe, figure, King Randor, Mattel, MOC **80.00**

Masters of the Universe, figure, Modulock, Mattel, MOC..**36.00**

Masters of the Universe, figure, Rokkon, Mattel, MOC ...**40.00**

Masters of the Universe, figure, Skeletor, Mattel, MOC .**115.00**

Masters of the Universe, figure, Teela, Mattel, MOC **70.00**

Masters of the Universe, figure, Two-Bad, Mattel, MOC .**32.00**

Micronauts, accessory, Alphatron, Mego, MIB **30.00**

Micronauts, accessory, Astro Station, EXIB **25.00**

Micronauts, accessory, Mega City, Mego, NMIB, from $30 to.**40.00**

Micronauts, figure, Baron Karza, Mego, EXIB **50.00**

Micronauts, figure, Biotron, Mego, NMIB **60.00**

Micronauts, figure, Lobros, Mego, NM **35.00**

Micronauts, horse, Pegasus, Mego, MIB.................................55.00

Planet of the Apes, figure, any, MIB, from $200 to **250.00**

Planet of the Apes, figure, any, MOC, from $100 to **125.00**

Planet of the Apes, figure, Peter Burke, MOC, from 100.00 to $125.00. (Photo courtesy Old Tyme Toy Store)

Pocket Super Heroes, figure, Batman or Robin, Mego, MOC, ea..........................**45.00**

Pocket Super Heroes, figure, Jor-El or Lex Luthor, MOC, ea..**25.00**

Six Million Dollar man, figure, Steve Austin, Kenner, 1976, MIB, $150.00. (Photo courtesy Jennifer Dobb)

Six Million Dollar Man, figure, Oscar Goldman, Kenner, 12", MIB...............................**125.00**

Space: 1999, figure, any except Zython Alien, Mattel, MOC..........**50.00**

Space: 1999, figure, Zython Alien, Mattel, MOC.................**215.00**

Stargate, accessory, Winged Glider, MIB....................**20.00**

Starsky & Hutch, figure, any, Mego, MOC, from $25 to **35.00**

Super Heroes, figure, Aquaman, Mego, 9", EX...................**35.00**

Super Heroes, figure, Batgirl, Mego, EX.......................**85.00**

Super Heroes, figure, Batman (Bend 'n Flex), Mego, 5", NM **30.00**

Super Heroes, figure, Catwoman, Mego, M........................**125.00**

Super Heroes, figure, Catwoman, Mego, MOC **400.00**

Super Heroes, figure, Green Goblin, Mego, MOC **600.00**

Super Heroes, figure, Iron Man, Mego, MIB....................**130.00**

Super Heroes, figure, Iron Man, Mego, MOC **425.00**

Super Heroes, figure, Lizard, Mego, MIB....................**175.00**

Super Heroes, figure, Lizard, Mego, MOC **425.00**

Super Heroes, figure, Penguin, Mego, MOC **100.00**

Super Heroes, figure, Riddler (fist-fighting), Mego, M **120.50**

Super Heroes, figure, Shazam, Mego, M..........................**65.00**

Super Heroes, figure, Superman, Mego, MOC **100.00**

Super Heroes, figure, Tarzan, Mego, 8", EX...................**45.00**

Super Heroes, figure, Thing, Mego, MIB....................**160.00**

Super Heroes, figure, Thor, Mego, NM................................**100.00**

Super Powers, accessory, Batmobile, Kenner, 1985, MIB, from $80 to **95.00**

Super Powers, figure, Aquaman, NM................................**15.00**

Super Powers, figure, Brainiac, Kenner, MOC.................**25.00**

Super Powers, figure, Cyclotron, Kenner, complete, M **30.00**

Super Powers, figure, Dr Fate, Kenner, complete, NM...**20.00**

Super Powers, figure, Golden Pharaoh, Kenner, MOC.**100.00**

Super Powers, figure, Lex Luthor, Kenner, MOC.................**15.00**

Super Powers, figure, Mr Freeze, Kenner, MOC.................**70.00**

Super Powers, figure, Red Tornado, Kenner, MOC.**50.00**

Super Powers, figure, Superman, Kenner, MOC.................**55.00**

Wizard of Oz, accessory, Emerald City (for 8" figures), Mego, MIB................................**325.00**

Wizard of Oz, figure, Wicked Witch, Mego, 8", MIB, from $75 to............................**100.00**

Wizard of Oz, figure, Wizard, Mego, 8", MIB, from $225 to..**250.00**

Wonder Woman, figure, fly-away action, 12", MIB, from $235.00 to $250.00. (Photo courtesy Jennifer Dobb)

Wonder Woman, figure, Nubia, Mego, 1976, 12", MIB..**100.00**

Wonder Woman, figure, Steve Trevor, Mego, 1976, 12", MIB............................**100.00**

WWF, figure, Andre the Great, Hasbro, MOC.................**60.00**

WWF, figure, Hulk Hogan, Hasbro, MOC.................**15.00**

WWF, figure, Hulk Hogan (mail-in), Hasbro, MIP...........**55.00**

WWF, figure, Lex Lugar, Hasbro, MOC..............................**18.00**

WWF, figure, Undertaker, Hasbro, MOC..............................**25.00**

X-Men, figure, any, Toy Biz, MOC, from $10 to....................**25.00**

Advertising Collectibles

As far back as the turn of the century, manufacturers used characters that identified with their products. They were always personable, endearing, amusing, and usually succeeded in achieving just the effect the producer had in mind, which was to make their product line more visual, more familiar, and therefore one the customer would more often than not choose over the competition. Magazine ads, display signs, product cartons, and TV provided just the right exposure for these ad characters. Elsie the Cow became so well known that at one point during a random survey, more people recognized her photo than one of the president!

There are scores of advertising characters, and many have

been promoted on a grand scale. Today's collectors search for the dolls, banks, cookie jars, mugs, plates, and scores of other items modeled after or bearing the likenesses of their favorites, several of which are featured in our listings.

Condition plays a vital role in evaluating vintage advertising pieces. Our estimates are for items in at least near-mint condition, unless another condition code is present in the description. Try to be very objective when you assess wear and damage.

For more informaiton, we recomment *Antique and Contemporary Advertising* by B.J. Summers.

See also Breweriana; Bubble Bath Containers; Character and Promotional Glassware; Novelty Telephones; Pin-Back Buttons; Radios. See Clubs and Newsletters for information concerning *The Prize Insider* newsletter for Cracker Jack collectors; Peanut Pals, a club for collectors of Planters Peanuts; and The Soup Collector Club (Campbells Soups).

Aero Mayflower Transit Co, truck, Linemar, litho tin, friction, MIB..............................**350.00**
Alka-Seltzer, bank, Speedy figure, vinyl, 5½", EX, minimum value............................**200.00**
Alka-Seltzer, doll, Speedy, 1960, vinyl, 8", EX, from $500 to..........**700.00**
Allied Van Lines, truck, tin, friction, MIB......................**325.00**
Aunt Jemima, doll, Uncle Moses, 1940s-50s, stuffed oilcloth, 12"...............................**95.00**

Aunt Jemima, doll, 1940s-50s, stuffed oilcloth, 11", EX..**95.00**
Bazooka Bubble Gum, doll, Bazooka Joe, 1973, stuffed cloth, EX........................**20.00**
Bean Bag Bunch, doll, w/tag, Kellogg's, MIP.................**9.00**
Betty Crocker, doll, Kenner, 1974, stuffed cloth, 13", VG **20.00**
Big Boy, bank, figure holding hamburger, ceramic............**500.00**
Big Boy, bank, figure w/ or w/out, hamburger, vinyl, M, ea.**25.00**

Big Boy bank, soft-molded vinyl figure with removable head, 1973, 9", M, from $20.00 to $25.00.

Big Boy, doll, Dakin, complete w/hamburger & shoes..**150.00**
Borden, bank, Beauregard, Irwin, 1950s, red plastic figure, 5", EX...................................**65.00**
Borden, Elsie's Funbook Cut-Out Toys & Games, 1940s, EX.........**115.00**
Borden, figure, Elsie the Cow, PVC, 3½", M, from $10 to........**20.00**
Borden, hand puppet, Elsie's baby, vinyl w/cloth body, EX...**75.00**
Borden, push-button puppet, Elsie the Cow, wood, EX.......**125.00**
Bosco Chocolate, doll, Bosco the Clown, vinyl, NM..........**45.00**
Brach's Peppermint, wristwatch, 1980s, MIB...................**15.00**

Buster Brown, Treasure Hunt Game, shoe box, 1930s, unused, from $50 to......**75.00**

Buster Brown Shoes, kite, 1940s, NM......**40.00**

Calgon Soap, ring, M......**150.00**

Campbell's, dolls, Campbell Kids, 1970s, rag-type, MIB, pr......**75.00**

Campbell's, dolls, Campbell Kids, 1970s, vinyl, 9", MIB, pr......**125.00**

Campbell's, truck, metal w/decaled sides, copyright 1985, 19", VG......**200.00**

Cap'n Crunch, bank, 1973, figural, painted plastic, VG......**65.00**

Cap'n Crunch, bank, 1984, treasure chest, blue plastic, NM......**5.00**

Cap'n Crunch, Cap'n Crunch Cruiser, 1987, plastic, EX......**10.00**

Cap'n Crunch, doll, Quaker Oats Co, 1990, plush, 18"......**20.00**

Cap'n Crunch, figure, Soggy, 1986, nearly clear plastic, 1½", EX......**5.00**

Cap'n Crunch, figure, 1986, blue plastic, 1½", VG......**5.00**

Cap'n Crunch, kaleidoscope, 1965, cardboard, 7", EX......**35.00**

Cap'n Crunch, ring, plastic figure, NM......**85.00**

Cap'n Crunch, coloring book, Whitman, 1968, VG......**20.00**

Cheetos, doll, Chester Cheetah, stuffed plush, 18", EX....**20.00**

Cherry 7-Up, wristwatch, 1980s, M......**15.00**

Chevrolet, wristwatch, 1927, salesman's award, EX......**400.00**

Chips Ahoy, figure, Nabisco, 1990s, rubber, 5", M......**20.00**

Chucky Cheese Pizza, bank, vinyl Chucky Cheese figure, 7", EX......**10.00**

Coca-Cola, boomerang, 1950s, EX......**35.00**

Coca-Cola, car, Ford Taxi, Taivo, litho tin, friction, 9", MIB......**400.00**

Coca-Cola, doll, Frozen Coca-Cola mascot, 1960s, stuffed cloth, NM......**150.00**

Coca-Cola, game, Steps to Health, 1938, complete, 26x11", NM......**150.00**

Coca-Cola, jigsaw puzzle, Teenage Party, NMIB......**100.00**

Coca-Cola, kite, American Flyer, 1930s, bottle at end, EX......**400.00**

Coca-Cola, pocket radio, Leader Wave, M......**15.00**

Coca-Cola, truck, Marx, 1957, litho tin w/Sprite Boy logo, 17", NMIB......**625.00**

Coca-Cola, whistle, 1950s, plastic, Merry Christmas...Memphis Tenn, EX......**25.00**

Cracker Jack, airplane, tin, orange w/black & red circles......**45.00**

Cracker Jack, airplane, tin, yellow & green, NM......**55.00**

Cracker Jack, banjo, litho tin.**47.00**

Cracker Jack, circus animals, litho tin, 5 different, ea......**135.00**

Cracker Jack, coin, plastic, various colors, ea......**8.00**

Cracker Jack, dexterity puzzle, Gee Cracker Jack Is Good, NM......**125.00**

Cracker Jack, dog figure, plastic......**9.50**

Cracker Jack, figure, skunk, squirrel, etc, 1950s, plastic, EX, ea......**10.00**

Cracker Jack, garage, litho tin, NM 80.00

Cracker Jack, Indian headdress, Me For Cracker Jack ...230.00

Cracker Jack, pin, Pied Piper, metal 65.00

Cracker Jack, pin-back button, celluloid w/mirror back, NM ..125.00

Cracker Jack, plate, plastic 5.50

Cracker Jack, put-together clown, plastic 8.00

Cracker Jack, puzzle, Last Round-Up, 1940, paper, red & green, EX 30.00

Cracker Jack, sled, metal w/silver finish...............................18.00

Cracker Jack, Smitty badge, plastic 42.00

Curtiss, tractor trailer, Buddy L, 1950s, rear drop gate, 29", EX........635.00

Del Monte, bank, Big Top Bonanza Clown, 1985, plastic, 7", M, $10 to 15.00

Del Monte, doll, Shoo Shoo Scarecrow, 1983, stuffed plush, NM......................15.00

Doctor Pepper, dart game, 1943, EX 300.00

Dole Pineapple, yo-yo, 1980s, plastic w/paper seal, NM........6.00

Dunkin' Donuts, wristwatch, 1999, M...........................10.00

Dutch Boy Paints, coloring book, WDP, 1957 premium, unused, EX 20.00

Eggo Waffles, wristwatch, 1990, Eggosaurus, M 15.00

Energizer Batteries, squeeze light, Energizer Bunny figure, MIP.8.00

Esso, Happy bank, plastic, 7x3", NM 95.00

Florida Oranges, bank, Orange Bird, 1974, vinyl, MIP ...40.00

Gerber, boxcar, Bachmann, 1978, blue, HO scale, 6", MIB.95.00

Gerber, Sh-h-hh! Baby's Asleep, paper stock sign that hangs from door knob, 1950s, 5½x8', $15.00. (Photo courtesy Joan Stryker Grubaugh)

Gerber, truck, Nylint, 1978, GMC, 18-wheeler, pressed steel, 21", M.....................................85.00

Goodyear Tires, wristwatch, 1970s, revolving disk, G.............50.00

Green Giant, doll, ca 1975, vinyl, 9", EX..............................85.00

Green Giant, doll, cloth, 1966, 16", M (in original mailer), from $25 to 35.00

Green Giant, doll, Little Sprout, talker, MIP.....................55.00

Green Giant, doll, Little Sprout, 1974, stuffed cloth, 10½", NM 15.00

Green Giant, figure, Little Sprout, molded vinyl, movable head, 1960s, 6½", M, $15.00.

Green Giant, jump rope, Little Sprout handles, MIP **20.00**

Green Giant, truck, Tonka, pressed steel, rubber tires, 24", G **165.00**

Gulf Gasoline, yo-yo, 1960s, wood w/painted seal, 3-pc, NM .**22.00**

Hawaiian Punch, game, Mattel, 1978, complete, EX (EX box).....**30.00**

Hawaiian Punch, wristwatch, Punchy, 1970s, red strap, digital, VG **50.00**

Heinz 57, truck, Metalcraft, green w/ white stake bed, 13", G+.**1,300.00**

Hess Gasoline & Fuel Oils, truck, 1970s, plastic & tin, MIB.**50.00**

Icee, bank, Icee Bear w/drink in front of him, rubber, 7", EX **30.00**

Jack Frost, doll, Jack Frost, stuffed cloth, 17", M **50.00**

Jell-O, puppet, Mr Wiggle, 1966, red vinyl, M **150.00**

Jordache, doll, Jeans Man, 12", MIB **30.00**

Keebler, bank, Keebler Elf figure, ceramic, lg, NM **60.00**

Keebler, bank, Keebler Elf figure, ceramic, sm, NM **25.00**

Keebler, truck, Nylint, 1986, MIB.**85.00**

Keebler, wristwatch, Ernie the Keebler Elf, 1970s, G.....**50.00**

Kodak, doll, Colorkins, ca 1990, stuffed, 8" to 10", ea **20.00**

Kool-Aid, wristwatch, Goofy Grape, 1976, G **200.00**

Kraft Macaroni & Cheese, wristwatch, 1980s, M **10.00**

Livesavers, yo-yo, wood Livesaver shape w/painted seal, NM .**45.00**

M&M, bean bag toy, M&M shape, red, green, blue or yellow, 6", ea..**5.00**

M&M, bean bag toy, peanut shape, golfer or witch, 6", ea **10.00**

M&M, calculator, yellow w/different color M&M keys, MIB **10.00**

M&M, dispenser, M&M shape, 1991, brown, sm **5.00**

M&M, dispenser, M&M shape, 1991, red, lg **10.00**

M&M, dispenser, peanut shape, orange, green or yellow, sm, ea **2.00**

M&M, dispenser, peanut shape, 1991, brown, sm **2.00**

M&M, dispenser, peanut shape, 1995, football player, lg.**20.00**

M&M, dispenser, peanut shape, 1995, yellow, lg **10.00**

M&M, dispenser, peanut shape, 1997, basketball player .**15.00**

M&M, doll, M&M shape, plush, 4½" **5.00**

M&M, doll, M&M shape, plush, 8" **5.00**

M&M, doll, M&M shape, plush, 12" **10.00**

M&M, Easy Bake Set, w/M&M stencil & spoon, MIB **12.00**

Mack Trucks, doll, Mack Bulldog, stuffed plush, NM **40.00**

Meow Mix, figure, vinyl cat, EX .**35.00**

Michelin, figure, Mr Bib, plastic, 12", NM **75.00**

Michelin, figure, Mr Bib on motorcycle, plastic, EX.........**110.00**

Michelin, nodder, Mr Bib, attaches to dashboard, 2 styles, ea.....**18.00**

Michelin, ramp walker, Mr Bib windup, MIB **25.00**

Michelin, yo-yo, Mr Bib in black outline on white, EX......**10.00**

Mobilgas, truck, Cragstan, ½-cab, litho tin, friction, EX (EX box) **225.00**

Mott's Apple Juice, doll, Apple of My Eye Bear, 1988, stuffed plush, M **15.00**

Nestle Quik, doll, Quik Bunny, plush, 1980s, mail-in, M..............35.00

Nestle Quik, figure, Quik Bunny, bendable, 6", EX 10.00

Oreo Cookies, wristwatch, 1998, M...................50.00

Oscar Mayer, bank, Weinermobile, 1988, plastic, 10", M......25.00

Oscar Mayer, ring, Little Oscar, 1970s, red & yellow plastic, EX...................5.00

Pepsi-Cola, kite, 1960s, features Mary Poppins, EX........125.00

Pepsi-Cola, truck, Barclay, 1950s, metal, 2", M.................155.00

Pepsi-Cola, truck, Marx, 1940s, plastic, NMIB..............450.00

Peters Weatherbird Shoes, yo-yo, Alox, 1950s, wood w/decal seal, NM 30.00

Phillips 66, tanker truck, metal, Ralstoy 3, Made in USA, 7¾", VG.................125.00

Pillsbury, bank, Poppin' Fresh, 1980s, mail-in premium, ceramic, M.....................35.00

Pillsbury, decals, Poppin' Fresh, set of 18, MIP................10.00

Pillsbury, doll, Poppin' Fresh, 1970s, stuffed cloth, 14", VG 14.00

Pillsbury, doll, Poppin' Fresh, 1972, stuffed cloth, 11", EX, $15 to..............................20.00

Pillsbury, doll, Poppin' Fresh, 1982, stuffed plush, M, from $40 to............................50.00

Pillsbury, figure, Grandmommer, 1974, vinyl, 5", M, from $75 to....................................95.00

Pillsbury, figure, Grandpopper, 1974, vinyl, 5¼", M, from $75 to 95.00

Pillsbury, figure, Poppie Fresh, 1972, vinyl, 6", M..........20.00

Pillsbury, gumball machine, Poppin' Fresh, w/5 lbs of gum, MIB..............................125.00

Pillsbury, place mat, Poppin' Fresh border, M, $35.00.

Pillsbury, wristwatch, 1996, Doughboy, talker, M......15.00

Planters, costume, Mr Peanut, 1970s, cloth w/plastic mask, 2-pc, NMIB 75.00

Planters, dish set, child's, Melmac, 1970s, 3 pcs, MIB 20.00

Planters, doll, Mr Peanut, Chase Bag, 1967, cloth, 21", EX .40.00

Planters, doll, Mr Peanut, Chase Bag, 1970, cloth, 18", NM.25.00

Planters, frisbee, white plastic w/Heritage logo, M.........15.00

Planters, Mr Peanut Peanut Butter Maker, 1970s, 12", MIB....................................50.00

Planters, nodder, Mr Peanut, Lego, papier-mache, NM 150.00

Planters, radio backpack, Munch 'N Go, 1991, EX, from $35 to 40.00

Planters, train set, 1988, battery-operated, MIB 50.00

Planters, vender's costume, Mr Peanut, life-size, EX, from $800 to........................900.00

Planters, wristwatch, Mr Peanut, 1966, yellow face, VG 50.00

Planters, yo-yo, Mr Peanut, Humphrey, 1976, NM....**12.00**

Poll Parrot Shoes, figures, Bride & Groom, Sonsco, celluloid, 4", EX....................................**65.00**

Poll Parrot Shoes, ring, 1950s, brass w/embossed parrot, EX....................................**65.00**

Raid Bug Spray, wristwatch, Raid Bug, 1970s, revolving disk, EX..................................**150.00**

Red Goose Shoes, bank, 1920s, red-painted cast iron, 9", EX..................................**135.00**

Red Goose Shoes, wristwatch, 1960s, G........................**130.00**

Reddy Kilowatt, figure, 1930s, hard rubber, 3"................**8.00**

Reddy Kilowatt, wristwatch, 1930s, VG.....................**250.00**

Reese's, doll, Reese's Bear, 1989, in Reese's T-shirt, NM+..**10.00**

Ritz Crackers, wristwatch, 1971, MIB..............................**200.00**

Salamander Shoes, figures, vinyl, sm, set of 6, M..............**125.00**

Seven-Up, car, Taiyo, litho tin w/logo, friction, 10½", NMIB........**235.00**

Seven-Up, music box, can shape, plays Love Story, NM....**50.00**

Shoney's, bank, Shoney's bear, vinyl, M..........................**20.00**

Sinclair, truck, Marx, litho tin, 18½", VG......................**375.00**

Smokey Bear, bank, ceramic, white w/gold details, EX..**60.00**

Smokey Bear, doll, inflatable vinyl, MIP....................**245.00**

Smokey Bear, doll, 50th Anniversary, 12", MIB...**30.00**

Smokey Bear, magic slate, Watkins-Strathmore, 1969, EX....................................**85.00**

Sprite, doll, Lucky Lymon, 1990s, talker, vinyl, 7½", M......**25.00**

Squirt, figure, Squirt Boy, 1961, vinyl, 18", very rare, M..**200.00**

Stanley Powerlock, wristwatch, 1980s, M........................**45.00**

Star-Kist Tuna, bank, Charlie Tuna, Japan, ceramic figure, 10", MIB........................**35.00**

Star-Kist Tuna, wristwatch, Charlie Tuna, 1971, facing left, VG..........................**50.00**

Star-Kist Tuna, wristwatch, Charlie Tuna, 1986, 25th Anniversary, MIB.........**25.00**

Sunbeam Bread, yo-yo, 1980s, plastic w/paper sticker seal, NM..................................**4.00**

Swiss Miss Chocolate, wristwatch, 1981, EX........................**50.00**

Tastee Freeze, yo-yo, 1970s, wood w/die-stamp seal, NM....**15.00**

Texaco, fire engine, Buddy L, 24", EX (VG box) **550.00**

Texaco, Service Station, steel w/plastic accessories, MIB (sealed) **350.00**

Texaco, truck, Buddy L, 1960s, pressed steel, red w/white grille, MIB....................**375.00**

Tropicana Orange Juice, doll, Tropic-Ana, 1997, stuffed cloth, 17", NM **35.00**

Tupperware, doll, 1988, stuffs into satin Tupperware bowl, 13", M....................................**25.00**

Tyson Chicken, doll, Chicken Quick, stuffed cloth, 13", VG **15.00**

Welch's Grape Juice, wristwatch, 1989, M..........................**20.00**

Wilkins Coffee, hand puppet, Wontkins, 1958, painted rubber, 7", EX...................**100.00**

Advertising Tins

Attractive packaging has always been a powerful marketing tool; today, those colorful tin containers that once held products ranging from cookies and dog food to motor oil and tobacco are popular collectibles. There are several interesting books on this topic you may want to refer to: *Antique Tins, Books I, II, and III,* by Fred Dodge; and *Encyclopedia of Advertising Tins, Volume II,* by David Zimmerman. All are published by Collector Books.

Allied Flagship, Typewriter Ribbon, ¾x2½" dia.........**12.00**
Beach, Bro-Aspirin, ¼x1⅝x1⅝".**8.00**
Bucki Supreme, Typewriter Ribbon, ⅞x2½" **15.00**

Certified Aspirin, ⅜x1", $5.00. (Photo courtesy David Zimmerman)

Fralinger's Salt Water Taffy, 5½x3½", $10.00. (Photo courtesy Linda McPherson)

Feminex, Tablets, ¼x1¼x1½".**30.00**
Flents, Ear Plugs, ½x2x2¾"...**5.00**
Garfield, Digestive Tablets, 25¢, American Stopper, ½x1½x3".**75.00**
Gin, Kidney Pills, 1¼x2" dia.**20.00**

Gre-Solvent Hand Cleaner, sample, ⅝x2", $12.00. (Photo courtesy David Zimmerman)

Hall's Zinc Oxide, 1x1¼" **18.00**
Hamilton Beach, Motor Oil, 1⅞x2"..............................**35.00**
Ideal Cocoa, sample, Liberty Can, 1¼x1⅝x2½" dia............**155.00**
Johnson's, Prepared Wax, American Can Co #70-A, ⅞x2⅜" dia......................**75.00**
Kickapoo Indian Salve, 25¢, ⅝x1⅞" dia......................**90.00**
Killark, Auto Fuses, ¼x1¼x1¾".**12.00**
Kohler-Antidote, Pain Pills, 25¢, ⅜x1¼x1¾" **15.00**
Kreko, Typewriter Ribbon, ¾x2½" dia **18.00**
La-May, Face Powder, ½x2½" dia **18.00**
McCormick Banquet Tea, Orange Pekoe, sample, 1¾x2¼x2½".**30.00**
Millar's Coffee, Magnet Brand, sample, 2⅜x3" dia........**110.00**
Nyal, Hinkle Tablets, 1x1½" dia.**18.00**
Paradise Brand Pepper, 3¼x2¼x1¼", minimum value **25.00**
Perfection, Tire Repair Kit, Chicago Stamping, ½x4x2½" **70.00**
Pompeian, Day Cream, ⅜x1⅜".**5.00**

Prize Medal Ginger, 4¼x2¼x1¼", minimum value..............**18.00**

Rose/Vel, Great Healer, 1x2½" dia....................................**10.00**

Rydale's, Liver Tablets, 25¢, ⅜x2⅛" dia........................**40.00**

Shell, Extra Loud Needles (phonographic), 100 pcs, ¼x1¼x1¾"..........**35.00**

Smithies, condoms, ¼x1⅝x2⅛".**65.00**

Sunder, Phono Needles, ⅜x1¼x1¾"......................**25.00**

Walgreen, Adhesive Plaster, 1⅛x1¼"...........................**18.00**

Wiggins Wigg's, Cleanser, Hekin, 2x1½" dia........................**12.00**

Williams' Talc Powder, La Tosca Rose, ¾x2⅛"...................**75.00**

Aluminum

From the late 1930s until early in the 1950s, kitchenwares and household items were often crafted of aluminum, usually with relief-molded fruit or flowers on a hammered background. Today many find that these diversified items make an attractive collection. Especially desirable are those examples marked with the manufacturer's backstamp or the designer's signature.

You've probably also seen the anodized (colored) aluminum pitchers, tumblers, sherbet holders, etc., that were popular in the late '50s – early '60s. Interest in these items has exploded, as prices on eBay sales attest. Be sure to check condition, though, as scratching and wear reduce values drastically. The more uncommon

forms are especially collectible.

For more information refer to *Collectible Aluminum, An Identification and Value Guide* (Collector Books), by Everett Grist.

Anodized ice bucket on tripod base, 10', from $35.00 to $55.00.

Ashtray, flying duck scene, unmarked, 6" dia...........**10.00**

Basket, floral band at edge, fluted & serrated, Everlast, 6x9"...**10.00**

Basket, sailing ship, double wire handle w/square knot, Federal, 9" dia................**35.00**

Basket, tomato pattern at edge w/double wire handle, Everlast, 6x11"...............**10.00**

Bookends, leaping bass w/sprays, Bruce Cox, 7x5x3", pr..**185.00**

Bowl, anodized, Bascal, 6", set of 8, EX....................................**26.00**

Bowl, bittersweet pattern, notched rim, W August Forge, 1x5".........**25.00**

Bowl, chrysanthemum pattern, deep well, serrated edge, Federal, 1x9"..................**15.00**

Bowl, dogwood pattern, fluted/crimped rim, W August Forge, 2x7" dia...............**20.00**

Bowl, hammered effect w/uneven scalloped edge, McClelland, 1½x6"...............................**5.00**

Bowl, salad; wheat pattern, Palmer-Smith, 4x14"......**60.00**

Butter dish, bamboo pattern & finial, w/lid, Everlast, 7x4x4"......**10.00**

Candlestick, handled saucer w/removable socket, beaded edge, unmarked............**10.00**

Candlesticks, hammered w/scalloped base, fluted bobeche, 3x4" dia, pr...............**20.00**

Candy dish, double, butterfly pattern, gold anodized, Neocraft, 12"...............**15.00**

Candy dish, leaf shape, sailing ships (3), curlicue-tail handle, 6x8"...............**15.00**

Casserole, pea-vine pattern, pea-pod finial, Everlast, 4x7" dia ..**10.00**

Casserole, rose pattern, rose finial, World Hand Forged, 4x8".**5.00**

Casserole, tomato pattern, flower & leaf finial, Everlast, 5x9" ..**5.00**

Coaster, embossed beetle, W August Forge, 3½" dia...**35.00**

Coaster, grapes w/leaves, unmarked, 5" dia............**3.00**

Coaster set, bamboo pattern, trivet-type holder, Everlast, holds 4.....**20.00**

Compote, hammered effect, unmarked, 5x6" dia.......**10.00**

Compote, stylized flower, double wire curlique stem on base, 5x8" dia...........**5.00**

Compote, wild rose pattern, Continental, 5x5"..........**20.00**

Creamer & sugar bowl, hammered effect, fluted rim, open **5.00**

Crumber & tray, Greek Key pattern, unmarked...............**5.00**

Crumber & tray, leaf design, Everlast............**5.00**

Cup, anodized, Heller Hostess Ware, set of 8, MIP........**45.00**

Double boiler, polished, wood handle & finial, Pyrex liner, 7" dia...............**10.00**

Ice bucket, chrysanthemum, mushroom finial, ribbon handles, 9x8" dia...............**40.00**

Ice bucket, hammered, open, 'barbell' handles, fluted, Everlast, 5x10"...............**15.00**

Ice bucket, hammered effect, black handles & finial, Kromex, 12x8" dia...............**10.00**

Ice bucket, medieval helmet style, no pattern, Hong Kong, 16x10" dia...............**20.00**

Jelly jar w/ladle, Nekrassoff, 5" dia underplate...............**35.00**

Key chain, teddy bear, Demarsh Forge...............**12.00**

Lazy Susan, fruit & flower pattern, serrated edge, Cromwell, 16" dia...............**5.00**

Letter basket, world map pattern, gold & silver anodized, 6x5x7"..**175.00**

Matchbox cover, kitchen; shotgun & flying duck scene, W August Forge...............**75.00**

Mint dish, dogwood pattern, glass insert, W August Forge, 12" dia...............**45.00**

Mug, hammered effect, 'ear' handle, copper colored, unmarked, 3x3"..**1.00**

Napkin rings, anodized, narrow, set of 8, MIB...............**28.00**

Paperweight, flying ducks, W August Forge, 5x3"........**75.00**

Pitcher, hammered effect, flared top & bottom, Nasco Italy, 7x5"...............**5.00**

Pitcher, tulip pattern, skinny 'ear' handle, R Kent, 9x5".....**35.00**

Plate, child's; ABCs around edge, unmarked, 7" dia...........**30.00**

Plate, dogwood & butterfly design, crimped edge, A Armour, 10" dia **45.00**

Plate, dogwood pattern, W August Forge, 9" dia **30.00**

Plate, Grove City College, DePonceau, 11" dia **35.00**

Plate, Signing of Declaration of Independence, W August Forge, 9" dia **45.00**

Popcorn popper, duck scene, W August Forge, 9" dia **75.00**

Relish tray, flying goose pattern, 4 compartments, A Armour, 5x16" **75.00**

Relish tray, marked Cellini-Craft, Argental, 17" dia.........**165.00**

Salad set, fork & spoon, hammered effect, unmarked, 12", pr...................................**45.00**

Saucepan, flower band on lid, twist wire handle, unmarked, 9" dia...............................**10.00**

Snack tray, flying ducks, lipped, self handles, 6x4" **3.00**

Snack tray, sailboat pattern, W August Forge, 5x8" **45.00**

Tray, bar; anchor, rope & gulls, applied handles, Everlast, 9x15"...............................**30.00**

Tray, bar; water lily pattern, self-handled, Arthur Armour .**45.00**

Tray, bread; acorns & grapes in floral chain, W August Forge, 7x11"...............................**45.00**

Tray, bread; stylized flower pattern, 6x11".........................**5.00**

Tray, bread; wild rose pattern, Continental, 6x13".........**15.00**

Tray, sandwich; bittersweet pattern, W August Forge, 8x11".....**35.00**

Tray, sandwich; poppy pattern, W August Forge, 10" dia....**45.00**

Tray, sandwich; tennis player, Hyman Blum, Pittsburgh PA, 10x16"...........................**45.00**

Tray, serving; purple anodized, 14" dia...........................**15.00**

Tray, serving; rose spray pattern, applied handles, unmarked, 16x10"..............................**5.00**

Water set, hammered, no mark: Pitcher, 7", $15.00; Tumblers, 5", set of six for $18.00; Tray, $7.00.

Anchor Hocking

From the 1930s until the 1970s Anchor Hocking (Lancaster, Ohio) produced a wide and varied assortment of glassware including kitchen items such as reamers, mixing bowls, and measuring cups in many lovely colors. Many patterns of dinnerware were made as well. Their Fire-King line was formulated to produce heat-proof glassware so durable that it was guaranteed for two years against breakage caused by heat. Colors included jade-ite, azur-ite, turquoise and sapphire blue, ivory, milk white (often decorated with fired-on patterns), Royal Ruby, and forest green. For the most part, prices are relatively low, except for some of the rarer items. For more information, we recommend *Anchor Hocking's*

Fire-King & More, Second Edition, by Gene Florence (Collector Books).

Bubble, bowl, fruit; ruby, 4½" .**9.00**

Bubble, stem, cocktail; forest green, 3½-oz **14.00**

Bubble, tumbler, juice; crystal, 5-oz, 4" **3.50**

Bubble, tumbler, water; ruby, 9-oz...................................**9.00**

Charm, bowl, dessert; azur-ite, 4¾" **6.00**

Charm, creamer, forest green..**7.50**

Charm, cup and saucer, ruby, $8.50. (Photo courtesy Gene Florence)

Charm, plate, dinner; jade-ite, 9¾" **50.00**

Charm, saucer, ruby, 5⅜".......**2.50**

Charm, sugar bowl, azur-ite .**12.00**

Early American Prescut, bowl, console; crystal, #797, 9" **15.00**

Early American Prescut, bowl, crystal, smooth rim, #726, 4¼".**22.00**

Early American Prescut, cup, punch or snack; crystal, no star, 6-oz...........................**2.50**

Early American Prescut, double candlestick, #784, $32.00. (Photo courtesy Gene Florence)

Early American Prescut, plate, crystal, 11" **12.00**

Early American Prescut, relish, crystal, 5-part, 13½" **30.00**

Early American Prescut, tumbler, iced tea; crystal, #732, 15-oz, 6" **20.00**

Forest Green, ashtray, 4⅝" sq.**6.00**

Forest Green, pitcher, 22-oz.**25.00**

Forest Green, stem, juice; 5½-oz .**12.50**

Forest Green, tumbler, 9½"....**6.50**

Game Bird, ashtray, white w/decals, 5¼".................**18.00**

Game Bird, bowl, vegetable; white w/decals, 8¼".................**65.00**

Game Birds, iced tea, 11-ounce, $12.00; Dinner plate, $6.50; Mug, eight-ounce, $8.00. (Photo courtesy Gene Florence)

Gray Laurel, bowl, vegetable; 8¼"...............................**30.00**

Gray Laurel, plate, salad; 7⅜".**8.00**

Gray Laurel, sugar bowl, footed .**5.00**

Jane Ray, creamer, jade-ite..**10.00**

Jane Ray, plate, salad; jade-ite, 7¾" **12.00**

Jane Ray, sugar bowl, jade-ite.**10.00**

Laurel, cup, peach lustre, 8-oz ..**3.50**

Laurel, plate, dinner; peach lustre, 9⅛" **5.00**

Laurel, soup plate, peach lustre, 7⅝"..................10.00

Meadow Green, bowl, vegetable; white w/decal, 8¼"........12.00

Meadow Green, creamer, white w/decal..................3.00

Meadow Green, platter, white w/decal, 12x9"................8.00

Moonstone, bowl, dessert; opalescent hobnail, crimped, 5½".9.50

Moonstone, creamer, opalescent hobnail..................10.00

Moonstone, goblet, opalescent hobnail, 10-oz....................20.00

Moonstone, vase, bud; opalescent hobnail, 5½"..................18.00

Prescut (Oatmeal), cup & saucer, crystal..................4.00

Prescut (Oatmeal), sherbet, crystal, 5-oz..................1.50

Prescut (Oatmeal), tumbler, water; crystal, 9-oz.........2.00

Prescut (Pineapple), box, cigarette/dresser; crystal, 4¾"......15.00

Prescut (Pineapple), butter dish, crystal, round................15.00

Prescut (Pineapple), tumbler, iced tea; white, 10-oz..............8.00

Primrose, cake pan, white w/decal, 8" sq..................12.00

Primrose, custard, low or dessert; white w/decal, 6-oz...........3.50

Primrose, plate, dinner; white w/decal, 9⅛"..................7.00

Rainbow, cup & saucer, pastel.10.00

Rainbow, jug, primary color, 54-oz..................60.00

Rainbow, plate, dinner; pastel, 9¼"..................12.00

Rainbow, shakers, primary color, pr..................25.00

Rainbow, tumbler, primary color, straight, 12-oz, 4¾"........35.00

Restaurant Ware, bowl, deep, jade-ite, G300, 15-oz.....28.00

Restaurant Ware, plate, pie/salad; jade-ite, G297, 6¾"........12.00

Restaurant Ware, platter, jade-ite, oval, G307, 9½"..............55.00

Royal Ruby, beer bottle, 7-oz.25.00

Royal Ruby, cup, round.........6.00

Royal Ruby, plate, dinner; 9⅛".11.00

Royal Ruby, punch bowl base.40.00

Royal Ruby, stem, goblet; 9-oz.14.00

Royal Ruby, tilted pitcher, $50.00.
(Photo courtesy Gene Florence)

Royal Ruby, vase, either style, 9"..................17.50

Sandwich, bowl, crystal, smooth, 6½"..................7.50

Sandwich, bowl, desert gold, scalloped, 5¼"..................6.00

Sandwich, bowl, forest green, scalloped, 6½"..................60.00

Sandwich, bowl, pink, scalloped, 8¼"..................27.50

Sandwich, creamer, crystal....8.00

Sandwich, plate, dinner; crystal, 9"..................20.00

Sandwich, plate, sandwich; desert gold, 12"..................15.00

Sandwich, tumbler, water; forest green, 9-oz..................4.00

Sapphire Blue, baker, round, 1-pt..................8.00

Sapphire Blue, cup, measuring; 3-spout, 8-oz **30.00**

Sapphire Blue, loaf pan, deep, 9⅛x5⅛" **22.00**

Sapphire Blue, roaster, 8¾".**55.00**

Shell, bowl, dessert; jade-ite, 4¾" **12.00**

Shell, creamer, peach lustre, footed **10.00**

Shell, plate, dinner; white w/gold trim, 10" **6.00**

Shell, sugar bowl, peach lustre, footed **10.00**

Swirl, bowl, cereal; white or ivory, 5⅞" **24.00**

Swirl, creamer, azur-ite, flat .**10.00**

Swirl, platter, Golden Anniversary, 12x9" **12.00**

Swirl, soup plate, Sunrise, 7⅝".**18.00**

Swirl, sugar bowl, pink, flat, tab handles **8.00**

Thousand Line, bowl, crystal, handles, 6" **10.00**

Thousand Line, bowl, vegetable; crystal, 8" **12.00**

Thousand Line, fork & spoon, crystal..................................**15.00**

Thousand Line, plate, luncheon; crystal, 8" **10.00**

Thousand Line, vase, bud; crystal..............................**12.50**

Turquoise Blue, ashtray, 5¾" **14.00**

Turquoise Blue, cup & saucer .**6.50**

Turquoise Blue, mug, 8-oz....**10.00**

Turquoise Blue, plate, snack; w/cup indent, 9" **6.00**

Wexford, bowl, centerpiece, footed, 8" **12.00**

Wexford, bowl, serving; crystal, scalloped top, 14" **10.00**

Wexford, cake stand, domed ..**6.00**

Wexford, candle, votive, 2½" ..**2.50**

Wexford, cup, punch or snack; 7-oz....................................**2.00**

Wexford, ice bucket, w/cover .**15.00**

Wexford, oil lamp, $35.00. (Photo courtesy Gene Florence)

Wexford, pitcher, crystal, footed, 18-oz **10.00**

Wexford, plate, crystal, 6-sided, 7¾" **7.00**

Wexford, platter, serving; 14" dia **10.00**

Wexford, sherbet, stemmed, 7¼-oz.**1.50**

Wexford, tidbit, 2-tier, 6" & 11" plates **10.00**

Wexford, tray, no center ring, 5 part, 11"............................**9.00**

Wheat, bowl, chili; white w/decals, 5"....................................**25.00**

Wheat, cup, snack; white w/decals, 5-oz...................................**3.00**

Wheat, custard, low or dessert; white w/decals, 6-oz.........**3.00**

Wheat, tray, snack; white w/decals, 11x6"................**4.00**

Aprons

Vintage aprons evoke nostalgic memories — grandma in her kitchen, gentle heat radiating from the cookstove, a child tugging on her apron strings — and even if collectors can't relate to that scene personally, they still want to cherish and preserve those old aprons. Some are basic and functional, perhaps made of flour-sack material, while others are embroidered and trimmed with lace or appliqués. Commercial-made aprons are collectible as well, and if they retain their original tags, their prices are higher. Remember, condition is critical, and as a general rule, those that are made by hand are preferred over machine — or commercial-made aprons.

Bib style, embroidered design on white, blue trim, 1940s, EX..............**26.00**
Bib style, embroidered flowers on flour-sack cotton, 1920-30s, EX..................................**34.00**
Bib style, family barbeque scene on cotton, 1960s.............**12.00**
Bib style, Girl Scouts, pockets for pencils, spoons & recipes, 1960s.............................**17.00**
Bib style, lavender/white diamond pattern on cotton, back snap closure **12.00**

Bib style, printed autumn theme, 1950s, $50.00. (Photo courtesy Barbara Peoples)

Bib style, wraparound, ties in front, 1940-50s, EX........**22.00**
Bib style, yellow & blue violets, heart-shaped pocket w/yellow trim.................................**18.00**
Strapless bib, clear plastic w/colored flowers, gathered red trim, NM **100.00**
Waist style, blue gingham, round pocket w/lady's face, MN .**20.00**
Waist style, clear w/white roses & yellow trim on vinyl, 1 pocket, EX...................................**32.00**
Waist style, decorative silver strip at hem of baby blue rayon satin................................**18.00**
Waist style, Disneyland & scene printed on cotton canvas, 1950s, EX **36.00**
Waist style, gray & white striped, w/eyelet lace & sm black bows...............................**20.00**
Waist style, Hawaiian scenes on cotton, 1940-50s, EX......**20.00**
Waist style, lt pink polished cotton w/rose design, scalloped hem **26.00**
Waist style, multicolored butterflies w/red border, 1960s.**13.00**
Waist style, multicolored fruit printed on terry cloth, 1960s ...**11.00**
Waist style, orange & white checked w/black crisscross stitching.........................**14.00**
Waist style, Pepsi Cola vendor, 'Say Pepsi Please,' 1960s, EX .**18.00**
Waist style, pink & blue flowers on white plastic, green trim .**27.00**
Waist style, poodles on salmon fabric, 1950s, EX............**40.00**
Waist style, red & white checked w/embroidered pockets & hem, 1950 ....**12.00**

Waist style, red cotton w/green, blue, white & yellow daisies, 1960s..............**13.00**

Waist style, white sheer trimmed w/rose pink & aqua bunnies, 1950s..............**18.00**

Ashtrays

Even though the general public seems to be down on smoking, ashtrays themselves are beginning to be noticed favorably by collectors, who perhaps view them as an 'endangered species'! Some of the more desirable examples are those with embossed or intaglio designs, applied decorations, added figures of animals or people, Art Deco stying, an interesting advertising message, and an easily recognizable manufacturer's mark.

For further information we recommend *Collector's Guide to Ashtrays, Identification and Values,* by Nancy Wanvig. She is listed in the Directory under Wisconsin.

Advertising, Ball (Canning Jars), clear w/blue center, 3 rests, 3½"..............**18.00**

Advertising, Breyers Ice Cream, white w/logo, ceramic, 5½" dia..............**20.00**

Advertising, Cavalier, Flavor, Mildness, bronze tin, 3⅝" dia..............**8.00**

Advertising, Falstaff, pale amber glass, rings on bottom, 3½" dia..............**18.00**

Advertising, Havana Club (Cuba), plastic w/center picture, 5½" dia..............**15.00**

Advertising, Olympia, black amethyst glass, stackable, 4⅛" dia..............**9.50**

Advertising, Reese Padlock, figural, cast aluminum, 3¾" L......**17.00**

Advertising, Resistol Hats, brown plastic, ad on top of brim, 4¾" L..............**25.00**

Advertising, Rubbermaid, 25th Anniversary, 1934-59, dustpan shape, 5"..............**20.00**

Advertising, University of Michigan, cream china, Wedgwood, 4⅜" dia........**11.00**

Art Deco, Egyptian woman, pewter-like metal, 3¾"..**39.00**

Art Deco, nude, bronze on chrome base, 2⅝"..............**70.00**

Casino, Nob Hill, clear glass w/white center, Casino-Las Vegas, 3½"..............**5.00**

Decorative, cranberry iridescent, round w/12-ball border, 5⅛" dia..............**17.00**

Decorative, Imari-type bowl, three rests on center top edge, Japanese mark, 6½", $15.00. (Photo courtesy Nancy Wanvig)

Decorative, pewter w/tile of grape harvest in center, 4½" W **30.00**

Decorative, squirrel on log, bronze-coated pot metal, 3⅛" **15.00**

Fraternal, Lions International, white plastic w/trademark & name, 9" dia.......................................**12.50**

Novelty, apple shape, pale yellow, Daisy & Button, 1 rest, 4¼" L.....................................**20.00**

Novelty, big-mouth hobo smokers, each from $35.00 to $38.00. (Photo courtesy Nancy Wanvig)

Novelty, canoe shape, amber, Daisy & Button, 1 rest ea end, 6½" L **17.00**

Novelty, life raft, yellow w/2 rests inside, 6⅝" L **15.00**

Novelty, Presidental pictures, through Lyndon Johnson, 7½" dia **18.00**

Novelty, seated Indian figural, composition w/glass inserts, 5" **20.00**

Tire Ashtrays

Tire ashtrays were introduced in the teens as advertising items. The very early all-glass or glass-and-metal types were replaced in the early 1920s by the more familiar rubber-tired varieties. Hundreds of different examples have been pro-duced over the years. They are still distributed (by the larger tire companies only), but no longer display the detail or color of the pre-World War II tire ashtrays. Although the common ones bring modest prices, rare examples sometimes sell for several hundred dollars.

For more information we recommend *Tire Ashtray Collector's Guide* by Jeff McMcVey; he is listed in the Directory under Idaho.

Armstrong Rhino-Flex, name in gold, glass insert w/rhino & name, 6"..........................**35.00**

Bridgestone, D-Lug, Tubeless, clear insert w/logo, 3x8¾" **30.00**

Cooper Cobra Radial GT 75th Anniversary, clear imprinted insert **25.00**

Dunlop Gold Seal 78 Twin Belt, clear imprinted insert....**30.00**

Falls Evergreen Tube That Sentenced Air..., Weller Pottery insert...............**175.00**

Firestone, High Speed, amber insert, Century of Progress 1934, 5¾"........................**85.00**

Firestone, red & black plastic insert, 3 extended rests, 6" **10.00**

General, Steelex Radial, black insert, black lettering, 6½" **17.50**

General, Streamline Jumbo, green insert w/Goes A Long..., 5" .**65.00**

Goodrich Silvertown, Lifesaver Radial HR-70-15, clear insert, 6" ..**20.00**

Goodyear, Hi-Miler Cross Rib, nylon, clear insert w/blue logo, 6¼" **20.00**

Goodyear Balloon All Weather 33x6.00, amber or green disc wheel insert...................**80.00**

Hood Arrow, Heavy Duty 6 Ply, 500-20, 6⅜"......................**65.00**

Kelly Springfield, Commercial Heavy Tread, clear insert, 6".........**35.00**

Kelly Springfield, Voyager, Aramid..., clear insert w/green decal, 6"...........................**20.00**

Mohawk, Akron O, glass insert w/yellow bottom, 1930s, 5⅜"......**45.00**

Pennsylvania Tires, pink glass insert, 5¼"......................**50.00**

Pennsylvania Vacuum Cup, all glass, $150.00. (Photo Courtesy Jeff McKey.

Pennsylvania Vacuum Cup 33x5, reproduction in modern colors, 6", ea........................**20.00**

Seiberling, Sealed-Aire, 760-15, clear insert, 5⅞".............**20.00**

Automobilia

Many are fascinated with vintage automobiles, but to own one of those 'classy chassis' is a luxury not all can afford! So instead they enjoy collecting related memorabilia such as advertising, owners' manuals, horns, emblems, and hood ornaments. The decade of the 1930s produced the items that are most in demand today, but the '50s models have their own band of devoted fans as well as do the muscle cars of the '60s.

Ashtray, Ford, shield logo in red & white on clear glass, sq, NM...............................**20.00**

Badge, chauffeur; Manitoba, 1922, VG+...............................**25.00**

Bank, Ford, shaggy dog figure w/Ford collar, Florence Ceramics, 8", EX...........**45.00**

Banner, North Bay Corvette Association, black on yellow, 13½x9"..........................**24.00**

Blotter, Dodge Brothers Trucks, 1929, 9x4", EX...............**35.00**

Book, Dodge Dynasty, Latham & Agresta, 1st edition, VG+.**15.00**

Book, My Days w/the Diesel, Clessie Cummins, 1967, EX (VG dust jacket)...........**160.00**

Book, 75 Years of Chevrolet, Dammann, 1986, EX.....**30.00**

Booklet, Lincoln V-8 Engine, 1950, 12 pages, EX.................**10.00**

Brochure, Aston Martin DB44, 1960s, 9x6", EX.............**35.00**

Brochure, Buick, 1955, 20 pages, VG.....................................**30.00**

Brochure, Lincoln Quick Facts, 1950s, 12 pages, VG......**12.00**

Brochure, 1916 Cadillac, worn cover, 32 pages, VG.....**120.00**

Calender, Nash, 1951, complete, EX.....................................**10.00**

Catalog, Alco/American Locomotive Co, 1913, 32 pages, EX.**350.00**

Chart, Tune-Up, 1956 Cadillac Eldorado, EX.................**25.00**

Clock, Packard, neon, 21" dia, EX.....................................**725.00**

Coaster/ashtray, Graham, aluminum, 3⅛" dia, EX **30.00**

Crank, Ford Model A, G **35.00**

Emblem, 1955 Ford Pickup, M in weathered box, $45.00. (Photo courtesy Chuck and Zandra Harral)

Emblem, BMW Isetta, 2⅜" dia, VG+ **25.00**

Emblem, Federal Knight, 1924-27, VG **150.00**

Emblem, hood; Cadillac, 1960s, EX **40.00**

Emblem, Pacific Coast Automobile Association, brass w/enamel, 3x4" **60.00**

Emblem, radiator; Cadillac, 1920s, 2⅛" dia, EX **150.00**

Emblem, radiator; Hupmobile 8, enamel, 1930s, 2⅛" dia, VG **120.00**

Emblem, radiator; 1920s Auburn, VG **50.00**

Gauge, gapping; Goodell-Pratt, from .005 to .010, VG **8.00**

Gauge, gapping; Millers Falls, VG- **12.00**

Gauge, tire; A Schrader's Son...NY EX **20.00**

Gearshift knob, glass w/brown & tan swirls, 2" dia, EX **50.00**

Handbook, Steam Turbines, 1924 Power Plant Engineering; 112 pages, VG **14.00**

Horn, Spartan SOS Deluxe, 6-volt, 16" L, EX **60.00**

Hubcaps, 1955 Oldsmobile, EX, pr **15.00**

Key case, Olds/Renault, brown leather, logo, 1960s, EX **5.00**

Key chain, '66 Olds Super Salesman, EX **15.00**

Key holder, Dodge, enameled logo on leather, EX **15.00**

Lapel pin, Rambler, metal, 2⅛x⅝", EX **20.00**

License plate frame topper, AAA, plastic w/aluminum back, 4¾x3½" ....:.**40.00**

Lighter, Downtown Ford Sales w/1950s-60s emblem, Zippo type, EX **20.00**

Lock & keys, Ford in script on brass padlock & 2 keys, 3x2x1", VG **70.00**

Manual, owner's; Buick, 1949, EX **30.00**

Manual, owner's; Cadillac Eldorado, 1979, EX..........**8.00**

Manual, owner's; Corvette, 1957, EX **180.00**

Manual, owner's; Corvette, 1965, EX **90.00**

Manual, owner's; Ford Mustang, 1967, EX **30.00**

Manual, owner's; Lincoln Continental, 1968, EX...**20.00**

Manual, owner's; 1932 Cadillac V-16, VG..........................**350.00**

Manual, owner's; 1940 Hudson, EX **30.00**

Manual, owner's; 1974 AMC Gremlin/Hornet/Javelin, EX **15.00**

Manual, service; Chevy Vega, 1972, EX **12.00**

Medallion, AAA, Cincinnati, some wear & repaint, 3x4½" ..**25.00**

Motometer, Boyce, VG..........**60.00**
Pamphlet, Buick, 1967, VG....**6.00**
Pin, Cadillac Craftsman, gold w/logo, 1947, EX **35.00**
Playing cards, Pontiac Sales & Service, 2 complete decks, EXIB **30.00**
Postcard, Buick Roadmaster, 1955, G **7.00**
Postcard, Dodge Brothers, Kind to Pocketbooks, 1930s, NM..**7.00**
Postcard, Kaiser-Darrin, 1953, lady standing admiring car, NM **20.00**

Poster, Chevrolet Impala, cardboard, 20½x34½", VG, $35.00. (Photo courtesy B.J. Summers)

Radiator cap, whippet dog figure, 4" L, EX **130.00**
Ruler, Chevrolet, celluloid, 1930s, 6", M **28.00**
Ruler, 1938 Pontiac, Indian head front w/new features on back, 15", VG **20.00**
Shoehorn, 1979 Chevrolet Theme Line, bow-tie logo, plastic, EX **8.00**
Sign, Effecto Auto Finishes, 7" dia, VG....................................**35.00**
Speedometer, Corbin Indian/Harley, 100 MPH, EX................**1,000.00**
Stock certificate, Studebaker-Packard, 100 shares, 1957, cancelled, EX.................**20.00**

Tape measure, Desoto Six, Product of Chrysler, 1½", EX......**50.00**
Token, 1955 General Motors Motorama, VG................**18.00**
Windshield scraper, Pontiac, 1957 ....**6.00**
Wrench, hubcap; Dodge Brothers, VG...................................**10.00**
Wrench, open end; Cadillac, marked Cadillac #3933, 6", VG.....................................**80.00**
Wrench, open end; Maxwell #1, 4⅞", VG **20.00**

Autumn Leaf

Autumn Leaf dinnerware was a product of the Hall China Company, who produced this extensive line from 1933 until 1978 for exclusive distribution by the Jewell Tea Company. The Libbey Glass Company made co-ordinating pitchers, tumblers, and stemware. Metal, cloth, plastic, and paper items were also available. Today, though very rare pieces are expensive and a challenge to acquire, new collectors may easily reassemble an attractive, usable set at a reasonable price. Hall has produced special club pieces (for the NALCC) as well as some limited editions for an Ohio company, but these are well marked and easily identified as such. Refer to *The Collector's Encyclopedia of Hall China* by Margaret and Kenn Whitmyer (Collector Books) for more information.

See Clubs and Newsletters for information concerning the *Autumn Leaf* newsletter.

Apron, oilcloth, from $600 to.**1,000.00**
Baker, French; 2-pt.............**175.00**
Blanket, Vellux, Autumn Leaf color, king size **200.00**
Book, Autumn Leaf Story.....**50.00**
Bowl, cream soup.................**35.00**
Bowl, fruit; 5½".......................**6.00**
Bowl, mixing; New Metal, 3-pc set **325.00**
Bowl, salad; 9".......................**20.00**
Bowl, vegetable; divided, Royal Glasbake, milk white ..**130.00**

Bowl, vegetable; oval, with lid, from $50.00 to $70.00.

Bowl lids, plastic, 8-pc set..**125.00**
Bread box, metal, from $400 to.**800.00**
Butter dish, ruffled lid, regular, ¼-lb, from $175 to............**250.00**
Calendar, 1920s-30s, from $100 to....................**200.00**
Canister, brown & gold **25.00**
Canister, copper top, 4-pc set, from $600 to.....................**1,200.00**
Casserole, w/lid, oval, Heatflow clear glass, Dunbar, 1½-qt, $50 to.............................**75.00**
Clock, electric, #11D831.....**550.00**
Coaster, metal, 3⅛" **8.00**
Coffeepot, electric percolator, all china, 4-pc....................**400.00**
Creamer & sugar bowl, Rayed, 1930s style.....................**80.00**
Cup, coffee; Jewell's Best **25.00**
Cup, St Denis.......................**37.50**

Dutch oven, metal & porcelain, w/lid, 5-qt.....................**160.00**
Gravy boat.............................**25.00**
Hot pad, metal back, round, 7¼", from $15 to.....................**25.00**
Lamp, hurricane; pr, minimum value...........................**500.00**

Marmalade, three-piece set, from $100.00 to $125.00.

Mug, Irish coffee.................**120.00**
Place mats, set of 8, from $150 to...................................**325.00**
Plate, cake; metal stand.....**180.00**
Plate, salad; 7¼", from $5 to .**10.00**
Plate, scarce, 8".....................**18.00**
Platter, oval, 13½" **28.00**
Playing cards, Autumn Leaf, double deck.........................**175.00**
Pressure cooker, Mary Dunbar, metal.............................**175.00**
Shelf liner, plastic...............**125.00**
Sifter, metal **400.00**
Stem, sherbet; gold & frosted on clear, footed, Libbey, 6½-oz..........**68.00**
Tablecloth, plastic, 54x54" .**135.00**
Teapot, Aladdin, from $50 to.**80.00**
Thermos, picnic jug.............**350.00**
Toy, Jewel Tea truck, green, from $350 to...........................**425.00**
Tray, coffee service; oval, 18¾".**100.00**
Tray, wood & glass **145.00**
Tumbler, Brockway, 13-oz....**45.10**

Tumbler, iced tea; frosted, Libbey,
5½" 20.00
Vase, bud; regular decal.....**250.00**

Banks

After the Depression, everyone was aware that saving 'for a
rainy day' would help during bad
times. Children of the '40s, '50s,
and '60s were given piggy banks in
forms of favorite characters to
reinforce the idea of saving. They
were made to realize that by saving money they could buy that
expensive bicycle or a toy they
were particularly longing for.

Today on the flea market cir-
cuit, figural banks are popular
collectibles, especially those that
are character-related — advertising characters and Disney in
particular.

Interest in glass banks has
recently grown by leaps and
bounds, and you'll be amazed at
the prices some of the harder-to-
find examples are bringing.
Charlie Reynolds has written the
glass bank 'bible,' called *Collector's
Guide to Glass Banks*, which you'll
want to read if you think you'd like
to collect them. It's published by
Collector Books. In our listings,
the glass banks we've included will
have punched factory slots or
molded, raised slots. There are
other types as well. Because of
limited space, values listed below
are mid range. Expect to pay as
much as 50% more or less than our
suggested prices.

Ceramic

Adult dog w/pups on books, porce-
lain, overpainted, ca 1930,
Japan, 5" **125.00**
Big-eyed man, low-fired pottery, ca
1930, Mexican, 6⅝".......**125.00**
Black & white cat, porcelain, ca
1930, Japan, 5" **100.00**
Black baby in washtub, pottery, ca
1930, US (?), 4" **175.00**
Black woman w/apron, pottery, ca
1940, US.......................**100.00**
Chicken on nest w/chicks, pottery, ca
1930(?), Guatemala, 3⅜".**125.00**
Dachshund, pottery, ca 1930, US
(?) **150.00**
Dutch boy, pottery, ca 1930,
Germany.......................**175.00**
Ebisu, god of fishermen, pottery,
ca 1930, Japan, 4¼".....**200.00**
Egg man w/green cap, pottery, ca
1940, US, 3¾" **100.00**
Egg man w/red cap, porcelain, ca
1930, Japan (?).............**100.00**
Elephant in tutu, pottery, ca 1940,
US **80.00**
Flowered elephant, porcelain, ca 1950,
Occupied Japan, 2¼"...........**85.00**
Girl's head, pottery, ca 1935, US
(?), 3⅞"..........................**100.00**
John Howard 1726-1790 Famed
Humanitarian, pottery, ca
1940-50, 8¾" **125.00**
King on throne, pottery, ca 1930,
US (?), 5" **150.00**
Maneki-Neko, pottery, ca 1930,
Japan, 5⅜" **350.00**
Mechanical cat, pottery, ca 1940,
Japan, 5" **300.00**
Oriental children, at plum bank,
porcelain, ca 1930, China (?),
3¾" **200.00**

Pig with bow, multicolor, USA, ca 1940, from $35.00 to $40.00. (Photo courtesy Tom and Loretta Stoddard)

Pig in counting house, porcelain, ca 1930, Germany, 3¼".....**100.00**

Scottie, pottery, ca 1935, US Tudor Potteries, Hollywood Ware, 4¾"..............................**200.00**

Snarling cat, pottery, ca 1935, US (?), 5⅛"..........................**100.00**

Stylized horse, porcelain, ca 1950, Occupied Japan, 3¼".....**80.00**

Trumpeting elephant, pottery, ca 1935, US (?), 5½"..........**80.00**

Glass

Baseball shape, clear w/gold tin lid, 3¼" dia, from $15 to.......**35.00**

Be Wise Owl, dark amber, Anchor Hocking, 6⅞", from $150 to..**300.00**

Ben Franklin Kite Experiment, purple, flask shape, 7¾".**25.00**

Boston Braves, baseball shape, white w/red letters, black base, 3½".....................**110.00**

Bunco Bucks, clear w/white plastic lid w/bear & 3 red dice, 6¼"....**25.00**

Canadian Bear w/hat, Archer & Archer Bath Scents, 6¼", from $35 to..............................**75.00**

Coal & Coke Oven, light green to amber, Coal & Coke Museum, 4⅝"..................................**55.00**

Girl-face jar, tin lid, heavy paper eyes & mouth, 4⅛", from $35 to.**75.00**

Honey Money Bear, clear w/plastic straw hat, red bow tie w/gold band..............................**100.00**

Lucky Barrel, clear w/embossed letters, raised slot, 4⅜", from $15 to.............................**35.00**

Mississippi Mud, Black & Tan Beer, plastic on glass bottom, 8¾".................................**25.00**

Pig Change Holder, clear pig figural w/cream plastic lid, 10¼"..............................**110.00**

Save For a Rainy Day, milk bottle shape, lid w/lock, 8¾", from $35 to...................**75.00**

Teddy Bear w/Bow Tie, seated, pink or clear, 6¼", from $75 to.................................**150.00**

Character Related

Andy Panda, cardboard, 1948, 6", EX....................................**30.00**

Baba Looey, plastic figure, 1960s, 9", EX..............................**35.00**

Batman, ceramic figural, 1966, EX **40.00**

Benny the Ball (Top Cat), ceramic figural, NM....................**65.00**

Betty Boop, figural, Japan, 7", MIB..................................**45.00**

Big Bird, plastic figure sitting on nest, 8", NM...................**15.00**

Bozo the Clown, plastic, 1972, NM **35.00**

Bullwinkle, clock bank, Larami, 1969, MOC **50.00**

Care Bears, Wish Bear on Star, composition, NM............**20.00**

Daffy Duck, painted metal figure standing by barrel, 4¼", NM..**85.00**

Donald Duck, Ucago, 1960s, MIB .**55.00**

Flintstones, Fred, hard plastic, Homecraft, 14", M..........**75.00**

Flintstones, Pebbles, vinyl figure sleeping, EX+ **25.00**

Huckleberry Hound, plastic, 1960, 10", EX............................**35.00**

Humpty Dumpty, litho tin figure, 5", EX..............................**50.00**

Li'l Abner, composition, Capp Enterprises, 1975, 7", M.**100.00**

Little Lulu, plastic figure, Play Pal Plastics, 7½", NM **50.00**

Marvin the Martian, Warner Bros, Made in China, 1994, M.**24.00**

Mickey Mouse in Car, multicolor ceramic figural, marked c Disney, Enesco, 4½", from $25.00 to $30.00. (Photo courtesy Jim and Beverly Mangus)

Miss Piggy, figural, Sigma, NM.**50.00**

Pac-Man, EX **20.00**

Peanuts, Lucy at desk, ceramic figural, NM.........................**30.00**

Planet of the Apes, Dr Zaius, Play Pal Plastics, 1967, 10", NM......**30.00**

Popeye, Daily Dime, metal register, KFS, 1956, 2⅝" square, EX.................................**100.00**

Popeye, sitting w/spinach can, Alan Jay, 1958, 8"..........**75.00**

Raggedy Ann & Andy, ceramic figural, musical, 4½", NM .**20.00**

Roadrunner, composition figure, VG+................................**25.00**

Smiling Jack, clear glass w/unpainted face, 8½", from $150 to.........................**300.00**

Smiling Jack, frosted glass w/painted head, 8½", from $300 to.........................**600.00**

Snoopy, figural as tennis player, Hat Series, 4", M **30.00**

Superman, composition, Enesco, 1987, MIB.....................**85.00**

Woodstock, ceramic figural, 6", M.**15.00**

Yogi Bear, plastic, 14", EX...**35.00**

Ziggy, Tom Wilson Earthenware, from $35 to.....................**50.00**

Barbie Dolls

Barbie doll was first introduced in 1959, and soon Mattel found themselves producing not only dolls but tiny garments, fashion accessories, houses, cars, horses, books, and games as well. Today's Barbie doll collectors want them all. Though the early Barbie dolls are very hard to find, there are many of her successors still around. The trend today is toward Barbie doll exclusives — Holiday Barbie dolls and Bob Mackie Barbie dolls are all very 'hot' items. So are special-event Barbie dolls.

When buying the older dolls, you'll need to do a lot of studying and comparisons to learn to distinguish one Barbie doll from another, but this is the key to making sound buys and good investments. Remember, though, collectors are sticklers concerning condition; compared to a doll mint in box, they'll often give an additional 20% if that box has never been opened! If you want a good source for study, refer to one of these fine books: *Barbie Fashions, Volume I, II,* and *III,* by Sarah Sink Eames; *Collector's Encyclopedia of Barbie Doll Exclusives and More, Vol. II,* by J. Michael Augustyniak; *The Story of Barbie, Second Edition,* by Kitturah Westenhouser; *The Barbie Doll Years* by Patrick C. and Joyce L. Olds; *Barbie, the First 30 Years, Second Edition,* by Stephanie Deutsch; and *Schroeder's Collectible Toys, Antique to Modern* (Collector Books).

Dolls

Barbie, Scottish, 1981, Dolls of the World, MIB (box not shown), $125.00.

Allan, 1964, painted red hair, straight legs, MIB, from $125 to **150.00**

Allan, 1965, bendable legs, NRFB **550.00**

Barbie, #5, 1961, red hair, original swimsuit, NM..............**375.00**

Barbie, American Airline Stewardess, 1963, NRFB....................**700.00**

Barbie, Angel Lights, 1993, NRFB **100.00**

Barbie, Ballerina Barbie on Tour, 1976, NRFB.................**125.00**

Barbie, Bay Watch (Black or White), 1995, NRFB, ea .**20.00**

Barbie, Busy Barbie, 1972, NRFB **200.00**

Barbie, Children's Doctor, 2000, NRFB............................**20.00**

Barbie, Cool Times, 1989, NRFB.**25.00**

Barbie, Dinner at Eight, 1964, NRFB..........................**600.00**

Barbie, Dorothy (Wizard of Oz), 1999, NRFB...................**18.00**

Barbie, Easter Party, 1995, NRFB **20.00**

Barbie, Eskimo, 1982, Dolls of the World, NRFB **100.00**

Barbie, Feelin' Groovy, 1987, NRFB..........................**175.00**

Barbie, Glinda (Wizard of Oz), 2000, NRFB...................**25.00**

Barbie, Great Shape (Black), 1984, NRFB..........................**25.00**

Barbie, Holiday, 1990, NRFB.**200.00**

Barbie, Holiday, 1993, NRFB.**175.00**

Barbie, Island Fun, 1988, NRFB..**20.00**

Barbie, Knitting Pretty (pink), 1964, NRFB **1,265.00**

Barbie, Lights 'n Lace, 1991, NRFB............................**30.00**

Barbie, Malt Shop, 1993, Toys R Us, NRFB **35.00**

Barbie, My First Barbie, 1981, NRFB............................**25.00**

Barbie, Nutcracker, 1992, Musical Ballet Series, NRFB **165.00**

Barbie, Oreo Fun, 1997, NRFB.**35.00**

Barbie, Peach Pretty, 1989, K-Mart, MIB **35.00**

Barbie, Phantom of the Opera, 1998, FAO Schwarz, NRFB......**150.00**

Barbie, Pink Sensation, 1990, Winn Dixie, NRFB........**25.00**

Barbie, Polly Pockets, 1994, Hill's, NRFB.............................**20.00**

Barbie, Quick Curl Miss America, 1976, MIB.....................**125.00**

Barbie, Rockettes, 1993, FAO Schwarz, NRFB...........**120.00**

Barbie, Safari, 1998, Disney, NRFB..............................**30.00**

Barbie, Scottish, 1981, Dolls of the World, NRFB **140.00**

Barbie, Snap 'n Play, 1992, NRFB .**20.00**

Barbie, Songbird, 1996, NRFB.**25.00**

Barbie, Super Star, 1979, NRFB .**25.00**

Barbie, Swan Lake Ballerina, 1991, NRFB.................**200.00**

Barbie, Swirl Ponytail, 1964, platinum hair, NRFB......**1,300.00**

Barbie, Ten Speeder, 1973, NRFB.**30.00**

Barbie, Twirly Curls, 1983, MIB.**45.00**

Barbie, Unicef, 1989, NRFB.**20.00**

Barbie, Yuletide Romance, 1996, Hallmark, NRFB **30.00**

Christie, Beauty Secrets, 1980, MIB................................**60.00**

Christie, Kissing, 1979, MIB.**65.00**

Christie, Sunsational Malibu, 1982, NRFB....................**30.00**

Francie, Busy, 1972, NRFB.**425.00**

Ginger, Growing Up, 1977, MIB.**95.00**

Kelly, Quick Curl, 1972, NRFB .**175.00**

Ken, Busy, with Holdin' Hands, 1972, NRFB, $175.00. (Photo courtesy Sara Sink Eames)

Ken, Arabian Nights, 1964, NRFB .**420.00**

Ken, Crystal, 1984, NRFB ...**40.00**

Ken, Hawaiian, 1979, MIB...**45.00**

Ken, Jewel Secrets, 1987, NRFB .**40.00**

Ken, Live Action, 1971, NRFB .**100.00**

Ken, Ocean Friends, 1996, NRFB.**20.00**

Ken, Sport & Shave, 1980, MIB..**40.00**

Ken, Superstar, 1977, MIB ..**95.00**

Ken, Western, 1982, MIB.....**35.00**

Midge, Ski Fun, Toys R US, 1990, MIB (box not shown), $30.00.

PJ, Deluxe Quick Curl, 1976, MIB..**65.00**

PJ, Gold Medal Gymnast, 1975, NRFB............................**120.00**

PJ, Malibu, 1978, MIB **55.00**

PJ, Sunsational Malibu, 1982, MIB................................**40.00**

Scott, Skipper's boyfriend, 1980, MIB................................**55.00**

Skipper, Music Lovin', 1985, NRFB............................**65.00**

Skipper, Super Teen, 1980, NRFB **35.00**

Skipper, Western, 1982, NRFB.**40.00**

Stacey, Twist 'n Turn, 1968, blond hair, NRFB..................**900.00**

Teresa, All American, 1991, MIB.**25.00**

Whitney, Nurse, 1987, NRFB.**80.00**

Cases

Barbie, Francie, Casey & Tutti, hard plastic, EX, from $50 to **75.00**

Barbie, 1961, red vinyl, pictured in 4 different outfits, EX, $30 to .**40.00**

Barbie, 1967, wearing All That Jazz surrounded by flowers, from $30 to **40.00**

Barbie & Stacey, 1967, vinyl, NM, from $65 to **75.00**

Barbie Goes Travelin', vinyl, rare, NM................................**100.00**

Barbie on Madison Avenue, FAO Schwarz, 1992, black w/pink handle, M **25.00**

Circus Star Barbie, FAO Schwarz, 1995, M...........................**25.00**

Fashion Queen Barbie, 1963, red vinyl, w/mirror & wig stand, EX................................**100.00**

Skipper and Skooter, made in France, blue or yellow background, EX, $100.00 each. (Photo courtesy Stefanie Deutsch)

Clothing and Accessories

Barbie, Brunch Time, #1628, 1965, complete, NM **125.00**

Barbie, Cloud Nine, #1489, 1969-70, complete, M............**200.00**

Barbie, Disco Dazzle, #1011, 1979, NRFB.............................**15.00**

Barbie, Fashion Luncheon, #1656, complete, EX...............**450.00**

Barbie, Flying Colors, #3492, 1972, complete, M........**300.00**

Barbie, Galaxy A Go-Go, #2742, 1986, NRFB....................**30.00**

Barbie, Graduation, #945, 1963, NRFB.............................**60.00**

Barbie, Jumpin' Jeans, Pak, 1964, NRFB.............................**85.00**

Barbie, Madras Mod, #3485, 1972, complete, M, $100.00.

Barbie, Madras Plaid, #3485, 1972, NRFB.................**120.00**

Barbie, Overall Denim, #3488, 1972, NRFB.................**110.00**

Barbie, Perfectly Pink, #4805, 1984, NRFB....................**10.00**

Barbie, Red Flair, #939, 1962, NRFB...........................**175.00**

Barbie, Sharp Shift, #20, 1970, NRFB...........................**110.00**

Barbie, Skin Diver, #1608, 1964, NRFB...........................**135.00**

Barbie, Teachers, #9085, 1985, NRFB...............................**5.00**

Barbie, Two-Way Tiger, #3402, 1971, NRFB.................**110.00**

Barbie, Yellow Go, #1816, 1967, NRFB...........................**800.00**

Francie, Calm Diggers, #1258, 1966, NRFB..................**185.00**

Francie, Hip Knits, #1265, 1966, NRFB............................**225.00**

Francie, Merry-Go-Rounders, #3446, 1971, NRFB **125.00**

Francie, Two for the Ball, #1232, MOC **225.00**

Julia, Brrr-Furrr, #1752, 1969, NRFB.............................**175.00**

Ken, Going Bowling, #1403, 1964, NRFB..............................**85.00**

Ken, Outdoor Man, #1406, 1980, NRFB..............................**15.00**

Midge, Orange Blossom, #987, 1967, NRFB....................**75.00**

Skipper, Goin' Sleddin', #3475, 1971, NRFB....................**75.00**

Skipper, Skating Fun, #1908, NRFB............................**175.00**

Skipper, Velvet Blush, #1737, 1970, NRFB....................**85.00**

Barbie Cookin' Fun Kitchen, MIB.............................**50.00**

Barbie Dream Bed & Nightstand, 1984, pink, MIB.............**25.00**

Barbie Dream House Kitchen Set, 1981, MIB........................**6.00**

Barbie's Apartment, 1975, MIB.**140.00**

Francie's House, 1966, complete, M...................................**150.00**

Go-Together Couch, 1964, MIB.**30.00**

Ice Capades Skating Rink, 1989, MIB.................................**70.00**

Magical Mansion, 1989, MIB.**125.00**

Skipper Dream Room, 1964, MIB.**300.00**

Suprise House, 1972, MIB .**100.00**

Susy Goose Ken Wardrobe, M.**50.00**

Tutti Playhouse, 1966, M...**100.00**

Gift Sets

Ballerina Barbie on Tour, 1976, MIB.............................**175.00**

Houses, Furnishings, and Vehicles

Barbie's Lively Livin' Room, MIB, $50.00. (Photo courtesy Paris and Susan Manos)

Barbie & Ken Little Theatre, 1964, complete, NMIB...........**600.00**

Barbie & the Rockers Dance Cafe, 1987, MIB.......................**50.00**

Barbie High Stepper Western Gift Set, 1995, NRFB, $100.00. (Photo courtesy J. Michael Augustyniak)

Barbie Loves Elvis, 1996, NRFB.**75.00**

Barbie's Olympic Ski Villiage, MIB.................................**75.00**

Dance Sensation Barbie, 1985, MIB.................................**35.00**

Happy Birthday Barbie, 1985, NRFB.............................**50.00**

Loving You Barbie, 1984, MIB.**75.00**

Malibu Barbie Fashion Combo, 1978, NRFB....................**80.00**

Pretty Pairs Nan 'n Fran, 1970, NRFB............................**250.00**

Superstar Barbie & Ken, 1978, MIB..............................**175.00**

Travelin' Sisters, 1995, NRFB.**70.00**

Contempo, teapot, beige **65.00**

Gloss Pastel Kitchenware, bowl, mixing; any color, #24, from $30 to............................**40.00**

Gloss Pastel Kitchenware, pitcher, ice water; pink, 2-qt, 6½x10" **95.00**

Bauer

The Bauer Company moved from Kentucky to California in 1909, producing crocks, gardenware, and vases until after the Depression when they introduced their first line of dinnerware. From 1932 until the early 1960s, they successfully marketed several lines of solid-color wares that are today very collectible. Some of their most popular lines are Ring, Plain Ware, and Monterey Modern. Refer to *The Collector's Encyclopedia of Bauer Pottery* by Jack Chipman (Collector Books) for more information.

Gloss Pastel Kitchenware, teapot, Aladdin, any color, eight-cup, from $160.00 to $200.00. (Photo courtesy Jack Chipman)

Brusche Al Fresco, bowl, fruit; speckled or solid, 5", from $10 to.....................................**12.00**

Brusche Al Fresco, mug, handled, solid colors, 8-oz, ea.......**10.00**

Brusche Al Fresco, plate, dinner; gray, 10" **10.00**

Cal-Art, flowerpot, Swirl #3, glossy, 3", from $20 to ...**25.00**

Cal-Art, swan, white matt, medium size, 9"......................**65.00**

Cal-Art, vase, 'Robot Midget,' burgundy, 4" **35.00**

Contempo, cup & saucer, Spice Green **12.00**

Hi-Fire, mixing bowl set, various colors, 4-pc, from $150 to.....**200.00**

Hi-Fire, Spanish pot #5, glossy white, 5" **35.00**

Hi-Fire, vase, chartreuse, #10 Stock..............................**125.00**

Hi-Fire, vase, garden; Fred Johnson, 18", minimum value........**750.00**

Hi-Fire, vase, Ring, cylinder, 10", from $125 to.................**175.00**

La Linda, bowl, cereal; from $15 to....................................**30.00**

La Linda, cup & saucer, from $35 to **45.00**

La Linda, cup & saucer, jumbo; glossy green....................**45.00**

La Linda, gravy boat, glossy colors, ea **25.00**

Matt Carlton, bowl, jade green, 3x6" sq **85.00**

Matt Carlton, vase, Carnation, jade green, 10" **350.00**

Monterey, cup & saucer, from $18 to **25.00**

Monterey, custard cup, orange-red **65.00**

Monterey, teapot, old style, 6-cup **85.00**

Monterey Moderne, teapot, 6-cup, from $65 to **95.00**

Oil jar, jade green, 16", minimum value **850.00**

Plain Ware, bean pot, individual, from $135 to **185.00**

Plain Ware, bowl, mixing; yellow, #3, 2-gallon...................**175.00**

Plain Ware, coffee server ...**115.00**

Plain Ware, ramekin, from $15 to................................**25.00**

Ring, ashtray, 4", from $65 to .**90.00**

Ring, bowl, low salad; light blue, 9"......................................**60.00**

Ring, carafe, orange-red, w/copper raffia-wrapped handle.....................**120.00**

Ring, coffee server, wooden handle, six-cup, from $75.00 to $100.00.

Ring, creamer & sugar bowl, midget...........................**250.00**

Ring, cup & saucer, cobalt....**50.00**

Ring, plate, dessert; Chinese yellow, 6½" **15.00**

Ring, plate, dinner; jade green, 9½"....................................**35.00**

Ring, salt & pepper shakers, jade green, squat style, pr.....**45.00**

Ring, sherbet, from $100 to.**150.00**

Ring, tumbler, cobalt, no handle, 12-oz **50.00**

Speckled Kitchenware, casserole, pink, 1½-qt, w/frame **40.00**

Speckled Kitchenware, Pelican pitcher, blue, 20-oz **45.00**

Speckled Kitchenware, teapot, Monterey Moderne style, green..............................**45.00**

Beanie Babies

Though everyone agrees Beanie Babies are on the downside of their highest peak, they're still a force to deal with, and you'll find Beanie Baby tables by the score in any large flea market field. New ones are being still being cranked out, thanks to collector demand — most of these current Beanies are valued at $5.00 to $7.00 or less, but a few are a little higher. See *Schroeder's Collectible Toys, Antique to Modern* or *Garage Sale and Flea Market Annual* for a comprehensive listing of retired Beanies as well as information on hang tags. (Both are published by Collector Books.) All of those we've listed here are retired; values reflect examples in mint condition.

Ally the Alligator, #4032 ......**35.00**

Almond the Bear, #4246, from $5 to **7.00**

Ants the Anteater, #4195, from $5 to **7.00**

Aurora the Polar Bear, #4271, from $5 to **7.00**

Baldy the Eagle, #4074, from $6 to **12.00**

Batty the Bat, #4035, pink or tie-dyed, from $5 to **8.00**

Beak the Kiwi Bird, #4211, from $5 to **7.00**

Bernie the St Bernard, #4109, from $5 to **8.00**

Blackie the Bear, #4011, from $8 to **20.00**

Blizzard the Tiger, #4163, white, from $9 to **13.00**

Brownie the Bear, #4010, w/swing tag, minimum value **1,500.00**

Bruno the Terrier, #4183, from $5 to **7.00**

Bucky the Beaver, #4016, from $10 to **15.00**

Bushy the Lion, #4285, from $5 to **7.00**

Canyon the Cougar, #4212, from $5 to **8.00**

Cassie the Collie, #4380, from $5 to **8.00**

Cheezer the Mouse, #4301, from $6 to **10.00**

Chilly the Polar Bear, #4012, minimum value **550.00**

Chipper the Chipmunk, #4259, from $5 to **7.00**

Chocolate the Moose, #4015, from $8 to **12.00**

Chops the Lamb, #4019, from $40 to **75.00**

Claude the Crab, #4083, tie-dyed, from $5 to **8.00**

Coral the Fish, #4079, tie-dyed, minimum value..............**40.00**

Crunch the Shark, #4130, from $5 to **7.00**

Curly the Bear, #4052, brown, from $8 to **10.00**

Dart the Blue Dart Frog, #4352 .**7.00**

Digger the Crab, #4027, 2nd issue, red, minimum value **25.00**

Doby the Doberman, #4110, from $6 to **10.00**

Doodle the Rooster, #4171, tie-dyed, from $6 to **10.00**

Early the Robin, #4190, from $5 to **7.00**

Ears the Rabbit, #4018, brown, from $10 to **20.00**

Eggbert the Baby Chick, #4232, from $5 to **7.00**

Ewey the Lamb, #4219, from $5 to **7.00**

Flash the Dolphin, #4021, minimum value **30.00**

Flashy the Peacock, #4339, from $8 to **10.00**

Flip the Cat, #4012, white, from $15 to **30.00**

Float the Butterfy, #4343, from $5 to **8.00**

Flutter the Butterfly, #4043, tie-dyed, minimum value..**300.00**

Frigid the King Penguin, #4270, from $6 to **8.00**

Frills the Hornbill Bird, #4367, from $6 to **10.00**

Garcia the Bear, #4051, tie-dyed, from $80 to **125.00**

Glory the Bear, #4188, from $15 to **20.00**

Gobbles the Turkey, #4034, $5.00 to $7.00. (Photo courtesy Amy Sullivan)

Goldie the Goldfish, #4023, from $15 to **30.00**

Gracie the Swan, #4126, from $5 to **8.00**

Groovy the Bear, #4256, from $5 to **7.00**

Grunt the Razorback Pig, #4092, red, minimum value **45.00**

Halo II the Angel Bear, #4269, from $7 to **10.00**

Happy the Hippo, #4061, gray, minimum value............**225.00**

Hippity the Bunny, #4119, mint green, from $7 to............**10.00**

Hissy the Snake, #4185, from $5 to **7.00**

Hoot the Owl, #4073, from $20 to **30.00**

Hoppity the Bunny, #4117, pink, from $6 to **10.00**

Hornsly the Triceratops, #4345, from $5 to **7.00**

Howl the Wolf, #4310, from $5 to **10.00**

Iggy the Iguana, #4038, all issues, from $6 to **8.00**

Jake the Mallard Duck, #4199, from $5 to **7.00**

Jolly the Walrus, #4082, from $5 to **7.00**

Kicks the Soccer Bear, #4229, from $6 to **8.00**

Kiwi the Toucan, #4070, minimum value **55.00**

Kuku the Cockatoo, #4192, from $5 to **7.00**

Lips the Fish, #4254, from $5 to .**7.00**

Lizzy the Lizard, #4033, tie-dyed, minimum value............**275.00**

Loosy the Canadian Goose, #4206, from $5 to **7.00**

Lurkey the Turkey, #4309, from $5 to **8.00**

Magic the Dragon, #4088, from $30 to **45.00**

Manny the Manatee, #4081, minimum value **45.00**

Mel the Koala Bear, #4162, from $5 to **7.00**

Morrie the Eel, #4282, from $5 to **7.00**

Mr the Groom Bear, #4363, from $5 to **9.00**

Mrs the Bride Bear, #4364, from $5 to **9.00**

Nanook the Husky Dog, #4104, from $5 to **7.00**

Nectar the Hummingbird, #4361, from $30 to **40.00**

Nibbly the Rabbit, #4217, brown, from $5 to **8.00**

Nip the Cat, #4003, 2nd issue, all gold, minimum value...**350.00**

Nuts the Squirrel, #4114, from $5 to **7.00**

Oats the Horse, #4305, from $5 to.**8.00**

Paul the Walrus, #4248, from $5 to **7.00**

Pecan the Bear, #4251, from $5 to......................................**7.00**

Peekaboo the Turtle, #4303, from $5 to **8.00**

Peking the Panda Bear, #4013, minimum value............**450.00**

Pounce the Cat, #4122, brown, from $5 to **7.00**

Princess the Bear, #4300, from $10.00 to $15.00. (Photo courtesy Amy Sullivan)

Prince the Bullfrog, #4312, from $5 to **8.00**

Puffer the Puffin, #4181, from $5 to **7.00**

Pugsly the Pug Dog, #4106, from $5.00 to $8.00. (Photo courtesy Amy Sullivan)

Radar the Bat, #4091, minimum value **45.00**

Ringo the Raccoon, #4014, from $10 to **15.00**

Roary the Lion, #4069, from $6 to....................................**8.00**

Rover the Dog, #4101, red, from $10 to **15.00**

Roxie the Reindeer, #4334, red or black nose, from $7 to ...**10.00**

Sakura the Bear, Japan exclusive, minimum value..............**70.00**

Sammy the Bear, #4215, tie-dyed, from $5 to **7.00**

Scat the Cat, #4231, from $5 to.**7.00**

Scorch the Dragon, #4210, from $5 to **8.00**

Scurry the Beetle, #4281, from $5 to **7.00**

Seamore the Seal, #4029, white, minimum value..............**45.00**

Sheets the Ghost, #4260, from $5 to **7.00**

Silver the Cat, #4242, gray, from $6 to..................................**8.00**

Slayer the Frilled Dragon, #4307, from $5 to **7.00**

Slither the Snake, #4031, minimum value **600.00**

Smooch the Bear, #4335, from $15 to **20.00**

Sneaky the Leopard, #4278, from $6 to..................................**8.00**

Snip the Siamese Cat, #4120, from $5 to..................................**7.00**

Snowball the Snowman, #4201, from $8 to......................**12.00**

Snowgirl the Snowgirl, #4333, from $8 to......................**12.00**

Spangle the Bear, #4245, red, white or blue face, from $8 to ...**20.00**

Sparky the Dalmatian, #4100, minimum value..............**30.00**

Spike the Rhinoceros, #4060, from $5 to..................................**7.00**

Spinner the Spider, #4036, from $5 to..................................**7.00**

Splash the Whale, #4022, minimum value **30.00**

Spooky the Ghost, #4090, orange ribbon, minimum value...............................**20.00**

Springy the Bunny, #4272, lavender, from $5 to.................**7.00**

Squealer the Pig, #4005, from $10 to **20.00**

Stilts the Stork, #4221, from $5 to **7.00**

Sting the Stingray, #4077, tie-dyed, minimum value....**40.00**

Stinger the Scorpion, #4193, from $5 to..................................**7.00**

Sunny the e-Beanie Bear, yellow-orange, from $8 to.........**10.00**

Swirly the Snail, #4249, from $5 to **7.00**

Tabasco the Bull, #4002, red feet, minimum value..............**40.00**

Teddy Bear, #4050, brown, new face, from $40 to **50.00**

Teddy Bear, #4051, teal, new face, minimum value............**550.00**

Teddy Bear, #4052, cranberry, new face, minimum value **550.00**

Teddy Bear, #4057, jade, new face, minimum value............**550.00**

The Beginning Bear, #4267, w/silver stars, from $10 to **15.00**

The End Bear, #4265, black, from $10 to **15.00**

Trap the Mouse, #4042, minimum value **465.00**

Tusk the Walrus, #4076, from $35 to **40.00**

Unity the Bear, #4606, TY Europe exclusive, from $20 to....**25.00**

Valentino the Bear, #4058, white w/red heart, from $8 to..**12.00**

Velvet the Panther, #4064, from $12 to..............................**20.00**

Waves the Whale, #4084, from $6 to **8.00**

Web the Spider, #4041, black, minimum value **225.00**

Whisper the Deer, #4187, from $5 to **7.00**

Wrinkles the Bulldog, #4103, from $6 to **8.00**

Zero the Penguin, #4027, w/Santa hat, from $5 to **7.00**

Zodiac Dog, #4326, from $6 to ..**8.00**

Zodiac Dragon, #4322, from $6 to..**8.00**

The Beatles

Beatles memorabilia is becoming increasingly popular with those who grew up in the '60s. Almost any item that could be produced with their pictures or logos was manufactured and sold by the thousands in department stores. Some have such a high collector value that they have been reproduced, so beware!

Balloon, white & beige or pink, MIP (sealed), ea **75.00**

Banjo, Mastro, 22", EX (EX box)......................**3,000.00**

Beatlephones, Koss Electronics, EX (EX box) **2,000.00**

Board game, Hullabaloo, 1965, VG (VG box)........................**75.00**

Book, Apple to the Core, softcover, NM **10.00**

Button, EX/NM, $50.00; G, $35.00. (Photo courtesy Barbara Crawford, Hollis Lamon, and Michael Stern)

Chair, Yellow Submarine, inflatable vinyl, NM **50.00**

Coin holder, red rubber squeeze type, 2x3", VG+..............**75.00**

Coloring book, Saalfield, unused, EX **85.00**

Decals, black & orange on yellow, unused, set of 11............**90.00**

Dolls, w/metal stands, Applause, 1988, 22", set of 4, M...**450.00**

Fan club booklet, black & white photo on cover, 20 pages, 1970, EX..........................**30.00**

Fan club picture cube, cardboard w/Apple logo on top, M (EX mailer)............................**75.00**

Figures, 'Hey Jude,' lead w/cardboard backdrop, EX.....**100.00**

Figures, cartoon style, resin, 6", set of 4, EX...................**125.00**

Figures, cartoon style, resin, 12", set of 4, EX...................**225.00**

Figures, Swingers Music Set, NMOC **125.00**

Film, Live at Shea Stadium, 8mm, EX..................................**30.00**

Flasher rings, set of 4, EX....**80.00**

Guitar, Big Six by Selcol, rare, 6-string version, EX **650.00**

Guitar, Red Jet by Selcol, electric, rare, 31", NM **1,500.00**

Guitar strings, Hofner, NMIP..**80.00**

Headband, Love the Beatles, Betterwear USA, MIP .**60.00**

Key chain, flashes from photo to lettering, Hong Kong, 1960s, NM..................................**70.00**

Magazine, Beatles on Broadway, Whitman, 1964, EX **18.00**

Magazine, Official Yellow Submarine, 49 pages, VG......................**45.00**

Notebook (paper), group in doorway, Westab, 11x8½", unused, EX..................................**90.00**

Ornaments, hand-blown glass, 4 different, EX, ea...........**200.00**

Pen, various colors w/The Beatles & names in silver, VG+.............................**90.00**

Pencil-By-Number Coloring Set, Kitfix, 1964, complete, rare, MIB..........................**2,250.00**

Pennant, I Love the Beatles, white & yellow on red felt, 29", EX...............................**230.00**

Photo album, Sgt Pepper's Lonely Hearts Club Band, lg, EX..**425.00**

Pillow, waist-length group pose, VG................................**160.00**

Punch-Out Portraits, Whitman, unused, complete, M....**200.00**

Record case, Disk-Go-Case, plastic w/group photo, brown, EX.**175.00**

Spatter toy, rare, 16", MIP.**380.00**

Squirt gun, yellow plastic submarine, 1960s, 6", EX.........**40.00**

Sunglasses, John Lennon, black, gold or silver frames, EX, ea **5.00**

Wig, Lowell, MIP (sealed)..**125.00**

Tray, multicolor with musical notes and star border, Great Britain, 13" square, VG, $50.00. (Beware of reproductions.) (Photo courtesy Bob Gottuso)

Beer Cans

Beer has been sold in cans since 1935, when the Continental Can Company developed a method of coating the inside of the can with plastic. The first style was the flat top that came with instructions on how to open it. Because most breweries were not equipped to fill a flat can, most went to the 'cone top,' but by the 1950s, even that was obsolete. Can openers were the order of the day until the 1960s, when tabtop cans came along. The heyday of beer can collecting was during the 1970s, but the number of collectors has since receded, leaving a huge supply of beer cans, most of which are worth no more than a few dollars each. The basic rule of thumb is to concentrate your collecting on cans made prior to 1970. Remember, condition is critical.

Values are based on cans in conditions as stated.

Bank top, Rod Schoen Dienst, Anheuser-Busch Inc, St Louis MO, 1970s, M.................**30.00**
Cone top, Becker's Beer, Unita Club, horse & cowboy, EX.......**250.00**
Cone top, Bergoff Beer, low profile, EX...................................**95.00**
Cone top, Breunig's Beer, VG.**110.00**
Cone top, Carling's Ale, EX.**110.00**
Cone top, Carling's Black Label, EX...................................**110.00**
Cone top, CB Fauerbach, Centennial Brew, Madison WI, EX.........................**175.00**
Cone top, Champagne Pilsner, Johnson Brewery, Lomira WI, EX...................................**195.00**
Cone top, Champagne Velvet Beer, CV, VG+ **75.00**
Cone top, E&B Special Beer, Detroit MI, EX.............**75.00**

Cone top, Falstaff, flat bottom, EX **65.00**
Cone top, Schmidt's Select, St Paul MN, EX.........................**120.00**
Cone top, Walter's Pilsner, Eau Claire WI, VG **195.00**
Flat top, Atlas Prager Beer, Atlas Brewing, Chicago IL, 1950s, EX...................................**30.00**
Flat top, Croft Cream Ale, Boston MA, VG+.......................**65.00**
Flat top, Falls City Beer, Louisville KY, EX-.........**70.00**
Flat top, Friar's Ale, South Bend IN, EX............................**30.00**
Flat top, Grand Prize Beer, Gulf Brewing, Houston TX, 1950s, EX...................................**45.00**
Flat top, Harvard, Export Green Label, Harvard, Lowell MA, EX...................................**70.00**
Flat top, Iron City Beer, Pittsburgh PA, EX.........**25.00**
Flat top, Krueger Beer, Cranston RI, VG............................**35.00**
Flat top, Manheim Beer, Reading PA, VG............................**20.00**
Flat top, Meister Brau, Fiesta, Peter Hand, Chicago IL, EX **275.00**
Flat top, Mile Hi Life, Tivoli Brewing, Denver, 1950s, EX..............**48.00**
Flat top, Nine-O-Five, Chicago IL, VG...................................**30.00**
Flat top, Pabst Blue Ribbon, Milwaukee WI, VG **35.00**
Flat top, Peter Hand Reserve, Chicago IL, EX...............**70.00**
Flat top, Schmidt's Bock Beer, Schmidt's, Philadelphia, 1950s, EX **40.00**
Flat top, Walter's Pilsner Beer, Pueblo CO, VG..............**45.00**

Flat top, Walters Pilsner Beer, Walter Brewing, Pueblo CO, 1950s, EX **30.00**

Flat top, Zing Beverage, Kingsbury Sheboygan WI, VG..........**30.00**

Pull tabs: Stallion XII Malt Liquor, Gold Medal Brewing, Wilkes-Barre, PA, 1960s, EX, $36.00; Hien Brau, Tivoli Brewing, Denver, CO, 1960s, NM, $12.00; Golden Lion Beer, Berger Meister Brewing, San Francisco, CA, 1960s, NM, $30.00.
(Photo courtesy Frank's Auctions)

Pull tab, Bausbrau Lager Beer, Maier Brewing, Los Angeles, 1960s, NM **55.00**

Pull tab, Big Cat Malt Liquor, zip top, EX............................**15.00**

Pull tab, Black Pride Beer, West Bend, West Bend WI, 1960s, NM................................**12.00**

Pull tab, Gex Premium Beer, EX..................................**15.00**

Pull tab, Iron City Beer, 1974 Pittsburgh football schedule, EX..................................**75.00**

Pull tab, Old Bohemian Draft, Eastern Brewing, Hammonton NJ, 1960s, EX..................**45.00**

Pull tab, Old Ranier Beer, Hornell Brewing, Trenton NJ, EX.**48.00**

Pull tab, Orbit Premium Beer, EX **35.00**

Pull tab, Ox Bow Beer, Walter Brewing, Pueblo Co, 1960s, NM..................................**32.00**

Pull tab, Regal Select Draft Beer, Maier, Los Angeles, 1960s, NM..................................**12.00**

Pull tab, Suntory Beer, Suntory Brewing, Japan, 1960s, NM..................**42.00**

Pull tab, 102 Continental Dark Beer, EX **125.00**

Pull tab, 102 Draft, EX.........**25.00**

Soft top, Iron City Beer, Pittsburgh Brewing, Pittsburgh PA, 1960s, EX........................**20.00**

Zip top, Kentucky Malt Liquor, Oertel Brewing, Louisville KY, 1960s, NM...............**38.00**

Zip top, Sebewaing Beer, Sebewaing Brewing, Sebewaing MI, 1960s, NM....................................**45.00**

1-gal, Kingsbury Draft, G Heileman La Crosse WI, flat top, VG **80.00**

Birthday Angels

Here's a collection that's a lot of fun, inexpensive, and takes relatively little space to display. They're not at all hard to find, but there are several series, so completing 12-month sets of them all can provide a bit of a challenge. Generally speaking, angels are priced by the following factors: 1) company — look for Lefton, Napco, Norcrest, and Enesco marks or labels (unmarked or unknown sets are of less value); 2) application of flowers, bows, gold trim, etc.,

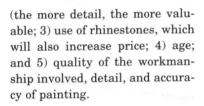

Enesco, Angel of the Month, June, holds flower bouquet, 4", from $15.00 to $18.00.

Lefton, #0489, June, girl with flowers, $30.00. (Photo courtesy Loretta DeLozier)

(the more detail, the more valuable; 3) use of rhinestones, which will also increase price; 4) age; and 5) quality of the workmanship involved, detail, and accuracy of painting.

#1294, angel of the month, white hair, 5", ea, from $18 to.**20.00**

#1600 Pal Angel, month series of both girl & boy, 4", ea, from $10 to..............................**15.00**

High Mountain Quality, colored hair, 7", ea, from $30 to.**32.00**

Kelvin, C-250, holding flower of the month, 4½", ea, from $15 to.....................................**20.00**

Lefton, #556, boy of the month, 5½", ea, from $25 to.......**30.00**

Lefton, #985, flower of the month, 5", ea, from $28 to..........**32.00**

Lefton, #1323, angel of the month, bisque, ea, from $18 to ..**22.00**

Lefton, #1987, angel of the month, ea, from $30 to **35.00**

Lefton, #3332, bisque, w/basket of flowers, 4", ea, from $25 to.**30.00**

Lefton, #6224, applied flower/birthstone on skirt, 4½", ea, $18 to..........**25.00**

Lefton, #6985, musical, sm, ea, from $40 to **45.00**

Lefton, AR-1987, w/ponytail, 4", ea, from $18 to **22.00**

Napco, A1917-1929, boy angel of the month, ea, from $20 to **25.00**

Napco, C1361-1373, angel of the month, ea, from $20 to ..**25.00**

Napco, S1291, day of the week 'Belle,' ea, from $22 to ...**25.00**

Napco, S1392, oval frame angel of the month, ea, from $25 to.......**30.00**

Norcrest, F-120, angel of the month, 4½", ea, from $18 to **22.00**

Norcrest, F-167, bell of the month, 2¾", ea, from $8 to.........**12.00**

Norcrest, F-23, day of the week angel, 4½", ea, from $18 to **22.00**

Norcrest, F-535, angel of the month, 4½", ea, from $20 to **25.00**

Relco, 6", ea, from $18 to......**22.00**

TMJ, angel of the month, w/flower, ea, from $20 to **25.00**

Ucagco, white hair, 5¾", from $12 to **15.00**

46

Black Americana

This is a wide and varied field of collector interest. Advertising, toys, banks, sheet music, kitchenware items, movie items, and even the fine arts are areas that offer Black Americana buffs many opportunities to add to their collections. Caution! Because some pieces have become so valuable, reproductions abound. Watch for a lot of new ceramic items, less detailed in both the modeling and the painting.

Book, Little Black Sambo, Gabriel, 1948, revised edition with color illustrations by M. L. Russell, 10x12", sixteen pages, EX, $150.00. (Photo courtesy Marvelous Books)

Album, Uncle Remus Stories, RCA Victor Youth series, 1940s, EX **49.00**

Ashtray, Afro Bar, drummer in red & white on clear glass, 1940s, 4" dia............................**45.00**

Ashtray, boy on clothesline w/3 open-top clothes, Japan, 2¼x3½" **40.00**

Ashtray, Dinah's Shack, lady's portrait on white, Japan, 5¼"..................................**95.00**

Ashtray, 2 babies on clothesline, Who Left This Behin', Japan, 2¼" **40.00**

Bell, Aunt Jemima in red w/white apron lettered New Orleans, 3¼"..................................**15.00**

Book, Little Alexander, B Schiff, hardcover, 1955, 10¾x8", EX **90.00**

Book, Little Black Sambo, Kellogg's Story Book of Games, 1931, EX **60.00**

Book, Little Washington's Holidays, LE Roy, 1925 1st edition, EX **50.00**

Book, Minstrel Parade, Charles George, Dennison & Co, 1950, 120-page **35.00**

Book, Treasury of S Foster, Random House, 1st edition, 1946, w/jacket **55.00**

Book, Two Black Crows in the AEF, CE Mack, Bobbs Merrill, 1928, EX **65.00**

Book, You Funny Little Noddy, E Blyton, hardbound, 1950, EX **29.00**

Brooch, lady's face, black turban w/rhinestones, green stone eyes, 2"..........................**35.00**

Brush, wooden Mammy figural, skirt forms brush, 1940s, 4½", EX **75.00**

Card game, Tops & Tails, ethnic caricature, 48 cards, EX **75.00**

Cookie jar, Coon Chicken Inn, caricature face, Copyright '92 USA **135.00**

Cookie jar, Mammy, Carol Gifford limited edition, 1986, 11".....................................**295.00**

Dolls, Golliwogg Bride & Groom, beanie type, J Robertson, 1999, pr.........................**95.00**

Figurine, angel boy, white robe, Shafford #8515C, 1950s, 3x3½"..............................**35.00**

Figurine, boy on alligator, unmarked, ca 1920-40, 2½x5"...............**50.00**

Figurine, guitar player in plaid jacket, ceramic, Italy, 3¾"......**50.00**

Figurine, Jungle Imp, comic character, McKay & Nye, #203, 4" L................................**75.00**

Figurine, native drummer, painted bisque, Japan, 1940s, 4¾".................................**36.00**

Figurine, native girl w/banjo, chenille, Japan, 1950s, 3¾".**15.00**

Figurine, 3-pc band on white sofa, Japan, 1930s, 2½x3"......**35.00**

Measuring cup, Aunt Jemima Pancake Mix, 1980s, ¼-cup...............**35.00**

Noisemaker, minstrel on litho tin, US Metal Toy Mfg, 5⅜x3", EX....................................**35.00**

Paper dolls, Oh Susanna, w/unbreakable record/color book, 1950, EX...............**65.00**

Paper plate, Aunt Jemima Days Are Here Again, 9¼", EX.....................................**30.00**

Perfume bottle, boy figural, clear glass w/cold paint, Germany, 2¼"...................................**55.00**

Picture record, Blue Tail Fly, banjo player sleeve, 1953, 78 rpm, EX..........................**40.00**

Place mat, Aunt Jemima Restaurant, Disneyland, 1955, 13¾x9¾", M.........**45.00**

Plaque, All God's Children, Holcombe, freestanding, 1988, 5½x8½"..........................**65.00**

Plate, Mammy's Shanty Restaurant, 7¼", NM.........................**30.00**

Postcard, Too Tough for the Alligator, Ark, used 1¢ stamp, EX................................**18.00**

Pottery, ethnic stereotype, cold paint on brown, USA, 3½".........**29.00**

Print, Catching Trout, Currier & Ives 1952 repro, 8½x13½" image..............................**18.00**

Shakers, Aunt Jemima & Uncle Mose, F&F Mold & Die Works, 3½", pr...............**55.00**

Shakers, boy & girl w/corn, ceramic, Japan, 3", pr, NM.....**80.00**

Shakers, boys riding ears of corn, Japan, 2¼x3¾", pr.......**100.00**

Shakers, ethnic caricature figures w/mortarboards, Japan, 1950s, pr.......................**165.00**

Shakers, Mammy and Chef, ceramic, black faces, yellow, with red and green trim, Souvenir of Boston, Mass, on skirt, 5", $55.00 pair.

Shakers, Mammy & Chef, light brown faces, Japan, 1940s, 2½", pr...........................**38.00**

Shakers, Mammy & Chef, painted chalkware, 2½", pr, EX .**28.00**

Shakers, man w/2 bottles (shakers), ceramic, Germany, #8195, 6⅜" **110.00**

Shakers, native boy & girl, ceramic, unmarked Japan, 1940s, 4¾", pr **75.00**

Shakers, native busts, unmarked California pottery, 1950s, 3¼", pr **95.00**

Shakers, native ladies w/bare shoulders, red Japan mark, 1950s, 4", pr **45.00**

Shakers, Native riding hippo, hand-painted details, Japan, 1950s, pr.......................**175.00**

Shakers, nude lady w/watermelon slice (shaker), nodder, Japan, 3½" **200.00**

Sheet music, Banjo Picker, ethnic cover, NL Wright, 1936, EX **13.00**

Sheet music, My Heart Belongs to You, Bette McLaurin cover, 1952, EX **8.00**

Sheet music, Shake Rattle & Roll, C Calhoun, J Turner cover, 1954, EX **10.00**

Tablecloth, printed caricature figures along yellow border, 51" sq, NM **225.00**

Table card, Aunt Jemima Restaurant, diecut, 1953, 3x4¾", NM **55.00**

Tile, Low Water in the Mississippi, Currier & Ives, early, 6½" dia................**85.00**

Towel, banjo player & children transfer, turquoise border, 1940s, NM **75.00**

Towel, linen w/embroidered Mammy w/cake, 1950s, 24x15", EX.**35.00**

Black Cats

This line of fancy felines was marketed mainly by the Shafford (importing) Company, although black cat lovers accept similarly modeled, shiny glazed kitties of other importing firms into their collections as well. Because eBay offers an over supply of mid-century collectibles, the value structure for these cats has widened, with prices for common items showing a marked decline. At the same time, items that are truly rare, such as the triangle spice set and the wireware cat face spice set have shot upwards to as much as $750.00 and $600.00 respectively! Values that follow are for examples in mint (or nearly mint) paint, an important consideration in determining a fair market price. Shafford items are often minus their white whiskers and eyebrows, and this type of loss should be reflected in your evaluation. An item in poor paint may be worth even less than half of given estimates. Note: Unless 'Shafford' is included in the descriptions, values are for cats that were imported by other companies.

Ashtray, flat face, Shafford, hard-to-find size, 3¾" **50.00**

Ashtray, head shape w/open mouth, Shafford, 3"........**22.00**

Cigarette lighter, Shafford, 5½", from $175 to **190.00**

Cookie jar, lg head cat, Shafford, from $80 to..................**100.00**

Creamer & sugar bowl, Shafford, from $40 to.....................**60.00**

Cruet, slender form, gold collar & tie, tail handle................**12.00**

Decanter, long cat w/red fish in mouth as stopper...........**75.00**

Decanter set, upright cat, yellow eyes, +6 plain wines......**45.00**

Grease jar, sm cat head, Shafford, scarce, from $150 to.....**175.00**

Stacking tea set, mama pot with kitty creamer and sugar bowl, yellow eyes, $85.00.

Milk pitchers, Shafford, 6½" and 6", from $120.00 to $140.00 each.

Mug, Shafford, 3½"...............**50.00**

Pincushion, cushion on cat's back, tongue measure..............**25.00**

Planter, cat & kitten in a hat, Shafford-like paint.........**30.00**

Planter, upright cat, Shafford-like paint, Mapco label, 6"....**20.00**

Salt & pepper shakers, range size, upright cats, Shafford, 5", pr.....................................**35.00**

Salt & pepper shakers, seated, blue eyes, Enesco label, 5¾", pr.....................................**15.00**

Spice set, 6 square shakers in wooden frame, Shafford, minimum..............................**175.00**

Spice set, 6 square shakers in wooden frame, yellow eyes.....**125.00**

Teapot, bulbous body, head lid, green eyes, Shafford, sm, 4"-4½"..................................**25.00**

Teapot, panther-like appearance, gold eyes, sm..................**15.00**

Teapot, yellow eyes, 1-cup....**25.00**

Toothpick holder, cat on vase, atop book, Occupied Japan....**12.00**

Tray, flat face, wicker handle, Shafford, scarce, from $75 to..................................**100.00**

Wall pocket, flat-backed 'teapot' cat, Shafford, minimum value..............................**185.00**

Wine, embossed cat's face, green eyes, Shafford, sm..........**50.00**

Blade Banks

In 1903 the safety razor was invented, making it easier for men to shave at home. But the old, used razor blades were troublesome, because for the next twenty-two years, nobody knew what to do with them. In 1925 the first patent was filed for a razor blade bank, a container designed to hold old blades until it became full, in which event it was to be thrown away. Most razor blade banks are 3" or 4" tall, similar to a coin bank with a slot in the top but no outlet in the bottom to remove the old blades. These banks were produced from 1925 to 1950. Some were issued by men's toiletry companies; many were made of tin and printed with an advertising message. An assortment of blade banks made from a variety of materials — ceramic, wood, plastic, or metal — could also be purchased at five-and-dime stores.

For information on blade banks as well as many other types of interesting figural items from the same era, we recommend *Collectibles for the Kitchen, Bath & Beyond* (featuring napkin dolls, egg timers, string holders, children's whistle cups, baby feeder dishes, pie birds, and laundry sprinkler bottles) by Ellen Bercovici, Bobbie Zucker Bryson, and Deborah Gillham (available through Antique Trader Books).

Barber holding pole, Occupied Japan, 4", from $50.00 to $60.00. (Photo courtesy Deborah Gillham)

Barber, wood w/Gay Blade on bottom, unscrews, Woodcraft, 1950, 6"...........................**75.00**
Barber, wood w/key & metal holders for razor & brush, 9", from $60 to.............................**80.00**
Barber chair, lg or sm, from $100 to...................................**125.00**
Barber pole w/barber head & derby hat, white, from $40 to.....................................**60.00**
Barber pole w/face, red & white, from $30 to.....................**40.00**

Barber pole, white ceramic with red stripes, marked Blades, 6", from $15.00 to $25.00. (Photo courtesy Amelio Potter)

Barber standing in blue coat & stroking chin, from $65 to.**85.00**
Barbershop quartet, 4 singing barber heads, from $95 to.**125.00**
Dandy Dans, plastic w/brush holders, from $25 to..............**35.00**
Frog, green, marked For Used Blades, from $60 to........**70.00**
Listerine donkey, from $20 to .**30.00**
Listerine elephant, from $25 to.**35.00**
Listerine frog, from $15 to ...**25.00**
Looie, right- or left-handed version, from $85 to..........**110.00**
Man shaving, mushroom shape, Cleminson, from $25 to .**35.00**
Razor Bum, from $85 to **100.00**

Safe, green, marked Razor on front, from $40 to...........**65.00**

Shaving brush, ceramic, wide style w/decal, from $45 to.......**65.00**

Tony the Barber, Ceramic Arts Studio, from $85 to........**95.00**

Bowl, Gay Plaid, 8" sq, from $20 to......................................**25.00**

Cookie jar, Gay Plaid, wooden lid, from $100 to.................**125.00**

Cup & saucer, Bird, from $30 to .**40.00**

Cup & saucer, Leaves, from $10 to......................................**12.00**

Blair Dinnerware

American dinnerware has been a popular field of collecting for several years, and the uniquely styled lines of Blair are very appealing, though not often seen except in the Midwest (and it's there that prices are the strongest). Blair was located in Ozark, Missouri, manufacturing dinnerware from the mid-1940s until the early 1950s. Gay Plaid, recognized by its squared-off shapes and brush-stroke design (in lime, green, brown, and dark green on white), is the pattern you'll find most often. Several other lines were made as well. You'll be able to recognize all of them easily enough, since most pieces (except for the smaller items) are marked.

Beer mug, Bird, from $90 to.**100.00**

Bowl, Gay Plaid, 6½" square, from $8.00 to $10.00.

Plate, dinner; Bamboo, square, $14.00.

Plate, dinner; Gay Plaid, from $10 to......................................**15.00**

Plate, dinner; Spiced Pear, from $30 to.............................**40.00**

Plate, salad; Bamboo, from $6 to ..**8.00**

Plate, salad; Brick, from $20 to .**25.00**

Salt & pepper shakers, Bamboo, short, pr, from $12 to.....**14.00**

Salt & pepper shakers, Gay Plaid, tall conical forms, pr, from $50 to......................................**60.00**

Tumbler, Bird, from $25 to ..**35.00**

Tumbler, Leaves, from $12 to.**15.00**

Blue Garland

This lovely line of dinnerware was offered as premiums through grocery store chains during the decades of the '60s and '70s. It has delicate garlands of tiny blue flowers on a white background trimmed in platinum. Rims are scalloped and handles are gracefully curved. Though the 'Haviland' backstamp might suggest otherwise, this china has no connection with the famous Haviland company of Limoges. 'Johann Haviland' (as contained in the mark) was actually the founding company that later became Philip Rosenthal & Co., the German manufacturer who produced chinaware for export to the USA from the mid-1930s until as late as the 1980s.

This line may also be found with the Thailand Johann Haviland backstamp, a later issue. Our values are for the line with the Bavarian mark; expect to pay at least 30% less for the Thailand issue.

Bell, from $35 to **50.00**
Beverage server, teapot/coffeepot, w/lid, 11", from $70 to ...**90.00**
Bowl, fruit; 5⅛", from $2.50 to .**3.00**
Bowl, oval, 10¾", from $50 to.**60.00**
Bowl, soup; 7⅝", from $9 to .**12.00**
Bowl, vegetable; 8½", from $28 to **35.00**
Butter dish, ¼-lb, from $70 to.**85.00**
Candlesticks, 3½x4", pr, from $80 to **100.00**
Casserole/tureen, w/lid, 12", from $70 to **85.00**
Chamberstick, metal candle cup & handle, 6" dia **75.00**
Coaster/butter pat, 3¾" dia, from $10 to **12.00**
Creamer, from $15 to...........**18.00**

Cup & saucer, flat, from $8 to.**12.00**
Cup & saucer, footed, from $8 to **12.00**

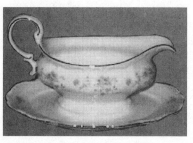

Gravy boat with undertray, from $35.00 to $45.00.

Plate, bread & butter; 6¼", from $2 to **3.00**
Plate, salad; 7¾", from $7 to ..**9.00**
Platter, 13", from $30 to **35.00**
Platter, 14½", from $35 to **45.00**
Platter, 15½", from $45 to **55.00**
Salt & pepper shakers, 4¼", pr, from $40 to **55.00**
Sugar bowl, w/lid, from $18 to .**22.00**
Teakettle, porcelain w/stainless steel lid **25.00**
Tidbit tray, 1-tier, from $35 to.**45.00**
Tidbit tray, 3-tier, from $45 to.**65.00**

Blue Ridge

Some of the most attractive American dinnerware made in the twentieth century is Blue Ridge, produced by Southern Potteries of Erwin, Tennessee, from the late 1930s until 1956. More than four hundred patterns were hand painted on eight basic shapes. Elaborate or appealing lines are represented by the high end of our range; use the lower side to evaluate simple patterns. The Quimper-like peasant-decorated line is one of the most treasured and should be priced at double the amounts recommended for the higher-end patterns. Refer to *Best of Blue Ridge Dinnerware* by Betty and Bill Newbound (Collector Books) for more information.

Ashtray, individual, from $18 to .**20.00**
Bowl, hot cereal; from $20 to.**25.00**
Butter dish, from $35 to **45.00**

Coffeepot, Ovoid Shape, from $150.00 to $160.00.

Creamer, demitasse; china, from $80 to **95.00**
Creamer, regular shape, from $12 to **18.00**
Cup & saucer, demitasse; earthenware, from $25 to...........**30.00**
Cup & saucer, regular shape, from $15 to **20.00**
Custard cup, from $18 to......**22.00**
Gravy boat, from $25 to........**35.00**
Pie baker, from $35 to **45.00**
Pitcher, Martha, earthenware, from $70 to **75.00**

Pitcher, Virginia, china, 6½", from $125 to **150.00**
Plate, aluminum edge, 12", from $40 to **45.00**
Plate, Christmas Tree, from $75 to **85.00**
Plate, dinner; 10½", from $20 to **25.00**
Plate, divided, heavy, from $40 to **50.00**
Plate, Forked-Tailed Flycatcher, from Colonial Birds salad set, from $75.00 ....**80.00**
Plate, 6", from $8 to **10.00**
Plate, 11½-12", from $50 to..**65.00**
Platter, 12½-13", from $25 to .**30.00**
Relish, T-handle, from $65 to .**75.00**
Salad fork, earthenware, from $50 to **60.00**
Salt & pepper shakers, Apple, 1¾", pr, from $40 to **45.00**
Sherbet, from $35 to **40.00**

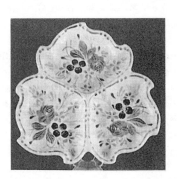

Snack tray, Irresistible, Martha shape, from $150.00 to $175.00. (Photo courtesy Betty and Bill Newbound)

Sugar bowl, Waffle, w/lid, from $15 to **20.00**
Teapot, Colonial, from $95 to .**150.00**
Teapot, Skyline, from $110 to.**125.00**
Teapot, Woodcrest, from $175 to.**200.00**

Tidbit tray, 2-tier, from $30 to ..**40.00**
Toast lid only, regular, from $75 to **100.00**
Vase, tapered, china, from $125 to **145.00**

Blue Willow

Inspired by the lovely blue and white Chinese exports, the Willow pattern has been made by many English, American, and Japanese firms from 1950 until the present. Many variations of the pattern have been noted — mauve, black, green, and multicolor Willow ware can be found in limited amounts. The design has been applied to tinware, linens, glassware, and paper goods, all of which are treasured by today's collectors. Refer to *Gaston's Blue Willow, 3rd Edition*, by Mary Frank Gaston (Collector Books) for more information. See also Royal China. See Clubs and Newsletters for information concerning *The Willow Review* newsletter.

Ashtray, Japan, Please Don't Burn Our Home, 6" L, from $55 to **75.00**
Ashtray, unmarked Japan, fish figural, 3x5", from $25 to **35.00**
Bell, unmarked, pattern in reserve, wooden handle, 8½", $35 to **45.00**
Bell, unmarked (Enesco label), 4", from $10 to **15.00**
Bowl, vegetable; unmarked (attributed to Homer Laughlin), w/lid, 10" **75.00**

Bowl, vegetable; Japan mark, 10½", from $35.00 to $40.00.

Butter dish, unmarked Japan, holds ¼-lb stick, 3½x7", from $75 to **85.00**
Butter warmer, unmarked Japan, candle holder beneath sm pot, from $100 to **125.00**
Canister, Japan, Instant Coffee, 6", from $55 to................**75.00**
Canisters, unmarked Japan, 3 stackable pcs w/lid.......**125.00**

Cheese keeper, slant lid, numbered, 7¾", $185.00.

Coffeepot, demitasse; unmarked Japan, from $50 to.........**75.00**
Compote, Shenango China, footed, 3½x7", from $60 to.........**75.00**
Creamer, Made in Japan, 3¼", from $15 to.....................**20.00**
Creamer, unmarked American, abbreviated border, 3", from $15 to **20.00**

Creamer & sugar bowl, demitasse; Japan, w/lid, 5", 3½", from $35 to **45.00**

Creamer & sugar bowl, unmarked Japan, 3¼", ea, from $15 to **20.00**

Cruets, Japan, marked Oil & Vinegar, 5¼", pr, from $55 to..............**65.00**

Cup, demitasse; Made in Japan, 2½", w/saucer, from $30 to.........**35.00**

Cup, soup; unmarked Japan, from $55 to **75.00**

Cup & saucer, chili; unmarked Japan, temple motif, 4x7½", from $50 to **55.00**

Egg cup, unmarked, variant pattern, handpainted, 3½", from $35 to **40.00**

Flour sifter, metal, 6", from $55 to **75.00**

Gravy dish, Shenango, traditional pattern, 6" L, from $15 to **25.00**

Jam jar, unmarked Japan, porcelain, bamboo handle, 1990s, from $15 to **20.00**

Juicer/reamer, 1990s, from $15 to **20.00**

Mug, farmer's; unmarked Japan, from $20 to **25.00**

Mustard pot, Japan, geometric border on handle, w/lid & spoon, from $75 to **80.00**

Napkin holder, unmarked Japan, 4½x4½", from $125 to..**145.00**

Pitcher, unmarked, Willow pattern on white frosted glass, ice lip, from $45 to..............**55.00**

Pitcher, unmarked Japan, 5", from $95 to **125.00**

Plate, grill; Shenango China, traditional border, 10", from $25 to **35.00**

Plate, grill; unmarked Japan, divided, 10½", from $15 to **20.00**

Plate, Jackson China, traditional border, 9", from $15 to...**18.00**

Plate, Japan, 6", from $15 to.**25.00**

Platter, Jackson China, oval, 12½", from $25 to...........**35.00**

Punch cup, unmarked, footed pedestal, 3", from $60 to.**65.00**

Relish, unmarked Japan, 3 divided sections, gold trim, 8", from $75 to **125.00**

Relish, Walker China, scalloped edge & ridges, 7¾", from $65 to..**75.00**

Salt & pepper shakers, Enesco label, gold trim, 2½", pr, from $25 to **35.00**

Salt & pepper shakers, Japan, varied shapes & sizes, pr, from $25 to **35.00**

Spoon rest, unmarked Japan, Spooner in center, hangs, from $25 to **35.00**

Tea set, Moriyama Japan, stackable pot, creamer & sugar bowl, from $175 to **225.00**

Tea strainer, unmarked Japan, modern, from $15 to **25.00**

Teacup & saucer, unmarked Japan, Temples II, from $35 to **45.00**

Teapot, unmarked Homer Laughlin, standard pattern, 5½", from $65 to.............**85.00**

Teapot, unmarked Japan, barrel shape, 7", from $75 to..**100.00**

Tumbler, unmarked Japan, 3¼", from $25 to **30.00**

Tureen, unmarked Japan, footed, w/ladle & tray, 10x6", from $175 to **225.00**

Umbrella stand, unmarked Japan, 1970s, 18x8½", from $75 to.**125.00**

Bookends

Bookends have come into their own as a separate category of collectibles. They are so diversified in styling, it's easy to find some that appeal to you, no matter what your personal tastes and preferences. Metal examples seem to be most popular, especially those with the mark of their manufacturer, and can still be had at reasonable prices. Glass and ceramic bookends by noted makers, however, may be more costly — for example, those made by Roseville or Cambridge, which have a crossover collector appeal.

Louis Kuritzky has written an informative book titled *Collector's Guide to Bookends*; he is listed in the Directory under Florida. See Clubs and Newsletters for information concerning the Bookend Collectors Club.

Elephants, painted cast iron, Connecticut Foundry, c 1930, 5¾", $75.00 for the pair. (Photo courtesy Louis Kuritzky)

Baby shoes, gray metal, marked Pat 1940, 5½", pr **75.00**

Catwalk, embossed lion, aluminum, ca 1970, 3½", pr................**25.00**

Colonial Trio, embossed figures, cast iron, ca 1925, 3", pr .**50.00**

Deco Bust, gray metal, Abbot, 1947, 7¼", pr................**150.00**

Elephant Terrain, gray metal, ca 1930, 6⅛", pr.................**95.00**

Empty Coach, cast iron, Champion, ca 1931, 3¼", pr **35.00**

Floral Design, openwork on flatiron shape, brass, ca 1925, 6", pr....................................**50.00**

Heraldic Eagle, Syroco, ca 1935, commonly found, 6", pr **30.00**

Knight Errant (on horse), bronze, ca 1925, 6¼", pr **95.00**

Lady's Face, clear glass, New Martinsville, 5¼", pr ...**200.00**

Lincoln Bust, cast iron, Verona, 6½", pr **65.00**

Looking Back, stylized horse, gray metal, Kraftware, 6½", pr.......................................**75.00**

Miles Standish (bust), gray metal, ca 1930, 7", pr **125.00**

Nuart Shepherd, seated dog, gray metal, Nuart shop mark, 7", pr....................................**90.00**

Nude w/Drape, iron, bronze-colored paint, Verona, 1920s, 6¾" **135.00**

Patriotic Eagle, chalkware, black & gold paint, ca 1970, pr **20.00**

Pink Lady, chalk on polished stone base, JBH (JB Hirsch), ca 1943, pr **125.00**

Scottish terrier embossed on painted cast iron, Connecticut Foundry, 1929, pr **50.00**

Seated Lincoln, bronze, marked Solid Bronze, 3¾", pr.....**90.00**

Syria Temple, embossed camel &
symbols, gray metal, 1930s,
5½", pr **75.00**
Trout, leaping, gray metal,
unmarked, 6½", pr.......**125.00**
Ye Olde Inn, Syroco Wood, ca
1940, 6¼", pr..................**45.00**

Bottles

Bottles have been used as
containers for commercial products since the late 1800s.
Specimens from as early as
1845 may still be occasionally
found today (watch for a rough
pontil to indicate this early production date). Some of the most
collectible are bitters bottles,
used for 'medicine' that was
mostly alcohol, a ploy to avoid
paying the stiff tax levied on
liquor sales. Spirit flasks from
the 1800s were blown in the
mold and were often designed to
convey a historic, political, or
symbolic message. Refer to
*Bottle Pricing Guide, Third
Revised Edition,* by Hugh
Cleveland (Collector Books) for
more information.

Dairy Bottles

The storage and distribution
of milk in glass bottles became
commonplace around the turn of
the twentieth century. They were
replaced by paper and plastic
containers in the mid-1950s.
Perhaps 5% of all US dairies are
still using some glass, and glass
bottles are still widely used in
Mexico and some Canadian
provinces.

Milk-packaging and distribution plants hauled trailer loads of
glass bottles to dumping grounds
during the conversion to the throw-
away cartons now in general use.
Because of this practice, milk bottles and jars are scarce today. Most
collectors search for bottles from
hometown dairies; some have completed a fifty-state collection in the
three popular sizes.

Bottles from 1900 to 1920 had
the name of the dairy, town, and
state embossed in the glass.
Nearly all of the bottles produced
after this period had the copy
painted and then pyro-glazed onto
the surface of the bottle. This
enabled the dairyman to use colors
and pictures of his dairy farm or
cows on the bottles. Collectors
have been fortunate that there
have been no serious attempts at
this point to reproduce a particularly rare bottle!

Bablin-Brook, clear, 1-pt, 7¼" .**6.00**
Badger Farms Creameries, orange
pyro, tall, 1-qt **15.00**
Baker & Son Dairy, Atlanta MI,
orange pyro, tall, 1-qt....**25.00**
Beaulac's Ideal Bakery, green
pyro, tall, 1-qt **14.00**
Beltz's Dairy, Palmerton PA, red
pyro, tall, 1-qt **32.00**
Blais Dairy Farm, Lewiston ME,
black & orange pyro, tall, 1-
qt...................................**24.00**
Borden's, Elsie image, red &
orange pyro, ½-pt...........**14.00**

Brown's Dairy, Cazenovia NY, red pyro, tall, 1-qt, from $20 to.**30.00**

Candlelight Goat Dairy, New Milford CT, green pyro, tall, 1-qt.....................**105.00**

Cloverleaf Blue Ribbon Farm, Stockton CA, cream top, red pyro, 1-qt.......................**25.00**

Cole Farm Dairy, Biddeford ME, black pyro, sq squat, ½-pt.**9.00**

Crystal Spring Dairy, green pyro, tall, 1-qt...........................**35.00**

Dodds Lakeview Farm, North Hero VT, orange pyro, tall, 1-qt.**60.00**

Douglaston Manor Dairy, Pulaski NY, black pyro, tall 1-qt.**35.00**

Dyke's Dairy, Youngsville-Warren PA, red pyro, tall, 1-qt...**25.00**

Ellerman Dairy, Athens WI, red pyro, tall, 1-qt.................**18.00**

Escanaba Dairy, red pyro, ½-pt..**25.00**

Fisher Dairy, Crystal Falls MI, black pyro, tall, 1-qt......**28.00**

FW White, orange pyro, tall, 1-qt.**35.00**

Gold Medal Farms, orange pyro, sq, 1-qt..............................**9.00**

Greenwood Dairy Farm, black pyro, Greenwood, SC, round quart, $40.00. (Photo courtesy Tyrrell's Antiques)

Harlow's Jerseydale Farm, Amherst MA, red pyro, tall, 1-qt.....................................**45.00**

Highland Dairy, Athol MA, green pyro, squat, 1-qt.............**20.00**

Highland Dairy, green pyro w/black Store banner, squat, 1-qt...................................**35.00**

Homestead Farm, Norwell MA, red pyro, sq, 1-qt............**12.00**

Indian Hill Farm, Greenville ME, orange pyro, tall, 1-qt....**28.00**

Lueck Dairy, Liverpool NY, orange pyro, 1-pt.......................**12.00**

Marble Farms Dairy, Marble Kid on back, orange pyro, sq, ⅓-qt...**9.00**

Melrose Dairy, Ormond FL, blue pyro, tall, 1-qt **34.00**

Mid Valley Farm Dairy, green pyro, sq, ½-pt **8.00**

Model Dairy, Waukon IA, red pyro, tall, 1-qt **22.00**

Natoma Farm, Hinsdale Il, orange pyro, cow & hen on front & back, tall, 1-qt...............**22.00**

North Chatham Dairy, North Chatham NY, maroon pyro, tall, 1-qt...........................**42.00**

Northland Milk, Hoppy Bottle, red pyro, sq, 1-qt **28.00**

O'Donnell's, Mattoon IL, orange pyro, tall, 1-qt **30.00**

Old Tavern Farm, Portland ME, red & black pyro, tall, 1-qt.....**32.00**

Rosebud Creamery, Plattsburg NY, maroon pyro, 1-qt............**10.00**

Shaw's Ridge Farm, Sanford ME, orange pyro, tall, 1-qt....**45.00**

Smith's Dairy Farm, Erie PA, maroon pyro, ½-pt **10.00**

St Mary's Dairy, George M Erich, St Mary's PA, brown pyro, tall, 1-qt.........................**35.00**

Stout's Valley Farm, Easton PA, black pyro, tall, 1-qt **35.00**

Sunshine Goat Milk, embossed standing goat, ½-pt........**70.00**

Vermont Country Egg Nog, Shelburne VT, maroon pyro, sq, 1-qt **12.00**

Witchita Natural Milk Producers, red pyro, tall, 1-qt **20.00**

Zenda Farms, Clayton NY, orange pyro, 1-qt **14.00**

3¢ Store, clear embossed, heavy, ¼-pt................................**14.00**

Soda Bottles With Applied Color Labels

This is a specialized area of advertising collectibles that holds the interest of bottle collectors as well as those who search for soda pop items; both fields attract a good number of followers, so the market for these bottles is fairly strong right now. See also Coca-Cola; Soda Pop.

Ace High, clear w/blue & white label, 12-oz **22.00**

All Star Kola, clear w/white label, 1940 ....**24.00**

Big Shot Beverages, clear w/red & white label, 12-oz **28.00**

Bull's Eye Sparkling Beverages, clear & blue & white label, 12-oz.....................................**24.00**

Cherry River, clear w/red & white label, 1956 ....**55.00**

Clicquot Club, clear w/yellow, black & red label, 9½"...**10.00**

Cuban Dry Beverages, clear w/red & white label, 9-oz **18.00**

Dad's Root Beer, amber w/yellow, red & blue label, 1-qt....**14.00**

Dad's Root Beer, yellow w/red, blue & yellow, Papa size, ½-gal **55.00**

Dillon Beverages, clear w/red & white label, 12-oz **18.00**

Dixie Dan, green w/blue & white label w/paddleboat **12.00**

Double Cola, clear w/red & white label, 8-oz **11.00**

FBI (Fisher Bros Inc), clear w/red, green & white label, 7-oz.**10.00**

Freshway Fresh Fruit...Beverages, amber w/blue & white label, 10-oz **15.00**

Frostie Root Beer, amber w/white, red, blue & black label, 10-oz **18.00**

Frosty Beverages, clear w/cream & green label, 9¾" **25.00**

Full Flavor Beverages, clear w/red & white label, 7-oz **28.00**

Garrison Hill Sparkling Beverages, green w/red & white label, 28-oz **25.00**

Grantman Beverages, clear w/red & white label, 8-oz **10.00**

Heep Good Beverages, clear w/orange & black label, 12-oz **24.00**

Hill Billy Joose, clear w/white label, 8¾-oz **40.00**

Jet-Up, green w/red & white label, 7-oz **24.00**

Kik, clear w/red, white & tan label w/sports figure, 12-oz **24.00**

Kool-Aid, First in Flavor, clear w/green label..................**15.00**

La Grape/La Orange Cola, clear w/red & white label, 9-oz.**24.00**

Leary Root Beer, clear w/yellow & brown label, 12-oz **12.00**

Liberty Club Beverages, green w/red & white label, 8-oz.**30.00**

Lindy Beverage, clear w/red & white label, 10-oz **24.00**

Lovie, A Great Mixer, green w/yellow & red label, 24-oz **24.00**

Madison Old Colonial Beverages, clear w/white & red label, 7-oz ..**18.00**

Mason's Quality Beverages, clear w/white label, 10-oz **18.00**

Moo Cho, clear w/white & red label, 7-oz **20.00**

Mountain Dew, green w/white & red label, Bob & Freda on front................................**18.00**

Mountain Dew, green w/white label, 7-oz **28.00**

Mr Nibbs, green w/white & red label, 7-oz **14.00**

Mr Up, green w/white label, 16-oz **42.00**

Polly's Soda Pop, clear w/parrot on perch in yellow & white..**55.00**

Ralph's, clear w/white label, 10-oz **12.00**

REO, clear w/white & red label, 12-oz **15.00**

Royal Crown Cola, aqua w/orange & yellow label, 12-oz.....**28.00**

Royal Crown Cola, clear w/red & yellow label, 1950 ....**15.00**

S&S Sweet Beverages, clear w/white & red label, 7-oz.**10.00**

Sheriff's Beverages, clear w/red & white label, white star...**60.00**

Sky High, clear w/red & white label, 12-oz **30.00**

Sky High, clear w/red & white label, 32-oz **50.00**

Sody-Licious Famous Brand, clear w/white label, 7-oz.........**25.00**

Spiffy, clear w/yellow, red & white label, 12-oz **25.00**

Springtime, clear w/yellow label, 7-oz **12.00**

Sun Spot, clear w/red & brown label, 12-oz **10.00**

Tiny Beverages, clear w/white label, 6-oz **10.00**

Tote A Pop, clear w/yellow label, 10-oz **10.00**

Twang Root Beer, clear w/white label, 7-oz **10.00**

Variety Club Junior, clear w/red & white label, 7½-oz..........**34.00**

Vic's Beverages, clear w/red & white label, 10-oz...........**34.00**

Waseca Quality Beverages, red and white label on clear, boating and fishing logo on back, seven-ounce, $30.00. (Photo courtesy Arvid and Barb Wallin)

Welchade, green w/white label w/purple grape clusters, 6-oz **24.00**

Western Beverage, clear w/red & white label of cowgirl.....**40.00**

Miscellaneous

Carter's Liver Bitters, C. M. Co. New York, dark amber, tooled mouth, some crudity, NM, $60.00. (Photo courtesy Pacific Glass Auctions)

Abbot's Bitters, amber, 6¼" ...**6.00**

Abell's White Pine Balsam, clear, rectangular, 4⅞" **4.00**

Anderson's Cough Drops, aqua, 3½".......................**4.00**

Ayer's Compound Extract Sarsaparilla, clear **10.00**

Bear's Oil, aqua, rectangular, 3".**8.00**

Bishop's Wahoo Bitters, amber, rectangular, 10"...........**100.00**

Combault's JE Caustic Balm, aqua, 6½".........................**10.00**

Crane's Extract Company, clear, 6-7", from $4 to **9.00**

Dr Carter's Compound, aqua, rectangular...........................**8.00**

Dr Ward's Cremola, lotion, clear, 5¼"......................................**8.00**

Espey's Fragrant Cream, clear, 4½"......................................**4.00**

Fenner's Kidney & Backache Cure, amber, oval, 10¼", from $20 to..............................**40.00**

Gilt Edge Shoe Polish, green, 4".**12.00**

Gomboult's Caustic Balsam, aqua, 8-sided, 6½"....................**10.00**

Herb Bitters, SB Caff's, aqua, 5½"......................................**20.00**

Holden's Cough Syrup, aqua, rectangular, 5" **6.00**

Johnson's Chill & Fever Tonic, clear, rectangular, 6".......**4.00**

NOSCO, The Natural Salt Co, amethyst, 3½" **7.00**

Porter's Pain Killer, pink or clear, rectangular, 6¾", ea $15 to **25.00**

Price's Delicious Flavoring Extracts, clear, 4½" **8.00**

Primley's Iron & Wahoo Tonic, amber, sq, 9" **20.00**

Ryder's Clover Bitters, amber, rectangular, 7¼" **60.00**

Sapo Elixir Dry Cleaner, clear, 6".......................................**3.00**

Sauer's Extracts, clear, 4¾" ...**4.00**

Star Anchor Bitters, amber, sq, 9"...................................**225.00**

Thomas Edison Special Battery Oil, Orange NJ, 4¾" **7.00**

Breweriana

Beer can collectors and antique advertising buffs alike enjoy looking for beer-related memorabilia such as tap knobs, beer trays, coasters, signs, and such. While the smaller items of a more recent vintage are quite affordable, signs and trays from defunct breweries often bring three-digit prices. Condition is important in evaluating early advertising items of any type.

Book, The Beer Book, by Will Anderson, 1973, NM+....**25.00**

Charger, Falstaff, tin w/tavern scene, 1970s, 24" dia, EX.**25.00**

Coaster, Busch, red & green logo, pressed paper, 3x3½", NM **5.00**

Decanter, Burgie Man, ceramic, Ceramarte, 1961, 10x3½", NM...................................**35.00**

Display, Grain Belt Beer, chalkware dog head, brown, 9", NM+..............................**50.00**

Door push, Pabst Blue Ribbon Beer, painted metal, 2x9", VG....................................**40.00**

Drinking glass, Anheuser-Busch, embossed pilsener, 6½", NM...............................**25.00**

Drinking glass, Goebel 22 Beer, footed, red-painted label, 1940s, M........................**15.00**

Drinking glass, Puritan Beer, etched goblet, pre-prohibition, EX+................................**20.00**

Foam scraper, Chief Oshkosh Beer, red on blue, 1940s, EX....**60.00**

Light & framed mirror, Rolling Rock Light, 1980s, 20x10", NM................................**16.00**

Light, Beck's Beer, Buffalo's Best, glass and metal, 9¾x14½", EX, from $195.00 to $225.00. (Photo courtesy Fink's Off the Wall)

Match holder, Busch Beer/John Busch Brewing Co, celluloid, VG................................**100.00**

Mechanical pencil, Budweiser, name & logo, 1940s, EX+ **18.00**

Miniature bottles, West Virginia Special, 1950s, EX+, pr .**40.00**

Model kit, Budweiser Clydesdales 8-Horse Hitch, AMT, 1970s, NMIB..............................**25.00**

Model sprint car, Budweiser, diecast metal, 1980s, 1/24th scale, MIB **35.00**

Mug, Hamm's, clear glass w/Hamm's bear & name, M **15.00**

Mug, Oldenberg Brewery, red & black on clear glass, 5¼", EX....................................**12.00**

Napkins, Camden Beer, paper, bottle graphics on white, 1950s, VG **3.00**

Patch, Ballantine Beer, ovoid, 7x7", EX+..........................**5.00**

Pocketknife, Utica Club Beer, pearl-like handles, 1930s, G+ **40.00**

Salt & pepper shakers, Coors, wooden barrels w/Coors in script, EX, pr.................**25.00**

Sign, Dick's Quincy Beer, tin on cardboard button, 1940s, 9", NM................................**140.00**

Sign, Marques, molded plastic, 1960s, 14½x12½", M......**30.00**

Sign, Rolling Rock, neon lettering w/oblong neon tube frame, 1960s, NM...................**150.00**

Steins, left to right: Budweiser/ Ceramarte, Christmas, 1989, $25.00; Budweiser/Ceramarte, Heroes of the Hardwood, 1990s, $25.00; Hamms/Ceramarte, Oktoberfest, 1973, $25.00. (Photo courtesy Fink's Off the Wall)

Stein, Anheuser-Busch, 10 Years Safe Service, 1978, 9"..**100.00**

Stein, Anheuser-Busch, 20 Years Safe Service, 1984, 13½".**100.00**

Stein, Anheuser-Busch Bevo Fox, ceramic figural, #CS-160, EXIB **85.00**

Stein, Anheuser-Busch/Albert Stahl, Budweiser Frog figural, 9½", EX..........................**150.00**

Stein, Anheuser-Busch/Black & Tan, #CS-314, MIB........**60.00**

Stein, Anheuser-Busch/Budweiser, Joe E Louis, #CS-206, MIB.**35.00**

Stein, Anheuser-Busch/Budweiser, #CS-53, MIB **65.00**

Stein, Anheuser-Busch/Ceramarte, Bavarian house, ½-litre ..**200.00**

Stein, Anheuser-Busch/Ceramarte, Bud Man, hollow head, ½-litre **250.00**

Stein, Anheuser-Busch/Ceramarte, Busch, #CS-44, 1980, EX.**100.00**

Stein, Anheuser-Busch/Ceramarte, Busch Gardens, blue/gray, 6½", EX **75.00**

Stein, Anheuser-Busch/Ceramarte, Centennial Olympic Games, 1996, EX.......................... **25.00**

Stein, Anheuser-Busch/Ceramarte, LA Olympic Committee, 1980, 10", EX **90.00**

Stein, Anheuser-Busch/Ceramarte, Mercedes Benz 1971, 7".**20.00**

Stein, Anheuser-Busch/Ceramarte, Statue of Liberty **25.00**

Stein, Anheuser-Busch/Michelob, #CS-54, MIB.................. **40.00**

Stein, Union/Shiller & Co, glass w/embossed pewter lid, 5¾", EX **160.00**

Tap knobs, left to right: Utica Club, Bakelite with metal and enamel insert, 1940s, EX, $22.00; Krueger Ale, Bakelite with plastic inserts (front and back), EX, $24.00; Ballantine Ale, metal and enamel insert, 1940s, NM, $36.00.
(Photo courtesy Fink's Off the Wall)

Tap knob, Berghoff 1887, Bakelite w/metal & enamel insert, 1940s, EX **26.00**

Tap knob, Stanton, Bakelite, 1940s, NM **65.00**

Tip tray, Hamm's Beer, shows the Hamm's bear, 1981, NM.**10.00**

Tip tray, Miller High Life, rectangular w/slanted sides, 1950s, VG+................................. **6.00**

Tumbler, Bud Light's Spuds MacKenzie, thermoplastic, 6¼", EX............................. **5.00**

Watch fob, Peru Beer Co, brass & enameled medallion, NM.**100.00**

Yardstick, Strohs Beer, painted wood trifold, red & yellow, 1960s, EX **15.00**

Breyer Horses

Breyer collecting has grown in popularity over the past several years. Though horses dominate the market, cattle and other farm animals, dogs, cats, and wildlife have also been produced, all with exacting details and lifelike coloration. They've been made since the early 1950s in both glossy and matt finishes. (Earlier models were glossy, but from 1968 until the 1990s when both glossy and semigloss colors were revived for special runs, matt colors were preferred.) Breyer also manufactures dolls, tack, and accessories such as barns for their animals.

For more information we recommend *Schroeder's Collectible Toys, Antique to Modern* (Collector

Books), and *Breyer Animal Collector's Guide* by Felicia Browell.

Arabian Foal, chestnut, 1973-82.**13.00**
Arabian Mare, bay, 1975-88...**9.00**
Balking Mule, matt liver chestnut, 1968-71..........................**100.00**
Bucking Bronco, black, 1966-73 & 1975-76..........................**42.00**
Citation, bay, 1975-81............**8.00**
Clydesdale Mare, light bay w/black mane & tail, 1990-91......**30.00**
Family Arabian Foal, bay w/black points, 1989-90...............**16.00**
Fighting Stallion, bay, 1961-87.**30.00**
Foundation Stallion, black, no markings, 1977-87.........**25.00**
Fury Prancer, woodgrain, 1958-62..................................**350.00**
Ginger (Toys R Us/Sweet Memories), brown appaloosa, 1997....**20.00**
Grazing Foal, palomino, 1964-81.................................**28.00**
Hobo (Hobo Gift Set), buckskin, 1975-81..........................**60.00**
Jumping Horse (Sears), seal brown w/black points, 1982-83..**80.00**
Kelso (Jeremy), brown, 1993-94.**20.00**
Legionario II, alabaster........**30.00**
Lipizzan Stallion, alabaster, 1975-80....................................**35.00**

Man O' War, Traditional Scale, #47, 1969 – 1995, $25.00. (Photo courtesy Carol Karbowiak Gilbert)

Mesteno, dark buckskin w/dark brown points, 1992-98 ...**15.00**
Morgan, bay, w/star, 1965-71.**120.00**
Mustang Stallion (Mustang Family), sorrel, 1976-90 .**15.00**
Old Timer, alabaster (w/hat), 1966-76..........................**50.00**
Polo Pony, bay w/black points, 1976-82..........................**40.00**
Proud Arabian Mare, glossy alabaster, 1956-60.......**125.00**

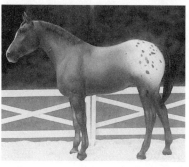

Quarter Horse Yearling (Appaloosa Yearling), sandy bay blanket appaloosa, Traditional Scale, 1971 – 1988, $40.00.

Quarter Horse Yearling, liver chestnut, 1970-80 ....**35.00**
Rearing Stallion, bay w/black points, 1965-80...............**25.00**
Running Mare, woodgrain, 1963-65 ....**150.00**
San Domingo, chestnut pinto, 1978-87..........................**35.00**
Seabiscuit, bay, 1976-90.........**9.00**
Sherman Morgan Prancing, black, 1991-92..........................**55.00**
Swamps (Black Silk), black, 1997 .**15.00**
Touch of Class, bay w/black points, 1986-88..........................**30.00**
Western Prancing Horse, smoke, 1961-76..........................**30.00**

Bubble Bath Containers

Figural bubble bath containers were popular in the 1960s and have become highly collectible today. The Colgate-Palmolive Company produced the widest variety called Soakies. Purex's Bubble Club characters were also popular. Most Soaky bottles came with detachable heads made of brittle plastic which cracked easily. Purex bottles were made of a softer plastic but lost their paint easier. Condition affects price considerably.

The interest collectors displayed in the old bottles prompted many to notice foreign-made products. Some of the same characters have been licensed by companies in Canada, Italy, the UK, Germany, and Japan, and the bottles they've designed have excellent detail. They're usually a little larger than domestic bottles and though fairly recent are often reminiscent of those made in the US during the 1960s.

For more information, we recommend *Schroeder's Collectible Toys, Antique to Modern*, published by Collector Books.

Alvin (Chipmunks), Colgate-Palmolive, w/puppet, neck tag & contents, M..................**50.00**
Alvin (Chipmunks), Soaky, Reckards, 6x6", M..........**30.00**

Aristocrats, Avon, 1971, NM..**8.00**
Atom Ant, Purex, 1965, rare, EX+.............................**40.00**
Auggie Doggie, Purex, 1967, rare, NM, from $50 to.............**60.00**
Baba Looey, Purex, 1960s, NM.**25.00**
Bambi, Colgate-Palmolive, 1960s, NM.................................**25.00**
Bamm-Bamm, Purex, 1960s, NM.................................**35.00**
Barney & Baby Bop, Kid Care, M......................................**8.00**
Barney Rubble, Milvern (Purex), 1960s, NM+.....................**35.00**
Betty Bubbles, Lander, 1950s, several variations, NM, ea .**35.00**
Big Bad Wolf, Tubby Time, 1960s, rare, NM.........................**35.00**
Blabber Mouse, Purex, 1960s, rare, NM.........................**125.00**
Bozo the Clown, Colgate-Palmolive, 1960s, NM ...**30.00**
Breezly the Bear, 1960s, rare, NM.................................**150.00**
Broom Hilda, Lander, 1977, rare, EX.................................**30.00**

Brutus and Popeye, Colgate-Palmolive, 1960s, NM, $35.00 each.

Bullwinkle, Fuller Brush, 1970, rare, NM........................**60.00**

Care Bears, AGC, 1984, several variations, NM, ea, from $5 to.....................................**10.00**

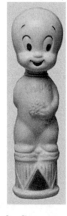

Left: Casper, Colgate-Palmolive, 1960s, EX+, $30.00.
Right: Lippy the Lion, Purex, 1962, $35.00. (Photo courtesy Greg Moore and Joe Pizzo)

Cecil Sea Serpent, Purex, 1962, NM.................................**40.00**

Creature From the Black Lagoon, Colgate-Palmolive, 1963, NM+..............................**125.00**

Dino, Purex, 1960s, rare, NM+.**85.00**

Droop-A-Long Coyote, Purex, 1960s, rare, EX+............**35.00**

Elmo, Softsoap, 1992, NM, from $5 to.....................................**10.00**

ET, Avon, 1984, NM..............**15.00**

Felix the Cat, Colgate-Palmolive, 1960s, EX+.....................**30.00**

Flintstones, Fun Bath, Roclar (Purex), 1970s, MIB (sealed)..............**75.00**

Goofy, Colgate-Palmolive, 1960s, w/car head, M.................**25.00**

Hot Wheels Race Car, Cosrich, 1993, NM.......................**15.00**

Huckleberry Hound, Milvern, 1960s, 15", M.................**40.00**

Humpty Dumpty, Avon, 1960s, NM, from $5 to..............**10.00**

Jinx w/Pixie & Dixie, Purex, 1960s, NM.....................**30.00**

Jurassic Park Dinosaur, Cosrich, 1992, NM, from $5 to **10.00**

Little Mermaid, Kid Care, 1991, tail up, NM.....................**10.00**

Little Orphan Annie, Lander, 1977, NM.......................**25.00**

Lucy (Peanuts), Avon, 1970, MIB................................**20.00**

Mighty Mouse, Lander, 1978, rare, VG+................................**20.00**

Miss Piggy, Calgon, Treasure Island outfit, M..............**10.00**

Mr Magoo, Colgate-Palmolive, 1960s, EX+.....................**25.00**

Paul McCartney, Soaky, 1965, EX...............................**75.00**

Peter Potamous, Purex, 1960s, M....................................**20.00**

Pokey, Novelty Packaging, 1987, NM................................**40.00**

Popeye, Colgate-Palmolive, 1977, rare, NM........................**35.00**

Quick Draw McGraw, Purex, 1960s, several variations, NM, ea **30.00**

Ricochet Rabbit, Purex, 1960s, EX................................**50.00**

Schroeder (Peanuts), Avon, 1970, MIB................................**25.00**

Scooby Doo, Colgate-Palmolive, 1977, NM.......................**45.00**

Skeletor (Masters of the Universe), Ducair Bio, NM+.............**15.00**

Smokey the Bear, Colgate-Palmolive, 1960s, NM ...**25.00**

Thumper, Colgate-Palmolive, 1960s, EX **25.00**

Wally Gator, Purex, 1963, rare,
M 50.00
Wendy, Colgate-Palmolive, NM .30.00
Yogi Bear, Purex, 1960s, several
variations, NM, ea 50.00

Cake Toppers

The first cake toppers appeared on wedding cakes in the 1880s and were made almost entirely of sugar. The early 1900s saw toppers carved from wood and affixed to ornate plaster pedestal bases and backgrounds. A few single-mold toppers were even made from poured lead. From the 1920s to the 1950s bisque, porcelain, and chalkware figures reigned supreme. The faces and features on many of these were very realistic and life-like. The beautiful Art Deco era was also in evidence.

Celluloid kewpie types made a brief appearance from the late 1930s to the 1940s. These were quite fragile because the celluloid they were made of could be easily dented and cracked. The true Rose O'Neill kewpie look-alike also appeared for awhile during this period. During and after World War II and into the Korean Conflict of the 1950s, groom figures in military dress appeared. Only a limited amount was ever produced; they are quite rare. From the 1950s into the 1970s, plastics were used almost exclusively. Toppers took on a vacant, assembly-line appearance with no specific attention to detail or fashion.

In the 1970s, bisque returned and plastic disappeared. Toppers were again more lifelike. For the most part, they remain that way today. Wedding cakes now often display elegant and elaborate toppers such as those made by Royal Doulton and Lladro.

Toppers should not be confused with the bride and groom doll sets of the same earlier periods. While some smaller dolls could and did serve as toppers, they were usually too unbalanced to stay upright on a cake. The true topper consisted of a small bride and groom anchored to (or a part of) a round flat base which made it extremely stable for resting on a soft, frosted cake surface. Cake toppers never did double-duty as play items.

Bride & groom, chalkware, arm-in-arm, 1920s, 3⅛" 80.00
Bride & groom, chalkware, 1920s, 4½", EX 100.00
Bride & groom, groom in Navy outfit, chalkware, 1930s-40s, EX 70.00

Bride and Groom, poured lead, single mold, 1920s, $45.00. (Photo courtesy Jeannie Greenfield)

Cinderella's Silver Coach, lights-up, Lefton, 8", EX **410.00**

Elvis w/Bride & Groom, lights-up, 6½x3½", EX..................**190.00**

Mickey & Minnie Mouse, WDW/ Wedgwood, 5½", MIB **65.00**

Military couple, flowers, leaves & 48-star flag.....................**60.00**

1900s couple on plaster, bower of cloth flowers w/painted center **50.00**

1930s couple on raised/sculpted base, columns w/floral trim, 10"....................................**75.00**

1930s porcelain kewpie, crepe-paper attire, plaster base, 3"....................................**50.00**

California Potteries

In recent years, pottery designed by many of the artists who worked in their own small studios in California during the 1940s through the 1960s has become highly sought after. Values continue to be impressive, though slightly compromised by the influence of the Internet. Among the more popular studios are Kay Finch, Florence Ceramics, Brayton, Howard Pierce, and Sascha Brastoff; but Matthew Adams, Marc Bellair, and deLee are attracting their share of attention as well, and there are others.

It's a fascinating field, one covered very well in Jack Chipman's *Collector's Encyclopedia of California Pottery, Second Edition* (Collector Books). Mike Nickel and Cynthia Horvath have written *Kay Finch Ceramics, Her Enchanted World* (Schiffer), a must for collectors interested in Kay Finch ceramics; and to learn more about Florence ceramics, you'll want to read *The Complete Book of Florence Ceramics: A Labor of Love*, written by Margaret Wehrspaun and Sue and Jerry Kline. They are listed in the Directory under Tennessee. See also Bauer; Cookie Jars; Franciscan; Metlox.

Adams, Matthew

Ashtray, elk on green, ovoid, 8x9".**45.00**

Ashtray, walrus, boomerang, free-form, 5¾x11¾" **65.00**

Creamer, polar bear, 4¾" **30.00**

Plate, Eskimo child in parka, #162, 7½"........................**50.00**

Salt & pepper shakers, igloos, gold trim, 3¾", pr..................**60.00**

Vase, Eskimo, 13½", minimum value $250.00. (Photo courtesy Jack Chipman)

Vase, Northern Lights & mountains, 7", EX **75.00**

Bellaire, Marc

Ashtray, Clown, multicolor on cream, 7"........................**65.00**

Bowl, Beachcomber, low teardrop shape, 12" L **100.00**

Bowl, dancing harlequins, footed, 7½" dia............................**80.00**

Figurine, Jamaican man playing guitar............................**300.00**

Platter, Friendly Island, 10".**135.00**

Tray, Jungle Dancer, figure on black & green, 12" dia.**145.00**

Tray, tribal figures in brown on gold, 15" long, $125.00.

Vase, Polynesian woman, 9".**100.00**

Brastoff, Sascha

Ashtray, peacock, 3 cigarette rests, 6¾" dia............................**28.00**

Ashtray, 5 partridges, multicolor w/gold birds on white, 5¾" sq....................................**30.00**

Creamer & sugar bowl, black w/gold, gold lid on sugar bowl.......**65.00**

Figurine, rooster, gold on speckled gold, 17x11"..................**165.00**

Pitcher, turquoise w/black & blue decor, #68, 10¾"............**80.00**

Pitcher, woman figural, 13", from $400.00 to $475.00.

Plate, Chi Chi Bird, 8½".....**200.00**

Vase, Roof Tops on white, #047, 8½"...............................**120.00**

Vase, turquoise w/blue & black decor, egg shape, 8x4¼"............................**50.00**

Brayton Laguna

Candle holder, Blackamoor seated on blue rug, 5"................**85.00**

Figurine, baby sitting in diaper, lg cowlick, blue eyes, 4", EX.**105.00**

Figurine, cow, purple, 5½x9".**200.00**

Figurine, donkey & cart, cart bottom & slats are wood, EX.......**130.00**

Figurine, Gay Nineties Bar, 3 men at bar, 8½x7½", from $100 to...................................**125.00**

Figurine, panther, snarling, #23-26, black w/jeweled collar, NM...............................**200.00**

Figurine, Pat (little girl) w/doll at back, 7", EX..................**135.00**

Figurine, Rosita, Spanish girl holding flower basket, 5½"...**100.00**

Figurine, rooster, ink stamp: Brayton - Calif USA, 8", $75.00. (Photo courtesy Lee Garmon)

Figurine, Sambo, Black boy, blue bibs, yellow hat, white shirt, 7¾"...............................**185.00**

Flower holder, Sally, freckled face, 7" **45.00**

Pitcher, orange-red w/green, early, 2⅝" **70.00**

Vase, white bonnet w/pink hand-painted roses & blue ribbon, 3x4" **35.00**

Cleminson Pottery

Bowl, Love Me on blue flowers & pink polka-dots, heart shape, 2¾" **15.00**

Button holder, lady figural, 6¾".**45.00**

Cigarette dispenser, wall hanging, 9x4" **25.00**

Cleanser shaker, Cleanser Kate, 6½" **40.00**

Creamer, rooster, 5½", from $40 to **50.00**

Cup, clown face w/hat lid, from $60 to **80.00**

Cup & saucer, jumbo; Mom..**16.00**

Darning egg, Darn It, girl form, original ribbon, 5", from $50 to **60.00**

Dish, 3-part, free-form, Galagray, 15x8" **22.50**

Marmalade, flowerpot with strawberry finial, 4", $25.00.

Mug, Morning After, Never Again inside, w/lid, 2¾" **22.00**

Soap dish, girl in tub, scarce, 4x5", EX **65.00**

String holder, heart shape, w/verse, 4½x5" **50.00**

Sugar shaker, represents girl, 3⅛x6" **30.00**

Wall plaque, apple decoration, 8¼" dia **22.00**

Wall plaque, mixed flowers, scalloped rim, 7" dia.............**12.50**

Wall pocket, kettle form, w/verse, 7¼" **30.00**

Wall pocket, salt crock, 5¾x6½" .**65.00**

Wall pocket, Take Time for Tea, 7¾x6⅝" **50.00**

DeForest of California

Bank, Goody, pig figural, brown or pink, 1956, from $225 to.**275.00**

Condiment, Horse Radish on hat, smiling face, from $25 to.**35.00**

Covered dish, peanut w/squirrel finial, from $15 to **20.00**

Creamer, pig figural, pink or brown, 1956, ea, from $20 to **25.00**

Hors d'oeuvres, pig figural w/holes in back, from $25 to.......**30.00**

Onion-head spice jars, set of six in wireware frame, NM, $235.00 (at auction). (Photo courtesy Janice Wise)

Plate, chop; Bar-B-Cutie, onion face, 15", from $65 to.....**75.00**

Plate, dinner; Bar-B-Cutie, onion face, 11", from $35 to.....**45.00**

Spoon rest, boy & girl faces form 2 rests, from $40 to..........**50.00**

deLee

Bank, Money Bunny, w/purse in right hand, from $90 to .**95.00**

Cookie jar, Cookie boy or girl chef, 12", from $250 to **400.00**

Figurine, Babe, girl holding starfish, round sticker, rare, 4" **85.00**

Figurine, Chesty, squirrel, 3½" **25.00**

Figurine, Danny, original sticker, 8½" **30.00**

Figurine, Dolores, incised mark, 8", from $75 to **100.00**

Figurine, Hank, green pants, leans against vase, EX **42.00**

Figurine, Joey, clown, 7½", from $110 to **150.00**

Figurine, lamb, 3½" **40.00**

Figurine, Miss Muffet, 5", from $90 to **125.00**

Figurine, Pedro, bongo player, from $75 to **125.00**

Figurine, Siamese cat, 4" L..**35.00**

Figurines, Grunt & Groan, pigs, floral decoration, pr **50.00**

Planter, Daisy, pink skirt, aqua top, pink clay, 8", NM....**30.00**

Planter/vase, crescent shape w/scalloped edge, 3½x6" .**32.50**

Wall pocket, bell w/cherries, black, red & green, 5½" **20.00**

Finch, Kay

Ashtray, Bloodhound head, #4773, 6½x6½" **150.00**

Ashtray, swan, #4958, 4½"...**70.00**

Candlesticks, turkey figural, #5794, 3¾", pr **225.00**

Figurine, Baby Ambrosia, cat, #5165, 5½" **200.00**

Figurine, Butch & Biddy, rooster & hen, #177 & #178, pr **175.00**

Figurine, choir boy, kneeling, #211, 5½" **65.00**

Figurine, elephant, Peanuts, #191, 8½" **350.00**

Figurine, guppy, fish, #173, 2½".**125.00**

Figurine, hippopotamus with bow, $400.00.

Figurine, long-eared donkey w/basket, #4769, 4"......**125.00**

Figurine, parakeet on perch, #5164, 5¾".....................**225.00**

Figurine, Scandie boy & girl, #126 & #127, 5¼", pr **150.00**

Figurine, Tubby, playful bear, #4847, 4¼"....................**225.00**

String holder, dog head, bow in hair, 4½x4"...................**400.00**

Wall plaque, sea horse, #5788, 16" L....................................**225.00**

Florence Ceramics

Note: The amount of applied decoration — lace, flowers, etc. — has a great deal of influence on values. Our ranges reflect this factor.

Abigail, beige dress w/red hair, 8", from $170 to.................**200.00**

Catherine, from $575.00 to $700.00.
(Photo courtesy Doug Foland)

Annette, 8¼", from $500 to..**550.00**
Irene, pink dress, 6", from $60 to......................................**70.00**
June, pink w/blue floral dress, flower holder, 7", from $50 to......................................**60.00**
Louise, 7½", from $175 to...**200.00**
Mimi, white dress w/gold trim, flower holder, 6¼", from $70 to......................................**80.00**
Scarlett, beige dress w/green trim, brown hair, 9", from $200 to......................................**250.00**
Yvonne, blue dress w/white purse & hat, gold trim, 8¾", $425 to......................................**500.00**

Keeler, Brad

Dish, green leaf shape w/red lobster, 2-section, #872, 12x7", from $40 to......................**50.00**

Divided dish, Tomato ware, green leaves form sections, $65.00.

Figurine, duck, browns & greens, #50, 4¾".........................**50.00**
Figurine, flamingo, head down, #31, 9½", from $85 to ..**100.00**
Figurine, swan, #704, 16½".**125.00**
Figurine, titmouse, yellow, on stump, #720F, 5½".........**40.00**
Figurines, Siamese mother, #7988, 7": kitten, #939, 1⅞", pr **50.00**
Plate, red crab on green scalloped shape, 12½x11½" **90.00**
Salt & pepper shakers, tomatoes, red, 1½", pr **30.00**

Schoop, Hedi

Bowl, shell form, ivory w/gold, black interior, 1950s, 12" L.......**42.50**
Candle holder, double, spiral-twist base & branches..............**45.00**
Figurine/planter, Balinese dancer w/fan (planter), gold trim, 12"................................**100.00**
Figurine/planter, Repose, lady sits w/long black hair, gold trim, 12"................................**180.00**
Figurines, Dutch boy & girl, pastel pinks & blues, 11½", 11", pr **175.00**

Figurines, Oriental couple with buckets, 11½", 13", from $135.00 to $160.00 for the pair.

Planter, horse w/saddle, must be signed, 7".........................**80.00**

Plate, poodle, black & gray on white, 7½" sq..................**85.00**

Twin Winton

Salt shakers, Cow, wood stain with hand-painted details, $40.00 for the pair. (Photo courtesy Lee Garmon)

Ashtray, kitten, 6x8" **100.00**

Bank, elf, 8"............................**50.00**

Bank, Hillbilly Line (Men of the Mountains), Mountain Dew Loot, 7" **75.00**

Candle holder, Strauss, 10x5".**15.00**

Canister, Bucket, Coffee, 5x6".**30.00**

Canister, Pot O' Tea, 5x4"....**20.00**

Creamer, Artist Palette, 4" dia.**40.00**

Figurine, Boo Boo bear, made for Idea Inc, 4".....................**75.00**

Figurine, elf in stump, 3".....**60.00**

Figurine, rabbit, lg smile, dated 1940-43, 6"......................**45.00**

Figurine, squirrel w/arms extended, 2½"............................**25.00**

Mug, Bamboo Line, 6" **20.00**

Mug, Hillbilly Line (Men of the Mountains), #H-102, 5" .**30.00**

Napkin holder, cow, 6x7"......**85.00**

Pitcher, Hillbilly Line (Men of the Mountains), #H-101, 7½"..**85.00**

Planter, fisherman's creel, 6" .**60.00**

Punch cup, Hillbilly Line (Men of the Mountains), #H-111, 3" **15.00**

Salt & pepper shakers, apple, pr.**75.00**

Salt & pepper shakers, cable car, pr....................................**50.00**

Salt & pepper shakers, cop, pr.**40.00**

Salt & pepper shakers, goose, pr **45.00**

Salt & pepper shakers, lion, pr.**45.00**

Salt & pepper shakers, poodle, pr....................................**50.00**

Salt & pepper shakers, teddy bear, pr....................................**50.00**

Spoon rest, elf, TW-17, 5x10".**40.00**

Tumbler, Wood Grain Line, 4"....................................**20.00**

Wall planter, lamb's head, TW-301, 5½"........................**100.00**

Weil Ware

Ashtray, Malay Bambu, 6x4".**15.00**

Bowl, Malay Blossom, 2¼x8½" sq....................................**20.00**

Bowl, serving; Malay Bambu, 11½"................................**30.00**

Cigarette box, Malay Bambu.**25.00**

Creamer and sugar bowl, brown roses on yellow, with lid, $25.00.

Cup & saucer, Malay Blossom.**15.00**

Flower holder, lady in blue stands between columns, #4027, 11"....................................**90.00**

Flower holder, lady in pink w/2 white baskets, #4024, 9½" **60.00**

Flower holder, lady in white
w/blue apron, pot on shoulder,
7".....................................**40.00**
Flower holder, Oriental lady seated
w/fan behind head, 9".....**65.00**
Pitcher, Rose, 6-cup, 6½"......**55.00**
Planter, Ming Tree, 3x5" sq .**25.00**
Plate, Malay Blossom, 5½" sq .**10.00**
Platter, Malay Blossom, rectangu-
lar, 11x7"........................**25.00**
Saucer, Malay Bambu, 6" dia.**7.00**
Tidbit, Malay Blossom, 1-tier,
metal handle, 9½"..........**20.00**
Vase, Ming Tree, 6" sq..........**30.00**

Yona

Christmas tree ornament, choir
boy, 4½"...........................**9.00**
Decanter, clown figural, cold-
painted, 13"....................**65.00**
Figurine, angel carrying dog in her
arms, gold trim, 5".........**30.00**

Figurine, angel, Count Your Blessings, gold trim, 5", $35.00.
(Photo courtesy Sandy Fienhold, Empty Clown Collectibles)

Figurines, Oriental man & lady,
#15 & #16, 9", pr............**50.00**
Pill jar, plump lady, hair is lid,
Shafford label, ca 1960..**45.00**

Pretzel jar, Country Club, cold-paint-
ed red stripes, #8741 ....**150.00**
Tumbler, Country Club, cold-
painted red stripes, 5", NM.**20.00**
Wall plaque, Egyptian faces, black
& gold, 11", pr................**55.00**

California Raisins

In the fall of 1986, the California
Raisins made their first commercials
for television. In 1987 the PVC figurines were introduced. Initially
there were four: a singer, two conga
dancers, and a saxophone player. At
this time, Hardee's issued similar
but smaller figures. Later that year
Blue Surfboard (horizontal), and
three Bendees (which are about 5½"
tall with flat pancake-style bodies)
were issued for retail sale.

In 1988 twenty one Raisins
were made for sale in retail stores
and in some cases used for promotional efforts in grocery stores:
Blue Surfboard (vertical), Red
Guitar, Lady Dancer, Blue/Green
Sunglasses, Guy Winking, Candy
Cane, Santa Raisin, Bass Player,
Drummer, Tambourine Lady
(there were two styles), Lady
Valentine, Male Valentine, Boy
Singer, Girl Singer, Hip Guitar
Player, Sax Player with Beret, and
four Graduates. The Graduates
are identical in design to the original four characters released in
1987 but stand on yellow pedestals
and are attired in blue graduation
caps and yellow tassels. Bass
Player and Drummer were initially distributed in grocery stores

along with an application to join the California Raisin Fan Club located in Fresno, California. Later that year Hardee's issued six more: Blue Guitar, Trumpet Player, Roller Skater, Skateboard, Boom Box, and Yellow Surfboard. As was true with the 1987 line, the Hardee's characters were generally smaller than those produced for retail sales.

Eight more made their debut in 1989: Male in Beach Chair, Green Trunks with Surfboard, Hula Skirt, Girl Sitting on Sand, Piano Player, 'AC,' Mom, and Michael Raisin. During that year the Raisins starred in two movies: *Meet the Raisins* and *The California Raisins — Sold Out*, and were joined in figurine production by five movie characters (their fruit and vegetable friends): Rudy Bagaman, Lick Broccoli, Banana White, Leonard Limabean, and Cecil Thyme.

The last release of Raisins came in 1991 when Hardee's issued four more — Anita Break, Alotta Style, Buster, and Benny. All Raisins issued for retail sales and promotions in 1987 and 1988, including Hardee's issues for those years, are dated with the year of production (usually on the bottom of one foot). Of those Raisins released for retail sale in 1989, only the Beach Scene characters are dated, and they are actually dated 1988. Hardee's Raisins, issued in 1991, are also undated. On Friday, November 22, 1991, the California Raisins were enshrined in the Smithsonian Institution to the tune of *I Heard It Through the Grapevine*. We recommend *Schroeder's Collectible Toys, Antique to Modern*, for more information.

Prices are down from their peak of a few years ago — hard hit, as many things have been, by the economy as well as eBay. Our prices reflect this downturn.

Beach Theme Edition, Boy in Beach Chair, orange glasses, 1988, M...........................**20.00**

Beach Theme Edition, Boy With Surfboard, brown base, 1988, M, $20.00.

Beach Theme Edition, Boy w/Surfboard, not connected to foot, 1988, M **10.00**

Beach Theme Edition, Hula Girl, yellow shoes/bracelet, 1988, M.....................................**20.00**

Christmas Issue, w/candy cane, 1988, M............................**9.00**

Christmas Issue, w/red hat, 1988, M.....................................**9.00**

Hardee's 2nd Promotion, Captain Toonz, w/blue boom box, 1988, sm, M...............................**2.00**

Hardee's 2nd Promotion, Waves Weaver I, foot on surfboard, 1988, sm **5.00**

Meet the Raisins 1st Edition, Lick Broccoli, w/guitar, 1989, M **20.00**

Meet the Raisins 1st Edition, Piano, red hair, green shoes, 1989, M............................**35.00**

Meet the Raisins 2nd Promotion, Cecil Thyme (Carrot), 1989, M...................................**250.00**

Post Raisin Bran Issue, Saxophone, inside sax painted red, 1987, M **2.00**

Special Edition, Michael Raisin, 1989, M............................**15.00**

Special Lover's Edition, Valentine, boy holding heart, 1988, M **8.00**

1st Commercial Issue, Guitar, w/red guitar, 1988, M **8.00**

1st Commercial Issue, Winky, hitchhiking pose & winking, 1988, M............................**5.00**

1st Key Chains, Saxophone, w/gold sax & no hat, 1987, M.....................................**5.00**

2nd Commercial Issue, Bass Player, w/gray slippers, 1988, M.....................................**8.00**

2nd Commercial Issue, Drummer, 1988, M............................**10.00**

2nd Commercial Issue, Girl w/Tamborine (Ms Delicious), 1988, M............................**15.00**

2nd Key Chains, Hip Band Guitarist (Hendrix), headband/guitar, 1988, M **65.00**

3rd Commercial Issue, Saxophone, black beret, blue eyelids, 1988, M............................**15.00**

Cameras

Whether buying a camera for personal use, adding to a collection, or for resale, use caution. Complex usable late-model cameras are difficult to check out at sales, and you should be familiar with the camera model or have confidence in the seller's claims before purchasing one for your personal use. If you are just beginning a camera collection, there are a multitude of different types and models and special features to select from in building your collection; you should have on hand some of the available guide books listing various models and types. Camera collecting can be a very enjoyable hobby and can be done within your particular funding ability.

Buying for resale can be a very profitable experience if you are careful in your selection and have made arrangements with buyers who have made their requirements known to you. Generally, buying low-cost, mass-produced cameras is not advisable; you may have a difficult time finding a buyer for such cameras. Of these low-cost types, only those that are mint or new in the original box have any appreciable appeal to collectors. Very old cameras are not necessarily valuable — it all depends on availability. The major criterion is quality; prices offered for mint-condition cameras may be double or triple those of average-wear items. You can expect to find that foreign-made cameras are preferred by most buyers because of the general perception that their lenses and shutters are superior. The German- and Japanese-made cameras dominate the 'classic' camera market. Polaroid cameras and movie cameras have yet to gain a significant collector's market.

The cameras listed here represent only a very small cross section of thousands of cameras available. Values are given for examples with average wear and in good working order; they represent average retail prices with limited guarantees. It is very important to note that purchase prices at flea markets, garage sales, or estate sales would have to be far less for them to be profitable to a resaler who has the significant expense of servicing the camera, testing it, and guaranteeing it to a user or a collector.

Canon Rangefinder IIS, ca 1955, from $200.00 to $400.00. (Photo courtesy C.E. Cataldo)

Canon F-1............................**225.00**
Canon III............................**250.00**
Canon J, 1939-44.............**5,000.00**
Canon S-II, 1947-49............**375.00**
Canon TL, from $40 to.........**60.00**
Canon VT, 1956-57.............**300.00**
Compass Camera, 1938, from $1,000 to....................**1,300.00**
Contex II or III, 1936, from $200 to...............................**400.00**
Eastman Folding Brownie Six-20......................................**12.00**
Eastman Kodak Bantam, Art Deco, 1935-38.................**35.00**
Eastman Kodak Box Hawkeye No 2A.......................................**8.00**
Eastman Kodak Medalist, 1941-48, from $140 to...........**175.00**
Eastman Kodak No 1 Folding Pocket camera...............**20.00**
Eastman Kodak Pony 135....**10.00**
Eastman Kodak Retina IIa..**80.00**
Eastman Kodak Retina IIIC, from $250 to..........................**375.00**
Eastman Kodak Signet 35....**20.00**
Eastman Kodak 35, 1940-51.**25.00**
Edinex by Wirgen.................**30.00**
Exakta VX, 1951...................**85.00**
FED-1 USSR, prewar, from $70 to................................**120.00**
Fujica AX-5.........................**125.00**

Agfa, box type, 1930-50, from $5 to....................................**20.00**
Agfa, Karat-35, 1940............**35.00**
Agroflex, Seventy-five, TLR, 1949-58.......................................**7.00**
Aires, 35III, 1958..................**35.00**
Ansco, Cadet...........................**5.00**
Ansco, Memar, 1954-58........**20.00**
Ansco, Speedex, Standard, 1950.**15.00**
Argus, A2F, 1940..................**20.00**
Argus, C4, 2.8 lens w/flash...**30.00**
Asahiflex 1, 1st Japanese SLR.**500.00**
Bell & Howell Dial-35...........**40.00**
Bolsey, B2..............................**20.00**
Burke & James, Cub, 1914..**20.00**
Canon AE-1, from $50 to......**80.00**
Canon F, 1958-61................**300.00**

Graflex Speed Graphic, various sizes, ea, from $100 to .**200.00**
Herbert-George, Donald Duck, 1946 ....**35.00**
Konica FS-1 ....**60.00**
Kowa H, 1963-67 ....**25.00**
Leica IID, 1932-38, from $250 to..........................**400.00**
Leica M3, 1954-66, from $500 to..........................**1,000.00**
Mamiyaflex TLR, 1951, from $100 to **150.00**
Minolta Autocord, TLR.......**100.00**
Minolta SR-7 ....**50.00**
Minolta SRT-202 ....**90.00**
Minolta XD-11, 1977..........**140.00**
Minolta-16, miniature, various models, ea, from $15 to .**30.00**
Miranda Automex II, 1963...**70.00**
Nikon EM, from $45 to.........**75.00**
Nikon FG **115.00**
Nikon S-2 Rangefinder, 1954-58, from $300 to **500.00**
Olympus OM-1 ....**120.00**
Olympus Pen EE, compact half-frame **35.00**
Pax, M3, 1957 ....**30.00**
Pentax ME............................**75.00**
Petri FT, FT-1000, FT & EE & similar models, ea..........**70.00**
Plaubel-Makina II, 1933-39.**200.00**
Polaroid SX-70 ....**35.00**
Polaroid 180, 185, 190, 195, ea, from $100 to **250.00**
Praktica Super TL **50.00**
Regula, King, various models, fixed lens, ea **25.00**
Ricoh Diacord 1, built-in meter, 1958 ....**75.00**
Ricoh Singlex, 1965 ....**80.00**
Rolleicord II, 1936-50, from $70 to..................................**90.00**
Rolleiflex SL35M, 1978 ......**100.00**

Samoca 35, 1950s................**25.00**
Spartus Press Flash, 1939-50.**10.00**
Tessina, miniature, from $300 to.**500.00**
Topcon Super D, 1963-74 ...**125.00**
Tower 45, w/Nikkor lens **200.00**
Univex-A, Univ Camera Co, 1933 ....**25.00**
Voigtlander Bessa, w/rangefinder, 1936 ....**140.00**
Voigtlander Vito II, 1950.....**40.00**
Yashica Electro-35, 1966......**25.00**
Yashicamat 124G, TLR, from $150 to **230.00**
Zeiss Ikon Juwell, 1927-39.**500.00**
Zenit A, USSR....................**35.00**

Zwiss Contaflex I, ca 1953 – 1958, Tessar 45/F.2.8 lens, from $60.00 to $90.00. (Photo courtesy C.E. Cataldo)

Candlewick

Candlewick was one of the all-time bestselling lines of The Imperial Glass Company of Bellaire, Ohio. It was produced from 1936 until the company closed in 1982. More than 741 items were made over the years; and though many are still easy to find today, some (such as the desk calendar, the chip and dip set, and the dresser set) are a challenge to

collect. Candlewick is easily iden-
tified by its beaded stems, han-
dles, and rims characteristic of the
tufted needlework of our pioneer
women for which it was named.
For a complete listing of the
Candlewick line, we recommend
*Elegant Glassware of the
Depression Era* by Gene Florence
(Collector Books).

Ashtray, heart, #400/172, 4½".**10.00**
Ashtray set, round, crystal or colored,
  nesting, #400/550, 3-pc.......**35.00**
Bowl, #400/7F, 8" **37.50**
Bowl, bouillon; handles, #400/
  126...............................**50.00**

Bowl, divided; handles, 6", $25.00.

Bowl, handles, #400/72B, 8½".**22.00**
Bowl, oval, #400/124A, 11".**275.00**
Bowl, relish; 2-part, #400/84,
  6½" **25.00**
Bowl, salad; #400/75B, 10½" .**40.00**
Bowl, sauce; deep, #400/243,
  5½"...............................**40.00**
Bowl, shallow, #400/17F, 12".**47.50**
Bowl, 3-toed, #400/205, 10" .**175.00**
Butter dish, #400/144, 5½" dia .**35.00**
Butter dish, bead top, #400/161,
  ¼-lb **30.00**
Candle holder, flower, sq,
  #400/40S, 6½" **75.00**
Candle holder, 3-toed, #400/207,
  4½"...............................**100.00**

Candle holder, 3-way, beaded
  base, #400/115..............**125.00**
Candy box, beaded, ftd, #400/
  140............................**395.00**
Celery tray, handles, oval,
  #400/105, 13½"...............**35.00**
Coaster, #400/78, 4"..............**10.00**
Compote, fruit; crimped, ftd,
  #40/103C, 10"...............**200.00**
Compote, 3-bead stem, #400/220
  5"................................**85.00**
Creamer, flat, bead handle,
  #400/126 ....**32.50**

**Creamer and sugar bowl on tray,
$60.00 for the set.**

Cup, coffee; #400/37 ....**7.50**
Cup, tea; #400/35 ....**8.00**
Fork & spoon set, #400/75....**40.00**
Ice tub, handles, #400/168, 7".**250.00**
Marmalade, beaded foot, w/lid &
  spoon, #400/1989, 3-pc...**45.00**
Mayonnaise, plate+divided bowl+2
  ladles, #400/84, 4-pc **45.00**
Mustard jar, w/spoon, #400/156 .**40.00**
Oil, bead base, #400/164, 4-oz .**55.00**
Oil, handle, bulbous bottom,
  #400/279, 6-oz **90.00**
Pitcher, beaded ft, #400/18, 80-oz..**250.00**
Pitcher, juice/cocktail; #400/19, 40-
  oz..................................**210.00**
Pitcher, low foot, #400/19, 16-oz.**250.00**
Pitcher, plain, #400/419, 40-oz.**50.00**
Plate, dinner; #400/10D, 10½".**45.00**
Plate, luncheon; #400/7D, 9".**15.00**
Plate, oval, #400/169, 8" **25.00**

Plate, serving; cupped edge, #400/92V, 13½" **47.50**

Plate, torte; #400/17D, 14" ...**50.00**

Punch ladle, #400/91 ....**30.00**

Salt cellar, #400/61, 2".........**11.00**

Shakers, bead foot, straight side, chrome top, #400/247, pr.**20.00**

Stem, cocktail; #3800, 4-oz...**25.00**

Stem, cocktail; #400/190, 4-oz .**22.00**

Stem, water goblet; #3800, 9-oz.**40.00**

Stem, wine; #3400, 4-oz........**26.00**

Sugar bowl, bead handles, #400/30, 6-oz **8.00**

Tidbit server, 2-tier, cupped, #400/2701 ....**60.00**

Tray, #400/29, 6½"...............**18.00**

Tumbler, #3800, 9-oz **30.00**

Tumbler, juice; #400/19, 5-oz.**12.50**

Tumbler, parfait; #3400, 6-oz.**70.00**

Tumbler, sherbet; #400/18, 6-oz .**60.00**

Vase, bud; bead foot, #400/28C, 8½"................................**110.00**

Vase, flat w/crimped edge, #400/287C, 6" **50.00**

Vase, footed, #400/193, 10".**250.00**

Vase, rolled rim, bead handles, #400/87R, 7" **45.00**

Cape Cod by Avon

Though now discontinued, the Avon company sold this dark ruby red glassware through their catalogs since the '70s, and there seems to be a good supply of it around today. In addition to the place settings (there are plates in three sizes, soup and dessert bowls, a cup and saucer, tumblers in two sizes, three different goblets, a mug, and a wine glass), there are many lovely accessory

items as well. Among them you'll find a cake plate, a pitcher, a platter, a hurricane-type candle lamp, a butter dish, napkin rings, and a pie plate server. Note: Mint-in-box items are worth about 20% more than the same piece with no box.

Bell, Hostess, unmarked, 1979-80, 6½"..................................**18.50**

Bell, Hostess; marked Christmas 1979, 6½"........................**22.50**

Bowl, dessert; 1978-90, 5" **14.50**

Bowl, rimmed soup; 1991, 7½" .**24.50**

Bowl, vegetable; marked Centennial Edition 1886-1986, 8¾" .**35.00**

Bowl, vegetable; unmarked, 1986-90, 8¾"............................**30.00**

Box, heart form, w/lid, 1989-90, 4" wide **20.00**

Butter dish, w/lid, 1983-84, ¼-lb, 7" L **25.00**

Candle holder, hurricane type w/clear chimney, 1985 ...**45.00**

Candlestick, 1983-83, 2½", ea .**10.00**

Candlesticks, 8¾", $25.00 for the pair.

Candy dish, 1987-90, 3½x6" dia.**19.50**

Christmas ornament, 6-sided, marked Christmas 1990, 3¼"............**15.00**

Creamer, footed, 1981-84, 4"..**12.50**

Cruet, oil; w/stopper, 1975-80, 5-oz....................................**12.50**

Cup & saucer, 15th Anniversary, marked 1975-90 on cup, 7-oz **24.50**

Cup & saucer, 1990-93, 7-oz..**19.50**

Goblet, champagne; 1991, 8-oz, 5¼"....................................**15.00**

Goblet, claret; 1992, 5-oz, 5¼".**14.00**

Goblet, water; 1976-90, 9-oz...**9.50**

Mug, pedestal foot, 1982-84, 6-oz, 5"......................................**12.50**

Napkin ring, 1989-90, 1¾" dia..**9.50**

Pie plate, server, 1992-93, 10¾" dia....................................**38.00**

Pitcher, water; footed, 1984-85, 60-oz **50.00**

Plate, bread & butter; 1992-93, 5½"......................................**9.50**

Plate, cake; pedestal foot, 1991, 3½"x10¾" dia...................**50.00**

Plate, dessert; 1980-90, 7½"...**8.00**

Plate, dinner; 1982-90, 11"...**30.00**

Platter, oval, 1986, 13".........**60.00**

Relish, rectangular, 2-part, 1985-86, 9½"............................**19.50**

Salt & pepper shakers, marked May 1978, ea....................**9.50**

Salt & pepper shakers, unmarked, 1978-80, ea **7.50**

Sauce boat, footed, 1988, 8" L.**29.50**

Sugar bowl, footed, 1980-83, 3½"....................................**12.50**

Tidbit tray, 2-tiered (7" & 10" dia), 9¾"......................................**55.00**

Tumbler, straight-sided, footed, 1988, 8-oz, 3½"...............**12.00**

Tumbler, straight-sided, 1990, 12-oz, 5½" **14.00**

Vase, footed, 1985, 8"............**24.00**

Wine goblets, 4½", $3.00 each; Decanter, 10½", $18.00.

Carnival Chalkware

Chalkware statues of Kewpies, glamour girls, assorted dogs, horses, etc., were given to winners of carnival games from about 1910 until the 1950s. Today's collectors especially value those representing well-known personalities such as Disney characters and comic book heroes. Refer to *The Carnival Chalk Prize* by Tom Morris for more information. Mr. Morris is in the Directory under Oregon.

Bear, bank, standing, 1940-50, 11"....................................**45.00**

Betty Boop, Max Fleischer Studios, 1930-40, 14½"...............**320.00**

Bird w/nest, ca 1940-50, 9½"..**40.00**

Bugs Bunny, standing behind tree, 1940-50, 16"....................**85.00**

Bulldog, sitting, chubby, ca 1935-45, 6¼"............................**25.00**

Chicken, flat back, ca 1935-50, up to 4"....................................**9.00**

Clown, bank, sitting behind drum, ca 1940-50, 12".............**65.00**

Clown, marked Happy, ca 1940-50, 7½".............**35.00**

Dog, sitting, flat back, 1935-50, up to 5".............**8.00**

Donald Duck, bank, head only, 1940-50, 10½".............**80.00**

Donkey, ca 1940 – 1950, 12", $40.00.
(Photo courtesy Tom Morris)

Elephant, standing, flat back, 1940-50, 10½".............**40.00**

Ferdinand the Bull, sitting, ca 1940-50, 10½".............**75.00**

Horse, standing w/western saddle, ca 1940-50, 10½".............**45.00**

Humpty Dumpty, sitting on fence, lg smile, 1940-50, 11" **45.00**

Indian chief on horseback, ca 1930-40, 11", from $50 to.........**65.00**

Lion, standing & growling, 1940-50, 9¼x12".............**45.00**

Majorette, marked El Segundo Novelty Co, 1949, 12" **65.00**

Owl on limb, bank, ca 1935-45, 10¼".............**55.00**

Popeye, boxing stance, 1940-50, 9¾".............**55.00**

Rabbit, sitting, flat back, ca 1945-50, 7½".............**20.00**

Scottie dog, sitting, ears pointed, ca 1935-45, 7".............**20.00**

Shirley Temple, full skirt, glows in the dark, 1935-50, 7".....**65.00**

Superman, wearing cape, S emblem on chest, 1940-50, 15".............**295.00**

Wimpy standing w/hands behind his back, 1930-50, 13½".**185.00**

Cat-Tail Dinnerware

Cat-Tail was a dinnerware pattern popular during the late 1920s until sometime in the 1940s. So popular, in fact, that ovenware, glassware, tinware, and even a kitchen table were made to coordinate with it. The dinnerware was made primarily by Universal potteries of Cambridge, Ohio, though a catalog from Hall China Co. circa 1927 shows a three-piece coffee service, and there may have been other pieces made by Hall as well. Cattail was sold for years by Sears, Roebuck and Company, and some items bear a mark with their name.

The pattern is unmistakable — a cluster of red cattails (usually six but sometimes only one or two) with black stems on creamy white. Shapes certainly vary; Universal used a minimum of three of their standard mold designs — Camwood, Old Holland, Laurella — and there were possibly others. Some pieces are marked 'Wheelock' on the bottom. Wheelock was a department store in Peoria, Illinois.

If you are trying to decorate a '40s vintage kitchen, no other design could afford you more to work with. To see many of the pieces that are available and to learn more about the line, read *The Collector's Encyclopedia of American Dinnerware* by Jo Cunningham (Collector Books).

Bowl, footed, 9½" **20.00**
Bowl, Old Holland shape, marked Wheelock, 6" **7.00**
Bowl, straight sides, 6¼" **12.00**
Bowl, w/lid, from ice box set, 4" .**12.00**
Bowl, w/lid, from ice box set, 6" .**18.50**
Butter dish, 1-lb **30.00**
Canister set, tin, 4-pc **60.00**

Chop plate, tab handles, 11", $30.00.

Coffeepot, electric...............**150.00**
Coffeepot, 3-pc **70.00**
Cookie jar, from $75 to **100.00**
Cracker jar, barrel shape, from $75 to **85.00**
Creamer...............................**20.00**
Cup & saucer, from $6 to **10.00**
Custard cup **9.00**
Gravy boat, from $18 to........**25.00**
Jug, ball; ceramic-topped cork stopper...........................**37.50**
Jug, canteen **38.00**
Jug, refrigerator; w/handle ..**38.00**
Jug, 1-qt...............................**25.00**
Match holder, tinware **35.00**

Pickle dish/gravy boat liner .**20.00**
Pie plate................................**30.00**
Pitcher, glass, w/ice lip, from $75 to **125.00**
Pitcher, milk/utility **22.00**
Pitcher, water........................**40.00**
Plate, chop; tab handles, 11" .**35.00**
Plate, sq, 7¼" **7.00**
Platter, 13½" **30.00**
Salad set (fork, spoon & bowl), from $50 to **60.00**
Saucer, from $3 to...................**6.00**
Scales, metal **37.00**
Stack set, 3-pc w/lids, from $35 to **40.00**
Sugar bowl, open, from $8 to.**10.00**
Sugar bowl, w/lid, from $20 to .**25.00**
Tablecloth **90.00**
Teapot, 4-cup.........................**35.00**
Tray, for batter set................**75.00**
Tumbler, juice; glass.............**30.00**
Tumbler, water; glass...........**35.00**
Waste can, tinware **35.00**

Ceramic Arts Studio

Whether you're a collector of American pottery or not, chances are you'll like the distinctive styling of the figurines, salt and pepper shakers, and other novelty items made by the Ceramic Arts Studio of Madison, Wisconsin, from about 1938 until approximately 1952. They're not especially hard to find — a trip to any good flea market will usually produce at least one good buy from among their vast array of products. They're easily spotted, once you've seen a few examples; but if you're not sure, check for the trademark — most are marked.

See the Directory for information concerning the CAS Collector's Association, listed under Clubs and Newsletters.

Ashtray, hippo, 5".............**135.00**
Bell, Lillibelle, 6½"............**165.00**
Bowl, Bonita, paisley shape, 3¾"
L....................................**65.00**
Candle holder, Hear No Evil, angel on cloud, 5".........**125.00**
Figurine, Alice in Wonderland, kneeling, 4½"..............**200.00**
Figurine, Aphrodite & Adonis, 7¾", 9", pr, from $650 to.......**695.00**
Figurine, birch-wood canoe, 8" L..............................**125.00**
Figurine, black bear cub, 2¼".**65.00**
Figurine, bunny baby, 2½"...**40.00**
Figurine, Burmese woman, 4½".**125.00**
Figurine, cat, kitten sleeping, 1"....................................**45.00**
Figurine, child w/towel, 5".**145.00**
Figurine, Colonial girl, 5".....**65.00**
Figurine, devil imp, sitting, 3½"..................................**150.00**
Figurine, dog, Collie pup playing, 2¼"..................................**45.00**
Figurine, dog, Pomeranian, standing, 3" **80.00**
Figurine, donkey, Dem, 4½".**125.00**
Figurine, duckling, 2¼".........**75.00**
Figurine, Egyptian man & woman, rare, 9½", pr.................**695.00**
Figurine, elephant, Elsie, 5"..**95.00**
Figurine, ewe, 2" L................**75.00**
Figurine, fish, straight tail, lg.**80.00**
Figurine, fox, sneering at goose, 3¼"...................................**95.00**
Figurine, girl praying, 3"......**50.00**
Figurine, guitar man on stool, scarce, 6½" **235.00**

Figurine, Isaac, 10"............**195.00**
Figurine, kangaroo mother, 4¾"..**90.00**
Figurine, leopards, fighting, 3½", 6¼" L, pr, from $250 to.**300.00**
Figurine, Little Bo Peep, 5½".**35.00**
Figurine, Lover Boy, 4½" **85.00**
Figurine, Peek-a-Boo pixie, 2½"..**65.00**
Figurine, Pioneer Sam & Pioneer Suzie, 5½", 5", pr **145.00**
Figurine, pixie sitting on bowl, 4½"..................................**145.00**
Figurine, rooster (fighting cock), 3¾"...................................**75.00**
Figurine, Santa Claus, 2¼".**145.00**
Figurine, Spring Sue, 5".......**85.00**

Figurines, Spanish Rhumba dancers, 7", 7½", $190.00 for the pair.

Figurines, Wee Eskimo boy & girl, 3¼", pr **35.00**
Head vase, Becky, 5¼" **195.00**
Head vase, Svea, 6" **215.00**
Metal accessory, arched window w/cross, 14"....................**80.00**
Metal accessory, pyramid shelf, flat back........................**75.00**
Miniature, pitcher, Diana Huntress, bisque, 3½" ...**65.00**
Miniature, teapot, applied swan, open **65.00**

Plaque, Blackamoor, 4¾" ...**495.00**
Plaque, Hamlet & Ophelia, 8¼",
pr **425.00**
Plaque, sprite, tail up, 4½"..**175.00**

**Salt and pepper shakers, camels,
$225.00 for the pair.**

Salt & pepper shakers, Calico Cat
& Gingham Dog, pr **125.00**
Salt & pepper shakers, dog & dog-
house, snuggle, pr........**165.00**
Salt & pepper shakers, fighting
cocks, pr, from $70 to **80.00**
Salt & pepper shakers, Paul
Bunyon & tree, pr........**200.00**
Salt & pepper shakers, Wee
Chinese boy & girl, pr ...**35.00**
Shelf sitter, canary, left (or right),
5" **95.00**
Shelf sitter, girl w/cat, 4½" ..**65.00**
Shelf sitter, Maurice & Michele,
7", pr, from $130 to......**165.00**
Shelf sitter, Persian mother, 4¼" .**50.00**

Character and Promotional Glassware

Once routinely given away
by fast-food restaurants and
soft- drink companies, these
glasses have become very collectible; and though they're
being snapped up by avid collectors everywhere, you'll still find
there are bargains to be had.
The more expensive are those
with Disney or Walter Lantz
cartoon characters, super-
heroes, sports greats, or personalities from Star Trek or the old
movies. For more information
refer to *The Collector's Guide to
Cartoon and Promotional
Drinking Glasses* by John
Hervey (L-W Book Sales). See
Clubs and Newsletters for information on *Collector Glass News*.

**Bugs Bunny 50th Anniversary,
from Ultramar (Canada), from
$8.00 to $10.00.** (Photo courtesy
Collector Glass News)

Al Capp, 1975, footed, Joe Btsfplk,
from $60 to **90.00**
Apollo Series, Marathon Oil,
carafe, from $6 to...........**10.00**
Arby's Stained Glass Series, late
1970s, carafe, from $6 to .**8.00**
Arby's Stained Glass Series, late 1970s,
5" or 6", ea, from $2 to **4.00**
Avoid the Noid, Domino's Pizza,
1988, 4 different, ea.........**7.00**
Avon Christmas Issues, 1969-
72, 4 different, ea, from $2
to **5.00**

BC Ice Age, Arby's, 1981, 6 different, ea, from $3 to............**5.00**

Beverly Hillbillies, CBS promotion, 1963, rare, NM..............................**200.00**

Cinderella, Disney/Libbey, 1950s-60s, set of 8...................**120.00**

Dallas Cowboys, Burger King, Dr Pepper, 6 different, ea, from $7 to...............................**15.00**

Dick Tracy, Domino's Pizza, M, from $75 to...................**100.00**

Dinosaur Series, Welch's, 1989, 4 different, ea.......................**2.00**

Disney's All-Star Parade, 1939, 10 different, ea, from $25 to...............................**50.00**

Donald Duck, Donald Duck Cola, 1960s-70s, from $10 to................................**15.00**

ET, Pizza Hut, 1982, footed, 4 different, from $2 to.............**4.00**

Goonies, Godfather's Pizza/Warner Bros, 1985, 4 different, from $3 to..................**5.00**

Hershey's Chocolate, A Kiss for You, from $3 to **5.00**

Hopalong Cassidy's Western Series, ea, from $25 to...**30.00**

James Bond 007, 1985, 4 different, ea, from $10 to **15.00**

Jungle Book, Disney/Pepsi, 1970s, Mowgli, unmarked, from $25 to.....................................**35.00**

Jungle Book, Disney/Pepsi, 1970s, Rama, unmarked, from $30 to **40.00**

Keebler Soft Batch Cookies, 1984, 4 different, ea, from $7 to **10.00**

King Kong, Coco-Cola/Dino De Laurentis Corp, 1976, from $5 to **8.00**

Mardi Gras, Burger King, 1989, black glass mug w/white logo, from $8 to **10.00**

McDonald's, McDonaldland Action Series, 1977, 6 different, ea, from $2 to **3.00**

McDonald's, McDonaldland Collector Series, 1970s, 6 different, ea......................................**2.50**

McDonald's, McVote, 1986, 3 different, ea, from $4 to **6.00**

Mickey Mouse, Happy Birthday, Pepsi, 1978, Daisy & Donald, from $5 to **10.00**

Night Before Christmas, Pepsi, 1982-83, 4 different, ea, from $4 to **6.00**

Pac-Man, Arby's Collector Series, 1980, rocks glass, from $2 to............**4.00**

PAT Ward, Pepsi, late 1960s, static pose, Boris and Natasha, from $20.00 to $25.00; Snidley Whiplash, from $15.00 to $20.00.

PAT Ward, Pepsi, late 1970s, static pose, Bullwinkle, 5", from $15 to **20.00**

PAT Ward, Pepsi, late 1970s, static pose, Dudley Do-Right, 5", from $10 to **15.00**

PAT Ward, Pepsi, late 1970s, static pose, Rocky, 5", from $10 to................................**15.00**

Peanuts Characters, milk glass mug, Snoopy on various poses, from $2 to........................**4.00**

Pocahontas, Burger King, 1995, 4 different, MIB, ea, from $1 to..**3.00**

Pochontas, Dairy Promo/Libbey, 1938-40, 12 different, ea, from $15 to..............................**25.00**

Popeye, Kollect-A-Set, Coco-Cola, 1975, Popeye, from $3 to......................................**5.00**

Ringling Bros Circus Clown Series, Pepsi, 1980s, 8 different, ea..............................**12.00**

Ringling Bros Circus Poster Series, Pepsi, 1980s, 6 different, ea..............................**20.00**

Roger Rabbit, McDonald's, 1988, plastic, ea, from $1 to......**2.00**

Roy Rogers Restaurant, 1883-1983 logo, from $3 to................**5.00**

Sleeping Beauty, American, late 1950s, 6 different, ea, from $15 to..............................**20.00**

Sleeping Beauty, Canadian, late 1950s, 12 different, ea, from $10 to..............................**15.00**

Snow White & the Seven Dwarfs, Bosco, 1938, ea, from $20 to **30.00**

Star Trek, Dr Pepper, 1976, 4 different, ea, from $15 to ...**20.00**

Star Trek, Dr Pepper, 1978, 4 different, ea, from $25 to ...**30.00**

Star Trek: Motion Picture, Coca-Cola, 1980, 3 different, ea, from $10 to......................**15.00**

Sunday Funnies, 1976, Broom Hilda, from $80 to........**100.00**

Super Heros, Marvel/7 Eleven, 1977, footed, Incredible Hulk, from $15 to.....................**20.00**

Walter Lantz, Pepsi, 1970s, Cuddles, from $40 to **60.00**

Walter Lantz, Pepsi, 1970s, Woody Woodpecker, from $7 to.**15.00**

Walter Lantz, Pepsi, 1970s-80s, Buzz Buzzard/Space Mouse, from $15 to.....................**20.00**

Western Heros, Lone Ranger, from $10 to..............................**15.00**

Wizard of Id, Arby's, 1983, 6 different, ea, from $7 to.....**10.00**

Wizard of Oz, Swift's, 1950s-60s, fluted bottom, Glinda, from $15 to..............................**25.00**

Ziggy, 7-Up Collector Series, 4 different, ea, from $3 to.......**5.00**

Character Collectibles

One of the most active areas of collecting today is the field of character collectibles. Flea markets usually yield some of the more common items. Toys, books, lunch boxes, children's dishes, and games of all types are for the most part quite readily found. Disney characters, television personalities, and comic book heroes are among the most sought after.

For more information, refer to *Schroeder's Collectible Toys, Antique to Modern*; *Cartoon Toys & Collectibles* by David Longest; *Collector's Guide to TV Toys & Memorabilia, 2nd Edition,* by Greg Davis and Bill Morgan; *Roy Rogers and Dale Evans Toys & Memorabilia* by P. Allan Coyle; *G-Men and FBI Toys and Collectibles* by Harry and Jody Whitworth; *Peanuts Collectibles* by Audrea Podley with Derrick Bang; and *The World of Raggedy Ann Collectibles* by Kim Avery. All are published by Collector Books.

See also Action Figures; Advertising; Banks; Bubble Bath Containers; California Raisins; Character and Promotional Glassware; Children's Books; Cookie Jars; Games; Garfield; Kliban Cat; Lunch Boxes; Novelty Telephones; Peanuts; Puzzles; Radios; Star Wars; Western Heroes.

A-Team, Grenade Toss, Placo, 1983, MIB (sealed).........**75.00**
Addams Family, figure, Remco, vinyl w/cloth outfit, 1964, NM **65.00**
Adventure Boy, finger puppet, w/Skymobile, Remco, 1970, MIB................................**65.00**
Aladdin, doll, dressed in white, Disney, MIB **40.00**
Alvin & the Chipmunks, harmonica, Plastic Inject Corp, 1959, 4", MOC **85.00**
Andy Brown, sparkler, Germany, push lever & eyes spark, tin, 1930s, NM **725.00**
Archie, hand puppet, plastic & vinyl, 1973, EX..............**45.00**
Archies, stencil set, 1983, MOC.**15.00**
Aristocats, Colorforms, 1960s, NMIB.............................**40.00**
Baby Huey, figure, Alvimar, inflatable vinyl w/bells inside, 1960s, EX **25.00**
Banana Splits, figure, Fleegle Sutton, 1973, MIP **80.00**

Banana Splits, Kut-Up Kit, Larami, 1973, MIP (sealed) **10.00**
Barney Google, figure, Syroco, 1944, 4", EX **65.00**
Batman, coins, Transogram, set of 20, 1966, MOC **50.00**
Batman, Fiddlesticks, Knickerbocker, 1979, complete, EXIB.........**45.00**
Batman, flicker ring, plastic, NM.**20.00**
Batman, magazine, Look, 1966, NM **50.00**
Batman, push-button puppet, Kohner, 1960s, NM......**100.00**
Batman, Thingmaker, Mattel, for rings or rubber stamps, 1965, EX **35.00**
Batman & Robin, pinball machine, Marx, 1966, 22x10", EX.**100.00**
Battlestar Galactica, ring, Lt Starbuck photo, MIB **75.00**
Beany & Cecil, Skill Ball Game, Pressman, 1961, NMIB.**145.00**
Beatle Baily, puffy stickers, Ja-Ru, 1983, MIP (sealed).........**20.00**
Betty Boop, figure, bendable, NJ Croce, 1988, 8", MOC **15.00**

Betty Boop, tambourine, lithographed tin, 1930s, 6" diameter, EX, $150.00.

Beverly Hillbillies, Colorforms Cartoon Kit, 1963, MIB, from $100 to **125.00**

Blondie & Dagwood, kazoo, tin sandwich shape, KFS, 1947, 6", NMIB **175.00**

Bozo the Clown, record player, Transogram, EX.............**65.00**

Bozo the Clown, Stitch-a-Story, Hasbro, 1967, MIB **50.00**

Brady Bunch, tambourine, Larami, 1973, MIP **25.00**

Brady Bunch, tea set, plastic, Larami, 1973, MOC.......**25.00**

Bugs Bunny, bank, Uncle Bugs, Great America, vinyl figure, 1978, EX..........................**25.00**

Bugs Bunny, figure, bendable, 1988, 8", EX **20.00**

Bugs Bunny, push-button puppet, Kohner, EX......................**20.00**

Bullwinkle's Supermarket Game, Whitman, 1976, NM **30.00**

Captain America, kite, Pressman, plastic w/full-color image, 1966, MIP.......................**65.00**

Captain Kangaroo, Finger Paint Set, Hasbro, 1956, complete, EXIB **55.00**

Captain Planet, tin container, 1990, 6½" dia, EX **15.00**

Casper the Ghost, baseball bat & ball set, inflatable vinyl, MOC .**15.00**

Care Bears, phonograph, 1983, MIB, $125.00. (Photo courtesy Martin and Carolyn Berens)

Charlie's Angels, AM Wrist Radio, Illco, 1977, MIB, from $250 to **300.00**

Charlie's Angels, magic slate, Whitman, 1977, M, from $25 to **30.00**

Chipmunks, figure, any character, PVC, NM, ea **5.00**

CHiPs, Emergency Medical Kit, Empire, 1980, MIB **30.00**

Cowboy Mickey Riding Pluto, windup, celluloid, EX ..**500.00**

Curious George, magic slate, Fairchild, 1968, 9x12", M.**10.00**

Dennis the Menace, figure, plastic w/movable arms, 1954, 5", EX **40.00**

Dick Tracy, finger puppet, marked Daily News Sync, 1961, EX.**25.00**

Dick Tracy, magnifying glass, Larami, 1979, MOC.......**20.00**

Donald Duck, train engine pull toy, Fisher-Price #450, 1940s, EX **200.00**

Dopey, bookends, Lamode, 1937, $375.00 for the pair. (Photo courtesy Joel Cohen)

Dr Dolittle, doll, Mattel, w/Pushmi-Pullyu & Polynesia, 1967, 6", MIB.................**90.00**

Dr Dolittle, periscope, Bat-Zam #609, NMIP **30.00**

Dr Kildare, scrapbook, 1962, 14x11", unused, NM **65.00**

Dr Suess, doll, Cat in the Hat, Coleco, stuffed plush, 1983, MIB **100.00**

Dukes of Hazzard, ID Set, Grand Toy, MOC **10.00**

Elmer Fudd, bank, Elmer standing beside barrel, painted metal, 5½" **85.00**

Elvira, makeup kit, MOC, from $15 to **20.00**

Emergency, fire helmet, plastic, Playco, 1975, EX+ **30.00**

ET, pillow, blue or purple, EX, ea **20.00**

Evel Knievel, bike flags, Schaper, 10x15", MIP **18.00**

Evel Knievel Formula 1 Dragster, 1975, Ideal, $125.00. (Photo courtesy June Moon Collectibles)

Family Affair, Buffy Fashion Wig, Amsco, 1971, MIB **100.00**

Family Affair, tea set, Buffy, plastic, Chilton Toys, 46 pcs, M **75.00**

Fat Albert, figure, vinyl, 1973, 7", VG **10.00**

Felix the Cat, Pencil Coloring by Numbers, Hasbro, 1958, MIP **50.00**

Figaro the Cat, windup, Louis Marx, 1939, EXIB **225.00**

Flash Gordon, beanie w/fins & goggles, 1950s, NM **400.00**

Flintstones, bubble pipe, Bamm-Bamm, Transogram, 1963, MOC **25.00**

Flintstones, Cockamamies, 1961, complete, NMIB **35.00**

Flintstones, coin purse, Barney, 1975, NM **25.00**

Flintstones, Crash Test Barney, 1993, MIB **15.00**

Flintstones, finger puppet, Fred, Knickerbocker, M (VG card) **20.00**

Flintstones, lamp, vinyl, Fred figure, 11", NM **55.00**

Flintstones, Play Fun Set, Whitman, 1965, complete, EXIB **65.00**

Flintstones, squirt gun, Fred, plastic head figure, 1974, EX **25.00**

Flintstones, yo-yo, Fred & Pebbles, litho tin, tournament shape, 1970s **20.00**

Flipper, Activity Box, Whitman, 1966, complete, MIB **40.00**

Flipper, magic slate, Whitman, 1967, NM **30.00**

Flipper, ukelele, Mattel, 1968, MIP **100.00**

Flying Nun, chalkboard, Hasbro, 1967, 16x24", MIP **75.00**

Flying Nun, Stich-a-Story, Hasbro, 1967, MIB **85.00**

Foghorn Leghorn, figure, ceramic, 1970s, NM **30.00**

Full House, doll, Michelle, talker, cloth & vinyl, 15", MIB..**40.00**

Green Hornet, Colorforms Cartoon Kit, 1965, complete, NMIB **100.00**

Green Hornet, kite, Roalex, 1967, MIP **200.00**

Gulliver's Travels, doll, King Little, Ideal, original decal, 12", EX........................**575.00**

Gumby & Pokey, Colorforms, 1988, MIB......................**10.00**

Happy Days, beanbag chair, Fonzie, red & white panels, 1970s, NM....................**125.00**

Happy Days, guitar, Fonzie, 1976, MIB (sealed)...................**75.00**

Hardy Boys & Nancy Drew, Cartoonarama, 1978, MIB .**60.00**

Hong Kong Phooey, candle, 1976, MIP..............................**25.00**

Howdy Doody, Bee-Nee Kit, NMIB **65.00**

Howdy Doody, doll, Howdy, stuffed cloth, Applause, 1988, 18", EX............................**30.00**

Howdy Doody, pen, posable plastic figure, Leadworks, 1988, 6", M......................................**5.00**

Howdy Doody, top, litho tin, LBZ/ West Germany, NM......**125.00**

Huckleberry Hound, Flip Show, 1961, EXIB....................**40.00**

I Dream of Jeannie, play suit, Ben Cooper, 1974, complete NMIB............................**60.00**

Incredible Hulk, Crazy Foam, 1979, VG+......................**25.00**

Incredible Hulk, Flip-It, Tillotson, 1977, MOC **50.00**

Indiana Jones & the Temple of Doom, sleeping bag, 1984, EX..................................**30.00**

James Bond, wallet, Glidrose Productions, vinyl, 1966, NM..................................**80.00**

Jetsons, Slate & Chalk Set, 1960s, unused, MIB **100.00**

Josie & the Pussycats, guitar, Larami, plastic, 1973, MOC....................................**75.00**

Knight Rider, sticker & album set, Goody Ind, MOC **8.00**

Land of the Lost, Direction Finder, Larami, 1975, MOC.......**30.00**

Land of the Lost, Safari Shooter, Larami, 1975, MIP **30.00**

Lassie, Trick Trainer, Mousely Inc, 1956, complete, NMIB..**175.00**

Laurel (from Laurel and Hardy), plastic figure, 1972, 14", $65.00. (Photo courtesy June Moon Collectibles)

Laverne & Shirley, iron-on transfers, several different, 1970s, MIP...............................**15.00**

Li'l Abner, figure, vinyl, 13", EX .**50.00**

Li'l Abner, Picto-Puzzles, set of 6, Plas-Trix, MOC............**100.00**

Little Audrey, doll, vinyl, unmarked, 13", EX **50.00**

Little Audrey, figure, vinyl, 13", EX **50.00**

Little Lulu, jewelry box, Larami, 1973, MIP......................**15.00**

Love Boat, Poster Art Kit, Craft Master, 1978, MIP.........**40.00**

Man From UNCLE, Foto Fantastiks Coloring Set, Faber, 1965, MIB.........**165.00**

Marvel Super Heros, Colorforms, 1983, complete, MIB......**20.00**

Mighty Mouse, Presto-Paints, Kenner, 1963, complete, EXIB..............................**65.00**

Mod Squad, Instant Intercom, Larami, white plastic walkie-talkies, MOC **50.00**

Mork & Mindy, sleeping bag, 1979, NM..................................**20.00**

Mr Ed, hand puppet, pull-string talker, Mattel, 1962, MIB......**200.00**

Munsters, doll, baby Herman, vinyl w/cloth clothes, Ideal, 1965, NM........................**65.00**

Muppets, oven mitt, Miss Piggy, 1981, NM........................**10.00**

Nancy Drew, fan club kit, FCCA, 1978, complete NM........**65.00**

New Zoo Revue, figure, vinyl, 1973, 3", EX **10.00**

Nightmare on Elm Street, doll, Maxx Fx, Matchbox, 12", MIB...............................**40.00**

Nightmare on Elm Street, figure, Stick-Up, 4", MOC **6.00**

Our Gang, rowboat, plastic, Mego, 1975, 12½", MIB............**40.00**

Peanuts, bank, Snoopy in yellow rain slicker & hat, ceramic, 1979, 5"...........................**25.00**

Peanuts, doll, Lucy w/hand out, red shirt, MIP **75.00**

Peanuts, doll, Snoopy, inflatable, 1969, 18", EX **10.00**

Peanuts, doll, Snoopy as baseball player, 1984, 8½", NM...**45.00**

Peanuts, jack-in-the-box, Snoopy, NMIB..............................**75.00**

Peanuts, megaphone, Charlie Brown, Chein, 1970, rare, EX.........**45.00**

Peanuts, top, litho tin, Chein, 1969, MIB.......................**75.00**

Pink Panther, Cartoonarama, 1970, complete, EXIB **60.00**

Pink Panther, slide-tile puzzle, Ja-Ru, 1981, MOC **15.00**

Pinocchio, figure, wood/compo, Multi Products, 1940, EX.........**225.00**

Pippi Longstocking, doll, Horsman, vinyl w/cloth clothes, MIB.**65.00**

Planet of the Apes, kite, Hi-Flyer, MIP.................................**75.00**

Popeye, Beach Boat, 1980, MOC.**50.00**

Popeye, boxing gloves, red, Everlast, 1950s, MIP.....**75.00**

Popeye, figure, Popeye, Syroco, 1944, 5", EX **60.00**

Popeye, mug, plastic head, thermo liner, 1990s, EX.............**20.00**

Porky Pig, ring, cloisonné, 1970s, M....................................**12.00**

Quick Draw McGraw, gloves, western-style cloth w/image, EX.....**25.00**

Raggedy Ann, Colorforms Pop-Up Tea Party, complete, MIB.**30.00**

Raggedy Ann, planter, William Hirsch, 1940s, EX.........**60.00**

Raggedy Ann & Andy, beach ball, Ideal, 1974, 20" dia, MIP.**30.00**

Raggedy Ann & Andy, camper, Buddy L, plastic & metal, 11", M...................................**100.00**

Raggedy Ann & Andy, crayon box, tin, Chein, 1974, VG+....**25.00**

Ricochet Rabbit, push puppet, Kohner, EX....................**40.00**

Rocky & Bullwinkle, Bullwinkle Electric Quiz, 1971, MOC (sealed) **40.00**

Saturday Night Live, doll, Ed Grimly, Tyco, talker, 1989, 18", MIB **125.00**

Scooby Doo, stamper, Hanna-Barbera, 1983, MOC........**6.00**

Sesame Street, figure set, PVC, set of 8, Applause, 1993, M.**20.00**

Simpsons, doll, any character, rag-type, Dandee, 11", NM, ea.**18.00**

Simpsons, Fun Dough Maker, MIB...............................**30.00**

Simpsons, Trace 'n Color Drawing Set, Toymax, complete NMIB **85.00**

Smurfs, bank, Peyo, molded plastic character, 1980s, NM.....**35.00**

Smurfs, figure, Papa Smurf, ceramic, VG....................**30.00**

Smurfs, Smurfs Village, ceramic, VG.................................**35.00**

Spider-Man, Code Breaker, Gordy, 1980, MOC **35.00**

Spider-Man, kazoo, Straco, MOC .**50.00**

Spider-Man, postcards, set of 10 different, EX...................**10.00**

Spider-Man, sunglasses, Nasta, 1986, MOC **10.00**

Spider-Man, TV chair, Carlin Playthings, inflatable vinyl, 1978, MIB.......................**75.00**

Starsky & Hutch, flashlight, Fleetwood, 1976, MOC ..**65.00**

Superman, crazy foam, American Aerosol, 1974, NM **50.00**

Superman, jointed wood doll with red cloth cape, Ideal, 1939, 12", EX, from $800.00 to $1,000.00.

Superman, kite, Hi-Flier, 1984, MIP................................**30.00**

Superman, pencil, #2 lead, 1978, M.....................................**20.00**

Superman, push-button puppet, Kohner, 1966, 4", NM....**15.00**

Superman, Radio Quiz Master, 1948, EX.........................**75.00**

Sylvester the Cat, roly-poly, EX.**25.00**

Tasmanian Devil, yo-yo, plastic, Magic Mountain souvenir, 1990, NM..........................**4.00**

Three Stooges, dolls, Presents, any character, 1988, 14", M, ea.**65.00**

Three Stooges, flasher rings, 3 different ones, EX, ea.........**25.00**

Tigger, handbag, front & rear pockets, Disney Store, M........**30.00**

Tom & Jerry, figures, either character, bendable, MOC, ea ...**10.00**

Tom & Jerry, ring, Jerry, cloisonné, 1970s, M...................**12.00**

Tweety Bird, charm, plastic figure, 1950s, ¾", NM................**15.00**

Underdog, bop bag, inflatable vinyl, MIB **50.00**

Underdog, pillow, inflatable vinyl, EX...............................**15.00**

V (TV series), Bop Bag, vinyl, 1970s, MIB.....................**30.00**

Waltons, farmhouse play set, Amsco, w/farmhouse, complete, 1975, MIB **75.00**

Welcome Back Kotter, Sweathogs Cartoon Set, Toy Factory, 1977, MIB.......................**40.00**

Welcome Back Kotter, Sweat-hog Calculator, Remco, #650, 1976, MOC, $35.00.

Winky Dink, paint set, Standard Toykraft, 1950s, EXIB...**85.00**

Wizard of Oz, cup holder, plastic, 1989, 7", M....................**10.00**

Wizard of Oz, flasher ring, Cowardly Lion or Tin Woodsman, M, ea..........**40.00**

Wolfman, figure, Playco Products, 1991, 10", MIB..............**12.00**

Wonder Woman, doll, inflatable vinyl, ca 1979, 24", MIP.**30.00**

Wonder Woman, hand puppet, cloth & vinyl, Ideal, 1966, 11", MIP..............................**225.00**

Wonder Woman, rub-on transfer, MIP................................**30.00**

Woody Woodpecker, harmonica, plastic figure, early, 6", EX.......**30.00**

Woody Woodpecker, movie, Witch Crafty, 8mm, black & white, 1960s, NMIB..................**15.00**

Woody Woodpecker, ring, cloisonné, 1970s, M....................**12.00**

Yogi Bear, camera, 1960s, MIB.**65.00**

Yogi Bear, pillow doll, w/bells inside, 1977, 15", EX.....**20.00**

Yogi Bear, pipe, red plastic figure, Transogram, 1963, MIP.**35.00**

Yogi Bear & Boo Boo, handkerchief, 1960s, 8" sq, EX...**10.00**

Ziggy, mirror, 1970s, MIP (sealed).**10.00**

Cherished Teddies

First appearing on dealer's shelves in the spring of 1992, Cherished Teddies found instant collector appeal. They were designed by artist Priscilla Hillman and produced in the Orient for the Enesco Company. Besides the figurines, the line includes waterballs, frames, plaques, and bells.

Seth and Sarabeth, retired, from $25.00 to $30.00.

#104029, No Celebration Is Complete Without Your Closest Friends..............**40.00**

#141313, Pat, Falling for You.**15.00**

#199869, I'm Always Good For a Soft Cuddle & a Warm Hug.....**50.00**

#203742, Darling Baby Cross, wall cross, 1996......................**15.00**

#2206, Daisy, Friendship Blossoms w/Love, 1999..................**145.00**

#269743, Spencer, I'm Head Over Skis for You, MIB..........**18.00**

#302694, A Decade of Teddy Bear Love **30.00**

#303097, I'm Sorry, miniature, 1½", 1997......................**15.00**

#476757, Friends Give You Wings To Fly **20.00**

#537195, Keep Good Friends Close to Your Heart, 1999.......**20.00**

#601659E, Neil (Armstrong) the Astronaut & a Moon Rock Figure, 2000 ....**40.00**

#624918, Teddy & Roosevelt, The Book of Teddies 1903-1993, 1993 ....**85.00**

#674044, A Mother Holds Her Children's...Hearts Forever, wall plaque....................**15.00**

#676888, You Can Always Trust Me To Be There, 2000 ...**20.00**

#706701, Wolfgang, The Spirit of Christmas Is in Us All, MIB .**20.00**

#789755, Nothing Is Better Than a Teddy Bear Hug, 2002...**25.00**

#848581, Nora, Brrrr, retired, MIB **25.00**

#916258, Holding On to Someone Special, 1993 ....**80.00**

#918686, Henrietta, A Basketful of Wishes, 1992 ....**20.00**

Children's Books

Books were popular gifts for children in the latter 1800s; many were beautifully illustrated, some by notable artists such as Frances Brundage and Maxfield Parrish. From this century tales of Tarzan by Burroughs are very collectible, as are those familiar childhood series books — for example, The Bobbsey Twins and Nancy Drew. For more information we recommend *Collector's Guide to Children's Books, Volumes I* and *II,* and *Boys' and Girls' Book Series* by Diane McClure Jones and Rosemary Jones (Collector Books).

Big Little Books

Probably everyone who is now fifty to sixty-five years of age owned a few Big Little Books as a child. Today these thick hand-sized adventures bring prices from $10.00 to $75.00 and upwards. The first was published in 1933 by Whitman Publishing Company. Dick Tracy was the featured character. Kids of the early '50s preferred the format of the comic book, and the Big Little Books were gradually phased out. Stories about super heroes and Disney characters bring the highest prices, especially those with an early copyright.

Adventures of Huckleberry Finn, Whitman #1422, NM **40.00**

Bambi's Children, Whitman #1497, 1943, EX.............**50.00**

Billy the Kid, Whitman #773, 1935, EX.........................**35.00**

Buck Jones & the Two-Gun Kid, Whitman #1404, 1937, EX.......................................**35.00**

Buck Rogers in City of Floating Globes, EX....................**150.00**

Convoy Patrol, Whitman #1469, NM.................................**35.00**

Cowboy Lingo, Whitman #1457, 1938, EX.........................**35.00**

Donald Duck Gets Fed Up, Whitman #1462, EX......**40.00**

Felix the Cat, Whitman #1129, 1936, EX.........................**55.00**

Frankenstein Jr, Whitman, 1968, NM.................................**20.00**

G-Man & the Gun Runners, Whitman #1469, EX+ **35.00**

Goofy in Giant Trouble, Whitman, 1968, NM+......................**10.00**

Hairbreath Harry in Dept QT, Whitman #1101, EX **25.00**

Jimmie Allen in the Air Mail Robbery, Whitman #1143, 1936, EX.........................**35.00**

Junior G-Men, Whitman #1442, 1937, EX......................**30.00**

Li'l Abner in New York, Whitman #1198, 1936, EX............**60.00**

Mickey Mouse & the Stolen Jewels, Whitman #1464, NM.......**75.00**

Once Upon a Time, Whitman #718, EX........................**35.00**

Our Gang on the March, Whitman #1451, NM.....................**65.00**

Popeye and Queen Olive Oyl, 1949, Bud Sagendorf, EX, $35.00.

Radio Patrol Trailing the Safeblowers, Whitman #1173, 1937, EX, $35.00.

Roy Rogers & the Deadly Treasure, Whitman #1473, VG...................................**40.00**

Skeezix Goes to War, Whitman #1414, NM.....................**50.00**

Sleeping Beauty, Golden All Star, 1967, EX+......................**15.00**

Snow White & the Seven Dwarfs, Golden Star, 1967, VG+.**15.00**

Tarzan the Terrible, Whitman #1453, EX+....................**40.00**

Two-Gun Montana, Whitman #1104, VG.....................**25.00**

Wyatt Earp, 1958, EX **15.00**

Little Golden Books

Little Golden Books (a registered trademark of Western Publishing Company Inc.), introduced in October of 1942, were an overnight success. First published with a blue paper spine, the later spines were of gold foil. Parents and grandparents born in the '40s, '50s, and '60s are now trying to find the titles they had as children. From 1942 to the early 1970s, the books were numbered from 1 to 600, while books published later had no numerical order. Depending on where you find the book, prices can vary from 25¢ to $30.00 plus. The most expensive are those with dust jackets from the early '40s or books with paper dolls and activities. The three primary series of books are the Regular (1 – 600), Disney (1 – 140), and Activity (1 – 52).

Television's influence became apparent in the '50s with stories like the Lone Ranger, Howdy Doody, Hopalong Cassidy, Gene Autry, and Rootie Kazootie. The '60s brought us Yogi Bear, Huckleberry Hound, Magilla Gorilla, and Quick Draw McGraw, to name but a few. Condition is very important when purchasing a book. You normally don't want to purchase a book with large tears, crayon or ink marks, or missing pages.

As with any collectible book, a first edition is always going to bring the higher price. To determine what edition you have on the 25¢ and 29¢ cover price books, look on the title page or the last page of the book. If it is not on the title page, there will be a code of 1/(a letter of the alphabet) on the bottom right corner of the last page. A is for 1st edition, Z would refer to the twenty-sixth printing.

There isn't an easy way of determining the condition of a book. What is 'good' to one might be 'fair' to another. A played-with book in average condition is generally worth only half as much as one in mint, like-new condition. To find out more about Little Golden Books, we recommend *Collecting Little Golden Books* (published by Books Americana) by Steve Santi.

A Year in the City, #48, A edition, 1948, VG 18.00
Baby's House, #80, A edition, 1950, VG+ 18.00
Captain Kangaroo, #261, A edition, 1956, EX+ 20.00
Chicken Little, #413, A edition, 1960, NM+ 8.00
Circus Time, #31, I edition, 1952, NM+ 15.00

Donald Duck & Santa Claus, #027, A edition, 1952, EX........**25.00**
Donald Duck Lost & Found, #86, A edition, 1960, EX **20.00**
Frosty the Snowman, #142, L edition, VG+ **6.00**
Helicopters, #357, A edition, 1959, NM+ **10.00**
Jack & the Beanstalk, #281, A edition, 1957, NM+ **10.00**
Little Red Hen, #6, M edition, 1952, VG........................**20.00**
Mickey Mouse & His Spaceship, #029, A edition, 1952, NM+.........**18.00**
New Pony, #410, A edition, 1961, VG....................................**8.00**
Party in Shariland, #360, A edition, 1958, NM+ **18.00**
Raggedy Ann & Fido, #585, 1st edition, 1972, NM+........**10.00**
Road Runner - A Very Scary Lesson, #122, 1st edition, 1974, EX **5.00**
Savage Sam, #0104, 1963, A edition, VG+ **10.00**
Smokey Bear & the Campers, #423, A edition, 1961, VG...........**8.00**
Three Little Kittens, #1, Q edition, 1951, EX+ **22.00**
What If?, #130, A edition, 1951, VG..................................**10.00**
Zorro, #068, D edition, 1965, NM+..............................**15.00**

Series

Everyone remembers a special series of books they grew up with: The Hardy Boys, Nancy Drew Mysteries, Tarzan — there were countless others. And though these are becoming very collectible today, there were many editions of each, and most are very easy to find. As a result, common titles are sometimes worth very little. Generally the last few in any series will be the most difficult to locate, since fewer were printed than the earlier stories which were likely to have been reprinted many times. As is true of any type of book, first editions or the earliest printing will have more collector value. Values in the listings below are general prices of books in a series, not specific titles. For further reading see *Boys' and Girls' Book Series* by Diane McClure Jones and Rosemary Jones (Collector Books).

Bill Bergson series, Lindren, Viking, Freeman illustrator, M w/jacket.......................**35.00**

Bobbsey Twins, LL Hope, Grosset, plain green hardcover, no jacket, EX.......................**15.00**

Camp-Fire Boys, L Hoover, AL Burt, hardcover, 1950s, EX........**15.00**

Christopher Cool Teen Agent, J Lancer, Grosset, 1960s, EX.**15.00**

Ellery Queen Jr, Grosset, 1950s, cloth-over-board hardcover, 1950s, EX.......................**40.00**

Fighters for Freedom, Whitman, ca 1940s, M w/dust jacket...**20.00**

Golden Stallion, R Montgomery, Little Brown, 1st edition, w/jacket, EX...................**35.00**

Kathy Martin Nurse, J James, Golden Press, yellow spine, 1960s, EX.......................**15.00**

Little League, CK Bishop, Steck Co/Lippincot, 1953-68, 13 titles, EX.......................**10.00**

Maxie, EB Gardner, Cupples & Leon, hardcover, 1932-39, M w/dust jacket..................**40.00**

Misery, Suzanne Heller, illustrated by author, Paul Eriksson, small blue and white oblong hardcover, 1964, $10.00 ($25.00 with dust jacket). (Photo courtesy Diane McClure Jones and Rosemary Jones)

Nancy Drew, Grosset & Dunlap, tweed cover, 1950+ unrevised version, EX....................**20.00**

Red Randall, Sidney Bowen, Grosset, hardcover, 1940s, EX.................................**15.00**

Skippy, Percy Crosby, Putnam, 1929-32, M w/dust jacket.**25.00**

Ted Wilford Mysteries, N Pallas, hardcover, 1951-67, 15 titles, EX.................................**10.00**

Uncle Bill, W James, Scribner, hardcover, later printing, M w/jacket.........................**30.00**

Walt Disney's Annette, D Schroeder, Whitman, 1960-63, EX.................................**15.00**

Whitman Tell-A-Tale Books

Though the Whitman Company produced a wide variety of children's books, the ones most popular with today's collectors (besides the Big Little Books which are dealt with earlier in this category) are the Tell-A-Tales. They were published in a variety of series, several of which centered around radio, TV, and comic strips.

becoming very collectible, especially those based on favorite TV and cartoon characters. Steve Santi's book *Collecting Little Golden Books* includes a section on Wonder Books as well.

Bible Stories, #828, 1947, EX.**8.00**
Bugs Bunny Hangs Around, 1957, NM..................................**15.00**
Circus Elephant, #2531, 1974, EX..................................**5.00**
Donald Duck & the Sticky Secret, 1976, EX..........................**10.00**
Frisker, #2426, 1956, EX........**5.00**
Grandpa's Police Friends, #2544, 1967, NM..........................**8.00**
Lassie & the Busy Morning, 1973, EX..................................**10.00**
Lassie Finds a Friend, 1960, VG.**10.00**
Little Red Riding Hood, #2670, 1960, EX..........................**10.00**
Night Before Christmas, #2517, 1969, VG..........................**5.00**
Princess Who Never Laughed, #2610, 1961, EX...............**5.00**
Roy Roger's Suprise for Donnie, #943, 1954, EX...............**20.00**
Suprise for Howdy Doody, #2573, 1950, EX..........................**30.00**
Try Again Sally, 1969, EX....**10.00**
Tweety, #2481, 1953, EX......**10.00**
Winnie the Pooh & Eeyore's House, #2620, 1976, EX.............**15.00**

Baby Bunny, #545, 1951, EX.**12.00**
Buzzy the Funny Cow, 1963, EX.**15.00**
Doll Family, #802, 1962, VG.**20.00**
Heckle & Jeckle Visit the Farm, 1958, EX..........................**25.00**
Hungry Baby Bunny, #847, 1951, EX..................................**10.00**
Kewtee Bear's Christmas, #867, 1956, EX..........................**8.00**
Little Cowboy's Christmas, 1951, EX..................................**20.00**
Make Believe Book, #634, 1959, VG..................................**15.00**
Nonsense Alphabet, #725, 1959, EX..................................**12.00**
Pony Engine, #626, 1957, EX.**8.00**
Romper Room, 1957, EX.......**10.00**

The Surprise Doll, #519, 1949, EX, $30.00. (Photo courtesy Laura Brink)

Visit to the Hospital, #690, EX.**5.00**
Who Likes Dinner?, #598, 1953, EX+..................................**10.00**

Wonder Books

Though the first were a little larger, the Wonder Books printed since 1948 have all measured 6½" x 8". They've been distributed by Random House, Grosset Dunlap, and Wonder Books Inc. They're

Miscellaneous

Bozo & His ABC Zoo, Saalfield, 1961, lg paperback, EX .**15.00**

Donald Duck & His Friends, Disney/Heath, 1939, NM.**50.00**

Gene Autry in Redwood Pirate, 1946, hardcover, EX **20.00**

Hansel & Gretel, Elf, 1960, EX.**10.00**

Here They Are, Disney/Heath, 1940, NM+......................**50.00**

Jack & the Beanstalk, Platt & Munk, 1934, softcover, VG+...........**30.00**

Little Pig's Picnic & Other Stories, Disney/Heath, 1939, NM+.**50.00**

Little Red Wagon, Jr Elf, 1949, VG+...............................**10.00**

Little Sallie Mandy and the Shiny Penny, Helen R. Van Derveer, Henry Altemus Co. publishers, 1926, 5½x4½", VG, $15.00. (Photo courtesy Diane McClure Jones and Rosemary Jones)

Meet Chitty-Chitty Bang-Bang, Random House, 1968, EX+ .**8.00**

Mickey Never Fails, Disney/ Heath, 1939, NM+.........**55.00**

Mighty Mouse, McGraw Hill, 1964, NM......................**20.00**

Mother Westwind Animal Friends, by Burgess, 1931, hardcover, VG..................................**10.00**

Mr Toys, Jr Elf, 1955, EX **10.00**

Perri, Big Golden Book, 1939, M.**22.00**

Popeye's How To Draw Cartoons, 1939, hardcover, EX+ **40.00**

Raggedy Ann Scratch & Sniff, 1976, hardcover, 9x9", EX.........**25.00**

Roy Rogers in Sundown Valley, 1950, hardcover, EX **20.00**

Tarzan, Golden, 1964, lg size, NM..................................**8.00**

Tom Sawyer, Little Big Classic, 1938, hardcover, EX **25.00**

Tom Terrific!, Pines #4, 1958, NM...............................**20.00**

Tuffy the Tugboat, Tip-Top, 1947, VG..................................**10.00**

Welcome to Upsy Downsy Land, Mattel, 1969, NM...........**30.00**

Zippy the Chimp, Rand McNally, 1956, 28 pages, NM **40.00**

Christmas

No other holiday season is celebrated to such an extravagant extent as Christmas, and vintage decorations provide a warmth and charm that none from today can match. Ornaments from before 1870 were imported from Dresden, Germany. They were usually made of cardboard and sparkled with tinsel trim. Later, blown glass ornaments were made there in literally thousands of shapes such as fruits and vegetables, clowns, Santas, angels, and animals. Kugles, heavy glass balls (though you'll sometimes find fruit and vegetable forms as well) were made from about 1820 to late in the century in sizes up to 14". Early Santa figures are treasured, especially those in robes other than red. Figural bulbs from the '20s and '30s are popular, those that are character related in particular. Refer to *Pictorial Guide to Christmas Ornaments and Collectibles* by George Johnson (Collector Books) for more information.

Beads, plastic chain, oval or round, Japan or China, 1960s-70s, 9'..............................**3.00**

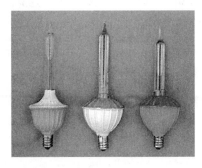

Bubble light styles in the C-7 base, old, each from $2.00 to $5.00. (New ones are $1.50 to $2.00 each.) (Photo courtesy George Johnson)

Bulb, bird, clear glass, exhaust tip in beak, 3-4", from $25 to **35.00**

Bulb, Bozo clown, milk glass, Japan, 1950s, 2½", from $25 to **35.00**

Bulb, bulldog on ball, clear glass, Japan, 2¼", from $15 to .**20.00**

Bulb, bunch of grapes, milk glass, 1950s, 2", from $6 to......**12.00**

Bulb, cat begging, milk glass, Japan, 2½", from $20 to .**30.00**

Bulb, cross on disc, milk glass, Japan, 1¾", from $25 to .**35.00**

Bulb, dog in polo outfit, milk glass, Japan, 1950s, 2¾", from $25 to....................**35.00**

Bulb, face on ball, milk glass, 2¼", from $20 to.....................**25.00**

Bulb, flower (generic), clear or milk glass, 1950s, 1½", from $8 to **12.00**

Bulb, Japanese lantern, milk glass, Japan, ca 1950, 2", from $5 to...............................**10.00**

Bulb, lantern, rounded top, clear glass, 2¼", from $8 to....**10.00**

Bulb, parrot, milk glass, Japan, 15V, 1¾", from $15 to....**20.00**

Bulb, Queen of Hearts, milk glass, 2¾", from $15 to.............**25.00**

Bulb, rose bud, milk glass, Japan, 1950s, 2½", from $10 to **12.00**

Bulb, snowman w/stick, milk glass, Japan, 2-4", ea, from $6 to **25.00**

Bulb, squirrel, milk glass, Japan, 1950s, 2", from $20 to....**25.00**

Candy container, basketball, paper, embossed ribs & lacing, 4".....................................**85.00**

Candy container, bell, chenille roping on cardboard, Japan, 4", from $90 to **100.00**

Candy container, parasol, paper w/fabric & lace, 2½" dia **175.00**

Candy container, Santa on skis, plastic, Rosbro, 1955, 4½"........**25.00**

Candy container, Santa w/pack, red plastic, Irwin USA, 1950s, 6".....................................**35.00**

Candy container, snowman, Rosbro , 1955, 5", from $12 to.........**15.00**

Decoration, candle in wreath, fluorescent plastic, 2-sided, 3¼"......**5.00**

Decoration, Glow-in-the-Dark plastic, lion, USA, 1940s-50s, 3¼" **8.00**

Decoration, pine tree, cardboard, easel back, Germany, 12", from $35 to **45.00**

Decoration, Santa in sled w/leaping deer, hard plastic, 1950s, 5" L **25.00**

Doll, Santa in sleigh, celluloid, Germany or Japan, 4", from $35 to **65.00**

Lantern, milk glass, double-faced Santa head, battery-op, Amico, 6" **40.00**

Lanterns, Japan, ca 1950s: snowman, 5", MIB, $50.00; Santa face, 5", MIB, $65.00.

Light, Royalite Snowman, hard plastic, ca 1955, 7½", from $25 to **35.00**

Light reflector, cardboard & glitter, 5½", from $2 to **3.00**

Light reflector, Mirostar, 5-pointed, Berwick, 2½", EX.................................**1.00**

Light reflector, multilayered foil, plain, US or Germany, 4", from $1 to **1.50**

Ornament, angel w/tree, mold-blown, Germany, 1980s, 4", from $90 to...................**100.00**

Ornament, ball, styrofoam w/satin or velvet cover, 1980s, 3" **50**

Ornament, barrel w/rose, mold-blown, Germany, 1½", from $15 to.............................**25.00**

Ornament, beaded airplane, made of blown beads, Japan, sm, from $15 to.....................**25.00**

Ornament, bear in leather shorts & suspenders, Germany, 1950s, 3½".....................**50.00**

Ornament, bell w/flowers, mold-blown, Germany, 2½", from $5 to...**10.00**

Ornament, bird & pine tree, mold-blown, 1950s, 2¾", from $10 to **12.00**

Ornament, birdhouse, mold-blown, Germany, 1950s, 1½", from $20 to.....................**30.00**

Ornament, bumpy heart, mold-blown, 1960s, 2¾", from $8 to **12.00**

Ornament, butterfly, flat metal, embossed details, 1980s, 2½"..............................**25.00**

Ornament, chalet, mold-blown, windows but no door, 1985, 2¾"................................**20.00**

Ornament, church w/short steeple, mold-blown, ca 1991, 3", from $8 to...............................**10.00**

Ornament, clown in drum, mold-blown, 1980s, lg or sm, from $8 to **10.00**

Ornament, clown on stump playing banjo, blown, 1980s, 4½", from $8 to......................**10.00**

Ornament, corn with leaves, mold-blown, Germany, 1990s, 3-3½", from $50 to **60.00**

Ornament, dog begging, mold-blown, 1980s, 3", from $12 to...............................**15.00**

Ornament, dog w/basket (begging), mold-blown, 1970s, 5", from $150 to **175.00**

Ornament, duck, mold-blown, bumpy body, Germany, 1950s & '70s, 3" **30.00**

Ornament, duck mold-blown, bumpy body, Germany, 1970s, 3", from $8 to..................**10.00**

Ornament, elephant on ball, mold-blown, W Germany, 1960s, 4¼" **12.00**

Ornament, flowerpot, blown, wire wrapped, w/fabric flower, 3½" **30.00**

Ornament, frog on leaf, mold-blown, Germany, 1991, 2½", from $35 to **50.00**

Ornament, heart w/embossed stars, mold-blown, Germany, 2", from $8 to..................**12.00**

Ornament, icicle, hollow-blown, silvered, 2-4", from $1 to **5.00**

Ornament, icicle, twisted plastic, ca 1960, 5", from 50¢ to...**1.00**

Ornament, Japanese bird, free-blown, plain & simple ball, 1950s, from $2 to **6.00**

Ornament, Nativity scene, cast metal, 3-D, Germany, 1980s, 2¾"....................................**45.00**

Ornament, owl in jacket, mold-blown, Germany, 1992, 8", from $8 to **10.00**

Ornament, pear, spun cotton, 1½-5", ea, from $15 to..........**50.00**

Ornament, purse, mold-blown, Radko, 1988, 3½", from $15 to **25.00**

Ornament, rabbit eating carrot, mold-blown, Germany, 1980s, 3" **70.00**

Ornament, rabbit w/carrot, mold-blown, 1980s, 3", from $10 to...........................**12.00**

Ornament, rosette, spun glass, sm Santa head scrap ea side, 2" dia **35.00**

Ornament, Santa head, scrap only, single head, 2¼", from $2 to **3.00**

Ornament, Santa on oval, mold-blown, 2½", from $25 to .**35.00**

Ornament, Santa w/book, scrap only, 4¾x2½", from $15 to..........**20.00**

Ornament, Santa w/tree, brass, recent, 2½", from $8 to..**10.00**

Ornament, singing dwarf, mold-blown, fat, Germany, 1980s, 2½" **85.00**

Ornament, songbird, blown w/spun glass wings, 1980s, 3½", from $10 to............**12.00**

Ornament, star frame, cast tin, flat, wire wrap, Germany, 2½" **40.00**

Ornament, table lamp, free-blown, 1980s, 3-4", from $10 to.**20.00**

Ornament, Virgin Mary, mold-blown, Germany, 1970s, 4", from $15 to **20.00**

Ornaments, house with pine roping, mold-blown, small, from $5.00 to $10.00; tall house, mold-blown, unsilvered with clear windows, from $15.00 to $20.00; square house, mold blown, small, from $10.00 to $15.00. (Photo courtesy George Johnson)

Toy, Santa, mechanical key-wind, Y (Japan), EX, from $50 to...............................**75.00**

Tree, green & white Visca (cellophane like), 3½-5', from $30 to.....................................**45.00**

Tree stand, cast iron, Merry Christmas cast in side, 12"...........................**25.00**

Tree stand, common type w/3 or 4 legs, 1850-90s, 32" leg spread............................**6.00**

Tree stand, standard metal style, 3 thumbscrews, 1950s-90s, from $3 to........................**5.00**

Tree with bubble lights, ca 1950s, 20", from $100.00 to $125.00. (Photo courtesy George Johnson)

Treetop, angel w/colored wings, Gem on base, 1940s-50s, MIB, from $20 to.....................**25.00**

Treetop, Krystal Star, metal & plastic, 5 arms w/plastic tips, 4½".................................**10.00**

Treetop, Santa w/tree, mold & free-blown, 1980s-90s, 11", from $20 to....................**25.00**

Treetop, spiked star, free-blown, Germany, 8", from $40 to .**50.00**

Treetop, star, foil, made to hold bulb, National Tinsel, 1940s, 9".......................................**2.00**

Treetop, star, 5-pointed, mold-blown, Rigby Co, 1990s, 6¾", $40 to.............................**45.00**

Treetop, star in indent center of point, plastic, Bradford, 1960s, 10"........................**3.00**

Cigarette Lighters

Pocket lighters were invented sometime after 1908 and were at their peak from about 1925 to the 1930s. Dunhill, Zippo, Colibri, Ronson, Dupont, and Evans are some of the major manufacturers. An early Dunhill Unique model if found in its original box would be valued at hundreds of dollars. Quality metal and metal-plated lighters were made from the 1950s to about 1960. Around that time disposable lighters never needing a flint were introduced, causing a decline in sales of figurals, novelties, and high-quality lighters.

The things that make a lighter collectible include novelty of design, type of mechanism (flint and fuel, flint and gas, battery, etc.), and manufacturer (and whether or not the company is still in business).

Advertising, Huddon's Credit Jewelers, tube style, Redlite, 3x⅜"...............................**25.00**

Advertising, Johnny Walker, bottle shape, 2⅜x⅝", from $15 to.....................**25.00**

Advertising, Lucky Strike, painted chromium, 1950s, 4⅜x3", from $20 to.............................**30.00**

Advertising, Mack Trucks, brass lift-arm butane, Korea, 1960s, 2½"....................................**15.00**

Advertising, Phillips 66, chromium & enamel, Park, 1960s, 2¼"..**20.00**

Aurora, camera form w/flashlight, chromium & leather, 1960s, 2x2½"..............................**30.00**

Colibri, chromium, butane, mid-1970s, 2½x⅞", from $25 to.**40.00**

Continental, chromium heart shape w/faux mother-of-pearl, 1950s, 2"........................**20.00**

Crown, gold-tone case, musical, ca 1948, pocket size, 2⅝", from $20 to **40.00**

DRP/Germany, chromium & leather, 1950s, table model, 3¼", from $45 to.............**60.00**

Evans, chromium, 1934, table model, 2x1⅞", from $25 to.............**35.00**

Figural, painted ceramic horse, table lighter, Japan, 1955, 5½x5½", from $15.00 to $25.00. (Photo courtesy James Flanagan)

Germany, butane pocket lighter, squeeze handle, late 1980s, 3", from $10 to **20.00**

Germany, saxophone form, butane, ca 1990, 3½", from $15 to **25.00**

Giv-A-Gift, candle shape, ceramic & brass, 1960s, 6¼", from $20 to **40.00**

Golden Wheel, chromium, lift-arm lighter, late 1940s, 1", from $20 to **30.00**

Golden Wheel, chromium & leather, lift-arm, windscreen, 2⅛", from $50 to.............**70.00**

Gulton, rechargeable electric pocket lighter, late 1950s, MIB, $50 to **75.00**

Japan, camel figural, metal, Japan, 1960s, 3½x4", from $20 to **30.00**

Japan, chromium & wood, 1970s, table model, 3x2⅛", from $10 to **15.00**

Japan, derringer shape, brass-plated, 4¼x8", from $10 to **20.00**

Japan, dinosaur figural, chromium, butane, 1988, 4¾x4", from $20 to **30.00**

Japan, pistol form, chromium & plastic, 1950s, 1⅜x2", from $15 to **25.00**

Japan, swan figural, chromium, early 1960s, 3x3¾", from $10 to .**20.00**

Magna, chromium, w/flashlight, battery, 1950s, 2¼x2", from $35 to **50.00**

Occupied Japan, silver-plated cowboy boot, ca 1950, 2⅞", from $50 to **70.00**

Penguin, chromium butane replica, lift-arm, late 1970s, 2⅝", from $10 to **20.00**

Pigeon, brass w/ivory-colored flower band, 1960s, 1⅜x1¾", from $20 to **25.00**

Prince, chromium crown w/gold, 1950s, table size, 2⅜", from $25 to **35.00**

Ronson, Comet, chromium & red plastic, late 1950s, 2¼", from $10 to..............................**15.00**

Ronson, Nordic, glass & chromium, ca 1955, 3½x3⅜", from $20 to **30.00**

Ronson, Princess, chromium w/green leather, 1950s, 1⅞x1½", MIB **50.00**

Ronson, Sport, chromium & blue leather, ca 1956, 2", M in gift box **40.00**

Ronson, Varaflame, chromium butane pocket lighter with gift box, made in France, 1964, 1½x2½", from $30.00 to $50.00. (Photo courtesy James Flanagan)

Royal Star, chromium & leather, ca 1954, 1⅝x1⅜", from $10 to **20.00**

Strikalite, elephant figural, painted metal, 1940s, 3x3½", from $25 to....................**35.00**

Strikalite, Scottie figural, painted metal, 2½x3", from $25 to.**40.00**

Wisner, Trickette, brass w/rhinestones, 1950s, 1½x1¾", from $25 to **40.00**

Yoshinaga Prince, Happy Days, brass finish, lift-arm butane, 1988, sm **10.00**

Zippo, chromium w/etched lady, ca 1993, 2¼", from $20 to ..**30.00**

Clothes Sprinkler Bottles

From the time we first had irons, clothes were sprinkled with water before ironing for the best results. During the 1930s and until the 1950s when the steam iron became a home staple, some of us merely took sprinkler tops and stuck them into old glass bottles to accomplish this task, while the more imaginative bought and enjoyed bottles made in figural shapes. The most popular, of course, were the Chinese men marked 'Sprinkle Plenty.' Some bottles were made by American Bisque, Cleminson of California, and other famous figural pottery makers. Many were made in Japan for the export market.

Clothespin, hand decorated, ceramic, from $150.00 to $200.00. (Photo courtesy Ellen Bercovici)

Cat, marble eyes, ceramic, American Bisque, from $300 to **400.00**

Cat, variety of designs & colors, homemade ceramics, from $75 to..................**150.00**

Chinese man, towel over arm, from $300 to................**400.00**

Dearie Is Weary, ceramic, Enesco, from $350 to................**500.00**

Dutch boy, green & white ceramic, from $175 to................**250.00**

Elephant, trunk forms handle, ceramic, American Bisque, from $400 to................**600.00**

Fireman............................**3,000.00**

Iron, blue flowers, ceramic, from $100 to.........................**150.00**

Iron, green ivy, ceramic, from $50 to....................................**75.00**

Iron, green plastic, from $35 to.**55.00**

Iron, souvenir of Wonder Cave, ceramic, from $250 to..**300.00**

Mammy, ceramic, possibly Pfaltzgraff, from $250 to.**350.00**

Mary Maid, all colors, plastic, Reliance, from $15 to.....**35.00**

Mary Poppins, ceramic, Cleminson, from $250 to...................**450.00**

Myrtle, ceramic, Pfaltzgraff, from $250 to..........................**350.00**

Poodle, gray & pink or white, ceramic, from $200 to..**300.00**

Rooster, green, tan & red detailing over white, ceramic, from $85 to....................................**125.00**

Coca-Cola

Introduced in 1886, Coca-Cola advertising has literally saturated our lives with a never-ending variety of items. Some of the earlier calendars and trays have been known to bring prices well into the four figures. Because of these heady prices and extreme collector demand for good Coke items, reproductions are everywhere, so beware! In addition to reproductions, 'fantasy' items have also been made, the difference being that a 'fantasy' never existed as an original. Don't be deceived. Belt buckles are 'fantasies.' So are glass doorknobs with an etched trademark, bottle-shaped knives, pocketknives, and there are others.

When the company celebrated its 100th anniversary in 1986, many 'centennial' items were issued. They all carry the '100th Anniversary' logo. Many of them are collectible in their own right, and some are already high priced.

If you'd really like to study this subject, we recommend these books: *Collector's Guide to Coca-Cola Items, Vols I* and *II,* by Al Wilson; *Coca-Cola Commemoratiave Bottles* by Bob and Debra Henrich; B.J. Summers' *Guide to Coca-Cola;* and *Pocket Guide to Coca-Cola.*

Ashtray, Drink..., round w/scalloped edge, 1950s, EX....**10.00**

Ashtray, metal w/bottle-shaped lighter in center, 1950s, EX...........**145.00**

Ashtray, wave logo, glass w/paper insert, Mexican, 1970s, EX.**5.00**

Blotter, couples at party, 1955, EX.................................**25.00**

Booklet, Profitable Soda Fountain Operation, 1953, EX......**75.00**

Boomerang, 1950s, EX **40.00**

Bottle, straight-sided w/diamond, 1st throw-away, 1960s, 10-oz, NM.............................**25.00**

Bottle, Super Bowl 2000, eight-ounce, with original single cardboard carton, NM, $75.00. (Photo courtesy B.J. Summers)

Display, cardboard diecut Santa, 1945, 14x9", EX, $225.00. (Photo courtesy B.J. Summers)

Calendar, sports scenes, full pad, 1980, M............................**20.00**
Calendar, The Pause That Refreshes, girl skier, 1957, VG **75.00**
Calendar, There's Nothing Like a Coke, full pad, 1956, EX......................................**125.00**
Calender, young lady w/boat oars, paper, 1957, 22x12¼", EX **20.00**
Carrier, 6-pack; King Size, plastic, red w/white letters, 1950s, EX **15.00**
Clock, counter; Drink..., light-up, 1950s, restored.............**850.00**
Clock, fishtail w/white background, light-up, 1960s, EX.......**195.00**
Comic book, Refreshment Through the Ages, 1951, EX **30.00**
Cooler, Drink..., red letters on stainless steel, 6-pack, 1950s, EX **425.00**
Cooler, Drink...in Bottles, metal, sm, 1950s, G.................**115.00**
Display case, for 20" bottle, 1950s, VG................................**180.00**

Doll, Barbie; After the Walk, 2nd in Fashion series, 1997, EX **125.00**
Door push, Coke Ads Life, wave logo, painted steel, 1970-80s, NM.................................**75.00**
Door push, Ice Cold in Bottles, red on white porcelain, 1960s, 30", EX.................................**325.00**
Fan, Compliments of Waycross Bottling Co, wicker, 1950s, 1950s, EX **95.00**
Ice pick, Drink..., red letters on wood handle, 1960s, EX .**12.00**
Knife, truck shape, from seminar, 1972, EX.........................**35.00**
Match book, King Size Coke, 1959, VG.....................................**5.00**
Menu board, w/clock, light-up, 1960s, EX **145.00**
Notebook, Coca-Cola Advertised Schedule, 1980, EX........**20.00**
Opener, bottle shape, flat metal, 1950s, EX **35.00**
Opener, 75th Anniversary from Columbus OH, plastic & metal, 1970s, EX...........**20.00**

Postcard, Coca-Cola Pavilion at World's Fair, 1964, 5½x3½", EX.................................**20.00**

Poster, Refresh, majorette, horizontal, cardboard, 1952, 36x20", VG.................**475.00**

Poster, So Delicious, snow ski scene, cardboard, 1954, 36x20", NM.................**600.00**

Poster, So Easy To Carry Home, woman in rain w/umbrella, 1942, EX.....................**400.00**

Poster, truck; Refreshing New Feeling, cardboard, 1960s, 67x32", EX...................**135.00**

Radio, cooler shape, lights up, musical, 1950s, EX......**900.00**

Sign, carton stuffer for Memorial Day, 1953, cardboard, 1953, EX.................................**55.00**

Sign, counter; 20-oz bottles, lights up, 1990s, 12x13", EXIB...........................**225.00**

Sign, diecut 6 pack, cardboard, 1954, EX.......................**750.00**

Sign, Drink Coca-Cola, white letters over wave logo, 1980s, 24x18", EX.....................**95.00**

Sign, Enjoy Coca-Cola, bottle rack, cardboard, red & white, 1970s, EX.....................**25.00**

Sign, Ice Cold, cup in center, metal, 1960s, 20x28", NM...............................**300.00**

Sign, Let's Watch for 'Em, girl running, cardboard, 1950s, 66x32", VG.................**500.00**

Sign, light-up; Have a Coke, beveled edge, 1950s, 18x12", EX...............................**775.00**

Sign, Pick Up the Fixins, Enjoy Coke, cardboard, 1957, 20x14", NM.................**55.00**

Sign, tin, 1964, 12x32", NM, $225.00. (Photo courtesy Muddy River Trading Co./Gary Metz)

Sign, woman shopper, French Canadian poster, cardboard, 1950s, EX.....................**160.00**

Sign, 6 pack w/6 for 25¢, die-cut cardboard, 1950s, 12", NM.....**575.00**

Sticker, Please Pay Cashier, 1960s, EX.......................**25.00**

Tablet, writing; Wildlife of USA, 1970s, G..........................**10.00**

Thermometer, Drink..., green on white, plastic/metal, 1960s, NM...............................**375.00**

Thermometer, Enjoy..., metal w/glass front, 1960s, 12" dia, EX................................**155.00**

Thermometer, round front dial, Pam, 1960s, 12" diameter, NM, $250.00. (Photo courtesy Muddy River Trading Co./Gary Metz)

Toy, bang gun, Santa on sleigh, 1950s, M.........................**20.00**

Toy car, friction, red & white, Taiyo, 1960s, EX..........**250.00**

Toy truck, Buddy L #5426, pressed steel, 1960s, 15", NMIB.**500.00**

Toy truck, tractor-trailer, Matchbox Super King, 1978, NMIB..............................**55.00**

Tray, serving; artwork of Lehigh Valley plant, 1981, EX ..**15.00**

Tray, serving; Goodwill Bottling, logo, rectangular, 1979, EX **15.00**

Tray, serving; pull cart w/picnic basket, 1958, 13¼x10½", EX **25.00**

Vending machine, Cavalier CS-72, 1950s, 24¾x21⅞", EX.**1,850.00**

Yo-yo, Drink Coca-Cola in Bottles in gold on red, wooden, EX.**110.00**

Coin Glass

Coin Glass was originally produced in crystal, ruby, blue, emerald green, olive green, and amber. Lancaster Colony bought the Fostoria Company in the mid-1980s and reproduced this line in crystal, green, blue, amber, and red. Except for the red and crystal, the colors are 'off' enough to be pretty obvious, but the red is so close it's impossible to determine old from new. Here are some (probably not all) of the items made in recent years: bowl, 8" diameter; bowl, 9" oval; candlesticks, 4½"; candy jar with lid, 6¼"; cigarette box with lid, 5¾" x 4½"; creamer and sugar bowl; footed comport; decanter, 10¼"; jelly; nappy with handle, 5¼"; footed salver, 6½"; footed urn with lid, 12¾"; and wedding bowl, 8¼". Know your dealer!

Emerald green is most desired by collectors. You may also find some crystal pieces with gold-decorated coins. These will be valued at about double the price of plain crystal if the gold is not worn. (When the gold is worn or faded, value is minimal.) Numbers included in our descriptions were company-assigned stock numbers that collectors use as a means to distinguish variations in stems and shapes. For further information we recommend *Collectible Glassware from the 40s, 50 & 60s*, by Gene Florence (Collector Books).

Ashtray, amber, center coin, #1372/119, 7½"..............**20.00**

Ashtray, crystal, round, #1372/124, 10"...............**25.00**

Ashtray/cover, green, #1372/110, 3"....................................**30.00**

Bowl, blue, footed, w/lid, #1372/212, 8½"............**175.00**

Bowl, blue, round, #1372/179, 8".**50.00**

Bowl, handled nappy, green, 5⅜", **$40.00. (Photo courtesy Gene Florence)**

Bowl, ruby, oval, #1372/189, 9".**50.00**

Bowl, wedding; amber, #1372/162, w/lid **70.00**

Candle holders, amber, #1372/326, 8", pr **60.00**

Candy box, crystal, #1372/354, w/lid, 4⅛"........................**30.00**

Cigarette urn, green, footed, #1372/381, 3⅜"...............**50.00**

Creamer, green, #1372/680 ..**30.00**

Jelly jar, blue, #1372/448 .....**25.00**

Lamp, courting; amber, oil burner, handle, #1372/310, 9¾".**110.00**

Lamp chimney, courting; blue w/handle, #1372/292......**65.00**

Nappy, crystal, #1372/495, 4½".**22.00**

Pitcher, amber or crystal, #1372/453, 32-oz, 6¼"....**55.00**

Pitcher, green, #1372/453, 32-oz, 6¼"................**195.00**

Plate, olive, #1372/550, 8" **20.00**

Punch cup, crystal, #1372/600.**35.00**

Punch cup, crystal, #1372/615.**35.00**

Stem, goblet; crystal, #1372/2, 10½"................**38.00**

Stem, sherbet; ruby, #1372/7, 9-oz, 5¼"................**100.00**

Stem, wine; ruby, #1372/26, 5-oz, 4"................**100.00**

Sugar bowl, blue, w/lid, #1372/673.**45.00**

Tumbler, highball/iced tea; #1372/64, 12-oz, 5⅛"......**37.50**

Tumbler, iced tea; olive, #1372/58, 14-oz, 5 3/16".................**40.00**

Tumbler, juice; crystal, #1372/81, 9-oz, 3⅝".........................**30.00**

Tumbler, scotch & soda; crystal, #1372/73, 9-oz, 4¼"........**30.00**

Urn, amber or olive, #1372/829, w/lid, footed, 12¾" **80.00**

Urn, green, #1372/829, w/lid, footed, 12¾".........................**200.00**

Vase, bud; amber, #1372/799, 8".**22.00**

Vase, crystal, #1372/818, footed, 10"................**45.00**

Coloring Books

Throughout the 1950s and even into the 1970s, coloring and activity books were produced by the thousands. Whitman, Saalfield, and Watkins-Strathmore were some of the largest publishers. The most popular were those that pictured well-known TV, movie, and comic book characters, and these are the ones that are bringing top dollar today. Condition is also an important worth-accessing factor. Compared to a coloring book that was never used, one that's only partially colored is worth from 50% to 70% less.

Adventures of Electro-Man, Lowe, 1967, unused, NM..........**20.00**

Annette, WDP, 1964, unused, EX.**15.00**

Atom Ant, Watkins-Strathmore, 1967, few pages colored, EX..........**10.00**

Baba Louie, Watkins-Strathmore, 1960, unused, EX...........**15.00**

Banana Splits, Whitman, 1969, unused, EX.....................**25.00**

Beatles, Saalfield, unused, EX.**125.00**

Beverly Hillbillies, Whitman #1137, unused, EX.........**30.00**

Black Hole, Whitman, 1979, unused, EX.....................**12.00**

Bobbsey Twins, Whitman, 1954, unused, VG....................**25.00**

Brady Bunch, Whitman, 1973, unused, EX, from $25 to .**35.00**

Buffy & Jody, Whitman, 1969, unused, NM....................**25.00**

Buzz Corry, Ralston Purina, 1953, few pages colored, scarce, EX.....................**75.00**

Casper & Nightmare, Saalfield, 1964, unused, EX...........**20.00**

Charlie Chaplin, Saalfield, 1941, unused, M......................**50.00**

Chatty Baby, Whitman, 1960s, unused, NM...................**25.00**

Dennis the Menace, Whitman, 1961, few pages colored, NM **20.00**

Dick Tracy, Saalfield, 1946, unused, EX......................**45.00**

Donna Reed, Saalfield, 1964, unused, NM....................**30.00**

Doris Day, Whitman, 1955, unused, EX......................**35.00**

Dumbo the Elephant, 1972, unused, M.......................**25.00**

Flintstones, Charlton, 1971, unused, EX, from $10 to.**15.00**

George of the Jungle, Whitman, 1968, unused, EX...........**30.00**

Gilligan's Island, Whitman, 1965, unused, EX......................**45.00**

Green Hornet, Whitman, 1966, unused, NM....................**60.00**

Gulliver's Travels, Saalfield, 1939, several pages colored, VG+.**45.00**

Gunsmoke, Whitman, 1959, few pages colored, EX...........**25.00**

Heckle & Jeckle, Treasure Books, 1957, unused, EX...........**15.00**

Howdy Doody, Whitman, 1952, pages slightly yellowed, VG..........**15.00**

John Wayne, Saalfield, 1951, few pages colored, rare, EX..**85.00**

Julia, A Coloring Book, Saalfield #9523, 1968, red or blue cover, NM, from $20.00 to $25.00. (Photo courtesy Greg Davis and Bill Morgan)

Land of the Lost, Whitman #1045, 1975, $25.00. (Photo courtesy Greg Davis and Bill Morgan)

Leave It to Beaver, Saalfield, 1958, unused, NM.........**65.00**

Little Orphan Annie, Artcraft, 1974, unused, NM.........**20.00**

Lucille Ball & Desi Arnez, Whitman, 1953, unused, EX............................**100.00**

Mr Beasley, Whitman, 1970, unused, NM....................**25.00**

Nanny & the Professor, Saalfield, 1971, unused, NM.........**20.00**

Pebbles & Bamm-Bamm, Charlton, 1971, unused, EX............**20.00**

Peter Pan, Whitman, 1952, unused, VG.....................**25.00**

Porky Pig, Leon Schlesinger, 1930s, unused, EX, from $150 to **175.00**

Rin-Tin-Tin, Whitman, 1955, unused, EX.....................**30.00**

Roger Ramjet, Whitman, 1966, unused, NM....................**40.00**

Shirley Temple Crosses the Country, Saalfield, 1939, unused, EX....................**75.00**

Six Million Dollar Man, Saalfield, 1976, unused, M **15.00**

Space Angel, Saalfield, 1963, unused, EX....................**35.00**

Straight Arrow, Stephens, 1949, few pages colored, EX....**30.00**

Tammy's Vacation, Watkins-Strathmore, 1960s, unused, EX..................................**20.00**

That Girl Artcraft, 1968, unused, NM.................................**25.00**

Thunderbirds, Whitman, 1968, unused, EX.....................**30.00**

Uncle Martin the Martian, Golden Press, 1964, few pages colored, EX+.........................**35.00**

Waltons, Whitman, 1975, unused, NM.................................**25.00**

Wizard of Oz, Whitman, 1962, unused, EX.....................**25.00**

101 Dalmatians, Whitman, 1960, unused, EX.....................**25.00**

Comic Books

Factors that make a comic book valuable are condition, content, and rarity, not necessarily age. In fact, comics printed between 1950 and the late 1970s are most in demand by collectors who prefer those they had as children to the earlier comics. Issues where the hero is first introduced are treasured. While some may go for hundreds, even thousands of dollars, many are worth very little; so if you plan to collect, you'll need a good comic book price guide such as Overstreet's to assess your holdings. Condition is extremely important. Compared to a book in excellent condition, a mint issue might be worth six to eight times as much, while one in only good condition should be priced at less than half the price of the excellent exam-ple. For more information see *Schroeder's Collectible Toys, Antique to Modern* (Collector Books).

Adventures of Mighty Mouse, St John #2, 1952, EX..........**55.00**

Andy Panda, Dell Four-Color #280, 1950, EX...............**25.00**

Archie Comics, Archie Publications #4, 1943, VG..................**325.00**

Avengers, Marvel #1, 1963, EX.**500.00**

Bat Masterson, Dell Four Color #1013, 1959, VG, $15.00. (Photo courtesy Bill Bruegman)

Beany & Cecil, Dell #2, 1962, rare, EX.....................................**25.00**

Beverly Hillbillies, Dell #5, NM, from $75 to....................**100.00**

Bonanza, Dell #210, 1962, EX.**125.00**

Bugaloos, Charlton #1, 1972, NM, from $20 to......................**30.00**

Captain Marvel, Fawcett #132, 1951, VG.........................**20.00**

Captain Midnight, Dell #37, EX.**85.00**

Cindy, Marvel #38, 1950, EX.**20.00**

Dark Shadows, Gold Key #15, 1972, EX..........................**15.00**

Dick Tracy Monthly, Dell #18, EX.**35.00**

Elmer Fudd, Dell #689, NM.**25.00**

Family Affair, Gold Key #1, 1970, NM..................................**40.00**

Flash, Why?, DC Comics, 1965, NM, from $30.00 to $40.00.

Flintstones, Bedrock Bedlam, Dell Giant #48, 1961, NM...**450.00**

Green Hornet, Dell #496, 1953, EX **35.00**

Hogan's Heroes, Dell #8, 1967, EX..**40.00**

Howdy Doody, Dell #4, 1950, EX...**40.00**

Howdy Doody, Dell #15, 1952, EX.**25.00**

Hunchback of Notre Dame, Dell #854, 1957, EX...............**40.00**

I Love Lucy, Dell #29, 1960, VG+..**35.00**

Iron Man, Dell #10, NM **25.00**

Josie & the Pussycats, Archie Comics #6, 1964, NM.....**20.00**

Justice League of America, Dell #6, VG............................**50.00**

Krofft Supershow, Gold Key #1, 1976, NM.......................**15.00**

Lawman, Dell #8, 1961, VG+ .**40.00**

Li'l Abner, Dell #61, 1947, NM.**195.00**

Lone Ranger, Dell #161, 1960, NM **75.00**

Man From UNCLE, Dell #8, VG..**15.00**

Marge's Little Lulu, Dell Four-Color #115, 1946, VG+ .**150.00**

Maverick, Dell #980, EX.......**40.00**

Mickey Mouse & the Mystery Sea Monster, Wheaties premium, 1950, NM.......................**15.00**

My Favorite Martian, Dell #3, EX **30.00**

Old Ironside w/Johnny Tremain, Dell #874, 1957, EX.......**15.00**

Peanuts, Gold Key #1, M......**25.00**

Raggedy Ann & Andy, Dell #452, 1952, NM, from $25 to ..**30.00**

Rawhide, Dell #1160, 1960, VG+............................**30.00**

Roy Rogers & Trigger, Dell #124, 1958, EX........................**35.00**

Sheena Queen of the Jungle, Jumbo Comics #140, VG **30.00**

Silver Surfer, Marvel #4, 1969, VG **65.00**

Six Million Dollar Man, Charlton #1, 1976, NM.................**15.00**

Space Ghost, Dell #1, NM ..**250.00**

Spider-Man, Marvel #1, 1966, VG **35.00**

Star Wars, Marvel #1, 1977, M.**45.00**

Superman, DC Comics #1, 1939, NM, minimum value .**10,000.00**

Superman's Girlfriend Lois Lane, Dell #13, NM, $100.00.

Tales of Suspense, Marvel Silver Age #46, 1964, VG+ **25.00**

Tarzan, Dell #27, 1951, EX ..**35.00**

Terry & the Pirates, Dell #6, 1936, oversized, NM **150.00**

Three Stooges, Dell #1170, 1961, VG..................................**30.00**

Tom Mix, Fawcett #2, VG ..**110.00**

Transformers, Marvel #78, 1991, EX+ **40.00**

Tweety & Sylvester, Dell #11, NM **20.00**

Uncle Scrooge, Dell #386, 1952, VG **75.00**

Walt Disney's Zorro, Dell #15, 1961, VG **45.00**

Wonder Woman, Dell #34, G .**30.00**

X-Men, Marvel #13, 1965, EX.**30.00**

77 Sunset Strip, Dell #1066, 1960, EX+ **30.00**

Compacts

Prior to World War I, the use of cosmetics was frowned upon. It was not until after the war when women became liberated and entered the work force that make-up became acceptable. A compact became a necessity as a portable container for cosmetics and usually contained a puff and mirror. They were made in many different styles, shapes, and motifs and from every type of natural and man-made material. The fine jewelry houses made compacts in all of the precious metals — some studded with precious stones. The most sought-after compacts today are those made of plastic, Art Deco styles, figurals, and any that incorporate gadgets. Compacts that are combined with other accessories are also very desirable.

For further information we recommend these books: *Collector's Encyclopedia of Compacts, Carryalls & Face Powder Boxes* by Laura M. Muller; and *Vintage & Vogue Ladies' Compacts* by Roselyn Gerson. Both are published by Collector Books. See Clubs and Newsletters for information concerning the *Powder Puff*.

Evans, gold-tone with pink cloisonné inset, hammered interior, framed mirror, 2⅝" square, from $50.00 to $65.00. (Photo courtesy Laura M. Mueller)

Biscay France, plastic w/copper-etched lady & lamb scene on lid **115.00**

Book form, green leather w/gold embossing, 2x3", from $80 to **125.00**

Brown leather, round, from $50 to **70.00**

Buick Eight logo applied to silver-tone lid, 3" dia, from $70 to........**85.00**

Coty, gold-tone vanity w/green enamel, raised gold-tone bow, 3" L **100.00**

Coty, gold-tone vanity w/rhinestones on wishbone & star, 3¾" **90.00**

Coty, polished nickel-finish octagonal vanity, from $60 to ...**80.00**

Damascene horseman scene on gold-tone, 1930s, from $40 to **60.00**

Disneyland souvenir, silver-tone w/gold-tone scene, 3½" dia, from $60 to **100.00**

Dorset, brushed gold-tone w/polished heart/I Love You, 2½", from $60 to **80.00**

E Arden, engraved silver-tone, powder sifter, 2½" dia, from $60 to **100.00**

Elgin American, Georgia state flag & flower on lid, 1950s, from $50 to **75.00**

Elgin American, gold-tone w/Eastern Star emblem, 3" dia, from $40 to..............**60.00**

Evans, silver-tone compact/watch combination, 1950s, from $100 to.....................................**150.00**

Fuller, plastic, sleeve for comb mounted on lid, from $40 to **60.00**

Fur covered, coin-purse snap closure, Argentina, from $55 to...............................**85.00**

Girl Scout emblem on satin gold-tone, from $60 to............**80.00**

Gold-tone compact/watch combination, Germany, from $125 to.....................................**175.00**

Gold-tone heart shape w/brocade lid, 1930s, from $40 to...**60.00**

Gold-tone triangle w/enameled birds, finger-ring chain, from $80 to............................**120.00**

Hand mirror shape, black enamel, floral disc on lid, 3½" L .**70.00**

Hand-mirror shape, engraved gold-tone, from $80 to..**100.00**

Harmony of Boston, tan box shape w/snap closure, from $50 to **60.00**

Hoechst, silver-plated hand mirror shape w/lipstick in handle, from $125 to.................**175.00**

Kigu, Cherie, gold-tone heart w/jeweled crown on lid, 1950s, from $50 to...................**80.00**

Kigu, gold-tone w/white enamel clock decor, 3¼" dia, from $40 to **60.00**

Lucite, photo placed behind removable mirror, 3¼" sq, from $60 to.....................**90.00**

Majestic, gold-tone egg shape, metal interior, 2x3", from $80 to....................................**100.00**

Marbleized metal w/portrait transfer, 2¾" sq, from $40 to ..**60.00**

Maroon leather, lipstick sleeve, 1930s, from $60 to **90.00**

Mini, green enamel w/gold-tone star, 1½" dia, from $75 to.......**100.00**

Mother-of-pearl w/petit-point border, sm, from $90 to **100.00**

Navy & white plastic, designed as officer's cap, 1940s, from $50 to **90.00**

Petit point scalloped crescent gold-tone vanity, 1930s, from $80 to.**125.00**

Pilcher, Slimpact, wood w/chess inlay, 1940-50s, from $60 to.........**80.00**

Plastic w/metal Scottie cutout on lid, w/cigarette holder, 1940s.**100.00**

Polished gold-tone, lock motif, 2½" dia, from $80 to............**100.00**

R Hudnut, gilt w/emb tulips, lipstick encased in lid cover, from $40 to **60.00**

Rex Fifth Ave, striped taffeta vanity pochette, mirror, 1940s, from $75 to **100.00**

Schildkraut, cloisonné enameled scene on gold-tone, 2¾", from $50 to **70.00**

Silver-tone w/orange/black/silver Deco design on lid, 2" dia, from $50 to **75.00**

Stratton, gold-tone w/scenic transfer on lid, 1950s, from $40 to **60.00**

Suitcase form, gold-tone w/blue enameling, snaps open, 3" L, from $80 to **120.00**

Tooled leather on gold-tone, Italy, sq, sm, from $30 to **50.00**

Vanity, black & white, mother-of-pearl w/attached lipstick, from $50 to **70.00**

Vanity, blue enamel w/Scottie transfer, compartments, sm, from $30 to **50.00**

Vanity, gilt mesh w/blue synthetic stone, metal mirror, 1940s, from $60 to **100.00**

Vanity, gold-tone w/black enameled USN insignia & gold heart, 1940s **100.00**

Vanity, lavender enamel w/floral decor, mirror, compartments, 2x1½"..............................**50.00**

Vanity clutch, navy moiré & gilt, w/compact/lipstick/comb, from $40 to **60.00**

Vanity pochette, brown suede, 1930s, from $70 to **90.00**

Volupte, brushed gold-tone w/red/white/blue stripes, 3x3", from $60 to **80.00**

Volupté, gold-tone with broad band lattice in high relief, puff with logo, glued-in mirror, 2⅜" square, from $25.00 to $40.00. (Photo courtesy Laura M. Mueller)

Volupte, Lucky Purse, brushed silver-tone, mirror, 3½", from $80 to **100.00**

Volupte, red anchor & blue rope enameled on white, 2½" dia, from $50 to **70.00**

Volupte, vanity pouch, light blue leather, collapses, 1930s, from $75 to **90.00**

Wedge shape, green enamel on gold-tone, interior light, 2¾x3¼"...........................**90.00**

Zell, maroon hatbox w/gold-tone anchor & USN emblem, 3" dia, from $150 to.........**175.00**

Cookbooks

Cookbook collecting can be traced back to the turn of the twentieth century. Good food and recipes on how to prepare it are timeless. Cookbooks fall into many subclassifications with emphasis on various aspects of cooking. Some specialize in regional or ethnic food; during the World Wars, conservation and cost-cutting measures were popular themes. Because this field is so varied, you may want to decide what field is most interesting and specialize. Hardcover or softcover, Betty Crocker or Julia Childs, Pillsbury or Gold Medal — the choice is yours!

For more information, we recommend *A Guide to Cookbook Collecting* by Colonel Bob Allen and *The Price Guide to Cookbook and Recipe Leaflets* by Linda Dickinson. Both are published by Collector Books.

All Doors Open to Jell-O, 1917, softcover **50.00**

American Domestic Cookbook for 1867, softcover **60.00**

American Girl Cook Book, 1966, hard cover **20.00**

Andre Simon's French Cook Book, 1938, hardcover **25.00**

Arthur Godfrey's Food & Fun, 1953, softcover **45.00**

Baker's Chocolate Choice Recipes, 1901 .... **20.00**

Baker's Chocolate and Cocoa recipes, 1931, $12.00. (Photo courtesy Col. Bob Allen)

Baker's Coconut Recipes, 1926. **20.00**

Ball Blue Book of Canning & Preserving Recipes, 1915, softcover **25.00**

Boston School Kitchen Text Book, 1887, hardcover, 237 pages. **90.00**

Breakfasts, Luncheons, Dinners, 1928, Mary D Chambers, hardcover **45.00**

Brer Rabbit's Modern Recipes for Modern Living, 1930s **15.00**

Budget Gourmet, 1962, Sylvia Vaughn Thompson, softcover **8.00**

Canning in a Wash Boiler, Ball Corp, 1915, color flyer ... **10.00**

Carnation, 100 Glorified Recipes, 1934 .... **14.00**

Cheese Recipes for Wartime Meals, Kraft, 1943, softcover **12.50**

Christmas Cookies, 1940, Hartford Electric Light Co **15.00**

Come Into the Kitchen Cookbook, 1969, hardcover **45.00**

Cook Book-Vegex, 1920s, shaped like a jar, softcover **20.00**

Dedicated to Home Makers Everywhere, Ruth Kerr, 1952, 56 pages **10.00**

Dr Miles Candy Book, 1910, softcover **20.00**

Eggs at Any Meal, 1931, US Dept of Agriculture, Leaflet #39, 8 pages **15.00**

Everyday Foods, 1930-32, Houghton Mifflin Co, hardcover, 550 pages **30.00**

Exciting World...Rice Dishes, 1959, General Foods, 20 pages, softcover **10.00**

Family Nurse, 1837, Lydia Child, hardcover **325.00**

Fireless Cooking, 1920s, softcover **20.00**

Fleischmann's The Young Cook's Bake-A-Bun Book, 1967 .. **8.00**

Food Treats for Keeps, 1957, Kerr Glass Mfg Co, 32 pages **3.00**

Gravenhurst Ladies Cook Book, 1900 .... **20.00**

How America Eats, Clementine Paddleford, 1st edition, hardbound, 1949, 495 pages, $25.00. (Photo courtesy Col. Bob Allen)

Jams, Jellies & Marmalades, Certo Suregel, 1924, Bradley, softcover **15.00**

Jell-O, Desserts of the World, 1909, softcover **75.00**

Jell-O Ice Cream Powder, 1906.**75.00**

Jell-O recipe booklet, copyright 1927, 10 pages, $15.00.

Kate Smith Chooses Her 55 Favorite Cake Recipes, 1952, softcover **10.00**

Kerr Economy Jar Home Canning Recipes, 1909, softcover.**25.00**

Kitchen Tested Recipes, 1933, Sunbeam Mixmaster, softcover.....................................**15.00**

Ladies Delight Cook Book, 1889, #2, 32 pages....................**30.00**

Lakes & Hills Cook Book, 1936, Branson MO Christian Church, 80 pages **15.00**

Libbey's Fancy Red Alaska Salmon, 1935, can shape, softcover **15.00**

Little Cookbook, Jean Allen tested recipes, Kroger, 1950s, 10 pages...............................**8.00**

Little Red Devil, 1920s, deviled ham, softcover, 30 pages.**20.00**

Low-Fat Cookery, 1959, Stead & Warren, hardcover.........**15.00**

Made Over Dishes, 1898, Sarah Tyson Rorer, hardcover.**55.00**

McCall's What To Serve at Parties, 1923, softcover.**14.00**

Oven Dinners-Menus & Recipes, Jean Allen, Kroger, 1930s, 8 pages...............................**12.50**

Pennsylvania Dutch Cooking, 1960, softcover **8.00**

Polly Put the Kettle On, We'll All Make Jell-O, 1924..........**65.00**

Pot Luck Cookery, 1955, Beverly Pepper, 190 pages, Pocket Cookbook **6.00**

Presidential Cook Book, 1907, hardcover.......................**30.00**

Rainbow Road to Health & Happiness, 1926, softcover.**20.00**

Ralston Purina Breakfast Around the World, 1940s............**12.50**

Recipes for New & Delicous Energy Dishes, Shredded Wheat, 1933 ....**12.00**

Recipes for War Breads, 1917, softcover **25.00**

Rumford, The Wholesome Baking Powder, 1907.................**25.00**

Sugar Spoon Recipes From the Domino Sugar Bowl Kitchen, 1962, spiral......................**8.00**

Sunkist Recipes, Oranges-Lemons, 1916, softcover................**20.00**

Teen Time Cooking w/Carnation, 1959 ....**8.00**

Tested Recipes w/Blue Ribbon Malt Extract, 1927, softcover.................................**18.00**

The I Hate To Cook Book, 1960, hardcover.......................**15.00**

Treasured Recipes of the Old South, 1941, softcover ...**12.50**

Watkins Almanac & Home Book, 1936 ....**14.00**

Wesson Oil Recipes, 1911, softcover **25.00**

When You Entertain, 1932, Coca-Cola, Ida Bailey Allen, softcover **25.00**

White Mountain Frozen Dainties, 1905 ....**24.00**

Who Says We Can't Cook, 1955, Women's National Press Club, hardcover........................**20.00**

Wines & Spirits, 1961, 1st edition, Massee, hardcover, 427 pages **15.00**

Woman's Day Cook Book of Relishes, 1963, softcover .**5.00**

Wonder Sandwich Book, 1928, softcover **20.00**

100 Old Fashion Cooking Recipes, 1910, softcover **25.00**

Cookie Cutters and Shapers

Cookie cutters have come into their own in recent years as worthy kitchen collectibles. Prices on many have risen astronomically, but a practiced eye can still sort out a good bargain. Advertising cutters and product premiums, especially in plastic, can still be found without too much effort. Aluminum cutters with painted wooden handles are usually worth several dollars each if in good condition. Red and green are the usual handle colors, but other colors are more highly prized by many. Hallmark plastic cookie cutters, especially those with painted backs, are always worth considering, if in good condition.

Be wary of modern tin cutters being sold for antique. Many present-day tinsmiths chemically antique their cutters, especially those done in a primitive style. These are often sold by others as 'very old.' Look closely, because most tinsmiths today sign and date these cutters. See Clubs and Newsletters for information concerning a collector's club, *Cookie Crumbs.*

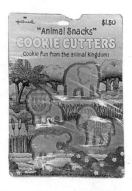

Animal Snacks Cookie Cutters, soft gold plastic, Hallmark, 1978, mini, set of four, MIP, $15.00.
(Photo courtesy Rosemary Henry)

American Flag (flying), tin, ca 1900, 4½x3¼", VG+ **50.00**

Cowboy, Aunt Chick's, mottled plastic, 5¼"....................**45.00**

Deer, recumbent, tin, flat back, 8x9½", EX......................**25.00**

Donald Duck, face, yellow plastic, marked Disney, Hallmark, 4½", EX..........................**25.00**

Donkey, Domar Life-Like Cookies, red plastic, Grant Mfg, 4", MOC **28.00**

Eagle, tin, 3⅞x2⅞"................**30.00**

Elephant, plastic, Kleeware, England, 3½x4½", EX ...**20.00**

Gingerbread man, copper, Pfaltzgraff, 10x5½", EX .**35.00**

Gingerbread man, tin, 8x6"..**40.00**

Goose, tin, Davis Baking Powder, 1920s, 3¾", EX **22.50**

Hansel & Gretel, tin, 1947, NM **35.00**

Heart, tin, strap handle, marked Fries, 3x2¼", EX **20.00**

Heart in circle, tin, ruffled edge, 3¼" dia **75.00**

Horse/squirrel/swan/bunny, aluminum w/wood handle, 8½" dia **40.00**

Mad Hatter, red plastic, unmarked, 3¾", EX **195.00**

MGM Cartoons, Tom, Jerry, Droopy & friends, set of 6, Loew's, 1956, EX **95.00**

Mickey Mouse (head only), handle embossed w/WDP, 4x4½" .**30.00**

Minnie Mouse, plastic, WDP, 4½", MIP **60.00**

Pig, aluminum, 4" **210.00**

Rabbit, Formay Shortening, 1930s, 6" **30.00**

Rabbit, jumping, tin, ca 1900, 2½x4" **30.00**

Rabbit, tin, Byrnes & Kiefer Co, ca 1902, 5½x3¼" **75.00**

Raggedy Ann w/teddy bear, Brown Bag Cookie Art, #25, M .**30.00**

Raggedy Ann and Andy, Ervan Guttman Co., $5.00. (Photo courtesy Rosemary Henry)

Ronald McDonald, yellow plastic, McDonald's, 1980, 3x3¼", EX **27.50**

Rooster, tin, Byrnes & Kiefer Co, ca 1902, 3¾x3½" **60.00**

Santa Claus, tin, Byrnes & Kiefer Co, ca 1900, 5⅞x3¼"......**75.00**

Scottie dog, metal w/red wood handle, 2½x2¾"...................**35.00**

Snoopy on pumpkin, orange plastic, Hallmark, 1972, 6½x5½".**45.00**

Star, copper, Martha Stewart, 8", M....................................**20.00**

State of Nebraska, tin, GM Thurnauer Co, 1956, EX (VG box) **55.00**

Trick or Treat, set of 6 Halloween figures, metal, 1950s, EXIB...**30.00**

Troll, Mirro Aluminum, 1965, 3¾", EX **25.00**

White Rabbit, Alice in Wonderland, red plastic, unmarked, 3½", EX .**280.00**

Cookie Jars

McCoy, Metlox, Twin Winton, Robinson Ransbottom, Brush, and American Bisque were among the largest producers of cookie jars in the country. Many firms made them to a lesser extent. Figural jars are the most common (and the most valuable), made in an endless variety of subjects. Early jars from the 1920s and 1930s were often decorated in 'cold paint' over the glaze. This type of color is easily removed — take care that you use very gentle cleaning methods. A damp cloth and a light touch is the safest approach.

For further information we recommend *Collector's Encyclopedia of Metlox Potteries* by Carl Gibbs, *Collector's Encyclopedia of McCoy Pottery* by Sharon and Bob Huxford, *Collector's Encyclopedia of Cookie Jars* by Joyce and Fred Roerig (there are three in the series), and *An Illustrated Value Guide to Cookie Jars* by Ermagene Westfall (all published by Collector Books). Values are for jars in mint condition unless otherwise noted. Beware of modern reproductions! See Clubs and Newsletters for information concerning *Cookie Jarrin' With Joyce: The Cookie Jar Newsletter.*

Abingdon, Bo Peep, #694, from $250 to............................**275.00**
Abingdon, Choo Choo, #651.**150.00**
Abingdon, Fat Boy, #495 ....**250.00**
Abingdon, Miss Muffet, #622.**205.00**
Abingdon, Pineapple, marked Abingdon USA #664, 1949..**95.00**

Abingdon, Pumpkin, #674, minimum value $325.00. (Photo courtesy Joyce Roerig)

American Bisque, After School Cookie Bus, from $150 to..............**175.00**

American Bisque, Chest, #CJ-562, from $150 to..................**175.00**
American Bisque, Churn, #CJ-756, from $25 to.............**35.00**
American Bisque, French Poodle, #CJ-751, from $100 to.**125.00**
American Bisque, Recipes, #CJ-563................................**100.00**

Brush, Elephant With Ice Cream Cone, has been reproduced, $500.00. (Photo courtesy Ermagene Westfall)

California Originals, Caterpiller, butterfly finial, #853, $75 to....**95.00**
California Originals, Donald Duck, cylinder, Disney ..**50.00**
California Originals, Man in Barrel, from $135 to **165.00**
California Originals, Yellow Taxi..**175.00**
Clay Art, Catfish, black or white, 1990 ....**45.00**
DeForest of California, Cocky (Dandee Rooster) **350.00**
DeForest of California, Lamb, For My Little Lamb on tummy.......**50.00**
DeForest of California, Pig, brown, 'Goodies' on tummy, 1956.**100.00**
Doranne of California, Cow on Moon, marked J 2 USA.**375.00**
Doranne of California, Hen w/Basket of Eggs, multicolor, #CJ-103 ....**50.00**

Doranne of California, Jack
Rabbit, green, 15".........**50.00**
Doranne of California, Seal, brown
& tan, marked USA 17..**35.00**
Enesco, Bear Pull Toy, 1996 ..**60.00**
Fitz & Floyd, Fat Lady, multicolor,
from $100 to................**150.00**
Fitz & Floyd, Holiday Cat..**130.00**
Fitz & Floyd, Strawberry Basket,
from $60 to....................**75.00**
Japan, Monk, brown robe, marked .**30.00**
Japan, Professor Owl, brown,
flower-like eyes..............**20.00**
Lefton, Bluebird, from $100 to.**125.00**
Maddux of California, Walrus .**65.00**
McCoy, Apples on Basketweave.**70.00**
McCoy, Black Lantern..........**65.00**
McCoy, Churn, 2 bands........**35.00**
McCoy, Corn, single ear, yellow.**175.00**
McCoy, Cylinder, w/red flowers.**45.00**
McCoy, Fortune Cookies.......**50.00**
McCoy, Kangaroo, blue.......**300.00**
McCoy, Little Clown.............**75.00**
McCoy, Milk Can, Spirit of '76.**45.00**

McCoy, Mouse on Clock, $40.00.

McCoy, Penguin, yellow or aqua .**200.00**
McCoy, Tepee, slant top **350.00**
McCoy, Wedding Jar.............**90.00**
Metlox, Apple, red, 3½-qt, 9½",
from $75 to.....................**85.00**
Metlox, Calico Cat, cream w/blue
ribbon, from $140 to **150.00**
Metlox, Circus Bear, from $400 to..**450.00**

**Metlox, Fido, white or beige, Made
in Poppytrail USA, $125.00.** (Photo
courtesy Fred and Joyce Roerig)

Metlox, Flamingo, minimum
value **750.00**
Metlox, Happy the Clown, 11",
minimum value............**350.00**
Metlox, Pinocchio Head, 10¾".**400.00**
Metlox, Salty the Pelican, from
$200 to.........................**225.00**
Metlox, Sammy the Seal, from
$475 to.........................**500.00**
Metlox, Watermelon, from $300
to................................**325.00**
Omnibus, Alley Cat w/Bowling
Ball **40.00**
Omnibus, Chili Cow..............**70.00**
Red Wing, Bob White......**200.00**
Red Wing, Crock, white........**80.00**
Red Wing, Friar Tuck, green,
marked **175.00**
Red Wing, Jack Frost, short,
unmarked.....................**250.00**
Red Wing, Pierre (chef), blue, brown
or pink, unmarked, ea ...**150.00**
Regal China, Cat, from $400 to.**450.00**
Regal China, Churn Boy,
unmarked.....................**375.00**
Regal China, Clown w/Cookie,
green collar, marked....**675.00**
Regal China, Hobby Horse, from
$250 to.........................**270.00**
Regal China, Quaker Oats .**115.00**
Regal China, Tulip, from $200
to....................................**225.00**

Robinson Ransbottom, Bud, Army man, 1942-43, 12", from $150 to **175.00**

Robinson Ransbottom, Hootie Owl, from $95 to **115.00**

Robinson Ransbottom, Ol' King Cole, multicolored w/black pipe & mug..................**425.00**

Shawnee, Cottage, marked USA #6 ....**1,350.00**

Shawnee, Drum Major, marked USA 10, 10"..................**600.00**

Shawnee, Fruit Basket, #84, 8" .**250.00**

Shawnee, Jill (name Cooky in gold), blue and white dress with gold flowers and trim, marked USA, minimum value $400.00. (Photo courtesy Ermagene Westfall)

Shawnee, Puss 'n Boots, short tail, marked, 10¼" **200.00**

Shawnee, Smiley the Pig, blue neckerchief, marked USA......**175.00**

Shawnee, Winnie the Pig, blue collar, marked USA..........**425.00**

Sierra Vista, Dog on Drum, from $85 to **100.00**

Sierra Vista, Train, smiling face .**65.00**

Sigma, Agatha....................**200.00**

Sigma, Cubs Bear **150.00**

Taiwan, Spuds, dog w/Mr Cookie on sweater **175.00**

Terrace Ceramics, Corn, yellow & green, #4299.................**45.00**

Treasure Craft, Cookie Balloon.**40.00**

Treasure Craft, Glass Bowl Santa, tummy is glass.............**195.00**

Treasure Craft, Grandpa Munster **275.00**

Treasure Craft, Nick at Nite Television, for Nickelodeon....................**600.00**

Treasure Craft, Smokey Bear, 50th Anniversary, 1994 limited edition......................**500.00**

Twin Winton, Baker, #67, 11x7" .**300.00**

Twin Winton, Butler, TW-60, $300.00. (Photo courtesy Mike Ellis)

Twin Winton, Cookie Churn, #72, 12x7"............................**100.00**

Twin Winton, Jack in the Box, #48, 13½x10"................**300.00**

Twin Winton, Keystone Cop, from $85 to **100.00**

Twin Winton, Snail, #37, 12x7½" .**250.00**

Vandor, Baseball...................**55.00**

Vandor, Mona Lisa **55.00**

Warner Bros, Porky Pig in TV, 1996, 12½".....................**75.00**

Copper Craft

Sold during the 1960s and 1970s through the home party plan, these decorative items are once again finding favor with the buying public. The Coppercraft Guild of Taunton, Massachusetts, made a wonderful variety of wall plaques, bowls, pitchers, trays, etc. Not all were made of copper, some were of molded plastic. Glass, cloth, mirror, and brass accents added to the texture. When uncompromised by chemical damage or abuse, the finish they used on their copper items has proven remarkably enduring. Collectors are beginning to take notice, but prices are still remarkably low. If you enjoy the look, now is the time to begin your collection.

Plaque, sailing vessel, coppertone plastic, 16x13", $12.00; 29x22", $25.00.

Bowl, footed, plain, 4⅛x8¾"..**12.50**
Bowl, footed, 4x7" dia **14.00**
Bowl, leaf shape, brass loop handle, 2x4x5¼" **8.50**
Bread tray, ornate etching in center, 12x6¾" **12.00**
Candle bowl, 2x4½" dia **15.00**
Dish, embossed floral rim, 1½x11" **15.00**
Flower bowl, 4-footed, 3⅞x9⅞" .**25.00**
Glasses, clear glass w/copper bands at bottom, set of 4, 5½" **13.50**

Gravy boat, w/stand & candle warmer, 8½" L **22.00**
Ice bucket, w/lid, 2 ring handles on sides, 5½x8"......................**9.00**
Mirror w/eagle finial, molded w/copper-tone finish, 21x14½" ..**35.00**
Mug, brass handle, sterling interior, 4 for **12.50**
Napkin holder, praying hands embossed on sides, 1¼x4¼x7"...................**7.00**
Plaque, embossed copper w/log cabin scene, 14"..............**14.00**
Serving dish, fluted, antique finish, 2¼x5¾" dia **15.00**
Tea set, demitasse; teapot, creamer & sugar bowl **30.00**
Tray, scalloped rim, 12" L....**10.00**

Crackle Glass

Most of the crackle glass you see on the market today was made from about 1930 until the 1970s. At the height of its popularity, almost five hundred glasshouses produced it; today it is still being made by Blenko, and a few pieces are coming in from Taiwan and China. It's hard to date, since many pieces were made for years. Some colors, such as red, amberina, cobalt, and cranberry, were more expensive to produce; so today these are scarce and therefore more expensive. Smoke gray was made for only a short time, and you can expect to pay a premium for that color as well. For more information we recommend *Crackle Glass, Books I* and *II,* by Stan and Arlene Weitman (Collector Books).

Basket, ruby, clear twist handle, Hamon/ Kanawha, 5¼", $50 to..........**75.00**

Bowl, amber w/applied serpentine, Kanawha, 2¾x4½", from $40 to.....................**45.00**

Bowl, Lemon Drop Yellow, handkerchief rim, Bischoff, 6", from $100 to.........................**125.00**

Candle holders, crystal w/aqua rosettes, Blenko, 3½", pr, from $100 to.........................**125.00**

Candy dish, green w/applied decor, Kanawha, 3x4½", from $45 to............................**55.00**

Creamer, blue, drop-over handle, Rainbow, 3", from $35 to.**40.00**

Cruet, blue, pulled-back handle, Pilgrim, 6¾", from $50 to.**75.00**

Decanter, amberina, double-gourd, 2-ball stopper, Rainbow, 8", from $100 to.................**125.00**

Decanter, amberina, long slim neck, flared base, Blenko, 1961, 17".......................**185.00**

Decanter, blue, conical, Rainbow, 7¾", from $85 to..........**100.00**

Decanter, crystal, clear ball stopper, Bonita, 6¼", from $85 to **100.00**

Decanter, green with royal blue pulled-back handle, Rainbow, 1940s – 1960s, 14½", from $100.00 to $125.00. (Photo courtesy Stan and Arlene Weitman)

Goblet, crystal, footed, unknown maker, 7½", from $50 to .**75.00**

Hat dish, turquoise, Blenko, 3", from $45 to **50.00**

Perfume bottle, gold, bulbous, atomizer, unknown maker, 3", $50 to.............................**75.00**

Perfume bottle, pink, atomizer, unknown maker, 3¾", from $50 to..............................**75.00**

Pitcher, amber, drop-over handle, Rainbow, 3½", from $40 to.**45.00**

Pitcher, amberina, crystal drop-over handle, Kanawha, 4¾", from $45 to **50.00**

Pitcher, cranberry, slim, crystal drop-over handle, Kanawha, 7¾"...............................**110.00**

Pitcher, lemon lime, green pulled-back handle, Rainbow, 5¼", from $60 to **80.00**

Pitcher, satin green, pulled-back frosted handle, Kanawha, 4¼" **55.00**

Rose bowl, topaz, folded rim, Blenko, 5x4½", from $95 to **110.00**

Swan dish, orange w/crystal head & neck, Kanawha, 6x7x5½", from $75 to **100.00**

Tumbler, crystal w/applied blue rosettes, Blenko, 2¼", from $50 to..............................**75.00**

Vase, amethyst, waisted, Blenko, 1960s, 4¾", from $60 to.**80.00**

Vase, cobalt satin, bulbous, unknown maker, 6", from $85 to....................................**110.00**

Vase, cranberry, trumpet neck, 4-scalloped rim, Rainbow, 5¼" **75.00**

Vase, crystal, Bischoff, 1942-63, 5", from $50 to................**75.00**

Vase, emerald green, waisted, Blenko, 4¾", from $45 to .**50.00**

Vase, green, applied green rigaree, ruffled, Kanawha, 3½" ..**50.00**

Vase, blue, Bischoff, 1940 – 1963, from $100.00 to $125.00. (Photo courtesy Stan and Arlene Weitman)

Vase, green, 4-scallop rim, Jamestown label, 5", from $40 to **45.00**

Vase, orange, ruffled rim, Rainbow, 1940s-60s, 5", from $45 to **50.00**

Vase, palest green, ruffled rim, attributed Bischoff, 5½x8¼".........**75.00**

Vase, tangerine/amberina, ruffled rim, footed, Blenko, 7¾", from $125 to **150.00**

Vase, yellow (deep), scalloped rim, slim, 5¼", from $45 to ...**50.00**

Czechoslovakian Glass

Czechoslovakia was established as a country in 1918. It was an area rich in the natural resources needed to produce both pottery and glassware. Wonderful cut and pressed scent bottles were made in a variety of colors with unbelievably well-detailed intaglio stoppers. Vases in vivid hues were decorated with contrasting applications or enamel work. See Clubs and Newsletters for information concerning the *Czechoslovakian Collectors Guild International.*

Bowl, cased autumn-colored mottle, sm foot, 4½" **60.00**

Bowl, crystal (bubbly) w/applied cobalt decor & foot, 4" .**375.00**

Candlestick, pale pink w/applied green serpentine trim, 8".**65.00**

Candlestick, red w/black & white enameled decor, 10½"....**85.00**

Candy basket, black w/silver mica, blue lining, black handle, 8" **350.00**

Candy basket, light green w/medium green stripes, green handle, 8"............................**200.00**

Cocktail shaker, green w/enameled rooster, chrome lid, 8¾".**125.00**

Cologne bottle, Hobnail, cranberry opalescent, 5½" **225.00**

Compote, white opaque, ruffled rim w/applied maroon trim, 6".**150.00**

Covered pitcher, Art Deco style, orange and green, 12½", with four 4⅞" matching tumblers, $500.00 for the set. (Photo courtesy Guy S. Forsythe)

Decanter, green (bubbly) w/hand-painted hunt scene, 9⅝".**175.00**

Decanter, orange cased, silver bird decor, footed, slim, 12"..**135.00**

Decanter, topaz stain, hand-painted carriage scene, 10¼"......**140.00**

Perfume bottle, amethyst, pyramidal with sm crystal stopper, 3½"..................................**135.00**

Perfume bottle, atomizer, crystal w/enamel decor, 7¾"....**125.00**

Perfume bottle, crystal, casket form w/blue fan stopper, 5¼"..............................**165.00**

Perfume bottle, pink, simple shouldered shape, sm crystal stopper, 5"....................**190.00**

Pitcher, orange cased, cobalt rim & handle, tricorner top, 5"..**85.00**

Puff box, blue satin, 3¼"......**95.00**

Puff box, Hobnail, cranberry opalescent, 3½"............**175.00**

Salt & pepper shakers, crystal w/porcelain duck-head tops, 2", pr...............................**45.00**

Trinket dish, polar bear on ice, crystal & frosted, 5¼"..**285.00**

Tumbler, orange w/enameled exotic bird & flowers, 5¼"....**85.00**

Vases: turquoise cased with mottled red, footed, flared rim, 6¾", from $60.00 to $70.00; vaseline with red, blue, and yellow mottled bottom, ruffled rim, waisted, from $65.00 to $70.00. (Photo courtesy Dale and Diane Barta and Helen M. Rose)

Vase, bud, yellow cased, black & silver decor, 9½"............**65.00**

Vase, cased mottle w/applied handles, 8⅜"......................**100.00**

Vase, cased mottled colors, fan form, 8¼"......................**200.00**

Vase, cobalt cased, multi-mottled base, 7"..........................**75.00**

Vase, crystal, intaglio cutting, ball form, 5"..........................**80.00**

Vase, crystal w/red overlay, footed, 8¼"................................**175.00**

Vase, frosted w/embossed wild horses, bulbous, 7".......**100.00**

Vase, jack-in-the-pulpit; yellow cased w/mottled colors, 7½".........**95.00**

Vase, mottled colors, stick form, 8½"................................**65.00**

Vase, orange cased, applied flower, ruffled rim, 7½"..........**100.00**

Vase, orange w/yellow overlay, footed fan form, 8".......**200.00**

Vase, pink cased w/white spiraling overlay, ruffled rim, 8½".**125.00**

Vase, red cased w/green aventurine, gourd shape, 7¼"............**180.00**

Vase, turquoise blue w/3 black buttressed feet, 9"........**125.00**

Vase, yellow cased, white interior, black serpentine decor, 9".**130.00**

Dakin

From about 1968 through the late 1970s, the R. Dakin Company produced a line of hollow vinyl advertising and comic characters licensed by companies such as Warner Brothers, Hanna-Barbera, and the Disney Corporation. Some figures had molded-on clothing; others had felt clothes and accessory items. Inspiration for characters came from TV cartoon shows, comic strips, or special advertising promotions. Dakins were offered in different types of packaging. Those in colorful 'Cartoon Theatre' boxes command higher prices than those that came in clear plastic bags. Plush figures were also produced, but the examples we've listed below are the most collectible. Assume all to be complete with clothes, accessories, and original tags unless otherwise noted. For further information and more listings we recommend *Schroeder's Collectible Toys, Antique to Modern* (Collector Books).

Baby Puss, Hanna-Barbera, 1971, NM..................................**80.00**

Bamm-Bamm, Hanna-Barbera, w/club, 1970, EX.............**30.00**

Benji, 1978, plush, EX..........**10.00**

Bugs Bunny, Warner Bros, 1971, MIP..................................**25.00**

Deputy Dawg, Terrytoons, 1977, EX...............................**50.00**

Dino Dinosaur, Hanna-Barbera, 1970, EX.........................**40.00**

Dream Pets, Bull Dog, cloth, EX..............................**10.00**

Dream Pets, Midnight Mouse, cloth, original tag, EX ...**15.00**

Elmer Fudd, Warner Bros, 1968, hunting outfit w/rifle, EX.**125.00**

Foghorn Leghorn, Warner Bros, 1970, EX+......................**75.00**

Goofy, Disney, cloth clothes, EX.**20.00**

Goofy Gram, Frog, Happy Birthday, EX..................**25.00**

Goofy Gram, Pepe Le Peu, You're a Real Stinker, 1971, EX ..**40.00**

Huckleberry Hound, Hanna-Barbera, 1970, EX+.......**60.00**

Jack-in-the-Box, bank, 1971, EX.**25.00**

Merlin the Magic Mouse, Warner Bros, 1970, EX+.............**25.00**

Monkey on a Barrel, bank, 1971, EX...................................**25.00**

Opus, 1982, cloth, w/tag, EX.**20.00**

Pinocchio, Disney, 1960s, EX.**20.00**

Porky Pig, Warner Bros, 1968, EX...............................**30.00**

Road Runner, Warner Bros, 1968, EX...............................**30.00**

Scooby Doo, Hanna-Barbera, 1980, EX...............................**75.00**

Scrappy Doo, Hanna-Barbera, 1982, EX.........................**75.00**

Sylvester, Warner Bros, 1968, EX...............................**20.00**

Elmer Fudd in tuxedo, Warner Bros., 1968, EX, $30.00.

Sylvester, Warner Bros., 1976, MIB (cartoon theatre box), $40.00.

Tasmanian Devil, Warner Bros,
1978, rare, NM............300.00
Tiger in Cage, bank, 1971, EX.25.00

Decanters

The James Beam Distilling
Company produced its first
ceramic whiskey decanter in
1953 and remained the only
major producer of these
decanters throughout the decade.
By the late 1960s, other companies such as Ezra Brooks,
Lionstone, and Cyrus Noble were
also becoming involved in their
production. Today these fancy
liquor containers are attracting
many collectors.

Barton, Black & Gold Apothecary,
2½ Million Barrel Commem-
orative............20.00
Beam, Casino Series, Harold's Club,
Covered Wagon, 1969........6.00
Beam, Casino Series, Statue of
Liberty, 1985............35.00
Beam, Centennial Series,
Laramie 7.00
Beam, Club & Convention Series,
Anaheim Convention #2...25.00
Beam, Club & Convention Series,
Gem City Club 27.00
Beam, Club & Convention Series,
Las Vegas Showgirl, #11,
brunette............45.00
Beam, Customer Series, Pon-
derosa Ranch............13.00
Beam, Executive Series, 1967
Prestige 18.00
Beam, Foreign Series, Australia,
Koalas............19.00

Beam, Fox Series, green coat.30.00
Beam, Organization Series,
Ducks Unlimited #1, Mallard,
1974............36.00
Beam, Organization Series, Ducks
Unlimited #12, Red Head,
1986 ....45.00
Beam, People Series, Captain &
Mate............20.00
Beam, Political Series, Donkey &
Elephant on football, pr.32.00
Beam, Sports Series, Bing's
29th 12.00
Beam, Sports Series, Kentucky
Derby, 98th 28.00
Beam, State Series, New Jersey,
blue 36.00
Beam, State Series, North
Dakota............39.00

**Beam, Statue of Liberty, 1975,
12½", $20.00.**

Beam, Train Series, Casey Jones
Caboose............25.00
Beam, Train Series, Casey Jones
Locomotive & tender 50.00
Beam, Trophy Series, Appa-
loosa............24.00
Beam, Trophy Series, Birds,
Eagle, 1966............15.00

Beam, Trophy Series, Birds, Woodpecker **9.00**

Beam, Trophy Series, Duck Decoy **25.00**

Beam, Wheel Series, 1913 Ford Model T, green **55.00**

Beam, Wheel Series, 1956 Thunderbird, gray or green, ea **100.00**

Beam, Wheel Series, 1968 Corvette, blue **60.00**

Brooks, American Legion, Chicago 1972 .... **49.00**

Brooks, American Legion, Miami Beach 1974 .... **9.00**

Brooks, FOE, Eagle 1979 ..... **25.00**

Brooks, General Stonewall Jackson **25.00**

Brooks, Iowa Statehouse **38.00**

Brooks, Panda **19.00**

Creative World, Romeo & Juliet, 1971, pr **69.00**

Double Springs, Excalibur Phaeton **22.00**

Early Times, Bicentennial Series, USA **59.00**

Famous Grouse, bisque finish, very rare **150.00**

Garnier, Valley Quail, California, no label **19.00**

Henry McKenna, stoneware, ½-gal jug **24.00**

Jack Daniels, Belle of Lincoln **.29.00**

Jack Daniels, Maxwell House. **59.00**

Kessler, Football Player **29.00**

Lionstone, Pheasant, 1977 ... **45.00**

Lord Calvert, Canadian Goose, #1 .... **46.00**

Lord Calvert, Canvasback, #3 **.16.00**

McCormick, Bicentennial Series, Ben Franklin **27.00**

McCormick, Bicentennial Series, George Washington **27.00**

Left: Lionstone, Fireman #1, $125.00. (Photo courtesy Roy Willis) **Right: McCormick, Frontiersman Series, Jim Bowie, 1975, $35.00.**

McCormick, Elvis, Aloha **169.00**

McCormick, Elvis, Karate, no box **319.00**

McCormick, Jimmy Durante, music box **69.00**

McCormick, Patrick Henry .. **19.00**

Old Barnstown, Christmas Card **14.00**

Old Barnstown, Tiger **29.00**

Old Commonwealth, Coal Miner Series, Coal Shooter, #5 .. **29.00**

Old Commonwealth, Coal Miner Series, Standing w/Shovel, #1 .... **95.00**

Old Commonwealth, Firefighter Series, Nozzleman, #2 ... **69.00**

Old Fitzgerald, South Carolina Tricentennial **11.00**

Old Mr Boston, FOE Spirit of '76 .... **9.00**

Old Mr Boston, West Virginia National Guard **28.00**

Paramount, Ohio Governor James Rhodes **25.00**

Ski Country, Animal Series, Badger **49.00**

Ski Country, Animal Series, Mountain Lion, miniature. **28.00**

Ski Country, Animal Series, Raccoon, 1975, $55.00.

Ski Country, Banded Waterfowl, Widgeon, 1979, 1.75 liters **149.00**

Ski Country, Bird Series, Bluejay........................**79.00**

Ski Country, Bird Series, Redwing Blackbird........................**45.00**

Ski Country, Christmas Series, Bob Cratchit..................**54.00**

Ski Country, Circus Series, Clown Bust **65.00**

Ski Country, Circus Series, Tiger on Ball **44.00**

Ski Country, Club Series, Raccoons, wall plaque.....................**79.00**

Ski Country, Customers Specialties, Clyde..............................**39.00**

Ski Country, Customers Specialties, Ladies of Leadville, blue..**24.00**

Ski Country, Domestic Animal Series, Holstein Cow **77.00**

Ski Country, Eagle Series, Birth of Freedom..........................**95.00**

Ski Country, Eagle Series, Hawk **129.00**

Ski Country, Falcon Series, Peregrine, 1-gal, 450 made **295.00**

Ski Country, Fish Series, Rainbow trout, miniature.............**35.00**

Ski Country, Hawk Series, Osprey........................**169.00**

Ski Country, Horned & Antlered Series, Bighorn Ram, 1973..................**45.00**

Ski Country, Indian Series, Ceremonial Dancers, Eagle......................**149.00**

Ski Country, Owl Series, Baby Snow Owl, miniature.....**65.00**

Ski Country, Owl Series, Speckled Owl **79.00**

Ski Country, Waterfowl Series, King Eider Duck............**55.00**

Wild Turkey, Series III Action, Turkey & Coyote, #10....**95.00**

Wild Turkey, Series III Action, Turkey & Eagle, #4 ....**95.00**

Wild Turkey, Series III Action, Turkey & Skunks, miniature...........**49.00**

Wild Turkey, Series III Action, Turkey in Flight, #1 ....**110.00**

Degenhart

Elizabeth Degenhart and her husband John produced glassware in their studio at Cambridge, Ohio, from 1947 until John died in 1964. Elizabeth restructured the company and hired Zack Boyd who had previously worked for the Cambridge Glass Company to help her formulate almost 150 unique and original colors which they used to press small-scale bird and animal figures, boxes, wines, covered dishes, and toothpick holders. Degenhart glass is marked with a 'D in heart' trademark. After her death and at her request, this mark was removed from the molds, some of which were bequeathed to the Degenhart museum. The remaining molds were acquired by Boyd, who added his own logo to them and continued to press glassware very similar to Mrs. Degenhart's.

Beaded Oval Toothpick, Crystal.......................**12.00**
Bird w/Cherry Salt, Daffodil.**20.00**
Bird w/Cherry Salt, Orchid..**20.00**
Buzz Saw Wine, Amberina/ Sunset.............................**20.00**
Chick Salt, Amber..................**15.00**
Chick Salt, Milk White..........**20.00**
Daisy & Button Toothpick, Baby Blue Slag.........................**20.00**
Forget Me Not Toothpick, Bluebell.............................**16.00**
Forget Me Not Toothpick, Old Lavender **20.00**
Gypsy Pot Toothpick Holder, Amberina **20.00**

Gypsy Pot Toothpick Holder, Bittersweet, $35.00.

Gypsy Pot Toothpick, Fawn .**17.50**
Hand, Sapphire.......................**6.00**
Hat, Amethyst Satin.............**18.00**
Hen Covered Dish, Custard, 5".**50.00**
Hen Covered Dish, Vaseline, 5".**30.00**
Hobo Baby Shoe, Caramel Custard Slag...................................**20.00**
Owl, Bernard Boyd's Ebony .**50.00**
Owl, Dark Heliotrope **75.00**
Owl, Lemon Opal...................**30.00**
Owl, Vaseline **25.00**

Portrait Plate, Cobalt...........**40.00**
Priscilla Doll, Amethyst **80.00**
Priscilla Doll, Dark Rose Marie **100.00**
Texas Boot, Amethyst...........**15.00**
Tomahawk, Crown Tuscan...**35.00**
Turkey Covered Dish, Dark Heliotrope.......................**75.00**

Department 56 Inc.

In 1976 this company introduced their original line of six handcrafted ceramic buildings. The Original Snow Village quickly won the hearts of young and old alike, and the light that sparkled from their windows added charm and warmth to Christmas celebrations everywhere. Accessories followed, and the line was expanded. Over the years, new villages have been developed — the Dicken's Series, New England, Alpine, Christmas in the City, and Bethlehem. Offerings in the '90s included the North Pole, Disney Parks, and Seasons Bay. Their popular Snowbabies assortment was introduced in 1986, and today they're collectible as well.

Amish Farm House, #59439, MIB **90.00**
Blythe Pond, Dickens Village, MIB **95.00**
Brick Abbey, Dickens Village, #65498, MIB.................**175.00**
Chocolate Shoppe, Christmas in the City, #5968-4, MIB..**80.00**
Christmas Pageant, Snowbabies, MIB...............................**95.00**

Church, Dickens Village, butterscotch version, #65161, MIB **90.00**

Cinema 56, Snow Village, MIB .**85.00**

Crystal Ice Palace, #56-58922, MIB **85.00**

Dinah's Drive-In, Snow Village, MIB **80.00**

Doctor's Office, Heritage Village, #5544-1, MIB **75.00**

Elvis Presley's Graceland, MIB .**85.00**

Fire Station #1, State Farm 65th Anniversary, MIB **75.00**

General Store, New England Village, #65307, MIB ...**185.00**

Glacier Park Pavillion, North Pole Series, MIB **80.00**

Grimsly Manor, Snow Village, #56-55004, MIB **85.00**

Halloween Haunted Barn, Snow Village, #55060, MIB **95.00**

Hank's Marker, Christmas in the City, MIB.......................**85.00**

Harley-Davidson Manufacturing Plant, Snow Village, #54948, 3 pcs, MIB **125.00**

Herod's Temple, Little Town of Bethlehem set, #56-56799, MIB...............................**80.00**

Hollydale's Department Store, Christmas in the City, MIB.......................**105.00**

Kensington Palace, #58309, 1998, MIB..............................**115.00**

Krispy Kreme Doughnut Shop, Snow Village, MIB.........**85.00**

Lego Warehouse & Forklift, North Pole Village, MIB.........**100.00**

Little Italy Restorante, Christmas in the City, #5538-7, MIB.....**90.00**

McDonald's, Snow Village, MIB **95.00**

Monopoly City Lights, complete, MIB..............................**130.00**

Old Queensbridge Station, Dickens Village, MIB.....**80.00**

Santa's Workshop, North Pole Building, #5600-6, 1993, MIB...........................**210.00**

Skating Pond, animated, MIB .**85.00**

Snowbell, snowbaby figural handle, 6¼"...........................**25.00**

Stone Cottage, #65188, green, MIB..............................**100.00**

Thatched Cottage, Heritage Village, #56-65188, 1985-88, MIB...............................**90.00**

Village Express Train Set, Heritage Village, #5980-3, 1988-1996, MIB **165.00**

Where Did You Come From, snowbaby, retired, M (EX box)..**45.00**

Wool Shop, Dickens Village, MIB **85.00**

Yankee Stadium, Christmas in the City Series, 2001, MIB, $70.00. (Photo courtesy Alexiy and Don Saint Michael)

Depression Glass

Depression glass, named for the era when it sold through dime stores or was given away as premiums, can be found in such varied colors as amber, green, pink, blue, red, yellow, white, and crystal. Mass produced by many different companies in hundreds of patterns, Depression glass is one of the most sought-after collectibles in the United States today. For more information, refer to *The Pocket Guide to Depression Glass; Collector's Encyclopedia of Depression Glass; Treasures of Very Rare Depression Glass;* and *Collectible Glassware of the 40s, 50s & 60s;* all are by Gene Florence (Collector Books). See also Anchor Hocking/Fire-King. See Clubs and Newsletters for information concerning the National Depression Glass Association.

Adam, bowl, oval, pink, 10"..**38.00**

Adam, cup, pink **30.00**

Adam, plate, sherbet; pink, 6".**12.00**

American Pioneer, candlesticks, green, 6½", pr...............**135.00**

American Pioneer, cup, green.**10.00**

American Sweetheart, bowl, cereal; pink, 6" **18.00**

American Sweetheart, plate, salvar; monax, 12" **24.00**

American Sweetheart, platter, oval, monax, 13".............**65.00**

Aunt Polly, bowl, berry; blue, 4⅜"................................**18.00**

Aunt Polly, creamer, green ..**35.00**

Aunt Polly, tumbler, blue, 8-oz, 3⅝" **38.00**

Aurora, bowl, cobalt, 4½" **65.00**

Aurora, cup, cobalt.................**17.00**

Avocado, bowl, salad; green, 7½" **72.00**

Avocado, cup, footed, pink....**35.00**

Avocado, sherbet, green........**65.00**

Beaded Block, bowl, round, green, 6½"...............................**25.00**

Beaded Block, creamer and sugar bowl, blue, $45.00 each. (Photo courtesy Gene Florence)

Beaded Block, creamer, opalescent **50.00**

Beaded Block, sugar bowl, green..........................**25.00**

Block Optic, bowl, cereal; pink, 5¼"...................................**30.00**

Block Optic, ice bucket, green.**45.00**

Block Optic, salt & pepper shakers, green, footed, pr......**45.00**

Cameo, bowl, salad; green, 7¼" ..**65.00**

Cameo, plate, dinner; green, 9½".**24.00**

Cameo, sugar bowl, green, 4¼".**32.00**

Cameo, vase, green, 8"..........**60.00**

Cherry Blossom, bowl, berry; green, 4¾" **22.00**

Cherry Blossom, creamer, pink.**25.00**

Cherry Blossom, pitcher, green, flat, 42-ounce, $75.00. (Photo courtesy Gene Florence)

Cherry Blossom, plate, dinner; green, 9" **28.00**

Cherry Blossom, sherbet, green .**20.00**
Chinex Classic, butter dish, ivory.............**55.00**
Chinex Classic, creamer, decorated.............**10.00**
Chinex Classic, plate, dinner; ivory, 9¼".............**4.00**
Chinex Classic, sugar bowl, decorated.............**10.00**
Circle, bowl, green, 8"..........**30.00**
Circle, pitcher, green, 80-oz .**35.00**
Circle, tumbler, green, 15-oz.**25.00**
Cloverleaf, bowl, cereal; green, 5".............**50.00**
Cloverleaf, cup, yellow..........**11.00**
Cloverleaf, plate, grill; green, 10¼".............**30.00**
Colonial, bowl, low soup; pink, 7".............**65.00**
Colonial, plate, dinner; green, 10".............**65.00**
Colonial, sugar, green, 5".....**16.00**
Colonial Block, bowl, green or pink, 7"............**22.00**
Colonial Block, butter tub, green or pink.............**45.00**
Colonial Block, pitcher, green or pink.............**45.00**
Colonial Fluted, bowl, deep salad; green, 6½".............**35.00**
Colonial Fluted, creamer, green.**10.00**
Columbia, bowl, ruffled edge, crystal, 10½".............**22.00**
Columbia, cup, pink.............**25.00**
Columbia, snack plate, crystal.**30.00**
Coronation, bowl, lg berry; red, 8".............**20.00**
Coronation, sherbet, pink.....**11.00**
Cremax, bowl, vegetable; ivory, 9".............**8.00**
Cremax, cup, demitasse; ivory.**15.00**
Cremax, plate, sandwich; ivory decorated, 11½".............**20.00**

Cube, candy jar w/lid, green, 6½".............**33.00**
Cube, tumbler, pink, 9-oz, 4".**75.00**
Diamond Quilted, creamer, blue.............**15.00**
Diamond Quilted, pitcher, green, 64-oz.............**50.00**
Diana, cup, pink.............**20.00**
Diana, plate, dinner; pink, 9½".**20.00**
Dogwood, cup, thin or thick, green.............**40.00**
Dogwood, plate, dinner; pink, 9¼".............**38.00**
Dogwood, sherbet, low foot, pink.............**35.00**
Doric, bowl, vegetable; pink, oval, 9".............**45.00**
Doric, candy dish, 3-part, green.**15.00**
Doric, cup, pink.............**12.00**
Doric, plate, grill; pink, 9"....**25.00**
Doric & Pansy, bowl, lg berry; pink, 8".............**30.00**

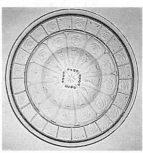

Doric and Pansy, dinner plate, green, 9", $40.00. (Photo courtesy Gene Florence)

Doric & Pansy, plate, salad; ultramarine, 7".............**40.00**
English Hobnail, bowl, cream soup; pink or green........**25.00**
English Hobnail, cup, pink or green.............**18.00**
English Hobnail, egg cup, pink or green.............**36.00**

English Hobnail, pitcher, pink or green, 23-oz **150.00**

Floral, bowl, berry; green, 4" .**24.00**

Floral, butter dish w/lid, green .**95.00**

Floral, plate salad; green, 8" .**15.00**

Floral & Diamond Band, creamer, green, 4¾" **20.00**

Floral & Diamond Band, tumbler, iced tea; pink, 5" **45.00**

Florentine No 1, ashtray, yellow, 5½" **22.00**

Florentine No 1, plate, dinner; green, 10" **20.00**

Florentine No 1, sugar bowl lid, yellow.............................**30.00**

Florentine No 2, bowl, green, 5½" **35.00**

Florentine No 2, cup, yellow .**10.00**

Florentine No 2, platter, oval, yellow, 11" **25.00**

Flower Garden w/Butterflies, creamer, pink or green ..**75.00**

Flower Garden w/Butterflies, cup, pink or green..................**75.00**

Flower Garden w/Butterflies, saucer, pink or green.....**25.00**

Fortune, bowl, rolled edge; pink, 5¼" **22.00**

Fortune, cup, pink **12.00**

Fruits, bowl, cereal; green, 5" .**35.00**

Fruits, sherbet, green **12.00**

Georgian, bowl, cereal; green, 5¾" **25.00**

Georgian, cup, green.............**10.00**

Georgian, plate, luncheon; green, 8"....................................**10.00**

Georgian, sugar lid, green, 3" .**50.00**

Hex Optic, bowl, lg berry; pink or green **15.00**

Hex Optic, bucket reamer, pink or green..............................**65.00**

Hex Optic, platter, round, pink or green, 11" **15.00**

Hex Optic, tumbler, footed, pink or green, 5¾" **10.00**

Hobnail, cup, crystal..............**4.50**

Hobnail, pitcher, crystal, 67-oz ..**28.00**

Hobnail, tumbler, iced tea; crystal, 15-oz˙..............................**16.00**

Homespun, bowl, cereal; pink, 5"................................**30.00**

Homespun, cup, pink............**14.00**

Indiana Custard, bowl, flat soup; ivory, 7½" **35.00**

Indiana Custard, cup, ivory .**37.50**

Iris, bowl, sauce; iridescent, 5" .**25.00**

Iris, cup, crystal **15.00**

Iris, vase, iridescent, 9" **27.00**

Jubilee, bowl, 3-footed, pink, 13" **250.00**

Jubilee, cup, pink.................**40.00**

Jubilee, sugar bowl, pink **35.00**

Laced Edge, bowl, fruit; blue or green, 4½" **30.00**

Laced Edge, cup, blue or green .**35.00**

Laced Edge, double candlestick, blue opalescent, $87.50. (Photo courtesy Gene Florence)

Laced Edge, saucer, blue or green............................**15.00**

Lake Como, bowl, cereal; 6" .**30.00**

Largo, bowl, blue or red, 5" ..**25.00**

Largo, candle holder, amber or crystal............................**25.00**

Laurel, bowl, jade, 11"..........**60.00**

Laurel, sherbet, ivory **12.00**

Lincoln Inn, bowl, cereal; red, 6" **15.00**
Lincoln Inn, plate, blue, 12".**65.00**
Lorain, bowl, cereal; green, 6"..**48.00**
Lorain, cup, yellow................**15.00**
Lorain, platter, green, 11½"..**30.00**
Madrid, bowl, soup; amber, 7"..**16.00**
Madrid, jam dish, green, 7"..**40.00**
Madrid, plate, relish; amber, 10¼" **15.00**
Manhattan, ashtray, round, crystal, 4" **15.00**
Manhattan, cup, crystal **20.00**
Manhattan, relish tray, 5-part, crystal, 14" **30.00**
Manhattan, vase, crystal, 8"..**25.00**

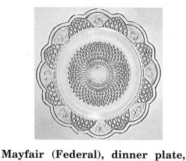

Mayfair (Federal), dinner plate, amber, 9½", $17.50. (Photo courtesy Gene Florence)

Mayfair (Federal), plate, dinner; green, 9½" **15.00**
Mayfair (Federal), plate, salad; green, 6¾" **9.00**
Mayfair (Federal), platter, oval, amber, 12" **30.00**
Mayfair (Open Rose), bowl, cereal; pink, 5½" **35.00**
Mayfair (Open Rose), pitcher, blue, 6"..........................**165.00**
Mayfair (Open Rose), plate, grill; pink, 9½" **52.00**
Miss America, bowl, berry; pink, 6¼" **30.00**
Miss America, cup, crystal **9.00**

Miss America, goblet, juice; crystal, 4¾" **27.00**
Miss America, sugar bowl, pink.**22.00**
Moderntone, bowl, berry; cobalt, 5" **28.00**
Moderntone, cup, amethyst..**12.00**
Moderntone, plate, dinner; cobalt, 8⅞" **18.00**
Moondrops, bowl, soup; red & blue, 6¾" **90.00**
Moondrops, creamer, colors other than blue or red, miniature, 2¾" **11.00**
Moondrops, goblet, cordial, red or blue, ¾-oz, 2⅞" **50.00**
Mt Pleasant, bowl, fruit; scalloped, black amethyst or cobalt, 10" **42.00**
Mt Pleasant, cup, black amethyst or cobalt..........................**12.00**
Mt Pleasant, leaf, black amethyst or cobalt, 11¼" **30.00**
Mt Vernon, spooner, crystal.**22.00**
New Century, ashtray/coaster, green, 5⅜" **28.00**
New Century, cup, green,.......**6.50**
New Century, plate, salad; green, 8½"...................................**15.00**
Newport, bowl, berry; cobalt, 4¼" **22.00**
Newport, salt and pepper shakers, fired-on colors, pr..........**22.50**
Newport, sugar, cobalt **14.00**
No 610 Pyramid, creamer, yellow **40.00**
No 610 Pyramid, pitcher, pink.**395.00**
No 612 Horseshoe, bowl, vegetable; yellow, 8½".........**38.00**
No 612 Horseshoe, relish, 3-part, footed, green...................**30.00**
No 616 Vernon, cup, green...**18.00**
No 616 Vernon, plate, luncheon; green, 8" **10.00**

No 616 Vernon, tumbler, footed, yellow, 5"........................**45.00**

No 618 Pineapple & Floral, ashtray, crystal, 4½"...........**16.00**

No 618 Pineapple & Floral, cup, amber..............................**10.00**

No 622 Pretzel, bowl, soup; crystal, 7½"...........................**10.00**

No 622 Pretzel, creamer, crystal.**5.00**

No 622 Pretzel, pitcher, crystal, 39-oz..............................**450.00**

Old Cafe, bowl, cereal; pink, 5½".**35.00**

Old Cafe, cup, red....................**8.00**

Old Cafe, lamp, pink...........**100.00**

Old Colony, bowl, salad; pink, 7¾"..................................**30.00**

Old Colony, compote, pink, 7".**32.00**

Old Colony, sugar bowl, pink.**30.00**

Orchid, bowl, square, red or blue, 4⅛"..................................**55.00**

Orchid, creamer, red or blue.**100.00**

Orchid, cup, decorated white.**12.50**

Orchid, sugar, red or blue..**100.00**

Ovide, candy dish, green, w/lid..........................**22.50**

Parrot, bowl, berry; amber, 5"...**23.00**

Parrot, cup, green.................**42.50**

Parrot, saucer, green............**15.00**

Patrician, bowl, cream soup; amber, 4¾".....................**18.00**

Patrician, plate, salad; green, 7½"..................................**18.00**

Patrick, goblet, juice; pink, 4¾"..................................**80.00**

Patrick, saucer, yellow.........**12.00**

Peacock & Wild Rose, cup, any color..............................**80.00**

Peacock & Wild Rose, plate, any color, 8"..........................**25.00**

Peacock Reverse, cup, any color.**145.00**

Peacock Reverse, plate, luncheon; any color, 8½"................**60.00**

Petalware, cup, pink..............**8.00**

Petalware, platter, oval, pink, 13"..................................**20.00**

Pillar Optic, mug, 12-oz, royal ruby..................................**30.00**

Pillar Optic, sugar bowl, crystal, footed..............................**50.00**

Primo, coaster/ashtray, yellow or green..................................**8.00**

Primo, saucer, yellow or green..**3.00**

Princess, ashtray, green, 4½"..**75.00**

Princess, plate, sherbet; pink, 5½"..................................**10.00**

Princess, relish, divided, pink, 7½"..................................**30.00**

Queen Mary, bowl, cereal; pink, 6"....................................**25.00**

Queen Mary, candy dish w/lid, crystal..............................**20.00**

Queen Mary, relish tray, 4-part, pink, 14"..........................**20.00**

Radiance, bonbon, amber, 6"..**15.00**

Radiance, bowl, celery; red or blue, 10"....................................**45.00**

Radiance, creamer, amber....**15.00**

Ribbon, bowl, berry; green, 4"....................................**35.00**

Ribbon, pitcher, crystal w/decoration, 80-oz, 8½"..............**35.00**

Ribbon, tumbler, green, 6"...**15.00**

Ring, decanter & stopper, crystal..............................**25.00**

Ring, vase, crystal, 8"...........**17.50**

Rock Crystal, cup, red, 7-oz..**70.00**

Rock Crystal, covered pitcher, pink, 9", $250.00.

Rock Crystal, lamp, electric, red............................**695.00**

Rock Crystal, salt cellar, crystal..**60.00**

Rose Cameo, plate, salad; green, 7"...................................**15.00**

Rose Cameo, tumbler, green, footed, 2 styles, ea, 5"...........**23.00**

Rosemary, cup, green..............**9.50**

Rosemary, platter, amber, oval, 12"....................................**15.00**

Roulette, bowl, fruit; pink, 9"..**25.00**

Roulette, sherbet, green.........**8.00**

Round Robin, bowl, berry; green, 4"......................................**10.00**

Round Robin, plate, sandwich; iridescent, 12"......................**10.00**

Roxana, bowl, yellow, 4½x2⅜"..**15.00**

Roxana, plate, yellow, 5½"...**12.00**

Royal Lace, candlesticks, pink, straight edge, pr.............**75.00**

Royal Lace, salt & pepper shakers, pink, pr...........................**70.00**

Royal Lace, tumbler, blue, 3½", 5-oz....................................**60.00**

S Pattern, cup, amber, thick or thin....................................**4.50**

S Pattern, plate, dinner; amber, 9¼"....................................**10.00**

Sandwich, bowl, salad; crystal, 7".......................................**7.00**

Sandwich, saucer, green.......**22.50**

Sandwich, sugar bowl, crystal, w/lid..................................**24.00**

Sharon, bowl, berry; pink, 5".**14.00**

Sharon, cup, pink..................**14.00**

Sharon, sugar lid, amber......**22.00**

Ships, ice bowl, blue/white...**40.00**

Ships, saucer, blue/white......**20.00**

Sierra, bowl, cereal; green, 5½"..**18.00**

Sierra, cup, pink...................**15.00**

Sierra, platter, green, oval, 11".**75.00**

Spiral, creamer, green, flat or footed....................................**9.00**

Spiral, pitcher, green, bulbous, 7⅝", $40.00.

Spiral, platter, green, 12".....**35.00**

Starlight, bowl, cereal; pink, 5½"....................................**14.00**

Starlight, creamer, crystal, oval............................**10.00**

Starlight, plate, sandwich; pink, 13"....................................**20.00**

Starlight, sugar bowl, crystal, oval....................................**10.00**

Strawberry, bowl, berry; pink or green, 4"........................**12.00**

Strawberry, plate, salad; pink or green, 7½".....................**18.00**

Strawberry, sugar bowl lid, pink or green.........................**65.00**

Sunburst, bowl, berry; crystal, 4¾"....................................**9.00**

Sunburst, relish, crystal, 2-part............................**12.00**

Sunflower, ashtray, pink, center design only, 5"...............**12.00**

Sunflower, saucer, green......**10.00**

Sunflower, tumbler, green or pink, footed, 4¾".....................**35.00**

Swirl, bowl, salad; pink, 9"...**20.00**

Swirl, salt & pepper shakers, ultramarine, pr..............**45.00**

Swirl, tumbler, pink, 4", 9-oz..**20.00**

Tea Room, bowl, finger; green or pink..............................**70.00**

Tea Room, creamer, green or pink, 4"....................................**28.00**

Tea Room, plate, luncheon; green, 8¼"....................................**35.00**

Thistle, plate, luncheon; green, 8"....................................**20.00**

Thistle, saucer, pink or green.**12.00**

Tulip, bowl, amethyst or blue, oval, 13¼"......................**110.00**

Tulip, creamer, green or crystal..**20.00**

Twisted Optic, basket, canary yellow, 10", $95.00. (Photo courtesy Gene Florence)

Twisted Optic, creamer, pink or green..................................**8.00**

Twisted Optic, plate, salad; pink or green, 7"........................**4.00**

Twisted Optic, sandwich server, pink or green, center handle **22.00**

Twisted Optic, sugar bowl, pink or green..................................**8.00**

US Swirl, butter dish, w/lid, green or pink...........................**120.00**

US Swirl, creamer, green or pink **20.00**

US Swirl, plate, sherbet; green or pink, 6⅛"..........................**2.50**

Victory, bowl, cereal; pink, 6½"..**14.00**

Victory, creamer, blue **50.00**

Victory, platter, pink, 12".....**30.00**

Vitrock, plate, dinner; white, 10"...**10.00**

Vitrock, plate, salad; white, 7¼"..**4.00**

Vitrock, platter, white, 11½"..**35.00**

Wakefield, basket, crystal w/red stain, 6" **65.00**

Wakefield, plate, crystal w/red stain, 6" **12.50**

Waterford, ashtray, crystal **7.50**

Waterford, plate, dinner; pink, 9⅝"....................................**28.00**

Waterford, sugar bowl, pink..**12.50**

Waterford, tumbler, pink, footed, 4⅞"....................................**28.00**

Windsor, bowl, vegetable; pink, oval, 9½"..........................**22.00**

Windsor, butter dish, crystal .**30.00**

Windsor, plate, dinner; pink, 9".**27.00**

Desert Storm

On August 2, 1990, Saddam Hussein invaded Kuwait, taking control of that small nation in less than four hours and capturing nearly a fourth of the world's oil supplies. President Bush set a January 15, 1991, deadline for the removal of Iraqui soldiers from Kuwait. January 16 saw the bombing of Baghdad and other military targets by U.S. forces, followed by SCUD missile attacks by Iraqi forces. The brief but bloody war ended in March, 1991, with Iraqi soldiers leaving Kuwait and US combat forces returning home.

Many Desert Storm related items were created as remembrances for this brief time in history. Topps published a series of Desert Storm trading cards, and Mattel got in on the action with Barbie and Ken in Desert Storm uniforms. Many other items were issued as well. Actual battle-related items are extremely scarce, but highly coveted by collectors.

Pocketknife, Case, two-blade, blue bone handle, lapel pin included, 1991, MIB, $35.00. (Photo courtesy William J. Williams)

Bayonet, M7, w/scabbard, EX .**35.00**
Bible, US Central Command, 6x4", M **15.00**
Book, Remembering the Gulf War, Keith F Girad, 120 pages, NM **20.00**
Coat, cold weather; 3-color camo, EX **45.00**
Coin, DS Veteran 1990-91/Persian Gulf War DS/Desert Shield, EX **30.00**
Field cap, Iraqi; khaki, cotton w/brass eagle pin on front, EX **80.00**
Gas mask, M25A1, worn by tank personel, complete, EX ..**80.00**
Hat, Special Forces Ranger Boony; camo, M **17.50**
Helmet, US, kevlar, camo cover, EX **75.00**
Incense burner, Aladdin's Lamp shape, brass, engraved, 4x6½", EX......................**25.00**
Model, AH-1 Super Cobra US Marines helicopter, 1:100 scale, M...........................**25.00**
Patch, Desert Storm F-111, jet, lightning bolt w/moon & sun, M **17.50**

Patch, Desert Storm 1991, Royal Air Force Station Fairford, B-52s, M **22.50**
Patch, VMA 542, jet & palm tree, M **30.00**
Patch, 596th Bombardment Squadron, Desert Storm, NM **20.00**
Patch, 806 Bomb Squadron Provisional, M **50.00**
T-shirt, I'd Fly 10,000 Miles To Smoke a Camel, jet w/camel, M **25.00**

Dollhouse Furnishings

Collecting antique dollhouses and building new ones is a popular hobby with many today, and all who collect houses delight in furnishing them right down to the vase on the table and the scarf on the piano! Flea markets are a good source of dollhouse furnishings, especially those from the 1940s through the 1960s made by Strombecker, Tootsietoy, Renwal, or the Petite Princess line by Ideal. For an expanded listing, see *Schroeder's Collectible Toys, Antique to Modern.*

Armoire, Mattel Littles **8.00**
Bed, blue or deep pink, Marx Newlywed, ea **15.00**
Bed, brown headboard w/yellow spread, Plasco **3.00**
Bunk bed, pink or blue, Best, ea..**5.00**
Cabinet, medicine; ivory, Tootsietoy **25.00**
Cabinet, Treasure Trove #4418-0, Ideal Petite Princess......**10.00**

Chair, barrel; hard plastic, red, Marx, ½" scale, from $3 to.**5.00**

Chair, dining room; ivory, Tootsietoy **7.00**

Chair, dining; reddish-brown swirl, Jaydon **2.00**

Chair, kitchen; red, Strombecker, ¾" scale **6.00**

Chaise, ivory w/bright pink, Marx Little Hostess **12.00**

Chest, 4-drawer; light brown, Blue Box **4.00**

Chest of drawers, hard plastic, blue or pink, Marx, ¾", ea **5.00**

Cradle, blue or pink, Ideal, ea.**45.00**

Crib, blue, Young Decorator.**45.00**

Dinette set, pedestal table and four chairs, Fisher-Price, 1978 – 1983, MIB, $10.00. (Photo courtesy Brad Cassity)

Dinette set, #251, Fisher-Price, M **4.00**

Fireplace, ivory, Marx Little Hostess **20.00**

Fireplace, rust, Reliable **45.00**

Highchair, blue or pink, Young Decorator........................**45.00**

Hutch, red or aqua, Allied/Pyro, ea.....................................**4.00**

Lamp, floor; black base, w/ivory shade, Strombecker **15.00**

Lawn bench, blue or red, Ideal, ea **18.00**

Lawn chair, yellow, soft plastic, Superior, sm....................**2.00**

Living room set, five-piece, Tootsietoy, NM, $65.00.

Plate or soup bowl, orange, Irwin, ea **3.00**

Range, #4507-0, no utensils, Ideal Petite Princess **3.00**

Range, counter-top; w/hood unit, Tomy Smaller Homes **18.00**

Refrigerator, white, soft plastic, Cheerio, sm **2.00**

Refrigerator, white, Young Decorator........................**55.00**

Seesaw, red or yellow horse heads, Acme/Thomas, ea...........**10.00**

Server, red w/opening drawer, Renewal..........................**15.00**

Shower curtain, light green, Irwin Interior Decorator............**4.00**

Sink, aqua or ivory, Strombecker, ea, ¾" scale......................**8.00**

Sink, bathroom; ivory w/black, Ideal................................**8.00**

Sink, bathroom; pink, Plasco .**4.00**

Sofa, Mattel Littles **8.00**

Stove, white, Donna Lee.........**6.00**

Stove, white, Young Decorator.**55.00**

Stove, white w/blue base, Plasco .**5.00**

Table, brown or caramel, Renwal, ea **8.00**

Table, coffee; pale green or red, Superior, ea.....................**8.00**

Table, kitchen, ivory, Ideal.....**6.00**

Table, kitchen; white, Ideal..**20.00**
Table, lowboy; red, Marx Little
Hostess **12.00**
Telephone, green, Tootsietoy .**45.00**
Toilet, ivory, Strombecker....**10.00**
Towel bar, ivory, Tootsietoy.**20.00**
Urn, green or yellow, Strombecker,
ea **10.00**

Dolls

Doll collecting is no doubt one of the most active fields today. Antique as well as modern dolls are treasured, and limited edition or artists' dolls often bring prices in excess of several hundred dollars. Investment potential is considered excellent in all areas. Dolls have been made from many materials — early to middle nineteenth-century dolls were carved of wood, poured in wax, and molded in bisque or china. Primitive cloth dolls were sewn at home for the enjoyment of little girls when fancier dolls were unavailable. In this century from 1925 to about 1945, composition was used. Made of a mixture of sawdust, clay, fiber, and a binding agent, it was tough and durable. Modern dolls are usually made of vinyl or molded plastic.

Learn to check your intended purchases for damage which could jeopardize your investment. In the listings values are for dolls in excellent condition unless another condition is noted in the line. They are priced 'mint in box' only when so indicated. Played-with, soiled dolls are worth from 50% to 75% less, depending on wear.

Patsy Moyer's books, *Modern Collector's Dolls, Volume IV* and *Volume V,* and *Doll Values* are filled with wonderful color photos and a wealth of valuable information; we recommend them highly. Also recommended is *Collector's Guide to Dolls of the 1960s and 1970s* by Cindy Sabulis and *Small Dolls of the 40s and 50s* by Carol Stover. All of these books are published by Collector Books. See also Action Figures; Advertising Collectibles; Character Collectibles; Holly Hobbie and Friends; Strawberry Shortcake Collectibles. See Clubs and Newsletters for information on *Doll Castle News* Magazine.

American Character

In business by 1918, this company made both composition and plastic dolls, all of excellent quality. Many collectors count them among the most desirable American dolls ever made. The company closed in 1968, and all of their molds were sold to other companies. The hard plastic dolls of the 1950s are much in demand today. See also Betsy McCall.

Annie Oakley, hard plastic walker, embroidered skirt, 14" **125.00**
Freckles, face changes, 1966, 13", EX **40.00**
Magic Make Up, vinyl, grow hair, 1965-66, 9", EX **75.00**
Miss America, 1963, EX **60.00**

Tiny Tears, molded painted hair, open mouth for bottle, 1950s, 12½".............................**185.00**

Toni, vinyl head, rooted hair, ca 1958, 10½"......................**50.00**

Toodles, box, wardrobe, accessories, ca 1960, 11".........**75.00**

Annalee

Annalee Davis Thorndike made her first commercially sold dolls in the late 1950s. They're characterized by their painted felt faces and the meticulous workmanship involved in their manufacture. Most are made entirely of felt, though Santas and rabbits may have flannel bodies. All are constructed around a wire framework that allows them to be positioned in imaginative poses. Depending on rarity, appeal, and condition, some of the older dolls have increased in value more than ten times their original price. Dolls from the 1950s carried a long white red-embroidered tag with no date. The same tag was in use from 1959 until 1964, but there was a copyright date in the upper right-hand corner. In 1970 a transition period began. The company changed its tag to a white satiny tag with a date preceded by a copyright symbol in the upper right-hand corner. In 1975 they made another change to a long white cotton strip with a copyright date. In 1982 the white tag was folded over, making it shorter. Many people mistake the copyright date as the date the doll was made — not so! It wasn't until 1986 that they finally began to date the tags with the year of manufacture, making it much easier for collectors to identify their dolls. Besides the red-lettered white Annalee tags, numerous others were used in the 1990s, but all reflect the year the doll was actually made.

For more information, refer to *Teddy Bears, Annalee's, and Steiff Animals,* by Margaret Fox Mandel, and *Garage Sale and Flea Market Annual.* Both are published by Collector Books. Values are given for dolls in clean, near-mint condition.

Beach girl w/towel, 1966, 10".**275.00**

Bride & groom mice, 1982, 12", pr..............................**300.00**

Ladybug kid, Halloween, 1992-93, 7"....................................**45.00**

Leprechaun, dk gray body, shamrock vest, 1977, 10", NM.**70.00**

Mouse (painted flat face), holds paint can and brush, 1968, 7", $250.00. (Photo courtesy Jane Holt)

Mr & Mrs Santa w/laundry basket for cards, 1972, 29", set..**145.00**

Skunk boy holds red heart, 1982, 12"..................................**115.00**

Tommy Turkey, tan body, yellow feet, 1989, 12" **80.00**

Betsy McCall

Tiny 8" Betsy McCall was manufactured by the American Character Doll Company from 1957 until 1963. She was made from fine quality hard plastic with a bisque-like finish and had hand-painted features. Betsy came with four hair colors — tosca, blond, red, and brown. She has blue sleep eyes, molded lashes, a winsome smile, and a fully jointed body with bendable knees. On her back is an identification circle which reads © McCall Corp. The basic doll could be purchased for $2.25 and wore a sheer chemise, white taffeta panties, nylon socks, and Mary Jane-style shoes.

There were two different materials used for tiny Betsy's hair. The first was soft mohair sewn onto mesh. Later the rubber skullcap was rooted with saran which was more suitable for washing and combing.

Betsy McCall had an extensive wardrobe with nearly one hundred outfits, each of which could be purchased separately. They were made from wonderful fabrics such as velvet, felt, taffeta, and even real mink fur. Each ensemble came with the appropriate footware and was priced under $3.00. Since none of Betsy's clothing is tagged, it is often difficult to identify other than by its square snap closures (although these were used by other companies as well).

Betsy McCall is a highly collectible doll today but is still fairly easy to find at doll shows. The prices remain reasonable for this beautiful clothes horse and her many accessories, some of which we've included below. For further information we recommend *Betsy McCall, A Collector's Guide,* by Marci Van Ausdall. See Clubs and Newsletters for information concerning the Betsy McCall's Fan Club.

Doll, American Character, Betsy McCall, all original, 29", M, $225.00; Sandy McCall, all original, 35", $500.00. (Photo courtesy McMasters Doll Auctions)

Outfit, Bar-B-Q, MOC, $125.00. (Photo courtesy Marci Van Ausdall)

Doll, American Character, metal barrettes in hair, ca 1960, 8" **175.00**

Doll, Horsman, w/makeup & other accessories, 1974, 12½", EX **50.00**

Doll, Ideal, original gray & white dress, 1953, 14".............**65.00**

Doll, Rothchild, 35th Anniversary Betsy, 1986, 12", EX......**45.00**

Doll, Uneeda, vinyl, rooted hair, 1964, 11½".....................**25.00**

Celebrities

Dolls that represent movie or TV personalities, fictional characters, or famous sports figures are very popular collectibles and can usually be found for well under $100.00. Mego, Horsman, Ideal, and Mattel are among the largest producers. Condition is vital. To price a doll in mint condition but without the box, deduct 50% to 60% from the value of one mint-in-the-box. Dolls in only good or poorer condition drop at a very rapid pace. For more information see *Collector's Guide to Celebrity Dolls* by David Spurgeon. For an expanded listing, see *Schroeder's Collectible Toys, Antique to Modern*.

Carrie Fisher as Princess Leia Organa, Hasbro, 1998, 11½", M.....................**20.00**

Damon Wayans as Homey the Clown, Acme, 1992, 24", M.............**50.00**

Dan Aykroyd as Elwood Blues, Toy Biz, 1997, 12½", MIB......**25.00**

Fran Drescher as Fran Fine, talking, Street Players, 1995, 11½", M **30.00**

James Arness as Matt Dillon, Exclusive Premier, 1997, 9", MIB...............................**25.00**

Joan Collins as Alexis Colby, World Doll, 1985, 19", MIB......**175.00**

Kate Jackson as Sabrina Duncan, Hasbro, 1977, 8½", M (no box)................................**25.00**

Max Baer Jr, as Jethro Bodine, Exclusive Premier, 1997, 9", MIB...............................**30.00**

Robert Vaugn as Napoleon Solo, Gilbert, 1965, 12½", M ..**200.00**

Left: Sonny Bono, Mego, 1976, all original, 12", $30.00. (Photo courtesy Jennifer Dobb)
Right: Suzanne Somers (Chrissy from Three's Company), Mego, 1970s, 12½", MIB, $85.00. (Photo courtesy Greg Davis and Bill Morgan)

Warren Beatty as Dick Tracy, Applause, 1990s, 14", M..**45.00**

William Shatner as Captain Kirk, Presents, 1991, 10", M w/tag **25.00**

Eegee

The Goldberger company made these dolls, Eegee (E.G.) being the initials of the company's founder. Dolls marked 'Made in China' were made in 1986.

Andy, molded painted hair, 1963, 12"..................................**35.00**

Annette, teen-type fashion, 1963, 11½", EX.........................**55.00**

Baby Carrie, w/carriage or carry seat, 1970, 24", EX.........**60.00**

Ballerina, hard plastic w/vinyl head, 1964, 31", EX.....**100.00**

Beverly Hillbillies, Granny Clampett w/gray rooted hair, 1960s, 14", EX................**65.00**

Georgie, Georgette, redheaded twins, 1971, 22", pr, EX..**50.00**

Little Debutantes, swivel waist w/high-heeled feet, 1958, 18", EX.....................................**50.00**

My Fair Lady, fashion type, 1958, 20", EX.............................**75.00**

Tandy Talks, pull-string talker, 1961, 20", EX **55.00**

some of the older dolls often bring $300.00 and up.

Alyssa, walker, rooted saran hair, ca 1960-61, 23"...............**90.00**

Baby Lisa Grows Up, in trunk w/wardrobe, 1983, EX..**150.00**

Champagne Lady, from Lawrence Welk's TV show, 1959, 23"..**85.00**

Humpty Dumpty, 1985, EX..**75.00**

Katie, molded hair, 1957, 8½" .**50.00**

Miss Chips, side-glancing eyes, 1966-81, 17", EX **35.00**

Patsy Ann, white organdy dress w/pink hair ribbon, 1959, 15" **100.00**

Polka Dottie, fabric body w/molded pigtails, 1954, 21", EX...**165.00**

Fisher-Price

Since the mid-1970s, this well-known American toy company has been making a variety of dolls. Many have vinyl heads, rooted hair, and cloth bodies. Most are marked and dated.

Baby Ann, vinyl/cloth, removable clothes, 1974-76, 13"......**25.00**

Natchez, vinyl, Pride of the South series, all original, ca 1981 13", $90.00. (Photo courtesy Patsy Moyer)

Effanbee

This company has been in business since 1910, continually producing high quality dolls, some of all composition, some composition and cloth, and a few of plastic and vinyl. In excellent condition,

My Friend Becky, #218, 1982 – 1984, M, $20.00. (Photo courtesy Brad Cassity)

Jenny, vinyl/cloth, rooted brown hair, 1974-76, 13" **25.00**

Mary, vinyl/cloth, rooted hair, removable apron & skirt, 1974-77, 13"...................**25.00**

My Friend Jenny, aerobics outfit & headband, gold purse, 1984-85 ....**20.00**

My Friend Jenny, vinyl, brunette hair, 1982-83, MIB **20.00**

My Friend Mikey, jeans, shirt, jacket & sneakers, 1982-84, MIB................................**30.00**

Horsman

During the 1930s, this company produced composition dolls of the highest quality. Today many of their dolls are made of vinyl. Hard plastic dolls marked '170' are also Horsmans. For more information see *Collector's Guide to Horsman Dolls* by Don Jensen.

Peggy Pen Pal, vinyl and hard plastic, rooted blond hair, blue painted eyes, all original, 1970s, 18", $25.00. (Photo courtesy Patsy Moyer)

Baby First Tooth, open/closed mouth w/tongue & 1 tooth, 1966, 16"..........................**40.00**

Baby Tweaks, cloth body w/inset eyes, ca 1967, 20", EX ...**30.00**

Cinderella, vinyl head w/plastic body, 1965, 11½", EX.....**30.00**

Gold Medal Doll, vinyl, molded hair, 1953, 26"................**45.00**

Police Woman, plastic fully articulated body, ca 1976, 9", EX...**35.00**

Ideal

For more than eighty years, this company produced quality dolls that were easily affordable by the average American family. Their Shirley Temple and Toni dolls were highly successful. They're also the company who made Miss Revlon, Betsy Wetsy, and Tiny Tears. For more information see *Collector's Guide to Ideal Dolls* by Judith Izen. See also Dolls, Shirley Temple and Tammy.

April Shower, battery operated, 1969, 14", EX **28.00**

Baby Crissy, foam-filled legs & arms, 1973-76, 24", EX.**150.00**

Chelsea,(Jet Set Doll), mod fashions, 1967, 24", EX.........**50.00**

Daddy's girl, 'Daddy's Girl' label on dress, 1961, 38".......**300.00**

Dennis the Menace, all-cloth, wearing overalls, 1976, 14", EX **20.00**

Hopalong Cassidy, in black cowboy outfit, 1949-50, 18", EX ..**80.00**

Little Miss Revlon, complete w/box, 1958-60, 10½" **75.00**

ed at the waist, heads, and wrists, so that they could be positioned at will with their musical instruments and other accessory items. Their clothing, their makeup, and their hairdos were wonderfully exotic, and their faces were beautifully molded. More information on Jem dolls may be found in *Modern Collectible Dolls* by Patsy Moyer (Collector Books).

Miss Revlon, 18", M with booklet and dress tag, $300.00. (Photo courtesy McMasters Doll Auctions)

Samantha, from TV show Bewitched, 1965-66, 12", EX..............**175.00**
Snoozie, cloth body w/Swiss music box, 1949, 11", EX..........**75.00**
Strawman, scarecrow in Wizard of Oz movie, yarn hair, 1939, 17"...........................**250.00**
Toni, Dupont nylon wig, P-90, 1949, 14"......................**125.00**
Velvet, grow hair, talker, pull-string, 1971-73, 15", EX..............**150.00**

Jem

The glamorous life of Jem mesmerized little girls who watched her Saturday morning cartoons, and she was a natural as a fashion doll. In 1985 Hasbro introduced the Jem line of 12" dolls representing her, the rock stars from Jem's musical group, the Holograms, and other members of the cast, including Rio, the only boy, who was Jem's road manager and Jerrica's boyfriend. Production was discontinued in 1987. Each doll was poseable, joint-

Doll, Pizzazz of the Misfits, 2nd issue, MIB, from $55.00 to $75.00. (Photo courtesy Jennifer Dobb)

Accessory, Backstager, M.....**25.00**
Accessory, KJEM Guitar, M..**25.00**
Accessory, New Wave Waterbed, M......................**35.00**
Accessory, Rock 'n Roadster, M..**65.00**
Doll, Aja (Hologram), 1st issue, 12½", M **45.00**
Doll, Ashley (Starlight Girl), 11", M......................**40.00**
Doll, Banee (Starlight Girl), 11", M......................**25.00**
Doll, Clash, MIB **25.00**

Doll, Danse (Holograms), M.**45.00**
Doll, Jem (Flash 'n Sizzle), M **30.00**
Doll, Jem (Glitter 'n Gold), M **60.00**
Doll, Jem/Jerrica, star earrings, M **35.00**
Doll, Jem/Jerrica, 1st issue, M **30.00**
Doll, Jetta, MIB **40.00**
Doll, Kimber (Holograms), 2nd issue, M **40.00**
Doll, Pizzazz (Misfit), 1st issue, M **50.00**
Doll, Raya (Holograms), M.**150.00**
Doll, Rio, 1st issue, M **25.00**
Doll, Rio (Glitter 'n Gold), NFRB **35.00**
Doll, Roxy, 2nd issue, MIB .**50.00**
Doll, Stormer (Misfits), 1st issue, M **50.00**
Doll, Synergy (Holograms), 12½", M **45.00**
Doll, Video, NFRB **35.00**
Outfit, Permanent Wave, MIB **30.00**
Outfit, Up & Rockin', MIB .**20.00**

Kenner

This company's dolls range from the 12" jointed teenage glamour dolls to the tiny 3" Mini-Kins with the snap-on changeable clothing and synthetic 'hair' ponytails. (Value for the latter: doll only, $8.00; doll with one outfit, $15.00; complete set, $70.00.)

Baby Bundles, white, 16", M.**20.00**
Butch Cassidy or Sundance Kid, 4", M, ea **15.00**

Darci Cover Girl, posable elbows & knees, jointed hands, 12½", M **55.00**
Erica Cover Girl, posable elbows & knees, jointed hands, 12½", M **100.00**
Gabbigale, Black, 1972, 18", M **45.00**
Rose Petal, scented, 1984, 7", M **20.00**
Steve Scout, 1974, 9", M.......**20.00**

Liddle Kiddles

Produced by Mattel between 1966 and 1971, Liddle Kiddle dolls and accessories were designed to suggest the typical 'little kid' in the typical neighborhood. These dolls can be found in sizes ranging from ¾" to 4", all with poseable bodies and rooted hair that can be restyled. Later, two more series were designed that represented storybook and nursery rhyme characters. The animal kingdom was represented by the Animiddles and Zoolery Jewelry Kiddles. There was even a set of extraterrestrials. And lastly, in 1979 Sweet Treets dolls were marketed.

Items mint on card or mint in box are worth about 25% more than one in mint condition but with none of the original packaging. Based on mint value, deduct 50% for dolls that are dressed but lack accessories. For further information we recommend *Dolls of the 1960s and 1970* by Cindy Sabulis, and *Schroeder's Collectible Toys, Antique to Modern*; both are published by Collector Books.

Baby Rockaway, #3819, MIP..**95.00**

Blue Funny Bunny, #3532, MIP **100.00**

Dainty Deer, #3637, complete, M **45.00**

Greta Grape, #3728, 1968-69, M **50.00**

Heart Pin Kiddle, #3741, complete, M...........................**65.00**

Howard Biff Biddle, #3520, complete, M...........................**75.00**

Kleo Kola, #3729, complete, M .**50.00**

Liddle Diddle, #3503, complete, M, $75.00. (Photo courtesy Cindy Sabulis)

Limey Lou Spoonfuls, #3815, MIP...............................**25.00**

Lorelei Locket, #3717, MIP ..**75.00**

Rolly Twiddle, #3519, complete, M **175.00**

Madame Alexander

Founded in 1923, Beatrice Alexander began her company by producing an Alice in Wonderland doll which was all cloth with an oil-painted face. By the 1950s there were over six hundred employees making dolls of various materials. The company is still producing lovely dolls today. For further infor-mation, we recommend *Madame Alexander Collector's Doll Price Guide* and *Madame Alexander Store Exclusives and Limited Editions* by Linda Crowsey; both are published by Collector Books.

Anatolia, straight legs, #524, 1987 only, 8".............................**65.00**

Cinderella, hard plastic, 'poor' outfit, 1966, 12"..................**675.00**

Daisy, #1110, Portrette Series, white lace over yellow, 1987 – 1988 only, 10", $75.00. (Photo courtesy Pat Smith)

Dearest, vinyl baby, 1962-64, 12" **125.00**

Goldilocks, floral dress, w/bear, #140500, 1994-95, 8" **75.00**

Lady Lee, Storybook Series, #442, 1988, 8"...........................**65.00**

Little Bo Peep, hard plastic, Wendy Ann, marked, #486, 1976-86, 8".....................**65.00**

Mary Had a Little Lamb, #14623, 1996, 8"...........................**75.00**

Nurse, all white dress, w/baby, #429, 1961, 8", minimum value **650.00**

Snowflake, ballerina in white/gold, Cissette, #1167, 1993 only, 10"...............**90.00**

Wicked Stepmother, #50002, 1996
limited edition, 21" **325.00**

Mattel

Though most famous, of course, for Barbie doll and her friends, the Mattel company also made celebrity dolls, Liddle Kiddles, Chatty Cathy, talking dolls, a lot of action figures (the Major Matt Mason line and She-Ra, Princess of Power, for example), and in more recent years, Baby Tenderlove and P.J. Sparkles. See also Barbie; Dolls, Liddle Kiddles.

To learn more about Mattel dolls, consult *Talking Toys of the 20th Century* and *Chatty Cathy Dolls, An Identification and Value Guide*, both by Kathy and Don Lewis. They are listed in the Directory under California.

Arnold Schwarzenegger as Jack
Slater, talking, 1993, 13",
MIB..............................**125.00**
Baby Beans, vinyl head, cloth
body, talking, 12", M **40.00**
Baby Love Light, battery operated, 16", M **18.00**
Baby Say 'N See, white dress w/pink
yoke, 1967-68, 17", M.......**35.00**
Big Josh, vinyl w/dark hair &
beard, 9½", M.................**35.00**
Captain Kangaroo, talker, Sears
only, 1967, 19", M..........**75.00**
Dancerina, Black, EX played with
(complete)......................**85.00**
Shrinkin' Violette, cloth w/yarn hair,
talker, 1964-65, 16", EX ...**50.00**
Tatters, cloth, talker, original rag
clothes, 1965-67, 19", EX..**30.00**

Nancy Ann Storybook

Nancy Ann Abbott was a multifaceted, multitalented Californian who seemed to excel at whatever was her passion at the moment. Eventually she settled on designing costumes for dolls. This burgeoned into a full-fledged and very successful doll company which she founded in 1937. Early on, her 5" dolls were imported from Japan; but very soon she was making her own dolls, first of which had jointed legs, while those made in the early '40s had legs molded as part of the body (frozen). But it was their costumes that made the dolls so popular. Many series were designed around various themes — storybook characters; the flower series; Around the World Dolls of every ethnic persuasion; the American girls; sports and family series; and dolls representing seasons, days of the week, and the months of the year. Ms. Abbott died in 1964, and within a year the company closed.

To learn more about this extensive line, we recommend *Encylopedia of Bisque Nancy Ann Storybook Dolls* by Elaine M. Pardee and Jackie Robertson (Collector Books).

Beauty (Beauty & Beast), lavender dress, frozen legs, #156,
M **45.00**
Girl For August..., flocked chiffon
dress, #194, M................**65.00**
Going a Milking, frozen legs, #126,
M **55.00**

Debut, Commencement Series, all original, 5", NM (NM box), minimum value, $75.00.

January Merry Maid..., striped dress, plastic arms/frozen legs, #187, M **45.00**

Little Betty Blue Wore Her Holiday Shoe, jointed legs, #109, M........................**135.00**

Mistress Mary Quite Contrary, frozen legs, #119, from $45 to **55.00**

Over the Hills, jointed legs, #114, M..................................**135.00**

School Days Dear Old Golden..., eyelet apron, jointed legs, #117, M........................**250.00**

See Saw Marjorie Daw, magenta & stripes on dress, frozen legs, #177, M........................**55.00**

Storybook Small Snow White, MIB, from $125.00 to $175.00. (Photo courtesy Robin Englehart/photo by Nancy Jean Mong)

Silks & Satin, fabric w/painted stripes, frozen legs, #168, M **45.00**

Raggedy Ann and Andy

Designed by Johnny Gruelle in 1915, Raggedy Ann was named by combining two James Whitcomb Riley poem titles, *The Raggedy Man* and *Orphan Annie*. The early cloth dolls he made were dated and had painted-on features. Though these dolls are practically nonexistent, they're easily identified by the mark, 'Patented Sept. 7, 1915.' P.F. Volland made these dolls from 1920 to 1934; theirs were very similar in appearance to the originals. The Mollye Doll Outfitters were the first to print the now-familiar red heart on her chest, and they added a black outline around her nose. These dolls carry the handwritten inscription 'Raggedy Ann and Andy Doll/Manufactured by Mollye Doll Outfitters.' Georgene Averill made them ca 1946 to 1963, sewing their label into the seam of the dolls. Knickerbocker dolls (1963 to 1982) also carry a company label. The Applause Toy Company made these dolls for two years in the early 1980s, and they were finally taken over by Hasbro, the current producer, in 1983.

Besides the dolls, scores of other Raggedy Ann and Andy items have been marketed, including books, radios, games, clocks, bedspreads, and clothing. Over the past several years, collector interest has really taken off, and just about any antique mall you visit today will have an eye-catching display. For more information see *The World of Raggedy Ann Collectibles* by Kim Avery.

Applause, 1986, 12", EX/NM, from $28.00 to $32.00 each. (Photo courtesy Kim Avery)

Applause, 8", EX, ea, from $8 to **12.00**

Applause, 20", EX, ea, from $45 to..................................**55.00**

Applause, 36", EX, ea, from $75 to **80.00**

Georgene, blue rompers, 1946-63, 22", EX, from $145 to ..**165.00**

Georgene, flowered dress, 1946-63, 19", EX, from $100 to ..**145.00**

Georgene, 1946-63, 15", EX, ea, from $180 to.................**210.00**

Knickerbocker, Korea, 15", EX, ea, from $30 to **40.00**

Knickerbocker, Taiwan, 15", EX, Ann: $40; Andy w/hang tag, from $50 to **65.00**

Knickerbocker, Taiwan, 19", EX, ea, from $40 to **45.00**

Remco

The plastic and vinyl dolls made by Remco during the 1960s and 1970s are gaining popularity with collectors today. Many have mechanical features that were activated either by a button on their back or batteries. The Littlechap Family of dolls (1964), Dr. John, his wife Lisa, and their two children, Judy and Libby, came with clothing and fashion accessories of the highest quality. Children found the family less interesting than the more glamorous fashion dolls on the market at that time, and as a result, production was limited. These dolls in excellent condition are valued at about $15.00 to $20.00 each, while their outfits range from about $30.00 (loose and complete) to a minimum of $50.00 (MIB).

Baby Grow a Tooth, 1968, 15", MIB................................**25.00**

Grandpa Munster, #1821, 1-pc plastic body, 1964, 4¾", EX ...**65.00**

Jumpsy, jumps rope, molded-on shoes & socks, 1970, 14", MIB **20.00**

Mimi, battery-operated singer, 1973, 19", MIB **50.00**

Pip, vinyl, blond rooted hair, all original, ca 1967, 6", $20.00. (Photo courtesy Patsy Moyer)

Sweet April, Black, 1971, 5½",
MIB..................................**15.00**
Tippy Tumbles, does somersaults,
1968, 16", MIB **55.00**

Shirley Temple

The public's fascination with Shirley was more than enough reason for toy companies to literally deluge the market with merchandise of all types decorated with her likeness. Dolls were a big part of that market, and the earlier composition dolls in excellent condition are often priced at a minimum of $600.00 on today's market. Many were made by the Ideal Company, who in the 1950s also issued a line of vinyl dolls.

Celluloid, Dutch Shirley Temple,
dimples in cheeks, ca 1937,
15".................................**100.00**
Composition, Hawaiian, black
yarn hair, grass skirt, 18",
NM.................................**950.00**

Composition head, open mouth with six upper teeth, original mohair wig and Scottie dress, replaced undies, shoes, and socks, Ideal, 18", $650.00. (Photo courtesy McMasters Auctions)

Porcelain, Danbury Mint, 1987,
16", EX............................**90.00**
Vinyl, 1973, 16", EX............**165.00**
Vinyl, marked 'Doll Dreams & Love,' 1984, 36"..............**75.00**
Vinyl, open/close eyes,
open/closed mouth w/teeth,
1957, 12', NM..............**275.00**

Tammy

In 1962 the Ideal Novelty & Toy Company introduced their teenage Tammy doll. Slightly pudgy and not quite as sophisticated as some of the teen fashion dolls on the market at the time, Tammy's innocent charm captivated consumers. Her extensive wardrobe and numerous accessories added to her popularity with children. Tammy had everything including a car, a house, and a catamaran. In addition, a large number of companies obtained licenses to issue products using the 'Tammy' name. Everything from paper dolls to nurse's kits were made to promote Tammy. Her success was not confined to the United States. She was also successful in Canada and in several European countries. Doll values listed here are for mint-in-box examples. (Loose dolls are generally about half mint-in-box value as they are relatively common.) Other values are for mint-condition items without their original packaging. (Such items with their original packaging or in less-than-mint condition would then vary up or down accordingly.)

Accessory, Model Miss outfit, #9173, MIP.....................**75.00**

Accessory, Tammy's 1963 Car, convertible, #9700, 1963-64, 18", MIB **250.00**

Accessory, Underwear Set outfit, #9091, 1962-64, MIP......**35.00**

Doll, Dad, 12½", MIB............**75.00**

Doll, Dodi, 1964, 9", MIB **75.00**

Doll, Mom, 1963, 12½", MIB..**75.00**

Doll, New Pepper, 1965, 9¼", MIB **75.00**

Doll, Pepper, standard playsuit, 1963, 8", MIB **50.00**

Doll, Pos'n Tammy, in formal feathers outfit, 12", MIB **100.00**

Doll, Tammy, Black, 1964, 12", MIB..............................**525.00**

Doll, Tammy, black hair, 12", M..**75.00**

Doll, Tammy, varying shades of blond hair, 1962, 12", M..**55.00**

Doll, Ted, 1963, 12½", MIB..**65.00**

Doll, Tammy's Mom, light or dark hair, EX, $45.00 each. (Photo courtesy Cindy Sabulis)

Vogue

This is the company that made the 'Ginny' doll famous. She was first made in composition during the late 1940s, and if you could find her in mint condition, she'd bring about $450.00 on today's market. (Played with and in relatively sad condition, she's still worth about $90.00.) Ginnys from the 1950s were made of rigid vinyl. The last Ginny came out in 1969. Tonka bought the rights in 1973, but the dolls they produced sold poorly. After a series of other owners, Dakin purchased the rights in 1986 and began producing a vinyl doll that resembled the 1950-style Ginny very closely.

Toddles Dutch boy and girl, five-piece composition bodies, EX original clothes, 7", $300.00 for the pair. (Photo courtesy McMasters Auctions)

Crib Crowd, baby w/curved legs, poodle-cut wig, 1950, 8".**175.00**

Ginette, open mouth w/painted eyes, 1955-69, 8" **50.00**

Ginny, painted hard plastic, tag on white w/blue letters, 1948-50, 8"...................................**100.00**

Ginny (baby), drink & wet doll, 1959-82, 12", EX **40.00**

Ginny (Sasson), slimmer body, 1981-82, 8", EX **35.00**

Jan, rigid body w/swivel waist, 1958-60, 10½", EX **150.00**

Jimmy, all-vinyl, opened mouth, 1958, 8", EX **60.00**

Miss Ginny, soft vinyl head that tilts, 1962-64, 15-16", EX **45.00**

Doorstops

Doorstops, once called door porters, were popular from the Civil War period until after 1930. They were used to prop the doors open during the hot summer months so that the cooler air could circulate. Though some were made of brass, wood, and chalk, cast iron was by far the most preferred material, usually molded in amusing figurals — dogs, flower baskets, frogs, etc. Hubley was one of the largest producers. Beware of reproductions! Assume all the examples in the listing that follows to be made of cast iron and with original paint; ranges reflect conditions from VG to M. See Clubs and Newsletters for information concerning the *Doorstop Collectors of America.*

Basket of Flowers, Hubley, #152, 7x5", from $75 to.......... **150.00**

Cat, arched back, Sculptured Metal Studios, 9x6¾", from $275 to.......................... **350.00**

Colonial Dame, Hubley, #37, 8x4½", from $200 to..... **275.00**

Colonial Woman, Littco Products (others), Pat Pend, 10¼", from $175 to.......................... **225.00**

Doberman Pinscher, full figure, 8x8½", from $400 to..... **550.00**

Doll on Base, full figured, solid, 5½x4⅞", from $75 to ..**125.00**

Donald Duck, w/stop sign, Walt Disney...1971, 8⅜", from $250 to **325.00**

Duck Head, 8x5¼", from $100 to **175.00**

Dutch Boy, hands in pockets, full figure, 8⅜x3⅜", from $275 to **350.00**

Dutch Girl, Hubley, #10, 9¼x5½", from $250 to **300.00**

Elephant, head down, S117, 6½x8¼", from $175 to..**250.00**

Fawn, stylized, No 6 c 1930 Taylor Cook, 10x6", from $250 to **375.00**

Fireplace, Eastern Specialty Co G1, 6¼x8", from $250 to **325.00**

French Basket, Hubley, #69, 11x6¾", from $125 to...**200.00**

Fruit Basket, Albany Foundry, 10⅛x7½", from $175 to **250.00**

Game Cock, full figure, 7x5⅜", from $275 to **350.00**

Geisha, full figure, Hubley, 7x6", from $200 to **275.00**

Horse on Base, 10½x12¼", from $125 to **200.00**

Japanese Spaniel, begging, cJo, #1267, 9x4½", from $200 to **375.00**

Li'l Bo Peep, 6¾x5", from $225 to **300.00**

Little Dutch Woman, full figure, solid, 4x2⅜", from $100 to............................ **125.00**

Mallard, full figure, 6¼x7½", from $275 to.......................... **350.00**

Narcissus, Hubley, #266, 7¼x6¾", from $150 to **225.00**

Organ Grinder, w/monkey, 9⅞x5¾", from $375 to..**450.00**

Oriental Man, hands over head, full figure, 9x7¼", from $225 to **275.00**

Parrot in Ring, B&H, 13¾x7¼", from $225 to **275.00**

Pelican on Dock, Albany Foundry, #113, 8x7¼", from $250 to **350.00**

Persian Cat, full figure, Hubley, 8½x6½", from $175 to **225.00**

Pied Piper, #120, 7¼x5", from $325 to **350.00**

Pine cones, wedge, 3⅝x6⅞", from $125 to **200.00**

Poppies & Daisies, Hubley, #491, 7¼x6", from $125 to.....**175.00**

Setter, pointing, full figure, Hubley, 8¾x15⅞", from $175 to **275.00**

Swan, 15¾x6¾", from $275.00 to $350.00. (Photo courtesy Jeanne Bertoia)

Terrier Pup, seated, full figure, 8¼x7½", from $275 to **350.00**

Topsy, wedge, Hubley, 6x4", from $275 to **300.00**

Tulips in Pot, LA-CS 770, 10½x5⅞", from $225 to **300.00**

Twin Penguins, 7¼x7½", from $175 to **250.00**

Windmill, National Foundry, #10 Cape Cod, 6¾x6⅞", from $100 to **150.00**

Dragon Ware

Dragon ware is fairly accessible and still being made today. The new Dragon ware is distinguishible by the lack of detail in the dragon, which will appear flat. In the older pieces, much detail work is done.

Background colors are primary. New pieces are shinier than old. New colors include green, lavender, yellow, pink, blue, pearlized, and orange as well as the classic blue/black. Many cups have lithophanes in the bottom. Nude lithophanes are found but are scarce. New pieces may have lithophanes; but again these tend to be without detail and flat.

Items listed below are unmarked unless noted otherwise. Ranges are given for pieces that are currently being produced. Be sure to examine unmarked items well; in particular, look for good detail. Remember, new pieces lack the quality of workmanship evident in earlier items and should not command the prices of the older ware. Use the low end to evaluate any item you feel may be new.

Aladdin lamp, orange, 3-leg, 6", from $20 to **35.00**

Box, dresser; footed, MIJ, 4½x5¼", from $30 to **60.00**

160

Condiment set, gray, no mark, tray w/8 pcs including lids, from $75 to.................**150.00**

Cup & saucer, black, unmarked, 2¼", 5½", from $12.50 to..**14.00**

Cup & saucer, demitasse; gold lustre, souvenir, from $10 to.........**15.00**

Cup & saucer, yellow, Made in Occupied Japan, 1½", 4", 4 for................................**175.00**

Incense burner, red, coralene (beaded) dragon, MIJ, 3", from $25 to..............................**40.00**

Luncheon set, shell form, HP MIJ, plates+cup+saucer, serves 8, from $125 to.................**200.00**

Sake cups, black, lithophanes, set of 6 ....**75.00**

Shakers, black lustre, pr, from $7.50 to............................**20.00**

Sherbet set, brown/yellow, cloverleaf plate w/sherbet cup, MIJ..**60.00**

Tea set, blue cloud, dragon spouts, Kutani, 24-pc, from $325 to **425.00**

Tea set, red, Japan, pot+creamer/sugar+6 cups/saucers, from $125 to..........................**275.00**

Vase, additional slip in yellow, MIJ, 4¾"..........................**17.50**

Vase, bud; pink, FL souvenir, MIJ, 5"......................................**7.50**

Vinegar bottle, gray, no mark...**22.50**

Egg Timers

The origin of the figural egg timer appears to be Germany, circa 1920s or 1930s, with Japan following their lead in the 1940s. Some American companies may have begun producing figural timers at about the same time, but evidence is scarce in terms of pottery marks or company logos.

Figural timers can be found in a wide range of storybook characters (Oliver Twist), animals (pigs, ducks, rabbits), career and vocational uniformed people (chef, London Bobby, housemaid), or people in native costume.

All types of timers were a fairly uniform height of 3" to 4". If a figural timer no longer has its sand tube, it can still be recognized by the hole which usually goes through the back of the figure or the stub of a hand. Most timers were made of ceramic (china or bisque), but a few are of cast iron or carved wood. They can be detailed or quite plain. Listings below are for timers with their sand tubes completely intact.

Bellhop, green, ceramic, Japan, 4½".................................**40.00**

Black chef standing w/frying pan, chalkware, Japan...........**95.00**

Boy, skiing, ceramic, German, 3", $50.00.

Boy w/black cloak & cane, German, 3¾" **50.00**

Chef, combination music box, wooden, lg......................**175.00**

Chicken on nest, green plastic, England, 2½".................**25.00**

Dutch boy standing, ceramic, German, 3½" **50.00**

Goebel, little girl w/chick on tip of her shoe, ceramic, from $95 to.................................**125.00**

Kitten w/ball of yarn, chalkware.**50.00**

Mouse, white apron says 'Chef,' ceramic, Josef Original.**35.00**

Penguin, chalkware, England, 3¾", from $25 to.............**40.00**

Sailboat, lustreware, German..**75.00**

Sailor, blue, ceramic German, 4" **50.00**

Sultan, ceramic, Japan, 3½"..**50.00**

Telephone, black glaze on clay, Japan, 2" **35.00**

Windmill w/dog on base, ceramic 3¾"....................................**85.00**

8-Track Tapes and Players

What CDs are to this generation, 8-Tracks were to the youth of the '60s, '70s, and '80s. Not only the tapes themselves but the players as well are now collectible. Just watch for signs of aging and wear. Condition is extremely important.

Tape, Wish You Were Here, Pink Floyd, NM, $15.00.

Case, tape holder; alligator cover, 1960s, EX **12.00**

Player, for 1968 Pontiac, black, M................................**255.00**

Player, Panasonic RS-8361, portable stereo, 1980s, EX working...........................**95.00**

Player, Sears NR 800.2106, w/AM/FM radio, portable, leather handle, EX.........**65.00**

Player, 1970 Chevelle factory option, EX working......**190.00**

Player/recorder, Realistic TR-884, 2 channel record levels, G working.........................**285.00**

Recorder, Fostex Model 80-8. EX w/manual......................**285.00**

Recorder, Fostex reel-to reel, EX, from $135 to **185.00**

Tape, Band on the Run, Paul McCartney & Wings, Quad, MIP..........**58.00**

Tape, Best of the Beach Boys, sealed, M **9.00**

Tape, Bob Dylan's Greatest Hits Vol 2, EX **6.00**

Tape, Briefcase Full of Blues, Blues Brothers, sealed, M...........**8.50**

Tape, Cheap Trick at Budokan, Epic 1978, 1979, EX **12.00**

Tape, Clapton, Eric Clapton, sealed, M **8.00**

Tape, Dark Side of the moon, Pink Floyd, EX...........**28.00**

Tape, Elvis Worldwide Gold Award Hits, Elvis Presley, sealed, M **7.50**

Tape, Eric Clapton at His Best, sealed, M **5.00**

Tape, Firebird, Tomita, RCA red seal recording pressure pads, EX **14.00**

Tape, Golden Dream, Hank Williams, EX **6.50**

Tape, Grateful Dead Live, sealed, M 8.50
Tape, Help!, Beatles, VG 12.50
Tape, Highway to Hell, AC/DC, sealed, M 9.00
Tape, Hotter Than Hell, KISS, sealed, M 9.00
Tape, I Will Survive, Ray Conniff, EX 6.50
Tape, Imagine, John Lennon, Quad, EX 78.00
Tape, King of Rock, Elvis, EX .4.00
Tape, Led Zeppelin, untitled IV album, Atlantic Records, 1971, sealed, M 38.00
Tape, Let It Be, Beatles, Capitol, EX 12.00
Tape, Like a Virgin, Madonna, NM 35.00
Tape, Love at First Sting, Scorpions, EX.................22.00
Tape, Love Gun, KISS, 1977, NM 6.00
Tape, Mercy, Ohio Express, sealed, M 12.00
Tape, Pet Sounds, Beach Boys, EX 8.00
Tape, Purple Rain, Prince, EX..12.00
Tape, Rubber Soul, Beatles, EX 5.00
Tape, Soul Men, Sam & Dave, sealed..............................12.00
Tape, Stampede, Doobie Brothers, EX 5.00
Tape, Station, David Bowie, sealed, M 10.00
Tape, Superman - The Movie, sealed, M 5.00
Tape, Tapestry, Carole King, Ode A&M 8Q-88009, VG 18.00
Tape, Thriller, Michael Jackson, sealed, M 8.50
Tape, Van Halen II, EX..........8.00

Tape, Venus & Mars, Paul McCartney, capital Q8W-11419, EX......................40.00

Elegant Glass

To quote Gene Florence, Elegant glassware 'refers mostly to hand-worked, acid-etched glassware that was sold by better departmant and jewelry stores during the Depression era through the 1950s, differentiating it from dime store and give-away glass that has become known as Depression glass.' Cambridge, Duncan & Miller, Fostoria, Heisey, Imperial, Morgantown, New Martinsville, Paden City, Tiffin, U.S. Glass, and Westmoreland were major producers. For further information we recommend *Elegant Glassware of the Depression Era* by Gene Florence (Collector Books).

Cambridge

Apple Blossom, bowl, pickle; crystal, 9" 30.00
Apple Blossom, plate, dinner; yellow or amber, 9½" 90.00
Apple Blossom, tumbler, crystal, 6" 25.00
Candlelight, bowl, crystal, 2-handled, footed, #3900/28, 11½" 85.00
Candlelight, creamer, crystal, #3900/41 ....25.00
Candlelight, plate, dinner; crystal, #3900/24, 10½"...............85.00
Caprice, bonbon, crystal, 2-handled, #154, 6" sq.............18.00

Caprice, cake plate, crystal, footed, #36, 13".........................**150.00**

Caprice, tumbler, blue or pink, footed, #11, 5-oz..............**50.00**

Chantilly, bowl, celery/relish; crystal, 3-part, 9"...................**38.00**

Chantilly, ice bucket, crystal, $100.00.

Chantilly, plate, salad; crystal, 8"..................................**12.50**

Chantilly, tumbler, tea; crystal, footed, #3779, 12-oz........**25.00**

Cleo, bowl, vegetable; blue, decagon oval, 9½"..........**145.00**

Cleo, candlestick, 3-light; blue.....................................**150.00**

Cleo, plate, grill; amber, green, pink or yellow, 9½"......**100.00**

Daffodil, bonbon, crystal, #1181..........................**30.00**

Daffodil, saucer, crystal, #1170..**5.00**

Daffodil, tumbler, crystal, footed, #1937, 5-oz......................**22.00**

Decagon, bowl, berry; blue, 10"..**50.00**

Decagon, ice tub, pastel colors..**45.00**

Decagon, tray, pickle; blue, 9"..**40.00**

Diane, bowl, baker; crystal, 10"..**60.00**

Diane, creamer, crystal........**20.00**

Diane, vase, bud; crystal, 10"..**65.00**

Elaine, basket, crystal, upturned sides, 2-handled, 6"........**30.00**

Elaine, cup, crystal...............**22.00**

Elaine, salt & pepper shakers, crystal, footed, pr...........**45.00**

Gloria, bowl, cereal; crystal, 6" sq................................**35.00**

Gloria, platter, crystal, 11½"..**75.00**

Gloria, tumbler, tea; crystal, #3135, 12-oz...................**32.00**

Marjorie, jug, crystal, #104, 30-oz...............................**165.00**

Marjorie, tumbler, crystal, #8851...........................**20.00**

Mt Vernon, bowl, amber or crystal, #135, oval, 11"...............**25.00**

Mt Vernon, plate, salad; amber or crystal, #5, 8½"...............**7.00**

Mt Vernon, sugar bowl, amber or crystal, #86....................**10.00**

Number 520, bowl, cream soup; peach blo or green..........**25.00**

Number 520, saucer, peach blo or green, #933......................**7.00**

Number 704, cheese plate, all colors, #468........................**35.00**

Number 704, cup, all colors, #933..............................**15.00**

Number 704, plate, all colors, 8".**15.00**

Portia, cup, crystal, round....**20.00**

Portia, plate, salad; crystal, 8"..............................**15.00**

Portia, vase, flower; crystal, 11"..............................**95.00**

Rosalie, bowl, blue, pink or green, 10"...................................**75.00**

Rosalie, celery dish, amber or crystal, 11"..........................**25.00**

Rosalie, vase, amber or crystal, 6"..................................**55.00**

Rose Point, bowl, fruit; crystal, #3500/10, 5"....................**85.00**

Rose Point, plate, luncheon; crystal, #3400/63, 9½"..........**42.00**

Rose Point, sugar bowl, crystal, #3500/14........................**25.00**

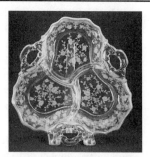

Rose Point, three-part relish, crystal, #3400/91, 8", $40.00.

Tally Ho, ashtray, amber or crystal, 4" **12.50**
Tally Ho, bowl, pan, forest green, 17"...................................**45.00**
Tally Ho, saucer, Carmen or Royal **5.00**
Valencia, bowl, crystal, #1402/82, 10"...................................**45.00**
Valencia, ice pail, crystal, #1405/52 ....**100.00**
Valencia, sugar bowl, crystal, #3500/14 ....**15.00**
Wildflower, cup, crystal, 3900/17 or #3400/54....................**22.00**
Wildflower, plate, crystal, #3400/62, 8½"................**18.00**
Wildflower, tumbler, water; crystal, #3121, 10-oz.............**30.00**

Duncan and Miller

Canterbury No 115, ashtray, crystal, 5" **12.00**
Canterbury No 115, candle holder, crystal, 3½" **15.00**
Canterbury No 115, ice bucket or vase, crystal, 7".............**35.00**
Canterbury No 115, vase, crystal, 8½x6"............................**50.00**
Caribbean, plate, crystal, 14"..**25.00**
Caribbean, saucer, blue..........**8.00**

Caribbean, tumbler, shot glass; crystal, 2-oz, 2¼"...........**25.00**

Caribbean, vase, blue, footed, 10", $145.00. (Photo courtesy Gene Florence)

First Love, candle holder, crystal, #115, 3½".......................**25.00**
First Love, cup, crystal, #115.**18.00**
First Love, egg plates; crystal, #30, 12".................................**150.00**
Lily of the Valley, ashtray, crystal, 3"....................................**25.00**
Lily of the Valley, bowl, crystal, 12"...................................**55.00**
Lily of the Valley, plate, crystal, 9" **45.00**
Nautical, ashtray, blue, 6" ...**40.00**
Nautical, creamer, crystal....**15.00**
Nautical, sugar bowl, crystal..**15.00**
Sandwich, oil bottle, crystal, 5¾" **35.00**
Sandwich, plate, dinner; crystal, 9½"...................................**40.00**
Sandwich, tray, crystal, oval, 8" **18.00**
Spiral Flutes, bowl, almond; amber, green or pink, 2"..............**13.00**
Spiral Flutes, platter, amber, green or pink, 11"..........**40.00**
Spiral Flutes, vase, amber, green or pink, 6½"...................**20.00**
Tear Drop, ashtray, crystal, 5"..**8.00**
Tear Drop, bowl, salad; crystal, 9" **30.00**

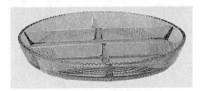

Tear Drop, six-part relish, crystal, 12", $40.00. (Photo courtesy Gene Florence)

Tear Drop, sugar bowl, crystal, 8-oz 8.00

Terrace, cup, cobalt or red....40.00

Terrace, plate, crystal or amber, 11".....................................30.00

Terrace, sugar lid, crystal or amber...............................12.50

Fostoria

American, covered candy dish, tall foot, 9½x5½", $37.50.

American, picture frame, crystal 15.00

American, platter, crystal, oval, 12"......................................55.00

American, rose, bowl; crystal, 5" 30.00

Baroque, bowl, vegetable; yellow, oval, 9½".........................65.00

Baroque, cup, blue 33.00

Baroque, vase, crystal, 7".....60.00

Brocade (Grape #287), whip cream pail, green, #2378 ....40.00

Brocade (Oakleaf 290), ice bucket, crystal, #2378..............100.00

Brocade (Paradise #289), plate, rose or green, #2419, 8" sq......35.00

Colony, bowl, fruit; crystal, 10"..40.00

Colony, candlestick, crystal, 7"..37.50

Colony, platter, crystal, 12"..52.50

Fairfax, ashtray, rose, blue or orchid, 4" 17.50

Fairfax, candlestick, amber, 3"..12.00

Fairfax, sugar pail, green or topaz.............................55.00

Fuchsia, bonbon, crystal, #2470 ....33.00

Fuchsia, oyster cocktail, Wisteria, #60064, 4½-oz 35.00

Fuchsia, saucer, crystal, #2440 ..7.50

Hermitage, icer, Azure, #2449 .30.00

Hermitage, plate, amber, green or topaz, #2449½, 9"..........20.00

Hermitage, vase, crystal, footed, 6"..................................22.00

June, ashtray, crystal...........25.00

June, bowl, bonbon; rose or blue 30.00

June, creamer, topaz, footed..20.00

Kashmir, ashtray, yellow or green.............................25.00

Kashmir, cup, blue................20.00

Kashmir, sugar lid, yellow or green...............................50.00

Lafayette, bowl, sweetmeat; crystal or amber, 4½"...........18.00

Lafayette, cup, Regal Blue ...35.00

Lafayette, plate, Wisteria, 6"..14.00

Navarre, console bowl, crystal, handled, footed, 10½", $95.00.

New Garland, bowl, fruit; amber or topaz, 5" **10.00**

New Garland, jelly dish, rose, 7" **18.00**

New Garland, sugar bowl, rose.**15.00**

Pioneer, ashtray, rose or topaz, 3¾" **20.00**

Pioneer, bowl, cereal; blue, 6"..**20.00**

Pioneer, plate, ebony, 6" **8.00**

Rogene, marmalade w/lid, crystal, #1968 ....**45.00**

Rogene, plate, crystal, 8" **15.00**

Rogene, vase, crystal, rolled edge, 8½" **95.00**

Royal, ashtray, #2350, 3½" ..**22.50**

Royal, bowl, soup; amber or green, #2350, 7¾" **30.00**

Royal, candlestick, amber or green, #2324, 4" **22.00**

Royal, egg cup, amber or green, #2350 ....**30.00**

Seville, ashtray, green, #2350, 4" **22.50**

Seville, comport, amber, #2350, 8" **27.50**

Seville, vase, amber, #2292, 8"..**75.00**

Sun Ray, cup, crystal............**12.00**

Sun Ray, jelly dish, crystal ..**16.00**

Sun Ray, plate, crystal, 16"..**70.00**

Trojan, candlestick, rose, #2394, 2" **25.00**

Trojan, comport, topaz, #2375, 7" **50.00**

Trojan, sauce plate, topaz, #2375 ....**45.00**

Versailles, ashtray, blue, #2350..................................**35.00**

Versailles, ice dish, pink or green, #2451 ....**45.00**

Versailles, sauce boat plate, yellow, #2375 ....**25.00**

Vesper, ashtray, amber, #2350, 4" **30.00**

Vesper, celery dish, green, #2350 ....**25.00**

Vesper, cup, blue, #2350.......**40.00**

Heisey

Charter Oak, bowl, finger; Moongleam, #3362.........**20.00**

Charter Oak (Acorn & Leaves), plate, luncheon; crystal, #1246, 8".........................**10.00**

Chintz, bowl, cream soup; Sahara **35.00**

Chintz, cup, crystal...............**15.00**

Chintz, plate, dinner; crystal; 10½" sq.........................**40.00**

Crystolite, coaster, crystal, 4"..**12.00**

Crystolite, cup, crystal.........**22.00**

Crystolite, plate, sandwich; crystal, 12" **45.00**

Empress, ashtray, Flamingo..**175.00**

Empress, bonbon, Sahara, 6"..**25.00**

Empress, cup, Moongleam....**35.00**

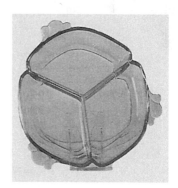

Empress, three-part relish tray, Flamingo, 10", $50.00.

Greek Key, coaster, crystal ..**20.00**

Greek Key, creamer, crystal.**50.00**

Greek Key, water bottle, crystal..........................**220.00**

Ipswich, creamer, crystal **35.00**

Ipswich, plate, pink, 7" sq....**60.00**

Ipswich, sugar bowl, crystal.**35.00**

Lariat, ashtray, crystal, 4"...**15.00**

Lariat, bowl, salad; crystal, 10½"...........................**40.00**

Minuet, bowl, shallow salad; crystal, 13½"........................**75.00**

Minuet, cup, crystal.............**30.00**

Minuet, vase, crystal, #4192, 10"...........................**110.00**

New Era, bowl, floral; crystal, 11"..............................**35.00**

New Era, cup, crystal...........**10.00**

New Era, sugar bowl, crystal .**37.50**

Octagon, basket, crystal, #500, 5"...............................**100.00**

Octagon, mayonnaise, Moongleam, footed, #1229, 5½".........**35.00**

Octagon, plate, Flamingo, 14"..**25.00**

Old Colony, cigarette holder, Sahara, #3390................**44.00**

Old Colony, cup, Sahara.......**32.00**

Old Colony, plate, Sahara, 8" sq...............................**24.00**

Old Sandwich, comport, crystal, 6"...............................**60.00**

Old Sandwich, floral block, Flamingo, #22 ....**25.00**

Old Sandwich, saucer, Moongleam....................**25.00**

Old Sandwich, tumbler, crystal, 10-oz **20.00**

Pleat & Panel, cup, Moongleam........................**17.50**

Pleat & Panel, plate, Flamingo, 6"...................................**8.00**

Pleat & Panel, vase, crystal, 8"............................**30.00**

Provincial, ashtray, crystal, 3" sq.............................**12.50**

Provincial, bowl, floral; crystal, 12"..................................**40.00**

Provincial, salt & pepper shakers, crystal, pr **40.00**

Queen Ann, ashtray, crystal.**30.00**

Queen Ann, bonbon, crystal, 6"............................**12.00**

Queen Ann, comport, crystal, footed, 6"..............................**25.00**

Queen Ann, cup, crystal.......**15.00**

Ridgeleigh, ashtray, crystal, 6" sq..................................**35.00**

Ridgeleigh, bowl, salad; crystal, 9"..................................**50.00**

Ridgeleigh, three-part relish, crystal, 11", $50.00. (Photo courtesy Gene Florence)

Ridgeleigh, vase, crystal, 8".**75.00**

Saturn, ashtray, crystal **10.00**

Saturn, comport, Zircon or Limelight, 7" **550.00**

Saturn, creamer, crystal.......**25.00**

Saturn, sugar bowl, crystal ..**25.00**

Stanhope, bowl, salad; crystal, 11" **90.00**

Stanhope, plate, crystal, 7" ..**20.00**

Stanhope, saucer, crystal **10.00**

Twist, baker, Marigold, oval, 9"...................................**60.00**

Twist, bowl, floral; Moongleam, 9" **50.00**

Twist, ice tub, Flamingo.....**125.00**

Twist, platter, crystal, 12"....**15.00**

Victorian, comport, crystal, 5"...**60.00**

Victorian, creamer, crystal...**30.00**

Victorian, vase, crystal, 4"....**50.00**
Waverly, bowl, salad; crystal, 7"..**25.00**
Waverly, cup, crystal **50.00**
Waverly, sugar bowl, crystal, footed **25.00**
Yeoman, bowl, baker; Moongleam, 9".....................................**45.00**
Yeoman, bowl, banana split; Hawthorne, footed **40.00**
Yeoman, plate, crystal, 6".......**3.00**

Imperial

Cape Cod, ashtray, crystal, #160/134/1, 4"................**14.00**
Cape Cod, bowl, fruit; crystal, #160/23b, 5½"................**10.00**
Cape Cod, bowl, jelly; crystal, #160/33, 3"......................**12.00**
Cape Cod, comport, crystal, #160/45, 6"......................**25.00**
Cape Cod, fork, crystal, #160/701 ....**12.00**

Cape Cod, pitcher, crystal, two-quart, $80.00.

Cape Cod, plate, crystal, #160/3d, 7".......................................**8.00**
Cape Cod, plate, crystal, #160/7d, 9"....................................**20.00**
Cape Cod, salt dip, crystal, #160/61 ....**20.00**

Cape Cod, tumbler, crystal, #160, 16-oz **35.00**
Cape Cod, vase, crystal, footed, #160/21, 11½"................**70.00**

Morgantown

Golf Ball, creamer, green or red..........................**175.00**
Golf Ball, schooner, green or red, 8½", 32-oz.....................**295.00**
Golf Ball, stem, cocktail; green or red, 3½-oz, 4½" **26.00**
Queen Louise, plate, salad; crystal w/pink..........................**150.00**
Queen Louise, stem, cocktail; crystal w/pink, 3-oz **375.00**
Queen Louise, stem, water; crystal w/pink, 9-oz..................**400.00**
Sunrise Medallion, cup, crystal..**40.00**
Sunrise Medallion, saucer, blue..**22.50**

Sunrise Medallion, sherbet, blue, $20.00; Sherbet plate, blue, 5⅞", $6.00. (Photo courtesy Gene Florence)

Sunrise Medallion, tumbler, pink or green, footed, 4-oz, 3½" ...**35.00**
Tinkerbell, bowl, finger; azure or green, footed.................**100.00**
Tinkerbell, stem, wine; azure or green, 2½-oz **135.00**
Tinkerbell, vase, azure or green, ruffled top, footed, #36 Uranus, 10" **400.00**

New Martinsville

Janice, basket, blue or red, 11"..**215.00**
Janice, bowl, crystal, 10"......**37.50**
Janice, plate, crystal, 15".....**40.00**

Janice, tall creamer and sugar bowl, red, $45.00 each; on matching handled red tray, $25.00. (Photo courtesy Gene Florence)

Meadow Wreath, bowl, crystal, crimped, #4220/26, 10"..**40.00**
Meadow Wreath, ladle, punch; crystal, #4226.................**55.00**
Meadow Wreath, plate, crystal, #42/26, 14".....................**45.00**

Paden City

Gazebo, bowl, pink, center handle, 9¼", $90.00. (Photo courtesy Gene Florence)

Black Forest, bowl, finger; green, 4½"...................................**40.00**
Black Forest, cake plate, amber, 2" pedestal **95.00**
Black Forest, egg cup, green .**150.00**
Black Forest, plate, luncheon; pink, 8" **40.00**

Black Forest, stem, water; crystal, 9-oz, 6"...........................**22.50**
Black Forest, whipped cream pail, amber...............................**95.00**
Gazebo, cake stand, crystal..**65.00**
Gazebo, creamer, crystal **22.50**
Gazebo, plate, crystal, 10¾".**45.00**
Gazebo, vase, crystal, 10¼"..**75.00**

Tiffin

Cadena, bowl, cream soup; crystal **25.00**
Cadena, oyster cocktail, pink or yellow.............................**30.00**
Cadena, plate, crystal, 9¼"..**45.00**
Cherokee Rose, bowl, finger; crystal, 5".............................**30.00**
Cherokee Rose, plate, luncheon; crystal, 8".......................**15.00**
Cherokee Rose, table bell, crystal.............................**75.00**
Classic, cup, crystal **65.00**
Classic, plate, crystal, 8"......**12.50**
Classic, vase, bud; crystal, 6½"..**27.50**
Flanders, celery dish, crystal, 11".............................**40.00**
Flanders, comport, yellow, 6"..**95.00**
Flanders, vase, bud; crystal .**50.00**
Flanders, vase, fan; pink....**250.00**
Fontaine, candlestick, amber, green or pink, #9758, low...........**35.00**
Fontaine, cup, Twilight, #8869 ....**125.00**
Fontaine, plate, Twilight, #8833, 8".....................................**35.00**
Fuchsia, bell, crystal, #15083, 5" **75.00**
Fuchsia, cup, crystal, #5813.**80.00**
Fuchsia, saucer, crystal, #5833..**15.00**
Julia, bowl, finger; amber **25.00**
Julia, plate, salad; amber.....**14.00**
Julia, sugar, amber..............**35.00**

June Night, bowl, crystal, crimped, 12"..................**75.00**

June Night, bowl, crystal, 3-part, 12½"..............................**65.00**

June Night, stem, parfait; crystal, 4½-oz **38.00**

Jungle Assortment, basket, #151, 6"....................................**95.00**

Jungle Assortment, tumbler, #444, 12-oz **32.00**

Jungle Assortment, vase, wall; #320 ....**75.00**

Psyche, pitcher, crystal with green handle, $395.00. (Photo courtesy Gene Florence)

Psyche, pitcher, crystal w/green handle, w/lid.................**495.00**

Psyche, stem, cocktail; crystal w/green stem..................**40.00**

Psyche, sugar bowl, crystal ..**65.00**

Elvis Presley Memorabilia

The king of rock 'n roll, the greatest entertainer of all time (and not many would disagree with that), Elvis remains just as popular today as he was in the height of his career. Over the past few years, values for Elvis collectibles have skyrocketed. The early items marked 'Elvis Presley Enterprises' bearing a 1956 or 1957 date are the most valuable. Paper goods such as magazines, menus from Las Vegas hotels, ticket stubs, etc., make up a large part of any Elvis collection and are much less expensive. His 45s were sold in abundance, so unless you find an original Sun label, a colored vinyl or a promotional cut, or EPs in wonderful condition, don't pay much! The picture sleeves are usually worth much more than the record itself! Albums are very collectible, and even though you see some stiff prices on them at antique malls, there's not many you can't buy for well under $25.00 at any Elvis convention.

Remember, the early mark is 'Elvis Presley Enterprises'; the 'Boxcar' mark was used from 1974 to 1977, and the 'Boxcar/Factors' mark from then until 1981. In 1982, the trademark reverted back to Graceland.

For more information, we recommend *Elvis Collectibles* and *Best of Elvis Collectibles* by Rosalind Cranor (Overmountain Press): see the Directory under Virginia for ordering information. Also available: *Elvis Presley Memorabilia* by Sean O'Neal (Schiffer).

Bracelet, charm; on card w/deep pink print, EPE, 1956 ..**150.00**

Cards set, Golden Boys, A&BC Gum, 1958, 36 cards......**80.00**

Cigarette lighter, Zippo, 1980s, 6 in series, ea, from $75 to....**100.00**

Clock, guitar shape, blue w/neon light border, 30x12", M **135.00**

Concert pin, laughing portrait, 3⅜"...................................**12.00**

Decanter, McCormick, 1978, Elvis Bust, no music box, 750 ml.................................**75.00**

Decanter, McCormick, 1979, Elvis Gold, plays My Way, 750 ml.......................**175.00**

Decanter, McCormick, 1981, Aloha Elvis, plays Blue Hawaii, 750 ml.................................**150.00**

Decanter, McCormick, 1982, Karate, musical, 14", MIB............**160.00**

Decanter, McCormick, 1984, Sgt Elvis Mini, plays GI Blues, 50 ml...................................**95.00**

Decanter, Yours Elvis, Elvis w/guitar, musical, 1977, MIB **60.00**

Doll, Celebrity Collection, World Doll, 1984, 21", MIB **110.00**

Doll, Comeback Special, black leather, Mattel, NRFB ..**40.00**

Doll, Comeback Special, Hasbro, 1993, NRFB....................**45.00**

Doll, in Army uniform, w/badges, dog tag & duffle bag, Mattel, 12", MIB **45.00**

Doll, in white jumpsuit, w/guitar, Eugene, 1984, 12", MIB...**60.00**

Doll, Teen Idol, Hasbro, 1993, NRFB..............................**42.50**

Figurine, Aloha From Hawaii, lights up, w/guitar, MIB.............**40.00**

Figurine, in white w/guitar, hands raised, Royal Orleans, 10", MIB..............................**55.00**

Flasher ring, 1957, EX minimum value **100.00**

Guitar, Lapin, 1984, MOC (sealed)..........................**75.00**

Hat, felt, 1950s, NM with original picture tag, $135.00. (Photo courtesy Tom Duncan)

Key chain, flasher, full figure on yellow background, 2½x2", EX **20.00**

Lamp, blue suede shoes, EPE, 13x9¼x9¼", M **45.00**

Lighter, w/bust of Elvis, signature on lid, Zippo, 1990, NRFB.............................**85.00**

Menu, Sahara Tahoe Hotel, Elvis photo cover, 1974, 8½x11", M..................................**60.00**

Necklace, Love Me Tender, EPE, 1956, from $175 to.......**225.00**

Ornament, gold figural, Hallmark Keepsake, 1979, MIB, from $20.00 to $25.00.

Ornament, w/guitar, plays Blue Christmas, Carlton Cards, 1995, MIB......................**55.00**

Overnight case, brown, EPE, 1956, 6½x12x9", M **650.00**

Paper doll book, Elvis St Martin's Press, 1982, uncut, EX ..**30.00**

Pen, Tickle Me, feather type, EX 35.00
Pennant, Birthpace Tupelo, EPE, 1962, M 30.00
Pin-back button, Vari-Vue, flicker type, 1960s 38.00
Pistol, black w/turquoise handle, non-working, Franklin Mint, MIB 175.00
Pocketknife, guitar form, portrait & 1935-77, 6" 45.00
Poster, Girl Happy, 1965, 41x27" 110.00
Poster, Trouble w/Girls, 1-sheet, 1969, EX 52.00
Ring, brass w/full-color image under clear bubble, 1956, EX 200.00
Scarf, concert giveaway, silky, M..40.00
Sideburn, sticker from gumball machine, 1950s, EX 55.00
Song book, #1, 15 songs, 15 pictures, 1956, 35-page, EX.............52.50
Tour photo, singing, down on 1 knee, full color, 8x10" 25.00

Enesco

Enesco is an importing company based in Elk Grove, Illinois. They're distributors of ceramic novelties made for them in Japan. There are several lines styled around a particular character or group, and with the emphasis collectors currently place on figurals, they're finding these especially fascinating. During the 1960s, they sold a line of novelties originally called 'Mother-in-the Kitchen.' Today's collectors refer to them as 'Kitchen Prayer Ladies.' Ranging from large items such as canisters and cookie jars to toothpick holders and small picture frames, the line was fairly extensive. Some of the pieces are very hard to find, and those with blue dresses are much scarcer than those in pink. Where we've given ranges, pink is represented by the lower end, blue by the high side. If you find a white piece with blue trim, add another 10% to 20% to the high end.

Another Enesco line that has become very collectible is called 'Kitchen Independence.' It features George Washington with the Declaration of Independence scroll held at his side and Betsy Ross wearing a blue dress and holding a large flag.

Both lines are pictured in *The Collector's Encyclopedia of Cookie Jars, Volumes 2* and *3*, by Joyce and Fred Roerig. See also Cookie Jars.

Air freshener, Kitchen Prayer Lady...............................125.00
Bank, Dear God Kids girl, 1982, from $40 to 45.00
Bank, Mother's Pin Money, Kitchen Prayer Lady, 5½"..........160.00
Banks, Lucy & Me, Prayer Bears, 1987, 5x4", pr..............120.00
Bell, Human Bean, 7 pictured on bell, 6"............................16.00
Bell, Kitchen Prayer Lady....75.00
Candy container, Dear God Kids, boy or girl, 1983, ea, from $45 to 50.00
Canister, Kitchen Prayer Lady, pink, ea........................300.00
Cookie jar, Kitchen Prayer Lady 250.00

Crumb tray or brush, Kitchen Prayer Lady, from $125 to...........**200.00**

Doll, Bong Bong, porcelain head & hands in clown clothes, 13", MIB.................**80.00**

Egg timer, windmill w/2 Dutch kids kissing, 4⅜", NMIB.........**68.00**

Figurine, Basil the Bassett Hound, standing & begging........**65.00**

Figurine, Dear God Kids, nurse, Let's Do Rounds Together, 1983, 4¾".........................**40.00**

Figurine, Eggbert Stacking Doll, Policeman, egg-shaped, set of 4, MIB............................**460.00**

Figurine, Eggbert the Dentist, 2x3", MIB **20.00**

Figurine, I'll...Treasure Your Friendship, Coral Kingdom #910970, 1995..............**110.00**

Figurine, Jeffrey, Bein' a Fireman Sure Is Hot & Thirsty Work, MIB................................**95.00**

Figurine, Mary Had a Little Lamb, 1995, 9", MIB **80.00**

Figurine set, Saints Marching Band, 9 pcs, from $6" to 8½", MIB.................................**95.00**

Figurine set, To Hog & To Hold, Little Piggy wedding set, 9 pcs, MIB **145.00**

Figurine set, Willowbrook Victorian Summer House, 1994, MIB......................**40.00**

Instant coffee jar, spoon-holder loop on side, Kitchen Prayer Lady..............................**120.00**

Jack-in-the-box, Snow White, NM (EX box)..........................**55.00**

Mug, Barbie Nurse, 1994, MIB **30.00**

Mug, coffee; Human Bean Loves Jelly Beans.....................**10.00**

Music box, Eggbert, Lovebird, plays Love Me Tender, 1989, 6½", MIB **240.00**

Music box, roller coaster, plays 6 tunes, MIB **100.00**

Music box, sewing machine w/mice, 6", MIB..............**90.00**

Music box, typewriter w/mice, 1991, EX.........................**90.00**

Napkin holder, pink, Kitchen Prayer Lady **25.00**

Night light, Wimbleduck, Eggbert coming out of tennis ball, 1989 ....**290.00**

North Pole Station, 1987......**80.00**

Ornament, Partners in Crime, dog & cat in shopping bag, 1994, 2½"..................................**30.00**

Ornament, Santa Knitting Scarf, 1994, 2¼"........................**25.00**

Ornament, The Tin Man, 50th Anniversary of Wizard of Oz, MIB................................**40.00**

Planter, Kitchen Prayer Lady ..**120.00**

Plate, Lucy & Me, 1982, 8½"..**125.00**

Ring holder, Kitchen Prayer Lady..............................**85.00**

Salt and pepper shakers, Dear God Kids, 4¾", from $75.00 to $85.00 for the pair. (Photo courtesy Judy Posner)

Snow dome, Eggbert in snow dome on top of golf ball.........**435.00**

Soap dish, Kitchen Prayer Lady.........................**35.00**

Spoon holder, Mary Poppins, musical, $175.00.

Sprinkler bottle, blue, Kitchen Prayer Lady, minimum value **600.00**

String holder, Kitchen Prayer Lady, wall mount.........**175.00**

Tea set, pot, sugar & creamer, Kitchen Prayer Lady ...**250.00**

Teapots, Mr & Mrs Humpty Dumpty, 1950s, 8" & 7", pr, M **160.00**

Vase, bud; pink, Kitchen Prayer Lady..............................**145.00**

Ertl Banks

The Ertl company was founded in the mid-'40s by Fred Ertl, Sr., and until the early 1980s, they produced mainly farm tractors. In 1981 they made their first bank, the 1913 Model T Parcel Post Mail Service #9647; since then they've produced thousands of models with the logos of countless companies. The size of each run is dictated by the client and can vary from a few hundred up to several thousand. Some clients will later add a serial number to the vehicle; this is not done by Ertl.

Other numbers that appear on the base of each bank are a four-number dating code (the first three indicate the day of the year up to 365, and the fourth number is the last digit of the year, '5' for 1995, for instance). The stock number is shown only on the box, never on the bank, so be sure to keep them in their original boxes. Our values are for banks that are mint and in their original boxes. For more information, see *Schroeder's Collectible Toys, Antique to Modern* (Collector Books).

Ace Hardware, 1918 Ford Model T, red w/black roof, white tires, NM...............................**160.00**

Ace Hardware, 1918 Ford Runabout, black, 1,600 made, M (NM+ box)...............**225.00**

American General, 1959 GMC Armoured Truck, M.....**340.00**

Anheuser Busch, 1918 Ford Runabout, #9766, MIB ..**60.00**

Aunt Jemima Pancakes, 1923 Ford Delivery Truck, MIB **40.00**

Batman, Joker Van, MIP, $12.00.

Bethlehem Steel, 1938 Chevy Panel Truck, #3, MIB **45.00**

Borden's Dairy, 1950 Divco Delivery Truck, MIB......**60.00**

Brinks, 1995 GMC Armored Truck, #0555F, MIB **110.00**

Budweiser, Clydesdales 8-Horse Hitch & Wagon, 4x19", MIB **65.00**

Budweiser, 1947 Studebaker Pick-Up, #H856, MIB.............**50.00**

Budweiser, 1954 GMC Delivery Tractor Trailer, #27170, MIB **75.00**

Chicago Bears, 1951 GMC Panel Van, NM **40.00**

Coca-Cola, 1923 Ford Delivery Truck, MIB.....................**40.00**

Conoco, 1926 Mack Tanker Truck, #9750, MIB....................**60.00**

Dairy Queen, 1951 GMC Panel Van, #2054, MIB............**40.00**

Federal Express, Grumman Stepvan, #9334, NM (EX box) **60.00**

Green Bay Packers, 1969 Ford Mustang, MIB...............**40.00**

Gulf Oil, 1925 Kenworth Wrecker, MIB................................**75.00**

Harley-Davidson, 1926 Mack Truck, #2, w/crates, NM (NM box) **210.00**

Iowa Hawkeyes, 1913 Ford Model T Delivery Van, #0933G, MIB **190.00**

John Deere Servicegard, #104, 1918 Ford Model T, MIB..........**50.00**

Lennox, 1905 Ford Delivery Truck, #4, MIB...............**55.00**

Michigan J Frog, Warner Brothers, 1917 Maxwell Touring Car, MIB.............................**105.00**

North Amercan Van Lines, 1917 Ford Delivery Van, MIB **40.00**

Penn State, 1912 Open Cab, MIB **45.00**

Pepe Le Pew & Penelope, Warner Brothers, VW Convertible, MIB................................**65.00**

Sinclair Oil, 1946 White Tilt-Cab Tanker, #8, MIB **50.00**

State Farm, 1913 Ford Delivery Van, EX **40.00**

State Farm, 1918 Ford Runabout, red w/black roof, MIB ...**90.00**

Texaco, The Texas Company, 1913 Model T Truck, #2128, MIB **1,075.00**

Texaco, The Texas Company, 1932 Ford Van, NM **75.00**

Texaco, Wings of Texaco 1929 Lockheed Air Express, Series #1, MIB.........................**175.00**

Texaco, 1926 Mack Tanker Truck, 1985, NM.....................**140.00**

Texaco, 1929 Mack Fire Truck, Collector Series #15, MIB **365.00**

Texaco, 1932 Ford Delivery Van, EX+ **75.00**

Texaco, 1934 Doodle Bug, #11, MIB, $25.00.

True Value, 1913 Ford Model T Delivery Van, #1482Z, NM **105.00**

True Value, 1926 Mack Delivery Van, MIB........................**80.00**

University of Kentucky, 1918 Ford Tanker Truck, blue & white, MIB.............................**105.00**

Washington Redskins, 1969 Ford Mustang, Goal Line Series #6, MIB.................................**70.00**

Watkins, 1957 Chevy, MIB ..**50.00**

25th Anniverary, 1957 Chevy Nomad, MIB..................**50.00**

Fenton

The Fenton glass company, organized in 1906 in Martin's Ferry, Ohio, is noted for their fine art glass. Over one hundred thirty patterns of carnival glass were made in their earlier years, but even their newer glass is considered collectible. Only since 1970 have some of the pieces carried a molded-in logo; before then paper labels were used. For more information we recommend *Fenton Art Glass, 1907 to 1939*, and *Fenton Art Glass Patterns, 1939 to 1980*, both by Margaret and Kenn Whitmyer. Two of their later lines, Hobnail and Silver Crest, are shown in Gene Florence's book called *Collectible Glassware of the 40s, 50s, and 60s*. All are published by Collector Books. See also Glass Animals; Glass Shoes. For information on Fenton Art Glass Collectors of America, see Clubs and Newsletters.

Apple Blossom, bonbon, 1960-61, 8", from $20 to.................**25.00**

Apple Blossom, candle holder, 1960-61, from $35 to......**42.50**

Aqua Crest, bowl, double crimped, #192, 1942-43, 10½", from $65 to........**70.00**

Aqua Crest, creamer, #680, 1949-54, from $40 to..............**45.00**

Basket Weave, bowl, lavender satin, #8222, 1977-78 ....**35.00**

Block & Star, creamer, milk glass, 1955-57, from $10 to......**12.00**

Block & Star, tumbler, milk glass, 1955-58, 12-oz, from $15 to..........................**22.00**

Bubble Optic/Honeycomb, vase, Apple Green, 1961-62, 5", from $35 to.....................**45.00**

Bubble Optic/Honeycomb, vase, Coral, pinched, 1961-62, 8", from $60 to.....................**85.00**

Burmese, tulip vase, hand-painted roses, #7255, 1977-80 ..**150.00**

Burmese, vase, hand-painted roses, #7251, 1973-76, 11".......**250.00**

Burred Hobnail, witch's kettle, milk glass, 1950-69, from $10 to....................................**12.00**

Cactus, basket, milk glass, 1959-60, from $25 to...............**35.00**

Cactus, basket, topaz opalescent, #3439, 1959-60, 9".......**165.00**

Cactus, creamer & sugar bowl, milk glass, w/lid, 1959-62, from $30 to.....................**40.00**

Cactus, cruet, milk glass, 1959-61, from $30 to....................**32.00**

Coin Dot, basket, lime opalescent, #1437, 1953 – 1954, 7", from $150.00 to $185.00. (Photo courtesy Margaret and Kenn Whitmyer)

Coin Dot, vase, topaz opalescent, #1442, 1959, 10".........**155.00**

Coin Dot, vase, topaz opalescent, #1458, 1959, 8".............**175.00**

Daisy & Button, basket, Colonial Green, oval, 1965-73, from $8 to.....................**10.00**

Daisy & Button, basket, milk glass, 1953-55, 4", from $18 to..**20.00**

Daisy & Button, basket, orange, oval, 1965-70, from $10 to.........**12.00**

Daisy & Button, bell, blue satin, 1973-80+, from $25 to....**35.00**

Daisy & Button, boot, Carnival, 1970-75, from $20 to......**22.00**

Daisy & Button, leaf ashtray, Colonial Amber, 1968-70, from $8 to.......................**10.00**

Daisy & Button, vase, Green Pastel, cupped/footed, 1954-56, 8", from $45 to.........**50.00**

Diamond Optic, candy jar, Colonial Amber, 1962-65, from $25 to.....................**35.00**

Diamond Optic, vase, Colonial Blue, 1962-64, 10½", from $45 to.......................**55.00**

Emerald Crest, bonbon, double crimped, #36, 1949-56, 5½", from $24 to.....................**28.00**

Empress, comport, Colonial Pink, footed, #9229, 1962-64...**16.00**

Empress, vase, black, #8252, 1968-69.....................**65.00**

Flame Crest, bowl, double crimped, #7321, 1963, 11½".........**95.00**

Hobnail, apothecary jar, green, 1964-70, from $55 to......**65.00**

Hobnail, ashtray, blue opalescent, oval, 1941-55, from $15 to................**18.00**

Hobnail, ashtray, orange, round, 1965-66, from $3 to.........**5.00**

Hobnail, banana bowl, topaz opalescent, 1959-60, from $150 to.........................**185.00**

Hobnail, basket, bluebells decor, #3839, 1971-72, 12".....**135.00**

Hobnail, basket, Colonial Amber, 1967-80+, 7", from $20 to................**25.00**

Hobnail, basket, milk glass, deep, 1963-78, 7", from $50 to.....................**60.00**

Hobnail, basket, Rose Pastel, 1954-57, 4½", from $25 to........**30.00**

Hobnail, bell, French opalescent, 1978-81, 6", from $35 to **45.00**

Hobnail, bonbon, Lime Green opalescent, double crimped, 1952-55, 6"......................**25.00**

Hobnail, bowl, Blue Marble, footed, 1970-74, 10", from $45 to.................**50.00**

Hobnail, bowl, cranberry, flared, oval, 1940-44, 7", from $35 to.................**40.00**

Hobnail, bowl, plum opalescent, 1959-63, 9", from $85 to **95.00**

Hobnail, candle bowl, blue opalescent, footed, 1978-79, from $40 to.............**45.00**

Hobnail, candle holder, ruby, 1972-80+, from $12 to....**14.00**

Hobnail, candy box, Colonial Blue, footed, 1966-70, from $35 to.....................**45.00**

Hobnail, cigarette box, milk glass, 1962-72, from $25 to......**35.00**

Hobnail, creamer & sugar bowl, French opalescent, 1940-57, from $35 to.....................**45.00**

Hobnail, fairy light, milk glass w/roses decor, #3608, 1974-75.........**40.00**

Hobnail, epergne, plum opalescent, three-lily, #371, made for Le Vay in 1984, $375.00. (Photo courtesy Lee Garmon)

Hobnail, jug, milk glass, 1964-80+, 70-oz, 9½", from $60 to.. **75.00**

Hobnail, rose bowl, blue opalescent, 1940-44, 4½", from $30 to. **35.00**

Hobnail, slipper, ruby, 1966-80, from $15 to **17.00**

Hobnail, toothpick holder, crystal, 1960s, from $4 to **6.00**

Hobnail, tumbler, cranberry opalescent, #3947, 1952-67, 12-oz. **40.00**

Hobnail, vase, Apple Green overlay, 1961-62, 8", from $40 to ... **45.00**

Hobnail, vase, cranberry opalescent, #189, 1947-51, 10" **145.00**

Hobnail, vase, Honey Amber, 1961-63, 11", from $65 to **85.00**

Hobnail, vase, orange, 1977-78, 11", from $30 to.............. **32.00**

Hobnail, vase, Rose Pastel, double crimped, 1954-57, 4½", $14 to **15.00**

Mandarin, vase, French opalescent, #8251, 1968 .... **155.00**

Mandarin, vase, milk glass, #8251, 1968-69 .... **85.00**

Melon Ribbed, pitcher, rose, #7464, 1960s, sm **55.00**

Mermaid, planter/vase, Carnival, #8254, 1970-72 .... **95.00**

Patriot, planter, Independence Blue Carnival, #8499, 1975 ..... **35.00**

Peach Crest, ewer, melon ribs, 9½", $65.00.

Peach Crest, vase, ruffled/crimped, #6059, 1956-59, 8½" **85.00**

Pinwheel, comport, ruby iridescent, #8227, 1976-77 ..... **45.00**

Rose, compote, black, #9222, 1979 .... **30.00**

Rose, compote, orange, double crimped, #9223, 1964-73.. **12.00**

Rose, shakers, Colonial Amber, #9206, 1967-58, pr **20.00**

Rose Crest, jug, #192-A, 1946-48, 9", from $125 to **150.00**

Silver Crest, bonbon, 2-tier, 1980+, from $35 to **42.00**

Silver Crest, cake plate, #680, 1952-80, 13", from $35 to **45.00**

Silver Crest, top hat, 1968-69, 8", from $100 to **145.00**

Spiral Optic, candy box, blue opalescent, 1979-80, from $75 to **85.00**

Spiral Optic, fairy light, cameo opalescent, 1979-80, from $45 to **55.00**

Spiral Optic, tumbler, cranberry, 1938-40, #187, 9-oz, from $45 to **50.00**

Thumbprint, anniversary bowl, Colonial Pink, #4484, 1963-66..................................**64.00**

Thumbprint, butter dish, Colonial Pink, #4477, 1965-66.....**22.00**

Thumbprint, compote, milk glass, w/lid, #4484, 1956..........**40.00**

Thumbprint, jug, Colonial Blue, ice lip, #4464, 1964-66, 2-qt..**60.00**

Thumbprint, salt shakers, Colonial Pink, #4408, 1963-67, pr **30.00**

Thumbprint, sherbet, Colonial Green, #4443, 1963-70.....**9.00**

Valencia, basket, orange, #8338, 1970-72, 8"......................**21.00**

Valencia, bowl, Colonial Green, flared, #8329, 1969-71...**20.00**

Violets in the Snow, bud vase, 1976-80, from $30 to......**35.00**

Violets in the Snow, comport, footed, #7429, 1968-83.........**45.00**

Violets in the Snow, vase, #7252, 1969-70, 7"......................**60.00**

Fiesta

Since it was discontinued by Homer Laughlin in 1973, Fiesta has become one of the most popular collectibles on the market. Values have continued to climb until some of the more hard-to-find items now sell for several hundred dollars each. In 1986 HLC reintroduced a line of new Fiesta that buyers should be aware of. To date these colors have been used: cobalt (darker than the original), rose (a strong pink), black, white, apricot (very pale), yellow (a light creamy tone), turquoise, sea mist (a light mint green), lilac, persimmon, periwinkle (country blue), sapphire (very close to the original cobalt), chartreuse (brighter), gray, juniper (teal), cinnabar (maroon), sunflower (yellow), plum (dark bluish-purple), and shamrock (similar to the coveted medium green). When old molds were used, the mark will be the same, if it is a molded-in mark such as on pitchers, sugar bowls, etc. The ink stamp differs from the old — now all the letters are upper case.

'Original colors' in the listings indicates values for three of the original six colors — light green, turquoise, and yellow. The listing that follows is incomplete due to space restrictions; refer to *Post86 Fiesta* by Richard Racheter and *The Collector's Encyclopedia of Fiesta, Ninth Edition*, by Sharon and Bob Huxford (Collector Books) for more information. See also Clubs and Newsletters for information on *Fiesta Collector's Quarterly*.

Coffeepot, demitasse; red, cobalt, or ivory, **$550.00**; original colors, **$425.00**; Cup, demitasse; red, cobalt, or ivory, **$80.00**; original colors, **$68.00**; '50s colors, **$375.00**.

Ashtray, original colors **48.00**
Bowl, covered onion soup; cobalt or
 ivory..............................**725.00**
Bowl, cream soup; '50s colors..**75.00**
Bowl, dessert; original colors,
 6"..............................**40.00**
Bowl, fruit; '50s colors, 5½"..**40.00**
Bowl, fruit; red, cobalt or ivory,
 4¾"..............................**35.00**
Bowl, individual salad; red,
 turquoise or yellow, 7½"..**90.00**
Bowl, nappy, original colors,
 8½"..............................**42.00**
Bowl, salad; footed, original col-
 ors..............................**340.00**
Candle holders, bulb; original col-
 ors, pr **110.00**
Casserole, French; yellow...**300.00**
Coffeepot, original colors....**195.00**
Compote, sweets; original col-
 ors..............................**80.00**
Creamer, '50s colors..............**40.00**
Creamer, original colors.......**22.00**
Egg cup, original colors **60.00**
Marmalade, original colors..**245.00**
Mixing bowl, #1, original colors.**180.00**
Mixing bowl, #2, original colors..**115.00**
Mixing bowl, #3, original colors..**125.00**
Mixing bowl, #4, original colors..**130.00**
Mug, Tom & Jerry, ivory w/gold
 letters **65.00**
Pitcher, disk juice; yellow.....**48.00**

**Pitcher, jug, two-pint, original col-
ors, $88.00; red, cobalt, or ivory,
$120.00; '50s colors, $150.00.**

Plate, '50s colors, 6"................**9.00**
Plate, '50s colors, 10"...........**52.00**
Plate, calendar; 1955, 9".......**50.00**
Plate, chop; original colors, 13"..**42.00**
Plate, compartment; red, cobalt or
 ivory, 10½" **45.00**
Plate, deep; '50s colors..........**58.00**
Plate, original colors, 9" **12.00**
Plate, red, cobalt or ivory, 10"..**40.00**
Platter, red, cobalt or ivory..**45.00**
Relish tray base, original colors..**75.00**
Relish tray side insert, original
 colors..............................**50.00**
Saucer, original colors **4.00**
Sugar bowl, yellow, individual.**125.00**
Syrup, original colors..........**375.00**
Teacup, original colors..........**25.00**
Teapot, original colors, lg...**210.00**
Teapot, red, cobalt or ivory,
 med **225.00**
Tray, utility; red, cobalt or ivory..**42.00**
Vase, bud; original colors **85.00**
Vase, red, cobalt or ivory, 8"..**700.00**

Kitchen Kraft

**Covered jug, light green or yellow,
$280.00; red or cobalt, $290.00.**

Bowl, mixing; light green or yellow, 10".........................**115.00**
Bowl, mixing; red or cobalt,
 10".............................**125.00**
Cake plate, light green or yel-
 low **55.00**

Casserole, light green or yellow, individual **150.00**

Casserole, red or cobalt, 7½"..**90.00**

Covered jar, red or cobalt, sm..**300.00**

Fork, light green or yellow.**125.00**

Pie plate, light green or yellow, 9" **45.00**

Platter, red or cobalt............. **75.00**

Spoon, light green or yellow ..**135.00**

Stacking refrigerator lid, light green or yellow............... **75.00**

Stacking refrigerator unit, red or cobalt **58.00**

Post '86 Line

Candle holder, bulb; lilac, pr ..**200.00**

Carafe, sapphire, from $40 to..**50.00**

Casserole, lilac, w/lid, 6x9½", from $85 to **95.00**

Clock, sapphire, made from plate, from $80 to **90.00**

Coffee server, lilac, from $175 to............................. **225.00**

Coffeepot, juniper, from $35 to **45.00**

Coffeepot, lilac, from $175.00 to $225.00.

Creamer & sugar bowl w/lid (handleless), lilac, from $110 to................................ **125.00**

Lamp, apricot, for JC Penney..**125.00**

Pitcher, disk water; apricot, from $40 to **50.00**

Pitcher, disk water; lilac, from $65 to **75.00**

Pitcher, mini disk; apricot, from $45 to **55.00**

Pitcher, mini disk; lilac, from $75 to **90.00**

Place setting, apricot, 5-pc, from $55 to **70.00**

Place setting, lilac, 5-pc...... **185.00**

Place setting, sapphire, 5-pc, from $180 to **200.00**

Plate, dinner; chartreuse, from $9 to **12.00**

Plate, dinner; sapphire, from $35 to **40.00**

Sauce boat, lilac, from $100 to **110.00**

Teapot, apricot, 7½", from $50 to **60.00**

Vase, lilac, 10", from $250 to .**300.00**

Vase, sapphire, 10", from $150 to **165.00**

Fishbowl Ornaments

Mermaids, divers, and all sorts of castles have been devised to add interest to fishbowls and aquariums. Many were made in Japan and imported decades ago to be sold in 5-&-10¢ stores along with the millions of other figural novelties that flooded the market after the war. The condition of the glaze is very important. For more information we recommend *Collector's Guide to Made in Japan Ceramics* by Carole Bess White (Collector Books). Unless noted otherwise, the examples in the listing that follows were produced in Japan.

Bathing beauty on turtle, red, tan & green on white, 2½"...**25.00**

Boy riding dolphin on wave, multicolored matt glazes, 3¾"..**25.00**

Castles, multicolored, left to right, black mark, 3¾"; unmarked, 4½", each from $15.00 to $20.00. (Photo courtesy Carole Bess White)

Castle w/arch, multicolored, 2½" or 3½", ea **20.00**

Colonade w/palm tree, green, blue & white, 3¾x4" **20.00**

Doorway, stone entry w/open aqua wood-look door, 2".........**15.00**

Fish riding waves, 2 white fish on cobalt waves, 3½x3".......**22.00**

Lighthouse, orange, yellow & brown, 2x2½" **16.00**

Lighthouse, tan, black, brown & green, 6½x4" **26.00**

Mermaid on sea horse, white, green & orange glossy glazes, 3¼" **25.00**

Mermaid on snail, 4", from $35 to **45.00**

Mermaid on 2 seashells, multicolored matt glazes, 3½", from $30 to............................**40.00**

Nude on starfish, bisque, 4½", from $40 to **50.00**

Pagoda, triple roof, blue, green & maroon, 5½x3¼" **20.00**

Sign on tree trunk, No Fishing, brown, black & white, 2½x4" **12.00**

Torii gate, multicolored glossy glazes, 3¾" **22.00**

Fisher-Price

Since about 1930 the Fisher-Price Company has produced distinctive wooden toys covered with brightly colored lithographed paper. Plastic parts were first added in 1949. The most valuable Fisher-Price toys are those modeled after well-known Disney characters and having the Disney logo. A little edge wear and some paint dulling are normal to these well-loved toys and to be expected; our prices are for toys in very good played-with condition. Mint-in-box examples are extremely scarce and worth from 20% to 40% more.

Our advisor for this category is Brad Cassity. For further information we recommend *A Pictorial Guide to the More Popular Toys, Fisher-Price Toys, 1931 – 1990,* by Gary Combs and Brad Cassity; *Fisher-Price, A Historical Rarity Value Guide,* by John J. Murray and Bruce R. Fox (Books Americana); and *Schroeder's Collectible Toys, Antique to Modern* (Collector Books). See also Dolls; Fisher-Price; and Clubs and Newsletters for information on the Fisher-Price Collectors Club.

#6 Ducky Cart, 1948-49........**50.00**

#102 Drummer Bear, 1931....**700.00**

#110 Puppy Playhouse, 1978-80..**10.00**

#118 Tumble Tower Game, 1972-75, w/10 marbles............**10.00**

#123 Roller Chime, 1953-60 & Easter 1961 ....**35.00**

#131 Toy Wagon, 1951-54 ....**225.00**

#140 Coaster Boy, 1941 ......**700.00**

#145 Musical Elephant, 1948-50 ....**200.00**

#150 Barky Budd, 1934-35 ....**600.00**

#152 Road Roller, 1934-35 ....**700.00**

#154, Frisky Frog, 1971 – 1983, $25.00. (Photo courtesy Brad Cassity)

#158 Katie Kangaroo, 1976-77, squeeze bulb & she hops ..**25.00**

#161 Looky Chug-Chug, 1949-52............................**200.00**

#175 Kicking Donkey, 1937-38 ....**450.00**

#177 Oscar the Grouch, 1977-84 ....**20.00**

#190 Gabby Duck, 1939-40 & Easter 1941 ....**350.00**

#198 Band Wagon, 1940-41 ....**350.00**

#210 Pluto the Pup, 1936-38 ....**150.00**

#300 Scoop Ladder, 1975-77 ....**15.00**

#305 Walking Duck Cart, 1957-64 ....**40.00**

#311 Bulldozer, 1976-77 ....**20.00**

#314 Husky Boom Crane, 1978-82 ....**25.00**

#338 Husky Power Tow Truck, 1982-84 ....**25.00**

#344 Copter Rig, 1981-84 .....**10.00**

#353 Adventure People Scuba Divers, 1976-81 ....**15.00**

#360 Go 'N Back Jumbo, 1931-34, windup..........................**900.00**

#375 Bruno Back-Up, 1932 ....**800.00**

#404 Bunny Egg Cart, 1949 ....**75.00**

#407 Chick Cart, 1950-53.....**50.00**

#423 Jumping Jack Scarecrow, 1979 ....**5.00**

#434 Ferdinand the Bull, 1939 ....**600.00**

#448, Mini Copter, blue lithograph, 1971 – 1984, $10.00. (Photo courtesy Brad Cassity)

#460 Movie Viewer, 1973-85, crank handle **8.00**

#473 Merry Mutt, 1949-54 & Easter 1955 ....**50.00**

#479 Donald Duck & Nephews, 1941-42 ....**400.00**

#494 Pinocchio, 1939-40 .....**600.00**

#500 Pushy Pig, 1932-35 ....**500.00**

#507 Pushy Doodle, 1933 ...**850.00**

#517 Choo-Choo Local, 1936....**550.00**

#530 Mickey Mouse Band, 1935-36 ....**800.00**

#600 Tailspin Tabby Pop-Up, 1947 ....**250.00**

#616 Chuggy Pop-Up, 1955-56....**75.00**

#628 Tug-A-Bug, 1975-77 ....**5.00**

#637 Milk Carrier, 1966-85..**15.00**

#642 Dinky Engine, 1959, black litho................................**60.00**

#656 Bossy Bell, 1961-63, no bonnet, new litho design **45.00**

#666 Creative Blocks, 1978-90 ....**10.00**

#700 Popeye, 1935 ....**700.00**
#703 Popeye the Sailor, 1936 ....**700.00**
#712 Johnny Jumbo, 1933-35 ....**550.00**
#723 Bouncing Bunny Cart, 1936...........................**350.00**
#728 Pound & Saw Bench, 1966-67....................................**25.00**
#740 Pushcart Pete, 1936-67....**600.00**
#757 Howdy Bunny, 1939-40....**350.00**
#760 Racing Ponies, 1936....**350.00**
#765 Dandy Dobbin, 1941-44....**175.00**
#773 Tip-Toe Turtle, 1962-77, vinyl tail **10.00**
#777 Pushy Bruno, 1933 ....**725.00**
#793 Jolly Jumper, 1963-64 & Easter 1965 ....**40.00**
#795 Mickey Mouse Drummer, 1937 ....**700.00**
#799 Duckie Transport, 1937....**400.00**
#845 Farm Truck, 1954-55.....**250.00**
#905 This Little Pig, 1959-62....**30.00**

#919, Movie Box Movie Camera, 1968 – 1970, $40.00. (Photo courtesy Brad Cassity)

#932 Ferry Boat, 1979-80.....**30.00**
#943 Lift & Load Railroad, 1978-79 ....**45.00**
#962 Woodsey's Airport, 1980-81, complete **10.00**
#979 Dump Truckers Playset, 1965-67 ....**75.00**

#990 Play Family A-Frame, 1974-76 ....**50.00**
#994 Play Family Camper, 1973-76 ....**50.00**
#2360 Little People Jetliner, 1986-88 ....**10.00**
#2504 Little People Garage, 1986, rare **55.00**
#4520 Highway Dump Truck, 1985-86 ....**15.00**
#4552 Jeep CJ-7 Renegade, 1985...........................**20.00**

Fishing Collectibles

Very much in evidence at flea markets these days, old fishing gear has become extremely collectible. Early twentieth-century plugs were almost entirely carved from wood, sprayed with several layers of enamel, and finished off with glass eyes. Molded plastics were of a later origin. Some of the more collectible manufacturers are James Heddon, Shakespeare, Rhodes, and Pflueger. Rods, reels, old advertising calendars, and company catalogs are also worth your attention. For more information we recommend *Nineteenth-Century Fishing Lures* by Arlan Carter; *Captain John's Fishing Tackle Price Guide* by John A. Kolbeck & Russell E. Lewis; *Fishing Lure Collectibles, Vol. One* by Dudley Murphy and Rick Edmisten; *Fishing Lure Collectibles, Vol. Two* by Dudley and Deanie Murphy; *The Heddon Legacy, A Century of Classic Lures* by Bill Roberts & Rob Pavey; *Modern Fishing Lure Collectibles, Vol. 1* and

2 by Russell E. Lewis; *Collector's Encyclopedia to Creek Chub Lures and Collectibles* by Harold E. Smith, MD; and *Commercial Fish Decoys* by Frank R. Baron. All are published by Collector Books.

Lures

Atlantic Lure, Frantic Antic, jitterbug-type, 2¾", from $10 to **12.00**

Bagley, Slo-dancer #4, flatfish type w/orange belly, 3½" **25.00**

Bagley Bait Co, Chatter Shad, black on chartreuse, 3", MOC.....**20.00**

Barracuda, Reflecto Spoon, #8, 2¾", MIB **10.00**

Burke, La-Z-Liz, 2 trebles, M, minimum value **25.00**

Butch Harris, Fas-Bak, staple hardware molded into casting, 2¼", M **15.00**

Diamond Jim, black & yellow marbleized paint, 2 trebles, 3¾" **17.50**

Fin-Wing, round decal type, 3", M, minimum value..............**50.00**

Garcia, Lippy Lure, 2 trebles, ¼-oz size, MIP.........................**20.00**

Herter's, minnow, shiny gold & black, 2 trebles, 3¼", MIP **10.00**

Hofschneider, Red Eye No 2P-C, 1950s, 2¼", MIB **20.00**

Lazy Ike, Skitter Ike, protruding eyes, 2 trebles, 3", from $8 to **10.00**

Les Davis, Hering Dodger #0, MOC, from $8 to **10.00**

Lucky Strike, Pi-Kee, 2-pc, 3 trebles, MIB, minimum value.......**50.00**

Makinen, Merry Widow, painted wood, no eyes, 2 trebles, 3¾", from $8 to **20.00**

Mille Mouse, wood, bead eyes, leather tail & ears, 2", 1½", M **90.00**

Normak, OK-doke, plastic, 2 trebles, MIB w/insert, minimum value **20.00**

Ozark Woodchopper, rainbow colored, ½-oz size, from $12 to..........**18.00**

Pflueger, Pal-O-Mine #5073, rainbow paint with carved eye, 4½", M, $30.00. (M with plastic-top cardboard box, $50.00+.) (Photo courtesy Russell E. Lewis)

Prez, plastic peanut-shaped spinner, 2 trebles, ⅓-oz class, MIB **25.00**

Rebel Brand (Pradco), Rattlin' Firetail Floater, plastic, from $8 to **12.00**

Shurebite, Shedevil, black & yellow, 1940s, from $15 to...**20.00**

Suick, Musky Thriller, plastic, 2 trebles, 4½", from $12 to.......**20.00**

Turner, Spoon #F1551, red & white, M in 2-pc box, from $20 to **30.00**

Reels

Pflueger Supreme, pair with double handles, good working order, $50.00 for the pair.

Abu-Ambassadeur 5000, common model, from $50 to **70.00**

Cardinal, spinning, mininum value **75.00**

Classic Pflueger Supreme, Patent Pending, M w/inserts etc in bag **100.00**

Shakespeare Criteron Level Winding, VG **45.00**

Shakespeare Marhoff Level Winding, MIB **45.00**

Shakespeare Model 2065 Spin Wonder, MIB, minimum value **50.00**

South Bend Bait Casting Cast-Oreno Model 16, M in bag, minimum value **30.00**

Utica Reel, early auto fly reel, values vary by models, from $20 to **60.00**

Miscellaneous

Casting weight, Abu-Carcia, ⅜-oz, 2⅛" L, from $5 to **15.00**

Creel, woven reed, round with square hole in top, unknown maker, 1950s, 6½x13x6½", EX, $75.00.

Decoy, Bear Creek, Ice King, plastic spearing type, MIB, from $50 to **75.00**

Fly line cleaner, Orvis, in EX tin container, from $5 to **10.00**

Hooks, Wright & McGill Eagle Claw Treble Hooks #375, ¼ gross, MIB **5.00**

Line, Ashaway, 2 unopened spools in cardboard box, from $15 to **22.00**

Line winder, boxwood w/bone spindles, 7", EX **22.00**

Rod, Kitkast Pocket Rod, extendable, M (G box)..............**33.00**

Tackle box, aluminum, embossed Gut Cast Box, 4½" dia ...**42.00**

Flashlights

The flashlight was invented in 1898 and has been produced by the Eveready Company ever since. Eveready dominated the flashlight market for most of this time, but more than one hundred twenty-five other U.S. flashlight companies have come and gone, providing competition along the way. Add to that number over thirty-five known foreign flashlight manufacturers, and you end up with over one thousand different models of flashlights to collect. They come in a wide variety of styles, shapes, and sizes. The flashlight field includes tubular, lanterns, figural, novelty, litho, etc. At present, over forty-five different categories of flashlights have been identified as collectible. For further information we recommend consulting the *Flashlight Collectors of America*, see Clubs and Newsletters.

Eveready, Masterlite, sq body, red, 7", EX.............................**20.00**

Eveready #2631, logo on butt end, EX **15.00**

Eveready, ca 1920s – 1930s, 7½", VG, $35.00. (Photo courtesy Bill Utley)

Genesy Electric Lantern Co Kansas MO, metal w/wood handle, EX......................**30.00**

Justrite, swivel head w/sq body, takes 8 D cells, VG+......**17.50**

Phillips, Red Head, 1925, EX..**80.00**

Ray-O-Vac, Patented December 3, 1929, working, G+.........**25.00**

Ray-O-Vac, Solid Copper, 1950s, VG..................................**25.00**

Siemens Handdynamo, squeeze action, VG (VG box).......**50.00**

Flower Frogs

Nearly every pottery company and glasshouse in America produced their share of figural flower frogs, and many were imported from Japan as well. They were probably most popular from about 1910 through the 1940s, coinciding not only with the heyday of American glass and ceramics, but with the gracious, much less hectic style of living the times allowed. Way before a silk flower or styrofoam block was ever dreamed of, there were fresh cut flowers on many a dining room sideboard or table, arranged in shallow console bowls with matching frogs such as

we've described in the following listings. For further information see *Collector's Guide to Made in Japan Ceramics, Identification and Values,* by Carole Bess White (Collector Books). See also specific pottery and glass companies.

Bird on grassy base, orange w/yellow & black wings, ceramic, 4x3".................................**22.50**

Bird on stump, dark blue & brown, ceramic, Made in Japan, 9x4"....................**40.00**

Bird on stump, shades of green with red crest, Made in Japan, 7¼", $30.00. (Photo courtesy Nada Sue Knauss)

Bird on stump, shiny multicolors, 3 holes, ceramic, Made in Japan, 4½" **36.00**

Butterfly on flower, multicolor, majolica-like pottery, 2x2½".........**30.00**

Fish lying flat, shiny blue, pottery, 5 holes in back, 1½x3¾".....**22.50**

Frog, shiny white w/details, ceramic, 3x4"..................**45.00**

Frog on lily pad, ceramic, Dept 56 B St John, 3x6½"...........**30.00**

Giraffe neck & head, ceramic, Roselane 603, 10", NM..**49.00**

Green Jade-ite, 1½x3" dia **40.00**

Hedgehog, blue & white, ceramic, marked Delft, 2¼" **48.00**

Loop holder, cast iron, marked JPO Patd, 1930s, 4½", VG **43.00**

Nude lady on rock, shiny white, ceramic, Made in Japan, 7x5x4" **28.00**

Nude lady w/hand to hair, white porcelain, Germany, #5911, 6¼" **110.00**

Nude sitting on rock putting up her hair, ceramic, Haeger, 7x4¾" **50.00**

Owl, brown w/white, ceramic, Made in Japan, 3¾" **18.00**

Parrot, blue w/multicolor feathers, ceramic, Made in Japan, 6¾" **40.00**

Parrot, red-orange w/green & yellow, ceramic, 5-hole, unmarked, 4½" **27.50**

Rooster, multicolor, ceramic, 14 holes, unmarked, 10½" ..**30.00**

Rose holder, double; lead, 1¾x4½x3", EX **72.00**

Sea gull (in flight), crystal glass, 10 holes, Cambridge, 10" **40.00**

Snowflake, cast iron, 12 sm holes, Japan, EX **35.00**

Turtle, cast iron, insert removes, 3x6" **60.00**

Water lilies, unmarked majolica, 1x5", pr **36.00**

'40s, '50s, and '60s Glassware

Remember the lovely dishes mother used back when you were a child? Many collectors do. With scarcity of the older Depression glassware items that used to be found in every garage sale or flea market, glass collectors have refocused their interests and altered buying habits to include equally interesting glassware from more recent years, often choosing patterns that bring back warm childhood memories. For an expanded listing and more information, see *Collectible Glassware from the 40s, 50s, and 60s,* by Gene Florence (Collector Books). See also Anchor Hocking.

Cambridge

Cascade, ashtray, crystal, 8" ..**20.00**

Cascade, candlestick, green, 5" ..**35.00**

Cascade, celery bowl, crystal, 3-part, 10" **20.00**

Cascade, creamer, yellow or green **20.00**

Cascade, plate, salad; crystal, 8½" **9.00**

Cascade, plate, torte; crystal, 4-footed, 14" **30.00**

Cascade, punch cup, crystal ...**7.50**

Cascade, shakers, crystal, pr ..**20.00**

Cascade, vase, green, 9½" **75.00**

Square, bowl, crystal, shallow, 12" **35.00**

Square, creamer, crystal **10.00**

Square, decanter, crystal, 32-oz..**95.00**

Square, stem, iced tea; crystal, 12-oz................................**12.00**

Square, two-part relish, crystal, 6½", **$17.50.** (Photo courtesy Gene Florence)

Square, tumbler, low sherbet; crystal **10.00**

Federal Glass Co

Golden Glory, bowl, dessert; white w/gold decor, 4⅝" **4.50**

Golden Glory, cup & saucer, white w/gold decor **4.00**

Golden Glory, plate, dinner; white w/gold decor, 10" **6.50**

Golden Glory, tumbler, white w/gold decor, footed, 9-oz **10.00**

Heritage, bowl, berry; blue or green, 5" **80.00**

Heritage, cup & saucer, crystal..**8.00**

Heritage, plate, dinner; crystal, 9¼" **12.00**

Park Avenue, ashtray, crystal, 4½" sq **7.00**

Park Avenue, candle holder, crystal, 5" **8.00**

Park Avenue, tumbler, iced tea; yellow, 12-oz, 5⅛" **14.00**

Pioneer, bowl, crystal, 7" **10.00**

Pioneer, bowl, pink/sprayed color, crimped, 11" **25.00**

Pioneer, plate, crystal, 12" ...**12.50**

Star, bowl, dessert; yellow, 4⅝" **7.00**

Star, bowl, salad; yellow, 6¼"..**6.00**

Star, cup & saucer, crystal.....**7.00**

Star, sugar bowl, crystal, w/lid **10.00**

**Yorktown, berry bowl, yellow, 5½",
$4.00.** (Photo courtesy Gene Florence)

Yorktown, bowl, fruit; crystal or yellow, footed, 10" **17.50**

Yorktown, mug, crystal or yellow, 5" **17.50**

Yorktown, sherbet, crystal or yellow, 7-oz **3.00**

Yorktown, vase, crystal or yellow, 8" **16.00**

Fostoria

Buttercup, bowl, baked apple; crystal, #2364, 6" **20.00**

Buttercup, candy dish, crystal, w/lid, #2364, 3¾" dia ...**135.00**

Buttercup, pickle dish, crystal, #2350, 8" **25.00**

Buttercup, plate, sandwich; crystal, #2364, 11" **35.00**

Buttercup, saucer, crystal, #2350 ....**5.00**

Buttercup, stem, low sherbet; crystal, #6030, 6-oz, 4⅜"........**17.50**

Buttercup, vase, crystal, footed, #4143, 6" **95.00**

Camellia, basket, crystal, wicker hdl, 10¼x6½" **95.00**

Camellia, bowl, crystal, flared, 8" **35.00**

Camellia, cracker plate, crystal, 10¾" **30.00**

Camellia, pitcher, crystal, 16-oz, 6⅛" **90.00**

Camellia, plate, dinner; crystal, 9½" **30.00**

Camellia, shakers, crystal, 3⅛", pr **50.00**

Camellia, tray, muffin; crystal, handles, 9½" **32.50**

Camellia, vase, crystal, footed, #6021, 6" **65.00**

Century, basket, crystal, wicker handle, 10¼x6½" **70.00**

Century, bowl, salad; crystal, 10½"...............................**32.50**

Century, comport, crystal, 4⅜"..**20.00**

Century, pitcher, crystal, 16-oz, 6⅛"..................................**60.00**

Century, plate, dinner; crystal, 10½"...............................**33.00**

Century, tray, crystal, center handle, 11½"...........................**30.00**

Chintz, bowl, bonbon, crystal, #2496, 7⅝".......................**32.50**

Chintz, candlestick, double; crystal, #6023........................**50.00**

Chintz, plate, luncheon; crystal, #2496, 9½"......................**21.00**

Chintz, relish, crystal, 3-part, #2496, 10x7½"................**40.00**

Chintz, tumbler, tea; crystal, footed, #6026, 13-oz.............**32.50**

Corsage, bowl, crystal, flared rim, #2496, 12".......................**55.00**

Corsage, cake plate, crystal, handles, #2440, 10½"..........**32.50**

Corsage, candlestick, crystal, duo, #2496...............................**45.00**

Corsage, plate, cracker; crystal, #2496, 11".......................**35.00**

Corsage, stem, water; crystal, #6014, 9-oz, 7⅜"............**25.00**

Corsage, sugar bowl, crystal, #2496, individual...........**12.50**

Heather, bowl, cereal; crystal, 6"..................................**25.00**

Heather, bowl, crystal, flared rim, 12"...................................**60.00**

Heather, pitcher, crystal, 16-oz, 6⅛"..................................**95.00**

Heather, shakers, crystal, 8⅛", pr **47.50**

Heather, tidbit tray, crystal, 2-tier, metal handle, 10¼"........**45.00**

Holly, creamer, crystal, #2666, individual **20.00**

Holly, finger bowl, crystal, #1769...........................**30.00**

Holly, mayonnaise ladle, crystal..**10.00**

Holly, relish, crystal, 2-part, #2364, 8¼"......................**20.00**

Horizon, bowl, salad; cinnamon, crystal or spruce, 10½"..**22.00**

Horizon, mayonnaise, cinnamon, crystal or spruce, 3-pc set..**25.00**

Horizon, plate, salad; cinnamon, crystal or spruce, 7"........**8.00**

Horizon, platter, cinnamon, crystal or spruce, oval, 12"...**22.00**

Jamestown, butter dish, amber or brown, #2791/300, ¼-lb...**24.00**

Jamestown, butter dish, green, #2719/300, $45.00. (Photo courtesy Gene Florence)

Jamestown, pickle dish, amethyst, crystal or green, 8⅜" **40.00**

Jamestown, stem, sherbet; pink, blue or ruby, 7-oz, 4⅛" ..**18.00**

Jamestown, tumbler, tea; amethyst, crystal or green, footed, 12-oz, 6"..............**21.00**

Lido, bowl, crystal, 3-cornered, handle, 4⅝" **14.00**

Lido, comport, crystal, 5½"...**25.00**

Lido, plate, crystal, 9½"........**32.50**

Lido, stem, claret; crystal, 4-oz ..**26.00**

Lido, tumbler, juice; crystal, footed, 5-oz............................**14.00**

Mayflower, bowl, bonbon; crystal, handle, 5¾x6¼" **20.00**

Mayflower, cake plate, crystal, #2560, 10½"....................**32.50**

Mayflower, candlestick, crystal, #2560, 4½".....................**25.00**

Mayflower, plate, lemon; crystal, handle, #2560, 6¼".........**6.00**

Mayflower, tumbler, water; crystal, footed, 9-oz...............**18.00**

Meadow Rose, bowl, crystal, tricornered, 4⅝"..................**15.00**

Meadow Rose, celery dish, crystal, 11"...................................**37.50**

Meadow Rose, plate, dinner; crystal, 9¾"............................**45.00**

Meadow Rose, tray, crystal, center handle, 11"......................**35.00**

Navarre, bowl, crystal, flared, #2496, 12".......................**62.50**

Navarre, bowl, crystal, handled, footed, #2496, 5".............**20.00**

Navarre, bowl, divided mayonnaise; #2496, 6½"...........**50.00**

Navarre, celery, crystal, #2440, 9".....................................**35.00**

Navarre, plate, crystal, #2496, 8".....................................**27.50**

Navarre, plate, dinner; crystal, #2440, 9½".......................**52.50**

Romance, bowl, crystal, footed, 12".....................................**55.00**

Romance, plate, crystal, 8"...**15.00**

Romance, plate, sandwich; crystal, 11"...................................**37.50**

Romance, stem, champagne; crystal, 6-oz, 5½"..................**16.00**

Romance, vase, crystal, footed, 7½"....................................**67.50**

Seascape, bowl, pansy; opalescent, 4½"....................................**35.00**

Seascape, mayonnaise, opalescent, 3-pc.....................................**55.00**

Seascape, salver, opalescent, footed, 12"...........................**135.00**

Wistar, bowl, crystal, triangular, handled, 4½".................**12.00**

Wistar, candlestick, crystal, 4"..**15.00**

Wistar, creamer, white, footed, 4".................................**12.50**

Wistar, tumbler, crystal, 12-oz..**12.50**

Hazel Atlas

Capri, ashtray, blue, 5" dia....**8.00**

Capri, creamer, blue, round.**12.50**

Capri, plate, blue, 8" sq..........**9.00**

Capri, stem, water; blue, 5½"..**9.00**

Capri, tumbler, Colony Swirl, blue, 12-oz, 5".................**10.00**

Colonial Couple, cup & saucer, Platonite w/trim.............**20.00**

Colonial Couple, egg cup, Platonite w/trim............................**20.00**

Colonial Couple, pitcher, milk; Platonite w/trim, 16-oz..**35.00**

Moderntone Platonite, bowl, cream soup; pastel color, 4¾"......**6.50**

Moderntone Platonite, cup, dark fired-on color, from $7 to..**8.00**

Moderntone Platonite, cup & saucer, white or w/stripes..**4.00**

Moderntone Platonite, dinner plate, white with stripes, 8⅞", $3.50. (Photo courtesy Gene Florence)

Moderntone Platonite, plate, dinner; Deco/Red or Blue Willow, 8⅞"...................................**25.00**

Moderntone Platonite, platter, dark fired-on color, 12", from $22 to..............................**32.00**

Moderntone Platonite, platter, pastel color, oval, 12".....**15.00**

Moderntone Platonite, tumbler, white or w/stripes, conical, footed **6.00**

Moroccan Amethyst, bowl, oval, 7¾"..................................**16.00**

Moroccan Amethyst, goblet, wine; 4 ½-oz, 4"........................**10.00**

Moroccan Amethyst, plate, salad; 7 /14"..............................**7.00**

Moroccan Amethyst, vase, ruffled, 8½"..................................**37.50**

Newport, bowl, berry; fired-on color, 8¼".........................**18.00**

Newport, plate, luncheon; white, 8½"..................................**3.00**

Newport, platter, fired-on color, oval, 11¾"........................**20.00**

Newport, tumbler, white **8.00**

Ovide, bowl, cereal; decorated white, deep, 5½".............**12.00**

Ovide, cup & saucer, Art Deco **30.00**

Ovide, plate, luncheon; fired-on color, 8"..............................**4.00**

Ovide, sugar bowl, white w/trim..**4.50**

Ripple, bowl, berry; any color, shallow, 5" **12.00**

Ripple, cup & saucer, any color..**5.00**

Ripple, sugar bowl, any color...**7.50**

Ripple, tumbler, any color, 20-oz, 6¼"..................................**10.00**

Heisey

Cabochon, bowl, dessert; crystal, #1951, 4½".........................**4.00**

Cabochon, candle holders, crystal, 2-light, #1951, pr **165.00**

Cabochon, plate, crystal, center handle, #1951, 13" **42.00**

Cabochon, sherbet, crystal, #1951 (pressed), 6-oz **4.00**

Cabochon, stem, cocktail; crystal, #6091, 4-oz **4.00**

Cabochon, tumbler, beverage; crystal #60092 (blown), 10-oz .**8.00**

Cabochon, tumbler, soda; crystal, #60092 (blown), 14-oz....**11.00**

Lodestar, bowl, Dawn, crimped, 11", $100.00. (Photo courtesy Gene Florence)

Lodestar, sauce dish, Dawn, 4½" **40.00**

Lodestar, tumbler, juice; Dawn, 6-oz.....................................**50.00**

New Era, celery tray, crystal, 13" **30.00**

New Era, creamer, crystal ...**37.50**

New Era, plate, luncheon; crystal, 9x7" **25.00**

Orchid, comport, crystal, blown, 5½" **95.00**

Orchid, plate, sandwich; crystal, 11"..................................**75.00**

Plantation, bowl, jelly; crystal, flared, 6½" **50.00**

Plantation, candlestick, crystal, 2-light **85.00**

Plantation, cup, punch; crystal..**40.00**

Plantation, stem, crystal, pressed or blown, 10-oz...............**50.00**

Rose, ashtray, crystal, 3".......**37.50**

Rose, bowl, gardenia; crystal, Waverly, 10"...................**75.00**

Rose, candy dish, crystal, footed, w/lid, Waverly, 5" **195.00**

Rose, stem, claret; crystal, 4-oz ..**135.00**

Imperial

Crocheted Crystal, basket, 12"..**75.00**

Crocheted Crystal, bowl, console; 12"...................................**32.50**

Crocheted Crystal, creamer and sugar bowl, flat, $30.00 each. (Photo courtesy Gene Florence)

Crocheted Crystal, mayonnaise bowl, 5¼"........................**12.50**

Crocheted Crystal, plate, 14"..**25.00**

Crocheted Crystal, punch cup, open handle......................**7.50**

Crocheted Crystal, stem, sherbet; 6-oz, 5"............................**20.00**

Crocheted Crystal, sugar bowl, footed **20.00**

Indiana Glass Co.

Christmas Candy, bowl, soup; teal, 7⅜"...................................**55.00**

Christmas Candy, creamer, crystal.....................................**8.00**

Christmas Candy, cup & saucer, crystal..............................**6.00**

Christmas Candy, tidbit server, crystal, 2-tier..................**17.50**

Constellation, cake stand, crystal.......................**50.00**

Constellation, creamer, crystal.**10.00**

Constellation, mug, crystal.**15.00**

Constellation, plate, salad; crystal **10.00**

Constellation, tumbler, crystal, flat, 8-oz......................**12.50**

Daisy, bowl, cream soup; green, 4½"................................**6.00**

Daisy, bowl, oval vegetable; red or amber, 10" **16.00**

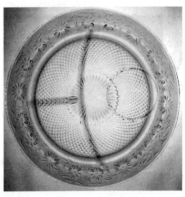

Daisy, grill plate with indent for cream soup, green, $14.00 (red or amber, $30.00). (Photo courtesy Gene Florence)

Daisy, plate, dinner; crystal, 9⅜"............................**5.00**

Daisy, plate, salad; green, 7⅜".**3.50**

Daisy, relish dish, red or amber, 3-part, 8⅜"..................**25.00**

Daisy, tumbler, crystal or green, footed, 12-oz................**20.00**

Diamond Point, ashtray, crystal w/ruby, 5½"...................**5.00**

Diamond Point, compote, crystal w/ruby, crimped rim, 7¼" **12.50**

Diamond Point, mug, crystal w/ruby **8.00**

Diamond Point, tumbler, crystal w/ruby, 9-oz 4.00

Orange Blossom, creamer, milk glass, footed..................5.00

Orange Blossom, sugar bowl, milk glass, footed 5.00

Pretzel, bowl, fruit cup; crystal, 4½"................................4.50

Pretzel, olive dish, crystal, leaf shape, 7" 5.00

Pretzel, plate, crystal, 3-part, indent, 7¼" sq 9.00

Pretzel, tumbler, crystal, 3½" 47.50

Sandwich, basket, amber or crystal, 10" 32.50

Sandwich, bowl, teal, hexagonal, 6", $14.00. (Photo courtesy Gene Florence)

Sandwich, candlesticks, amber or crystal, 3½", pr...............17.50

Sandwich, plate, sherbet; teal blue, 6" 7.00

Sandwich, puff box, amber or crystal......................16.50

Sandwich, wine, red, 4-oz, 3"..12.50

Wild Rose, bowl, sauce; crystal, milk glass or crystal satin, handles 4.00

Wild Rose, candle holder, sprayed & satinized colors 8.00

Wild Rose, sherbet, multicolored 12.50

Wild Rose, tray, iridescent, handles....................20.00

Jeannette

Camellia, bowl, nappy, crystal, handle..............................8.00

Camellia, candle holder, crystal..10.00

Camellia, cup & saucer, crystal..1.50

Camellia, sugar bowl, crystal, footed 7.50

Dewdrop, bowl, crystal, 4¾"...5.00

Dewdrop, butter dish, crystal..27.50

Dewdrop, cup, punch or snack; crystal..............................3.00

Dewdrop, plate, snack; crystal, indent for cup..................4.00

Dewdrop, tumbler, water; crystal, 9-oz 17.50

Dewdrop, tumbler, crystal, 12-ounce, 6", $25.00. (Photo courtesy Gene Florence)

Floragold, ashtray/coaster, iridescent, 4"..............................5.50

Floragold, candlesticks, iridescent, double-branch, pr...........60.00

Floragold, sugar bowl, iridescent 6.50

Floragold, tumbler, iridescent, footed, 10-oz or 11-oz, ea.......20.00

Harp, ashtray/coaster, crystal...5.00

Harp, cake stand, crystal, 9"...25.00

Harp, vase, crystal, 7½" 27.50

Holiday, bowl, lg berry; pink, 8½"..............................35.00

Holiday, pitcher, milk; iridescent, 16-oz, 4¾" 25.00

Holiday, plate, dinner; pink, 9"..**20.00**
Holiday, sandwich tray, irides-
cent, 10½".......................**15.00**
Iris & Herringbone, bowl, sauce;
crystal, ruffled rim, 5"...**10.00**
Iris & Herringbone, creamer, iri-
descent, footed................**14.00**
Iris & Herringbone, goblet, cock-
tail; crystal, 4-oz, 4½"....**24.00**
Iris & Herringbone, goblet, wine;
iridescent, 4" **28.00**
Iris & Herringbone, sherbet, iri-
descent, footed, 2½".......**15.00**
National, bowl, crystal, flat,
12"............................**15.00**
National, punch bowl, crystal,
12" **25.00**
National, shakers, crystal, pr...**9.00**
Shell Pink, bowl, pink opaque,
footed, Florentine, 10"...**30.00**

**Emerald Glo, condiment set: three
jars with metal lids, original
spoon, and handled tray, $80.00.**
(Photo courtesy Gene Florence)

Emerald Glo, cruet................**30.00**
Emerald Glo, oil bottle **30.00**
Emerald Glo, sugar bowl......**20.00**
Emerald Glo, tray, handled,
8½" **30.00**

US Glass

**Shell Pink, creamer and sugar
bowl, Baltimore Pear, with lid,
$17.50.** (Photo courtesy Gene Florence)

Shell Pink, creamer, pink opaque,
Baltimore Pear design...**15.00**
Shell Pink, relish, octagonal, Vinyard
design, 4-part, 12"..............**40.00**
Shell Pink, vase, 7"...............**35.00**

Paden City

Emerald Glo, candle holders, ball
w/metal cups, pr **40.00**
Emerald Glo, cocktail shaker, 26-
oz, 10" **60.00**

**King's Crown, cup and saucer,
ruby flashed, $16.00.** (Photo courtesy
Gene Florence)

King's Crown/Thumbprint, bowl,
mayonnaise, ruby flashed,
5" **50.00**
King's Crown/Thumbprint, bowl,
ruby flashed, crimped,
4½x11½"......................**125.00**
King's Crown/Thumbprint, candle
holder, ruby flashed, 2-light,
5½" **110.00**
King's Crown/Thumbprint, plate,
salad; 7⅜".......................**14.00**
King's Crown/Thumbprint, sugar
bowl, ruby flashed **22.50**

Viking

Prelude, bonbon, crystal, 3-footed, 6"......................................**22.00**

Prelude, butter dish, 8½", $35.00.
(Photo courtesy Gene Florence)

Prelude, butter dish, crystal, oval, 6½".....................................**37.50**
Prelude, candy box, crystal, closed knob, 6".............................**50.00**
Prelude, compote, cheese; crystal...............................**15.00**
Prelude, oil bottle, crystal, 4-oz..**45.00**
Prelude, plate, dinner; crystal, 10"......................................**40.00**
Prelude, relish, crystal, 3-part, handles, 7"........................**15.00**
Prelude, sugar bowl, crystal, flat...............................**12.50**

Franciscan

When most people think of the Franciscan name, their Apple or Desert Rose patterns come to mind immediately, and without a doubt these are the most familiar of the hundreds of lines produced by Gladding McBean. Located in Los Angeles, they produced quality dinnerware under the trade name Franciscan from the mid-1930s until 1984, when they were bought out by a company from England. Many marks were used; most included the Franciscan name. An 'F' in a square with 'Made in USA' below it dates from 1938, and a double-line script F was used later. Some of this dinnerware is still being produced in England, so be sure to look for the USA mark. For an expanded listing, see *Schroeder's Antiques Price Guide* (Collector Books).

Desert Rose, salt and pepper shakers, tall, $75.00; syrup pitcher, $75.00.

Apple, ashtray, individual....**12.00**
Apple, bowl, mixing; sm **155.00**
Apple, bowl, vegetable; 8".....**32.00**
Apple, butter dish **45.00**
Apple, coffeepot **75.00**
Apple, cup & saucer, demitasse ..**45.00**
Apple, mug, barrel, 12-oz **35.00**
Apple, pitcher, milk **65.00**
Apple, plate, 6½"....................**6.00**
Apple, salt & pepper shakers, tall, pr....................................**45.00**
Apple, soup ladle...................**75.00**
Apple, tile, sq **45.00**
Coronado, bowl, casserole; w/lid, from $45 to **90.00**
Coronado, bowl, rim soup; from $14 to **25.00**
Coronado, pitcher, 1½-qt, from $25 to **45.00**
Coronado, plate, 9½", from $10 to **15.00**
Coronado, teapot, from $45 to ..**75.00**

Desert Rose, bell, dinner **95.00**

Desert Rose, bowl, fruit..........**7.00**

Desert Rose, bowl, rimmed soup..**25.00**

Desert Rose, candle holders, pr..**95.00**

Desert Rose, coffeepot, individual **395.00**

Desert Rose, cup & saucer, coffee **85.00**

Desert Rose, egg cup.............**35.00**

Desert Rose, mug, cocoa; 10-oz..**95.00**

Desert Rose, plate, chop; 14"..**95.00**

Desert Rose, plate, 9½" **20.00**

Desert Rose, tumbler, juice; 6-oz..**45.00**

El Patio, bowl, cream soup; w/underplate, from $25 to **40.00**

El Patio, butter dish, from $25 to **40.00**

El Patio, plate, individual crescent salad; from $22 to..........**32.00**

El Patio, plate, 9½", from $10 to..**15.00**

El Patio, teacup & saucer, from $8 to **12.00**

Forget-Me-Not, cup & saucer, coffee **85.00**

Forget-Me-Not, sherbet **20.00**

Ivy, bowl, fruit.........................**8.50**

Ivy, creamer, regular.............**18.00**

Ivy, plate, 10½".....................**22.00**

Ivy, tumbler, 10-oz................**38.00**

Meadow Rose, bowl, rimmed soup............................**25.00**

Meadow Rose, candy dish, oval .**225.00**

Meadow Rose, cup & saucer, demitasse................................**45.00**

Meadow Rose, plate, 9½"......**20.00**

Meadow Rose, tile, sq **35.00**

Poppy, bowl, cereal **22.50**

Poppy, sugar bowl..................**38.00**

Starburst, bowl, soup/cereal.**13.00**

Starburst, creamer.................**15.00**

Starburst, cup & saucer **25.00**

Starburst, lemon nappy/jam-jelly................................**22.00**

Starburst, coffeepot, $150.00.

Starburst, oil cruet **75.00**

Starburst, plate, dinner........**12.00**

Starburst, salt & pepper shakers, sm, pr.............................**20.00**

Frankoma

Since 1933 the Frankoma Pottery Company has been producing dinnerware, novelty items, vases, etc. In 1965 they became the first American company to produce a line of collector plates. The body of the ware prior to 1954 was a honey tan that collectors refer to as 'Ada clay.' A brick red clay (called 'Sapulpa') was used from then on, and this and the colors of the glazes help determine the period of production.

For more information refer to *Frankoma and Other Oklahoma Potteries* by Phyllis and Tom Bess (Schiffer), and *Frankoma Pottery, Value Guide and More,* by Susan N. Cox. See Clubs and Newsletters for information on the Frankoma Family Collectors Association.

Ashtray, Tulsarama, Desert Gold, red clay, 1957, 7¾" **50.00**

Bowl, Desert Gold, red clay, #214, 1950-74, 12".....................**30.00**

Catalog, 1950 ....**35.00**

Christmas card, 1967 ....**70.00**

Jug, Iowa Sunshine, Prairie Green, Ada clay, 1950s, 6½" **60.00**

Match cover, w/out matches, G-..**11.00**

Mug, Donkey, Carter Mondale, 1977 ....**40.00**

Mug, Elephant, 1974, from $30 to...................................**40.00**

Pipe rest, #454, black, ca 1935-40 ....**175.00**

Pitcher, eagle, Dusty Rose, Ada clay..................................**35.00**

Plate, Conestoga Wagon, Pale Blue, 1971, 2,000 made **200.00**

Plate, Helen Keller **60.00**

Plate, Symbols of Freedom, Bicentennial, 1976.........**40.00**

Plate, Teenagers of the Bible, Jesus the Carpenter, $35.00.

Postcards, of Frankoma family, factory, color, ea.............**18.00**

Sculpture, Circus Horse, White Sand, #138, 4½" **195.00**

Sculpture, Puma, seated, White Sand...............................**75.00**

Table bell, brown satin, #817, 1982-92, 6".....................**25.00**

Teapot, Wagon Wheel, Prairie Green, 2-cup, #94C **40.00**

Trivet, Cherokee Alphabet, Flame **6.50**

Vase, boot w/star, Ada clay ..**30.00**

Vase, collector; V-12, black & Terra Cotta, 1980, 13"...**65.00**

Vase, cylinder, Prairie Green, Ada clay, #28, 6" **45.00**

Vase, leaf handles, early glaze, #71, 1942, 10"...............**125.00**

Wall mask, Maiden, Ada clay, Prairie Green, #132, 4½"..**75.00**

Wall pocket, Phoebe, #730, 1948-49, 7½"..........................**100.00**

Wall pocket, Wagon Wheel, Red Bud, #94Y, 7" **75.00**

Fruit Jars

Some of the earliest glass jars used for food preservation were blown, and corks were used for seals. During the nineteenth century, hundreds of manufacturers designed over 4,000 styles of fruit jars. Lids were held in place either by a wax seal, wire bail, or the later screw-on band. Jars were usually made in aqua or clear, though other colors were also used. Amber jars are popular with collectors, milk glass jars are rare, and cobalt and black glass jars often bring $3,000.00 and up, if they can be found! Condition, age, scarcity, and unusual features are also to be considered when evaluating old fruit jars. For more information see *1,000 Fruit Jars* by Bill Schroeder.

Acme (on shield w/stars & stripes), qt, clear............................**2.00**

Atlas, E-Z Seal, qt, green **15.00**

Atlas, Strong Shoulder Mason, pt, blue................................**12.00**

Atlas Easy Seal, quart, light blue with glass lid and wire bale, $20.00; another example in red-amber, $40.00; Swayzee's Improved Mason, quart, medium green, NM, $80.00. (Photo courtesy Pacific Glassworks Auctions)

Atlas (HA in Strippled Circle) Mason, pt, clear **5.00**

Atlas Mason Improved, qt, sky blue **25.00**

Ball & Refrigator & Freezer Jar, pt, clear............................**3.00**

Ball Improved, ½-gal, aqua **15.00**

Ball Improved Ghost Mason, pt, aqua **20.00**

Ball Perfect Mason, ½-gal, black, 9 ribs **15.00**

Ball Perfect Mason, 40-oz, blue ..**25.00**

Ball Sanitary Sure Seal, qt, blue **5.00**

Ball Special (8 ribs), pt, clear, round or square................**5.00**

Ball Sure Seal, ½-gal, black **12.00**

Ball 3 L Loop Improved Mason, pt, aqua **7.00**

Bamberger's Mason Jar (in circle), pt, blue............................**30.00**

Bernardin (Script) Underlined Mason, pt, clear **10.00**

Brockway Sure-Grip Mason, qt, clear, zinc lid....................**8.00**

Clark's Peerless, ½-gal, aqua.....**18.00**

Cleveland Fruit Juices, ½-gal, clear **6.00**

Conserve Jar, qt, clear............**5.00**

Corona Jar, pt, clear, made in Canada **3.00**

Double Seal, qt, clear...........**15.00**

Drey Square Mason (in carpenter's square), ½-gal, clear **20.00**

Gem on base, Pat Nov 26 67, ½-gal, aqua........................**15.00**

Genuine (Mason script in flag), ½-gal, light green...............**25.00**

Hazel-Atlas Lightning Seal, qt, aqua **25.00**

Ideal Wide Mouth (in shield), 24-oz, clear, made in Canada...........................**18.00**

Ivanhoe on base, pt, clear.......**4.00**

Jewel Jar, qt, clear, made in Canada **5.00**

Jewel Jar (block letters in frame), qt, clear...........................**15.00**

Kerr 'Self Sealing' Trade Mark Patented Mason, ½-gal, clear **5.00**

Knox (K in Keystone) Mason, pt, clear, regular zinc lid.......**2.00**

Lamb Mason, qt, clear, zinc lid ..**3.00**

Leotric (sm mouth), qt, green ..**15.00**

Lockport Mason Improved, ½-gal, clear **20.00**

Lustre R E Tongue & Bros Inc Phila (in circle), pt, blue..**7.00**

Mason (star) Jar, pt, clear......**1.00**

Mason's Patent, ½-gal, aqua.....**10.00**

Mrs Chapin's Mayonnaise Boston Mass, pt, clear..................**6.00**

New Gem (Gem is in script), pt, clear **17.00**

Princess, qt, clear.................**18.00**

Putnam (base), 1½-pt, aqua......**30.00**

Putnam (on base), aqua, 7⅜"..**75.00**

Safe Seal (in circle), pt, blue ..**5.00**

Superior A G Co (in circle), pt, aqua **12.00**

Sure Seal, made for L Bamberger
Co, pt, black **25.00**
TM Lightning, ½-gal, aqua....**15.00**
TM Lightning Registered US Patent
Office, ½-gal, aqua............**15.00**
Trade Mark Banner WM
Warranted, qt, blue **7.00**
Trade Mark Lightning Putnam,
24-oz, aqua **75.00**
Victory on lid, pt, clear, twin side
clamps.............................**6.00**

Games

The ideal collectible game is
one that combines playability (i.e.,
good strategy, interaction, surprise, etc.) with interesting graphics and unique components.
Especially desirable are the very
old games from the nineteenth and
early twentieth centuries as well
as those relating to early or popular TV shows and movies. As
always, value depends on rarity
and condition of the box and playing pieces. For a greatly expanded
list and more information, see
*Schroeder's Collectible Toys,
Antique to Modern* (Collector
Books).

$10,000 Pyramid, Milton Bradley,
1972, EX (EX box)..........**15.00**
ABC Education, card game, ED-
U Cards, 1959, EX+ (EX
box)..............................**10.00**
Adventures of Lassie, Whiting,
1955, EX (EX box)..........**50.00**
Adventures of Robin Hood, Bettye-
B, 1956, EX (VG box).....**65.00**
Alien, Kenner, 1979, EXIB...**50.00**

Alvin & the Chipmunks, Acorn
Hunt, Hasbro, 1960, EX (EX
box) **35.00**
Angela Cartwright's Buttons &
Bows, Transogram, 1960,
EXIB **50.00**
Archie Bunker Poker, Cadeaux,
1972, EX (EX container).**30.00**
Automobile Race, McLoughlin Bros,
1904, EX (EX box)......**1,800.00**
Baretta, Milton Bradley, 1976, EX
(EX box).........................**20.00**
Bat Masterson, Lowell, 1958,
NMIB..............................**75.00**
Batman & Robin Target, Hasbro,
1966, MIB....................**200.00**
Batman Shooting Arcade, Marx,
1966, EX (EX box) **250.00**
Beach Head Invasion, Built-Rite,
1950s, EX (EX box)........**40.00**

**Beany and Cecil Match It, Mattel,
1961, MIP, $65.00. (Photo courtesy
June Moon)**

Beany & Cecil Ring Toss, Pressman,
1961, EX (EX box)............**50.00**
Beverly Hillbillies, Standard
Toykraft, 1963, NMIB ...**50.00**
Boots & Saddles, Gardner, 1958,
EX (EX box)....................**50.00**

Brady Bunch, Whitman, 1973, MIB................................**100.00**

Bugaloos, Milton Bradley, 1971, MIB, from $50 to **60.00**

Cabby, Selchow & Righter, 1950s, EX (EX box)....................**75.00**

Camp Granada, Milton Bradley, 1965, NMIB....................**50.00**

Candyland, Milton Bradley, 1962, VG (VG box)....................**50.00**

Captain Kangaroo TV Lotto, Ideal, 1961, EX (EX box)..........**25.00**

Captain Kidd, Lowell, 1950s, EX (EX box)...........................**50.00**

Championship Baseball, Lansing, 1966, EX (EX box)..........**35.00**

Chase Back, Milton Bradley, 1962, MIB (sealed)...................**15.00**

Chutes Away, Gabriel, 1978, EX (EX box)...........................**65.00**

Cinderella, Parker Bros, 1964, EXIB...............................**50.00**

Cold Feet, Ideal, 1967, EX (EX box) **35.00**

Cootie House, Schaper, 1966, EX (EX box)...........................**35.00**

Crosby Derby, Fishlove, 1947, EX (EX box)...........................**65.00**

Dancing Princess, Hasbro, 1964, EX (EX box)....................**35.00**

Dark Shadows, Milton Bradley, 1969, NMIB....................**40.00**

Dating Game, Hasbro, 1967, EX (EX box)...........................**30.00**

Davy Crockett Adventures, Gabriel, 1955, NM (EX box)..........**95.00**

Davy Crockett Radar Action, Ewing, 1955, EX (EX box)............**85.00**

Dick Tracy, Crimestopper, Ideal, 1963, NM (EX box) **75.00**

Dick Van Dyke, Standard Toykraft, 1964, EX (EX box) **75.00**

Diver Dan Tug-O-War, Milton Bradley, 1961, EX (EX box).....................................**50.00**

Don't Spill the Beans, Schaper, 1967, MIB (sealed).........**25.00**

Donald Duck Wagon Train, 1977, NMIB..............................**25.00**

Dragnet, Transogram, 1955, NMIB..............................**50.00**

Dukes of Hazzard, Ideal, 1981, EXIB **25.00**

Electric Baseball, Electric Game Co, 1940s, EX (EX box)..**35.00**

Ellsworth Elephant, Selchow & Righter, 1960, EX (EX box)..**50.00**

Emergency, Milton Bradley, 1973, NMIB..............................**20.00**

Family Ties, Applestreet, 1986, EXIB **30.00**

Felix the Cat, target game, Lido, 1960, EX (EX box)..........**60.00**

Fireball XL5, Milton Bradley, 1964, EX (EX box)..........**95.00**

Flea Circus, Mattel, 1964, EX (EX box) **35.00**

Flintstones Beake Ball, Whitman, 1962, EX (EX box)..........**85.00**

Flintstones Pitch 'N Bowl, Transogram, 1961, EX (EX box) **55.00**

Flip-It 7-11, Aurora, 1973, EX (EX box) **45.00**

Flying the Beam, Parker Bros., 1941, MIB, $60.00. (Photo courtesy Rick Polizzi)

Flying Nun, Milton Bradley, 1968, NMIB..............................**50.00**

Fortune's Wheel, Parker Bros, 1903, EX (EX box) **175.00**

Fugitive, Ideal, 1964, EX (EX box)..............................**125.00**

Game of Politics, Parker Bros, 1952, VG (VG box)........**40.00**

Gang Busters, Whitman, 1939, EX (EX box).........................**75.00**

Garroway's Game of Possessions, Remco, 1955, EX (EX box) **45.00**

Giant Cootie, Schaper, 1950s, EX (EX box)..........................**85.00**

Gomer Pyle, Transogram, 1964, EX (EX box)....................**50.00**

Great Shakes Charlie Brown, Golden, 1988, MIB.........**12.00**

Groucho's TV Quiz, Pressman, 1954, EXIB.....................**75.00**

Gunfight at OK Corral, Ideal, 1973, EX (EX box)..........**75.00**

Gusher, Carrom, 1946, EX (EX box) **75.00**

Have Gun Will Travel, Parker Bros, 1959, EXIB...........**75.00**

Hearts, card game, Whitman, 1951, NM (EX box) **10.00**

High Dice, Bettye-B, 1956, EX (EX box) **40.00**

Hollywood Squares, Ideal, 1974, EX (EX box)....................**25.00**

Hopalong Cassidy, Milton Bradley, 1950, EX (EX box) **85.00**

Hopalong Cassidy Chinese Checkers, Milton Bradley, 1951, EX (EX box)..........**50.00**

Hoppity Hopper, Milton Bradley, 1964, NMIB...................**75.00**

Howdy Doody's Own Game, Parker Bros, 1949, EX (EX box) **75.00**

Hunt for Red October, 1988, EXIB.............................**30.00**

Ironside, Ideal, 1967, EX (EX box)...............................**95.00**

Jack the Giant Killer, Lowell, 1950s, EX (EX box)........**40.00**

Jetsons Fun Pad, Milton Bradley, 1963, EX (EX box)..........**75.00**

King of the Cheese, Milton Bradley, 1959, EX (EX box)...........**40.00**

Knight Rider, Parker Bros, 1983, NM (EX box) **20.00**

Kreskin's ESP, Milton Bradley, EXIB..............................**10.00**

Land of the Giants, Ideal, 1968, NM (NM box)...............**200.00**

Laverne & Shirley, MIB (sealed).......................**25.00**

Let's Face It, Hasbro, 1955, NMIP...........................**35.00**

Limbo Legs, Milton Bradley, 1969, EX (EX box)...................**35.00**

Little Rascals Clubhouse Bingo, Gabriel & Sons, 1958, complete, scarce, NM (NM box), $100.00.

Liz Taylor Hollywood Starlet, Ideal, 1963, EX (EX box)............**35.00**

Lone Ranger Double Target, Marx, 17", EX (EX box)..........**200.00**

Looney Tunes, Milton Bradley, 1968, EX (EX box)..........**50.00**

Lost Heir, Milton Bradley, 1905, EX (G box)....................**135.00**

Love Boat, Ungame, 1980, VG (VG box) **20.00**

M*A*S*H, Milton Bradley, 1981, MIB **30.00**

Magilla Gorilla, Ideal, 1964, NMIB **100.00**

Man From UNCLE, target game, Marx, 1966, EX (EX box)..**300.00**

Mary Hartman, Mary Hartman, Reiss, 1977, NM (EX box)..**40.00**

Melvin the Moon Man, Remco, 1959, NMIB....................**65.00**

Mentor, Hasbro, 1961, EX (EX box) **40.00**

Miami Vice, Pepper Lane, 1984, EX (EX box)....................**25.00**

Mickey Mouse, Bagatelle, Marx Bros, NM **700.00**

Mickey Mouse Circus, Marx Bros, EX (EX box)..................**650.00**

Mickey Mouse Pop Game, Marks Bros, 1930s, EX (EX box) **650.00**

Mighty Hercules, Hasbro, 1963, NMIB...........................**300.00**

Mr Machine, Ideal, 1961, EX (EX box) **75.00**

OK Telegraph, 1910, EX (VG box) **300.00**

Peter Potamus, Ideal, 1964, EX (EX box).......................**185.00**

Petticoat Junction, Standard Toy Craft, EX (EX box), $100.00. (Photo courtesy John and Sheri Pavone)

Poison Ivy, Ideal, 1969, VG (VG box) **40.00**

PT Boat 109, Ideal, 1963, VG (G box) **35.00**

Rin-Tin-Tin, Transogram, EX (G box) **25.00**

Snagglepuss, Transogram, 1961, EX (EX box)....................**40.00**

Space Pilot, Cadaco, 1951, EXIB **75.00**

Stingray Underwater Maze, Transogram, 1966, EX (EX box) **150.00**

Talking Football, Mattel, 1971, EX (EX box).........................**100.00**

Treasure Island, Harett-Gilmer, 1955, EX (EX box)..........**45.00**

Walt Disney Fantasyland, Parker Bros, 1950s, MIB **50.00**

77 Sunset Strip, Lowell, 1960, NM (EX box).........................**35.00**

Garfield

America's favorite grumpy cat, Garfield has his own band of devotees who are able to find a good variety of merchandise modeled after his likeness. Garfield was created in 1976 by Jim Davis. He underwent many changes by the time he debuted in newspaper in 1978. By 1980 his first book was released, followed quickly in 1981 by lines of collectibles by Dakin and Enesco. The stuffed plush animals and ceramic figures were a huge success. There have been thousands of items made since, with many that are hard to find being produced in Germany, the Netherlands, England, and other European countries.

Banks, displays, PVCs, and figurines are the most desirable items of import from these countries.

Bank, bowling, Enesco, NM, from $35 to **45.00**

Bank, football player, Enesco, from $35.00 to 45.00.

Bank, piggy shape, Paws, MIB.**45.00**
Bank, seated in green chair, Enesco, 9", M..................**35.00**
Christmas Village Post Office, Danbury Mint, 1995-96, 6½x8¾", NM **60.00**
Cookie jar, seated w/cookie jar, #E-5932, Made in Japan, 1978, MIB................................**55.00**
Doll, as Canadian Mountie w/flag, Dakin, 9", NM (original tags) **42.50**
Doll, dressed as a pineapple, plush, w/tags, 9½", NM.............**75.00**
Figure, as Frankenstein, Enesco, 3¼", NM **40.00**
Figure, fishbowl in belly, plastic, 18", M **45.00**
Figure, Garfield's Retreat, tree house, Danbury Mint, M..**35.00**
Figure, Let's Get Fiscal, w/Odie, Enesco, 1978, M.............**50.00**

Figure, Let's Play Doctor, dressed as doctor, Enesco, 1978, NM .**45.00**
Figure, seated on dresser looking in mirror w/Odie & Pookie Bear, NM........................**35.00**
Figure, w/Odie, All He Does Is Stare & Slobber, Enesco, 1978, EX........................**45.00**
Nodder, Wacky Wobbler, 7½", MIB **60.00**
Pasta container, image on white, ceramic, 4x12" dia, EX ..**65.00**
Salt & pepper shakers, head w/lg teeth, Enesco, 1978, pr..**90.00**
Teapot, porcelain enamel on steel, PAWS, 2½-qt, M............**35.00**
Toothbrush holder, figural, hole in back, Enesco, 1981, M ...**45.00**

Gas Station Collectibles

From the invention of the automobile came the need for gas service stations, who sought to attract customers through a wide variety of advertising methods. Gas and oil companies issued thermometers, signs, calendars, clocks, banks, and scores of other items emblazoned with their logos and catchy slogans. Though a rather specialized area, gas station collectibles encompass a wide variety of items that appeal to automobilia and advertising collectors as well. For further information we recommend *Antique and Contemporary Advertising* by B.J. Summers and *Value Guide to Gas Station Memorabilia* by B.J. Summers and Wayne Priddy.

Both are published by Collector Books.

Ashtray, United Gasoline Super Charged, glass, 4 rests, sq..**10.00**

Bank, Atlas Batteries, battery shape, red & black, metal, 3".......**30.00**

Bottle, Mobil Window Spray, glass w/paper label..................**40.00**

Can, Beaver Petrolatum, red & white on green, tin, 13"..**45.00**

Can, En-Ar-Co Motor Oil, tin, ca 1935 – 45, quart, EX, $35.00. (Photo courtesy B.J. Summers and Wayne Priddy)

Can, Fisk Motor Tune-Up, boy w/tire, tin, 16-oz, 3¾x5⅞"..............**45.00**

Can, Johnson Motor Oil, Time Tells, black/orange & white, tin, 5-qt..........................**40.00**

Can, Mobilgrease No 4, red, white & blue, tin, 100-lb..........**45.00**

Can, Polarine Transmission Lubricant, red & black on yellow, tin, 5x8"..................**65.00**

Can, Pyro, Completely Denatured Alcohol, tin, 1-gal, 10¼x8"...**40.00**

Clock, Cadillac Service, logo in center, glass lens in plastic case...........................**175.00**

Clock, Firestone Tires, wood frame w/glass front, 15¼" sq...**200.00**

Clock, Studebaker Batteries, red & blue on glass, metal frame, 15" sq...........................**150.00**

Clock, Wolf's Head Motor Oil & Lubes, red, black, green & white, round.................**165.00**

Display rack, Mohawk Tires, painted tin, 13x9"..........**75.00**

Figure, Sinclair Dinosaur, inflatable vinyl.......................**25.00**

Flag, Atlantic Refining Co, cloth, logo on black, 54x87", EX..........**70.00**

Gas cart, Bowser, w/transfer can............................**450.00**

Gas mileage finder, Texaco, on key chain, EX.......................**10.00**

Globe, Gaylor, red & yellow lens w/white band, 3-pc, 13½"..**375.00**

Globe lens, Mobilgas, red pegasus w/black letters, 16½", pr..**75.00**

Hood Tire Dealer, red, black & white man in uniform, die-cut porcelain....................**2,750.00**

Map rack, Atlantic, Flying A logo, red & white, metal, 36x8½"...**110.00**

Paperweight/mirror, Phillips 66, black & white, 1955, 3½" dia......**120.00**

Penzbest Kendall Motor Oils, red, white & blue, porcelain, 36" dia...............................**500.00**

Plate, Golden Tip Gasoline, blue & cream, Taylor, Smith & Taylor...........................**75.00**

Radio, Champion Spark Plugs, spark plug shape, red, white & gray, 14"....................**75.00**

Shell Gasoline, red & yellow, clam logo, 24"........................**650.00**

Sign, Bell Oil Lubricants, white bell & letters on red, porcelain, 4x27"...................**700.00**

Sign, Cooper Tires, red, white & blue w/helmet, tin, oval, 32½x12"........................**150.00**

Sign, Golden-Tip Gasoline, yellow on blue, arrow-shape, 48" L..**600.00**

Sign, Jenny Aero, red, white & blue, porcelain, 12x9"..**150.00**

Sign, Phillips 66, orange & black shield, porcelain, 1950s, 48x48".........................**600.00**

Sign, pump; Sinclair Oils, black on white, porcelain, round..**400.00**

Sign, Service Entrance, blue & white, arrow shape, porcelain, 42x10".........................**200.00**

Sign, Tenneco, red, white & blue, porcelain, 14¾x9½" **35.00**

Sign, We Fit Lodge Spark Plugs, red, yellow & black on tin, 18x12".........................**60.00**

Thermometer, Amalie Motor Oil, red, black & white, glass front, 9" dia **85.00**

Thermometer, Mobilgas Friendly Service, porcelain, 1920-30, 35x4½".........................**250.00**

Thermometer, Mobiloil, shield logo, 23x8" **250.00**

Thermometer, Penzoil Motor Oil, glass face with Liberty Bell in center, NM, $200.00. (Photo courtesy B.J. Summers and Wayne Priddy)

Thermometer, Texaco, red & blue on white, glass face, 12" dia **500.00**

Tire gauge, Schrader, black on red, 1920-30s, 14¾x6" dia...**160.00**

Toy, Texaco Fire Chief's Hat, red & white, plastic w/center logo, 8"....................................**75.00**

Toy truck, Shell Tanker, Tootsietoy, pressed steel, 1¾x6" **75.00**

Uniform hat, winter; Marathon, runner on patch, EX....**135.00**

Gay Fad

This company started out on a very small scale in the late 1930s, but before long, business was booming! Their first products were hand-decorated kitchenwares, but it's their frosted tumblers, trays, pitchers, and decanters that are being sought out today. In addition to souvenir items and lines with a holiday theme, they made glassware to coordinate with Royal China's popular dinnerware, Currier and Ives. They're also known for their 'bentware' — quirky cocktail glasses with stems that were actually bent. Look for an interlocking 'G' and 'F' or the name 'Gay Fad,' the latter mark indicating pieces from the late 1950s to the early 1960s. See also Anchor Hocking/Fire-King.

Ashtray, Trout Flies, clear **8.00**

Batter bowl, Fruits, milk white, signed w/F (Federal Glass), handled..........................**55.00**

Bent tray, Stylized Cats, clear, signed Gay Fad, 11½" dia **24.00**

Bowl, chili; Fruits, 2¼x5".....**14.00**

Canister set, Red Rose, red lids, white interior, 3-pc **60.00**

Casserole, Fruits, w/lid, Fire-King, 1-qt....................................**35.00**

Cocktail shaker, full-figure ballerina, frosted, 28-oz, 9"......**35.00**

Cocktail shaker, The Last Hurdle (fox hunting scenes), 32-ounce, $35.00. (Photo courtesy Donna McGrady)

Cruet set, Oil & Vinegar, Cherry, clear **17.00**

Goblet, Bow Pete, Hoffman Beer, 16-oz **15.00**

Ice tub, Gay '90s, frosted......**21.00**

Loaf pan, Apple, Fire-King Ivory **35.00**

Mug, Fruits, stackable, Fire-King, 3".......................................**15.00**

Mug, Notre Dame, frosted, 16-oz **15.00**

Pitcher, Currier & Ives, blue & white, frosted, 86-oz **60.00**

Pitcher, juice; Ada Orange, frosted, 36-oz...........................**22.00**

Pitcher, Rosemaling (tulips), white inside, 32-oz **28.00**

Plate, Fruits, lace edge, Hazel Atlas, 8½".......................**17.50**

Range set, Rooster, frosted w/red metal lids, 8-oz, 4-pc....**120.00**

Salt & pepper shakers, Fruits, 3½", pr, MIB..................**50.00**

Stem, bent cocktail, Beau Brummel, clear, signed Gay Fad, 3½-oz.....................**12.00**

Tom & Jerry set, Christmas bells, milk white, marked GF, bowl & 6 cups..........................**70.00**

Tumbler, Christmas Greetings From Gay Fad, frosted, 4-oz.......**17.00**

Tumbler, Hors D'oeuvres, clear, 14-oz **10.00**

Tumbler, Ohio Presidents, frosted, 12-oz, set of 8 ....**60.00**

Tumbler, Oregon state map on pink picket fence, clear, marked GF **6.00**

Vanity set, butterflies in meadow, pink inside, 5-pc.............**60.00**

Vase, Red Poppy, clear, footed, 10" **24.00**

Wine set, Grapes, decanter & 4 2½-oz stemmed wines, clear, 5-pc **40.00**

Geisha Girl China

More than sixty-five different patterns of tea services were exported from Japan around the turn of the century, each depicting geishas going about the everyday activities of Japanese life. Mt. Fuji is often featured in the background. Geisha Girl porcelain is a generic term collectors use to identify them all. Many of our lines contain reference to the color of the rim bands, which collectors use to tentatively date the ware.

Bowl, Boat Festival, pale cobalt blue, 9½"..........................**35.00**

Bowl, Boy's Processional, red-orange w/yellow, 9½".....**40.00**

Bowl, Dragonboat, blue w/gold, 6-lobed **25.00**

Bowl, Feather Fan, pierced handles, 8" **35.00**

Bowl, nut; Basket A, apple green, footed, 6", $25.00. (Photo courtesy Elyce Litts)

Bowl, rice; Carp D, red **15.00**

Butter pat, Fan A, red border, 4¼".....................................**8.00**

Cocoa pot, Battledore, ewer shape, yellow-green, 9"..............**85.00**

Cookie jar, Checkerboard, 3-footed, cobalt blue **85.00**

Creamer, Basket A, bulbous, red-orange w/gold buds **10.00**

Creamer, Boy w/Scythe, #20, cobalt blue w/gold **15.00**

Creamer, toy; Chrysanthemum Garden, red **10.00**

Cup & saucer, AD; Chrysanthemum Garden, J#16, red.............**25.00**

Cup & saucer, tea; Bamboo Trellis, dark green......................**12.00**

Cup & saucer, tea; Blue Hoo..**14.00**

Dresser box, Boat Festival, red-orange, #19, 6" dia **30.00**

Egg cup, Cloud A, red...........**20.00**

Hair receiver, Battledore, red-orange w/gold.................**25.00**

Hair receiver, Boat Dance, ribbed, grass green w/gold **24.00**

Mint dish, Bamboo Trellis, scalloped, red-orange **6.00**

Mug, Boy's Processional, red w/yellow lacing...............**25.00**

Mustard jar, Child Reaching for Butterfly, red **15.00**

Nut dish, master; Duck Watching, red w/gold, footed...........**28.00**

Plate, Bamboo Tree, 6" **5.00**

Plate, Blue Hoo, J#39, 7½"...**10.00**

Plate, Duck Watching, #62, gold, 7".....................................**14.00**

Plate, toy; Bird Cage, pine green w/white **12.00**

Powder jar, Carp A, deep brownish-red w/gold.................**26.00**

Puff box, Field Laborers, red w/gold **10.00**

Salt & pepper shakers, Basket B, apple green, pr...............**25.00**

Salt & pepper shakers, Dressing, red, pr...........................**10.00**

Salt & pepper shakers, Waterboy, blue w/gold leaf design, 2¾", pr.....................................**15.00**

Salt dish, Cloud A, red-orange w/flowers **14.00**

Sugar bowl, Carp C, ribbed, red w/gold **25.00**

Tea tile, Feather Fan, #12....**50.00**

Teapot, Cloud B, melon ribbed, red-orange w/yellow.......**30.00**

Teapot, Dressing, red w/gold..**25.00**

Teapot, Fan Dance A, red & cobalt blue, melon ribbed **45.00**

Teapot, toy; Blind Man's Bluff, red-orange w/gold buds.........**35.00**

Toothpick holder, Circle Dance, cylindrical, red **12.00**

Vase, Fan A, red neck, modern, Japan paper sticker, 3" ...**5.00**

GI Joe

Introduced by Hasbro in 1964, 12" GI Joe dolls were offered in four basic packages: Action Soldier, Action Sailor, Action Marine, and Action Pilot. A Black figure was included in the line, and there were representatives of many nations as well. Talking dolls followed a few years later, and scores of accessory items such as vehicles, guns, and uniforms, were made to go with them all. Even though the line was discontinued in 1976, it was evident the market was still there, and kids were clamoring for more. So in 1982, Hasbro brought out the 'little' 3¾" GI Joe action figures, each with his own descriptive name. Sales were unprecedented. The small figures are easy to find, but most of them are loose and played with. Collectors prefer old store stock still in the original packaging; such examples are worth from two to four times more than those without the package, sometimes even more.

For more information we recommend *Schroeder's Collectible Toys, Antique to Modern* (Collector Books).

12" Figures and Accessories

Accessory, Astronaut boots, plastic, VG+, pr.....................**25.00**
Accessory, Big Trapper, cardboard seat & side panels, EX..**200.00**
Accessory, Binoculars, red w/string, 1960s, EX **14.00**

Accessory, Combat Jeep Set, #7000, w/motor sound, complete, EX.......................**175.00**
Accessory, Demolition, #7370, M (EX+ box)......................**175.00**
Accessory, First Aid Pouch, green cloth w/snap closure, EX..**50.00**
Accessory, Green Beret Weapons Pack, MIP (sealed).......**115.00**
Accessory, Helmet Set, #7507, M (NM card)......................**110.00**
Accessory, jacket & trousers, Airborne MP, green, VG..**85.00**
Accessory, Jet Helicopter, Irwin, #5395, EX (EX box), from $160 to..........................**185.00**
Accessory, Medal, Australian, Victoria Cross, Action Man, EX.................................**10.00**
Accessory, Scuba Suit, orange w/front zipper, MIP **580.00**
Accessory, Sleeping Bag, #7515x140, 1964, MOC......................**185.00**
Accessory, Sten Gun, British, Action Man, EX.............**60.00**
Figure, Action Marine, #7700, complete, EXIB **350.00**
Figure, Action Nurse, #8060, MIB (sealed) **5,000.00**
Figure, Action Sailor, complete, NM (EX box) **300.00**

Figure, Adventure Team Talking Commander, EX (VG box), $300.00.
(Photo courtesy McMaster's Doll Auctions)

Figure, Adventure Team Air Adventurer, complete, EX..**150.00**

Figure, Adventure Team Mike Power Atomic Man, MIP, from $80 to............................**100.00**

Figure, Air Adventurer, #7403B, EX (VG box), $250.00. (Photo courtesy Cotswold Collectibles, Inc.)

Figure, Air Adventurer, EX.**150.00**

Figure, Australian Jungle Fighter, complete, EX **375.00**

Figure, Canadian Mountie, NM **775.00**

Figure, Combat Engineer, M .**950.00**

Figure, Dangers of the Depths, complete, M, from $425 to ...**500.00**

Vehicle, Sears Sandstorm Survival Jeep, EX, $350.00. (Photo courtesy Old Tyme Toy Store)

Figure, Japanese Soldier (Basic), complete, EX **300.00**

Figure, Landing Signal Officer, #7410, rare blue outfit, EX (EX box).......................**375.00**

Figure, Smoke Jumper, complete, M **375.00**

Figure, Tank Commander, complete, EX **795.00**

3¾" Figures and Accessories

Figure, Heavy Duty, 1990, complete, M, $6.00. (Photo courtesy Myla Perkins)

Accessory, Combat Jet Skystriker Mp-14F, 1983, MIB **250.00**

Accessory, SAS Parachutist Attack, Action Force, MIP **35.00**

Accessory, Transportable Tactical Battle Platform, 1985, NM .**30.00**

Accessory, USS Flagg Aircraft Carrier, 1986, EX, from $250 to **280.00**

Figure, Ace, 1983, w/accessories, NM **20.00**

Figure, Annihilator, 1989, NMOC **25.00**

Figure, Barbeque, 1985, MOC ..**50.00**

Figure, Big Boa, 1987, EX....**18.50**

Figure, Blast-Off, 1993, w/accessories, NM **6.00**

Figure, Breaker, 1982, swivel-arm, EX **20.00**

Figure, Chuckles, 1987, MOC..**30.00**

Figure, Cobra Commander, 1986, battle armor, MOC **45.00**

Figure, Crimson Guard, 1985, MOC **95.00**

Figure, Drop-Zone, 1990, MOC..**25.00**

Figure, Grunt, 1982, straight arms, w/accessories & file card, NM.........................**22.50**

Figure, Iceberg, 1986, complete w/rifle, NM **10.00**

Figure, Raptor, 1987, MOC..**36.00**

Figure, Red Dog, 1987, w/accessories, NM **8.00**

Figure, Ripper, 1985, complete w/accessories, EX...........**12.00**

Figure, Road Pig, 1988, w/accessories & file card, EX.....**18.00**

Figure, Sci-Fi, MOC, $40.00. (Photo courtesy Old Tyme Toy Store)

Figure, Snake Eyes, 1985, w/accessories & file card, NM ...**75.00**

Figure, Stalker, 1982, straight arms, w/accessories & file card, NM.........................**35.00**

Figure, Techno-Viper, 1987, MOC **23.00**

Figure, Tunnel Rat, 1987, MOC.**45.00**

Figure, Voltar, MOC, $35.00. (Photo courtesy Old Tyme Toy Store)

Glass Animals and Birds

Nearly every glasshouse of note has at some point over the years produced these beautiful models, some of which double for vases, bookends, and flower frogs. Many were made during the 1930s through the 1950s and 1960s, and these are the most collectible. But you'll also be seeing brand new examples, and you need to study to know the difference. A good reference to help you sort them all out is *Glass Animals* by Dick and Pat Spencer (Collector Books). See also Fenton.

Airedale, crystal, Heisey .**1,400.00**

Angelfish, black, Viking, 6½"..**150.00**

Bear, carnival, sitting, Fenton ..**30.00**

Bird, crystal satin, Cambridge, 2¾" L **35.00**

Buddha, amber, Cambridge, 5½".........................**250.00**

Bull, amber, Imperial, very rare.........................**725.00**

Butterfly, crystal, Westmoreland, 4½"..................................**45.00**

Cardinal, Green Mist, Westmoreland **20.00**

Cardinal head, ruby, Fenton, 6½" **175.00**

Cat, green, sitting, Viking, 8"..**55.00**

Cat, lt blue, Fostoria, 3¾"....**35.00**

Cat, Sassy Suzie, milk glass, Tiffin **300.00**

Chick, frosted, New Martinsville, 1"......................................**35.00**

Clydesdale, Salmon, Imperial..**200.00**

Colt, amber, kicking, Heisey ..**650.00**

Colt, amber, standing, Heisey, $650.00. (Photo courtesy Lee Garmon and Dick Spencer)

Colt, cobalt, kicking or rearing, Heisey, ea...................**1,500.00**

Colt, Silver Mist, standing, Fostoria **45.00**

Cygnet, black, Imperial, 2½"..**45.00**

Dolphin, blue, Fostoria, 4¾"..**35.00**

Donkey, caramel slag, Imperial..**55.00**

Donkey, crystal, Heisey......**295.00**

Duck, ashtray, crystal, Duncan & Miller, 4"..........................**20.00**

Duck, mama, crystal, Fostoria..**30.00**

Duck, vaseline, Viking, 5"....**40.00**

Elephant, amber, Heisey, lg or med, ea.....................**2,400.00**

Elephant, bookend, crystal, New Martinsville, 5½", $90.00.

Elephant, bookend, ebony, Fostoria, 6½", ea..........**150.00**

Filly, crystal, head backwards, Heisey........................**1,500.00**

Fish, bookend, Rosalene, Fenton, ea **95.00**

Fish, bookend, ruby, Imperial, ea...............................**340.00**

Fish, crystal, solid, Tiffin, 8¾x9" **350.00**

Fish, match holder, crystal, Heisey, 3x2¾" **180.00**

Frog, crystal satin, Cambridge ..**35.00**

Gazelle, Rosalene, Fenton..**125.00**

Giraffe, crystal, head to side, Heisey..........................**275.00**

Goose, crystal, LE Smith, 2½"..........................**25.00**

Hen, crystal, LE Smith, 5"...**75.00**

Heron, crystal, Cambridge, lg, 12" **150.00**

Heron, crystal, Duncan & Miller......................**150.00**

Horse, bookend, crystal, Fostoria, 7¾", ea..........................**45.00**

Horse, crystal, rearing, Paden City **150.00**

Hound dog, crystal, Viking, 8"..**50.00**

Irish setter, ashtray, crystal, Heisey..........................**30.00**

King fish, aquarium, green, LE Smith, 7¼x15"..............**325.00**

Mallard, crystal, wings half, Heisey............................**225.00**

Mermaid, crystal, Fostoria, 11½"............................**125.00**

Owl, Hootless; caramel slag, Imperial..........................**50.00**

Piglet, ruby, standing, Imperial .**35.00**

Plug horse, cobalt, Heisey..**1,200.00**

Polar bear, crystal, Fostoria, 4⅝"............................**65.00**

Polar bear, topaz, Fostoria, 4⅝" **125.00**

Pony, black, Paden City, 12"..**350.00**

Rabbit, mama, crystal, New Martinsville..................**350.00**

Robin, pink, Westmoreland, 5⅛"..**25.00**

Rooster, amber, Heisey, 5⅜"..**2,500.00**

Rooster, Elegant; light blue, Paden City, 11"........................**225.00**

Rooster, orange, Viking's Epic Line, 1960s, 9½", from $60.00 to $65.00.

Rooster, pink, fighting, Imperial..**175.00**

Rose Lady, flower frog, amber, Cambridge, 8½" **225.00**

Scottie, bookends, crystal, hollow, Cambridge, pr..............**175.00**

Scottie, crystal, Heisey.......**170.00**

Seal, topaz, Fostoria, 3⅞"...**125.00**

Ship, bookend, crystal, New Martinsville, ea..............**45.00**

Swan, amber, #1 style, Cambridge, 10½"..............................**875.00**

Swan, candle holder, red, Duncan & Miller, 7" **80.00**

Swan, Carmen, Cambridge, 6½"............................**225.00**

Swan, crystal, Heisey......**1,300.00**

Swan, ebony, Cambridge, 3"..**65.00**

Swan, emerald, Cambridge, 8½"............................**125.00**

Swordfish, crystal, Duncan & Miller............................**275.00**

Tiger, paperweight, caramel slag, Imperial..........................**95.00**

Turkey, blue, w/lid, Cambridge..**550.00**

Turtle, flower block, amethyst, Fenton, 4" L **85.00**

Two Kids, flower frog, crystal, Cambridge, 9¼" **200.00**

Wood duck, crystal, floating, Heisey..........................**225.00**

Wood duckling, standing, Ultra Blue, Imperial................**45.00**

Wren, Crystal Mist, Westmoreland, 2½"....................................**20.00**

Glass, Porcelain, and Pottery Shoes

While many miniature shoes were made simply as whimseys, you'll also find thimble holders, perfumes, inkwells, salts, candy containers, and bottles made to resemble shoes of many types. For more information we recommend *Collectible Glass Shoes, 2nd Edition,* by Earlene Wheatley (Collector Books). See also Degenhart.

Glass

Boot, amber, Daisy & Button on top w/alligator foot, 2⅜x2½" ..**25.00**

Boot, black, cuffed, spur, ca 1900, 4x3¼" **85.00**

Boot, blue w/leather strap, embossed cow & star, handled **45.00**

Boot, clear w/painted scene, pale green toe, ca 1900, 3x5½"..**55.00**

Boot, crystal, etched Murphy...Peel St, 2½" **40.00**

Boot, Daisy & Button, blue w/clear,solid toe & heel, 3⅜" **125.00**

Boot, Daisy & Button, crystal, Duncan & Sons, 4¾"......**95.00**

Boot, purple slag, cuffed.......**85.00**

Boot, transparent pink, marked France, 2⅜x2½" **25.00**

Boot, yellow, 1970s, 4¼x6½" .**25.00**

Boot pitcher, pink & white slag, 1⅜" **30.00**

Boot w/turned-up toe, gold opalescent, Venetian, 3⅜"........**50.00**

Dutch style, blue, 8¼" **125.00**

Golf shoe, crystal, Waterford, 5¾x2¼" **85.00**

High shoe roller skate, diamond pattern, crystal **75.00**

Santa-style boot, cobalt blue, 1930s, 2½x2¾" **20.00**

Shoe, crystal w/ruby-stained heel, toe & buttons, 4¾x2½"..**100.00**

Shoe, Daisy & Button, mesh sole, blue, Duncan, lg.............**55.00**

Shoe, frosted multicolor millefiori w/crystal heel, Murano, 5⅝"..**90.00**

Shoe, high heel w/round heel plate, amethyst, 1880s, 3¾"...**110.00**

Slipper, blue & white w/crystal ruffle & heel, 5¾x2¾"..**100.00**

Slipper, blue millefiori w/crystal ruffle & heel, 5⅛x2".....**100.00**

Slipper, crystal w/3-D Cinderella on steps, Disney, 7¼x3"......**125.00**

Slipper, Daisy & Button, w/perfume bottle, Duncan, 5¾x3" **75.00**

Kitten Slipper, Hobnail, blue opalescent, Fenton, 3x5⅞", $25.00.

Porcelain and Pottery

Baby shoes, white w/gold laces, marked Block Pottery, pr................**65.00**

Boot, tan, Franklin Pottery Co, 2½"..................................**40.00**

Boot, white over gold w/applied grape cluster, bisque, Germany.........................**40.00**

Boot, white over gold w/applied grape cluster, Germany, 3x3½"............................**40.00**

Boot, white w/gold butterfly on branch, Germany, 4x3½" **85.00**

Bootee, tan, holes around top, 3x2½" **25.00**

Brogan-type shoe, white w/Country Rose decor, 6x3½" **35.00**

Shoe, white w/gold buckle & George Washington on toe, Mt Vernon, 3¾".....................**35.00**

Shoe w/laces, pink, marked McCoy, ca 1941, 5x3¼"..**40.00**

Slipper, Bowness of Windermere, pink flowers, New Devon Pottery, 4x2" **35.00**

Slipper, green, marked Metlox, 1930s, 6x3½" **60.00**

Slipper, green lustre w/gilding, Germany, 1920s, 4x2½"..**65.00**

Slipper, white w/gold lace & flowers, Heirlooms of Tomorrow, 5½".........................**45.00**

Slipper, 2 cherubs sit on blue & white bow, 6x2½".........**200.00**

Slipper on back of cherub, white w/applied flowers, #242, 9½" **550.00**

Golden Foliage

If you can remember when this glassware came packed in boxes of laundry soap, you're telling your age. Along with 'white' margarine, Golden Foliage was a product of the 1950s. It was made by the Libbey Glass Company, and the line was rather limited; as far as we know, we've listed the entire assortment here. The glassware features a satin band with various leaves and gold trim. (It also came in silver.)

Drink set, includes 6 jiggers & brass-finished caddy......**49.00**

Drink set, includes 8 tumblers (9-oz), ice tub & brass-finished caddy...............................**75.00**

Goblet, cocktail; 4-oz...............**6.00**

Goblet, cordial; 1-oz **9.50**

Goblet, pilsner; 11-oz.............**9.50**

Goblet, sherbet; 6½-oz............**4.50**

Goblet, water; 9-oz..................**6.50**

Ice tub, in metal 3-footed frame ..**22.50**

Pitcher, 5¼", w/metal frame..**16.50**

Salad dressing set, includes 3 bowls (4") & brass-finished caddy.............................**19.50**

Tumbler, beverage; 12½-oz **9.50**

Tumbler, cooler; 14-oz **9.50**

Tumbler, jigger; 2-oz..............**7.00**

Tumbler, juice; 6-oz **5.00**

Tumbler (water), 10-ounce, $7.50; goblet (water), 9-ounce, $6.50.

Tumbler, old fashioned; 9-oz ..**6.00**

Graniteware

Graniteware is actually a base metal with a coating of enamel. It was first made in the 1870s, but graniteware of sorts was made well into the 1950s. In fact, some of what you'll find today is brand new. But new pieces are much lighter in weight than the old ones. Look for seamed construction, metal handles, and graniteware lids on such things as tea- and coffeepots. All these are indicators of age. Colors are another, and swirled pieces — cobalt blue and white, green and white, brown and white, and red and white — are generally older, harder to find, and therefore more expensive. For a comprehensive look at this popular collectible, we recommend *The Collector's Encyclopedia of Graniteware* by Helen Greguire (Collector Books).

Baking pan, blue & white fine mottle, cobalt trim, 19x12x2¼", EX..........................**145.00**

Baking pan, cobalt and white large swirl, oblong with handles and ribbed bottom, G, $225.00.

Bean pot, blue solid, white interior, perforated lid, 7¾x5¾"..**125.00**

Bowl, fruit; cobalt & white lg mottle, ped ft, 7½x8", EX ..**145.00**

Bucket, berry; cream w/green, wire bail, seamless, 5x3½", EX **145.00**

Bucket, green veins w/white lumpy effect, green trim, 10x8¼", EX...................**325.00**

Chamber pot, black & white lg swirl w/black trim, seamless, 12"................................**295.00**

Coal hod, black-gray solid, seamed, 15x10½x18", EX...........**250.00**

Coffeepot, light blue & white med swirl, black trim & handle, 6¾"................................**160.00**

Coffeepot, red inside & out, black trim & handles, bulbous, 9", NM.............................**105.00**

Coffeepot, sea green to moss green, seamless, 9x5¼"...........**395.00**

Corn pot, solid yellow w/brown trim & lid, ceramic on steel, 1988, M........................**20.00**

Cup, custard; cream w/green trim, 2¼x3⅜".........................**55.00**

Cup, custard; shaded blue, Bluebelle Ware, 2½x3⅞", EX...........**75.00**

Dustpan, gray lg mottle, Haberman's Steel Enamel Ware label, 14", G+ **850.00**

Foot tub, dark gray mottle, seamed, oval, 9x19x13", EX........**195.00**

Fry pan, red & white lg swirl w/black trim & handle, 1970s, 6⅜"................................**185.00**

Funnel, blue & white mottle, gray interior, seamless, 3¼" dia, EX...............................**165.00**

Grater, dark gray solid, 11¾x4⅞", EX...............................**675.00**

Measure, aqua & white lg swirl w/cobalt trim, riveted/seamed, 4⅞"................................**450.00**

Mold, ribbed tube, cobalt w/white interior, 2⅞x8¼", EX.....**95.00**

Mold, ring, yellow w/white interior, 2¼x8⅛", EX..............**65.00**

Mug, blue & white swirl w/black trim, white interior, 3½", NM.....**95.00**

Mug, camp/mush; blue & white wavy mottle w/black trim, 4⅜x6"............................**175.00**

Mug, dark green & white mottle w/cobalt trim, Chrysolite, 2¾", EX...............................**135.00**

Pail, water; black & white lg mottle, white interior, wood bail, 9x11"............................**275.00**

Pail, water; gray lg mottle, seamless, wooden bail, 9⅜x12", EX................................**95.00**

Pitcher, milk; brown w/white specks & fine mottle, 8½x5⅜"..**200.00**

Pitcher, molasses; white solid w/cobalt handle & trim, 5½x3½" EX..................**175.00**

Potty, gray lg mottle, EL-AN-GE...label, child size, 3¾x6½".......................**145.00**

Pudding pan, red solid w/black trim, narrow rim, 2¾x9¾".........**30.00**

Pudding pan, white w/cobalt trim, Tru-B1 Quality...label, 7"..**35.00**

Roaster, red solid w/cobalt trim & handles, wire inset, w/lid, 11⅝".............................**110.00**

Roaster, solid red lid w/ridges, black bottom, 6½x9½", EX........**65.00**

Spoon, solid med blue, white interior, 2⅜x5¼", NM........**155.00**

Tea steeper, blue and white large swirl, 6", G, $350.00.

Tea strainer, gray med mottle, pierced bottom, 4" dia, NM...............**95.00**

Teakettle, solid white w/black trim & knob, wooden bail, 8", NM..............................**95.00**

Teapot, dark red & white swirl w/black trim, 1950s, 7¾x4¾", NM..............................**195.00**

Teapot, yellow & white swirl w/black trim, 1960s, lightweight, 8", EX..............**120.00**

Tube mold, solid cobalt w/white interior, Turk's head turban, 9", EX..............................**95.00**

Griswold

Cast-iron cooking ware was used extensively in the nineteenth century, and even today a lot of folks think no other type of cookware can measure up. But whether they buy it to use or are strictly collectors, Griswold is the name they hold in highest regard. During the latter part of the nineteenth century, the Griswold company began to manufacture the finest cast-iron kitchenware items available at that time. Soon after they became established, they introduced a line of lightweight, cast-aluminum ware that revolutionized the industry. The company enjoyed many prosperous years until its closing in the late 1950s. You'll recognize most items by the marks, which generally will include the Griswold name; for instance, 'Seldon Griswold' and 'Griswold Mfg. Co.' But don't overlook the 'Erie' mark, which the company used as well.

See Clubs and Newsletters for information on the Griswold and Cast Iron Cookware Association.

Ashtray, #00, PIN 570, round, w/matchbook holder, from $10 to.....................................**15.00**

Cake mold, lamb, PIN 866, from $75 to............................**100.00**

Dutch oven, #8, Early Tite-Top, Block trademarks, full writing on lid..............................**50.00**

Dutch oven, Favorite Piqua Ware #7, stylized trademark, from $40 to.............................**60.00**

Gem pan, #1, slant/EPU trademark, PIN 940, from $200 to **250.00**

Gem pan, #18, popover, wide handle, 6 cups, from $50 to..**70.00**

Gem pan, #24, Breadstick, PIN 957, from $400 to **450.00**

Gem pan, #100, heart & star, 5 cups, from $600 to **800.00**

Griddle, #8, Slant/EPU trademark, X bar support, hdl, from $20 to **40.00**

Griddle, #12 Gas or Vapor, marked Erie Gas Griddle, from $275 to **325.00**

Patty molds, #2, MIB, set, from $25 to **35.00**

Roaster, #3, oval, block trademarks, marked lid, from $475 to **525.00**

Skillet, #3, Block trademark, no heat ring, from $10 to....**20.00**

Skillet, #3, Square Fry, PIN 2103 (reproduced), from $75 to..**125.00**

Skillet, #4, wood handle, block trade mark, no heat ring, Pattern #758, $600.00. (Photo courtesy Grant S. Windsor)

Skillet, #5, sm trademark, grooved handle, from $10 to..........**15.00**

Skillet, #8, sm trademark, extra deep, w/hinge, from $35 to **45.00**

Skillet, #12, Block trademark, from $75 to **100.00**

Skillet, #15, oval, from $250 to..**300.00**

Skillet lid, #3, high smooth, from $150 to **200.00**

Teakettle, #8, Spider trademark top, from $400 to..........**500.00**

Waffle iron, #2, sq, from $650 to **700.00**

Guardian Ware

The Guardian Service company was in business from 1935 until 1955. They produced a very successful line of hammered aluminum that's just as popular today as it ever was. Sold through the home party plan, special hostess gifts were offered as incentives. Until 1940 metal lids were used, but during the war when the government restricted the supply of available aluminum, glass lids were introduced.

Be sure to judge condition when evaluating Guardian Service. Wear, baked-on grease, scratches, and obvious signs of use devaluate its worth. Our prices range from pieces in average to exceptional condition. To be graded exceptional, the interior of the pan must have no pitting, and the surface must be bright and clean. An item with a metal lid is worth 25% more than the same piece with a glass lid.

Ashtray, glass, w/knight & stars logo, hostess gift, from $25 to **30.00**

Beverage urn (coffeepot), glass lid, w/screen & dipper, 15" ..**50.00**

Can of cleaner, unopened **15.00**

Cookbook, Guardian Service or Pressure Cooker, from $20 to **35.00**

Dome cooker, 1-qt, glass lid, w/handles, 6¾" dia, from $25 to **45.00**

Fryer, breakfast; glass lid, 10", from $45 to **60.00**

Gravy boat and undertray, from $30.00 to $50.00. (Photo courtesy Dennis McAdams)

Handle, clamp-on style, from $10 to **15.00**

Ice bucket, glass lid, liner & tongs, 9", from $50 to **90.00**

Pressure cooker, from $125 to ..**165.00**

Roaster, turkey; glass lid, no rack, 16½" L, from $100 to ...**135.00**

Tray, serving; hammered center, w/handles, 13" dia, from $20 to **30.00**

Tureen, bottom; glass lid, from $40 to **65.00**

Tureen, casserole; glass lid, from $65 to **90.00**

Tureen, top; glass lid, from $30 to **45.00**

Gurley Candles

Santas, choir boys, turkeys, and angels are among the figural candles made by this company from the 1940s until as late as the 1960s, possibly even longer. They range in size from 2½" to nearly 9", and they're marked 'Gurley' on the bottom. Because they were so appealing, people were reluctant to burn them and instead stored them away and used them again and again. You can still find them today, especially at flea markets and garage sales. Tavern candles (they're marked as well) were made by a company owned by Gurley; they're also collectible.

Christmas, First Noel, NMIB, $18.00. (Photo courtesy Melissa Katcher)

Christmas, angel, marked Gurley, 3" **3.50**

Christmas, Black caroler man w/red clothes, 3"...............**8.50**

Christmas, choir boy or girl, 2¾",
ea **6.00**
Christmas, grotto w/shepherd &
sheep.............................**14.50**
Christmas, reindeer, marked
Tavern, 3½" **2.50**
Christmas, Santa, 6¼" **12.00**
Christmas, snowman running
w/red hat, 3"....................**8.50**
Christmas, 3" deer standing in
front of candle, 5".............**6.50**
Easter, pink birdhouse w/yellow
bird, 3" **7.50**
Easter, pink egg w/squirrel inside,
3"....................................**12.00**
Easter rabbit, pink or yellow, 3"..**5.00**
Halloween, black cat (4") w/orange
candlestick beside it **18.00**
Halloween, pumpkin w/black cat,
2½" **8.00**
Halloween, white ghost, 5"...**18.00**
Halloween, witch w/black cape,
3½" **8.50**
Other Holidays, birthday boy,
marked Tavern, 3"...........**6.00**
Other Holidays, Eskimo girl & igloo,
marked Tavern, 2-pc........**10.00**

**Thanksgiving turkey, 6½", M,
$20.00.**

Thanksgiving, acorns & leaves,
3½".................................**6.50**
Thanksgiving, Indian boy & girl,
brown & green clothes, 5",
pr..................................**30.00**
Thanksgiving, turkey, 2½" **2.50**
Thanksgiving, turkey, 5¾"...**15.00**

Hall

Most famous for their exten-
sive lines of teapots and colorful
dinnerwares, the Hall China
Company still operates in East
Liverpool, Ohio, where they were
established in 1903. Refer to *The
Collector's Encyclopedia of Hall
China* by Margaret and Kenn
Whitmyer (Collector Books) for
more information. See Clubs and
Newsletters for information on the
Hall China Collector's Club. For
listings of Hall's most popular din-
nerware line, see Autumn Leaf.

Aladdin, teapot, Marine Blue with
gold trim, from $75.00 to. **90.00**
Arizona, bowl, vegetable; open,
Tomorrow's Classic, 8¾" sq ..**25.00**
Arizona, plate, Tomorrow's
Classic, 11".....................**13.00**
Autumn Flowers, bean pot, New
England, #4 ....**130.00**
Beauty, bowl, Thin Rim, 6" ..**22.00**
Blue Blossom, ball jug, #3..**150.00**
Blue Blossom, water bottle,
Zephyr **800.00**
Blue Bouquet, bowl, Thick Rim,
6" **20.00**
Blue Bouquet, spoon...........**130.00**
Blue Garden, custard, Thick
Rim............................**24.00**

Blue Garden, drip jar, #1188, open **55.00**

Blue Willow, ashtray **35.00**

Bouquet, casserole, Tomorrow's Classic, 1¼-qt **45.00**

Bouquet, platter, Tomorrow's Classic, 17" **45.00**

Buckingham, bowl, salad; Tomorrow's Classic, lg, 14½" **45.00**

Buckingham, plate, Tomorrow's Classic, 8" **9.50**

Cactus, cookie jar, Five Band..**350.00**

Cameo Rose, bowl, cream soup; E style, 5" **90.00**

Cameo Rose, saucer, E style ..**1.50**

Caprice, bowl, celery; Tomorrow's Classic, oval **22.00**

Caprice, saucer, AD; Tomorrow's Classic **3.50**

Christmas Tree & Holly, cup, E style **20.00**

Crocus, bowl, Radiance, 9" ...**37.50**

Crocus, creamer, modern...... **19.00**

Crocus, pretzel jar............... **190.00**

Dawn, bowl, open baker; Tomorrow's Classic, 11-oz...................... **24.00**

Dawn, platter, Tomorrow's Classic, 17" **40.00**

Eggshell, baker, fish-shape, Swag, 13½" **85.00**

Eggshell, shirred egg, Dot **32.00**

Fantasy, bowl, fruit; Tomorrow's Classic, footed, lg........... **40.00**

Fantasy, sugar bowl, Tomorrow's Classic, w/lid **20.00**

Fern, ashtray, Century........... **8.00**

Fern, plate, Century, 8".......... **4.50**

Five Band, batter bowl, red or cobalt **60.00**

Flair, bowl, celery; Tomorrow's Classic, oval **24.00**

Flair, teapot, Tomorrow's Classic, 6-cup **210.00**

Flamingo, syrup pitcher, $125.00; batter bowl, 8", $100.00. (Photo courtesy Margaret and Kenn Whitmyer)

Flare-Ware, bowl, Gold Lace, 8¾"................................. **10.00**

Flare-Ware, cookie jar, Autumn Leaf................................ **37.00**

French Flower, creamer, Bellevue...................... **25.00**

Frost Flowers, ashtray, Tomorrow's Classic **9.00**

Game Bird, ball jug #3, E style..**275.00**

Game Bird, plate, E style, 10"..**70.00**

Garden of Eden, casserole, Century **55.00**

Garden of Eden, sugar bowl, Century, w/lid **15.00**

Gold Label, baker, French....**18.00**

Golden Glo, casserole, hen on nest............................... **50.00**

Golden Glo, Welsh rarebit, 15-oz **25.00**

Golden Oak, bowl, flat soup; 8½" **8.00**

Golden Oak, bowl, straight-sided, 7½"................................. **15.00**

Harlequin, platter, Tomorrow's Classic, 15".................... **37.00**

Harlequin, vinegar bottle, Tomorrow's Classic **95.00**

Heather Rose, bowl, cereal; E style, 6¼"...................... **10.00**

Heather Rose, jug, Rayed.....**25.00**

Holiday, ladle, Tomorrow's Classic..............22.00
Holiday, plate, Tomorrow's Classic, 8"..............9.00
Homewood, bowl, fruit; D-style, 5½"..............5.50
Homewood, coffeepot, Terrace..70.00
Lyric, candlestick, Tomorrow's Classic, 4½"..............32.00
Lyric, egg cup, Tomorrow's Classic..............55.00
Medallion, bowl, Chinese Red, #4, 7¼"..............20.00
Medallion, jug, Lettuce, ice lip, 5-pt..............47.00
Mulberry, egg cup, Tomorrow's Classic..............55.00
Mulberry, marmite, w/lid, Tomorrow's Classic........35.00
Mums, drip jar, w/lid, Medallion..............45.00
Mums, plate, 8¼"..............7.50
Mums, pretzel jar..............225.00
No 488, bowl, Radiance, 9"...32.00
No 488, creamer, Art Deco...25.00
No 488, cup..............18.00
No 488, jug, Rayed..............70.00
Orange Poppy, canister, Radiance..............450.00
Orange Poppy, cup..............30.00
Orange Poppy, salt & pepper shakers, Novelty Radiance, pr..90.00
Orange Poppy, soap dispenser..165.00
Pastel Morning Glory, bowl, oval..............40.00
Pastel Morning Glory, casserole, Radiance..............45.00
Pastel Morning Glory, stack set, Radiance..............125.00
Peach Blossom, coffeepot, Tomorrow's Classic, 6-cup..............105.00
Peach Blossom, onion soup, w/lid, Tomorrow's Classic........35.00

Pinecone, teapot, Tomorrow's Classic, six-cup, $125.00. (Photo courtesy Margaret and Kenn Whitmyer)

Pinecone, egg cup, Tomorrow's Classic..............45.00
Radiance, canister, red or cobalt, 2-qt..............65.00
Radiance, casserole, ivory....25.00
Red Poppy, custard..............20.00
Red Poppy, pie baker..............45.00
Red Poppy, platter, D style, 13¼"..............30.00
Red Poppy, sifter, metal, 2 styles, ea..............75.00
Ribbed, onion soup, Chinese Red, w/lid..............45.00
Ribbed, ramekin, Russet, 4½-oz..............5.50
Sear's Arlington, bowl, E style, oval, 9¼"..............20.00
Sear's Arlington, saucer, E style..1.50
Sear's Fairfax, creamer, E style..7.00
Sear's Fairfax, sugar bowl, w/lid, E style..............14.00
Sear's Monticello, bowl, cereal; E style, 6¼"..............9.00
Sear's Monticello, plate, E style, 8"..............7.50
Sear's Richmond/Brown-Eyed Susan, cup..............6.50
Sear's Richmond/Brown-Eyed Susan, saucer..............1.50
Serenade, bowl, fruit; D style, 5½"..............5.00

Serenade, fork......................**120.00**

Silhouette, coffeepot, glass dripper, Five Band..............**100.00**

Silhouette, gravy boat, D style..........................**30.00**

Silhouette, tea tile, 6"...........**90.00**

Spring, bowl, fruit; Tomorrow's Classic, 5¾"......................**6.50**

Springtime, bowl, Thick Rim, 7½"................................**14.00**

Springtime, pie baker............**20.00**

Springtime, plate, D style, 6".**4.00**

Sundial, batter jug, Art Glaze colors.................................**225.00**

Sundial, coffee server, red or cobalt.............................**550.00**

Sunglow, butter dish, Century..**125.00**

Sunglow, salt & pepper shakers, Century, pr......................**32.00**

Tulip, plate, D style, 9".........**12.00**

Tulip, waffle iron, metal.....**120.00**

Wildfire, coffee dispenser, metal...........................**30.00**

Wildfire, custard, straight sided.............................**25.00**

Wildfire, gravy boat, D style..**25.00**

Yellow Rose, creamer, Norse..**20.00**

Yellow Rose, plate, D style, 8¼"..**9.00**

Hallmark

Since 1973 the Hallmark Company has made Christmas ornaments, some of which are today worth many times their original price. Our suggested values reflect the worth of those in mint condition and in their original boxes. See Clubs and Newsletters in the Directory for information regarding *The Baggage Car.*

A Matchless Christmas, QX132-7, 1979................................**85.00**

Animal House, QX149-6, 1987.**175.00**

Baby Partridge, QX452-5, 1989................................**15.00**

Baby's 1st Christmas, QX131-5, 1977................................**75.00**

Baby Unicorn, QX548-6, 1990.**25.00**

Beauty of Friendship, QX303-4, 1980................................**65.00**

Behold the Star, QX255-9, 1979................................**39.50**

Betsy Clark, 250HD100-2, 1973................................**85.00**

Birds of Winter, Cardinals, QX205-1, 1976................**85.00**

Brass Carousel, QX707-1, 1984................................**95.00**

Brother, QX468-4, 1992........**16.50**

Candyville Express, QX418-2, 1981................................**95.00**

Charmers, QX109-1, 1974....**45.00**

Christmas Joy, QX624-1, 1996.**30.00**

Christmas Time, QX226-1, 1980...............................**30.00**

Christmas Together, QX269-6, 1978................................**35.00**

Cool Swing Penguin, QX487-5, 1989................................**35.00**

Cows of Bali, QX599-9, 1995.**19.50**

Currier & Ives, QX164-1, 1975................................**55.00**

Dove, QX190-3, 1978...........**85.00**

Drummer Boy, QX312-2, 1977.**65.00**

Elfin Engineer, LX720-9, 1991................................**25.00**

Faithful Firefighter, QX578-2, 1993................................**20.00**

Fun On a Big Scale, QX513-4, 1992................................**23.50**

Godchild, QX603-5, 1981......**22.50**

Good Cheer Blimp, QX704-6, 1987................................**60.00**

Goody Gumballs, QLX736-7, 1995 ....**33.00**
Grandmother, QX204-1, 1980 .**20.00**
Here Comes Santa, QX155-9, 1979 ....**595.00**

Hooked on Santa, Julia Lee, QX410-9, 1991, $20.00.

Icicyle Bicycle, QX583-6, 1993.**20.00**
Jingle Bears, QLX732-3, 1991 .**57.50**
Jolly Dolphin, QX468-3, 1990 **37.50**
Journey to Bethlehem, QXM403-6, 1994 ....**17.50**
Joyous Carolers, QLX729-5, 1989 ....**70.00**
Jump-long Jackolope, 2250, QX575-6, 1994 ....**22.50**
Love, QX255-4, 1984 ....**25.00**
Mickey's Long Shot, Disney, golf, QXD641-2, 1997 ....**22.00**
Mountains, QX158-2, 1977...**45.00**
Nativity, QX253-6, 1978 .....**150.00**
Our Christmas Together, QX580-9, 1995 ....**19.50**
Peace on Earth, Nostalgia, QX131-1, 1975 ....**165.00**
Perfect Catch, QX569-3, 1990.**20.00**
Puppy Love, QX406-2, 1981 .**40.00**
Rapid Delivery, QX509-4, 1992.**25.00**
Ready for Christmas, QX133-9, 1979 ....**150.00**
Rudolph & Santa, QX213-1, 1976 ....**95.00**

Santa Pipe, QX494-2, 1985 ..**25.00**
Santa's Arrival, QX702-4, 1984 ....**65.00**
Son, QX502-4, 1992 ....**26.50**
Special Delivery, QX432-5, 1989 ....**25.00**
St Louie Nick, QX453-9, 1987 .**30.00**
Star of Wonder, QX598-2, 1993 .**22.50**
The Stocking Mouse, QX412-2, 1981 ....**115.00**
Trumpet Panda, QX471-2, 1985.**25.00**

Halloween

Halloween items are fast becoming the most popular holiday-related collectibles on the market today. Although originally linked to pagan rituals and superstitions, Halloween has long since evolved into a fun-filled event; and the masks, noise-makers, and jack-o'-lanterns of earlier years are great fun to look for.

Pamela E. Apkarian-Russell (the Halloween Queen), has written several books on the subject: *Collectible Halloween; Salem Witchcraft and Souvenirs; More Halloween Collectibles; Halloween: Decorations and Games; Anthropomorphic Beings of Halloween;* and *The Tastes and Smells of Halloween.* She is listed in the Directory under New Hampshire. See Clubs and Newsletters for information concerning *The Trick or Treat Trader.*

Bendee, pumpkin-face man, Burger King premium ...**10.00**
Book & record set, Georgie's Halloween, by Robert Bright, EX **25.00**

Bank, Schultz, Whitman Candy, modern, $14.00. (Photo courtesy Pamela Apkarian-Russell)

Candy box, cardboard w/image of owl on branch, EX **45.00**

Candy container, beet-headed clown, composition, Germany, 3½" **200.00**

Candy container, devil head w/veggie body, composition, 6", EX............................**250.00**

Candy container, pumpkin-head policeman, glass...........**800.00**

Candy container, tree trunk, pressed cardboard, NM..................**150.00**

Candy holder, cat pulls pumpkin coach, cardboard, 2-sided, EX **45.00**

Costume, Bart Simpson, Ben Cooper (Canadian), MIB..**12.00**

Costume, Beatles, any member, Ben Cooper, 1960s MIB, ea...**400.00**

Costume, Bionic Woman, Ben Cooper, 1975, MIB, from $30 to **40.00**

Costume, Dick Tracy, Ben Cooper, 1967, complete, EX........**50.00**

Costume, Lucy (Peanuts), Collegeville, 1980s, MIB..**15.00**

Costume, Snoopy, Determined, 1960s, MIB **25.00**

Cup, witch head in cone-shape hat, Malibu on hat & removable glasses **20.00**

Decoration, bat w/movable wings, paper................................**6.00**

Decoration, cat, cardboard, jointed arms, Beistle, 1930s, 27", VG **50.00**

Decoration, owl, cardboard w/fold-out paper wings **30.00**

Diecut, devil w/pitch fork, heavily embossed cardboard, Germany, lg **150.00**

Diecut, flying witch, heavily embossed cardboard, Germany.........**145.00**

Figure, ghost on jack-o'-lantern, Hallmark Merry Miniature, EX **15.00**

Figure, witch, painted bisque, Japan, 1950s, 3", EX **40.00**

Figure, witch holding black cat, VC/USA, celluloid, 4½", VG **250.00**

Hat, orange felt w/black cat & jack-o'-lantern, EX.........**20.00**

Hat, orange felt w/painted black cat & jack-o'-lantern, conical **15.00**

Horn, cardboard litho, wooden mouthpiece **65.00**

Jack-o'-lantern, paper on wire frame, folds up, EX........**25.00**

Jack-o'-lantern, pulp, eyes crossed, pug nose, American, 1940s, 5", NM **150.00**

Jack-o'-lantern, soft plastic, battery-operated, Japan, 1950s, 4", MIB **65.00**

Lantern, owl, cast iron, openwork feathers, original............**85.00**

Lantern, pumpkin face, pressed cardboard w/paper insert, Germany......................**125.00**

Lantern, witch & owl on 4 panels, cardboard/tissue paper, EX **65.00**

Mask, Batgirl, Ben Cooper, 1977, NM **8.00**

Mask, Raggedy Ann, Collegeville, 1991, M, $25.00. (Photo courtesy Kim Avery)

Noisemaker, black cat, cardboard, wood handle, Germany, 1920s, 6", EX **75.00**

Noisemaker, drum-type w/hanging bells, wood & paper **95.00**

Nut cup, jack-o'-lantern, papier-mache **20.00**

Postcard, pumpkin-face children & black cat, easel back **22.00**

Rattle, plastic witch head atop wooden handle, 1950s, 8", EX **40.00**

Squeeze toy, Crying Pumpkin, Made in Boston USA, EX...........**45.00**

Tambourine, laughing devil's face, tin, EX **110.00**

Yo-yo, jack-o'-lantern, tin, modern **8.00**

Yo-yo, skulls & crossbones, litho tin, 1960s, MIP **10.00**

Handkerchiefs

Lovely to behold, handkerchiefs remain as feminine keepsakes of a time past. Largely replaced by disposable tissues of more modern times, handkerchiefs found today are often those that had special meaning, keepsakes of special occasions, or souvenirs. Many collectible handkerchiefs were never meant for everyday use, but intended to be a feminine addition to the lady's total ensemble. Made in a wide variety of styles and tucked away in grandmother's dresser, handkerchiefs are now being brought out and displayed for their dainty loveliness and fine craftsmanship. For further information we recommend *Handkerchiefs, A Collector's Guide,* by Helene Guarnaccia and Barbara Guggenheim; and *Ladies' Vintage Accessories, Identification & Value Guide,* by LaRee Johnson Bruton (Collector Books).

Batiste, white, w/3-D pink hearts hanging at corners, 1930, 12½" **35.00**

Batiste, white w/blue & green dots, monogram, 14" **25.00**

Batiste, white w/lg monogram, vintage, 15x15" **25.00**

Cotton, cat w/rhinestone eyes, w/original label, 1950, 10" **30.00**

Cotton, fine voille printed, Regency lady in ea corner, 1950s, 15" **30.00**

Cotton, lg initial w/embroidered satin leaves, 16" **30.00**

Cotton, peach, hand-embroidered, lace design in corner, from $5 to **12.00**

Cotton, w/pretty initial, 1920s, 11" **25.00**

Cotton, w/wide lace border, 1950s, 10" **30.00**

Cotton, white, w/'Mother' & spray of flowers sewn in silk threads, 12"..................**30.00**

Cotton, white w/blue printed waves & anchor, WWII era, 13".................................**32.50**

Cotton, white w/embroidery & monogram, 1940s, 12"...**25.00**

Irish linen, w/tag: Arrow 100% Irish Linen, 17"..............**15.00**

Irish linen, white, edged in green crochet trim, from $5 to..**15.00**

Lawn, white, hemstitched w/fine hairpin lace, from $25 to..........................**55.00**

Linen, initial & 3-D flower in corner, 1930s, 13"..............**30.00**

Linen, pale blue w/hand-appliqued & embroidered satin initial, 18"..................................**30.00**

Linen, pale green w/white Belgian Princess lace corners & edges, 12"..................................**30.00**

Linen, pink, filet lace butterfly in one corner, from $25 to..**55.00**

Linen, sq w/hand-embroidered initial in corner, 1920........**25.00**

Linen (various colors) with crochet trim or lace, each from $5.00 to $10.00. (Photo courtesy LaRee Johnson Bruton)

Linen, w/pink embroidered initial in corner, hand-stitched hem, 1930s.............................**20.00**

Linen, white, bordered w/fine Battenburg-type lace, from $65 to..............................**85.00**

Linen, white, white embroidered initial, 1920s, 12"...........**30.00**

Linen & lace, w/label: Made in Switzerland attached, 13"..**30.00**

Madeira lace, black w/multicolored butterflies, vintage, 16"..**25.00**

Princess lace, ecru, on net background, from $25 to.......**55.00**

Silk, aqua, deep embroidered sheer silk border, 14" sq, from $15 to..............................**25.00**

Silk, yellow-gold w/'Mother' & US Army Eagle stamped in corner, 11"............................**15.00**

Voille, pale lemon w/hand-crocheted lace Crinoline lady, 1930s, 12"......................**25.00**

Voille, w/pink embroidered initial, 1920s, 12"......................**25.00**

Wedding, fine lawn w/wide machine-lace border, ca 1900, 17", from $25 to..............**35.00**

Hartland

Hartland Plastics Inc. of Hartland, Wisconsin, produced a line of Western and Historic Horsemen and Standing Gunfighter figures during the 1950s, which are now very collectible. Using a material called virgin acetate, they molded such well-known characters as Annie Oakley, Bret Maverick, Matt Dillon, and many others, which they painted with highest attention to detail. In addition to these, they made a line of sports greats as well as one featuring religious figures.

Gunfighter, Bat Masterson, standing, NMIB **500.00**

Gunfighter, Bret Maverick, NMIB **600.00**

Gunfighter, Dan Troop, standing, NM..............................**600.00**

Gunfighter, Paladin, standing, NM..............................**400.00**

Horseman, Bill Longley, NM..**600.00**

Horseman, Buffalo Bill, NM, $600.00.

Horseman, Cactus Pete, NM .**150.00**

Horseman, Cheyenne, w/tag, NM **190.00**

Horseman, Commanche Kid, NM...........................**150.00**

Horseman, Dale Evans, purple, NM..............................**250.00**

Horseman, General Robert E Lee, NMIB...........................**175.00**

Horseman, Jim Hardy, NMIB..**300.00**

Horseman, Lone Ranger, rearing, NMIB...........................**300.00**

Horseman, Rebel, NMIB..**1,200.00**

Horseman, Roy Rogers, walking, NMIB...........................**300.00**

Horseman, Tonto, semi-rearing, rare, NM......................**650.00**

Sports, Babe Ruth, 1960s, NM, from $175 to.................**200.00**

Sports, Dick Groat, 25th Anniversary, M (NM box)........................**45.00**

Sports, Eddie Matthews, 1960s, NM, from $125 to........**150.00**

Sports, Hank Aaron, 1960s, EX, from $175 to.................**190.00**

Sports, Harmon Killebrew, 1960s, EX...............................**290.00**

Sports, Lou Gerhrig, 1960s, NMIB **200.00**

Sports, Mickey Mantle, 1960s..**350.00**

Sports, Nellie Fox, 1960s, NM, from $200 to.................**250.00**

Sports, Roger Maris, 1960s, NM, from $350 to.................**400.00**

Sports, Ted Williams, 1960s, NM............................**235.00**

Sports, Washington Redskins, 1960s, EX, from $275 to..............**310.00**

Sports, Willie Mays, NM, from $225 to..........................**250.00**

Sports, Yogi Berra, w/mask, NM, from $175 to.................**250.00**

Hawaiian Shirts

Vintage shirts made in Hawaii are just one of many retro fads finding favor on today's market. Those with the tag of a top designer can bring hefty prices — the more colorful, the better. Shirts of this type were made in the states as well. Look for graphics that shout 'Hawaii!' Fabrics are typically cotton, rayon, or polyester (poly in our lines).

Hale Hawaii, beach scene w/flowers & palm trees, bamboo buttons, poly, M.................**120.00**

Jam World Collectors Edition, red & yellow floral on blue & green, rayon **95.00**

Lauhala, maroon w/yellow & tan orchid sprays, coconut buttons, EX..........................**75.00**

Leighton, maroon w/green & white floral, shell buttons, 1950s, EX..................................**90.00**

Made in Hawaii, 100% cotton, bright print, $100.00. (Photo courtesy/copyright John Dowling)

McGregor, tan w/surfer on red board, 1950s, EX..........**465.00**

Reyn Spooner's Jimmy Buffett, Air Margaritaville, M...........**70.00**

RJC Ltd, tiki tribal w/turtles, fish, men & floral, cotton, EX..**65.00**

Rossini by Cali-Fame, surfers, hula dancers, volcanos & flowers, rayon, M **230.00**

Royal Hawaiian, yellow & white flowers on brown, EX **55.00**

Scoggins Golfer, maroon w/under-the-sea theme, EX **100.00**

Shahleen, off-white w/2 red fish, poly/cotton, EX.............**130.00**

Somerset, Penney's, blue & white birds flying on gray-toned clouds, NM **55.00**

Tommy, light blue huts on dark blue, EX.........................**50.00**

Head Vases

Many of them Japanese imports, head vases were made primarily for the florist trade. They were styled as children, teenagers, clowns, and famous people. There are heads of religious figures, Blacks, Orientals, and even some animals. One of the most common types are ladies wearing pearl earrings and necklaces. Refer to *Head Vases, Identification and Value Guide,* by Kathleen Cole and *Collecting Head Vases* by David Barron (Collector Books) for more information. See Clubs and Newsletters for information concerning the *Head Hunter's Newsletter.*

Baby, Enesco #2185, pink bonnet w/blue bow, w/phone, 5".......................................**45.00**

Baby, Relpo #K1866, blond w/pink bonnet w/blue bow, 7"....**75.00**

Baby, unmarked, blond in ruffled bonnet, lg pale blue bow, 5½" **65.00**

Baby, Velco #3797, light brown hair, w/pink bow, sitting on pillow, 7".........................**75.00**

Boy, Inarco #E1575, blond, head bowed & hands in prayer, 5¾" **85.00**

Boy fireman, Inarco label, #5 on hat, 5" **75.00**

Clown, Inarco #E5071, white w/red nose & mouth, sm black hat, 4½" **85.00**

Famous people, Ben Franklin, white shirt & black collar, 6" **125.00**

Famous people, Inarco #E1852, Jackie Kennedy, black glove, 5½"................................**650.00**

Girl, Inarco #E1247, blond in Christmas hat & coat, 4"..**65.00**

Girl, Inarco #E1579, blond w/hands in prayerful pose, 6"........**45.00**

Girl, Inarco #E2965, pigtails, yellow scarf & bodice, 7" **58.00**

Girl, unmarked, blond, pink bonnet w/flower, flowered bodice, 5"....................................**65.00**

Girl, unmarked, winking, black hat, blue & white bow at neck, 6"....................................**50.00**

Girl, Wales label, Japan, brown hair updo w/flowers & ponytail, 6" **95.00**

Girl with umbrella, unmarked, 4½", $60.00. (Photo courtesy Kathleen Cole)

Lady, Lefton (paper label) #1343B, wide-brimmed hat, 6", $90.00; Lady, Napco #C4414C, green hat, bow at chin, 1959, 6", $65.00. (Photo courtesy Kathleen Cole)

Lady, Inarco #1608, light brown updo, double pearls, 10"..**675.00**

Lady, Lefton's #2705, blond in pink, hand up, 6½" **75.00**

Lady, Lefton's #2900, flower on hat, strapless bodice, hands up, 6" **85.00**

Lady, marked Glamour Girl, white w/gold trim, 6½".............**20.00**

Lady, Nancy Pew, blond w/blue bow, pearls, yellow bodice, hand up, 6"...................**125.00**

Lady, Napco #C5046, blond, gloved hands folded, flat hat, 4½"................................**95.00**

Lady, Napco #C5708, white ringlets, ruffled sq neckline, 1962, 6"........................**200.00**

Lady, Napcoware #CF6060, blond, pearl earrings, gold trim, 3½"......................**35.00**

Lady, Relpo A-1229, blond, floral pillbox hat, gloved hands up, 6½"................................**75.00**

Lady, Reubens #4121, blond, yellow hair bows & bodice, pearls, 5½" **85.00**

Lady, unmarked, blond in ruffled bonnet, thick lashes, 5½" **175.00**

Lady, Vcagco, blond w/pink hat, pearl earrings, 5½" **75.00**

Lady, Velco #10759, side-swept hair, yellow bodice, 5½"..**75.00**

Madonna & Child, Napcoware label #R7076, pastels, 6½".......**50.00**

Man, unmarked, black hair, winking, green hat, bow tie, 4½"......**45.00**

Nun, Relpo, prayerful pose w/hands crossed, thick lashes, 6½" **35.00**

Oriental lady, Japan, ornate headdress, pastels w/gold, 5" ..**50.00**

Oriental lady, unmarked, ornate headdress & bodice, 8½"..**125.00**

Teen girl, #4796, blond braids, flat pink bow, 5¾" **50.00**

Teen girl, Caffco label, blond frosted flip, bow at neck, 7" **225.00**

Teen girl, Enesco, brunette, flower at shoulder, 5¾"............**50.00**

Teen girl, Inarco #E2967, blond w/black head band & bodice, 5½"..................................**80.00**

Teen girl, Inarco #E3523, blond w/curls & bows, ruffled collar, 7"....................................**265.00**

Teen girl, Inarco #E5623, blond curls, dark eyes, pearls, 6½" **125.00**

Teen girl, Relpo #K1694/S, blond w/pink coat, gloved hand, 5½" **95.00**

Teen girl, unmarked, blond ponytail, brown derby hat, hand up, 6½" **90.00**

Teen girl graduate, Napco #C4072G, blond w/diploma, 6".........**100.00**

Uncle Sam, unmarked, pastel green overall, 6½"..........**45.00**

Holly Hobbie and Friends

About 1970 a young homemaker and mother, Holly Hobbie, approached the American Greeting Company with some charming country-styled drawings of children. Since that time over four hundred items have been made with almost all being marked HH, H. Hobbie, or Holly Hobbie.

Clock, Start Each Day in a Happy Way, wall type, battery operated, MIB **45.00**

Cradle, wood frame, quilted coverlet, fits 16-21" dolls, EX..**38.00**

Cross-stitch kit, baby quilt, 1980, 33x45", +sham, nearly completed, EX......................**50.00**

Doll, Grandma Holly, Knickerbocker, cloth, 24", MIB **30.00**

Doll, Holly Hobbie, all vinyl with painted eyes, marked KTC 1975/ Made in Taiwan on head and back, Knickerbocker, 11", from $12.00 to $15.00. (Photo courtesy Patsy Moyer)

Doll, Holly Hobbie, Heather, Amy or Carrie, Knickerbocker, 6", MIB, ea...........................**10.00**

Doll, Holly Hobbie, Heather, Amy or Carrie, Knickerbocker, 9", MIB, ea...........................**15.00**

Doll, Holly Hobbie, Heather, Amy or Carrie, Knickerbocker, 16", MIB................................**25.00**

Doll, Holly Hobbie, Heather, Amy or Carrie, Knickerbocker, 27", MIB................................**35.00**

Doll, Holly Hobbie, Heather, Amy or Carrie, Knickerbocker, 33", MIB................................**45.00**

Doll, Holly Hobbie, 1988, scented, clear ornament at neck, 18", NRFB............................**40.00**

Doll, Holly Hobbie Dream Along, Holly, Knickerbocker, 12", MIB **20.00**

Doll, Holly Hobbie Talker, cloth, 4 sayings, 16", MIB **30.00**

Doll, Little Girl Holly, Knickerbocker, cloth, 1980, 15", MIB **30.00**

Doll, Robbie, Knickerbocker, cloth, 9", MIB **20.00**

Doll, Robbie, Knickerbocker, cloth, 16", MIB **30.00**

Dollhouse **300.00**

Figurine, Grandmother's Keepsake, American Greetings, on base, 1985 ....**100.00**

Figurine, Mother's Bouquet, American Greetings, 1984, 5½" **85.00**

Plate, Country Morning, Collectors Edition Series II, 1982 ....**55.00**

Platter, transfer on white porcelain, gold trim, 14½x10½" **35.00**

Playset, Gazebo, w/sm Knickerbocker doll & picnic basket, 1976, NRFB **60.00**

Sewing Machine, Durham, plastic & metal, battery-op, 1975, 5x9", EX..........................**40.00**

Sing-A-Long, Electric Parlor Player, Vanity Fair, 1970s, complete, NMIB **45.00**

Tea set, china, Chilton Toys, 1960, serves 4, 15-pc, MIB **48.00**

Holt Howard

Collectors search for the pixie kitchenware items from the late 1950s such as cruets and condiments, all with flat, disk-like pixie heads for stoppers. In the '60s the company designed and distributed a line of roosters — egg cups, napkin holders, salt and pepper shakers, etc. Items with a Christmas theme featuring Santa or angels, for instance, were sold from the '50s through the '70s, and you'll also find a line of white cats collectors call Kozy Kitten. These are only a sampling of the wonderful novelties imported by this company. Most are not only marked but dated as well.

Christmas, planter, reindeer, $25.00; salt and pepper shakers, reindeer, $30.00. (Photo courtesy Pat and Ann Duncan)

Blue Willow, mugs, set of 4..**45.00**

Bride & Groom, candle holders, 4", pr......................................**50.00**

Butler (Jeeves), martini shaker, 9" **200.00**

Butler (Jeeves), tray, 4¾" wide **150.00**

Christmas, butter pats, holly leaves & berries, 2¾", set of 4.....**32.00**

Christmas, candle holder, double; 3 choir boys hold lg song book **38.00**

Christmas, candle holders, camel figurals, 4", pr **50.00**

Christmas, Christmas tree, electric, 10" **70.00**

Christmas, cookies/candy jar, roly-poly Santa figure, 3-pc, from $120 to **150.00**

Christmas, dish, Santa face, 7¼x5½" **20.00**

Christmas, match holder, Santa w/bongo drum, 4½" **30.00**

Christmas, place card holders/figurines, elves, 3", set of 4 ....**55.00**

Christmas, salt & pepper shakers, angels, 3½", pr **22.00**

Christmas, salt & pepper shakers, Santa & his bag, Santa: 3", pr **35.00**

Christmas, salt & pepper shakers, standing Santas, 5½", pr **18.00**

Christmas, salt & pepper shakers, stylized deer figurals, 1 buck & 1 doe, pr **30.00**

Christmas, tray, Santa beard forms tray, 7¾", from $25 to......**30.00**

Christmas, votive candle holder, Santa, dated 1968, 3" **20.00**

Coin Kitty, bank, bobbing head finial, from $100 to **150.00**

Dandy Lion, bank, bobbing head, from $100 to **150.00**

Goose & Golden Egg, salt & pepper shakers, pr **40.00**

Honey Bunnies, candle climbers, w/bases, 4-pc set **50.00**

Hot Stuff, super scooper, red & white, w/lid, 6" **50.00**

Kozy Kitten, bud vase, cat in plaid cap & neckerchief, from $75 to **100.00**

Kozy Kitten, butter dish, cats peeking out on side, ¼-lb, from $100 to **150.00**

Kozy Kitten, cookie jar, head form, from $40 to **50.00**

Kozy Kitten, cottage cheese keeper, cat knob on lid, from $45 to **55.00**

Kozy Kitten, creamer & sugar bowl, stackable, from $85 to ..**100.00**

Kozy Kitten, salt & pepper shakers, cat's head, pr...........**30.00**

Kozy Kitten, salt & pepper shakers, tall cats, w/noisemakers, pr....................................**45.00**

Kozy Kitten, spice set, stacking; from $150 to **175.00**

Kozy Kitten, spice shaker, cat head w/loop atop for hanging, 2½x3" **35.00**

Kozy Kitten, string holder, head only, from $40 to............**50.00**

Kozy Kitten, tape measure, cat on cushion **85.00**

Kozy Kitten, wall pocket, cat's head, from $30 to..........**40.00**

Moo Cow, salt & pepper shakers, working 'mooing' mechanism, 3¼", pr..........................**42.50**

Nursery Rhymes, mug, footed, verse printed in wide graphic band...............................**25.00**

Pig, votive candle holder, pastel, dated 1958, 5½" **45.00**

Pixie Ware, candlesticks, pr, from $50 to **65.00**

Pixie Ware, cherries jar, flat head finial, w/cherry pick or spoon.........................**150.00**

Pixie Ware, chili sauce, rare, minimum value **350.00**

Pixie Ware, cocktail cherries, from $160 to **175.00**

Pixie Ware, cocktail onions, onion-head finial, from $160 to ..**175.00**

Pixie Ware, cruets, oil & vinegar; Sally & Sam, pr, minimum value **250.00**

Pixie Ware, French dressing bottle, minimum value, from $160 to.........................**175.00**

Pixie Ware, honey, very rare, from $400 to.........................**500.00**

Pixie Ware, Italian Dressing bottle, round head, from $160.00 to $190.00. (Photo courtesy Pat and Ann Duncan)

Pixie Ware, jam & jelly jar, flathead finial on lid, from $65 to..................................**85.00**

Pixie Ware, mustard jar, yellow head finial on lid, from $80 to..................................**110.00**

Pixie Ware, onion jar, flat onion-head finial, 1958..........**200.00**

Pixie Ware, relish jar, green flat head on lid....................**250.00**

Pixie Ware, Russian dressing bottle, minimum value **200.00**

Pixie Ware, spice set, stacking; from $135 to.................**150.00**

Ponytail Princess, lipstick holder, from $50 to.....................**65.00**

Ponytail Princess, tray, double; 2 joined flower cups, girl between...........................**60.00**

Poodle & Cat, salt & pepper shakers, 4½", 4", pr................**40.00**

Rake 'N Spade, plate, MIB ...**20.00**

Rock 'N Roll Kids, salt & pepper shakers, heads on springs, pr...**125.00**

Rooster, candle holders, $15.00 each; Bud vase, from $25.00 to $30.00; Syrup pitcher, $30.00; Mustard jar, $35.00; Dish, figural with open body receptacle, $20.00.

Rooster, ashtray/tea bag holders, set of 4, from $35 to........**40.00**

Rooster, bowl, cereal; 6"..........**9.00**

Rooster, coffeepot, electric, from $50 to..............................**70.00**

Rooster, coffeepot, embossed rooster.....................................**85.00**

Rooster, cookie jar, embossed rooster **150.00**

Rooster, creamer & sugar bowl, embossed rooster, from $30 to..................................**45.00**

Rooster, cup & saucer............**15.00**

Rooster, egg cup, double; figural rooster **25.00**

Rooster, jam & jally jar, embossed rooster, from $40 to........**50.00**

Rooster, ketchup jar, embossed rooster, w/lid..................**50.00**

Rooster, mustard jar, embossed rooster, w/lid..................**35.00**

Rooster, napkin holder.........**40.00**

Rooster, pincushion, 3¼x4", from $65 to.............................**75.00**

Rooster, plate, embossed rooster, 8½", from $15 to.............**22.00**

Rooster, tray, facing left, from $15 to....................................**20.00**

Rooster, trivet, tile w/rooster in iron framework, from $40 to...**50.00**

Tiger, salt & pepper shakers, big smile, 3½", pr.................**25.00**

Homer Laughlin

The Homer Laughlin China Company has produced millions of pieces of dinnerware, toiletry items, art china, children's dishes, and hotel ware since its inception in 1874. On most pieces the backstamp includes company name, date, and plant where the piece was produced, and nearly always the shape name is included. We have listed samples from many of the decaled lines; some of the more desirable patterns will go considerably higher. Refer to *The Collector's Encyclopedia of Homer Laughlin China* by Joanne Jasper; *Homer Laughlin China Company, A Giant Among Dishes,* by Jo Cunningham; and *The Collector's Encyclopedia of Fiesta, Ninth Edition,* by Sharon and Bob Huxford. See Clubs and Newsletters for information concerning *The Laughlin Eagle,* a newsletter for collectors of Homer Laughlin dinnerware. See also Fiesta.

Brittany Shape (available in Lady Alice, Emerald, Sylvan, and Hemlock)

Bowl, deep, 6".......................**18.00**
Creamer.................................**16.00**
Dish, 15"...............................**30.00**
Nappy, w/lid, 9"....................**57.00**
Plate, 10"..............................**15.00**
Saucer, cream soup................**8.00**
Sugar bowl, w/lid.................**26.00**
Teapot...................................**55.00**

Cavalier Shape (available in Berkshire, Crinoline, Jade Rose, and Turquoise Melody)

Casserole, w/lid.....................**60.00**

Dinner plate, from $12.00 to $14.00; Teacup and saucer, from $12.00 to $14.00 (each in Turquoise Melody pattern). (Photo courtesy Joanne Jasper)

Plate, rim soup; deep............**15.00**
Plate, 6"..................................**8.00**
Plate, 9"................................**15.00**
Platter, 11"...........................**25.00**
Salt & pepper shakers, Jubilee shape, pr........................**30.00**
Saucer, tea..............................**7.00**
Teapot...................................**75.00**

Debutante Shape (available in Blue Mist, Champagne, Gray Laurel, and Wild Grapes)

Casserole, w/lid 35.00
Coffeepot...........................60.00
Creamer.............................14.00
Dish, 15" 25.00
Nappy, 7"...........................12.00
Pie server..........................30.00
Plate, 10" 9.00
Plate, 9" 8.00

Empress Shape, early 1900s (available in Flying Bluebirds, Pink Moss Rose, Rose and Lattice, Others

Baker, 8"............................18.00
Bone dish...........................10.00
Casserole, 9".......................45.00
Cup, coffee; AD.....................18.00
Egg cup, Boston 25.00
Ladle, rare..........................22.00
Plate, coupe; 7".....................9.00
Plate, 6" 7.00
Sauce boat 28.00
Teapot...............................95.00

Kwaker Shape, 1920s (available in Dream Poppy, Vestal Rose, Vandemere, Presidential)

Baker, 8"............................20.00
Bowl, fruit; 5" 6.00
Bowl, oyster; 1¼-pt..............20.00
Casserole, w/lid 55.00
Creamer.............................18.00
Dish, 12" 24.00
Nappy, 9"...........................20.00
Plate, 10" 14.00
Plate, 6" 7.00
Sugar bowl, w/lid 28.00

Liberty Shape (available in Calirose, Dogwood, Greenbrier, and Stratford)

Baker, oval 30.00
Bowl, cream soup; rare.........40.00
Bowl, fruit............................9.00
Bowl, oatmeal; 6" 16.00
Bread plate, rare..................45.00
Casserole, w/lid 75.00
Egg cup, double, Cable 100.00
Jug, 5"...............................95.00
Mug, coffee 40.00
Plate, rare, 8" 12.00
Plate, rim soup; deep............15.00
Plate, 9" 15.00
Sugar bowl, w/lid 28.00
Teapot...............................75.00

Nautilus Regular Shape, 1930s (available in Cardinal, Colonial, Old Curiosity Shop, Magnolia)

Baker, 10"...........................28.00
Bowl, coupe soup..................11.00
Bowl, oatmeal; 6" 10.00
Casserole, w/lid 62.00
Cup, coffee; AD.....................24.00
Dish, 15½" 32.00
Plate, 7" 10.00
Sugar bowl, w/lid 28.00

Newell: 1927 design (available in Yellow Glow, Puritan, Song of Spring, Southern Pride, Poppy)

Baker, 7".............................18.00
Bowl, fruit; 5" 7.00
Bowl, oyster; 1¼-pt..............20.00
Cake plate, 11".....................25.00
Nappy, 7"............................18.00
Plate, 6" 8.00
Saucer, coffee; rare 8.00

Republic Shape (available in Jean, Calais, Priscilla, and Wayside)

Baker, 9" **20.00**
Bowl, deep, 1⅜-pt **20.00**

Coffeepot (Priscilla pattern), from $85.00 to $95.00.

Dish, w/lid, 8" **40.00**
Dish, 13" **28.00**
Jug, 30s, 2½-pt **32.00**
Nappy, 9" **24.00**
Plate, 10" **15.00**
Teacup **10.00**

Rhythm Shape (available in Allegro, Daybreak, Rybaiyat, and Something Blue)

Bowl, soup/cereal; 5½" **10.00**
Creamer **20.00**
Dish, 15½" **32.00**
Nappy, round **25.00**
Plate, 9" **15.00**
Sauce boat **30.00**
Teapot **55.00**

Swing Shape (available in Blue Flax, Chinese Three, Moss Rose, and Pate Sur Pate)

Butter dish, Jade **85.00**
Dish, 13" **40.00**
Egg cup, double **30.00**

Muffin cover **80.00**
Plate, 6" **10.00**
Salt & pepper shakers, pr **55.00**
Sauce boat **35.00**
Teapot **125.00**

Virginia Rose, 1930 (Pink Wild Rose, Rose and Daisy, Patrician, Nosegay; Add 20% for JJ59 and VR128)

Bowl, coupe soup **25.00**
Bowl, cream soup; rare **40.00**
Bowl, deep, 5" **30.00**
Cake plate, rare **50.00**

Covered casserole (Wild Rose pattern), from $30.00 to $35.00. (Photo courtesy Joanne Jasper)

Creamer **30.00**
Dish, 15½" **55.00**
Jug, w/lid, rare, 7½" **195.00**
Nappy, 9" **30.00**
Plate, rare, 8" **35.00**
Saucer, tea **8.00**

Wells, 1930 (Flight of the Swallows, Cosmos, Flowers of the Dell, Gold Stripe, Hollyhock)

Bowl, bouillon **20.00**
Bowl, cream soup **28.00**
Bowl, fruit **10.00**
Butter dish **90.00**
Jug, w/lid, 42s **50.00**
Plate, 10" **18.00**

Sauce boat **35.00**
Saucer, tea **7.00**

Yellowstone 1927 (available in Moss Rose, Poppy Pastel, Golden Rose, Buttercup, Floral Spray)

Baker, oval, 5½" **12.00**
Bowl, oatmeal; 36s **14.00**
Butter dish, w/lid **75.00**
Creamer, individual **14.00**
Jug, 48s **25.00**
Plate, deep, 9" **12.00**
Plate, 5" **8.00**
Sugar bowl, individual **16.00**

Hot Wheels

An instant success in 1968, Hot Wheels are known for their racy style and custom paint jobs. Kids loved them simply because they were the fastest model cars on the market. Keeping up with new trends in the big car industry, Hot Wheels also included futuristic vehicles, muscle cars, trucks, hot rods, racers, and some military vehicles. A lot of these can still be found for very little, but if you want to buy the older models (collectors call them 'Redlines' because of their red sidewall tires), it's going to cost you a little more, though many can still be found under $25.00. By 1971, earlier on some models, black-wall tires had become standard.

Though recent re-releases have dampened the collector market somewhat, cars mint in the original packages are holding their values and still moving well. Near-mint examples (no

package) are worth about 50% to 60% less than those mint and still in their original package, excellent condition about 65% to 75% less. For more information see *Hot Wheels, The Ultimate Redline Guide, 1968 – 1977, Vol. 1* and *Vol. 2,* by Jack Clark and Robert Wicker.

'32 Ford Delivery, 1989, black walls, yellow, MIP **22.50**
'57 Chevy, yellow w/flame accents, MIP **12.00**
'65 Mustang Convertible, red w/tan interior, MIP **8.00**
Alive '55, 1979, redline, chrome, M **45.00**
American Tipper, 1976, redline, red, M **55.00**
Backwoods Bomb, 1975, redline, light blue, NM+ **55.00**

Beatnik Bandit, 1968, redline tires, metallic green, NM+, $30.00. (Photo courtesy June Moon)

Brabham Repco FI, redline, aqua or blue, NM+ **30.00**
Bugeye, 1973, redline, pink, EX **75.00**
Cargoyle, 1986, black walls, orange, M **5.00**
Chapparal 2G, 1969, redline, yellow, NM+ **45.00**
Classic '31 Ford Woody, 1969, redline, aqua, NM+ **50.00**
Classic '31 Ford Woody, 1969, redline, red, M **40.00**

Classic '32 Ford Vicky, 1968, redline, gold, NM+ **50.00**

Classic '32 Ford Vicky, 1969, redline, aqua, NM+ **50.00**

Classic Cord, 1971, redline, green, NM- **225.00**

Classic Nomad, 1970, redline, purple, NM+ **145.00**

Cockney Cab, 1971, redline, red, NM+ **75.00**

Custom AMX, 1969, redline, magenta, NM+ **125.00**

Custom Barracuda, 1968, redline, aqua, NM+ **85.00**

Custom Charger, 1969, redline, aqua, M **195.00**

Custom Charger, 1969, redline, purple, NM+.................**250.00**

Custom Continental Mark III, 1969, redline, gold, NM+............**50.00**

Custom Corvette, 1968, redline, red w/gold interior, NM+.....**130.00**

Custom Eldorado, 1968, redline, light blue w/black interior, NM+...........................**185.00**

Custom Firebird, 1968, redline, light green w/white interior, NM+..............................**170.00**

Custom Fleetside, 1968, redline, blue, NM+ **165.00**

Custom T-Bird, 1968, redline, purple w/white interior, NM+ **200.00**

Custom Volkswagen, 1968, redline, blue, M **50.00**

Double Header, 1973, redline, dark blue, NM+............**155.00**

Dumpin' A, 1983, black walls, gray, M **30.00**

El Ray Special, 1974, redline, dark blue, NM+ **400.00**

Emergency Squad, 1982, black walls, red, MIP...............**10.00**

Ferrari 512P, 1973, redline, light blue, NM.......................**120.00**

Fiero 2M4, white w/red, black & yellow accents, MIP.........**8.00**

Flashfire, black w/red interior, MIP................................**10.00**

Ford Dump Truck, 1982, black walls, green, NM+............**5.00**

Ford J-Car, 1968, redline, white, NM+................................**55.00**

Formula PACK, 1978, black walls, black, NM+.....................**15.00**

Gremlin Grinder, 1975, redline, green, NM+ **50.00**

Gun Slinger, 1975, redline, light olive, M...........................**55.00**

Heavy Chevy, 1974, redline, yellow, NM+.......................**110.00**

Heavyweight Dump Truck, 1970, redline, white, NM.......**200.00**

Highway Robber, 1973, redline, red, NM+ **120.00**

Hot Heap, 1968, redline, pink w/white interior, NM+..**325.00**

Ice T, 1973, redline, light blue, NM+...............................**180.00**

Indy Eagle, 1969, redline, aqua w/blue interior, NM+.....**35.00**

Inside Story, 1980, black walls, yellow, MIP **27.00**

Lamborghini Diablo, red, MIP **5.00**

Light My Firebird, 1970, redline, purple w/brown interior, NM+ **90.00**

Mantis, 1970, redline, red w/white interior, NM+ **35.00**

Mercedes 380 SEL, 1982, black walls, metal-flake gray, MIP.........**8.00**

Mighty Maverick, 1970, redline, rose, NM+.....................**120.00**

Mongoose Funny Car, 1970, redline, red, NM+..............**100.00**

Old Number 5, 1982, black walls, red, NM+ **10.00**

Open Fire, 1972, redline, magenta, NM+..............................**175.00**

Paramedic, 1977, black walls, yellow, NM+ **20.00**

Peterbilt Dump Truck, 1983, black walls, yellow, MIP **10.00**

Porsche 917, 1970, redline, yellow, NM+...............................**50.00**

Prowler, 1976, redline, chrome, M **60.00**

Python, 1968, redline tires, metallic blue, based on *Car Craft Magazine's* 'Dream Car,' designed by Bill Cushenberry, M, $50.00. (Photo courtesy June Moon)

Python, 1968, redline, yellow w/white interior, NM+...**38.00**

Rescue Ranger, 1988, black walls, red, NM **4.00**

Rocket Bye Baby, 1971, redline, aqua, NM+ **65.00**

Short Order, 1972, redline, dark blue, NM+ **90.00**

Six-Shooter, 1971, redline, magenta, EX.............................**50.00**

Sol-Aire CX4, 1989, black walls, black, MIP **6.00**

Spoiler Sport, 1980, black walls, green, MIP......................**16.00**

Super Cannon, 1985, black walls, olive, MIP **7.00**

T-4-2, 1971, redline, magenta, EX **50.00**

Thrill Drivers Torino, 1977, black walls, white, NM- **75.00**

Tricar X8, 1982, black walls, white, MIP.......................**7.00**

Turbo Streak, 1988, black walls, white, EX.........................**6.00**

Turismo, 1981, black walls, red, MIP **8.00**

Wind Splitter, 1984, black walls, metallic blue, MIP **9.00**

Hull

Established in Zanesville, Ohio, in 1905, Hull manufactured stoneware, florist ware, art pottery, and tile until about 1935, when they began to produce the lines of pastel matt-glazed artware which are today very collectible. The pottery was destroyed by flood and fire in 1950. The factory was rebuilt and equipped with the most modern machinery which they soon discovered was not geared to duplicate the matt glazes. As a result, new lines — Parchment and Pine and Ebb Tide, for example — were introduced in a glossy finish. During the '40s and into the '50s, their kitchenware and novelty lines were very successful. Refer to *Robert's Ultimate Encyclopedia of Hull Pottery* and *The Companion Guide,* both by Brenda Roberts (Walsworth Publishing), for more information. Brenda also has authored a third book, *The Collector's Encyclopedia of Hull Pottery,* which is published by Collector Books.

Bow-Knot, teapot, #B-20, 6", from $450 to............................**650.00**

Butterfly, ewer, #B11, 8¾", from $155 to............................**215.00**

Calla Lily, bowl, #500/32, 10", $215 to............................**260.00**

Capri, basket, #48, 12¼", from $80 to.................................**120.00**

Capri, urn vase, #50, 9 ", from $45 to **65.00**

Capri, vase, #58, 13¾", from $55 to **75.00**

Continental, basket, #55, 12¾", from $145 to.................**215.00**

Continental, bud vase, #66, 9½", from $35 to.....................**50.00**

Dogwood, low bowl, #521, 3¾", from $160 to.................**195.00**

Dogwood, window box, #508, 10½", from $250 to.................**310.00**

Ebb Tide, basket, #E-ll, 16½", from $210 to............................**265.00**

Fantasy, window box, #74, 12½", from $18 to.....................**24.00**

Fiesta, basket, #44, 6½", from $75 to **105.00**

Fiesta, flowerpot, #40, 4¼", from $20 to............................**30.00**

Fiesta, vase, #50, 9", from $80 to............................**110.00**

House and Garden, chip & dip, 15 x 11" **$200.00.** (Photo courtesy Brenda Roberts)

Imperial, bowl, #117, 9", from $8 to **10.00**

Imperial, swan, #81, 10½", from $55 to............................**95.00**

Iris, console bowl, #409, 12", from $125 to............................**155.00**

Iris, ewer, #401, 8", from $280 to............................**325.00**

Iris, jardiniere, #413, 9", from $475 to............................**575.00**

Magnolia, gloss; console bowl, #H-23, 13", from $125 to ...**165.00**

Magnolia, gloss; ewer, #H-16, 12½", from $370 to **465.00**

Magnolia, matt; teapot, #23, 6½", from $240 to.................**275.00**

Magnolia, matt; vase, #16, 15", from $475 to.................**600.00**

Mardi Gras/Granada, basket, #65, 8", from $140 to **170.00**

Mardi Gras/Granada, vase, #215, 9", from $50 to................**80.00**

Novelty, bandana duck, #74, 7x9", from $80 to **115.00**

Novelty, basket, #72, 8", from $80 to **125.00**

Novelty, dancing girl, #955, 7", from $60 to **85.00**

Novelty, dog w/yarn planter, #88, 5½x8", from $30 to.........**35.00**

Novelty, goose planter, #411, 12¼", from $55 to...........**85.00**

Novelty, leaf dish, #85, 13", from $35 to **45.00**

Novelty, lovebirds, #93, 6", from $40 to **60.00**

Novelty, planter, cat, #63, 5⅜" high, $75.00.

Novelty, pig bank, #196, 6", from $85 to............................**125.00**

Novelty, rooster, #951, 7", from $50 to..............................**80.00**

Novelty, vase, #73, 10½", from $35 to.....................................**50.00**

Novelty, wall pocket, #112, 10½", from $55 to......................**75.00**

Open Rose, cornucopia, #101, 8½", from $175 to................**215.00**

Orchid, basket, #305, 7", from $750 to..........................**800.00**

Orchid, jardiniere, #317, 4¾", from $225 to..........................**265.00**

Parchment & Pine, ashtray, #S-14, 14", from $145 to.........**185.00**

Parchment & Pine, teapot, #S-15, 8", from $175 to...........**225.00**

Poppy, basket, #601, 6½", from $1,300 to.....................**1,600.00**

Poppy, wall pocket, #609, 9", from $360 to..........................**460.00**

Rosella, ewer, #R-11, 7", from $140 to....................................**175.00**

Rosella, vase, #R-15, 8½", from $135 to..........................**165.00**

Serenade, beverage pitcher, #S21, 10½", from $225 to **275.00**

Serenade, candy dish, #S3, 8¼", from $155 to.................**200.00**

Sueno Tulip, vase, #100-33, 10", from $275 to.................**325.00**

Sunglow, pitcher, #55, 7½", from $155 to..........................**205.00**

Sunglow, salt shaker, #54, 2¾", from $15 to.....................**20.00**

Tropicana, vase, #54, 12½", from $450 to..........................**550.00**

Tuscany, leaf dish, #10, 13", from $30 to..............................**50.00**

Tuscany, urn, #5, 5½", from $40 to **60.00**

Water Lily, candle holder, #L-22, 4½", from $85 to **125.00**

Water Lily, console bowl, #L-21, 13½", from $260 to **300.00**

Water Lily, jardiniere, #L-24, 8½", from $365 to.................**425.00**

Wildflower, ewer, #W-2, 5½", from $105 to..........................**140.00**

Wildflower, sugar bowl, #74, 4¾", from $240 to.................**275.00**

Woodland, cornucopia, #W2, 5½", from $105 to.................**145.00**

Woodland, double bud vase, #W15, 8½", from $225 to **265.00**

Woodland, ewer, #W3, 5½", from $130 to..........................**175.00**

Woodland, planter, #W19, 10½", from $175 to.................**235.00**

Dinnerware

Avocado, coffee cup, 7-oz **6.00**

Centennial, mug, unmarked, 4"..**50.00**

Crestone, bowl, 9-oz, from $4 to..**6.00**

Crestone, pitcher, 6¾", $45.00.

Crestone, plate, 10¼", from $10 to....................................**12.00**

Gingerbread Man, child's bowl..**80.00**

Gingerbread Man, server, brown, 10x10"............................**30.00**

Mirror Almond, bud vase, 9", from $16 to............................**22.00**

Mirror Almond, Dutch oven, 3-pt, from $30 to **40.00**

Mirror Brown, bowl, divided vegetable; #542, 10¾", from $25 to **35.00**

Mirror Brown, bowl, 10¼", from $20 to **30.00**

Mirror Brown, casserole, w/lid, #544, 10", from $35 to ...**50.00**

Mirror Brown, cookie jar, #523, 94-oz, from $50 to **75.00**

Mirror Brown, custard, from $4 to....................................**5.00**

Mirror Brown, gravy boat, 16-oz, from $35 to **50.00**

Mirror Brown, mug, #502, 9-oz, from $4 to **6.00**

Mirror Brown, plate, 10", from $8 to **12.00**

Mirror Brown, sugar bowl, 12-oz, from $12 to **15.00**

Mirror Brown, teapot, #549, 5-cup, from $25 to **35.00**

Rainbow, cup, 6-oz, from $4 to..**6.00**

Rainbow, plate, 10½", from $8 to **10.00**

Ring, creamer & sugar bowl.**24.00**

Ring, platter, oval **18.00**

Tangerine, coffeepot, 8-cup ..**45.00**

Tangerine, steak plate, oval, 11¾" **15.00**

Indiana Carnival Glass

Though this glass looks old, it really isn't. It's very reminiscent of old Northwood carnival glass with its grape clusters and detailed leaves and vines, but this line was actually introduced in 1972! Made by the Indiana Glass Company, Harvest (the pattern name

assigned by the company) was produced in blue, lime green, and marigold. Although they made a few other carnival patterns in addition to this one, none are as collectible or as easy to recognize.

This glassware is a little difficult to evaluate as there seems to be a wide range of 'asking' prices simply because some dealers are unsure of its age and therefore its value. If you like it, now is the time to buy it!

Harvest values given below are based on items in blue. Adjust them downward a price point or two for lime green and even a little more so for marigold. For further information we recommend *Garage Sale and Flea Market Annual* (Collector Books).

Iridescent Amethyst (Heritage)

Basket, footed, 9x5x7" **40.00**

Butter dish, 5x7½" dia, from $40 to **60.00**

Candle holders, Harvest, embossed grapes, from $22.00 to $28.00 for the pair.

Center bowl, 4¾x8½", from $30 to....................................**40.00**

Goblet, 8-oz, from $15 to **22.00**

Pitcher, 8¼", from $40 to......**60.00**

Punch set, 10" bowl & pedestal, 8 cups, w/ladle, 11-pc, $175 to **225.00**

Swung vase, slender & footed w/irregular rim, 11x3", from $30 to..............................**40.00**

Iridescent Blue

Butter dish, Harvest, embossed grapes, ¼-lb, 8" L, from $25 to **40.00**

Candy box, Harvest, embossed grapes w/lace edge, w/lid, 6½", $20 to..............................**35.00**

Canister/Candy jar, Harvest, embossed grapes, 7", from $15 to **35.00**

Canister/Candy jar, Harvest, embossed grapes, 9", from $80 to **150.00**

Canister/Snack jar, Harvest, embossed grapes, 8", from $60 to...................................**125.00**

Garland bowl (compote), paneled, 7½x8½" dia, from $15 to .**20.00**

Goblet, Harvest, embossed grapes, 9-oz, from $10 to............**12.00**

Hen on nest, from $15.00 to $25.00.

Pitcher, Harvest, embossed grapes, 10½", common, from $25 to **40.00**

Plate, Bicentennial; American Eagle, from $10 to **15.00**

Punch set, Princess, complete w/ladle & hooks, 26-pc, from $60 to............................**125.00**

Wedding bowl (sm compote), Thumbprint, footed, 5x5", from $10 to **15.00**

Iridescent Gold

Basket, Monticello, lg faceted allover diamonds, sq, 7x6", $30 to..............................**35.00**

Canister/Snack jar, Harvest, embossed grapes, 8", from $40 to **60.00**

Cooler (iced tea tumbler), Harvest, 14-oz, from $8 to............**12.00**

Egg relish plate, 11", from $15 to **35.00**

Goblet, Harvest, embossed grapes, 9-oz, from $8 to **12.00**

Hen on nest, 5½", from $10 to..**20.00**

Pitcher, Harvest, embossed grapes, 10½", from $24 to **30.00**

Relish tray, Vintage, 6 sections, 9x12¾", from $15 to.......**18.00**

Wedding bowl, Harvest, embossed grapes, 8x8½", from $22.00 to $28.00.

Wedding bowl (sm compote), 5x5", from $9 to **12.00**

Iridescent Lime

Canister/Snack jar, Harvest, embossed grapes, 8", from $40 to **60.00**

Compote, Harvest, embossed grapes, 7x6", from $15 to.**20.00**

Egg/relish tray, 12¾", from $15 to..................................**25.00**

Goblet, Harvest, embossed grapes, 9-oz, from $10 to **15.00**

Hen on nest, from $10 to......**25.00**

Pitcher, Harvest, embossed grapes, 10½", from $30 to............**40.00**

Punch set, Princess, complete w/ladle & hooks, 26-pc, from $60 to............................**125.00**

Iridescent Sunset (Amberina)

Basket, footed, 9x5x7", from $30 to **50.00**

Basket, sq, 9½x7½", from $50 to................................**60.00**

Bowl, crimped, 3¾x10", from $40 to **50.00**

Butter dish, 5x7½" dia, from $35 to **40.00**

Creamer & sugar bowl **40.00**

Goblet, 8-oz, from $12 to **18.00**

Pitcher, 8¼", from $40 to......**50.00**

Rose bowl, 6½x6½", from $25 to..**35.00**

Tumbler, 3½", from $10 to ...**15.00**

Japan Ceramics

Though Japanese ceramics marked Nippon, Noritake, and Occupied Japan have long been collected, some of the newest fun-type collectibles on today's market are the figural ashtrays, pincush-ions, wall pockets, toothbrush holders, etc., that are marked 'Made in Japan' or simply 'Japan.' In her books called *Collector's Guide to Made in Japan Ceramics* (there are five in the series), Carole Bess White explains the pitfalls you will encounter when you try to determine production dates. Collectors refer to anything produced before WWII as 'old' and anything made after 1952 as 'new.' You'll find all you need to know to be a wise shopper in her books.

See also Black Cats; Blue Willow; Egg Timers; Enesco; Fishbowl Ornaments; Flower Frogs; Geisha Girl; Head Vases; Holt Howard; Lefton; Moss Rose; Nippon; Noritake; Occupied Japan; Rooster and Roses; Sewing Items; Toothbrush Holders; Wall Pockets.

Ashtray, calico baby & mother bird, multicolored, 2¾", from $25 to **40.00**

Ashtray, calico dog on side, 2¾", from $18 to **28.00**

Ashtray, calico dog w/card suit heart, 2¾", from $18 to .**28.00**

Ashtray, clown w/banjo at side, multicolored, 3¼", from $30 to **65.00**

Ashtray, dog & dish form, multi-colored lustre, 2½", from $20 to....................................**30.00**

Ashtray, dog & doghouse, w/snuffers, multicolored, 2¼", from $20 to.....................**30.00**

Ashtray, dog w/water barrel form, white & multicolored, 4", from $150 to.........................**200.00**

Ashtray, elephant at side of mottled green base, 4½", from $22 to **35.00**

Ashtray, frog in water, multicolored, 5", from $18 to **28.00**

Ashtray, house form, multicolored w/tan lustre, 3½", from $15 to **22.00**

Ashtray, set of 4 stacking card suite, multicolored lustre, 3", $25 to **45.00**

Ashtray, smoker boat, multicolored, w/original sticker, 3", $10 to **18.00**

Ashtray, sombrero couple, multicolored, 3¾", from $15 to **22.00**

Ashtray, stylized house, multicolored lustre, 3¼", from $15 to **22.00**

Ashtrays, card suit shapes w/floral decor, 2¾-3¼", 4 for **80.00**

Bell, colonial lady figural, multicolored, 3½", from $12 to....**20.00**

Biscuit jar, floral on multicolored, w/handle, 4", from $15 to **25.00**

Biscuit jar, floral on orange & white, sm handles, 6¼", from $48 to **68.00**

Biscuit jar, mixed fruit on cream crackle, 7", from $48 to **68.00**

Biscuit jar, white basketweave, w/flower finial, 6¼", from $48 to **68.00**

Bookends, Asian man & woman, multicolored, 5½", from $28 to **48.00**

Bookends, colonial man & woman w/blue rhinestone eyes, 6¼", from $25 to **40.00**

Bookends, trains in black on tan body, 5½", from $20 to...**30.00**

Bowl, candle holders in rim, rosebud flower frog, 6" diameter, from $35.00 to $45.00.

Bowl, fruit; multicolored on tan lustre, basket handle, 8½", from $65 to **95.00**

Bowl, house in yellow, multicolored/shiny, handles, 8", from $65 to **85.00**

Bowl, house scene, multicolored on teal lustre, lug handles, from $25 to **55.00**

Bowl, house scene, white on multicolored lustre, 8", from $65 to **85.00**

Cake plate, floral on multicolored lustre, 9½", from $35 to **55.00**

Candlesticks, floral, blue & white on orange, 5½",pr, from $30 to **50.00**

Comport, floral decor on shiny, handled, 6¾", from $35 to **55.00**

Comport, house, white on multicolored lustre, handled, from $60 to **75.00**

Condiment set, girl w/flowers at center of tray, 3¾", from $125 to **150.00**

Creamer & sugar bowl, dog figurals, w/yellow eyes, 6¾", from $100 to **150.00**

Creamer & sugar bowl, floral w/multicolored lustre, +7" tray, from $55 to **96.00**

Creamer & sugar bowl, green oil spots, handles, 7½" tray, from $35 to **50.00**

Figurine, barefoot boy fishing, multicolored, 4¾", from $35 to **50.00**

Figurine, colonial lady, multicolored, 7", from $30 to **45.00**

Figurine, doll w/wig & blue dress, bisque, 6½", from $35 to **55.00**

Figurines, musician trio, multicolored, 2¾", set of 3, from $10 to **18.00**

Flower bowl, circle of swans, blue & tan lustre, 8½", from $85 to...................................**135.00**

Flower bowl, floral, white on blue, w/handles, 8¾", from $20 to............................**30.00**

Flower frog, bird, multicolored lustre, 7½", from $30 to......**45.00**

Incense burner, bird-handled w/liner, multicolored, 5¾", from $35 to **55.00**

Incense burner, Japanese lady w/dog, multicolored, 4¾", from $40 to..............................**50.00**

Lamp, sailboat on shiny white, 6¾" to top of ceramic post, from $25 to **35.00**

Lemon server, floral, white on orange, bird handle, 6", from $25 to **35.00**

Lemon server, Mexican decor, multicolored, 5½", from $25 to **35.00**

Liquor flask, girl & dog, multicolored, bisque, 4", from $75 to **135.00**

Marmalade pot, mixed fruit decor, w/handles, 4¾", from $25 to **35.00**

Marmalade, strawberry form, unmarked, 4½", from $20.00 to $25.00.

Match holder, 2 men at sides, multicolored, 4½", from $75 to **125.00**

Pitcher, multicolored floral w/orange handle, 7¾", from $45 to..............................**75.00**

Sandwich server, floral on teal & blue, center handle, 10", from $45 to..............................**75.00**

Sandwich server, floral w/tan & lavender, center handle, 10", from $45 to **75.00**

Teapot, blue & tan lustre, w/floral decor, 6½", from $35 to..**50.00**

Teapot, multicolored/shiny, 5", w/cream-colored tile, from $68 to **78.00**

Teapot, river scenic w/multicolored lustre, dome lid, 7", from $35 to..............................**50.00**

Teapot, white w/gold lustre, ring handle, 4½", from $35 to ..**50.00**

Vase, blue shiny w/handles, 5¾", from $25 to **40.00**

Vase, floral, multicolored on cream lustre, 6¾", from $50 to..**75.00**

Vase, floral, multicolored on tan lustre, handles, 7", from $50 to **75.00**

Vase, stylized dog at side, shiny maroon, 6¼", from $25 to .**40.00**

Jewelry

Anyone interested in buying gems will soon find out that antique gems are the best values. Not only are prices from one-third to one-half less than on comparable new jewelry, but the older pieces display a degree of craftsmanship and styling seldom seen in modern-day jewelry. Costume jewelry from all periods is popular, especially Art Nouveau and Art Deco examples. Signed pieces are particularly good, such as those by Miriam Haskell, Eisenberg, Trifari, Hollycraft, and Weiss, among others.

There are some excellent reference books available if you'd like more information. Marcia 'Sparkles' Brown has written *Unsigned Beauties of Costume Jewelry* and *Signed Beauties of Costume Jewelry, Vol. I* and *Vol. II;* Lillian Baker has written several: *Plastic Jewelry of the Twentieth Century; 50 Years of Collectible Fashion Jewelry;* and *100 Years of Collectible Jewelry.* Books by other authors include *Costume Jewelry* and *Collectible Silver Jewelry* by Fred Rezazadeh; *Collector's Encyclopedia of Hairwork Jewelry* by C. Jeanenne Bell, G.G.; *Collectible Costume Jewelry* by Cherri Simonds; *Brilliant Rhinestones* by Ronna Lee Aikens; *Painted Porcelain Jewelry and Buttons* by Dorothy Kamm; *Vintage Jewelry for Investment and Casual Wear* by Karen L. Edeen; and *Christmas Pins* by Jill Gallina. All are published by Collector Books. See Clubs and Newsletters for information on the *Vintage Fashion & Costume Jewelry* newsletter and club.

Bracelet, Coro, flexible w/lg topaz-colored jewel amid pearls, from $50 to.....................**70.00**
Bracelet, M Haskell, 3 strands of white glass beads w/rhinestones...........................**135.00**
Bracelet, unmarked, gold-plated wrap w/red sq rhinestones.......................**105.00**
Bracelet, unmarked, hinged, covered in red & smoky rhinestones, from $75 to........**95.00**
Bracelet, unmarked, hinged, gold-plated w/tiger-eye cabochon in mesh **35.00**
Bracelet, unmarked, single line of pearls & topaz rhinestones..........................**30.00**
Bracelet, unmarked, sm sq white rhinestones in 7 rows, recent, from $25 to.....................**35.00**
Bracelet, unmarked, tourist type w/letters topped w/rhinestones...........................**22.00**
Bracelet, unmarked, 2 strands of faux pearls w/fine clasp..**15.00**
Bracelet, unmarked, 7 rows of rhinestones w/lg stones centered, wide.....................**45.00**
Bracelet & earrings, Marvella, faceted iridescent glass beads, from $50 to **70.00**
Bracelet & earrings, unmarked, multicolor pastel stones, from $40 to **70.00**
Bracelet & earrings, unmarked, red & clear rhinestones w/faux pearls.................**60.00**

Brooch, Art, gold-tone dragonfly w/enamel flowers, from $50 to **75.00**

Brooch, Baldwin, silver leaf w/autumn-like enameling, from $30 to **40.00**

Brooch, Beaucraft, silver musical note, lg, +matching earrings, $40 to **65.00**

Brooch, butterfly, gold-tone covered in white rhinestones, lg, from $45 to **65.00**

Brooch, Castlecliff, crown, sterling with red & white rhinestones, 2" **170.00**

Brooch, Coro, faux pearls & rhinestones form flower, lg, from $50 to................... **85.00**

Brooch, Danecraft, silver floral design, from $35 to **45.00**

Brooch, Gerry's, gold-tone rooster w/enameled details, from $12 to **35.00**

Brooch, Hollycraft, pastel multicolor stones, lg, from $60 to............................... **95.00**

Brooch, KJ Lane, fish jade bodies with rhinestones, golden fins................................. **80.00**

Brooch, Mazer Bros, bucktoothed rabbit, gold-plated metal **80.00**

Brooch, Reja, silver bug w/multicolor rhinestones, lg, from $75 to **100.00**

Brooch, S Coventry, clear rhinestones form lg snowflake, from $25 to **35.00**

Brooch, Trifari, silver floral design w/faux pearls, from $40 to **60.00**

Brooch, unmarked, enameled firefly **14.00**

Brooch, unmarked, gold-plated Christmas tree w/glued-in rhinestones..................... **38.00**

Brooch, unmarked, gold-plated 5-petal flower w/colored rhinestones............................ **48.00**

Brooch, unmarked, gold-tone cat figural w/enameling, sm, from $15 to.............................. **20.00**

Brooch, unmarked, gold-tone elephant w/flowers in trunk, sm................................ **22.00**

Brooch, unmarked, rhinestone swan w/enamel touches .**80.00**

Brooch, unmarked, sterling vermeil w/lg emerald-cut topaz ...**62.00**

Brooch, unmarked, turtle w/pave head, green stone, rhinestones, pearls **25.00**

Brooch, unmarked, white rhinestones on silver-tone snowflake, lg.**42.00**

Brooch, Weiss, faceted rhinestones of varied shapes, lg, from $80 to................................... **100.00**

Brooch and earrings, aurora borealis chatons in three layers swedged to gold-plated flower petals, matching earrings, $45.00 for the set.
(Photo courtesy Marcia Brown)

Brooch & earrings, red stone w/red aurora borealis rhinestones **60.00**

Brooch & earrings, Trifari, gold-plate w/white rhinestones...........**95.00**

Brooch & earrings, unmarked, black & iridescent rhinestones, from $50 to **75.00**

Brooch & earrings, Weiss, enameled daisies, from $50 to **75.00**

Cuff links, Cellini, cornucopia enameling on silver, pr, from $35 to **50.00**

Earrings, Albion, gold-washed metal leaves w/faux pearls, pr, from $10 to **15.00**

Earrings, Boucher, gold-tone metal flower, clip, pr, from $50 to **80.00**

Earrings, Kramer, grape cluster, clear rhinestones, sm, pr, $25 to **30.00**

Earrings, M Haskell, turquoise birds w/rhinestones, pr..**60.00**

Earrings, red rhinestones in gold-tone circle, sm, pr, from $15 to **25.00**

Earrings, Robert Originals, faux pearls with pink and blue rhinestones, blue and gold bead drops, $90.00 for the pair. (Photo courtesy Marcia Brown)

Earrings, Schiaparelli, sculptured stones & pearl accents, pr, from $60 to **90.00**

Earrings, unmarked, aurora borealis rhinestone cluster, pr........**38.00**

Earrings, unmarked, black & frosted glass, Deco style, 2", pr...................................**55.00**

Earrings, unmarked, black Bakelite crescent w/clear rhinestones, pr...............**35.00**

Earrings, unmarked, blue beads, buttons, rhinestones & flowers, pr **35.00**

Earrings, unmarked, blue iridescent navette & chaton rhinestones, pr........................**38.00**

Earrings, unmarked, clear rhinestone bowling shoe w/red eyelets, pr **55.00**

Earrings, unmarked, faux emerald amid faux pearls, screwbacks, pr **12.00**

Earrings, unmarked, faux turquoise drops w/antique-silver look, pr **26.00**

Earrings, unmarked, gray & red rhinestones form dome, pr **45.00**

Earrings, unmarked, green rhinestone teardrops, prong set, 1", pr....................................**30.00**

Earrings, unmarked, lavender & purple rhinestone buttons, 2" dia, pr **45.00**

Earrings, unmarked, pearl w/rhinestone accents, pr **15.00**

Earrings, unmarked, red button amid clear rhinestones, pr, from $12 to **18.00**

Earrings, unmarked, yellow plastic flower w/rhinestone center, pr...................................**14.00**

Earrings, unmarked, yellow rhinestones, prong-set dangles, 4", pr...................................**50.00**

Earrings, unmarked, 3 rows of aurora borealis stones, 1x⅝", pr......................**50.00**

Earrings, unmarked (Czech), brass w/green glass dangles, 2", pr..............................**42.50**

Earrings, unmarked (Czech), molded glass, Egyptian Revival style, pr.............**58.00**

Earrings, Weiss, flower w/white glass petals and black center, pr......................................**40.00**

Earrings, Weiss, w/tiger's eye & cultured pearl, pr, from $35 to **50.00**

Necklace, Avon, gold-tone with faux pearl inserts, from $15 to **20.00**

Necklace, BSK, gold-tone w/floral design & pink rhinestones, from $30 to....................**45.00**

Necklace, double strand of pearls with baroque pearl clasp, $28.00. (Photo courtesy Marcia Brown)

Necklace, Hollywood Stars, carved wooden beads.................**40.00**

Necklace, Kramer, faux pearls set in gold-plated chain.......**88.00**

Necklace, Pam, floral design w/iridescent stones & enameling, from $40 to.....................**60.00**

Necklace, unmarked, colored rhinestones form teardrop-shaped pendant..............**38.00**

Necklace, unmarked, gold-tone chain w/rhinestone fringe, EX quality **40.00**

Necklace, unmarked, pink & fuchsia faceted beads w/red rhinestones..............................**35.00**

Necklace, unmarked, silver & abalone shells, 1950s, from $50 to..............................**85.00**

Necklace, unmarked, tiny single strand of clear rhinestones **15.00**

Necklace, unmarked, 2 strands of faux pearls w/Baroque clasp............................**28.00**

Necklace & earrings, Trifari, gold-tone w/plastic inserts & enameling................................**75.00**

Necklace & earrings, Trifari, green beads & crystals, 6-strand **80.00**

Necklace & earrings, unmarked, white stones & clear rhinestones..............................**40.00**

Pendant, Art, silver-tone metal w/red opaque stones, from $45 to......................................**65.00**

Pendant, Vendome, red & blue rhinestones form flower, from $80 to............................**140.00**

Ring, Ciner, silver w/lg faceted green crystal stone, from $45 to **65.00**

Rings: Double-cut sky blue rhinestones, $54.00; Gold-plated faux pearls with silver pavé leaves, $42.00; Gold-plated with seven topaz rhinestones, $38.00. (Photo courtesy Marcia Brown)

Ring, Eisenberg Ice, lg yellow topaz teardrop stone amid rhinestones...............**125.00**

Ring, Emmons, turquoise & faux pearls, from $30 to........**45.00**

Ring, Judy-Lee, green marquise stone amid sm green rhinestones, from $25 to **40.00**

Ring, Sarah Coventry, silver w/hematite stone, from $25 to...............................**35.00**

Ring, unmarked, silver set w/lg turquoise stone, from $75 to **100.00**

Ring, unmarked, silver w/mother-of-pearl scorpion-like design...........................**25.00**

Ring, unmarked, silver w/multicolor faux gem stones.........**36.00**

Ring, unmarked, silver-tone band w/rhinestone flower design **85.00**

Ring, unmarked, 10k yellow gold w/round carnelian stone ..**50.00**

Ring, unmarked, 10k yellow gold-filled band w/Deco faux topaz stone **75.00**

Ring, unmarked, 14k overlay sterling, garnet stone...........**95.00**

Ring, unmarked, 18k white gold w/rhinestones & faux emeralds, lg **50.00**

Johnson Brothers

Dinnerware marked Johnson Brothers, Staffordshire, is bought and sold with considerable fervor on today's market, and for good reason. They made many lovely patterns, some scenic and some florals. Most are decorated with multicolor transfer designs, though you'll see blue or red transferware as well. Some, such as Friendly Village (one of their most popular lines), are still being produced, but the lines are much less extensive now, so the secondary market is being tapped to replace broken items that are no longer available anywhere else.

Some lines are more valuable than others. Unless a pattern is included in the following two categories, use the values below as a guide. One-Star patterns are basically 10% to 20% higher and include Autumn's Delight, Coaching Scenes, Devonshire, Fish, Friendly Village, Gamebirds, Garden Bouquet, Hearts and Flowers, Heritage Hall, Indies, Millstream, Olde English Countryside, Rose Bouquet, Sheraton, Tulip Time, and Winchester. Two-Star lines include Barnyard King, Century of Progress, Chintz-Victorian, Dorchester, English Chippendale, Harvest Fruit, His Majesty, Historical America, Merry Christmas, Old Britain Castles, Persian Tulip, Rose Chintz, Strawberry Fair, Tally Ho, Twelve Days of Christmas, and Wild Turkeys. These patterns are from 25% to 35% higher than our base values.

For more information refer to *Johnson Brothers Dinnerware* by Mary J. Finegan. She is listed in the Directory under North Carolina.

Bowl, rimmed or coupe soup ..**14.00**

Bowl, soup; round or sq, 7"...**12.00**

Bowl, soup/cereal **10.00**
Bowl, vegetable; round or oval..**30.00**
Bowl, vegetable; w/lid **90.00**
Cake plate, 12" **50.00**
Coffeepot...............................**90.00**
Creamer................................**30.00**
Cup & saucer, jumbo **30.00**
Cup & saucer, tea **15.00**
Egg cup.................................**15.00**
Mug, coffee **20.00**
Pitcher/jug............................**45.00**
Plate, buffet; 10½-11" **26.00**
Plate, dinner..........................**14.00**
Plate, luncheon **12.00**
Plate, salad; round or sq **10.00**
Platter, lg, 14"+ **60.00**
Platter, sm, up to 12"............**35.00**

Platter, turkey; Friendly Village pattern, 20½", $220.00.

Salt & pepper shakers, pr **40.00**
Sauce boat base/relish **20.00**
Sauce boat/gravy..................**40.00**
Sugar bowl, w/lid **40.00**
Teapot...................................**90.00**

Kentucky Derby Glasses

Kentucky Derby glasses are the official souvenir glasses that are filled with mint juleps and sold on Derby Day. The first glass (1938), picturing a black horse within a black and white rose garland and the Churchill Downs stadium in the background, is said to have either been given away as a souvenir or used for drinks among the elite at the Downs. This glass, the 1939, and two glasses said to have been used in 1940 are worth thousands and are nearly impossible to find at any price.

1940, aluminum **800.00**
1941-44, plastic Beetleware, ea, from $2,500 to **4,000.00**
1945, jigger.....................**1,000.00**
1945, regular...................**1,600.00**
1945, tall...........................**425.00**
1946-47, ea **100.00**
1948, clear bottom **225.00**
1948, frosted bottom...........**250.00**
1949 ....**225.00**
1950 ....**450.00**
1951 ....**650.00**
1952 ....**225.00**
1953 ....**175.00**
1954 ....**200.00**
1955 ....**150.00**
1956, 1 star, 2 tails.............**275.00**
1956, 1 star, 3 tails.............**400.00**
1956, 2 stars, 2 tails **200.00**
1956, 2 stars, 3 tails **250.00**
1957, gold & black on front..**125.00**
1958, Gold Bar **175.00**
1958, Iron Leige **225.00**
1959-60, ea **100.00**
1961 ....**100.00**
1962, Churchill Downs, red, gold & black on clear...........**110.00**
1963 ....**70.00**
1964 ....**55.00**
1965 ....**75.00**
1966-68, ea **60.00**

1969 ....**65.00**
1970 ....**70.00**
1971 ....**50.00**
1972 ....**45.00**

1973, $55.00. (Photo courtesy Betty L. Hornback/Photographer Dean Langdon)

1974, Federal, regular or mistake, ea **200.00**
1974, mistake (Canonero in 1971 listing on back) **18.00**
1974, regular (Canonero II in 1971 listing on back) **16.00**
1975 ....**16.00**
1976 ....**16.00**
1976, plastic **16.00**
1977 ....**14.00**
1978-79, ea **16.00**
1980 ....**22.00**
1981-82, ea **14.00**
1983-85 ....**12.00**
1986 ....**14.00**
1986 ('85 copy).......................**20.00**
1987-89, ea **12.00**
1990-92, ea **10.00**
1993-95, ea **9.00**
1996-97, ea **8.00**
1998-99, ea **6.00**
2000-02, ea **5.00**
2003 mistake, 1932 incorrectly listed Derby Triple Crown Winner...........................**8.00**
2003-2004, ea **3.00**

Kitchen Collectibles

From the early patented apple peelers, cherry pitters, and food choppers to the gadgets of the '20s through the '40s, many collectors find special appeal in kitchen tools. Refer to *Kitchen Antiques, 1790 – 1940,* by Kathryn McNerney and *Kitchen Glassware of the Depression Years* by Gene Florence for more information. Both are published by Collector Books.

Unless noted otherwise, our values are for glassware and ceramic items that are in mint condition, and appliances, tools, and miscellaneous items in excellent condition.

See also Aluminum; Clothes Sprinkler Bottles; Cookie Cutters; Egg Timers; Enesco; Graniteware; Griswold.

Bowl, green transparent glass, with lid, Jeannette, 9", $50.00. (Photo courtesy Gene Florence)

Apple peeler, Little Star, cast iron **65.00**
Batter jug, cobalt, McKee...**160.00**
Biscuit cutter, Stover's Pride, tin, 2½x3".............................**50.00**
Blender, Nutone In-Built, pink triangular shape w/gray lid, 9", EX **50.00**

Boiler, Oriental Deco, Porcelier, 6-cup or 8-cup, ea..............**65.00**

Bowl, mixing; glass, Delphite Blue, Jeannette, 9" **100.00**

Broiler, lg frame, Faberware, 1960s, cooking surface: 8½x12"...**24.00**

Broiler, Maxim Barbeque Model EB-7, stainless, MIB......**12.50**

Butter box, glass, green, Jeannette, 2-lb **200.00**

Cake turner, red wood handle, 1950s, 7½" **10.00**

Can opener, Dazey Push Button, 1950s, MIB **32.50**

Can opener, Edlund Co Edlund Junior, red wood handle..**7.00**

Can opener, Libby's Can-O-Matic, Amsco, 1950s, MIB **30.00**

Canister set, polished chrome, sq sides, Garner Ware, 1950s, 4 for.....................................**25.00**

Canisters, Country Life, Porcelier, ea **35.00**

Cheese slicer, wire type w/red wood handle, 8½"..............**8.00**

Chopper, bell-shaped metal, red wood handle, 6"..............**18.50**

Chopper, curved blade, wishbone shank, wood handle.......**30.00**

Churn, Dazey #40 ....**150.00**

Coffeepot, Basketweave Floral, decorated dripper, Porcelier, 6-cup **55.00**

Crimper/noodle cutter, brass & iron w/turned wood handle, 7¼"...............................**60.00**

Cutter, French fry; red handle, 2 blades, Ekco, 9"..............**25.00**

Donut maker, Sears Maid of Honor, metal, M in (G box).........**15.00**

Egg beater, Vandeusen Egg Whip, CA Chapman...1894, all metal, 11" **15.00**

Egg cooker, aluminum, Hankscraft, circa 1950 ....**15.00**

Egg cooker, aluminum, Sunbeam, holds 3, 8".....................**25.00**

Flour sifter, Androck Handi-Sift, mother & children tin litho, M **50.00**

Glass knife, Cryst-O-Lite, crystal, 8½", MIB **12.00**

Glass knife, Dur-X, 3 leaf, crystal, MIB.................................**25.00**

Glass knife, Vitex, pink, 8½"..**28.00**

Glass knife, Vitex (Star & Diamond), crystal **15.00**

Glass knife, Westmoreland, thumb guard, crystal, painted handle, 9¼"............................**45.00**

Grater, nutmeg; Pat Date Dec 26 77, crank handle, spring loaded, EX....................**175.00**

Grinder, Griswold #1, cast iron, w/4 blades, 40" **25.00**

Hot plate, single burner, Rival, 750 watt, standard 110-volt plug........**35.00**

Ice bucket, Hex Optic, green, reamer top, Jeannette ...**45.00**

Juicer, Juice King #JK-54-6, red & chrome, 1950s **30.00**

Kettle, General Electric, chrome half-oval w/cream handle, 1950s, 11" **25.00**

Masher, twisted heavy wire, red wood handle, made in USA...........**8.00**

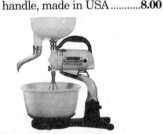

Mixer, Hamilton Beach, complete with Seville Yellow bowls, $200.00. (Photo courtesy Gene Florence)

Measuring cup, crystal, Glasbake, McKee, 1-cup.................**25.00**

Mixer, Mary Dunbar Handymix, 1940s, 11x8"...................**30.00**

Mixer, Oster #210, black enamel on cast iron, stainless containers, EX...........................**100.00**

Percolator, Kenmore Automatic, Bakelite handle, 1950s..**22.50**

Popcorn popper, Kenmore, aluminum, glass finial, 1951....................................**10.00**

Reamer, Coke-bottle green, unmarked, w/pitcher.....**25.00**

Reamers, Hazel Atlas, green, 2-pc, footed, mark A&J, 4-cup....................................**45.00**

Refrigerator dish, Blue Dots on custard, McKee, 4x5".....**28.00**

Refrigerator dish, yellow opaque, 7¼"....................................**35.00**

Rolling pin, glass, white clambroth w/wooden handles........**125.00**

Sieve, Foley Food Mill, tin w/wood handles............................**12.00**

Strainer, woven wire, wood handle, 8¾".............................**6.00**

Toaster, Estate Stove Co #177, chrome, Bakelite switch on cord...................................**55.00**

Toaster, McGraw Electric Co #1B8, chrome & Bakelite, 7x10"...............................**55.00**

Waffle iron, chrome w/Bakelite lid, General Electric, 12".................**35.00**

Waffle iron, red wood handles, Rogers Electric Laboratories Co....................................**22.50**

Waffle iron, Silhouette, Porcelier....................**225.00**

Water bottle, Forest Green, Owens-Illinois................**22.50**

Kliban

B. Kliban, artist and satirist, was extremely fond of cats and usually had more than one in his California home. This affinity led to his first book (published in 1975), simply titled *Cat*. The popularity of the Kilban cat led to sales of various types of merchandising featuring his likeness. Among the items you may encounter are calendars, mugs, note pads, Christmas cards, and stuffed toys, the majority of which are of recent production.

Apron, mice & cheese printed on white, EX.......................**20.00**

Bank, cat wearing red sneakers, 1979, 6½", from $40.00 to $55.00. (Photo courtesy Marbena Fyke)

Book, Never Eat Anything Bigger than Your Head, 1976, 1st edition, EX **15.00**

Bowl, cat in red sneakers on white, Kiln Craft Tableware Ironstone, 6"......................................**15.00**

Candle holder, cat climbing tree, Sigma, 8¼", from $30 to...............................**50.00**

Clock, wearing red sneakers, battery-operated, 8½" dia...............**30.00**

Creamer, red bow on tail, Sigma Tastetester, 7x4¾", from $50 to.....................................**60.00**

Jigsaw puzzle, 100-pc, 7x7, MIB...........................**20.00**

Mug, as lifeguard, California below, Gift Creations, 1989, MIB................................**35.00**

Mug, Peace, Santa peeking in window, ceramic...................**12.50**

Paperweight, Aloha Cat, steel..**8.00**

Picture frame, Love a Cat, 3-D cat by 7½x5" frame, Sigma...**65.00**

Pillow, stuffed figure, 22".....**22.50**

Pillow cases, wearing red sneakers, pr **30.00**

Poster, Momcat, 1977, 24x18"..**15.00**

Rubber stamp, Butterfly Cats..**15.00**

Sheet, flanel, flat, twin size ..**25.00**

Sheets (1 fitted/1 flat), full size, 2-pc set................................**45.00**

Sleeping bag, cat in red sneakers, 78", M **20.00**

T-shirt, Florida Yacht Cats, SS Feliner **35.00**

T-shirt, Sashimi, w/fish & chopsticks..............................**20.00**

Teapot, dressed in tuxedo, unmarked, 8½" **135.00**

Tumbler, plastic, 4½" **29.00**

Kreiss

These novelties were imported from Japan during the 1950s. There are several lines. One is a totally off-the-wall group of caricatures called Psycho Ceramics. There's a Beatnik series, Bums, and Cave People (all of which are strange little creatures), as well as some that are very well done and tasteful. Others you find will be inset with colored 'jewels.' Many are marked either with an ink stamp or an in-mold trademark (some are dated).

Values are lower than we reported in the last editon; this is only one of many collectibles that have been affected by the Internet.

Ashtray, girl in bathtub, rectangular, 4x8½".......................**18.00**

Ashtray, Queen of Hearts, Bridge set, 7"..............................**30.00**

Ashtray, smiling man's head w/outstretched arms as bowl, 6"......................................**22.50**

Ashtray, white w/baseball player & umpire, 2½x6"................**20.00**

Bank, grumpy Santa, 7".......**25.00**

Bank, pink winking pig w/You Save...Pig's Eye on belly, 4x5x6"..............................**25.00**

Bell, choir angel, 'spaghetti' decor on dress, 4⅝"..................**15.00**

Bells, male & female angels, 4½", pr.....................................**30.00**

Candle holder, boy & girl angel w/Noel banner, 3¼x6" ...**25.00**

Condiment set, ketchup & mustard, girl head finials, pr..........**30.00**

Cup & saucer, white w/queen on 1 side, king on other, Bridge set..................................**17.50**

Decanter/bank, hillbilly stands by keg, hat is lid, musical, 12".........**22.50**

Egg cups, Mr & Mrs Santa Claus, 2¼", pr.............................**20.00**

Figurine, angry Santa, What Do I Look Like-Rin Tin Tin?, 6".**20.00**

Figurine, angry Santas face-to-face, Which 1 of Us...Phoney?, 5x5"................................**25.00**

Figurine, blue guy w/lg eyes, 5".................................**15.00**

Figurine, caveman w/wooly mammoth, 2½", 5"...................**40.00**

Figurine, chubby guy on scales that read 700 pounds, 5x4½" **18.50**

Figurine, Daffy Bell, white coat w/blue stripes, blue & tan hat, 5"......................................**28.00**

Figurine, drunk with elephant, either size, $55.00. (Photo courtesy Phil and Nyla Thurston)

Figurine, Elegant Heirs, woman on hands & knees w/bone in mouth **15.00**

Figurine, female dancer in yellow, white dress w/black stripes **30.00**

Figurine, gray mouse w/spring tail, 5"............................**18.50**

Figurine, lady in red & white Christmas dress, 5½" **20.00**

Figurine, pixie girl, seated, in cream attire, 3½x4".......**18.50**

Figurine, purple man w/stitches allover, rhinestone eyes.**18.00**

Figurine, Santa holding candle, 'spaghetti' hat & coat, 7½" **25.00**

Figurine, Santa w/sleigh & reindeer................................**40.00**

Figurine, turtle, head turned, marked Kreiss 1957, 3x3½"............**25.00**

Figurine, 3 Santa's stacked like a totem, 7½" **20.00**

Figurines, cocker spaniel mom w/2 pups chained to her, 7½"..**20.00**

Figurines, Hawaiian couple, dancing, 1950s, 8", pr............**85.00**

Figurines, Mr & Miss Mistletoe angels/fairies, 4½", pr....**28.00**

Figurines, Siamese cats, 1 lg & 2 sm chained to mom........**15.00**

Figurines, 'spaghetti' poodles, 1 lg w/2 sm attached w/chain.**30.00**

Hors d'oeuvres holders, white pigs w/holly, 3¼x5½", pr.............**30.00**

Mug, Christmas Cheer, white w/leaves & berries, candy cane handle, 4"...............**30.00**

Mug, Santa, rhinestone eyes, 2½" **10.00**

Mug, Santa head, winking, 2-sided..............................**20.00**

Napkin doll, blonde in pink dress, fan in hand (candle holder), 10"......................................**50.00**

Napkin doll, yellow & green dress, candle holder hat, 10", on tray............................**55.00**

Napkin doll, yellow & green dress, holds tray, 10", +pr 4¾" shakers **100.00**

Shakers, happy reindeer, seated, 4", pr **20.00**

Shakers, Mistletoe Men, 4", pr.**20.00**

Shakers, Mr & Mrs Snowman, 4½", 4", pr.....................**18.50**

Lava Lamps

These were totally cool in the '60s — no self-respecting love child was without one. Like so many good ideas, this one's been revived and is popular again today. In fact, more are being sold this time around than were sold forty years ago. We've listed only vintage examples.

Aluminum base, gold top, red lava, Century series, Simplex..**60.00**

Aluminum base & top, blue-green lava, 14", VG (scratches)..**55.00**

Aluminum base w/flower tray, red lava, Simplex Corp #800-N, 16½"..............................**65.00**

Candle powered, 13½", from $100.00 to $125.00. (Photo courtesy Teresa Wagner)

Gold base & top, red lava, Leviton on switch, 1960s.............**45.00**

Gold base & top, red lava, shape resembles rocket ship, 1960s **75.00**

Lantern shape (aka coach lantern), red lava, att Mathmos, 1970s, 19" ...**135.00**

Pepsi special edition bottle, white lava in blue liquid, 15" overall **60.00**

Silver base & top, blue lava, 1960s, 18x5¾" **125.00**

Lefton China

Since 1940 the Lefton China Co. has been importing and producing ceramic giftware which may be found in shops throughout the world. Because of the quality of the workmanship and the beauty of these items, they are eagerly sought by collectors. Lefton pieces are usually marked with a fired-on trademark or a paper label.

Loretta DeLozier, author of *Collector's Encyclopedia of Lefton China, Books I, II,* and *III,* and *Lefton China Price Guide* is listed in the Directory under Iowa. See Clubs and Newsletters for information concerning the National Society of Lefton Collectors.

Bank, lady in mink coat, Money Is Everything, 7½", from $35.00 to $45.00. (Photo courtesy Loretta DeLozier)

Bell, White Holly, #6053 ......**10.00**

Bowl, Only a Rose, swan shape, #425, 7½" **90.00**

Candy box, Misty Rose, #5538, 4¾" **47.50**

Coffeepot, Green Heritage, #3065 ....**140.00**

Compote, Floral Chintz, #8043, 7" **20.00**

Cookie jar, bunny in egg house, #4484, 8¾"....................**200.00**

Cookie jar, Dutch Boy, #22072, 9¼".................................**350.00**

Cookie jar, girl's head, #397, 8" ..**275.00**

Creamer & sugar bowl, Rose Chintz, #663....................**40.00**

Cup & saucer, Poinsettia, #4392.........................**30.00**

Cup & saucer, tea; floral design, #976 ....**30.00**

Dish, Green Holly, tree shape, #2688, 11¾"....................**20.00**

Egg cup, Rose Chintz, #658, 7" **25.00**

Figurine, angels w/flowers, glazed, #00780, pr **15.00**

Figurine, Country Doctor, #5687, 6¾"..................................**70.00**

Figurine, George Washington, #1108, 8"........................**90.00**

Figurine, Kewpie sitting on leaf, #2992, 3½"......................**30.00**

Figurine, man & woman w/jugs, #5641, 8", pr.................**125.00**

Figurine, Old Shoemaker, #4718, 6¾"..................................**90.00**

Figurine, red squirrel, #4492, 8"..............................**90.00**

Figurine, Ruffed Grouse, #2668, 5", pr **70.00**

Figurine, Simple Simon, #1255, 6¼"..................................**90.00**

Figurine, Valentine Girl, #033, 4"..................................**17.50**

Figurine, Victorian lady w/umbrella, #1570, 6¼" **135.00**

Jam jar, Cuddles, seated cat, #1451 ....**30.00**

Jam jar, Festival, #2617, w/tray & spoon...............................**40.00**

Jam jar, To a Wild Rose, #2579 ..**40.00**

Lamp, bluebird, #6143, 6¼"..**40.00**

Mug, Stonewall Jackson, #1112..**42.50**

Mug, White Christmas, #1387..**7.50**

Night light, mouse w/mushroom, #7920, 6"........................**25.00**

Pin holder, Magnetic Bobby, #993, #993, 4½"......................**50.00**

Pitcher, Brown Heritage Fruit, #3115 ....**125.00**

Planter, beagle pup, #6974, 6" ..**25.00**

Planter, clown's head, #4498, 4" **40.00**

Planter, double heart shape w/Cupid, #2995, 4"........**20.00**

Planter, Home Tweet Home, birdhouse, pink, #50261, 5"...**42.50**

Planter, watering can, Floral Bisque Bouquet, #6968, 6" **25.00**

Plate, cake; #608, 7½" **15.00**

Punch bowl, Green Holly, #1367 .**45.00**

Salt & pepper shakers, Dark Green Heritage, #30132, pr **25.00**

Salt & pepper shakers, Fruits of Italy, #1207, pr **13.50**

Snack set, Misty Rose, #5690..**20.00**

Teabag holder, Violet Chintz, #1793 ....**30.00**

Teapot, Paisley Fantasia, #6797, miniature........................**40.00**

Teapot, Thumbelina, #1695..**170.00**

Teapot, rose design, #2117, $55.00.
(Photo courtesy Loretta DeLozier)

Tumble cup, To a Wild Rose, #2582 ....**60.00**

Vase, Brown Heritage Fruit, #3117, 8¾" **65.00**

Vase, Only a Rose, #420, 6"..**70.00**

Wall pocket, Sweet Violets, #2894, 6½" **15.00**

Letter Openers

Here's a chance to get into a hobby that offers more than enough diversification to be both interesting and challenging, yet requires very little room for display. Whether you prefer the advertising letter openers or the more imaginative models with handles sculpted as a dimensional figure or incorporating a gadget such as a penknife or a cigarette lighter, you should be able to locate enough for a nice collection. Materials are varied as well, ranging from silver plate to wood.

Advertising, brass, Diversified Industries, Inc, stamped B & B.................................**22.00**

Advertising, bronze, Life & Casualty Ins Co **25.00**

Advertising, bronze, The Robbins & Meyers Co, Springfield, OH **35.00**

Advertising, gold-plated, Holiday Inns of America...............**6.00**

Bone w/purple wood handle, painted scene, Mexico **15.00**

Brass, lion w/wings on pillar.**10.00**

Brass, magnifying pineapple top **10.00**

Brass, Revolutionary patriot on horse, back marked England **10.00**

Brass, Roman soldier w/shield, marked Italy **12.00**

Brass, seashell, stamped w/anchor & PM at Flukes...............**8.00**

Brass, 3-D grasshopper, paperweight handle **20.00**

Bronze, griffin over lion head ..**12.00**

Bronze, rampant lion w/sceptor, royal seal **10.00**

Cast metal, knight in armor..**12.00**

Copper, swordfish, Florida, Made in Japan............................**8.00**

Enamel & chrome, dragon w/green tassel...............................**25.00**

Enamel & steel, yellow flowers w/red tassel **15.00**

Gold-colored pot metal, lobster handle...............................**8.00**

Gold-plated, eagle handle.......**8.00**

Ivory, carved dragon, double-sided **55.00**

Leather handle, floral, gold, orange & green, Germany............**8.00**

Leather handle, w/gold stamp, marked Italy **6.00**

Lucite handle w/2 1976 US pennies, Las Vegas **12.00**

Mother-of-pearl, w/brass handle, floral, Victorian..............**50.00**

Plastic, bathing beauty w/flocked suit.................................**20.00**

Celluloid and steel with penknife handle, Little White House, Warm Springs, Georgia, Made in Germany, $40.00. (Photo courtesy Everett Grist)

Silver-plated, Boston, The Midnight Ride of Paul Revere **10.00**

Stag & bone, artist signed, Koras...........................**15.00**

Stag handle, steel blade **10.00**

Steel, golfer, made in Italy...**12.00**

Steel, marked on reverse w/soldier w/sword & shield **4.00**

White metal, letter holder in handle, Mailway....................**6.00**

Wood, African native head...**10.00**

Wood, sailboat, laser carved...**8.00**

Wood handle, sea horse w/palm tree..................................**8.00**

Liberty Blue

'Take home a piece of American history!,' stated an ad from the 1970s for this dinnerware made in Staffordshire, England. Blue and white depictions of George Washington at Valley Forge, Paul Revere, Independence Hall — fourteen historic scenes in all — were offered on different pieces. The ad goes on to describe this 'unique...truly unusual...museum-quality...future family heirloom.'

For every five dollars spent on groceries you could purchase a basic piece (dinner plate, bread and butter plate, cup, saucer, or dessert dish) for fifty-nine cents on alternate weeks of the promotion. During the promotion, completer pieces could also be purchased. The soup tureen was the most expensive item, originally selling for $24.99. Nineteen completer pieces in all were offered along with a five-year open stock guarantee. For more information we recommend Jo Cunningham's book, *The Best of Collectible Dinnerware.*

Teapot, from $95.00 to $145.00.

Bowl, cereal; 6½", from $12 to..**15.00**

Bowl, flat soup; 8¾", from $20 to..............................**22.00**

Bowl, fruit; 5", from $6 to.......**6.50**

Bowl, vegetable; oval, from $40 to..................................**45.00**

Bowl, vegetable; round, from $40 to....................................**45.00**

Butter dish, w/lid, ¼-lb.........**55.00**

Casserole, w/lid...................**125.00**

Coaster...................................**12.50**

Creamer, from $18 to...........**22.00**

Creamer & sugar bowl, w/lid, original box..........................**80.00**

Cup & saucer, from $7 to **9.00**

Gravy boat, from $32 to........**38.00**

Gravy boat liner, from $22 to ..**30.00**

Mug, from $10 to...................**12.00**

Pitcher, 7½"..........................**125.00**

Plate, bread & butter; 6", from $4 to **4.50**

Plate, dinner; 10", from $6 to..**8.00**

Plate, luncheon; scarce, 8¾" ..**24.00**

Plate, scarce, 7", from $9 to..**12.00**

Platter, 12", from $35 to.......**45.00**

Platter, 14" **95.00**

Salt & pepper shakers, pr, from $38 to **42.00**

Soup ladle, plain white, no decal, from $30 to **35.00**

Soup tureen, w/lid..............**425.00**

Sugar bowl, no lid **10.00**

Sugar bowl, w/lid **28.00**

License Plates

Early porcelain license plates are treasured by collectors and often sell for more than $500.00 per pair when found in excellent condition. The best examples are first-year plates from each state, but some of the more modern plates with special graphics are collectible too. Prices given below are for plates in good or better condition.

1934 (all), Washington, $40.00 for the pair; Alaska, $200.00; Arizona, $80.00.

Alabama, 1984-87, ea **3.50**
Alaska, 1953...........................**75.00**
Arizona, 1933, copper **100.00**
Arkansas, 1986-89, ea **3.50**
California, 1931.....................**20.00**
Delaware, 1982 ....**5.50**
Florida, 1938 ....**30.00**
Georgia, peach, 1990..............**3.50**
Hawaii, 1972 ....**8.50**
Idaho, 1990, mountains..........**2.50**
Illinois, 1940...........................**9.50**
Indiana, 1948 ....**9.50**
Iowa, 1967 ....**4.00**
Kentucky, 1961 ....**10.50**
Maine, 1990, lobster **4.50**
Massachussetts, 1918-19, ea ..**25.00**
Michigan, 1970........................**2.50**
Mississippi, 1974....................**5.50**
Montana, 1063 ....**7.50**
Nebraska, 1941 ....**40.00**
Nevada, 1997, Silver State.....**3.50**
New Jersey, 1923..................**15.50**
New Mexico, 1999, cactus.......**2.50**
New York, 1961, tab **3.00**
North Carolina, 1975, First in Freedom...........................**3.50**
North Dakota, 1988, Teddy....**9.50**
Ohio, 1962 ....**6.50**
Oklahoma, 1986, Sun **4.50**
Oregon, 1996, Trail...............**15.00**
Pennsylvania, 1938...............**11.50**
Rhode Island, 1941 ....**15.50**
South Carolina, 1977 ....**5.00**
Tennessee, 1961 ....**10.50**
Texas, 1974.............................**3.50**
Utah, 1947, some rust **14.50**
Vermont, 1995.......................**10.50**
Virginia, 1966.........................**4.50**
Washington, 1996 ....**3.50**
West Virginia, 1996 ....**7.50**
Wisconsin, 1955 ....**12.50**
Wyoming, 1969.......................**5.50**

Little Red Riding Hood

This line of novelties and kitchenware has always commanded good prices on the collectibles market. In fact, it became valuable enough to make it attractive to counterfeiters, and now you'll see reproductions everywhere. They're easy to spot, though, watch for one-color eyes. Though there are other differences, you should be able to identify the imposters armed with this information alone.

Little Red Riding Hood was produced from 1943 to 1957. The Regal China Company was by far the major manufacturer of this line, though a rather insignificant number of items were made by the Hull Pottery of Crooksville, Ohio, who sent their whiteware to the Royal China and Novelty Company (a division of Regal China) of Chicago, Illinois, to be decorated. For further information we recommend *The Collector's Encyclopedia of Hull Pottery* by Brenda Roberts and *The Collector's Encyclopedia of Cookie Jars, Vol I*, by Joyce and Fred Roerig. Both are published by Collector Books.

Bank, standing, from $900 to..**1,350.00**
Butter dish, from $350 to...**400.00**
Canister, salt....................**1,100.00**
Canisters, coffee, sugar or flour, ea, from $600 to...........**700.00**
Cookie jar, full skirt, from $750 to................................**850.00**

Cookie jar, open basket, from $400 to....................................**500.00**
Cookie jar, stars on apron, minimum value **675.00**
Creamer, side pour, from $150 to **225.00**
Creamer, top pour, no tab handle, from $400 to.................**425.00**

Jug, batter, $450.00. (Photo courtesy Pat and Ann Duncan)

Lamp, from $2,000 to **2,650.00**
Mustard jar, w/spoon, from $375 to **460.00**
Pitcher, 8", from $550 to **850.00**
Shakers, 3¼", pr, from $95 to ..**140.00**
Shakers, 5½", pr, from $180 to ..**235.00**
Sugar bowl, crawling, no lid, from $300 to.............................**450.00**
Sugar bowl, standing, from $175 to **225.00**
Sugar bowl, w/lid, from $350 to...........................**425.00**
Teapot, from $400 to...........**450.00**
Wolf jar, red base, from $925 to **1,000.00**
Wolf jar, yellow base, from $750 to **850.00**

Lu Ray Pastels

Introduced in 1938 by Taylor, Smith, and Taylor of East

Liverpool, Ohio, Lu-Ray Pastels is today a very sought-after line of collectible American dinnerware. It was first made in these solid colors: Windsor Blue, Surf Green, Persian Cream, and Sharon Pink. Chatham Gray was introduced in 1948 and is today priced higher than the other colors.

Individual sugar and creamer, $92.00 each; individual coffeepot, $200.00; four-part relish, $95.00. (Photo courtesy Kathy and Bill Meeham)

Bowl, '36s oatmeal **60.00**
Bowl, cream soup **70.00**
Bowl, fruit; Chatham Gray, 5"..**16.00**
Bowl, lug soup; tab handled ..**24.00**
Bowl, mixing; 7" **125.00**
Bowl, mixing; 10¼" **150.00**
Bowl, salad; yellow **55.00**
Butter dish, any color other than Chatham Gray, w/lid **50.00**
Butter dish, Chatham Gray, rare color, w/lid **90.00**
Casserole **140.00**
Coffee cup, AD......................**20.00**
Creamer..................................**8.00**
Egg cup, double....................**30.00**
Jug, water; footed **150.00**

Muffin cover, w/8" underplate **165.00**
Pitcher, juice **200.00**
Plate, cake **70.00**
Plate, chop; 15" **38.00**
Plate, 6" **3.00**
Plate, 8" **25.00**
Plate, 10" **25.00**
Platter, oval, 13" **24.00**
Sauce boat **28.00**
Saucer, coffee; AD **8.50**
Saucer, tea..............................**2.00**
Sugar bowl, AD; w/lid, individual **40.00**
Teacup **8.00**
Teapot, curved spout, w/lid..**125.00**
Teapot, flat spout, w/lid......**160.00**
Tray, pickle...........................**28.00**
Tumbler, water **80.00**

Lunch Boxes

In the early years of this century, tobacco companies often packaged their products in tins that could later be used for lunch boxes. By the 1930s oval lunch boxes designed to appeal to school children were being produced. The rectangular shape that is now popular was preferred in the 1950s. Character lunch boxes decorated with the faces of TV personalities, super heroes, Disney, and cartoon characters are especially sought after by collectors today. Our values are for lunch boxes only (without the Thermos, unless one is mentioned in the line).

Refer to *Collector's Guide to Lunchboxes* by Carole Bess White and L.M. White for more information. For an expanded listing, see *Schroeder's Collectible Toys, Antique to Modern* (Collector Books).

A-Team, metal, 1983, VG.....**20.00**
Adam-12, metal, 1972, VG...**35.00**
Airport Control Tower, vinyl, 1972, EX.......................**150.00**
Animal Friends, metal, 1975, EX..............................**30.00**
Atom Ant, metal, 1966, G **40.00**
Ballerina on Lily Pad, vinyl, 1960s, EX.....................**100.00**
Banana Splits, vinyl, 1969, w/Thermos, NM...........**450.00**
Barbie, vinyl, 1972, pink, w/Thermos, VG+.............**60.00**
Batman, plastic, 1982, blue, VG...**5.00**
Battle of the Planets, metal, 1979, EX...................................**30.00**
Beany & Cecil, vinyl, 1961, w/Thermos, NM...........**200.00**
Beatles, metal, 1965, w/Thermos, NM...............................**600.00**
Bonanza, metal, 1963, VG....**50.00**
Bozo the Clown, metal, 1963, dome top, NM.......................**250.00**
Brave Eagle, metal, 1957, w/Thermos, NM...........**250.00**

Bullwinkle and Rocky, metal, 1962, blue background, NM, $600.00.

Cabbage Patch Kids, plastic, 1983, yellow, w/Thermos, EX..**10.00**
California Raisins, vinyl, 1988, EX **20.00**
Campbell Kids, metal, 1975, NM **275.00**
Cartoon Zoo Lunch Chest, metal, 1962, EX.....................**175.00**
Chavo, metal, 1979, M........**100.00**
CHiPs, plastic, 1977, dome top, NM................................**30.00**
Davy Crockett, metal, 1955, green rim, VG+.........................**60.00**
Dawn, vinyl, 1970, w/Thermos, EX..............................**175.00**
Disney Express, metal, 1979, EX..**20.00**
Dr Seuss, metal, 1970, VG+..**70.00**
Dr Seuss, plastic, 1996, EX..**15.00**
Dream Boat, vinyl, NM **125.00**
Dynomutt, metal, 1976, EX..**35.00**
Flipper, metal, 1967, EX **100.00**
Garfield, plastic, red, 1980s, EX.............................**15.00**
Get Smart, metal, 1966, EX .**135.00**
Goofy, metal, 1984, EX+.......**25.00**
Gunsmoke, metal, 1959, EX..**175.00**
Hee Haw, metal, 1970, EX...**70.00**

Hogan's Heroes, metal, 1966, dome top, VG, $150.00.

Hogan's Heroes, metal, 1966, dome top, w/Thermos, EX......**200.00**
Hulk Hogan, plastic, 1989, EX..**10.00**

Incredible Hulk, metal, 1978, EX.............................**50.00**

Keebler Cookies, plastic, 1987, w/Thermos, M **50.00**

Knight Rider, metal, 1983, EX..**35.00**

Lassie, metal, 1978, VG........**35.00**

Lawman, metal, 1961, VG....**45.00**

Li'l Jodie, vinyl, 1985, EX **40.00**

Lone Ranger, metal, 1954, VG.**100.00**

Looney Tunes, plastic, 1977, EX...............................**10.00**

Marvel Super Heroes, metal, 1976, VG+.................................**25.00**

Mary Poppins, vinyl, 1973, VG...**50.00**

Mighty Mouse, plastic, 1979, EX+.............................**20.00**

Miss America, metal, 1972, VG+ **40.00**

Monroes, metal, 1967, EX..**150.00**

Munsters, metal, 1965, w/Thermos, NM.................................**250.00**

Nestle's Quik, plastic, 1980, NM.**25.00**

Pac Man, metal, 2 swing handles, 1980, NM+......................**30.00**

Pepsi-Cola, vinyl, 1980, yellow, EX **50.00**

Pete's Dragon, metal, 1978, EX..**35.00**

Play Ball, metal, 1969, VG w/Thermos, EX+ **35.00**

Princess, vinyl, 1963, yellow, w/Thermos, EX..............**50.00**

Rambo, metal, 1985, NM+ ...**25.00**

Rap It Up, plastic, 1992, EX..**15.00**

Sabrina, vinyl, 1972, NM ...**200.00**

Scooby Doo, metal, 1973, w/Thermos, NM.................................**175.00**

Six Million Dollar Man, plastic, 1974, M...........................**35.00**

Smokey Bear, metal, 1975, NM **350.00**

Space: 1999, metal, 1974, G..**25.00**

Star Trek the Motion Picture, metal, 1979, EX+ **60.00**

Super Friends, metal, 1976, w/Thermos, EX...............**50.00**

Superman, plastic, phone booth scene, 1986, EX..............**25.00**

Tarzan, metal, 1966, w/Thermos, NM...............................**150.00**

Tic Tac Toe, vinyl, 1970s, EX ..**50.00**

Tony Tiger (Kellogg's Frosted Flakes), metal, 1969, VG+...............**150.00**

Twiggy, vinyl, 1967, w/Thermos, EX **175.00**

UFO, metal, 1973, VG **50.00**

Underdog, vinyl, 1963, yellow, w/Thermos, EX...............**50.00**

Underdog, vinyl, 1972, with Thermos, NM, $300.00.

Voltron, plastic, 1984, w/Thermos, NM.................................**15.00**

Wild Frontier, metal, 1977, EX..**40.00**

Wizard in the Van, vinyl, 1978, orange, VG+ **60.00**

Woody Woodpecker, metal, 1972, w/Thermos, NM **200.00**

World of Barbie, vinyl, 1971, pink, EX **50.00**

Ziggy, vinyl, 1979, EX...........**50.00**

Zorro, metal, 1958, VG **90.00**

Magazines

Some of the most collectible magazines are *Life* (because of the celebrities and important events they feature on their covers, *Saturday Evening Post* and *Ladies' Home Journal* (especially those featuring the work of famous illustrators such as Parrish, Rockwell, and Wyeth), and *National Geographics* (pre-WWI issues in particular). As is true with any type of ephemera, condition and value are closely related. Unless they're in fine condition (clean, no missing or clipped pages, and very little other damage), they're worth very little; and cover interest and content are far more important than age. For more information refer to *Old Magazines* by Richard E. Clear.

Agricultural Digest, 1934, November, Parrish cover, NM **60.00**

American Cinematographer, 1979, January, NM **30.00**

American Heritage, 1968, April, Mickey Mouse cover, VG.. **25.00**

American Needlewoman, 1926, May **3.00**

Art Photography, 1956, April, Sophia Loren, VG **10.00**

Baseball Digest, 1951, April, Joe DiMaggio, VG **30.00**

Better Homes & Gardens, 1935, September, EX **30.00**

Cad, 1965, June, VG **20.00**

Camera Craft, 1925, July, EX.. **15.00**

Child Life, 1954, December, Norman Rockwell, EX ... **20.00**

Collier's, 1945, June, Harry Truman, EX **7.00**

Collier's, 1955, November, Bette Davis, EX **20.00**

Collier's, 1955, November 11, Agatha Christie, EX **10.00**

Cosmopolitan, 1936, July, Crandall, EX **12.00**

Cosmopolitan, 1955, October, Audrey Hepburn article, EX **11.00**

Cosmopolitan, 1969, August, Elizabeth Taylor, VG+..... **8.00**

Cue, 1953, June 27, Marilyn Monroe, NM **35.00**

Esquire, 1943, May, Vargas illustrations, VG+ **30.00**

Esquire, 1960, November, Lenny Bruce article, EX **10.00**

Esquire, 1973, March, Fat City Follies, EX+ **8.00**

Family Circle, 1942, October 16, Judy Garland, EX **20.00**

Family Circle, 1946, April 26, Marilyn Monroe, EX.... **350.00**

Famous Models, 1950, April-May, VG **28.00**

Fortune, 1930s-40s, ea, from $8 to **75.00**

Fortune, 1948, railroad cover, EX **30.00**

Garden & Home Builder, 1920s, VG, from $6 to **8.00**

Good Housekeeping, 1937, October, Pearl Buck, Petty art ads, EX **15.00**

Good Housekeeping, 1945, August, baby cover, EX+ **8.00**

Gourmet, 1940s-50s, VG-EX, from $3 to **5.00**

Gourmet, 1965, April, Lucius Beebe/Along the Boulevards, VG+ **4.00**

Highway Traveler, 1940s-50s, VG, from $3 to **5.00**

House Beautiful, 1959, October, Frank Lloyd Wright, EX **12.00**

Inside Sports, 1993, March, swimsuit issue, EX **5.00**

Jack & Jill, 1961, May, Roy Rogers, EX......................**10.00**

Ladies' Home Journal, 1934, January, reclining lady on cover, NM.......................**12.00**

Ladies' Home Journal, 1947, May, Eleanor Roosevelt article, EX..............................**4.00**

Ladies' Home Journal, 1960, January, Pat Boone, EX ..**5.00**

Ladies' Home Journal, 1967, June, Twiggy, VG.......................**2.00**

Life, April 2, Gus Grissom & John Young, VG......................**16.00**

Life, 1917, July 23, Clint Eastwood, EX+...............**25.00**

Life, 1938, February 7, Gary Cooper, Fair **20.00**

Life, 1939, December 11, Betty Grable, G...........................**8.00**

Life, 1940, September 2, Dionne Quintuplets, EX.............**35.00**

Life, 1942, November 16, NC Wyeth art for corn ad, EX.....................................**16.00**

Life, 1944, December 11, Judy Garland, EX....................**35.00**

Life, 1947, November 17, Howard Hughes, EX.....................**15.00**

Life, 1949, August 1, Joe DiMaggio, EX.................**75.00**

Life, 1951, Gina Lollobrigida, EX...............................**10.00**

Life, 1953, July 20, Senator John Kennedy, EX...................**10.00**

Life, 1960, February 1, Dinah Shore cover & article, EX.............**4.00**

Life, 1961, May 17, Alan B Shepard **12.00**

Life, 1964, August 28, Beatles cover & article, EX **40.00**

Life, 1969, April 18, Mae West, VG.................................**10.00**

Life, 1968, April, Martin Luther King, NM, $50.00. (Photo courtesy P.J. Gibbs)

Life, 1971, March 19, Ali/Frazier, EX....................................**35.00**

Life, 1981, May, Reagan's attempted assassination, EX+ **12.00**

Literary Digest, 1918, April 27, NC Wyeth cover art, EX......**20.00**

Look, 1937, May, Jean Harlow, Prohibition, EX..............**15.00**

Look, 1939, December 5, Hitler, VG+................................**10.00**

Look, 1940, February 27, Superman article, VG+...**90.00**

Look, 1941, May 20, Gale Storm, EX....................................**8.00**

Look, 1946, May 28, Nagasaki, EX **10.00**

Look, 1950, December 5, Esther Williams, EX.................**20.00**

Look, 1954, June 1, Jackie Gleason, EX....................**12.00**

Look, 1956, November, James Dean, EX **18.00**

Look, 1958, June 24, Hugh O'Brien, EX....................**12.00**

Look, 1963, January 9, Beatle article, EX **28.00**

Look, 1964, July 28, NY Nightlife, EX **8.00**

Look, 1967, February 6, John Kennedy, EX **6.00**

McCall's, 1932, February, Zane Grey article, EX **8.00**

McCall's, 1940-49, EX, ea, from $2 to **5.00**

McCall's, 1960, April, Marilyn Monroe, EX **19.00**

McCall's, 1968, June, Jacqueline Kennedy, EX **6.00**

Modern Photography, 1956, September, glamour issue, EX **10.00**

Modern Screen, 1939, Deanna Durbin, EX **30.00**

Movie Classic, 1936, October, Glenda Farrell, G...........**22.00**

Movie Life, 1968, October, Elvis, EX **20.00**

Movie Stars Parade, 1950, May, June Allyson, EX **20.00**

National Geographic, 1915-16, ea **15.00**

National Geographic, 1917-24, ea **9.00**

National Geographic, 1925-29, ea **8.00**

National Geographic, 1930-45, ea **7.00**

National Geographic, 1946-55, ea **6.00**

National Geographic, 1956-67, ea **5.50**

National Geographic, 1968-69, ea **4.50**

National Geographic, 1990-present, ea **2.00**

New Yorker, 1953, April 6, VG **10.00**

Newsweek, 1941, September 8, Hitler, VG.......................**10.00**

Newsweek, 1957, July 1, Stan Musial, EX **25.00**

Newsweek, 1975, June 16, Nolan Ryan, EX **20.00**

Newsweek, 1989, June 26, Batman, NM **8.00**

Parade, 1962, June, Elizabeth Taylor, NM....................**25.00**

Parents, 1942, September, EX..**5.00**

Penthouse, 1985, September, Madonna, EX **20.00**

People Weekly, 1976, July 7, Paul McCartney, NM **8.00**

Photoplay, 1966, April, Peyton Place cast, NM **8.00**

Playboy, 1955, February, Jayne Mansfield, EX **150.00**

Playboy, 1956, college edition, NM, $100.00.

Playboy, 1958, May, Tina Louise, EX **24.00**

Playboy, 1964, January, Marilyn Monroe nude photo, EX..**35.00**

Playboy, 1964, July, Bridgette Bardot, EX.....................**24.00**

Playboy, 1974, April, Jane Fonda, EX **14.00**

Playboy, 1981, September, Bo Derek, EX......................**12.00**

Playgirl, 1976, August, Robert Redford, EX+.................**32.00**

Police Gazette, 1940, April, Carol Landis, EX......................**7.00**

Popular Song Hits, 1947, May, Betty Grable, VG.............**9.00**

Redbook, 1934, November, Herbert Hoover, EX.........**8.00**

Redbook, 1936, June, Tunney & Louis, EX.........................**8.00**

Redbook, 1954, November, Grace Kelly, EX........................**15.00**

Redbook, 1955, July, Marilyn Monroe............................**55.00**

Redbook, 1955, October, Jackie Gleason, EX.....................**6.00**

Rolling Stone, 1968, April 27, Beatles, NM.................**100.00**

Rolling Stone, 1968, February 24, #6, Janis Joplin, EX+..**185.00**

Rolling Stone, 1969, #37, Elvis Presley, EX....................**20.00**

Rolling Stone, 1974, March 14, #156, Bob Dylan, M.......**20.00**

Rolling Stone, 1975, #198, Bob Dylan, EX.........................**8.00**

Rolling Stone, 1984, #415, Beatles, EX......................................**7.00**

Rolling Stone, 1985, May 9, Madonna, M, from $6 to..**8.00**

Rolling Stone, 1987, February 12, Pee Wee Herman, EX......**5.00**

Saturday Evening Post, 1956, October 13, Eisenhower article, EX **24.00**

Saturday Evening Post, 1957, April 20, Yogi Berra, EX **40.00**

Saturday Evening Post, 1964, February 15, Sophia Loren, EX **12.00**

Screen Guide, 1936, Ginger Rogers, EX....................**20.00**

Screen Guide, 1951, March, Betty Grable, Roy Rogers, etc, NM **15.00**

Screenland, 1939, October, Claudette Colbert, EX+..**25.00**

Silver Screen, 1958, June, Mitzi Gaynor, EX.....................**12.00**

Sporting News, 1947, December 3, Joe DiMaggio, EX.........**38.00**

Sports Illustrated, 1954, August 23, Yankee cards, EX..**325.00**

Sports Illustrated, 1956, April 23, Billy Martin, EX............**15.00**

Sports Illustrated, 1964, Sandy Koufax, EX....................**32.00**

Sports Illustrated, 1969, October 20, World Series, M.......**10.00**

Sports Illustrated, 1978, February 27, Leon Spinks, EX........**5.00**

Sports Illustrated, 1980, February 4, Christie Brinkley, EX **40.00**

Sports Illustrated, 1988, March 21, Larry Bird, EX.........**10.00**

Tattler, 1930s-40s, EX, ea, from $4 to **6.00**

Time, 1938, Frank Cappa, EX..**28.00**

Time, 1944, July 17, Ernie Pyle, EX+ **8.00**

Time, 1955, Oppenheimer, EX..**10.00**

Time, 1971, March 8, Ali/Frazier, EX **12.00**

Time, 1973, January 22, Marlon Brando, EX.....................**5.00**

True Crime, 1955, May, VG...**5.00**

True Story, 1935, April, Zoe Martin art cover, EX **30.00**

Tuff Stuff, 1990, July, Nolan Ryan, VG..............................**5.00**

TV Star Parade, 1960, November, Debbie Reynolds, EX.......**6.00**

Vogue, 1895, October 10, golf issue, EX.......................**70.00**

Who, 1941, April, Vol 1 #1,
Winston Churchill, VG..**20.00**
Woman's Home Companion, 1950,
March, VG+......................**3.00**
Woman's Home Companion, 1956,
December, VG..................**2.00**
Yatchsman's Magazine, 1942,
May, EX.........................**20.00**

Marilyn Monroe

Her life was full of tumult, her career short, and the end tragic, but in less than a decade she managed to establish herself as the ultimate Hollywood sex goddess; and though there have been many try, none has ever came close to evoking the same devotion movie goers have always felt for Marilyn Monroe. Her sexuality was innocent, almost unintentional. She was one of the last from the era when stars wore designer fashions, perfectly arranged hair styles, and flawless makeup. Her relationships with the men in her life, though all were unfortunate, only added to the legend. Fans today look for the dolls, photographs, and various other collectibles that have been produced over the years.

Calendar, 1954, pinup pose with lace overlay, complete, 15x9", NM, $80.00.

Calendar, 1955, nude photos, complete, 10x17" w/8x10" picture, EX....................................**30.00**
Cookie jar, bust from Seven Year Itch, Clay Art, 1996, MIB.**45.00**
Cookie jar, seated on chest, Clay Art, 1997, 13", MIB.......**45.00**
Decanter, McCormick, Seven Year Itch pose, 7", M............**180.00**
Doll, Barbie Hollywood Premiere, NMIB..............................**50.00**
Doll, dressed in movie costume, porcelain, Franklin Mint, 24"..............................**310.00**
Doll, Gentlemen Prefer Blondes, Franklin Mint, 19", NMIB, from $125 to................**175.00**
Doll, River of No Return, 21st Century Fox Movie Collection, MIB................................**65.00**
Doll, Spotlight Slender Marilyn, American Beauty Classic, 1993, MIB.....................**75.00**

Blanket, image of postage stamp, 53x65", M **45.00**
Book, The Marilyn Monroe Story, 1st edition, EX.............**300.00**
Book, The Strange Death of Marilyn Monroe, Frank Capell, 1964, EX............**50.00**
Calendar, 1953, nude pose, Golden Dreams, 13x8", EX **60.00**

Magazine, Night & Day, August 1954, cover photo, EX....**65.00**
Magazine, Playboy, on cover, 1953, EX............................**2,750.00**

Ornament, Hallmark Keepsake, 1998, NMIB.....................**15.00**

Plate, A Star Is Born, Norma Jean, Hamilton, 8", MIB.........**55.00**

Plate, Her Day in the Sun, Hamilton, 1994, MIB.....**85.00**

Plate, Isn't It Delicious, Bradford Exchange, 8¼"...............**65.00**

Plate, My Heart Belongs to Daddy, Delphi, 8½", 1990, MIB..**60.00**

Plate, Seven Year Itch, Delphi, 8½", EX..........................**75.00**

Plate, Sweet Sizzle, Bradford Exchange #3113A, 1996, EXIB..............................**45.00**

Plates, Reflections of Marilyn, set of 8, Bradford Exchange, EXIB.............................**110.00**

Postage stamps, 20 stamp sheet, 1995, M...........................**45.00**

Poster, for theatre, Bus Stop, 1-sheet, framed, EX+......**260.00**

Puzzle, Playboy Centerfold pose, Alskog Inc, 1973, EXIB.**70.00**

Salt & pepper shakers, gold shoe shape, pr, EX.................**15.00**

Salt & pepper shakers, TV w/picture, on stand, 1950s, Vandor, MIB.................................**20.00**

Sculpture, Reflection, Franklin Mint, 10½", M................**45.00**

Statue, caricature, Continental Studios, 1970s, 20¾", EX..**130.00**

Thimble, name & image, ceramic, England, 1¼", EX..........**10.00**

Watch, gold-tone bezel w/faux signature, Fossil, 1995, NMIB ..**45.00**

Matchbox Cars

Introduced in 1953, the Matchbox Miniatures series has always been the mainstay of the company. There were seventy-five models in all but with enough variations to make collecting them a real challenge. Larger, more detailed models were introduced in 1957. This series, called Major Pack, was replaced a few years later by a similar line called King Size. To compete with Hot Wheels, Matchbox converted most models over to a line called SuperFast that sported thinner, low-friction axles and wheels. (These are much more readily available than the original 'regular wheels,' the last of which was made in 1959.) At about the same time, the King size series became known as Speed Kings; in 1977 the line was reintroduced under the name Super Kings.

Another line that's become very popular is their Models of Yesteryear. These are slightly larger replicas of antique and vintage vehicles. Values of $20.00 to $60.00 for mint-in-box examples are average, though a few sell for even more.

Sky Busters, introduced in 1973, are small-scale aircraft measuring an average of 3½" in length. Models currently being produced sell for about $4.00 each.

To learn more we recommend *Matchbox Toys, 1947 to 1999,* and *Toy Car Collector's Guide* by Dana Johnson; and a series of books by Charlie Mack: *Lesney's Matchbox Toys* (there are three: Regular Wheels, SuperFast Years, and Universal years).

To determine values of examples in conditions other than given in our listings, based on MIB or MOC prices, deduct a minimum of 10% if the original container is missing, 30% if the condition is excellent, and as much as 70% for a toy graded only very good.

Key:
reg: regular wheels
    (Matchbox Miniatures)
SF: SuperFast

King Size, Speed Kings, and Super Kings

K-12-A, Heavy Breakdown Wreck Truck, 1963, 4¾", MIB, from $30.00 to $40.00. (Photo courtesy Dana Johnson)

K-1-A, Weatherhill Hydraulic Shovel, 1960, MIP, from $60 to **75.00**
K-3-B, Hatra Tractor Shovel, 1965, MIP, from $25 to..**30.00**
K-4-C, Leyland Tipper, orange-red, 1970, MIP, from $15 to...**20.00**
K-5-C, Muir Hill Tractor Trailer, yellow, 1972, MIP, from $18 to.....................................**22.00**
K-8-D, Animal Transport, 1980, MIP, from $20 to............**30.00**

K-10-A, Aveling-Barford Tractor Shovel, 1963, MIP, from $30 to **40.00**
K-13-A, Foden Ready-Mix Concrete Truck, 1963, MIP, from $30 to **40.00**
K-16-B, Petrol Tanker, green cab w/Texaco tampo, 1974, MIP, from $75 to **100.00**
K-22-A, Dodge Charger, 1969, MIP, from $15 to............**20.00**
K-27-A, Camping Cruiser, 1971, MIP, from $12 to............**15.00**
K-31-B, Peterbilt Refrigerator Truck, red, Coca-Cola tampo, 1978, MIP......................**45.00**
K-39-A, Milligan's Mill, 1973, MIP, from $12 to............**15.00**
K-49-A, Ambulance, white, 1973, MIP, from $12 to............**15.00**
K-76-A, Volvo Ralley Set, 1981, MIP, from $30 to............**35.00**
K-117-A, Toyota 4x4 Hi-Lux, white, 1989, MIP, from $15 to.................................**20.00**
K-118-A, Road Construction Set, 1985, MIP, from $30 to **40.00**

Models of Yesteryear

Y-1-B, Ford Model T, silver plated, 1965, MIP, from $20 to **25.00**
Y-2-C, Prince Henry Vauxhall, blue w/red seats, 1970, MIP, from $900 to **1,200.00**
Y4-A, Sentimental Steam Wagon, unpainted metal wheels, 1956, MIP......................**55.00**
Y-5-C, 1907 Peugeot, bronze w/bronze roof, 1969, MIP, from $20 to **25.00**

Y-3-D, 1912 Ford Model T Tanker, 1982, blue and white with gold-spoked wheels, Express Diary, MIB, from $15.00 to $20.00. (Photo courtesy Dana Johnson)

Y-6-C, 1913 Cadillac, silver plated, 1967, MIP, from $125 to **150.00**

Y-10-B, Mercedes Benz 360/220, cream, 1963, MIP, from $75 to **80.00**

Y-13-B, Daimler, yellow, 1966, MIP, from $30 to...........**40.00**

Y-17-A, 1938 Hispano Suiza, green, 1973, MIP, from $20 to..................................**25.00**

Y-19-B, Fowler B6 Snowman's Engine, 1986, MIP, from $20 to **25.00**

Y-23-A, 1922 AEC S Type Omnibus, red w/The RAC tampo, 1982, MIP **17.50**

Y-33-A, 1920 Mack Truck, 1990, MIP, from $15 to...........**20.00**

Y-48-A, 1931 Garrett Steam Wagon, 1996, MIP, from $50 to **60.00**

Skybusters

SB-01-A, Lear Jet, white w/G-JCB tampo, 1973, MIP **7.00**

SB-05-A, Starfighter F104, 1973, MIP...............................**9.00**

SB-07-a, Junkers 87B, black w/swastikas, 1973, MIP...**85.00**

SB-21-A, Lightning, 1977, MIP..**9.00**

SB-23-A, SST Super Sonic Transport, white w/Singapore tampo, 1979, MIP **17.50**

SB-27-A, Harrier Jet, white & red, 1981, MIP.......................**7.00**

SB-40-A, Boeing 737-300, 1992, MIP **4.50**

1-75 Series

4-H, Gruesome Twosome, gold w/purple windows, 1971, MIB...............................**70.00**

5-F, Seafire Boat, white deck w/blue hull, 1975, MIB....**6.50**

6-E, Ford Pickup, SF, 1970, MIB...............................**14.00**

7-H, Volkswagen Ruff Rabbit, 1983, MIB.......................**5.00**

8-A, Caterpillar Tractor, light yellow w/red driver, 1955, MIB **90.00**

9-F, Ford Escort, white w/red interior, Phantom labels, 1978, MIB..................................**5.00**

9-G, Fiat Abarth, white w/Alitalia tampo, 1982, MIB..............................**3.00**

10-E, Leyland Pipe Truck, silver grill, black wheels, 1970, MIB **17.50**

11-K, Chrysler Atlantic, gold, 1997, MIB.......................**3.00**

12-C, Safari Land Rover, green w/brown luggage rack, 1965, MIB..............................**10.00**

14-F, Rallye Royale, 1973, MIB.**7.50**

14-I, Corvette Convertible, metallic silver w/red interior, 1983, MIB..................................**4.00**

16-E, Badger Exploration Truck, olive drab, w/radar, 1974, MIB..............................**40.00**

17-B, Austin London Taxi, maroon w/silver wheels, 1960, MIB **70.00**

18-D, Caterpillar Crawler Bulldozer, silver plastic rollers, 1964, MIB..........**95.00**

19-F, Road Dragster, purple, 1970, MIB...............................**17.50**

20-B, ERF 686 Truck, Eveready For Life, blue w/black wheels, 1959, MIB......................**40.00**

21-F, Rod Roller, yellow w/red rear wheels, 1973, MIB **15.00**

23-D, Volkswagen Camper, 1970, turquoise with opening roof, M, $12.00. (Photo courtesy Dana Johnson)

23-H, Honda ATCC, red, 1985, MIB................................**10.00**

24-G, Datsun 280ZX 2+2, black w/gold stripes, 1983, MIB **3.00**

25-A, Bedford Dunlop 12CWT Van, 1956, MIB..............**45.00**

26-C, GMC Tipper Truck, reg, 1968, MIB........................**8.00**

28-f, Stoat Armoured Truck, SF, metallic gold, 1974, MIB..**10.00**

29-A, Bedford Milk Delivery Van, 1956, MIB......................**50.00**

31-C, Lincoln Continental, SF, green-gold, 1969, MIB...**22.50**

32-A, Jaguar XK140 Coupe, red, 1957, MIB......................**85.00**

32-E, Maserati Bora, gold, 1972, MIB..............................**32.50**

34-B, Volkswagen Caravette Camper, light green, 1962, MIB **45.00**

36-A, Austin A50 Sedan, blue-green, metal wheels, 1957, MIB................................**40.00**

38-C, Honda Motorcycle w/trailer, orange w/no decals, reg, 1967, MIB................................**22.50**

41-A, D-Type Jaguar, green, #41 decal, metal wheels, 1957, MIB................................**35.00**

43-D, Pony Trailer, yellow, SF, 2 horses, 1970, MIB..........**17.50**

44-E, Boss Mustang, yellow, 1972, MIB...................................**7.00**

46-C, Mercedes Benz 300SE, green, regular, 1968, MIB..........**10.00**

46-F, Ford Tractor, dark blue, 1978, MIB......................**45.00**

48-A, Meteor Sports Boat & trailer, tan deck, blue hull, MIB..**45.00**

48-F, Sambron Jack Lift, yellow w/Sambron tampo, 1977, MIB **180.00**

50-B, John Deere Tractor, gray plastic tires, 1964, MIB..**27.50**

50-G, Harley-Davidson Motorcycle, 1980, MIB........................**5.00**

53-B, Mercedes Benz 220 SE, maroon w/gray wheels, 1963, MIB..............................**27.50**

53-E, Tanzara, orange w/chrome interior, 1972, MIB........**13.00**

55-A, DUKW Army Amphibian, metal wheels, 1958, MIB..**40.00**

56-G, Peterbilt Tanker, blue w/white tank, Milk tampo, 1982, MIB.........................**5.00**

57-A, Wolseley 1500 Sedan, pale green w/silver grille, 1958, MIB.................................**45.00**

59-A, Ford Thames Singer Van, green w/gray plastic wheels, 1958, MIB........................**35.00**

60-F, Mustang Piston Popper, yellow w/red interior, 1982, MIB **9.00**

62-E, Mercury Cougar Rat Rod, Wildcat, doors open, 1970, MIB................................**22.50**

64-F, Caterpillar Bulldozer, yellow w/black blade & canopy, 1979, MIB..................................**9.00**

67-A, Saladin Armoured Car, olive green w/black wheels, 1959, MIB................................**35.00**

68-F, Dodge Caravan, burgundy w/black stripes, England cast, 1984, MIB.......................**18.00**

69-C, Rolls Royce Silver Shadow Convertible Coupe, 1969, metallic blue, SuperFast wheels only, 3", MIB, from $15.00 to $20.00. (Photo courtesy Dana Johnson)

71-C, Ford Heavy Wreck Truck, Esso, regular, amber windows, 1968, MIB **65.00**

72-E, Maxi Taxi Mercury Capri, 1973, MIB........................**10.00**

75-A, Ford Thunderbird, cream & pink, gray plastic wheels, 1960, MIB.......................**55.00**

McCoy

A popular collectible with flea market goers, McCoy pottery was made in Roseville, Ohio, from 1910 until the late 1980s. They are most famous for their extensive line of figural cookie jars, more than two hundred in all. They also made amusing figural planters, etc., as well as dinnerware, and vases and pots for the florist trade. Though some pieces are unmarked, most bear one of several McCoy trademarks. Beware of reproductions made by a company in Tennessee who until recently used a very close facsimile of the old McCoy mark. They made several cookie jars once produced by McCoy as well as other now-defunct potteries. Some of these (but by no means all) were dated with the number '93' below the mark.

For more information refer to *The Collector's Encylopedia of McCoy Pottery* by Sharon and Bob Huxford, *McCoy Pottery Wall Pockets and Decorations* by Craig Nissen, and *McCoy Pottery, Collector's Reference & Value Guide,* Volumes I, II, and III, by Margaret Hanson, Craig Nissen, and Bob Hanson (all available from Collector Books). See also Cookie Jars. See Clubs and Newsletters for information concerning the newsletter *NM (Nelson McCoy) Xpress.*

Ashtray, brown w/white interior, 1948, 6½", from $25 to ..**30.00**

Ashtray, Sunburst Gold, shell form, 1957, 6¼x4½", from $60 to **70.00**

Bank, Seaman's, sailor w/bag over shoulder, no mark, 5¾", from $75 to **90.00**

Bean pot, apple decal, w/4 serving bowls, 1967, from $65 to..**75.00**

Beer stein, boot shape, 1971, 8¼", from $35 to **50.00**

Bookend/planter, dog w/bird in mouth, natural colors, 1955, 6x6", pr **150.00**

Bookends, Lily Bud, pastel matt colors, marked NM, 5¾", pr..**150.00**

Bookends, rearing horse, brown, 1942, pr, from $125 to ..**175.00**

Bowl, red rose decal on white, 1950s-1960s, 10", from $30 to..................................**35.00**

Candle holder, floral decal, w/chimney, 1982, from $40 to **50.00**

Candlestick, blue sponging on white, 1982, from $15 to..**18.00**

Canister set, blue windmill decal, 4-pc set, 1974, from $75 to **100.00**

Casserole, Brocade, black & pink spatter, in metal frame, 3-pt **60.00**

Centerpiece, antelope form, black or green base, 1955, 12" **400.00**

Coffee server, Grecian, 1956, 10½", from $100 to **125.00**

Console bowl, floral decal, w/handles, 1950s, 9", from $40 to **50.00**

Dog dish, green w/embossed letters, flaring sides, 1940s, 6" **70.00**

Flower bowl ornament, peacock, white, no mark, 4¾", from $100 to **125.00**

Flower holder, turtle form on sq base, yellow, marked NM, 4x2" **90.00**

Flowerpot, embossed basket-weave on blue, 1940, 3½x5", from $35 to **40.00**

Flowerpot & saucer, red rose decal, 1950s-1960s, 6", from $20 to **25.00**

Grease jar, cabbage form, 1950s, 7", from $100 to **125.00**

Ice jug, Antique Rose on white, 48-oz, 1959, from $40 to **50.00**

Jardiniere, basketweave w/embossed handle-like medallions, 1950, 6"......................................**40.00**

Jardiniere, blue onyx, 1930s, 6", from $30 to **40.00**

Jardiniere, fluting and leaves, 6x7½", $30.00.

Jardiniere, red rose decal on white, 1950s, 6", from $30 to **35.00**

Lamp, Hyacinth, 1950, 8", from $800 to **1,000.00**

Lamp, leaves & berries, 1930s, 5½", from $175 to **225.00**

Lamp, Sunburst Gold, rearing horse, no mark, from $65 to........**95.00**

Oil & Vinegar set, yellow w/red stoppers, 1950s-1960s, from $15 to **20.00**

Pitcher, elephant form, white, 1940s, 7", from $350 to ..**400.00**

Pitcher, fish form, green/brown combination, 1949, 7", from $650 to **800.00**

Pitcher & bowl set, blue sponge-ware, 1982, from $40 to ..**50.00**

Planter, Antique Rose, 1959, 15½", from $40 to **50.00**

Planter, baby rattle w/pink bow, 1954, 5½x3", from $90 to.............**110.00**

Planter, bird, head up, singing, aqua, 1940s, 7x6¾", from $35 to **45.00**

Planter, dog w/cart, black, 1950s, 8½", from $80 to.............**90.00**

Planter, fish form, rare, 1955, 12x7", from $1,000 to..............**1,200.00**

Planter, frog, green w/yellow trim, no mark, 1950s, 6x7½"..**30.00**

Planter, frog w/separate umbrella, 1954, 5½x7½", from $125 to.................................**175.00**

Planter, hunting dog with bird in mouth, ca 1955, 12½" long, from $150.00 to $175.00.

Planter, Liberty Bell, 1954, 10x8", from $200 to **300.00**

Planter, puppy, 1 eye closed, sitting, natural colors, 1959, 6x6" **60.00**

Planter, rabbit & stump, w/gold trim, 1951, 5½", from $150 to................................**200.00**

Planter, squirrel w/nut, brown w/decorated nut, 1955, 5x4½"............................**25.00**

Planter, Sunburst Gold, footed, 1950s-60s, 6", from $25 to..............**30.00**

Planter, Village Smithy, from $45 to **75.00**

Planter, 2 ducks perched on 2 eggs, 1940s, 6x3"............**30.00**

Platter, fish form in yellow & blue, 1973, 18x8¼", from $150 to **200.00**

Serving dish, shell form, blue sponging on white, 1970s, from $10 to **25.00**

Skillet, white w/green interior, 1950s, 10", from $25 to **30.00**

Spoon rest, penguin form, yellow, 1953, 7", from $100 to .**150.00**

Stretch animal, lion, pastel matt colors, no mark, 7½x5½", $225 to **275.00**

Tea set, embossed pine cones on blue, 1940s-50s, from $100 to **125.00**

Teapot, floral decal, 1960s, 36-oz, from $40 to **50.00**

Vase, Blossomtime, rectangular, 1946, 8", from $50 to **60.00**

Vase, Butterfly, butterfly form, blue, USA, 7½x5½"........**90.00**

Vase, Butterfly, tulip rim & base, long handles, USA, 10", $150 to **225.00**

Vase, cornucopia; ribbed w/dimensional flowers at base, white, 7½" **40.00**

Vase, Early American, footed, 1967, 8½", from $50 to ..**60.00**

Vase, hand form, original cold paint on fingernails, 1940s, 6½"...............................**175.00**

Vase, Harmony, 12", from $30 to................................**40.00**

Vase, Hobnail, tulip rim, pastel matt colors, marked NM, 9"....................**125.00**

Vase, Hyacinth, pink or blue, 1950, 8", from $100 to............**125.00**

Vase, peacock pair embossed on aqua, handles, 1948, 8"..**40.00**

Vase, Ram's Head, black, 1950s, 9½".................................**75.00**

Vase, Rustic, V-shape w/swooping lip, embossed berries, footed, 8"....................................**50.00**

Vase, Uncle Sam, white, 7½", from $50 to..............................**60.00**

Wall pocket, Butterfly, pastel matt colors, marked NM, 7x6"............................**500.00**

Wall pocket, clock, weights on chains, bird in peak, yellow, 8"...................................**150.00**

Wall pocket, cornucopia, 1950s, 8", from $70 to.....................**85.00**

Wall pocket, iron on trivet backsplash, 1950s, 8½", from $50 to.....................................**75.00**

Wall pocket, lady w/bonnet, 1940s, 8", from $75 to **200.00**

Wall pocket, Lily, yellow lily w/green leaves at base, 1940s, 6½"..................................**95.00**

Wall pocket, pear on leafy backsplash, natural colors, from $70 to..............................**85.00**

Wall pocket, umbrella form w/yellow handle, 1950s, 8¾" **175.00**

Window box, Rustic, pine cone feet, 1945, 7½" **20.00**

Metlox Dinnerware

Since the 1940s, the Metlox company of California has been producing dinnerware, cookie jars, novelties, and decorative items, and their earlier wares have become very collectible. Some of their best-known dinnerware patterns are California Provincial (the dark green and burgundy rooster), Red Rooster (in red, orange, and brown), Homestead Provincial (dark green and burgundy farm scenes), and Colonial Homestead (farm scenes done in red, orange, and brown). See also Cookie Jars.

Carl Gibbs Jr. is listed in the Directory under Texas; he is the author of *Collector's Encyclopedia of Metlox Potteries* (Collector Books), highly recommended if you'd like to learn more about this company.

California Ivy, sugar bowl and creamer, $25.00 to $30.00 each; plate, 9¼", $15.00.

California Ivy, bowl, cereal; 6¾" **20.00**

California Ivy, bowl, soup; 6¾"..**22.00**
California Ivy, Lazy Susan..**175.00**
California Ivy, mug, 7-oz......**30.00**
California Ivy, pepper mill...**50.00**
California Ivy, pitcher, lg, 2½-qt..**75.00**
California Ivy, plate, bread & butter; 6½"...........................**10.00**
California Provincial, ashtray, sm, 4½"...............................**20.00**
California Provincial, bowl, salad; 11⅛"..............................**110.00**

California Provincial, bowl, vegetable; 10", $65.00. (Courtesy Old Tyme Toy Store)

California Provincial, butter dish, w/lid................................**80.00**
California Provincial, cruets, oil & vinegar; w/lids, 7-oz, pr ..**45.00**
California Provincial, egg cup ..**45.00**
California Provincial, kettle casserole warmer, med, metal..**50.00**
California Provincial, pitcher, milk; med, 1-qt...............**85.00**
California Provincial, platter, turkey; 22½".................**325.00**
California Provincial, saucer, 6⅛"...............................**6.00**
California Provincial, sugar canister, w/lid.........................**90.00**

California Strawberry, baker, oval, 11"..........................**50.00**
California Strawberry, bowl, fruit; 5⅜"..................................**14.00**
California Strawberry, bowl, soup; 6¾"..................................**18.00**
California Strawberry, creamer, 10-oz.............................**28.00**
California Strawberry, pitcher, med, 1¼-pt.....................**55.00**
California Strawberry, platter, oval, sm, 9½".................**35.00**
California Strawberry, salt & pepper shakers, pr...............**25.00**
California Strawberry, sauce boat, 1¼-pt..............................**40.00**
California Strawberry, saucer, 6"...................................**4.00**
California Strawberry, tea canister, w/lid.........................**45.00**
California Strawberry, tumbler, 12-oz..............................**30.00**
Grape Arbor, baker, oval, 10¼"..**50.00**
Grape Arbor, bowl, cereal; 7⅜".......................................**16.00**
Grape Arbor, bowl, soup; 8½"..**22.00**
Grape Arbor, bowl, vegetable; divided, med, 9½"..........**50.00**
Grape Arbor, creamer, 10-oz..**28.00**
Grape Arbor, cup, 7-oz..........**12.00**
Grape Arbor, mug, 8-oz........**25.00**
Grape Arbor, plate, bread & butter; 6⅜"...........................**10.00**
Grape Arbor, platter, oval, sm, 9⅝"...................................**40.00**
Grape Arbor, salt & pepper shakers, pr.............................**25.00**
Homestead Provincial, bowl, vegetable; sm, 7⅛"...............**55.00**
Homestead Provincial, bread server, 9½"...........................**80.00**
Homestead Provincial, cookie jar, w/lid..............................**125.00**

Homestead Provincial, egg cup..**45.00**

Homestead Provincial, gravy boat, 1-pt................**50.00**

Homestead Provincial, saucer, 6⅛"................**6.00**

Homestead Provincial, soup tureen, w/ladle...............**65.00**

Homestead Provincial, sprinkling can **105.00**

Homestead Provincial, steeple crock **110.00**

Homestead Provincial, sugar canister, w/lid **90.00**

Red Rooster, butter dish, decorated or red, w/lid...............**65.00**

Red Rooster, coaster, decorated or red, 3¾", ea **22.00**

Red Rooster, cookie jar, w/lid, decorated or red, ea...........**110.00**

Red Rooster, creamer, decorated or red, 6-oz **28.00**

Red Rooster, cruet, oil; w/lid, decorated or red, 7-oz, ea......**40.00**

Red Rooster, cup, decorated or red, 7-oz, ea................**12.00**

Red Rooster, pepper mill, decorated or red, ea **45.00**

Red Rooster, pitcher, decorated or red, sm, 1½-pt, ea.........**50.00**

Red Rooster, plate, dinner; decorated only, 10"................**14.00**

Red Rooster, tea canister, w/lid, decorated or red, ea.......**60.00**

Red Rooster, tumbler, red only, 11-oz................**40.00**

San Fernado, baker, oval, 11¼"................**45.00**

San Fernado, bowl, fruit; 6" ..**14.00**

San Fernado, bowl, salad; 12½"................**70.00**

San Fernado, buffet server, 14¼" dia................**60.00**

San Fernado, cup, 6-oz **10.00**

San Fernado, pitcher, med, 1-qt................**55.00**

San Fernado, plate, salad; 7½"................**10.00**

San Fernado, platter, oval, lg, 13¾"................**40.00**

San Fernado, soup tureen, w/lid, 3-qt................**165.00**

San Fernado, tumbler, 10-oz..**30.00**

Sculptured Daisy, bowl, soup; 8¼" **20.00**

Sculptured Daisy, bowl, vegetable; sm, 7"................**35.00**

Sculptured Daisy, butter dish, w/lid................**55.00**

Sculptured Daisy, casserole, w/lid, 1½-qt................**90.00**

Sculptured Daisy, pitcher, sm, 1 ½-pt................**50.00**

Sculptured Daisy, plate, luncheon **22.00**

Sculptured Daisy, platter, oval, sm, 9½"................**35.00**

Sculptured Daisy, salt & pepper shakers, pr **25.00**

Sculptured Daisy, sauce boat, 1-pt **40.00**

Sculptured Daisy, saucer, 6¼"..**4.00**

Sculptured Daisy, teapot, w/lid, 7-cup **100.00**

Sculptured Grape, buffet server, 12⅛" dia................**80.00**

Sculptured Grape, butter dish, w/lid................**65.00**

Sculptured Grape, compote, footed, 8½"................**80.00**

Sculptured Grape, flour canister, w/lid **85.00**

Sculptured Grape, mug, 8-oz..**28.00**

Sculptured Grape, plate, bread & butter; 6⅜" **11.00**

Sculptured Grape, plate, dinner; 10½"................**18.00**

Sculptured Grape, tumbler, 12-oz **38.00**

Miller Studio

Brightly painted chalkware plaques, bookends, thermometers, and hot pad holders modeled with subjects that range from Raggedy Ann and angels to bluebirds and sunfish were the rage during the 1950s and 1960s, and even into the early 1970s you could buy them from the five-&-dime store to decorate your kitchen and bathroom walls with style and flair. Collectors who like this 'kitschy' ambience are snapping them up and using them in the vintage rooms they're re-creating with period appliances, furniture, and accessories. They're especially fond of the items marked Miller Studio, a manufacturing firm located in New Philadelphia, Pennsylvania. Most but not all of their pieces are marked and carry a copyright date. If you find an unmarked item with small holes on the back where stapled-on cardboard packaging has been torn away, chances are very good it's Miller Studio as well. Miller Studio is still in business and is today the only American firm that continues to produce hand-finished wall plaques.

Angels, cherub's face, orange, 1954, pr, from $18 to **10.00**
Animals, bunny toothbrush holder, yellow & black, from $30 to **32.00**

Animals, cat mother & 3 kittens, 1960, she: 8½", they: 3½" **25.00**
Animals, elephant, pink & red, 1972, 4-pc set, from $18 to..........**24.00**
Animals, horse head, black w/flaxen manes, 3-color eyes, 1959, 7", pr **25.00**
Animals, horse head, brown, 1951, from $12 to **14.00**
Animals, pig, blue & white, sm, from $10 to **12.00**

Animal, poodle, black and white, 1969, from $12.00 to $15.00.

Animals, poodle plaques, pink & blue, sq, 1972, pr, from $12 to....................................**15.00**
Animals, Siamese cats, pink bows & green eyes, 1976, 10½x3½", pr......................................**30.00**
Birds, bluebird, blue & yellow, 1970, sm, pr, from $8 to ..**10.00**
Birds, cardinal, red, 1972, pr, from $8 to..............................**10.00**
Birds, flying pheasants, M36, red, 3-pc set, from $25 to **30.00**
Birds, parrot, tropical colors, 1967, 8x13" **18.00**

Birds, swan, pink, oval, 1965, pr, from $8 to **10.00**

Birds, swan plaques, pink & white, round, 1958, pr, from $14 to **16.00**

Figures, Raggedy Ann & Andy, blue & orange, pr, from $28 to **32.00**

Fish, family, blue, 1950s, 4-pc set, 9", from $16 to **20.00**

Fish, gaping mouths, pink, pr w/bubbles, 4-pc set, 7", from $10 to **14.00**

Fish, male & female, black, 1954, pr, from $12 to **14.00**

Fruit, bunch, brown & yellow, round, 1968, from $6 to ...**8.00**

Fruit, carrot bunch, orange & green, 1971, from $6 to **8.00**

Fruit, grapes on wood, gold, 1964, from $10 to **12.00**

Fruit, lg mushrooms, yellow & brown, 1977, pr, from $13 to **16.00**

Hot pad holder, Campbell Soup Kid boy & girl, yellow, 1964, pr.....................................**25.00**

Hot pad holder, peach w/funny face, yellow, 1972, pr, from $8 to **10.00**

Note pad, bird, Make a Note, yellow & red, 1954, from $17 to **20.00**

Note pad, fruit, Don't You Forget It, blue & red, 1968, from $10 to **15.00**

Note pad, owl w/pencil holder, red & yellow, 1970, from $12 to **15.00**

People, man & lady (faces), red, yellow & green, 1950, 4x3", pr **25.00**

Seasons, black w/gold, 1966, 5½" dia, 4+Four Seasons plaque, 5-pc **25.00**

Thermometer, fruit bunch, multicolor, 1981, from $10 to **12.00**

Thermometer, mermaid, aqua & white, 1976, from $14 to............................**17.00**

Thermometer, Sniffy Skunk, M55, black & yellow, from $28 to **30.00**

Model Kits

The best-known producer of model kits today is Aurora. Collectors often pay astronomical prices for some of the character kits from the 1960s. Made popular by all the monster movies of that decade, ghouls like Vampirella, Frankenstein, and the Wolfman were eagerly built up by kids everywhere. But the majority of all model kits were vehicles, ranging from 3" up to 24" long. Some of the larger model vehicle makers were AMT, MPC, and IMC. Condition is very important in assessing the value of a kit, with built-ups priced at about 50% lower than one still in the box. Other things factor into pricing as well — who is selling, who is buying and how badly they want it, locality, supply, and demand. For additional listings we recommend *Schroeder's Collectible Toys, Antique to Modern* (Collector Books).

Adams, Chuck Wagon, 1958, MIB **40.00**

Addar, Super Scenes, Jaws, 1975, MIB **40.00**

AEF, Aliens, Ferro #AM-11, 1980s, 1/35, MIB **26.00**

Airfix, Coldstream Guardsman #205, 1960s, 1/12, MIB..**15.00**

Airfix, Lunar Module #3013, 1991, 1/72, MIB (sealed)..........**10.00**

Airfix, Skeleton #3541, 1979, 1/6, MIB **14.00**

AMT, '69 Chevelle SS 396 Hardtop, MIB.................**35.00**

AMT, '74 Corvette, MIB **40.00**

AMT, Farrah's Foxy Vette, 1977, MIB **35.00**

AMT, Interplanetary UFO #960, 1970s, 1/635, MIB (sealed).....................**130.00**

AMT, Man From UNCLE Car #912, 1967, 1/25, MIB ..**220.00**

AMT, Star Trek, Mr Spock, 1967, MIB **135.00**

AMT/Ertl, Batmobile, 1989, MIB (sealed) **20.00**

AMT/Ertl, Star Trek, USS Enterprise, chrome set, special edition, MIB **30.00**

AMT/Ertl, Star Trek (TV), Kirk, 1994, 12", MIB (sealed) ..**25.00**

Arii, Macross, Quilted-Queleual Ship #332, 1/2000, MIB.............**30.00**

Arii, Southern Cross, ATAC-Bowie Emerson, MIB................**25.00**

Aurora, Alfred E Newman, 1965, EXIB **120.00**

Aurora, Batboat, 1968, MIB, from $400 to..........................**500.00**

Aurora, Batplane, 1967, MIB..**200.00**

Aurora, Captain Kidd, MIB (sealed) **150.00**

Aurora, Comic Series, Spider-Man, assembled, NM...**100.00**

Aurora, Dick Tracy, 1967, MIB **150.00**

Aurora, Famous Fighters, Vikings #K6, 1958, 1/8, MIB.....**350.00**

Aurora, Godzilla, 1969, glow-in-the-dark, MIB (sealed).........**350.00**

Aurora, Gullotine, 1964, original issue, MIB **650.00**

Aurora, King Kong, 1964, assembled, EX...........................**75.00**

Aurora, Lunar Probe, 1960s, MIB **175.00**

Aurora, Monsters of the Movies, Dracula, 1975, MIB **250.00**

Aurora, Phantom of the Opera, Canadian issue, MIB...**200.00**

Aurora, Prehistoric Scenes, Jungle Swamp, 1971, MIB **100.00**

Aurora, Prince Valiant, 1959, MIB **200.00**

Aurora, Scene Machines, Butterfly Catcher, MIB **40.00**

Aurora, Tonto, 1974, MIB (sealed) **275.00**

Aurora, Wolf Man #450, 1972, 1/8, MIB..............................**120.00**

Aurora, Wolf Man's Wagon, 1965, MIB, $250.00. (Photo courtesy Rick Polizzi)

Aurora, Zorro, 1965, assembled, EX **125.00**

Bachmann, Birds of the World, Barn Swallow, 1950s, MIB **30.00**

Bandai, Thunderbird #536188, 1984, MIB......................40.00

Billiken, King Kong, MIB.....95.00

FX, Tales From the Darkside, Gargoyle, resin, 17", MIB 120.00

Hawk, Convair Manned Satellite, 1960s, MIB...................100.00

Horizon, Dracula, 1988, MIB..50.00

Horizon, Mole People, 1988, MIB 50.00

Horizon, Wolf Man, MIB......60.00

Imai, Orguss, Dr Doom, 1991, MIB...............................40.00

Life-Like, Moorish North African Rifle, MIB......................45.00

Lindberg, Brontosaurus, MIB..15.00

Lindberg, Lucky Loser, 1965, MIB, $20.00. (Photo courtesy June Moon)

Lindberg, SST Continental, 1958, MIB...............................175.00

Monogram, Dracula, 1991, MIB (sealed) 30.00

Monogram, Luminators, King Kong, MIB......................40.00

Monogram, Snoopy Is Joe Cool, 1970, MIB....................135.00

Monogram, Superman, 1978, MIB (sealed) 35.00

MPC, Alien, 1979, MIB 75.00

MPC, CB Freak, 1975, MIB ..50.00

MPC, Fonz & His Bike, 1976, MIB 50.00

MPC, Ironside's Van, 1970, MIB 80.00

MPC, Six Million Dollar Man #602, 1975, 1/12, MIB ...50.00

MPC, Sweat Hogs Dream Machine, 1976, MIB 50.00

Palmer, Brontosaurus Skeleton, 1950s, MIB....................60.00

Pyro, Classic Auburn Speedster, MIB...............................85.00

Pyro, Peacemaker 45, 1960, MIB (sealed) 100.00

Pyro, Surf's Up, Surf Trailer Bicycle, 1970, MIB........50.00

Revell, Astronauts in Space, 1968, MIB...............................100.00

Revell, Corporal Missile, 1958, MIB...............................100.00

Revell, Eastern Airlines Golden Falcon, 1950s, MIB........75.00

Revell, F-89D Scorpion USAF Jet, 1950s, MIB 75.00

Revell, Happy Days '29 Model Pickup, 1982, MIB.........30.00

Revell, Lacross Missile #1816, 1958, 1/70, MIB 200.00

Revell, Robotech, Nebo #1400, 1984, 1/72, MIB..............30.00

Revell, Space Pursuit, 1989, MIB 240.00

Revell, Teddy the Koala Bear, MIB...............................40.00

Screamin', London After Midnight Vampire, MIB 100.00

Screamin', Werewolf, MIB..100.00

Superior, Seeing Eye, 1959, MIB............................35.00

Testors, Top Gun, A-4 Aggressor, 1987, MIB......................10.00

Toy Biz, Storm, 1996, MIB (sealed)..........................30.00

Tsukuda, Metaluna Mutant, MIB...........................100.00

Mood Indigo

Quite an extensive line, this ware was imported from Japan during the 1960s. It was evidently quite successful, judging from the amount of it still around today. It's inexpensive, and if you're into blue, this is for you! It's a deep, very electric shade, and each piece is modeled to represent stacks of various fruits, with handles and spouts sometimes turned out as vines. All pieces carry a stamped number on the bottom which identifies the shape. There are more than thirty known items to look for, more than likely others will surface.

Ashtray, 5¾x4¼".....................**5.00**
Bell, 5", from $5 to...............**15.00**
Cake plate, 9½".....................**25.00**
Candle holder, goblet shape, 4½",
    pr...................................**28.00**
Cookie jar/canister, E-2374, 8"..**18.00**
Creamer & sugar bowl, w/lid, from
    $10 to.............................**12.00**

Cruet, $17.50.

Gravy boat, 6½" **15.00**
Ladle, 9¾"............................**25.00**
Mug, coffee; 4⅛" **5.00**
Pitcher, footed, 6".................**15.00**
Salt & papper shakers, 3½", pr..**12.00**
Teapot, 8" **15.00**
Tray, 8½x5¾".......................**28.00**
Trivet, 6" dia **10.00**

Moon and Star

A reissue of Palace, an early pattern glass line, Moon and Star was developed for the market in the 1960s by Joseph Weishar of Island Mould and Machine Company (Wheeling, West Virginia). It was made by several companies. One of the largest producers was L.E. Smith of Mt. Pleasant, Pennsylvania, and L.G. Wright (who had their glassware made by Fostoria and Fenton, perhaps others as well) carried a wide assortment in their catalogs for many years. It is still being made on a very limited basis, but the most collectible pieces are those in red, blue, amber, and green — colors that are no longer in production. The values listed here are for pieces in red or blue. Amber, green, and crystal prices should be 30% lower.

Ashtray, moons at rim, star in
    base, 6-sided, 5½" **14.00**
Ashtray, moons at rim, star in
    base, 6-sided, 8½" **20.00**
Bell, pattern along sides, plain rim
    & handle.......................**35.00**

Bowl, allover pattern, footed, crimped rim, 7½" **25.00**

Butter/cheese dish, patterned lid, plain base, 7" dia, from $45 to **55.00**

Cake plate, allover pattern, low collared base, 13" dia, from $50 to **60.00**

Candle bowl, allover pattern, footed, 8", from $25 to..........**30.00**

Candle holders, allover pattern, flared base, 4½", pr, from $20 to **25.00**

Candle lamp, patterned shade, clear base, 2-pc, 7½", from $20 to **25.00**

Canister, allover pattern, 1-lb or 2-lb **12.00**

Canister, allover pattern, 3½-lb or 5-lb **18.00**

Cheese dish, patterned base, clear plain lid, 9½"..................**60.00**

Compote, allover pattern, footed, flared crimped rim, 5" ...**15.00**

Compote, allover pattern, scalloped rim, footed, 5½x8" **28.00**

Compote, allover pattern, scalloped rim, footed, 7x10" **35.00**

Creamer, allover pattern, raised foot w/scalloped edge, 5¾x3"...**30.00**

Cruet, vinegar; 6¾", from $65 to **75.00**

Epergne, allover pattern, 2-pc, 9" **65.00**

Goblet, water; plain rim & foot, 5¾"...................................**12.00**

Goblet, wine; plain rim & foot, 4½"....................................**9.00**

Lamp, miniature; amber, from $115 to...........................**125.00**

Lamp, miniature; blue, from $165 to **190.00**

Lamp, miniature; green **135.00**

Lamp, miniature; milk glass, from $200 to...........................**225.00**

Lamp, miniature; red, from $175 to **200.00**

Lighter, allover patterned body, metal fittings, from $40 to.............**50.00**

Nappy, allover pattern, crimped rim, 2¾x6", from $12 to..**15.00**

Pitcher, water; 7½", from $65.00 to $75.00; Tumbler, iced tea; 5", $18.00.

Plate, patterned body & center, smooth rim, 8"................**30.00**

Relish bowl, 6 lg scallops form allover pattern, 1½x8"...**30.00**

Relish dish, allover pattern, 1 plain handle, 2x8" dia, from $35 to **35.00**

Salt cellar, allover pattern, scalloped rim, sm flat foot **6.00**

Soap dish, allover pattern, oval, 2x6"....................................**9.00**

Sugar shaker, allover pattern, metal top, 4½x3½".........**45.00**

Toothpick holder, allover pattern, scalloped rim, sm flat foot ..**9.00**

Tumbler, no pattern at rim or on disk foot, 7-oz, 4¼".........**12.00**

Mortens Studios

Animal models sold by Mortens Studios of Arizona during the 1940s are some of today's most interesting collectibles. Hundreds of breeds of dogs, cats, and horses were produced from a plaster-type composition material constructed over a wire framework. They range in size from 2" up to about 7", and most are marked. Crazing and flaking are nearly always present to some degree. Our values are for animals in excellent to near-mint condition, allowing for only minor crazing.

Airedale, standing, black & tan, #741, 5¾x4¾".................**80.00**
Arabian horse, wall plaque .**125.00**
Bengal tiger, 6x8"...............**175.00**
Boxer, sitting, 4½", from $90 to.............................**110.00**
Brahma bull, blond version, #401.............................**150.00**
Chihuahua pup, sitting, 3½x2¾".......................**60.00**
Cocker spaniel, begging, red, #764, 5"......................................**75.00**
Collie, sitting, tan & cream, #791, 5¾".....................................**110.00**
Dalmatian pup, sitting, #812, 3¼".................................**65.00**
Doberman pinscher, sitting, 6½x5½".........................**145.00**
Fox terrier, tan & cream, smooth coat, #772b, 5¼".............**75.00**
German shepherd, standing, tan & black, #755, 6½"...........**100.00**

Great Dane, 8½x8"..............**95.00**
Horse, gray, #652, 4½x5".....**85.00**

Lion, bookends, $175.00 for the pair.

Lynx.....................................**175.00**
Old English sheep dog, foil sticker, 6" L...............................**150.00**
Pekingese, standing, red & tan, #740, 4½x3½".................**75.00**
Persian cat, silver tabby, 3¾x4½".......................**100.00**
Samoyed (Husky), 2¼".........**50.00**
Scottie dog, sitting, hard to find, 4½"..............................**150.00**
Swedish lady, bookends, #311, pr..............................**145.00**
Wolfhound, 6¼x7¼".............**145.00**

Moss Rose

Though the Moss Rose pattern has been produced by Staffordshire and American pottery companies alike since the mid-1800s, the lines we're dealing with here are all from the twentieth century. Much was made from the late 1950s into the 1970s by Japanese manufacturers. Even today you'll occasionally see a tea set or a small candy dish for sale in some of the chain stores. (The collectors who are already picking this line up refer to it as Moss Rose, but we've seen it advertised as Victorian Rose, and some companies called their lines Chintz Rose or French Rose; but for now, Moss Rose seems to be the accepted terminology.

Rosenthal made an identical pattern, and prices are generally higher for examples that carry the mark of that company. The pattern consists of a briar rose with dark green mossy leaves on stark white glaze. Occasionally, an item is trimmed in gold. In addition to dinnerware, many accessories and novelties were made as well.

For further information on items made by Lefton, see *The Collector's Encyclopedia of Lefton China* by Loretta DeLozier (Collector Books). Refer to *Garage Sale and Flea Market Annual* for more a more extensive listing.

Platter, Ucagco, rare, 12", from $65.00 to $85.00. (Photo courtesy Pam Kozak)

Bowl, Japan, 1950s, 4x7"......**20.00**

Candle holders, Japan, 3", pr..**15.00**
Creamer, footed, 4".............**13.00**
Cup, gold trim, footed, 2½x3½" **12.00**
Dinnerware set, Japan, 1960s, child size, 38-pc, MIB..**165.00**
Flower frog, 5½x6"..............**50.00**
Lamp, Aladdin; gold trim, 5¾" **18.00**
Lamp, oil, 2 handles, Japan, 7½"...........................**30.00**
Lamp, oil; frosted chimney, round base, 8" **36.00**
Salt & pepper shakers, pr **18.00**
Sugar bowl, gold trim, w/lid, 4x5½"............................**13.00**
Teapot, gold trim, locking lid, electric, 6x6".........................**30.00**
Teapot, musical, plays Tea For Two **55.00**
Teapot, whistling, electric, Japan, 6"....................................**15.00**
Tidbit tray, 2-tier, Japan......**20.00**
Tidbit tray, 3-tier, gold trim, EX **25.00**
Trinket box, gold trim, 3x4½x2½" **20.00**
Vase, bud; 8" **23.00**

Music Boxes

So many of the music boxes you'll find at flea markets today are related to well-known characters or special holidays. These have a cross-over collectible appeal, and often are priced in the $75.00 to $100.00 range — some even higher. Many are animated as well as musical.

Most modern music boxes are figural, but some have been made by children's toy companies to look like grandfather clocks or radios, for instance. Fisher-Price in particular made many styles.

Anri, Cinderella & mice, plays Honey, Reuge movement, 1971, MIB......................**145.00**

Anri, hula girl, Tiny Bubbles, 6½", M...................................**110.00**

Anri, Peanuts characters in shadowbox, wall mount, 1971, 8½x8", NM **285.00**

Anri/Hummel, Chick Girl, Voices of Spring, limited edition, 1988, MIB.....................**145.00**

Anri/Thorens, girl w/pie, dog & 2 light posts, I Could Have Danced..., M **85.00**

Breyer 50th Anniversary Carousel Horse, Carousel Waltz, 13x12", M **135.00**

Disney/Jaymar, Three Little Pigs, fiddler and fifer are animated, plays Who's Afraid of the Big Bad Wolf, 1950s, 10x11½", EX, $70.00. (Photo courtesy Angel Palmer)

Disney, Jiminy Cricket, shelf sitter figural, 5½" (seated), M **85.00**

Disney, Sleeping Beauty's Castle, Once Upon a Dream, gold trim, 6", M......................**85.00**

Disney/Schmid, Little Mermaid, Under the Sea, MIB **85.00**

Disney/Schmid, Pinocchio & J Crickett, When You Wish, 1995, 8", M **98.00**

Disney/Schmid, Uncle Scrooge McDuck, You've Got a Friend, 7", MIB **110.00**

Disney/Willets, Winnie the Pooh, Let It Snow, 1990, 3", MIB.....................................**85.00**

Enesco, Magic Dragon, 2 knights & castle, Puff the Magic Dragon, MIB **90.00**

Enesco, Shave & Haircut (Santa & elves), Jolly Old St..., 1993, M **160.00**

Enesco, Small World of Music, Dachshund, Edelweiss, MIB **100.00**

Fisher-Price, Change-A-Tune Carousel, #170, 3-tune, 1981-83, M...............................**30.00**

Fisher-Price, Do-Re-Mi Pocket Radio, #759, 1969-73, EX.**20.00**

Fisher-Price, Music Box Record Player, #2205, 1988-92, EX.....................**6.00**

Fisher-Price, Music Box Teaching Clock, #998, 1968-83, EX **40.00**

Josef, Special Graduation, girl in blue, Impossible Dream, 1984, 6", M **75.00**

Land of Oz, Wizard of Oz, Somewhere Over the Rainbow, retired, M.....**110.00**

Marshall Fields, Uncle Mistletoe & Aunt Holly, ca 1960, 7½", pr...................................**235.00**

Mr Christmas Gold Label, Inspirational Symphonique, 10 songs, M **75.00**

Precious Moments, Guardian Angel, Silent Night, 1980, E5642, M **215.00**

Reuge, ballerina dancer, The Magic Flute, 22-note, inlaid box, M **250.00**

San Francisco Music Box Co, Kaleidoscope, 2 color wheels, M **100.00**

San Francisco Music Box Co, Phantom of Opera, Music of Night, #99, M **110.00**

San Francisco Music Box Co, Rhett & Scarlett, Tara's Theme, 8", MIB **75.00**

Sanyo Japan, Smokey the Bear, Perfect Harmony, 7¾x5", M **110.00**

Schmid, Snoopy & Woodstock at piano, #254, 1960s, MIB **115.00**

Schmid/Beatrix Potter, Little Old Woman Who Lived in Shoe, 1983, M **110.00**

Sigma, Kilban cat, 1970s, 7⅜x5¼x4½", EX.......... **220.00**

Susy Goose/Mattel, Barbie Music Box Piano, +bench & candelabra, 1964, EX **190.00**

T Kinkade, Sweetheart Cottage II, Always, limited edition, 4¼", MIB **95.00**

T Pacconi Classics, animated winter scene, wooden cabinet, 9x10x11", M **85.00**

Waterford, Joseph, Mary, Jesus & star on lid, Silent Night, 1996, MIB............................. **265.00**

Willets, Snoopy Corvette, Puppy Love, 1988, 10½" long, NM **150.00**

Niloak

Produced in Arkansas by Charles Dean Hyten from the early 1900s until the mid-1940s, Niloak (the backward spelling of kaolin, a type of clay) takes many forms — figural planters, vases in both matt and glossy glazes, and novelty items of various types. The company's most famous product and the most collectible is their Swirl or Mission Ware line. Clay in colors of brown, blue, cream, red, and buff are swirled within the mold, the finished product left unglazed on the outside to preserve the natural hues. Small vases are common; large pieces or unusual shapes and those with exceptional coloration are the most valuable. Refer to *The Collector's Encyclopedia of Niloak, A Reference and Value Guide,* by David Edwin Gifford (Collector Books) for more information.

Note: The terms '1st' and '2nd art mark' used in the listings refer to specific die-stamped trademarks. The earlier mark was used from 1910 to 1924, followed by the second, very similar mark used from then until the end of Mission Ware production. Letters with curving raised outlines were characteristic of both; the most obvious difference between the two was that on the first, the final upright line of the 'N' was thin with a solid club-like terminal.

Ashtray, Arkansas state shape w/symbol, 4¼x3½" **100.00**

Ashtray, swan figural, ivory, Niloak block letters, 5"..**75.00**

Basket, Ozark Blue, Niloak low relief, 3½"......................**35.00**

Bowl/flower frog, Ozark Blue, scalloped rim w/figural duck, 3½x10"...........................**100.00**

Cup & saucer, Ozark Blue, petal design, lg 2nd art mark, 3", 6" dia...................................**75.00**

Ewer, Ozark Blue, Crown design by Peterson, incised mark, 16½"..............................**125.00**

Figurine, bulldog, lying down, blue & tan, Niloak low releif, 5¾".....................................**75.00**

Figurine, dog, long floppy ears, brown, 2"........................**100.00**

Figurine, frog, blue-green, open mouth, 1st Hywood by Niloak, 3¼"...............................**100.00**

Figurine, Indian canoe, Ozark Dawn II, Niloak block letters, 3½x11"............................**55.00**

Figurine, rocking horse, Ozark Blue, Niloak low relief, 6¼".....**100.00**

Figurine, Southern belle, standing w/hat, Ozark Dawn II, 7¼"................................**125.00**

Figurine, Trojan horse, ivory, lg 2nd art mark, 8¾".......**175.00**

Flower frog, turtle, Canary Yellow, sm Niloak block letters, 4¾".......................**100.00**

Jug, Canary Yellow, miniature, Niloak #71, hand thrown, 4½"................................**45.00**

Mug, Mission/Swirl, 1st art mark, 4"....................................**350.00**

Pitcher, bull's-eye; Ozark Blue, unmarked, 9¼"............**100.00**

Pitcher, maroon, Lewis glaze, long spout, 2"........................**15.00**

Pitcher, Ozark Dawn II, 1st Hywood by Niloak, 6"....**50.00**

Pitcher, Peacock Blue II, petal design, Lewis glaze, unmarked, 8¾"...........**125.00**

Plant bowl, fish form, 4¾x5x9", from $35.00 to $45.00.

Planter, bird, turned head, Ozark Dawn II, Niloak low relief, 3x3"................................**25.00**

Planter, camel, sitting, unmarked, 3¾"................................**75.00**

Planter, deer in grass, Ozark Blue, Niloak low relief, 8".......**35.00**

Planter, elephant, black, 2nd art mark, 3¾"....................**100.00**

Planter, rabbit, ivory, Niloak block letters, 3½"....................**25.00**

Planter, swan, Ozark Blue, Alley design, 6½"....................**25.00**

Plate, dinner; Ozark Blue, Niloak block letters, 10" dia....**100.00**

Plate, salad; Ozark Dawn II, unmarked, 8" dia...........**75.00**

Salt & pepper shakers, geese, heads down, Ozark Dawn II, 2", pr..............................**45.00**

Salt & pepper shakers, penguins, Ozark Blue, 2¾", pr.......**45.00**

Tankard, Mission/Swirl, straight sides, 1st art mark, 13½" **1,200.00**

Teapot, French; Ozark Dawn II, lg 2nd art mark, 9"..........**100.00**

Tumble up, Mission/Swirl, first art mark, 9", from $600.00 to $800.00.

Vase, cabinet; green & tan matt, Hywood incised, 2¾"......**25.00**
Vase, fan; Ozark Dawn II, unmarked, 7"..................**75.00**
Vase, horn of plenty; Ozark Blue, Lewis glaze, Hywood, 7"..**75.00**
Vase, Mission/Swirl, hourglass shape, 1st art mark, 8"..**275.00**
Vase, Mission/Swirl, straight sides, 1st art mark, 9¼".........**325.00**
Vase, Missionware, solid white, incurvate rim, 6¼".......**250.00**

Nippon

In complying with American importation regulations, from 1891 to 1921 Japanese manufacturers marked their wares 'Nippon,' meaning Japan, to indicate country of origin. The term is today used to refer to the highly decorated porcelain vases, bowls, chocolate pots, etc., that bear this term within their trademark. Many variations were used. Refer to *The Collector's Encyclopedia of Nippon Porcelain* (there are seven volumes in the series) by Joan Van Patten (Collector Books) for more information. See Clubs and Newsletters for information concerning the International Nippon Collectors Club.

Ashtray, blown-out reclining dog, 5½" diameter, $465.00. (Photo courtesy Joan F. Van Patten)

Ashtray, golfer, 3 rests, 4½" dia...........................**550.00**
Bowl, bird & floral scene w/3-D figural bird on side, 7".....**325.00**
Bowl, camel w/rider in desert, 2 tab handles, 6½"..........**150.00**
Box, cigarette; sailing ship on lid, 4½"...............................**450.00**
Box, trinket; floral decor on lid, 4" L....................................**225.00**
Box, trinket; floral on white, 1¾" dia....................................**75.00**
Box, trinket; sailing boat scene on lid, heart shape, 3"......**165.00**
Box, white & yellow bands, butterflies on lid, 3" dia.........**165.00**
Cake dish, windmill scene, blue & gold border, green mark, 10¾"..............................**500.00**
Celery dish, butterflies on blue, 2-handled, 12" L..............**250.00**
Dresser tray, bird in tree, #106..**115.00**
Dresser tray, tan butterflies on white, 11¼" L................**110.00**

Ewer, owl on branch, handled, tapered, 11¼".............**1,600.00**

Hatpin holder, blue bird on white, tapered sides, 4¾".........**130.00**

Humidor, gold dragon on smoke, sq, w/lid, 6¾"..................**850.00**

Humidor, lady w/2 red aces, w/lid, 5½"..............................**1,800.00**

Humidor, pink flowers on green, squirrel finial, 7".........**1,000.00**

Humidor, puppies playing on cobalt, w/lid, 5½"..........**600.00**

Humidor, swans swimming, 3 gold handles, w/lid, 6½".......**700.00**

Humidor, 2 elk in woods, 3 ball feet, w/lid, 5½"..............**700.00**

Mug, The Cardinal, portrait, 5¼"..............................**950.00**

Mug, windmill scene, 7½"..**400.00**

Pitcher, white dragon on black, 5"................................**300.00**

Plate, 2 asparagus spears on white, cobalt blue & gold border, 7½"........................**300.00**

Plate, maple leaf mark, 8¾", from $350.00 to $425.00. (Photo courtesy Joan Van Patten)

Platter, game; pheasants strutting, ornate border, 17" L.....**900.00**

Ring holder, plate w/floral decor w/white 3-D hand, 3¾" dia...............**135.00**

Shaving mug, red roses in grass, gold handle, 3½".........**225.00**

Sugar shaker, sailboat scene, cobalt & gold borders, 4½".....**300.00**

Tea strainer, floral w/cobalt blue & gold borders, handled, 1½"............................**375.00**

Teapot, gold on cobalt, ornate handle, 6½".......................**400.00**

Tray, sailing ships w/cobalt & gold border, blue mark, 12½" L.................................**700.00**

Vase, floral; roses, blue & gold top/bottom, green mark, 5½"............................**500.00**

Vase, lilac tapestry, gold borders, 9"................................**1,750.00**

Vase, Moriage, flying geese scene, squat shape, 3".........**1,100.00**

Vase, red & white floral, slight center taper, 8½".........**500.00**

Vase, swans on water w/floral decor, 2-handled, 6"..**1,200.00**

Vase, white dragon on black, 2 ring handles, 6½".........**450.00**

Wall plaque, elk bedded down, sunset background, 10" dia..**650.00**

Wall plaque, fruit w/tree background, 11" dia.............**500.00**

Wall plaque, 2 ducks fly over field, 8½" dia **400.00**

Wall plaque, 2 hunters stand in field w/2 geese overhead, 10" dia.................................**700.00**

Noritake

Since the early 1900s, the Noritake China Company has been producing fine dinnerware, occasional pieces, and figural items decorated by hand in delicate florals, scenics, and wildlife studies. Azalea and Tree in the Meadow are two very collectible lines of dinnerware. We've listed several examples. Refer to *Early Noritake* by Aimee Neff Alden (Collector Books) for more information.

Azalea

Bowl, deep, #310 .... **68.00**
Bowl, vegetable; divided, #439, 9½"............................... **295.00**
Butter chip, #312, 3¼"........ **120.00**
Celery tray, closed handles, 10".......................... **330.00**
Compote, #170...................... **98.00**
Cup & saucer, #2 .... **20.00**
Gravy boat, #40..................... **48.00**
Pitcher, milk jug; #100, 1-qt .. **225.00**
Plate, breakfast/luncheon; #98 .. **28.00**
Plate, salad; 7⅝" sq **85.00**
Platter, #17, 14" **60.00**

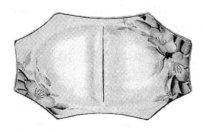

Relish, two-compartment, #171, $58.00.

Salt & pepper shakers, bell form, #11, pr **30.00**
Salt & pepper shakers, individual, #126, pr **32.00**
Spoon holder, #189, 8"........ **115.00**
Teapot, #15.......................... **110.00**

Vase, fan form, footed, #187 . **185.00**
Whipped cream/mayonnaise set, #3, 3-toed, 3-pc............... **38.50**

Tree in the Meadow

Bowl, cream soup; 2-handled .. **35.00**
Bowl, soup **38.00**

Candy dish, #318, $350.00. (Photo courtesy Joan Van Patten)

Celery dish **35.00**
Cruets, vinegar & oil; cojoined, #319 .... **325.00**
Egg cup................................. **30.00**
Lemon dish............................ **15.00**
Plate, salad; 8" **12.00**
Platter, 11¾x9" **58.00**
Relish, divided....................... **35.00**
Teapot.................................. **95.00**

Miscellaneous

Chocolate pot, gold decoration on white, blue mark, 9¾", $225.00.

Bowl, winter scene w/cabin, 3-handled, red M mark, 6½"...**65.00**

Bowl, 2 parakeets in floral wreath, green M mark, 7"..........**50.00**

Chocolate pot, gold overlay on white, 9".......................**200.00**

Compote, autumn scene w/creek, M mark, 2-handled, 9"...**75.00**

Compote, floral on cream, red M mark, 2-handled, 9¾"....**90.00**

Condiment set, 2 birds on red, green M mark, 4 pcs, 6¾" tray..............................**130.00**

Dresser tray, jester juggling balls, red M mark, 6¾" dia ...**275.00**

Lemon dish, lemon in center, orange border, red M mark, 5¾" dia...........................**35.00**

Plaque, dog beside river, green M mark, 7½" dia **175.00**

Plaque, lg steamship, M mark, 10" dia.................................**200.00**

Potpourri jar, floral on blue, green M mark, 6½".................**115.00**

Tea tile, building & tree along creek, green M mark, 5" sq.........**50.00**

Toast rack, bird finial, green M mark, 5½" L **110.00**

Tray, white w/fruit border, 2-handled, red M mark, 11"..**100.00**

Tray, 2 horse's heads behind trees, green M mark, 12".........**90.00**

Vase, ballerina in white on orange, red mark w/#29612, 8½"..**325.00**

Wall pocket, 2 butterflies on tan, red M mark, 9".............**120.00**

Novelty Telephones

Novelty telephones representing well-known advertising or cartoon characters are proving to be the focus of a lot of collector activity — the more recognizable the character, the better. Telephones modeled after product containers are collectible as well. For more information refer to *Schroeder's Collectible Toys, Antique to Modern* (Collector Books).

AC Spark Plug, EX...............**35.00**

Alvin (Chipmunk), 1984, MIB..**50.00**

Bart Simpson, Columbia Tel-Com, 1990s, MIB, $35.00.

Batmobile (Batman Forever), MIB, from $25 to **35.00**

Bugs Bunny, Warner Exclusive, MIB, from $60 to **70.00**

Cabbage Patch Girl, 1980s, EX, from $65 to **75.00**

Crest Sparkle, MIB, from $50 to **75.00**

Garfield, MIB **50.00**

Ghostbusters, MIB................**30.00**

Little Green Sprout, EX **75.00**

Mario Bros, 1980s, MIB **50.00**

Mickey Mouse, Western Electric, 1976, MIB....................**200.00**

Oscar Meyer Wiener, EX......**65.00**

Raggedy Ann & Andy, Pay Phone, 1983, MIB......................**75.00**

Raggedy Ann & Andy, Pay Phone, 1983, 7½", EX **40.00**

Snoopy as Joe Camel, 1980s, MIB..............**55.00**

Spider-Man, REC Sound, 1994, MIB..............**30.00**

Strawberry Shortcake, MIB..**75.00**

Superman, early rotary dial, M..........................**500.00**

Ziggy, 1989, MIB..................**75.00**

Occupied Japan

Items with the 'Occupied Japan' mark were made during the period from the end of World War II until April 1952. Porcelains, novelties, paper items, lamps, silver plate, lacquer ware, and dolls are some of the areas of exported goods that may bear this stamp. Because the Japanese were naturally resentful of the occupation, it is felt that only a small percentage of their wares were thus marked. Although you may find identical items marked simply 'Japan,' only those with the 'Occupied Japan' stamp command values such as we have suggested below. For more information we recommend *Occupied Japan Collectibles* written by Gene Florence for Collector Books. Items in our listings are ceramic unless another material is noted, and figurines are of average, small size. See Clubs and Newsletters for information concerning The Occupied Japan Club.

Ashtray, house on lake scene, 6-sided, blue rim w/3 red rests **10.00**

Ashtray, Wedgwood type, blue & white, 2⅝" **10.00**

Basket, pink w/angel on handle, red mark, 5" **60.00**

Bell, Dutch girl figural, orange lustre skirt, sm **20.00**

Bookend, Dutch boy & girl seated, deep colors, pr..............**40.00**

Bookends, penguins, 4", pr...**25.00**

Candle holder, Colonial figure seated between 2 flower cups, 4", pr..............................**55.00**

Child's tea set, 2 place settings, 9 pcs..................................**45.00**

Child's tea set, 6 place settings, 26 pcs..................................**125.00**

Crumb butler, metal, souvenir of Washington DC..............**10.00**

Cup & saucer, floral on white w/gold rim, red mark.....**20.00**

Cup & saucer, flower on pink, Trimont China **22.00**

Doll, celluloid, baby in snow-suit..............................**35.00**

Doll, celluloid, pink crocheted dress, 6"..........................**40.00**

Figurine, ballerina, net dress, 5¾" **40.00**

Figurine, ballerina on tiptoe, 5¾"..............................**40.00**

Figurine, boy & girl on fence, cat at feet, 4", pr **35.00**

Figurine, boy w/saxophone, blue pants, red hair, 4⅝" **10.00**

Figurine, boy w/truck, 2½".....**5.00**

Figurine, bride & groom on base, 6⅛"..................................**50.00**

Figurine, Cinderella & Prince Charming on base, Mariyama, 8¼"................................**175.00**

Figurine, Colonial lady mandolin player, 10¼" **50.00**

Figurine, cowboy, gun on hip, yellow hat, 5⅛" **15.00**

Figurine, dog pushing 2 puppies in basket-like buggy, 3" **15.00**

Figurine, East Indian man winding turban, 6" **20.00**

Figurine, girl holding doll, Hummel-like, 4¼" **18.00**

Figurine, lady bug w/bat, 4" ..**17.00**

Figurine, lady dancer, arms behind head, red mark, 5" **17.50**

Figurine, Oriental lady w/fan, 5" **20.00**

Figurine, peacock w/plume tail cascading down, 5" **20.00**

Figurine, rooster & hen on base, 5", pr **35.00**

Lamp, 10", $40.00. (Photo courtesy Gene Florence)

Lamp base, Colonial couple, bisque, 11" **50.00**

Pencil holder, dog figural **10.00**

Planter, baby buggy, black, 5¼" **10.00**

Planter, couple w/rabbits, bisque, Paulux, 5¼x7¼" **150.00**

Planter, dog, comic look, 3⅝" ..**8.00**

Planter, dog sticks out tongue beside top hat, 3⅝" **8.00**

Planter, lady standing beside lg open flower, bisque, Paulux, 6" **75.00**

Plaque, mallard in flight, wings wide, 6½" **25.00**

Plate, flower center, lattice rim, Rosetti Chicago USA, 6" ..**25.00**

Plate, fruit center on white w/gold trim, Ohata China, 6" **20.00**

Shaker, Dutch girl, red mark, 3" **8.00**

Shelf, corner; lacquerware, folding type, 9¼" **45.00**

Shoe, cowboy boot, 4⅜" **8.00**

Shoe, rabbit stands beside, 2⅜" ..**8.00**

Tablecloth, linen, paper label, 32" sq, +4 10½" linen napkins **90.00**

Teapot, windmill, 5", $40.00. (Photo courtesy Gene Florence)

Toby pitcher, man holding 2 mugs, red mark, 4⅞" **40.00**

Vase, cherub seated beside, pastel w/gold, red mark, 3⅜" ...**15.00**

Vase, cornucopia; silver-tone metal, 8", pr **35.00**

Vase, snake charmer couple stands before vase, 5½" **30.00**

Old MacDonald's Farm

Made by the Regal China Co., items from this line of novelty ware were designed around characters and animals from Old MacDonald's Farm. They're not easily found, and though prices had softened for awhile, they're back on the rise again. The milk pitcher is especially hard to find. Items are marked Pat Pending with a 300 or 400 series number.

Butter dish, cow's head, from $175 to..................................**200.00**
Canister, flour, cereal or coffee, med, ea, from $225 to..**275.00**
Canister, pretzels or popcorn, lg, ea, from $325 to...........**375.00**
Canister, salt, sugar or tea, med, ea, from $225 to...........**275.00**
Canister, soap or cookies, lg, ea, from $350 to.................**425.00**
Cookie jar, barn, from $295 to..**325.00**
Grease jar, pig, from $200 to..**250.00**
Pitcher, milk; from $425 to..**450.00**
Salt & pepper shakers, boy & girl, pr....................................**80.00**
Salt & pepper shakers, churns, gold trim, pr **95.00**

Salt and pepper shakers, feed sacks with sheep, from $150.00 to $195.00.

Spice jar, assorted lids, sm, ea, from $125 to.................**150.00**

Sugar bowl, hen **135.00**

Paper Dolls

Though the history of paper dolls can be traced even farther back, by the late 1700s they were being mass produced. A century later, paper dolls were being used as an advertising medium by retail companies wishing to promote sales. But today the type most often encountered are in book form — the dolls on the cardboard covers, their wardrobe on the inside pages. These have been published since the 1920s. Celebrity and character-related dolls are the most popular with collectors, and condition is very important. If they have been cut out, even if they are still in fine condition and have all their original accessories, they're worth only about half as much as an uncut doll. In our listings, if no condition is given, values are for mint, uncut paper dolls. For more information, we recommend *Price Guide to Lowe and Whitman Paper Dolls* by Mary Young (see the Directory under Ohio). For an expanded listings of values, see *Schroeder's Collectible Toys, Antique to Modern* (Collector Books). See Clubs and Newsletters for information concerning the *Paper Doll News.*

Airline Stewardess, Lowe #2742, 1959, uncut, M...............**35.00**
Annette in Hawaii, Whitman #1969, 1961 ....**60.00**

Army & Navy Wedding Party, Saalfield #2446, 1943 ..**125.00**

Baby Sparkle Plenty, Saalfield #2500, 1948, uncut, M...**50.00**

Betsy McCall, Whitman #1969, 1971 ....**25.00**

Blondie, Saalfield #4434, 1968 ....**75.00**

Bride Doll, Lowe #1043 ....**55.00**

Cinderella, Saalfield #2590, 1950..............................**75.00**

Connie Francis, Whitman #1956, 1963 ....**85.00**

Darling Dolls, Saalfield #6169, 1964 ....**30.00**

Debbie Reynolds, Whitman #1955, 1955, uncut, M.............**100.00**

Dinah Shore, Whitman #1963, 1958 ....**75.00**

Elizabeth, Lowe #2750, 1963 ....**30.00**

Flying Nun, Saalfield #6069, 1969, uncut, MIB, from $50 to....................................**60.00**

Giselle MacKenzie, Saalfield #4421, 1957 ....**90.00**

Hayley Mills in Summer Magic, Whitman #1966, 1963 ...**60.00**

Hedy Lamarr, Saalfield #2600, 1951 ....**125.00**

Hello Patti, Lowe #1877, 1964, uncut, M **12.00**

I Love Lucy Packaway Kit, Whitman #5624, 1953, EX, $125.00. (Photo courtesy Bill Bruegman)

Jane Russell, Saalfield #4328, 1955 ....**95.00**

Janet Lennon, Whitman #1964, 1958 ....**60.00**

Julia, Saalfield #4435, 1968 .**60.00**

June Allyson, Whitman #1956, 1955 ....**90.00**

Kewpies, Saalfield #1332, 1963 ....**60.00**

Lace & Dress Puppy or Kitty, Lowe #8902 or #8903, ea........**18.00**

Let's Play House, Lowe #2708, 1957, uncut, M **20.00**

Mary Poppins, Whitman #1982, 1964, uncut, M **40.00**

Mopsy & Popsy, Lowe #2713, 1971 ....**10.00**

Oklahoma!, Whitman #1954, 1956 ....**125.00**

Paper Doll's Beauty Contest, Lowe #1026, 1941 ....**95.00**

Princess Diana, Whitman #1530, 1985, uncut, M **50.00**

Quintuplets, Saalfield #1352, 1964 ....**60.00**

Rita Hayworth, Dancing Star, Merrill #3478, 1942..............................**300.00**

Rosemary Clooney, Lowe #2569, 1956 ....**125.00**

Seven & Seventeen, Merrill #3441, 1945 ....**125.00**

Story Princess, Saalfield #2761, 1957 ....**70.00**

Teen Queens, Lowe #2710, 1957, uncut, M **20.00**

Tricia (Nixon), Saalfield #4248, 1970 ....**45.00**

Victory Volunteers, Merrill #3424, 1942 ....**125.00**

Walt Disney's Mary Poppins, Whitman #1982, 1964, uncut, M................................**40.00**

Wishnik Cut-Outs, Whitman #1954, uncut, M, from $30.00 to $40.00.

Wishnik Cut-Outs, Whitman #1965, 1965 ....**40.00**

Peanuts Collectibles

First introduced in 1950, the Peanuts comic strip soon became the world's most widely read cartoon, ultimately appearing in about 2,200 daily newspapers. From that funny cartoon about kids (that seemed to relate to readers of any age) sprung an entertainment arsenal featuring movies, books, Broadway shows, toys, theme parks, etc. At any flea market you'll always spot several Peanuts collectibles. United Media, the company that syndicates and licenses the Peanuts comic strip, estimates there are approximately 20,000 new products produced each year. If you want to collect, you should know that authenticity is important. The United Features Syndicate logo and copyright dates

must appear somewhere on the item. In most cases the copyright date simply indicates the date that the character and his pose as depicted on the item first appeared in the comic strip.

For more information we recommend *Peanuts Collectibles* by Andrea Podley with Derrick Bang (Collector Books).

Pendulum clock, Japan, #QH2457-1, 13", $135.00. (Photo courtesy Andrea Podley)

Bank, Snoopy, seated, Italian, 1965, 8½x7", EX.............**65.00**
Bank, Snoopy lying on 1982 penny, 6", M **75.00**
Bathtub, characters on sides, ceramic, Determined, 1960s, NM+...............................**95.00**
Bell, Snoopy on cracked Liberty bell, Schmid, 1976, 5", MIB **35.00**
Bowl, clear w/etched characters, Waterford, MIB..............**30.00**
Christmas train, characters on train cars, Danbury Mint, MIB...............................**85.00**
Cookie jar, clear glass w/Snoopy & cookies decal, Anchor Hocking, NMIB..............**70.00**
Doll, pocket; Charlie Brown, rubber, Determined, 7", NMIP ..**115.00**

Doll, Snoopy Astronaut, 1969, complete, NMIB..........**500.00**

Figurine, Charlie Brown, plastic, Hungerford, 1958, 9", EX................**175.00**

Figurine, Pig Pen, Peanuts Memory Lane by Playing Mantis, MIP..................**80.00**

Figurine, Snoopy as Flying Ace at cafe table, Determined, 1971, 5", EX..............**70.00**

Game, Monopoly, Peanuts version, MIB................**35.00**

Music box, Linus w/blanket, wooden, Anri, 1972, 5½", EX................**175.00**

Nightlight, Linus sucking thumb, holding blanket, ceramic, 7", EX..................**30.00**

Nodder, Schroeder, Lego, 1950s, EX................**220.00**

Ornament, Peppermint Patty w/guitar, Determined, 1976, EX................**45.00**

Ornament, Snoopy as magician, Determined, 1977, 3", NM................**65.00**

Ornament, Snoopy lying on hamburger, Made in Japan, 1958, 1½", EX................**165.00**

Plate, O Christmas Tree, characters around tree, Schmid, MIB................**35.00**

Plate, Snoopy kissing Lucy, Mother's Day, 1975, 7¼", M (EX box)................**40.00**

Plate, Woodstock watches as Snoopy blows bubbles, Valentines 1980, MIB....**35.00**

Puppet, Snoopy, Pelham, 1965, NM (EX box)................**165.00**

Push puppet, Snoopy as magician, Ideal, 1970s, 4", EX.......**30.00**

Puzzle, A Charlie Brown Christmas, Springbok, 500 pcs, MIB................**35.00**

Tea set, characters on pcs, Chein, complete, EXIB............**215.00**

Thingmaker, Peanuts characters, Mattel, 1969, complete, EX (VG box)................**95.00**

Pennsbury

From the 1950s through the 1970s, dinnerware and novelty ware produced by the Pennsbury company was sold through tourist gift shops along the Pennsylvania turnpike. Much of their ware was decorated in an Amish theme. A group of barbershop singers was another popular design, and they made a line of bird figures that were very similar to Stangl's, though today much harder to find.

Ashtray, Pennsbury Commemorative, 1961, 5"............**25.00**

Ashtray, Pennsbury Inn, 8"..**45.00**

Bank, Hershey Kiss, brown, 4"................**20.00**

Bank, jug shape, pig w/Stuff Me underneath, 7"............**200.00**

Basket, desk; Lafayette, 4"...**60.00**

Bowl, Dutch Talk, 9"............**90.00**

Bowl, pretzel; Gay Ninety, 12x8"................**95.00**

Butter dish, Red Rooster, w/lid, 5x4"................**40.00**

Candle holders, rooster figurals, 4", pr................**85.00**

Coaster, Doylestown Trust Co, 1896–1958, 5"................**25.00**

Cookie jar, Red Barn, w/lid..**225.00**

Cruets, Amish man's and lady's head stoppers, 7", $150.00 for the pair.

Cruets, oil & vinegar; Black Rooster, pr....................**150.00**
Cup & saucer, Hex................**30.00**
Figurine, Barn Swallow, #123, 6¼"..............................**375.00**
Figurine, Blue Jay, #108, 10½"..**400.00**
Figurines, hen & rooster, brown & yellow, pr......................**450.00**
Mug, Bucks County Fire Department, William Penn, 5"....................................**40.00**
Mug, coffee; Eagle, 3¼"........**20.00**
Pitcher, Amish woman, miniature, 2½"....................................**30.00**
Pitcher, Tulip, 4"..................**40.00**
Plaque, CP Huntington, 1863, 7½"x5½"..........................**125.00**
Plaque, eagle, #P214, 22"...**175.00**
Plaque, Iron Horse Ramble, Reading Railroad, 1960, 7¼"x5¼"..........................**60.00**
Plaque, Kissing Over Cow, 6"..**50.00**
Plaque, United States Steel, 12+13 Club, 1954, 8" dia..........**40.00**
Plaque, Walking to Homestead, 6"....................................**40.00**
Plaque, Washington Crossing the Delaware, 5" dia............**25.00**

Plate, Blue Dowry, 10".........**35.00**
Plate, bread; Give Us This Day Our Daily Bread, 8" dia..........**40.00**
Plate, chip & dip; Red Rooster, 11"................................**85.00**
Plate, Neshaminy Woods, 11½"......................**120.00**
Plate, Red Rooster, 10".........**35.00**
Tumbler, lady w/tall sunflower, 3¾"................................**55.00**
Wall pocket, clown w/yo-yo, trimmed in pink, 6½"....**75.00**

Wall pocket, lady looking over shoulder, 6½", $150.00.

Wall pocket, ship w/brown border, signed LE, 6½" sq..........**50.00**

Pez Dispensers

Originally a breath mint targeted for smokers, by the '50s Pez had been diverted toward the kid's candy market, and to make sure the kids found them appealing, the company designed dispensers they'd be sure to like — many of them characters the kids could easily recognize. On today's collectible market, some of those dispensers bring astonishing prices!

Though early on collectors preferred the dispensers with no feet, today they concentrate primarily on the character heads. Feet were added in 1987, so if you want your collection to be complete, you'll need to buy both styles. For further information and more listings, see *Schroeder's Collectible Toys, Antique to Modern* (Collector Books). Our values are for mint dispensers. Very few are worth collecting if they are damaged or have missing parts. See Clubs and Newsletters for information concerning *Pez Collector News*.

Angel, no feet 50.00
Baloo, w/feet...........................20.00
Barney Bear, w/feet..............30.00
Batman, no feet.....................10.00
Betsy Ross, no feet..............150.00
Boy, w/feet, brown hair..........3.00
Bozo, no feet, diecut............175.00
Bubble Man, w/feet.................5.00
Captain America, no feet....100.00
Casper, no feet 175.00
Charlie Brown, w/feet & tongue..20.00
Chick in Egg, no feet 15.00
Clown, w/whistle head............6.00
Cool Cat, w/feet.....................75.00
Daffy Duck, no feet 15.00
Daniel Boone, no feet..........175.00
Doctor, no feet.....................200.00
Donald Duck, no feet, diecut..150.00
Donkey, w/feet, whistle head..6.00
Eerie Spectres, Air Spirit, Diabolic or Zombie (no feet), ea..200.00
Fireman, no feet....................95.00
Frankenstein, no feet 300.00
Garfield, w/feet, from $1 to 3.00
Goofy, no feet, ea...................10.00
Henry Hawk, no feet 65.00

Indian Brave, no feet, yellow head-dress 90.00
Jerry Mouse, w/feet, painted face................................6.00
Lamb, no feet 15.00
Lion w/Crown, no feet.........100.00
Mary Poppins, no feet.........700.00
Mexican, no feet..................250.00
Miss Piggy, w/feet & eyelashes..15.00
Nurse, no feet, brown hair..175.00
Panda, w/feet, whistle head ...6.00
Penguin (Batman), no feet, soft head...............................175.00
Pilgrim, no feet 150.00
Pluto, no feet 10.00
Practical Pig (B), no feet.......30.00
Psychedelic Flower, no feet..300.00
Raven, no feet, yellow beak..70.00

Roadrunner, no feet, $20.00; Uncle Sam, no feet, $175.00.

Rudolph, no feet....................50.00
Santa Claus (A), no feet, steel pin.............................125.00
Scrooge McDuck (A), no feet..35.00
Smurf, w/feet..........................5.00
Space Trooper Robot, no feet, full body 325.00
Spike, w/feet...........................6.00
Sylvester (A), w/feet, cream or white whiskers, ea...........5.00
Thumper, w/feet, no copyright..45.00
Tinkerbell, no feet...............275.00

Tweety Bird, no feet **10.00**
Wile E Coyote, w/feet............**60.00**
Wolfman, no feet.................**300.00**
Zorro **75.00**

Pfaltzgraff Pottery

Since early in the seventeenth century, pottery has been produced in York County, Pennsylvania. The Pfaltzgraff Company that operates there today is the outgrowth of several of these small potteries. A changeover made in 1940 redirected their efforts toward making the dinnerware lines for which they are now best known. Their earliest line, a glossy brown with a white frothy drip glaze around the rim, was called Gourmet Royale. Today collectors find an abundance of good examples and are working toward reassembling sets of their own. Village, another very successful line, is tan with a stencilled Pennsylvania Dutch-type floral design in brown. It was all but discontinued a few years ago (they do make a few pieces for collectors now), and already Village fans are turning to secondary market sources to replace and replenish their services. The line is very extensive and offers an interesting array of items.

Giftware consisting of ashtrays, mugs, bottle stoppers, a cookie jar, etc., all with comic character faces was made in the 1940s. This line was called Muggsy, and it is also very col-

lectible, with the more common mugs starting at about $35.00 each. For more information refer to *Pfaltzgraff, America's Potter*, by David A. Walsh and Polly Stetler, published in conjunction with the Historical Society of York County, York, Pennsylvania.

Christmas Heritage, bowl, soup/cereal; #009, 5½", from $2 to **3.50**
Christmas Heritage, pedestal mug, #290, 10-oz **3.00**
Gourmet Royale, ashtray, #321, 7¾", from $9 to...............**12.00**
Gourmet Royale, baker, #321, oval, 7½", from $8 to......**10.00**
Gourmet Royale, bean pot, #11-1, 1-qt, from $10 to **12.00**
Gourmet Royale, bean pot, #11-3, 3-qt..................................**25.00**
Gourmet Royale, bean pot, #30, w/lid, lg, from $30 to......**40.00**
Gourmet Royale, bowl, #241, oval, 7x10", from $10 to.........**12.00**
Gourmet Royale, bowl, mixing; 6", from $8 to **10.00**

Gourmet Royale, chip 'n dip two-piece set, with stand, #306, from $22.00 to $25.00.

Gourmet Royale, bowl, soup; 2¼x7¼", from $4 to..........**6.00**

Gourmet Royale, bowl, vegetable; #341, divided.................**10.00**

Gourmet Royale, canister set, 4-pc.................................**60.00**

Gourmet Royale, casserole, stick handle, 1-qt, from $9 to..**12.00**

Gourmet Royale, casserole, stick handle, 4-qt, from $25 to.......................................**35.00**

Gourmet Royale, cheese shaker, bulbous, 5¾", from $12 to.....**15.00**

Gourmet Royale, creamer, #382, from $4 to.........................**5.00**

Gourmet Royale, cup & saucer, from $4 to.........................**6.00**

Gourmet Royale, egg/relish tray, 15" L, from $18 to..........**22.00**

Gourmet Royale, gravy boat, w/stick handle, 2-spout, from $8 to................................**12.00**

Gourmet Royale, jug, #386, ice lip, from $25 to.....................**30.00**

Gourmet Royale, ladle, 3½" dia bowl w/11" handle, from $12 to....................................**15.00**

Gourmet Royale, mug, #391, 12-oz, from $5 to.........................**7.00**

Gourmet Royale, pie plate, #7016, 9½", from $10 to.............**12.00**

Gourmet Royale, plate, grill; #87, 3-section, 11", from $9...**12.00**

Gourmet Royale, plate, steak; 12", from $9.......................**12.00**

Gourmet Royale, platter, #337, 16", from $18 to.............**20.00**

Gourmet Royale, relish dish, #265, 5x10"................................**9.00**

Gourmet Royale, roaster, #326, oval, 16", from $20 to.....**25.00**

Gourmet Royale, salt & pepper shakers, bell shape, pr....**9.00**

Gourmet Royale, shirred egg dish, #360, 6", from $7 to.......**10.00**

Gourmet Royale, sugar bowl, from $4 to.................................**6.00**

Gourmet Royale, tray, 3-part, 15½" L.............................**25.00**

Heritage, cup & saucer, #002-002, 9-oz....................................**3.00**

Muggsy, ashtray.................**125.00**

Muggsy, cigarette server....**125.00**

Muggsy, clothes sprinkler bottle, Myrtle, white..............**250.00**

Muggsy, mug, Black action figure...............................**125.00**

Muggsy, shot mug, character face, ea, from $40 to..............**50.00**

Planter, donkey, brown drip, common, 10", from $15 to....**20.00**

Village, baker, #24, oval, 10¼", from $7 to.........................**9.00**

Village, bean pot, 2½-qt, from $22 to...................................**28.00**

Village, bowl, batter; w/spout & handle, 8", from $35 to.................**42.00**

Village, bowl, rim soup; #012, 8½".................................**6.00**

Village, bowl, soup/cereal; #009, 6".................................**4.50**

Village, bread tray, 12", from $15 to...................................**18.00**

Village, canisters, #520, 4-pc set, from $50 to.....................**60.00**

Village, coffee mug, #89F, 10-oz, from $5 to.......................**7.00**

Village, creamer & sugar bowl, #020, from $9 to.............**12.00**

Village, flowerpot, 4½", from $12 to...................................**15.00**

Village, pedestal mug, #90F, 10-oz......................................**3.50**

Village, plate, dinner; #004, 10¼", from $3 to.........................**4.50**

Village, quiche, 9", $16.00; measuring cups, from $6.00 to $8.00 each.

Village, spoon rest, #515, 9" L, from $6 to **7.50**

Pie Birds

What is a pie bird? It is a functional and decorative kitchen tool most commonly found in the shape of a bird, designed to vent steam through the top crust of a pie to prevent the juices from spilling over into the oven. Other popular designs were elephants and black-faced bakers. The original vents that were used in England and Wales in the 1800s were simply shaped like funnels.

From the 1980s to the present, many novelty pie vents have been added to the market for the baker and the collector. Some of these could be obtained from Far East Imports; others have been made in England and the US (by commercial and/or local enterprises). Examples can be found in the shapes of animals (dogs, frogs, ele-

phants, cats, goats, and dragons), people (policemen, chefs with and without pies, pilgrims, and carolers), or whimsical figurals (clowns, leprechauns, and teddy bears). A line of holiday-related pie vents was made in the 1990s.

Consequently a collector must be on guard and aware that these new pie vents are being sold by dealers (knowingly in many instances) as old or rare, often at double or triple the original cost (which is usually under $10.00). Though most of the new ones can't really be called reproductions since they never existed before, there's a black bird that is a remake, and you'll see them everywhere. Here's how you can spot them: they'll have yellow beaks and protruding white-dotted eyes. If they're on a white base and have an orange beak, they are the older ones. Another basic tip that should help you distinguish old from new: older pie vents are air-brushed versus being hand painted. Please note that incense burners, one-hole pepper shakers, dated brass toy bird whistles, and ring holders (for instance, the elephant with a clover on his tummy) should not be mistaken for pie vents. See Clubs and Newsletters for information concerning *Pie Birds Unlimited Newsletter*.

Advertisement, TG Green, on pie funnel, England, 1993 to present **10.00**
Benny the Baker, all white, Far East Imports, 4¾"........**150.00**

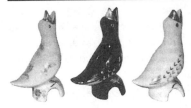

Songbirds, gold trim, Chick Pottery, Zanesville, Ohio, 1936 – 1961, from $125.00 to $150.00 each.
(Photo courtesy Linda Fields)

Bird, cobalt, stoneware, New Hampshire pottery, new, 4¼".................................**20.00**

Black chef, yellow, red & white attire, brown spoon, Taiwan, 4½"..................................**10.00**

Blackbird, 2-pc, marked Royal Worchester, England, 1960 to mid-1980s.......................**75.00**

Blackbird on log, marked Artone Pottery England.............**50.00**

Bluebird, black speckles, heavy pottery, US, 1950s.........**60.00**

Boy w/'Pie Boy' painted down leg, USA **300.00**

Canary, yellow w/pink lips...**40.00**

Crow dressed as chef, holds pie, marked SB, England, new **30.00**

Elephant on drum, marked CCC (Cardinal China), solid pink base...............................**120.00**

Funnel, Pyrex glass **30.00**

Funnel, white, unmarked, England **15.00**

Green Willow, decaled, new .**15.00**

Humpty Dumpty...................**50.00**

Morton 'patches' pie bird, USA.....................................**30.00**

Pelican on stump, yellow bill & feet, England.................**52.50**

Rooster, multicolor, Cleminson..**45.00**

Royal Commemorative pie funnel, England..........................**35.00**

Snowman w/pie, dressed in hat, scarf & mittens, ceramic..**45.00**

Witch, holding pie, w/painted bird flying out, marked SB ...**40.00**

Pin-Back Buttons

Because most of the pin-backs prior to the 1920s were made of celluloid, collectors refer to them as 'cellos.' Many were issued in sets on related topics. Some advertising buttons had paper inserts on the back that identified the company or the product they were advertising. After the 1920s lithographed metal buttons were produced; they're now called 'lithos.'

See also The Beatles; Elvis Presley; Political.

Audubon Society, Red-Headed Woodpecker, celluloid, ⅞" **23.50**

Aunt Jemima Breakfast Club, 1" **25.00**

Buick Fireball 8, 1941 Buick, 1¾"................................**60.00**

Ceresota, Best Flour on Earth, 1¼"..................................**75.00**

Collect Crayola Crayons & Markers, crayon pack shape, 1980s, 2x3".....................**30.00**

Dizzy Dean, metal, ⅞"........**100.00**

Dupont Smokeless Powder, bird in center, celluloid, 1¼" **90.00**

Free Tom's Toasted Peanuts, 3"..**15.00**

Hires R-J Root Beer, A Treat in Every Bottle, 2".............**20.00**

Hopalong Cassidy, photo in red star on blue, 2¼"............**55.00**

In Memoriam of Queen Victoria, center photo, Whitehead & Hoag, 1¾".......................**17.50**

Infant of Prague, Badge-a-Minit, 2¼"................................**21.50**

John Wayne, black & white photo on blue, 1940s-1950s, 1¼".....**14.00**

Miss Bardahl, Seattle Washington, boat & driver, 1960s-70s, oval, 3x2"..................................**17.50**

Popeye, Member Electric Theatre Club, Parisian Novelty, 1935, ⅞"....................................**22.50**

Raggedy Ann & Andy, 1971, 1¼"............................**15.00**

Santa, Ackers Candles, Christmas, celluloid, 1¼"................**140.00**

Santa, Merry Christmas/Happy New Year, celluloid........**55.00**

Shirley Temple, The World's Darling, celluloid, Ideal Novelty, 1¼"...................**75.00**

Soupy Sales Society, Charter Member, 3½"..................**12.50**

Spider-Man Official Member Super Hero Club, Button World, 1966, 3", MIP, $50.00. (Photo courtesy Bill Bruegman)

Superman of America, celluloid, 1948, 1¼".......................**30.00**

Use Peters Semi Smokeless Cartridges, Bastion Brothers, 1"....................................**30.00**

USS Stethem DDG 63, Seabee fighting bee logo, 2¼"....**15.00**

Yellow Kid, #2, High Admiral Cigarettes, 1894.............**50.00**

You're Nothing But a Hound Dog, w/dog, Elvis Presley Enterprises, 1"...............**20.00**

Zorro/7-Up, Walt Disney Productions, 1957, 1¼"..**20.00**

Pep Pins

In the late '40s and into the '50s, some cereal companies packed a pin-back button in each box of their product. Quaker Puffed Oats offered a series of movie star pin-backs, but Kellogg's Pep Pins are probably the best known of all. There were eighty-six different Pep pins, so theoretically if you wanted the whole series, as Kellogg hoped you would, you'd have to buy at the very minimum that many boxes of their cereal. Pep pins came in five sets, the first in 1945, three more in 1946, and the last in 1947. They were printed with full-color lithographs of comic characters licensed by King Features and Famous Artists — Maggie and Jiggs, the Winkles, and Dagwood and Blondie, for instance. Superman, the only D.C. Comics character, was included in each set. Most Pep pins range in value from $10.00 to $15.00 in NM/M condition; for a complete listing we recommend *Garage Sale and Flea Market Annual* (Collector Books).

Corky, NM............................**16.00**

Fat Stuff, NM.......................**15.00**

Flash Gordon, NM **30.00**

Jiggs, NM **25.00**
Kayo, NM **20.00**
Maggie, NM..........................**25.00**

Moon Mullins, NM, $10.00. (Photo courtesy Doug Dezso)

Pat Patton, NM.....................**10.00**
Rip Van Winkle, NM **20.00**
Toots, NM.............................**15.00**
Uncle Walt, NM **12.50**
Winkles Twins, NM **90.00**

Pinup Art

Collectors of pinup art look for blotters, calendars, prints, playing cards, etc., with illustrations of sexy girls by artists who are famous for their work in this venue: Vargas, Petty, DeVorss, Elvgren, Moran, Mozert, Ballantyne, Armstrong, and Davis among them. Though not all items will be signed, most of these artists have a distinctive style that is easy to recognize.

Bracelet, inlayed concho shell & onyx, marked Vargas, ¾x7", EX **40.00**

Calendar, 1948, Mac Therson, 12½x9½", $35.00.

Calendar, Elvgren, Doggone Good, October-December, 1961, 33x16", EX...................**130.00**

Calendar, Esquire 1952, complete, EX...................................**35.00**

Calendar, Marilyn Monroe, December (only), 1954, EX...................**45.00**

Calendar, Moore, Esquire, 1950, complete, EX **45.00**

Calendar, Petty, Esquire, 1955, 11x8¼", MIP..................**60.00**

Calendar, Vargas, Esquire, 1942, 12x9", EX.....................**110.00**

Calendar, Vargas, Esquire, 1947, complete, EX (w/VG original envelope) **95.00**

Calendar sheet, Beautiful Pearls, Playboy Playmate Margaret Scott, NM **30.00**

Lighter, Memphis Bell, silkscreen on brass, Zippo, 1977, MIB ...**65.00**

Lighter, Vargas girl on both sides, Gibson, VG+ **30.00**

Magazine, Beauty, August 1924, Vargas cover, complete, EX **530.00**

Magazine, Esquire, December 1941, Christmas, 306 pages, EX **40.00**

Magazine, Petty/Vargas, Esquire, Back to School, September 1941, EX......................**25.00**

Magazine, Playboy's Vargas Girls, Playboy Press, 1972, EX ..**80.00**

Magazine page, lady w/2 Borzoi dogs, from Playboy, 1966, 11x8", EX........................**60.00**

Mutoscope card, Golden Hours, nude, Moran, 1945, 5¼x3¼", EX.................................**55.00**

Necktie, mauve w/geometric designs, blonde in purple inside, 1950s, EX...........**35.00**

Playing cards, brunette in stockings, West End Sunoco, M (sealed box).....................**35.00**

Playing cards, Comme Ci Comme Ca, Vargas, double deck, NM..................**140.00**

Playing cards, Peppy, Naughty But Nice Comic Cards, 54 cards, NMIB..................**35.00**

Poster, The Petty Girl (the movie), ca 1955, EX..................**170.00**

Print, AC Schultz, nude, lithograph, 1930s, 30x27", EX..........**135.00**

Print, Elvgren, cowgirl sits on fence w/smoking gun, 15x18", EX.................................**50.00**

Print, Moran, nude redhead looking up, color, 1940s, 11x15" +frame...........................**85.00**

Print, Roy Best, nude dancing, 1930s, 26x19", NM.........**55.00**

Print, Sheer Elegance, from 1941, published in 1980s, 24x36", EX.................................**25.00**

Playing Cards

Here is another collectible that is inexpensive, easy to display (especially single cards), and very diversified. Variations are endless.

Some backs are printed with reproductions of famous paintings or pinup art. Others carry advertising messages, picture tourist attractions, or commemorate a world's fair. Early decks are scarce, but those from the 1940s on are usually more attractive anyway, so pick an area that interests you most and have fun! Though they're usually not dated, you may find some clues that will help you to determine an approximate date. Telephone numbers, zip codes, advertising slogans, and patriotic messages are always helpful. See also Pinup Art.

Air Canada, Graphica, M (sealed box)...................................**9.00**

Airplane Spotter, USPC, 52+Joker+extra card, wide, EX (EX box)....................**25.00**

Canary Islands, 54 Views, 52+2 Jokers+2 extra cards, M (EX box)...............................**12.00**

Cap 'N Crunch, Quaker Oats Cereal, 52+Joker, ca 1976, M...............................**16.00**

City of Chicago, B&B, 52+Joker, NM (EX box).................**10.00**

Cola Clan 4th Annual National Convention, 1978, M (sealed box)...............................**10.00**

Dallas Cowboys Cheerleaders, Trans Media Inc, M (sealed box)...................................**8.00**

Denver & Rio Grande Western, Interstate, 52+Joker, NM (EX box)...............................**45.00**

Enjoy Coke, White Hen Pantry, basketball deck, M (sealed box)...............................**20.00**

Epcot Center, M (sealed wrap) .**6.00**

Ford Motor, Arrco, 52+2 Jokers, M (EX box)...........................**15.00**

Golf Is Better Than Sex, Big Fun, 52 no Joker, wide, M (EX box)................................**5.00**

Hand Sign Reading, 52+Joker+2 extra cards, M (EX box).**14.00**

Indians of the Southwest, Fred Harvey, 52+Joker, NM (EX box)...............................**200.00**

Jerry's Nuggets, USPC, 52+Joker, no box, VG.........................**5.00**

Melitta, Obergs, 52+Joker, M (EX box)................................**12.00**

Michelin, BP Grimaud, 52+Joker, M (EX box).....................**14.00**

New York City, USPCC, 52+Joker, ca 1900, NM (EX box)....**85.00**

New Zealand Views, GB Scott, 52+2 extra cards, M (EX box)............................**12.00**

On the Spot, C. James Plumbing, Saturday Evening Post, double deck, EX, from $20.00 to $25.00.

Pennsylvania Railroad, pinochle, M (sealed box)................**10.00**

Pep Boys, Arrco, 52+Joker+extra card, M (NM+ box).........**75.00**

Pokeman, USPC, 52+extra card, no Joker, wide, M (EX box)...**4.00**

Reynolds Wrap Aluminum, 52+Joker+extra card, NM (EX box)..............................**20.00**

San Diego Zoo, B&B, 52+Joker, narrow, EX (EX box)......**20.00**

Scenes from Venice, Italy, WPCC, 52+Joker, gold edge, M (EX box)................................**10.00**

Schlitz Beer, M (sealed)..........**6.00**

South Africa Railways & Harbors, gold edges, 52+joker, EX+ (worn box).......................**50.00**

SS President Cleveland, 52+Joker, M (partial box)...............**15.00**

XIII Olympic Winter Games, Lake Placid 1980, TDC M (sealed box)..................................**5.00**

Plush Toys

Always popular with the children, soft and cuddly plush toys are gaining the interest of adult collectors as well. Character-related plush toys seem to be most popular, especially characters that are movie or Disney related. Condition is everything. Look for items that are in the finest and cleanest condition possible. There is little or no interest in plush items that are soiled, damaged, or faded.

Alf the Alien, talking, Coleco, 1986, 18", M...................**25.00**

Big Henry the Dog, Animal Fair, 1960s, 20", EX................**55.00**

Bull's Eye (horse), from Toy Story 2, bendable, Disney, 14", M...........................**40.00**

Buzz Lightyear from Toy Story, in pajamas, Disney, 18", M..............................**40.00**

Catbert from Dilbert, Gund, 6", M w/tags...........................**30.00**

Curious George, felt eyes, vintage, Commonwealth Toy Co, 15", EX **90.00**

Duck from Old Bear & Friends stories, Jane Hissey, jointed legs, M **65.00**

Horton the Elephant, Dr Seuss Enterprises, over 20", M ..**22.50**

Huckleberry Hound, Knickerbocker, 1959, NM **30.00**

Lion from the Wizard of Oz, Exclusive by Presents, c 1939, Ren. 1966...1987 Turner Entertainment, 15", $20.00.

Mouse, Rushton Co, 10", EX ..**25.00**

Pac Man, purple shirt: Score w/Me, 1980s **25.00**

Rabbit from Winnie the Pooh, Disney, 18", M **30.00**

Snoopy, United Features Syndicate, Korea, 1968, 11½", MIB **30.00**

Sonic the Hedgehog, 13", M...**40.00**

Spider Man, Ultimate Marvel Kellytoy, 58", M w/tags...**55.00**

Sponge Bob Square Pants, 38", NM **35.00**

Sponge Bob Square Pants, 42", M **95.00**

Spyro the Dragon, 11", EX ...**25.00**

Stitch (Lilo & Stitch), says 35 phrases, Disney, MIB **45.00**

Sully from Monsters Inc, 12x10", M **24.00**

Tiger, battery-operated growler, Steiff, 36x72", M **95.00**

Woody from Toy Story 2, Disney, 30", M **45.00**

Yertle the Turtle and Thidwick Moose (Dr. Suess), 1983, large, $75.00 each. (Photo courtesy June Moon)

Political Collectibles

Pennants, posters, badges, pamphlets — in general, anything related to a presidential campaign or politicians — are being sought by collectors who have an interest in the political history of our country. Most valued are items from a particularly eventful period or those things having to do with an especially colorful personality.

Celluloid pin-back buttons ('cellos') were first widely used in the 1896 presidential campaign; before that time medals, ribbons, and badges of various kinds predominated. Prices for political pinbacks have increased considerably in the last few years, more due to speculative buying and selling rather than inherent scarcity or unusual demand. It is still possible, however, to find quality collectible items at reasonable prices. In flea markets, recent buttons tend to be overpriced; the goal, as always, is to look for less familiar items that may be priced more reasonably. Most buttons issued since the 1964 campaign, with a few notable exceptions, should be in the range of $2.00 to $10.00. Condition is critical: cracks, scratches, spots, and brown stains ('foxing') seriously reduce the value of a button.

Prices are for items in excellent condition. Reproductions are common; many are marked as such, but it takes some experience to tell the difference. The best reference book for political collectors is Edmund Sullivan's *Collecting Political Americana, 2nd Edition.*

Our advisors for this category are Michael and Polly McQuillen; they are listed in the Directory under Indiana. See Clubs and Newsletters for information concerning Political Collectors of Indiana.

Badge, John Kennedy multicolor portrait button above flasher of White House and Capitol, Inauguration information on purple ribbon, 1961, 7¼", EX, $20.00.

Bank, peanut w/Jimmy Carter smile, Cardinal, 11½", EX............**20.00**

Bobbin' head, Jimmy Carter, Bosley Bobbers, 7", MIP..............**17.50**

Bobbin' head toy, Nixon & Mao playing ping-pong, NM.........**150.00**

Bookends, JFK busts, bronzelike metal w/marble base, 6¾", pr.........................**35.00**

Bottle, Coca-Cola; Commemorating Jimmy Carter, 1985, NM.**80.00**

Bust, Gerald Ford, Bronzite, w/metal nameplate, 7", M..............**35.00**

Christmas card, sent by Gerald Ford & family, 1976, M..**55.00**

Christmas card, sent by Senator John F Kennedy & family, 1950s, EX.....................**120.00**

Cigar, Kennedy & Johnson on white & gold, 10½x1¼", MIP............................**25.00**

Doll, JFK, Franklin Mint, MIB.....................................**80.00**

Doll, JFL in rocking chair, Japan, EX...................................**55.00**

Doll, Ronald Reagan Hosts State Reception, Horsman Toys, 19", MIB.........................**65.00**

Doll, window cling; Ronald Reagan caricature, EX................**28.50**

Figurine, Lyndon B Johnson w/lg white hat, Remco, 1964, 6", M.....**25.00**

Fishing lure, peanut shape w/Jimmy Carter smile, Cordell, MIB...................**20.00**

Golf ball, Ronald Reagan logo, Top Flite, 1981, MIP.............**90.00**

Halloween mask, Jimmy Carter, EX...................................**20.00**

Menu, Official State Dinner, 1984, NM...............................**160.00**

Model kit, JFK, Aurora #851, 1965, M (EX box)...........**90.00**

Paperweight, Ronald Reagan faux signature & Presidential seal, M **25.00**

Paperweight medallion, Jimmy Carter profile, Schmid, ½x3½", MIB .**15.00**

Plate, At the Helm, JFK on boat, Franklin Mint, M.........**35.00**

Plate, Lyndon B Johnson w/Family, white w/gold band, 9¼".....**23.50**

Plate, Ronald Reagan & George Bush, A New Beginning, Hagel, 1981, M...............**35.00**

Plate, The Torch Is Passed, JFK w/seal background, Franklin Mint, M...........................**30.00**

Radio, Jimmy Carter head coming out of peanut, M (EX box) **30.00**

Ramp walker, peanut shape w/Jimmy Carter face, Wolfe, 1970s, 5", MIB **15.00**

Salt & pepper shakers, JFK seated on chair, 2-pc, EX **90.00**

Salt & pepper shakers, Mr & Mrs JFK portraits on white ceramic, 3", pr **30.00**

Teapot, Ronald Reagan caricature, Hall, 1980, 10" **210.00**

Tie, Jimmy Carter faces w/peanuts on blue, polyester, EX ...**25.00**

Tie clasp, gold-tone w/blue faux signature & seal, EX **25.00**

Watch, President Jimmy Carter riding a donkey on face, EX..**25.00**

Toy, The Prez or Ross the Boss, noise activated, 1996, $20.00 each. (Photo courtesy Michael McQuillen)

Precious Moments

Precious Moments, little figurines with inspirational captions, were created by Samuel J. Butcher and are produced by Enesco Inc. in the Orient. They're sold through almost every gift store in the country, and the earlier, discontinued models are becoming very collectible. Unless noted otherwise, our prices are for mint in the box examples. For more information see *Official Precious Moments Collector's Guide to Company Dolls* by John and Malinda Bomm.

Figurine, God Understands, E-1379B, 1978, suspended in 1984, fish mark, 5", no box, M, $85.00.

Egg, A Reflection of His Love, #529095, 1994 ....**30.00**

Egg, I Will Cherish the Old Rugged Cross, #523534, 1991 ....**35.00**

Figurine, A King Is Born, #532088, no mark, 1994................**30.00**

Figurine, Bless You Two, E9255, fish mark, 1983 ....**55.00**

Figurine, But Love Goes on Forever, E3115, hourglass mark, 1982 ....**60.00**

Figurine, camel, E2363, hourglass mark, 1982 ....**45.00**

Figurine, cow w/bell around neck & bird on back, E5638, no mark, 1981 ....**55.00**

Figurine, Death Can't Keep Him in the Ground, no mark, 1994 ....**40.00**

Figurine, donkey, E5621, no mark, 1981 ....**35.00**

Figurine, He Is My Inspiration, no mark, 1991 ....**70.00**

Figurine, He Is Not Here, For He Is Raised As He Said, no mark, 1993 ....**120.00**

Figurine, He Restoreth My Soul, no mark, 1998 ....**60.00**

Figurine, Heaven Must Have Sent You, #135992, no mark, 1996...............................**60.00**

Figurine, His Presence Is Felt in the Chapel, no mark, 1996 ....**30.00**

Figurine, Hogs & Kisses, Country Lane Series, no mark, 1998.................**100.00**

Figurine, I'll Play My Drum For Him, #2360, fish mark, 1983......**45.00**

Figurine, Jesus Loves Me, E9279, fish mark, 1983 ....**35.00**

Figurine, Love Beareth All Things, E7158, fish mark, 1983 ..**50.00**

Figurine, Love Is Sharing, E3110G, hourglass mark, 1982 ....**45.00**

Figurine, Mother Sew Dear, E3106, fish mark, 1983 ....**50.00**

Figurine, Nativity Boy, #2395, fish mark, 1983 ....**160.00**

Figurine, Rejoicing w/You, E4724, hourglass mark, 1982....**60.00**

Figurine, Seeds of Love From The Chapel, #271586, no mark, 1997 ....**45.00**

Figurine, Surely Goodness & Mercy Shall..., #523410, no mark, 1998 ....**60.00**

Figurine, The Lord Bless Us & Keep Us, E3114, fish mark, 1983 ....**60.00**

Figurine, The Purr-Fect Gramdma, E3109, fish mark, 1983 ....**40.00**

Figurine, Thou Art Mine, E3113, triangle mark, 1981.......**55.00**

Figurine, Two Section Wall, E5644, fish mark, 1983 ....**135.00**

Figurine, Walking by Faith, E3117, fish mark, 1983..**95.00**

Figurines, Come Let Us Adore Him, E2800, fish mark, 9-pc, 1983 ....**150.00**

Figurines, They Follow the Stars, E5624, fish mark, 3-pc, 1983.....................**270.00**

Figurines, Wee Three Kings, E5635, hourglass mark, 3-pc, 1982 ....**105.00**

Ornament, But the Greatest of These Is Love, #527734, 1992 ....**35.00**

Ornament, Christmas Is Ruff Without You, #520462, 1989 ....**35.00**

Ornament, I'm Nuts About You, #520411, 1992 ....**25.00**

Ornament, Surround Us w/Joy, E-0513, fish mark, 1983....**75.00**

Thimble, Love Is the Best Gift of All, #109843, 1987 ....**40.00**

Thimble, Time To Wish...Merry Christmas, #115312, 1988..**35.00**

Princess House Glassware

The home party plan of Princess House was started in Massachusetts in 1963 by Charlie Collis. His idea was to give women an opportunity to have their own business by being a princess in their house, thus the name for this company. Though many changes have been made since the 1960s, the main goal of this company is to better focus on the home party plan.

Most Princess House pieces are not marked in the glass — they carry a paper label. Heritage is a crystal cut floral pattern, introduced not long after the company started in business. Fantasia is a crystal pressed floral pattern, introduced about 1980. Both lines continue today; new pieces are being added, and old items are continually discontinued.

Heritage, casserole, three-quart, MIB, $75.00.

Apple, cookie jar, 10x9" **50.00**
Bordeaux, stem, water goblet; 7", 4 for.................................**50.00**

Bordeaux, stem, wine; 6"......**58.00**
Empress, table lamp, 3-column, pr...................................**60.00**
Fantasia, plate, lilac, scalloped edge, 8", set of 4, MIB ...**65.00**
Fantasia, plate, 8", 6 for.......**50.00**
Fantasia, punch bowl, w/ladle & 12 matching cups........**120.00**
Fantasia, sleigh & 2 reindeer (candle holders), retired **110.00**
Fantasia, stem, iced beverage; sapphire blue, set of 4, MIB...**45.00**
Fantasia, stem, margarita/dessert; set of 8 ....**50.00**
Figurine, bald eagle, Wonders of the Wild, #6503, 8½", $55 to..**65.00**
Figurine, bass, Wonders of the Wild, retired..................**50.00**
Figurine, bull, Wonders of the Wild **48.00**
Figurine, Cassie cocker spaniel, retired, 3½", MIB...........**50.00**
Figurine, elephant, Wonders of the Wild **45.00**
Figurine, grizzly bear, Wonders of the Wild, #996, MIB **85.00**
Figurine, jaguar, Wonders of the Wild, #899, 5½", MIB **55.00**
Figurine, lion, Wonders of the Wild, 4½x6½"................**60.00**
Figurine, Nativity set, 5-pc, #739, MIB...............................**60.00**
Figurine, snail, 2½x3" **68.00**
Figurine, stag........................**55.00**
Figurine, stallion, 7½x6¼" ...**55.00**
Figurine, trout, Wonders of the Wild, limited edition, 5", MIB............................**90.00**
Figurine, wolf, 7x6", MIB **55.00**
Floor vase, Pat O'Brien, blown/cut, footed, 21½x8"................**80.00**
Garden Mist, stem, goblet, 9", pr **55.00**

Garden Mist, stem, iced tea; 7⅞",
pr, MIB, from $45 to.....**60.00**
Heritage, cafe mug, #6147, 14-oz,
5x3¾", 4 for....................**60.00**
Heritage, coke glass, 5x3", 4
for............................**60.00**
Heritage, mug, Irish coffee; set of
4, MIB............................**30.00**
Heritage, pitcher, icer/liner; #346A,
retired hostess gift..........**65.00**
Heritage, salad set, 9-pc, MIB.**55.00**
Heritage, stem, champagne; blue
stem, 4 for......................**70.00**
Heritage, stem, goblet/wine; 11-oz,
set of 4, MIB....................**60.00**
Heritage, stem, wine; #420,
6", set of 4, MIB, from $50
to............................**55.00**
Heritage, sundae/parfait, footed, 4
for..................................**58.00**
Heritage, teapot, blown, 5-pc, 1998
hostess item, 7¼"+warmer
base..............................**60.00**
Heritage, tumbler, juice; set of 12,
MIB..................................**60.00**
Heritage, tumbler, 7¼", 6 for..**60.00**
Orchard Medley, pitcher, #241B
hostess gift, 9"................**50.00**
Pastel Scallop, plate, dessert; 8¾",
set of 4, MIB....................**65.00**
Romance, night lamp, hostess gift,
#971, 10½x6"..................**50.00**
Tulip, cake plate, w/lid.........**55.00**

Purinton

Popular among collectors
due to its 'country' look, Purinton
Pottery's dinnerware and
kitchen items are easy to learn to
recognize due to their bold yet
simple designs, many of them of
fruit and flowers, created with
basic hand-applied colors on a
creamy white gloss.

Bowl, fruit; Apple, scalloped bor-
der, 12"..........................**45.00**
Bowl, vegetable; Maywood,
w/lid............................**35.00**
Canister, Normandy Plaid, apart-
ment size, 5½"................**45.00**
Coffeepot, Apple, 8-cup.........**75.00**
Coffeepot, Fruit, 8-cup..........**25.00**
Cup & saucer, Pennsylvania
Dutch............................**20.00**

Jam and jelly dish, Apple, 5½",
$45.00. (Photo courtesy Susan Morris)

Jug, Dutch; Fruit, 5-pt.........**25.00**
Jug, honey; Ivy, 6¼", from $15
to................................**18.00**
Jug, honey; Petals, 6¼"........**15.00**
Jug, Kent; Normandy Plaid.**25.00**
Mug, beer; Heather Plaid.....**40.00**
Pitcher, beverage; Apple.......**40.00**
Plate, breakfast; Cactus, desert
scene, 8½"......................**95.00**
Plate, chop; Brown Intaglio,
12"..............................**20.00**
Plate, dinner; Palm Tree,
9½"..............................**175.00**
Plate, dinner; Provincial Fruit,
9½"..............................**35.00**

Plate, dinner; Tea Rose, 9½"..**75.00**

Plate, dinner; Turquoise Intaglio, 9½".................................**20.00**

Plate, salad; Apple, 6¾" **15.00**

Plate, salad; Ming Tree, 6¾".**25.00**

Platter, Apple, 11" **15.00**

Platter, Brown Intaglio, 12"..**20.00**

Platter, Saraband, 12"..........**20.00**

Salt & pepper shakers, Maywood, mini jug, pr **35.00**

Salt & pepper shakers, Peasant Garden, mini jug, pr......**95.00**

Salt & pepper shakers, Pennsylvania Dutch, Pour & Shake, pr ..**75.00**

Teapot, Cactus Flower, 2-cup ..**125.00**

Puzzles

Of most interest to collectors of vintage puzzles are those made of wood or plywood, especially the early hand-cut examples. Character-related examples and those representing a well-known personality or show from the early days of television are coming on strong right now, and values are steadily climbing in these areas. For an expanded listing, see *Schroeder's Collectible Toys, Antique to Modern* (Collector Books).

Aquaman, jigsaw, Whitman, 1968, 100 pcs, MIB **50.00**

Aristocats, image around chair, frame-tray, 1970s or 1980s, MIP...............................**15.00**

Batman, jigsaw, Whitman, 1966, 150 pcs, 14x18", NMIB **30.00**

Beverly Hillbillies, cast on stairs, jigsaw, 1963, VG+IB......**45.00**

Bionic Woman, jigsaw, Whitman, 1976, complete, MIB, from $40 to..............................**50.00**

Buffalo Bill Jr, w/female co-star, frame-tray, Built-Rite, 1958, NM+..............................**10.00**

Casper the Friendly Ghost, frame-tray, 1992, 8x11", EX.....**10.00**

Charlie's Angels, jigsaw, H-G Toys, 1976, 150 pcs, MIB, from $25 to **30.00**

Cheyenne, jigsaw, Milton Bradley, 1957, set of 3, EXIB.......**40.00**

Cloud Strife, jigsaw, Final Fantasy 7, Japan, 7x10½", MIB (sealed)..................**35.00**

Daniel Boone, jigsaw, The Shawnees Attack, Jaymar, 1961, NMIB...................**20.00**

David Cassidy, jigsaw, APC, 1972, MIB, from $35.00 to $45.00. (Photo courtesy Greg Davis and Bill Morgan)

Donald Duck, jigsaw, Whitman, 1965, 100 pcs, 8½x11", M (sealed box)....................**40.00**

Donnie & Marie, jigsaw, Whitman, 1976, complete, MIB......**35.00**

Fantastic Four, jigsaw, Third Eye, 1971, 500 pcs, MIB **100.00**

Flash Gordon, frame-tray, Milton Bradley, 1951, set of 3, VG+IB **65.00**

Flipper, jigsaw, Whitman, 1965, 100 pcs, MIB **20.00**

GI, jigsaw, Battle 1 or Battle 2, 1985, EXIB, ea **15.00**

Impossibles, frame-tray, fight scene, Whitman, 1967, EX+ **25.00**

KISS, jigsaw, Casse-Tete, 1977, NMIB **25.00**

Land of the Lost, jigsaw, Whitman #4609, 1975, NMIB........**20.00**

Lassie, frame-tray, Whitman, 1966, complete, NM.......**20.00**

Marlin Perkins Wild Kingdom, jigsaw, Sparrow Hawk, 1971, VG (VG box)...........................**15.00**

Mr Jinks, frame-tray, w/Pixie & Dixie on high wire, Whitman, 1961, EX+ **15.00**

Mr Magoo, frame-tray, 1965, complete, NM.......................**20.00**

Pink Panther, jigsaw, playing violin, 1979, VGIB **15.00**

Raggedy Ann & Andy, frame-tray, Whitman, 1976, complete, 11x8", MIP......................**10.00**

Roadrunner, frame-tray, 1966, complete, NM **15.00**

Roadrunner, frame-tray, 1973, EX **10.00**

Snow White, Whitman, 1938, complete, (VG box), $125.00.

Six Million Dollar Man, frame-tray, APC, 1976, complete, MIP **35.00**

Skippy, jigsaw, Consolidated Paper, 1933, set of 3, M (EX box) **125.00**

Spider-Man, frame-tray, Playskil, 1981, EX **18.00**

Starsky & Hutch, jigsaw, HG Toys, 1976, complete, MIB, from $25 to **30.00**

Super Six, jigsaw, Whitman, 1969, NMIB..............................**30.00**

Sword in the Stone, frame-tray, Whitman #4456, 1963, G+....................**10.00**

Tammy & Pepper, jigsaw, Ideal, 100 pcs, VG (VG box).....**25.00**

Underdog, frame-tray, Whitman #4522, 1965, MIB (sealed) **23.00**

Wizard of Oz, frame-tray, photo image, 1988, EX.............**15.00**

Radios

Novelty radios are those that carry an advertising message or are shaped like a product bottle, can, or carton; others may be modeled after the likeness of a well-known cartoon character or disguised as anything but a radio — a shoe or a car, for instance. It's sometimes hard to recognize the fact that they're actually radios.

Transistor radios are collectible as well. First introduced in 1954, many feature space-age names and futuristic designs. Prices here are for complete, undamaged examples in at least very good condition. If you have vintage radios you need to evaluate, see *Collector's Guide to Antique Radios, Fifth Edition,* by John Slusser and the staff of *Radio Daze* (Collector Books).

Novelty Radios

Firestone Steel Belted Radial-721, Hong Kong, distributed by PRI, 5" diameter, from $35.00 to $45.00. (Photo courtesy Bunis and Breed)

Agaay Power Max Battery, clip-on antenna, EX **45.00**

Bart Simpson, riding skateboard, JPI, China, 6½x8", EX ..**50.00**

Baseball, Texas Rangers & Gatorade, 3½" dia, EX...**40.00**

Baseball Player, bat on shoulder, many teams, Sutton, 9x4¾", EX, ea **50.00**

Big Bird, dancing on base, FM, Justin, Korea, 1989, 12x6", EX **45.00**

Blinking Elephant, blue w/hair ribbon, 6⅜x5", EX..........**25.00**

Bullwinkle, plastic 3-D, PAT World Prod, Hong Kong, 11⅞x6¼", EX................**250.00**

Butterfinger, AM/FM, Hong Kong, 3½x6", EX......................**35.00**

Dick Tracy Wrist Watch, Creative Creations, Japan, 1975, EX......................**225.00**

Elmer Fudd & Bugs Bunny, turtle shape, Warner Bros, 1973, EX.................................**50.00**

Fanta Orange, 1 side French/other English, EX.....................**35.00**

GTE, headphone radio, China, EX **35.00**

Guitar, plastic figure w/metal accents, Federal, Taiwan, 11x4", EX.......................**60.00**

Gulfpride Multi-G Motor Oil, can, EX **35.00**

Incredible Hulk, Marvel Comics, Amico, 1978, 7x5½", EX..**75.00**

Marlboro Cigarettes, Japan, 13¼x8⅞", EX................**100.00**

Mickey Mouse, head figural, Radio Shack, 5½x7", EX **50.00**

Minizoo, Mickey Mouse as lion tamer, lion shape, WDP, EX..........**50.00**

Paint Can, Wet Paint w/footprints, by Heritage, Taiwan, EX **50.00**

Pooch, w/clock in belly, AM/alarm, Power Tronics, 1986, 7½x4½" **40.00**

Radio Bag, tote bag, clear plastic, 15x13", EX......................**60.00**

Skinner's Enriched Macaroni, Short Cut Elbow, Hong Kong, 5x3½".............................**60.00**

Snow White & Seven Dwarfs, flying bird shape, WDP, EX **50.00**

Starforce Robot, plastic w/movable arms, Hong Kong, 6x3¾", EX **50.00**

Texaco Super Unleaded, gas pump, EX **45.00**

True Value, Chicago Cubs, EX..**25.00**

Twix Cookies-n-Creme/Chocolate Fudge Billboard, 2-sided, China, 4x12"..................**75.00**

Wilson's Dry Ginger Ale, GE, Hong Kong, EX..............**35.00**

Yoohoo Chocolate, AM/FM, China, 5x3", EX.........................**45.00**

7-Up Vending Machine, AM/FM, Markatron #2001, Hong Kong, EX..............**100.00**

Transistor Radios

Admiral, Y2351X, horizontal, 8 transistors, AM, battery, 1963..............**15.00**

Admiral, 7M16, horizontal, 7 transistors, AM, battery, 1958.....**50.00**

Airline, GEN-1202A, horizontal, 6 transistors, AM, battery, 1962..............**35.00**

Aiwa, AR-102, horizontal, 8 transistors, AM, battery, 1964...**15.00**

Aladdin, AL65, vertical, 6 transistors, AM, battery, 1962..**125.00**

America, ST-6Z, vertical, 6 transistors, AM, battery, 1962..**35.00**

Arvin, 60R23, horizontal, 6 transistors, AM, battery, 1960..............**25.00**

Bradford, AR-121, vertical, 10 transistors, AM, FM, battery, 1965..............**15.00**

Bulova, 660, vertical, 8 transistors, AM, battery, 1959..........**85.00**

Columbia, 400B, vertical, 4 transistors, AM, battery, 1960...**55.00**

Continental, 160, vertical, 6 transistors, AM, battery, 1959...**75.00**

Dewald, K-544A, horizontal, 4 transistors, AM, battery, 1957..............**65.00**

Eico, RA-6, horizontal, 6 transistors, AM, battery, 1960...**15.00**

Emerson, 555, horizontal, 4 transistors, AM, battery, 1959...**75.00**

Futura, 366, vertical, 6 transistors, AM, battery, 1963..........**50.00**

General Electric, CT455A, horizontal, 6 transistors, AM, battery, 1960.......................**20.00**

General Electric, 675, horizontal, 5 transistors, AM, battery, 1955..............**100.00**

Hitache, KH-903, horizontal, 9 transistors, AM, FM, battery, 1964..............**20.00**

Hitache, TH-667, horizontal, 6 transistors, AM, battery, 1960..............**80.00**

Jaguar, 6T-250, vertical, 6 transistors, AM, battery, 1960..**175.00**

Kent, TR-605, vertical, 6 transistors, AM, battery, 1965..**15.00**

Knight, KN-2400, horizontal, 9 transistors, AM, FM, battery, 1964..............**25.00**

Lloyd's, TR-6P, vertical, 6 transistors, AM, battery, 1965..............**10.00**

Marvel, 6YR-05, vertical, 6 transistors, AM, battery, 1961..**75.00**

Motorola, 6X39A-1, horizontal, 6 transistors, AM, battery, 1958..............**125.00**

Norelco, L0X95T/62R, horizontal, 7 transistors, AM, battery, 1961..............**30.00**

Panasonic, DT-495, horizontal, 6 transistors, AM, battery, 1962..............**25.00**

RCA, 1-T-4J, vertical, 8 transistors, AM, battery, 1959..**35.00**

RCA, 4RG51, vertical, 8 transistors, AM, battery, 1963..**30.00**

Seminole, 600, vertical, 6 transistors, AM, battery, 1962..**20.00**

Sharp, BX-326, horizontal, 10 transistors, AM, battery, 1961 ....**35.00**

Silvertone, 3229, horizontal, 13 transistors, AM, FM, battery, 1963 ....**20.00**

Silvertone, #5205, seven transistors, AM, battery, $15.00. (Photo courtesy Marty and Sue Bunis)

Toshiba, 3TP-315Y, vertical, 3 transistors, AM, battery, 1959 ....**150.00**

Transitone, TR-1645, vertical, 6 transistors, AM, battery, 1963 ....**10.00**

Ramp Walkers

Ramp walkers date back to at least 1873 when Ives produced a cast-iron elephant walker. Wood and composite ramp walkers were made in Czechoslovakia and the USA from the 1920s through the 1940s. The most common were made by John Wilson of Watsontown, Pennsylvania. These sold worldwide and became known as 'Wilson Walkies.' Most are two-legged and stand approximately 4½" tall.

Plastic ramp walkers were manufactured primarily by the Louis Marx Co. from the 1950s through the early 1960s. The majority were produced in Hong Kong, but some were made in the USA and sold under the Marx logo or by the Charmore Co., a subsidiary of Marx.

The three common sizes are small premiums about 1½" x 2"; the more common medium size, 2¾" x 3"; and large, approximately 4" x 5". Most of the smaller walkers were unpainted, while the medium and large sizes were hand or spray painted. Several of the walking types were sold with wooden or colorful tin lithographed ramps. For more extensive listings and further information, see *Schroeder's Collectible Toys, Antique to Modern* (Collector Books.)

Astro, Hanna-Barbera........**150.00**

Astro and George Jetson, $75.00. (Photo courtesy Randy Welch)

Bear, plastic **20.00**

Big Bad Wolf & Mason Pig, Marx **50.00**

Bison w/Native, Marx **40.00**

Bull, plastic **20.00**

Chipmunks carrying acorns, plastic **35.00**

Donald Duck, pulling nephews in wagon, Marx **35.00**

Donald Duck & Goofy, riding go-cart, Marx.......................**40.00**

Elephant, plastic w/metal legs, sm...................................**30.00**

Fred & Wilma on Dino, Hanna-Barbera...........................**60.00**

Frontiersman w/Dog, plastic..**95.00**

Goofy, riding hippo, Marx **45.00**

Horse, circus style, plastic....**20.00**

Horse w/English rider, plastic, lg **50.00**

Mama duck w/3 ducklings, plastic...................................**35.00**

Mickey Mouse, pushing lawn roller, Marx **35.00**

Monkey carrying bananas, plastic..................................**60.00**

Pigs, 2 carrying 1 in basket, plastic **40.00**

Pluto, plastic w/metal legs, sm, Marx **35.00**

Popeye, Irvin, celluloid, lg....**60.00**

Santa, w/gold sack **45.00**

Sheriff facing outlaw, plastic....................................**65.00**

Spark Plug.........................**200.00**

Records

Records that made it to the 'Top Ten' in their day are not always the records that are prized most highly by today's collectors, though they treasure those which best represent specific types of music: jazz, rhythm and blues, country and western, rock 'n roll, etc. Many search for those cut very early in the career of artists who later became superstars, records cut on rare or interesting labels, or those aimed at ethnic groups. A fast-growing area of related interest is picture sleeves for 45s. These are often worth more than the record itself, especially if they feature superstars from the 1950s or early 1960s.

Condition is very important. Record collectors tend to be very critical, so learn to watch for loss of gloss; holes, labels, or writing on the label; warping; and scratches. Unless otherwise noted, values are for records in like-new condition — showing little sign of wear, with a playing surface that retains much of its original shine, and having only a minimal amount of surface noise. EP (extended play 45s) and LPs (long-playing 33⅓ rpm 'albums') must have their jackets (cardboard sleeves) in nice condition free of tape, stickers, tears, or obvious damage. *The American Premium Record Guide* by Les Docks is a great source for more information. Mr. Docks is listed in the Directory under Texas. Note: When two condition codes are present in our descriptions, the first gives the condition of the record itself, the second is for the sleeve.

Children's Records

Adventures of Batman & Robin, Leo/MGM, 33⅓ rpm, EX/EX **30.00**

Adventures of Mighty Mouse, Rocking Horse, 78 rpm, 1978, EX/EX **15.00**

Bozo & His Rocket Ship, Capitol, 78 rpm, 1947, EX/EX, from $15 to **20.00**

Flipper the Fabulous Dolphin, Golden, 45 rpm, 1962, EX/EX, from $4 to **6.00**

Gabby Hayes 1001 Western Nights, RCA, 78 rpm, 1950s, EX/VG **35.00**

It's Howdy Doody Time, RCA Victor, 1951, EX (EX cover), from $50.00 to $60.00. (Photo courtesy Peter Muldavin)

Little Engine That Could, RCA, 78 rpm, 1949, EX/EX, from $15 to **20.00**

Mickey & the Beanstalk, Capitol, 78 rpm, 1948, w/booklet, EX/EX **25.00**

Pinky Lee, Decca Records, 78 rpm, ca 1954, EX/NM **30.00**

Planet of the Apes Book & Record, Power Record Co, 45 rpm, EX/EX+, ea **15.00**

Popeye-Where There Is a Way, Peter Pan, 45 rpm, 1962, EX/EX **12.00**

Rover the Strong Man, Voco, 78 rpm, 1948, NM, from $30 to......**40.00**

Rusty in Orchestraville, Capitol, 78 rpm, 1947, EX/EX, from $10 to **20.00**

Ten Little Indians, Voco, 1948, 78 rpm, NM, 16", from $15 to **25.00**

The Fox, Talking Book Corp, 78 rpm, 1917, very rare, 4", EX/NM **130.00**

Wonder Woman, Christmas Island, 45 rpm, 1978, EX/EX **25.00**

LP Albums

Blues Brothers, Briefcase Full of Blues, Atlantic SD19217, 1978, $20.00.

Atkins, Chet; Session, RCA Victor 1090, EX **25.00**

Big Bopper, Chantilly Lace, red label, Mercury MG-20402, EX **25.00**

Cannon, Freddie; Steps Out, Swan 511, EX...........................**40.00**

Chantays, Pipeline, stereo, Dot 25516, EX.......................**35.00**

Cleftones, Heart & Soul, Gee 705, EX..................................**85.00**

Dimensions, My Foolish Heart, Coral 757430, EX...........**65.00**

Dorsey, Lee; Ya Ya, Fury 1002, EX **40.00**

Everly Brothers, Songs Our Daddy Taught Us, Cadence 3016, EX **25.00**

Five Royales, Sing for You, King 616, EX...........................**85.00**

Four Knights, Spotlight Songs, Capital 346, EX..............**65.00**

Goodman, Dickie; Many Faces of..., Rori 3301, EX.........**40.00**

Hawkins, Ronnie; Mr Dynamo, Roulette 25102, EX........**40.00**

Husky, Ferlin; Born To Lose, Capitol 1204, EX............**17.50**

Jordan, Louis; Go Blow Your Horn, Score 4007, EX....**85.00**

Lewis, Jerry Lee; Jerry Lee Lewis, Sun 1230, EX **42.50**

Lowe, Jim; Wicked Women, Dot 3114, EX.........................**25.00**

Miller, Jody; Queen of the House, Capitol 2349, EX............**12.50**

Nelson, Ricky; Ricky Sings Again, Imperial 9061, EX **35.00**

Piano Red, In Concert, Groove 1002, EX......................**125.00**

Raney, Wayne; Songs From the Hills, King 588, EX........**35.00**

Scott, Jack; Burning Bridges, Capitol 2135, EX............**50.00**

Sons of the Pioneers, One Man's Songs, RCA Victor 1483, EX.......**12.50**

US Bonds, Gary; Twist up Calypso, Legrand 3002, EX...........**25.00**

Valens, Ritchie; In Concert at Pacoima Jr High, Del-Fi 1225, EX **35.00**

45 rpms

Adams, Jo Jo; Didn't I Tell You, Chance 1127...................**90.00**

Anka, Paul; Dance On Little Girl, ABC-P10220, EX/EX **10.00**

Audrey, Dear Elvis, Plus 104, EX/EX.............................**12.50**

Avalon, Frankie; Why/Swinging on a Rainbow, Chancellor 1045, M/EX.....................**10.00**

Baez, Joan; Be Not Too Hard, Vanguard 35055, NM/EX..**15.00**

Beach Boys, Getcha Back/Male Ego, CS 493, M/M............**2.50**

Beach Boys, Surfin', Candix 301, EX/EX.............................**65.00**

Beatles, Let It Be/You Know My Name, Apple 2764, EX/EX..**15.00**

Beatniks, Blue Angel, Key-Lock 913, EX...........................**15.00**

Bergeron, Shirley; French Rockin Boogie, EX/EX................**12.50**

Big Five, Blue Eyes, Shad 5019, EX/EX.............................**10.00**

Boone, Pat; Ain't That a Shame, Dot 15377, M/EX **15.00**

Boone, Pat; Bernardine/Love Letters in the Sand, Dot 15570, NM/EX.................**8.00**

Bowles, Doug; Cadillac Baby, Tune 206, EX/EX...........**20.00**

Buchanan, Wes; Give Some Love My Way, Pep 114, EX/EX.......**35.00**

Cannon, Freddy; Way Down Under in New Orleans, Swan 4043, NM/EX....................**6.00**

Capris, The; It Was Moonglow, Gotham 7306, EX **40.00**

Cardinals, I'll Always Love You, Atlantic 952, EX/EX **40.00**

Chandler, Wayland; Little Lover, 4 Star 1716, EX/EX **10.00**

Clefs, The; We Three, Chess 1521, EX/EX **65.00**

Continentals, It Doesn't Matter, Hunter 3502, EX/EX......**25.00**

Cruisers, Cryin' Over You, V-Tone 213, EX/EX.....................**10.00**

Davis, Dale & The Tomcats; Gotta Rock, Stardale 100/101, EX/EX **20.00**

Denson, Lee; High School Bop, Kent 306, EX/EX...........**25.00**

Domino, Fats; Poor Poor Me, Imperial 5197, EX **30.00**

Donn, Larry; Honey-Bun, Vaden 113, EX/EX....................**35.00**

Dunn, Webster Jr; Go Go Baby, Dunmar 101, EX/EX......**35.00**

Ermines, The; True Love, Loma 701, EX/EX.....................**25.00**

Everly Brothers, Walk Right Back/ Ebony Eyes, Warner Bros. 5199, EX/ VG, from $10.00 to $20.00.

Fabian, Hound Dog Man/This Friendly World, Chancellor 1044, M/EX....................**12.50**

Fender, Freddie; Mean Woman, Duncan 1000, EX/EX.....**17.50**

Fender, Freddie; Wasted Days & Wasted Nights, Duncan 1001, EX **15.00**

Five Rovers, Down to the Sea, Music City 798, EX/EX...**17.50**

Fleetwoods, Mr Blue, Dolton 2001, EX **20.00**

Four Gents, On Bended Knee, Park 113, EX/EX...........**50.00**

Garner, Gabby; Smokin' Heart, Erald 2052, EX/EX **25.00**

Gilley, Mickey; Susie-Q, Astro 104, EX **20.00**

Glenn, Glen; Goofin' Around, Dore 523, EX/EX.....................**10.00**

Halo, Johnny; Little Annie, Angletone 538, EX/EX...**10.00**

Head, Don; Goin' Strong, Dub 2840, EX/EX...................**12.50**

Hooker, John Lee; Walkin' the Boogie, Chess 1513, EX/EX **90.00**

Infatuators, I Found My Love, Destiny 504, EX/EX.......**12.50**

Ink Spots, Ebb Tide, King 1297, EX **15.00**

Jay, Dale; Shakin' All Over, Raven 001, EX/EX.......................**8.50**

Jumpintones, I Wonder, Raven 8004, EX/EX.....................**8.50**

Kodaks, Teenager's Dream, Fury 1007, EX **20.00**

Landon, Buddy; Foxy, Hollywood 1052, EX/EX...................**10.00**

Lauren, Rod; If I Had a Girl/No Wonder, RCA 7645, NM/NM.........**10.00**

Lewis, Bobby; Memphis Blues, Chess 1518, EX/EX........**40.00**

Long Hairs, Go-Go-Go, Memphis 110, EX/EX.....................**17.50**

Magnets, You Just Say the Word, Groove 0058, EX/EX **12.50**

329

Majestics, Unhappy & Blue, Chex 1004, EX..........................**15.00**

McDonald, Jim; Let's Have a Ball, KCM 3700, EX/EX.........**10.00**

Miller, Carl; Rhythm Guitar, Lu 503, EX/EX.....................**32.50**

Morris, Bob; Party Time, Cascade 5907, EX/EX.....................**8.50**

Nelson, Rick; Fools Rush In/Down Home, Decca 31533, M/EX **12.50**

Nelson, Rick; Stood Up/Waitin' in School, Imperial 5483, NM/EX...........................**12.50**

Nolen, Jimmy; Let's Try Again, Imperial 5363, EX/EX **8.50**

Orioles, If You Believe, Jubilee 5161, EX..........................**15.00**

Pat & Dee, Gee Whiz, Dixie 2006, EX/EX.............................**20.00**

Paul & Paula, Ba-Hey-Be/Young Lovers, Philips 40096, NM/EX.............................**6.00**

Plaids, My Pretty Baby, Nasco 6011, EX/EX.....................**6.50**

Premiers, Diary of Our Love, Herald 577, EX/EX........**10.00**

Presley, Elvis; Are You Lonesome Tonight/I Gotta Know, RCA 1781, EX/EX.....................**8.00**

Presley, Elvis; I Got a Woman, RCA 6637, EX...............**20.00**

Presley, Elvis; Stuck on You/Fame & Fortune, RCA 47-7740, M/NM **18.00**

Rebels, The; Wild Weekend, Marlee 009, EX/EX........**12.50**

Robbins, Eddie; A Girl Like You, Power 214, EX/EX **17.50**

Robbins, Marty; Long Tall Sally, Columbia 40679, EX......**20.00**

Russel, Ted; Bright Lights, Terock 1000, EX/EX....................**8.50**

Shakey Jake, Respect Me Baby, The Blues 303, EX/EX.....**8.50**

Smith, Gene; I'm Gone, Rem 458, EX/EX.............................**17.50**

Sparks, Jerry; My Tears, Fidelity 4058, EX/EX.....................**6.50**

Star Combo, Mr Rock & Roll, Skippy 102, EX/EX........**20.00**

Starr, Ringo; It's All Down to Goodnight Vienna, Apple 1882, NM/VG, $5.00.

Teardrops, The Stars Are Out Tonight, Josie 766, EX **75.00**

Tempo Mentals, Dearest, Ebb 112, EX/EX.............................**17.50**

Texiera, John; Strike It Rich, G&G 100, EX/EX.....................**17.50**

Tillotson, Johnny; Earth Angel/Pledging My Love, Cadence 1377, EX/EX......**8.00**

Vale, Blackie; If I Had Me a Woman, Hurricane 100, EX/EX.............................**42.50**

Vernon, Ray; Evil Angel, Rumble 1349, EX/EX...................**10.00**

Whitley, Ray; Yessirree-Yessirree, Vee Jay 433, EX/EX.........**8.50**

Whitman, Slim; China Doll, Imperial 8156, EX **15.00**

Williams, Billy; Smoke From Your Cigarette, Coral 61363, EX/EX.............................**5.00**

Woods, Bill; Crazy Man, Fire 100, EX/EX **25.00**

78 rpms

Anderson, Maybelle; Moanful Wailin' Blues, Supertone 9429, EX/EX **175.00**

Baker, Buddy; Box Car Blues, Victor 40017, EX/EX **17.50**

Blues Birdhead, Harmonica Blues, Okeh 8824, EX/EX **65.00**

Butcher, Dwight; By a Little Bayou, Victor 23794, EX/EX **25.00**

Childre, Lew; The Old Gray Mare, Gennett 7312, EX/EX **50.00**

De Witte, Charles M; My Kentucky Cabin, Champion 16658, EX/EX **42.50**

Erby, Jack; Hey Peter, Columbia 14570-D, EX/EX **45.00**

Green, Ruth; Sad & Lonely Blues, Okeh 8140, EX/EX **42.50**

Greene, Amos; Just a Lonely Hobo, Supertone 9709, EX/EX **15.00**

Hopkins, Doc; Methodist Pie, Broadway 8337, EX/EX ...**8.50**

Hudson, Hattie; Black Hand Blues, Columbia 14279-D, EX/EX **50.00**

Johnson, Louise; On the Wall, Paramount 13008, EX/EX ..**200.00**

Mack, Bill; Play My Boogie, Imperial 8174, EX/EX **8.50**

Maxwell, Claude; Bad Woman Blues, Sterling 3006, EX/EX **8.50**

McLaughlin's Melody Makers, Mississippi Shadows, Victor 5296, EX/EX **12.50**

Mississippi Mudder, Meat Cutter Blues, Decca 7009, EX/EX ..**42.50**

Oakley, Jessie; Aged Mother, Supertone 9243, EX/EX ..**10.00**

Pickett, Dan; Lemon Man, Gotham 201, EX/EX **20.00**

Rand & Foster, Only a Step to the Grave, Supertone 9373, EX/EX **10.00**

Sanders, Dilliard; I'll Never Be Yours, Supertone 9247, EX/EX **10.00**

Smith, Bessie; Oh Daddy Blues, Columbia A-3888, EX/EX..**10.00**

Stone, Jimmy; Midnight Boogie, Imperial 8137, EX/EX **8.50**

Taylor, Edna; Good Man Blues, Paramount 12057, EX/EX **175.00**

Washington, Booker T; Cotton Club Blues, Bluebird 8378, EX/EX **17.50**

Weber, Dan; Fair Florella, Supertone 2527, EX/EX..**32.50**

Wilson, Leola; Down the Country, Paramount 12444, EX/EX **125.00**

Red Glass

Ever popular with collectors, red glass has been used to create decorative items such as one might find in gift shops, utilitarian bottles and kitchenware, figurines and dinnerware lines such as were popular during the Depression era.

Ashtray, standing clown, Venetian, 1998, 4" **25.00**

Basket, Barred Oval pattern, Fenton, ca 1985-85, 7½"..**35.00**

Basket, bird of paradise pattern, LE Smith, 1980, 13½" ...**40.00**

Basket, sq w/crystal rim, foot & handle, made in Italy, 5¾".....**75.00**

Bell, ruby overlay, decorative metal handle, Poland, 1970 ......**20.00**

Bell, Victorian girl, Imperial, ca 1980s, 4" **95.00**

Bowl, fruit; Grape, w/pedestal, unknown maker, 8¼x10" **35.00**

Bowl, ruffled rim, Blenko, 9½" **25.00**

Box, heart-shaped, bird in flight design on lid, Mosser, 1980,3" **8.00**

Butter dish, pressed star pattern, w/cover, A A Imports, 1991, 5" **20.00**

Cake plate, water lilies design in silver overlay, Cambridge, 14½" **95.00**

Candle holder, Cape Cod, w/hurricane globe, Avon, 1985, 11" **45.00**

Candlesticks, lustre cut-prism design, Cambridge, 1930s, 10" **80.00**

Candy dish, leaf form, Blenko, ca 1970s-80s, 6¾" **10.00**

Centerpiece bowl, plain w/gold edge & rim, footed, Italian, 1950, 16" **250.00**

Coaster, Bubble (underside), Duncan & Miller, 1930, 3½" **20.00**

Decanter, milk glass stopper, w/base & handle, made in Italy, 17" **80.00**

Figurine, baby bootie w/Daisy & Button pattern, Summit, 1980, 4¼" **15.00**

Figurine, Colonial man, Boyd's Crystal Art Glass, 1990, 4¼" **15.00**

Gravy pitcher, dophin design w/dolphin finial, 2-pc, ca 1991 ....**25.00**

Molasses jug, w/crystal handle, Blenko, 1980, 5½" **20.00**

Open salt, tulip form, Summit, 1980, 1" **6.00**

Paperweight, tiger form, Imperial Glass, 1980, 8" **200.00**

Pie server, Cape Cod, red handle, Avon, ca 1981-84, 8" **15.00**

Pitcher, English Hobnail pattern, footed w/lip, Westmoreland, 38-oz **150.00**

Plate, pineapple pattern w/floral decor, Indiana Glass, 1970, 8" **15.00**

Salt & pepper shakers, metal caps, LG Wright, ca 1970s, 3½"..**40.00**

Tray, Regina pattern, Paden City, 1936, 13¼x7¾" **40.00**

Tumbler, Georgian pattern, handmade, Imperial Glass, 1930, 9-oz.....................................**10.00**

Vase, daffodil w/ruffled edge, Fenton, 1989, 7¾" **35.00**

Vase, painted floral decor, Venetian, 1982, 11½" **55.00**

Vase, pedestal foot, unknown pattern and maker, 9", $30.00. (Photo courtesy Naomi Over)

Vase, Victorian style, unknown makers, ca early 1900s, 12" **60.00**

Water glass, silver stripe accents, Macbeth & Evans, 8-oz...**10.00**

Red Wing

Taking their name from the location in Minnesota where they located in the late 1870s, the Red Wing Company produced a variety of wares, all of which are today considered noteworthy by pottery and dinnerware collectors. Their early stoneware lines, Cherry Band and Sponge Band (Gray Line), are especially valuable and often fetch prices of several hundred dollars per piece on today's market. Production of dinnerware began in the '30s and continued until the pottery closed in 1967. Some of their more popular lines — all of which were hand painted — were Bob White, Lexington, Tampico, Normandie, Capistrano, and Random Harvest. Commercial artware was also produced. Perhaps the ware most easily associated with Red Wing is their Brushware line, unique in its appearance and decoration. Cattails, rushes, florals, and similar nature subjects are 'carved' in relief on a stoneware-type body with a matt green wash its only finish.

For more information, we recommend *Collector's Encyclopedia of Red Wing Art Pottery* and *Red Wing Art Pottery, Book II,* by B.L. Dollen. To learn about their stoneware production, refer to *Red Wing Stoneware, An Identification and Value Guide,*

and *Red Wing Collectibles,* both by Dan and Gail de Pasquale and Larry Peterson. All are published by Collector Books.

Artware

Vase, #1102, from $40.00 to $50.00.

Bowl, boat shape, pink, #H18, 11½", from $42 to...........**60.00**
Bowl, brown w/orange interior, flat, #414, 7", from $32 to.......**44.00**
Bowl, flecked Zephyr Pink, spiked edges, #1483, 18", from $48 to...................**60.00**
Bowl, Mandarin, green, 8-sided, #331, 8x12", from $52 to...............................**65.00**
Bowl, pink, sq w/incurvate sides, #1037, 7½", from $30 to...............................**38.00**
Candle holders, white, scalloped edges, #1619, 4½", pr, from $30 to.............................**40.00**
Compote, ivory, pedestal foot, #M1597, 7", from $30 to...**36.00**
Jardiniere, leaf design, Walnut Green, 9x10", from $90 to.............**130.00**
Planter, lamb figural, blue, 6½", from $110 to.................**145.00**

Planter, swan shape, matt white, #259, 6", from $42 to **55.00**

Urn, pitcher; Vintage, ivory w/brown wipe, #616, 11", from $90 to **125.00**

Vase, blue, swirled decor, #952, 6", from $48 to **60.00**

Vase, Brushed Ware, bronze tan, 7", from $65 to................**90.00**

Vase, coral w/tan interior, #445, 8", from $72 to................**85.00**

Vase, cornucopia; blue w/yellow interior, #1097, 5¾", from $36 to **48.00**

Vase, cornucopia; ivory w/brown wash, #1098, 8½", from $42 to **58.00**

Vase, Egyptian; Glazed Ware, light green, #154, from $110 to **135.00**

Vase, fan; ivory w/green interior, #982, 7½", from $36 to ..**48.00**

Vase, horn of plenty, white, #K8, 12", from $46 to..............**58.00**

Vase, Indian, Ocean Green, scalloped top, #291, 5½", from $55 to **72.00**

Vase, ivory, contoured, #M1447, 12½", from $28 to...........**36.00**

Vase, lustre blue w/coral interior, purple leaf decor, #1105, 8" **84.00**

Vase, Magnolia, ivory w/brown wash, handled, #1012, 7", from $58 to **75.00**

Vase, Magnolia, ivory w/brown wash, tapered, #1213, 9", from $72 to **95.00**

Vase, petal shape, salmon w/yellow interior, #1625, 10", from $44 to **56.00**

Vase, pink w/ivory interior, angels & floral decor, #1159, 8", $72 to **86.00**

Vase, shell shaped, orange w/white interior, #1295, 7", from $36 to **48.00**

Vase, vory w/green interior, #1056, 9½", from $84 to.............**98.00**

Wall pocket, ivory w/brown wash, #1630, 7", from $125 to **175.00**

Wall pocket, sconce (shell) shape, pink w/ivory interior, #1254, 7"......................................**95.00**

Water cooler, Tampico, 2-gal, w/stand, from $600 to..**750.00**

Dinnerware

Blossom Time, cup, decor inside, from $6 to........................**8.00**

Blossom Time, plate, dinner; 10½", from $20 to **26.00**

Blossom Time, saucer, from $6 to **8.00**

Bob White, cookie jar, w/lid, from $125 to..........................**175.00**

Bob White, plate, dinner; 11", from $22 to **32.00**

Bob White, salt & pepper shakers, bird shape, pr, from $42 to...................................**48.00**

Bob White, water cooler, 2-gal, w/stand, from $625 to..**775.00**

Brittany, plate, dinner; 10", from $18 to **22.00**

Capistrano, plate, dinner; 10½", from $22 to **26.00**

Hearthside, relish tray, metal center handle, from $26 to..**38.00**

Iris, plate, dinner; 10½" sq, from $30 to **35.00**

Lotus, cup, decor inside, from $6 to **8.00**

Lotus, plate, salad; 7", from $8 to **12.00**

Orleans, French casserole, $45.00.

Pink Spice, bowl, buffet; irregular shape, 10½", from $46 to ..**54.00**

Plain, cruet, oil; yellow w/white interior, slight swirl, 4", $40 to **55.00**

Plain, salt & pepper shakers, teapot shape, blue, 3", pr, from $22 to **30.00**

Random Harvest, casserole, w/lid, from $36 to **40.00**

Random Harvest, gravy boat, from $25 to **30.00**

Random Harvest, relish tray, from $26 to **34.00**

Spruce, plate, dinner; 10½", from $30 to **35.00**

Village Green, beverage server, w/lid, 8-cup, from $30 to ..**40.00**

Village Green, mug, from $18 to **25.00**

Village Green, pitcher, 10-cup, from $32 to **46.00**

Village Green, sugar bowl, w/lid, from $18 to **20.00**

White & Turquoise, bean pot, w/lid, wire coiled handle, 2-qt, $42 to **48.00**

Willow Wind, plate, dinner; 10½", from $26 to **30.00**

Restaurant China

Restaurant china is specifical-ly designed for use in commercial food service. Not limited to restaurants, this dinnerware is used on planes, ships, and trains as well as hotel, railroad, and airport dining rooms. Churches, clubs, department stores, and drug stores also put it to good use.

The popularity of good quality American-made heavy gauge vitrified china with traditional styling is very popular today. Some collectors look for transportation system top-marked pieces, others may prefer those with military logos, etc. It is currently considered fashionable to serve home-cooked meals on mismatched top-marked hotel ware, adding a touch of nostalgia and remembrances of elegant times past. For a more thorough study of the subject, we recommend *Restaurant China, Identification & Value Guide for Restaurant, Airline, Ship & Railroad Dinnerware, Volume 1* and *Volume 2,* by Barbara Conroy (Collector Books). She is listed in the Directory under California.

Ashtray, Amelio's, white & brown trim, Econo-Rim (Syracuse), 1955 .... **18.00**

Ashtray, Diplomat Resorts & Country Club, Royal Copenhagen, 1940s **12.00**

Ashtray, Inter-Continental Hotels, ivory w/gold, Apilco, 1980 .... **8.00**

Ashtray, President Hotel, white w/blue trim, Noritake, 1970s **12.50**

Ashtray, Seaview Country Club, cream w/gold, Hall, 1950s, 5½".....................**15.00**

Ashtray, Trans-Europe Express (RR), white w/TEE, Langenthal, 1976............**30.00**

Baker, Hotel Dennis, open, Haviland, 1914, 7" L......**30.00**

Celery dish, The Montauk, white w/logo, Greenwood, 1902, 11¾" L **80.00**

Cup, Hyatt Hotels, white w/brown band & logo, Villeroy & Boch, 1980s.................................**18.00**

Cup, Star Clippers, Star Flyer pattern, Victoria, 1990s......**20.00**

Cup & saucer, AD; Canadian Pacific RR, Calgary, Minton, minimum value............**375.00**

Cup and saucer, AD; Fairmont Hotel (San Francisco), Syracuse, 1951 date code. (Photo courtesy Barbara Conroy)

Mug, Denver & Rio Grande Western RR, peach lustre, Fire-King, 1960s **12.50**

Mug, Dunkin' Donuts, white w/brown & black, Bel-Terr, 1980s.................................**35.00**

Mug, Sear's Restaurant, Syracuse, 1973 ....**16.00**

Plate, Al Dowd's, white w/red trim, Caribe, 1964, 7" **15.00**

Plate, Anvil Club, Syralite (Syracuse), 1967, 9¾"....**16.00**

Plate, Apostleship of the Sea, white w/logo, Sampsonite, 1987, 6"............................**20.00**

Plate, Clinton Hotel, white w/blue, Grindley Hotel Ware, 1930s, 9".......................................**15.00**

Plate, Fallen Leaf Lodge, white w/green leaf, Buffalo, 1930s, 6¾"....................................**18.00**

Plate, fruit; Hotel Astor, Haviland, ca 1910............................**40.00**

Plate, ivory w/multicolored lines, Iroquois, 1960s, 8".........**12.00**

Plate, Lee Seymour's Fisherman's Wharf, Syracuse, 1972, 11½"...**35.00**

Plate, Little Joe's, cream w/logo, Tepco, 1960s, 7" **24.00**

Plate, menu; Houston Club, Shenango, 1958, 10¾"...**30.00**

Plate, Miramar Hotel, logo on white, rose border, Mayer, 1940s, 7¼" **22.00**

Plate, Montgomery Ward, white w/blue trim & logo, 1972, Syracuse, 9"....................**20.00**

Plate, San Jose's Prime Rib, tan w/logo, Tepco, 1960s, 8¾" **25.00**

Plate, Santa Barbara Yacht Club, white w/logo, Jackson, 1979, 5¼"...................................**15.00**

Plate, Schuler's Family Restaurants, tan, Iroquois, 1950s, 5½" **18.00**

Plate, service; Condado Beach Hotel, Iroquois, 1950s, 10¾"............................**40.00**

Plate, service; Surfside Hotel, center logo, Iroquois, 1930s, 10¾" **50.00**

Plate, Washington State University, logo on white, Laughlin, 1993, 11" **24.00**

Sauce boat, Adam, green transfer, Buffalo, 1932.................**18.00**

Sauce boat, Panelli's, Toltec by Walker, 1953.................**22.00**

Sugar bowl, Autumn Leaves pattern, w/lid, Shenango, 1940s..........................**24.00**

Sugar bowl, Plaza, knob finial, Hall #331, 1950s............**25.00**

Sugar packet holder, Golden Glo, Hall #716, 1950s............**10.00**

Tankard, The Berghoff, Hall #592, 1960s, 14-oz...................**24.00**

Teapot, aqua blue, w/lid, marked Chefsware by HF Coors, 1960s.............................**24.00**

Teapot, Chesapeake & Ohio RR, Geo Washington, Buffalo, 1932, minimum............**600.00**

Tray, Atlantic Hotel, white w/green, Hutschenreuther, 1920s, 4½" L...................**10.00**

Tray, Hotel Bologna, white w/brown image, Ridgway, 1960s, 4" sq.....................**9.00**

Tray, Parliament Hotel, white w/logo, Wedgwood, 1977, 4½" dia.....................................**8.00**

Rock 'n Roll

Concert posters, tour books, magazines, sheet music, and other items featuring rock 'n roll stars from the '50s up to the present are today being sought out by collectors who appreciate this type of music and like having these mementos of their favorite performers around to enjoy.

See also Elvis Presley; Records.

Abba, annual, 1978, NM **25.00**

Alice Cooper, LP album, Pretties for You, NM....................**25.00**

Alice Cooper, resin figure, Lil' Goblins, 6".......................**35.00**

Alice Cooper, shot glass, Lace & Whiskey on clear glass ..**45.00**

Animals/Pink Floyd, concert tour program, 1977................**50.00**

Bee Gees, puzzle set, On Stage, sealed.............................**24.00**

Bobby Sherman, photo, pointing, color, 8x10"......................**10.00**

Bobby Sherman, sheet music, Goin' Home, photo cover, NM **22.50**

Bobby Vinton, poster, Surf Party, 1-sheet, 1964, NM..........**70.00**

Dave Clark 5, lobby card, Having a Wild Weekend, 11x14", EX..**22.00**

David Cassidy, Colorforms, Partridge Family, 1972, NM (EX box)..........................**80.00**

David Cassidy, photo badge, 1970s, 3", M (sealed)......**24.00**

Dick Clark, writing tablet, 1950s, EX, $20.00.

Dick Clark, picture patch, 1950s, MOC **20.00**

Everly Brothers, guitar pick, photo, 5-point star cutout, M **20.00**

Everly Brothers, tour book, 1985, NM.................................**24.00**

Grateful Dead, poster, Fox Theater, St Louis MO, 1973, 17½x23", EX.................**275.00**

Herman's Hermits, poster, Hold On!, 1966, 41x27", EX....................................**32.00**

KISS, backstage pass, pictures band wearing makeup.....**9.00**

KISS, belt buckle, logo on brass, 1970s..............................**28.00**

KISS, guitar pick, Psycho Circus, Gene, Paul or Ace, ea **15.00**

KISS, lighter, KISS Army, Zippo, w/litho sleeve..................**22.50**

KISS, magazine, Rock Scene, September, 1978............**12.00**

KISS, masks, full head, rubber w/lifelike hair, set of 4 ....**130.00**

KISS, necklace, gold letters, vending machine item.............**4.00**

KISS, pass, Revenge, laminated, 1992 ....**15.00**

KISS, pens (far right and far left), MOC, $80.00 each; pencils (center), set of four, MIP, $60.00. (Photo courtesy Bob Gottuso)

KISS, program, 1984 World Tour............................**50.00**

KISS, slippers, Peter Criss, pr, w/original Spencer Gifts tag.............................**30.00**

Marie Osmond, Hair Care Set, Gordy, 1976, MOC.........**25.00**

Moby Grape, Country Joe & Fish, poster, Mari Tepper, 1968, 21x14", NM **90.00**

Monkees, book, Monkees Go Mod, softcover, 1967, EX........**12.00**

Monkees, fan club kit complete w/magazine, in folder, 1967, EX, $75 to.....................**100.00**

Monkees, puzzle, Fairchild, 340 pcs, 1967, NMIB **60.00**

Partridge Family, bus, Johnny Lightning, diecast metal, 3"...............................**10.00**

Paul McCartney & Wings, book, Tony Jasper, hardcover w/dust jacket, EX...........**20.00**

Ricky Nelson, photo, 1960s, double-matted to fit 10x12" frame **15.00**

Ricky Nelson, Picture Patch, 1950s, MOC....................**20.00**

Rolling Stones, backstage pass, from $5 to **10.00**

Rolling Stones, blue jeans jacket, '98 Tour, NM..................**90.00**

Rolling Stones, book, Ultimate Guide Book, 1962-65, EX....................**45.00**

Rolling Stones, concert ticket, New York, 1972, unused......**165.00**

Rolling Stones, mobile, Voodoo Lounge, poster board material, complete **47.50**

Rolling Stones, poster, Altamont, 14x22", M, from $10 to **20.00**

Rolling Stones, poster, Oakland Stadium, 1989, 31x23", from $20 to **50.00**

Rolling Stones, poster, Veterans Stadium, 1997, M, from $15 to **25.00**

Rolling Stones, rub-off transfers, 27 lip logos, unopened **5.00**

Rolling Stones, song book, Exile on Main St, 102 pages, 1972, EX **38.00**

Rolling Stones, T-shirt, Flat Tongue tour, M, from $15 to **30.00**

Rolling Stones, T-shirt, Voodoo Lounge, M, from $15 to....**25.00**

Rolling Stones, tie, Some Girls, embossed silk, by RM Style, M...................................**100.00**

Rolling Stones, tour book, 1972..**22.50**

Rolling Stones, wall clock, Musidor BV Clock Works, MIB................................**40.00**

Three Dog Night, poster, 1970s, 22x14", EX.....................**30.00**

Rooster and Roses

Rooster and Roses is a quaint and provincial line of dinnerware made in Japan from the '40s and '50s. The rooster has a yellow breast with black crosshatching, a brown head, and a red crest and waddle. There are full-blown roses, and the borders are yellow with groups of brown diagonals. Several companies seem to have made the line, which is very extensive — more than seventy-five shapes are known. For a complete listing of the line, see *Garage Sale and Flea Market Annual* (Collector Books).

Ashtray, rectangular, 3x2" **9.50**

Ashtray, sq, lg, from $35 to..**40.00**

Biscuit jar, w/wicker handle, from $65 to..............................**95.00**

Bowl, cereal; from $14 to......**25.00**

Bowl, 8", from $45 to............**55.00**

Butter dish, ¼-lb, from $20 to ..**25.00**

Candy dish, w/3-dimensional leaf handle, from $25 to........**45.00**

Canister set, sq, 4-pc, from $100 to **150.00**

Carafe, no handle, w/stopper lid, 8", from $65 to................**85.00**

Casserole dish, w/lid, from $65 to **85.00**

Chamberstick, saucer base, ring handle, from $25 to........**35.00**

Cigarette box w/2 trays, hard to find, from $65 to **75.00**

Coffee grinder, minimum value......................**150.00**

Cookie jar, ceramic handles, from $85 to............................**100.00**

Creamer & sugar bowl on rectangular tray, from $65 to ..**75.00**

Cruets, oil & vinegar; sq, lg, pr, from $30 to **35.00**

Cup and saucer, $25.00; dinner plate, from $25.00 to $35.00; side salad, crescent shape, hard to find, from $50.00 to $60.00. (Photo courtesy Jacki Elliot)

Demitasse pot, w/6 cups & saucers, minimum value **175.00**

Egg cup on tray, from $35 to ..**45.00**

Flowerpot, buttress handles, 5", from $35 to **45.00**

Instant coffee jar, spoon-holder tube on side, rare...........**45.00**

Jam jar, attached underplate, from $35 to **45.00**

Lamp, pinup, made from match holder or salt box, ea, from $75 to.............................**100.00**

Match holder, wall mount, from $65 to..............................**85.00**

Mug, round bottom, med, from $20 to **25.00**

Napkin holder, from $30 to ..**40.00**

Pitcher, 3½", from $15 to......**20.00**

Platter, 12", from $55 to.......**80.00**

Relish tray, 3 wells w/center handle, from $55 to..............**65.00**

Salt box, wooden lid..............**60.00**

Snack tray w/cup, oval, 2-pc, minimum value **45.00**

Toast holder, minimum value ..**75.00**

Wall pocket, scalloped top, bulbous bottom, from $55 to....................................**65.00**

Roselane Sparklers

A line of small figures with a soft shaded finish and luminous jewel eyes was produced during the late 1950s by the Roselane Pottery Company who operated in Pasadena, California, from the late 1930s until possibly the 1970s. The line was a huge success. Twenty-nine different models were made, including elephants, burros, raccoons, fawns, dogs, cats, and fish. Not all pieces are marked, but some carry an incised 'Roselane Pasadena, Calif.,' or 'Calif. U.S.A'; others may have a paper label.

Angelfish, 4½", from $20 to..**25.00**

Basset hound, sitting, 4", from $15 to **18.00**

Basset hound pup, 2", from $12 to **15.00**

Bulldog, fierce expression, looking right, 2", from $12 to **15.00**

Bulldog, sitting, slender body, looking right, 6" **25.00**

Cat, Siamese, sitting, facing forward, jeweled collar, 7", from $40 to **50.00**

Cat, sitting, head turned right, tail out behind, from $25 to ..**28.00**

Chihuahua, sitting, left paw raised, looking straight ahead, 6½".................................**28.00**

Cocker spaniel, 4½" **20.00**

Deer, standing, head turned right, looking downward, 5½"..**25.00**

Deer w/antlers, standing, jeweled collar, 4½", from $22 to..**28.00**

Elephant, sitting on hind quarters, 6".....................................**28.00**

Elephant, trunk raised, striding, jeweled headpiece, 6".....**28.00**

Fawn, legs folded under body, 4x3½"..............................**25.00**

Fawn, upturned head, 4x3½" ..**20.00**

Fawn, 4½x1½"......................**20.00**

Kangaroo mama w/babies, from $40 to.............................**45.00**

Kitten, sitting, 1¾" **12.00**

Owl, very stylized, lg round eyes, teardrop-shaped body, lg.................................**25.00**

Owl, 3½" **15.00**

Owl, 5¼" **25.00**
Owl, 7" **30.00**
Owl baby, 2¼", from $12 to..**15.00**
Pig, lg..................................**25.00**

Pouter pigeon, 3½", $20.00. (Photo courtesy Lee Garmon)

Raccoon, standing, 4½", from $20 to **25.00**
Whippet, sitting, 7½", from $25 to..................................**28.00**

Rosemeade

Novelty items made by the Wapheton Pottery Company of North Dakota from 1941 to 1960 are beginning to attract collectors of American pottery. Though smaller items (salt and pepper shakers, figurines, trays, etc.) are readily found, the larger examples are scarce and can be very expensive. The name of the novelty ware, 'Rosemeade,' is indicated on the paper labels (many of which are still intact) or by the ink stamp.

Ashtray, chickadee at side of green tray, 4 rests, 5", from $200 to **250.00**

Ashtray, mallard on side, North Dakota, green, 5".........**225.00**
Bank, black bear, 3¼x5¾", minimum value **400.00**
Candy dish, shell form, white & ice blue, 2¾x4½"..................**50.00**
Cotton dispenser, rabbit, 4¾x2½", from $150 to.................**200.00**
Covered dish, hen on basket, black & white, 5½x5½", $350 to **400.00**
Figurine, cock strutting, white, red comb/green base, 3¾", $125 to..........................**150.00**
Figurine, frog, solid, green w/black spots, 1¼x1¼", from $150 to **175.00**
Figurine, potato, 1½x2½", from $100 to..........................**125.00**
Jam jar, barrel w/strawberries finial, 5".......................**150.00**
Pitcher, 2-color swirl, 3", from $150 to..........................**200.00**
Planter, circus horse, light blue, 5x6½"............................**100.00**
Plaque, lg-mouth bass, 3½x6", from $300 to.................**500.00**
Salt & pepper shakers, bear cubs, 3½", 3", pr......................**75.00**

Salt and pepper shakers, standing pigs, 3¾", from $125.00 to $150.00 for the pair. (Photo courtesy Darlene Hurst Dommel)

Salt & pepper shakers, cocks fighting, mini, 1", 1½", pr ...**100.00**

Salt & pepper shakers, ducklings, black, 2¼", 2½", pr.......**100.00**

Salt & pepper shakers, flamingos on nests, 3", 3¾", pr, $200 to **250.00**

Spoon rest, tulip, many colors, 5", ea, from $80 to **100.00**

TV Lamp, panther, forest green or black, 7x13", minimum value.............................**700.00**

Wall pocket, deer, aqua or pink, 5", from $40 to **60.00**

Roseville

This company took its name from the city in Ohio where they operated for a few years before moving to Zanesville in the late 1890s. The're recognized as one of the giants in the industry, having produced many lines in art pottery from the beginning to the end of their production. Even when machinery took over many of the procedures once carefully done by hand, the pottery they produced continued the fine artistry and standards of quality the company had always insisted upon.

Several marks were used along with paper label. The very early art lines often carried an applied ceramic seal with the name of the line under a circle containing the words Rozane Ware. From 1910 until 1928 an Rv mark was used. Paper labels were common from 1914 until 1937. From 1932 until closure in 1952, the mark was Roseville in script or R USA, Pieces marked RRP Co Roseville, Ohio, were not made by Roseville Pottery but by Robinson Ransbottom of Roseville, Ohio. Don't be confused. There are many jardinieres and pedestals in a brown and green blended glaze that are being sold at flea markets and antique malls as Roseville that were actually made by Robinson Ransbottom as late as the 1970s and 1980s. That isn't to say they don't have some worth of their own, but don't buy them for old Roseville.

If you'd like to learn more about the subject, we recommend *The Collector's Encyclopedia of Roseville Pottery Revised Edition, Vols. 1* and *2,* by Sharon and Bob Huxford and Mike Nickel. Mr. Nickel is listed in the Directory under Michigan.

Note: Watch for reproductions! They're flooding the market right now; be especially wary at flea markets and auctions. These pieces are usually marked only Roseville (no USA), though there are exceptions. These have a 'paint by number' style of decoration with little if any attempt at blending.

See Clubs and Newsletters for information concerning *Rosevilles of the Past* newsletter.

Apple Blossom, bowl vase, #342-6, blue, 6", from $325 to ..**375.00**

Artwood, planter set, #1051-6, 2 side sections, ea 4", & 6" $110 to **125.00**

Baneda, vase, #603, green, 4½",
from $625 to **675.00**
Baneda, vase, #603, pink, 4½",
from $525 to **625.00**
Bittersweet, basket, #809-8, 8½",
from $200 to **250.00**
Bittersweet, vase, #884-8, 8", from
$150 to **175.00**

**Blackberry, vase, 5", $440.00. (Photo
courtesy Jackson's Auctions)**

Blackberry, vase, 6", from $550
to **600.00**
Bleeding Heart, candlesticks,
#1139-4½, blue, pr, from $275
to **325.00**
Bushberry, double cornucopia,
#115-8, blue, 6", from $200
to **225.00**
Bushberry, vase, #157-8, blue, 8",
from $250 to **275.00**
Bushberry, vase, #157-8, orange,
8", from $200 to **225.00**
Carnelian I, vase, w/handles, 10",
from $200 to **250.00**
Clemana, vase, #112, blue, 7½",
from $450 to **500.00**
Clemana, vase, #112, tan, 7½",
from $300 to **350.00**
Clematis, center bowl, #456-6,
green or brown, 9", from $125
to **150.00**

Clematis, vase, #102-6, blue, 6½",
from $110 to **130.00**
Dahlrose, bud vase, #78, 8", from
$175 to **225.00**
Dogwood II, bowl, 2½x7", from
$125 to **150.00**
Donatello, basket, 7½", from $350
to **400.00**
Donatello, bowl, 6", from $75 to..**95.00**
Early Pitchers, Grape, natural col-
ors, 6", from $150 to **175.00**
Early Pitchers, Landscape, 7½",
from $150 to **175.00**
Florentine, vase, 8", from $175
to **225.00**
Foxglove, tray, #414, blue, 15",
from $300 to **350.00**
Foxglove, vase, #47-8, green/pink,
8½", from $275 to **325.00**
Freesia, vase, #212-8, blue, 8",
from $200 to **225.00**
Freesia, vase, #212-8, green, 8",
from $225 to **250.00**
Fuchsia, vase, #898-8, blue, 8",
from $475 to **525.00**
Futura, jardiniere, #616, 6", from
$550 to **650.00**
Futura, vase, #382, 7", from $375
to **450.00**
Gardenia, vase, #686-10, 10½",
from $225 to **250.00**
Hyde Parke, ashtray, Made in
USA, #1900, 8½", from $30
to **40.00**
Imperial I, compote, 6½", from
$175 to **225.00**
Iris, vase, #924-9, pink or tan, 10",
from $350 to **400.00**
Ivory II, vase, w/handles,
stepped wide base, 7", from
$75 to **95.00**
Jonquil, vase, w/handles, #529, 8",
from $500 to **600.00**

Juvenile, Baby's Plate, rolled edge, various decals, 8", ea, from $250 ....**300.00**

Juvenile, Goose creamer, 4", from $450 to **500.00**

Juvenile, Rabbit custard, 2½", from $300 to **350.00**

Juvenile, Skinny puppy plate, 8", from $125 to **150.00**

La Rose, jardiniere, 6½", from $125 to **175.00**

La Rose, wall pocket, 12", from $350 to **400.00**

Laurel, vase, #676, gold, 10", from $550 to **650.00**

Lotus, planter, #L9-4, 3½x4", from $100 to **125.00**

Luffa, vase, #689, green or brown, 8", from $650 to **750.00**

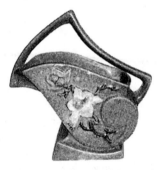

Magnolia, basket, 3386-12, from $275.00 to $325.00.

Magnolia, vase, #180-6, 6", from $95 to **110.00**

Magnolia, vase, #91-8, 8", from $125 to **150.00**

Ming Tree, basket, #509-12, 13", from $275 to **300.00**

Ming Tree, conch shell, #563, 8½", from $90 to **110.00**

Mostique, vase, 6", from $175 to **225.00**

Peony, tray, 8", from $75 to..**100.00**

Peony, vase, #58-14, 14", from $300 to **350.00**

Peony, wall pocket, 8", from $400 to **450.00**

Persian, jardiniere, creamware w/pastel floral, 8", from $450 to **500.00**

Pine Cone, basket, #353-11, green, 11", from $425 to **475.00**

Pine Cone, vase, #850-14, blue, 14½", from $1,500 to..**1,750.00**

Pine Cone, vase, #850-14, green, from $650 to **750.00**

Raymor, covered butter dish, #181, 7½", from $75 to **100.00**

Raymor, gravy boat, #190, 9½", from $30 to **35.00**

Raymor, pitcher, #189, 10", from $100 to **150.00**

Raymor, vegetable bowl, #160, 9", from $30 to **40.00**

Rosecraft Hexagon, vase, blue, 6", from $450 to **500.00**

Rosecraft Hexagon, vase, 6", brown, from $250 to **300.00**

Rozane (1917), vase, 8", from $150 to **175.00**

Silhouette, vase, #780-6, 6", from $90 to **110.00**

Silhouette, vase, #783, with nude, 7", from $400.00 to $500.00.

Snowberry, ewer, #1TK-15, green, from $525 to **575.00**

Snowberry, vase, #1UR-8, blue or pink, 8½", from $225 to...**250.00**

Sunflower, vase, 5", from $600 to **700.00**

Thorn Apple, bowl vase, #305-6, 6½", from $200 to **250.00**

Thorn Apple, wall pocket, 8", from $700 to..........................**800.00**

Water Lily, candlesticks, #1155, rose w/green, 5", pr, from $225 to...................................**250.00**

Water Lily, hanging basket, 9", from $375 to.................**425.00**

White Rose, double bud vase, #148, 4½", from $85 to ..**95.00**

White Rose, vase, #987-9, 9", from $150 to..........................**200.00**

White Rose, wall pocket, 8½", from $450 to..........................**500.00**

Wincraft, ewer, #218-18, 19", from $650 to..........................**750.00**

Zephyr Lily, vase, #202-8, blue, from $250 to.................**275.00**

Zephyr Lily, vase, #202-8, green, 8½", from $200 to **225.00**

Royal China

Several lines of the dinnerware made by Royal China (Sebring, Ohio) are very collectible. Their Currier and Ives pattern (decorated with scenes of early American life in blue on a white background) and the Blue Willow line are well known, but many of their others are starting to take off as well. Since the same blanks were used for all patterns, shapes and sizes will all be the same from line to line. Both Currier and Ives and Willow were made in pink as well as the more familiar blue, but pink is hard to find and not especially collectible in either pattern. See Clubs and Newsletters for information on Currier & Ives Dinnerware Collector Club.

Blue Willow

Ashtray, 5½"...........................**12.00**

Bowl, fruit nappy; 5½"............**6.50**

Bowl, vegetable; 10".............**22.00**

Creamer.................................**6.00**

Gravy boat............................**22.00**

Plate, dinner; 10" **8.00**

Platter, oval, 13" **32.00**

Salt & pepper shakers, pr **25.00**

Teapot, unmarked, $125.00.

Colonial Homestead

Bowl, cereal; 6¼"...................**15.00**

Bowl, soup; 8¼".....................**12.00**

Casserole, angle handles, w/lid..**75.00**

Cup & saucer..........................**5.00**

Pie plate................................**25.00**

Plate, chop; 12" **18.00**

Plate, salad; rare, 7¼"............**7.00**

Platter, serving; tab handles, 11"..............................**15.00**

Sugar bowl, w/lid **15.00**

Currier and Ives

Sugar bowl, flared top, no handle, $48.00; candle lamp, from $250.00 to $300.00; creamer, tall, round handle, $48.00. (The rare creamer and sugar bowl were restyled in the 1960s for Montgomery Ward.) (Photo courtesy Jack and Treva Hamlin)

Tab gravy and white tab underplate, rare, $125.00. (Photo courtesy Jack and Treva Gamblin)

Ashtray, 5½"...........................**18.00**
Bowl, fruit nappy; 5½"............**5.00**
Bowl, salad/cereal; tab handles, 6¼"...................................**48.00**
Bowl, vegetable; deep, 10"....**35.00**
Butter dish, Fashionable decal, ¼-lb, from $40 to................**55.00**
Casserole, tab handles, w/lid..**200.00**
Clock plate, blue numbers, 2 decals............................**200.00**
Creamer, angle handle **8.00**
Gravy boat, pour spout.........**20.00**
Gravy ladle............................**45.00**
Pie baker, 9 decals, 10", ea...**30.00**
Plate, calendar; ca 1969-86, ea ..**20.00**
Plate, chop; Rocky Mountains, 11½"..............................**65.00**

Plate, luncheon; 9"................**25.00**
Platter, oval, 13"...................**35.00**
Salt & pepper shakers, pr **30.00**
Sugar bowl, no handles, straight sides, w/lid.....................**30.00**
Tumbler, juice; glass, 5-oz, 3½", from $8 to.......................**12.00**
Tumbler, water; glass, 4¾" ..**12.00**

Memory Lane

Bowl, cereal; 6¼"...................**15.00**
Bowl, soup; 8½".....................**12.00**
Butter dish, ¼-lb..................**35.00**
Gravy boat.............................**18.00**
Gravy ladle, plain, white for all sets, from $45 to **65.00**
Plate, chop; 12" **25.00**
Plate, dinner..........................**8.00**
Plate, salad; rare, 7" **10.00**
Platter, tab handles, 10½"....**15.00**
Sugar bowl, w/lid **15.00**
Tumbler, juice; glass..............**9.00**

Old Curiosity Shop

Bowl, fruit nappy; 5½"............**5.00**
Bowl, vegetable; 9"................**22.00**
Casserole, w/lid.....................**90.00**
Cup & saucer...........................**5.00**
Plate, bread & butter; 6⅜".....**3.00**
Platter, tab handles, 10½"....**15.00**
Sugar bowl, w/lid **12.00**
Teapot..................................**115.00**

Royal Copley

Produced by the Spaulding China Company of Sebring, Ohio, Royal Copley is a line of novelty planters, vases, ashtrays, and wall pockets modeled after appealing puppy dogs, lovely birds, innocent-eyed children, etc. The decoration is airbrushed and underglazed; the line is of good quality and is well received by today's pottery collectors.

Joe Devine is the editor of *Royal Copley, Books I* and *II*, originally published by Leslie Wolfe; Mr. Devine is listed in the Directory under Iowa. See Clubs and Newsletters for information concerning *The Copley Currier*.

Bank, Farmer Pig, flat unglazed bottom, paper label, 5½"..**80.00**
Bank, Teddy Bear, black & white, 8"..................................**175.00**
Coaster, hunting dog scene, 4⅝"............................**40.00**
Creamer, rose & yellow w/green handles, raised letters, 3" **35.00**

Figurine, Blackamoor, 8½", from $24.00 to $26.00.

Figurine, blue sparrow, paper label, 5½"........................**65.00**
Figurine, cockatoo, white w/gold trim, 7" **40.00**
Figurine, finch, paper label, 5"..**40.00**
Figurine, kinglet, paper label, 3½"................................**28.00**

Figurine, pouter pigeon, paper label, 5¾"......................**25.00**
Figurine, wren, paper label, 3½" **32.00**
Figurines, hen & rooster, black & white, white base, paper label, pr **125.00**
Figurines, hen & rooster, teal colored breasts, paper label, med, pr **150.00**
Lamp base, cocker spaniel, sitting up begging, 10" **125.00**
Lamp base, Flower on Tree Trunk, paper label, 8½".............**60.00**
Lamp base, Thorup's Rose, paper label, 10½"......................**75.00**
Pitcher, Floral Beauty, green stamped bottom, 8"........**50.00**
Planter, bamboo, oval, paper label, 5¾" **15.00**
Planter, birdhouse w/bird, 8"..**110.00**
Planter, cockatiel, kidney shaped, paper label, 8½".............**60.00**
Planter, Island Lady, 8" **125.00**

Planter, kitten and boot, from $50.00 to $60.00.

Planter, poodle, white, sitting by basket, 7⅛"....................**50.00**
Planter/candle holder, star shaped, paper label, 4¾".............**25.00**
Plaque planter, Valentine, gold stamp, 5" **35.00**

Plate, Oriental boy w/basket on ground, raised letters, 7¾"..**25.00**

Vase, bamboo, cylindrical, paper label, 8"............................**20.00**

Vase, Carol's Corsage, cobalt w/green stamp on bottom, 7" **30.00**

Vase, cornucopia, gold stamped bottom, 8¼"....................**30.00**

Vase, floral decal, cylindrical, 8" **45.00**

Vase, Floral Elegance, raised letter mark, 8"....................**25.00**

Vase, Pome Fruit, green stamp, 8"................................**100.00**

Vase, stylized leaf decor, 8¼"...**15.00**

Royal Haeger, Haeger

Manufactured in Dundee, Illinois, Haeger produced some very interesting lines of artware, figural pieces, and planters. Their animal figures designed by Royal Hickman are well known. These were produced from 1938 through the 1950s and are recognized by their strong lines and distinctive glazes. For more information we recommend *Haeger Potteries Through the Years* by David Dilley (L-W Books); he is listed in the Directory under Indiana.

Ash bowl, #2057, ball shape, Brown Earth Graphic Wrap, 3¾x3¾"............................**20.00**

Ashtray, #R-449, leaf shape, Mauve Agate, 3½x4½x1"............**10.00**

Ashtray, #110-H, leaf shape, Jade Crackle, 13¾x7½x2½" ...**10.00**

Bookends, #R-132, ram figural, no marks, 8½x8x4", pr **150.00**

Bookends, R-475, Calla Lily, amber, 4½x4½x6⅛", pr..**75.00**

Bowl, #R-1402-C, stylized bird shape, Ebony Cascade, 17½x4x8"........................**60.00**

Bowl, #R-297, shell shape, chartreuse & Silver Spray, 14x7½x2¾" **30.00**

Bowl, #329-H, pheasant figural, Gold Tweed, 21¼x7¼x5½" **40.00**

Bowl, #373-H, Mandarin Orange, 15x7x4"...........................**20.00**

Bowl/planter, #R-293, violin, Mallow, 16x5¾x1⅝".......**60.00**

Candle holder, #243, Peach Agate, twisted stem, ca 1927, 7½x4¼"..........................**50.00**

Candle holder, #3277, bow tie, blue, ca 1947, 7½x3¼" ..**60.00**

Compote, #5, blue, 3-footed, ca 1914, no marks, 1⅞x6¼" dia......**35.00**

Cookie jar, #8198, Gleep, yellow-orange, head is lid **200.00**

Cookie jar, Keebler Treehouse, 11x7¼"........................**125.00**

Dish, #9-H, Mandarin Orange, w/lid, 7½x3¼" dia **40.00**

Figurine, #F-3, duck, head up, white, ca 1941, 5x3x2"...**10.00**

Figurine, #R-284, fish, amber, no marks, 4x3½".................**60.00**

Figurine, #R-379, bull, Mallow, ca 1941, 6½x12"................**500.00**

Figurine, #R-413, fawn, sitting, dark brown, ca 1949, no marks, 6½"......................**30.00**

Figurine, #R-777, cocker spaniel, recumbent, no marks, 3x5½" **40.00**

Figurine, #R-784, elephant, chartreuse & honey, 8¼x3¾x6" **40.00**

Figurine, #495, panther, ebony, 24½x5½".........**40.00**

Figurine, #502-H, bull fighter, Haeger Red, 13x5½"....**100.00**

Figurine, #612, rooster, red w/black & green accents, 11x8½".........**50.00**

Figurine, #649 & #650, doves (pigeons), 8½", 9½", pr ..**30.00**

Figurine, #3248, rabbit, blue, no marks, ca 1940s, 4x4x5"..**20.00**

Figurine, #8296, Toe Tapper w/violin, brown textured, 9¼x3¾".........**50.00**

Flower frog, #R-363, nude astride fish, yellow, 10", $100.00. (Photo courtesy David Dilley)

Goblet, #3928, gold, 1962-69, 9⅜".........**15.00**

Planter, #B3322, stork & baby bed, light pink, 7¾x5x10"......**20.00**

Planter, #R-182L, swan, Peach Agate, no marks, 7¾x3⅛x7½".........**35.00**

Planter, #R-281, sphere w/3 feather plumes, Mauve Agate, 5½x9".........**100.00**

Planter, #R-321, conch shell, Cloudy Blue, no marks, 4½x3x8".........**25.00**

Planter, #R-334, fan-tail Pouter Pigeon, Peach Agate, 9x8x8"..........**150.00**

Planter, #R-453, peacock figural, Mauve Agate, 9¾x3⅛x10"...**75.00**

Planter, #R-540, turtle, Green Agate, 13½x9½x4".........**45.00**

Planter, #R-3107, lamb, pink, no marks, 3x3½x4½".........**15.00**

Planter, #616, teddy bear beside drum, chartreuse, no mark, 7x3¼x5".........**15.00**

Planter, #3296, donkey & cart, blue, ca 1943, 5x3x3".....**15.00**

Planter, #5025, elephant, Playful Critter, Bennington Brown Foam, 6x9".........**30.00**

Planter, #5073, raccoon w/bucket, Bennington Brown Foam, 9x5½".........**40.00**

Planter/bookend, #R-641, stallion head, 5½x3½x8¾", pr....**50.00**

Sign, Haeger logo; brown, 8¾" L.........**25.00**

Table lighter, #899, Mandarin Orange, ribbed, foil label, 5x3" dia.........**15.00**

Table lighter, #8054, boot shape, Rust Brown, 4¼x2x9¼".........**15.00**

Vase, #R-1460, double leaf, Antique, no marks, 8¾x3¾x10¾".........**20.00**

Vase, #3220, rooster, white, no marks, 7x4x14".........**95.00**

Russel Wright Dinnerware

Dinnerware with a mid-century flair was designed by Russel Wright, who was at one time one of America's top industrial engineers.His most successful lines are American Modern, manufactured by the Steubenville Pottery Company (1939 – 1959), and Casual by Iroquois, introduced in 1944. He also introduced several patterns of melmac dinnerware and an interesting assortment of spun aluminum serving and decorative items such as candle holders, ice buckets, vases, and bowls.

To calculate values for items in American Modern, use the high end for Cedar, Black Chutney, and Seafoam; add 50% for Bean Brown, White, Glacier Blue, and Cantaloupe. For patterned lines, deduct 25%. In Casual, Brick Red, Cantaloupe and Aqua items go for about 200% more than any other color, while those in Avocado Yellow are priced at the low end of our range of suggested values. Other colors are in between, with Oyster, White, and Charcoal at the higher end of the scale. Glassware prices are given for Flair in Crystal and Pink; other colors are higher. Add 100% for Imperial Pinch in Cantaloupe. Ruby is very rare, and market value has not yet been established. For more information refer to *The Collector's Encyclopedia of Russel Wright Designs* by Ann Kerr (Collector Books).

Ashtray, White Clover, clover decor, from $40 to **45.00**
Bowl, baker; American Modern, from $40 to **50.00**
Bowl, cereal; Meladur, rare, from $10 to **12.00**

Bowl, covered vegetable; American Modern, from $65.00 to $85.00. (Photo courtesy Ann Kerr)

Bowl, fruit; Country Garden, from $100 to **115.00**
Bowl, fruit; Flair, #707 .... **18.00**
Bowl, lug soup; Residential, #706 .... **10.00**
Bowl, salad; Iroquois Casual, 52-oz, 10", from $35 to **45.00**
Bowl, Spun Aluminum, from $75 to **95.00**
Bowl, vegetable; Iroquois Casual, open, 36-oz, 8½", from $25 to **30.00**
Butter spreader, Pinch, from $100 to **110.00**
Casserole, Country Garden, hinged lid, from $350 to **400.00**
Casserole, Iroquois Casual, 2-qt, 8", from $35 to **45.00**

Coffeepot, after dinner; Iroquois Casual, 4½", from $100.00 to $125.00. (Photo courtesy Ann Kerr)

Coffeepot, Theme Formal, from $600 to............................**650.00**

Creamer, Everlast Gold Aluminite, from $50 to..**60.00**

Creamer, Flair, #711 ....**12.00**

Cup, Residential, #701 ....**6.00**

Fork & spoon, salad; Oceana, from $275 to............................**350.00**

Goblet, iced tea; Old Morgantown, 15-oz, 5¼", from $25 to..................**30.00**

Goblet, juice; Imperial Pinch, 6-oz, from $30 to......................**35.00**

Goblet, old fashioned; Imperial Twist, rare, from $35 to..**50.00**

Goblet, water; Imperial Flair, 11-oz, from $50 to **65.00**

Gravy boat, American Modern, from $30 to......................**40.00**

Ice bowl, Chase, w/tongs, #28002, from $175 to..................**185.00**

Ice fork, Spun Aluminum, from $75 to..............................**100.00**

Knife, Pinch, from $125 to .**150.00**

Ladle, Country Garden, from $125 to....................................**175.00**

Mug, Iroquois Casual, restyled, scarce, from $70 to.........**85.00**

Pitcher, beer; Devonshire, #90025, from $225 to..................**250.00**

Pitcher, cherry; Spun Aluminum, from $250 to.................**275.00**

Plate, bread & butter; American Modern, 6", from $6 to.....**8.00**

Plate, chop; White Clover, clover decor, 11", from $40 to **50.00**

Plate, compartment; Meladur, rare, 9½", from $15 to ...**18.00**

Plate, dinner; Knowles Esquire, 10¾", from $15 to...........**18.00**

Plate, dinner; White Clover, clover decor, 9¼", from $18 to..**20.00**

Plate, salad; Meladur, rare, 7¼", from $10 to.....................**12.00**

Plate, salad; Theme Formal, from $75 to............................**100.00**

Platter, Flair, #710 ....**28.00**

Relish, Oceana, 1-handled, from $500 to..........................**600.00**

Saucer, Knowles Esquire, from $4 to..**6.00**

Teapot, Knowles Esquire, from $250 to..........................**300.00**

Tumbler, Everlast Gold Aluminite, from $65 to..**75.00**

Tumbler, Flair, #715.............**18.00**

Salt Shakers

You'll probably see more salt and pepper shakers during your flea market forays than T-shirts and tube socks! Since the 1920s salt and pepper shakers have been popular souvenir items, and have been issued by companies to advertise their products. These advertising shakers are always good, and along with miniature shakers (1½" or under) are some of the more valuable. Of course, those that have a crossover interest into other categories of collecting — Black Americana, Disney, Rosemeade, Shawnee, Ceramic Arts Studios, etc. — are often expensive as well. There are many good books on the market; among them are *Florence's Big Book of Salt and Pepper Shakers* by Gene Florence; and *Salt & Pepper Shakers, Identification & Values, Books I, II, III,* and *IV,* by Helene Guarnaccia; All are published by Collector Books. See also

Advertising Collectibles; Ceramic Arts Studio; Character Collectibles; Disney; Gas Station Collectibles; Shawnee; Rosemeade.

Bahama police, ceramic, 1950s, 4⅜", pr **38.00**

Ballerina bears, ceramic, PY, 3½", pr......................................**35.00**

Baseball boy & girl, painted bisque, vintage, 2¾", pr **24.00**

Baseballs, pottery, realistic appearance, 1950s, 2½", pr.........**15.00**

Bowling ball & pin, ceramic, no mark, from $8 to.............**10.00**

Boxers, 1 punching, 2nd w/black eye, ceramic, pr, from $15 to ...**35.00**

Boy on cotton bale, ceramic, Parkcraft, 3½x2½", pr ...**250.00**

Bugs Bunny, shiny porcelain, Warner Bros, 1960s, pr...**165.00**

Candlesticks, ceramic, Arcadia, 1½", pr **30.00**

Cave man & woman, ceramic, unmarked, vintage, 4", pr..**60.00**

Chicks in a basket, unmarked, $12.00.
(Photo courtesy Helene Guarnaccia)

Cigarettes & lighter, ceramic, vintage, pr **26.00**

Circus horses, Salty & Pepper, ceramic, vintage, 4", pr..**24.00**

Coffee grinder & coffeepot, ceramic, no mark, pr, from $18 to...**22.00**

Doughnut & cup of coffee, ceramic, no mark, pr, from $15 to..**18.00**

Dutch boy & girl kissing, ceramic, pr, from $10 to **12.00**

Fingerhut truck, 2-pc truck, 1¾x3¾", EX....................**35.00**

Fish (realistic Muskellunge), Relco paper label, 5¾" L, pr **35.00**

Frying pan, orange plastic w/black trim, from $8 to..............**10.00**

Ft Pitt Beer bottles, glass, 3", pr, EX **20.00**

Groom carrying bride, ceramic, pr, from $10 to **45.00**

Gun & bullet, ceramic, no mark, vintage, 4", pr.................**24.00**

Ham slice in skillet, ceramic, no mark, from $18 to **22.00**

Horse heads, ceramic, Japan paper label, 3½", pr **15.00**

Humpty Dumpty w/bow tie, wood, Chrissy Japan, 1950-60s, 3⅜", pr, VG **14.00**

Kansas (state) & flower, ceramic, Victoria Ceramics, 1950s, pr.................................**24.00**

Louisiana (state) & cotton ball, ceramic, Parkcraft, 1950s, pr.................................**50.00**

Mammy & Chef, ceramic, black Japan ink stamp, older set, 2½", pr **55.00**

Mary Had a Little Lamb, ceramic, Relco (Japan), 1950s-60s, 4", pr.................................**45.00**

Oriental boy & girl, porcelain w/gold trim, Germany, 1¾", pr.................................**35.00**

Pandas (playful), ceramic, red Japan mark, 3½", pr......**12.00**

Peanuts, white hard plastic, Hong Kong, 1970s, 3½", pr........**9.00**

Pebbles & Bamm-Bamm, ceramic, Harry James, 4", pr.......**65.00**

Penguins, painted wood, 1950s, 2½x2", pr **12.00**

Photo album & camera, ceramic, no mark, pr, from $22 to **26.00**

Pineapple slices, ceramic, no mark, from $10 to..........**12.00**

Pixie heads, shiny porcelain, marked #6981 Japan, 3¼", pr **32.00**

Prager Beer bottles, glass w/metal tops, pr...........................**28.00**

Roller skates, multicolored plastic, pr, from $8 to **10.00**

Squirrel & acorn, pottery (heavy), no mark, 3½", pr............**10.00**

Stagecoach & saloon, ceramic, Arcadia, 1¼x1½", pr......**90.00**

Strawberries in white basket, ceramic, no mark, from $8 to......**10.00**

Tappan chefs, ceramic, Japan, 4¼", pr............................**25.00**

Thanksgiving, Pilgrim boy & girl, ceramic, Hallmark, 1970, pr........................**15.00**

Toaster & toast (stacking), ceramic, USA Pottery, 1950s, 3⅞", pr....................................**20.00**

Washington Monument, Bakelite, 4¼", pr **65.00**

Sad Sack, copyright George Baker, Norcrest, paper label, ca 1949, 4", from $250.00 to $300.00. (Photo courtesy Helene Guarnaccia)

Scarecrow couple, ceramic, vintage American, 3", pr.............**28.00**

Sea horses, ceramic, Leyden Arts, California, 4¼", pr.........**22.00**

Shlitz Beer bottles, glass w/paper labels, metal tops, 4¼", pr..........................**28.00**

Singing Towers, silver-tone metal, Lake Wales FL, 3¼", pr ..**55.00**

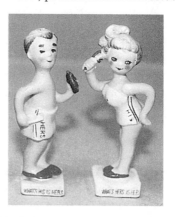

What's His Is Hers, from $45.00 to $55.00. (Photo courtesy Judy Posner)

Yosemite Sam, ceramic, Lego paper label, 1960s, pr..**125.00**

Zodiac girls, ceramic, red Japan ink stamp, 4½", pr.........**55.00**

Scottie Dogs

An amazing array of Scottie dog collectibles can be found in a wide range of prices. Collectors might choose to specialize in a particular area, or they may enjoy looking for everything from bridge tallies to original portraits or paintings. Most of the items are from the 1930s and 1940s. Many were used for advertising purposes; others are simply novelties. For further information we recommend *A Treasury of Scottie Dog Collectibles* by Candace Sten Davis and Patricia Baugh (there are three in the series by Collector Books).

Ashtray, metal/bronze wash, Aberdeen terrier, 4¼x3¼", $40 to 60.00

Bookends, cast iron, Hubley #263, 1940s, from $125 to 150.00

Candy dish, crystal glass/frosted, embossed Scottie dogs, 5½x5½x1" 25.00

Cookie cutter, aluminum, Purple Puma Cookie Co, 1990s, 2½x2½" 12.00

Covered dish, silver on frosted glass, 1940s, 3½x2⅞x2", $60 to 80.00

Frame, ceramic, dog sits beside, 1980s, 4x5", from $5.00 to $15.00.
(Photo courtesy Candace Sten Davis and Patricia Baugh)

Hanger, wood, marked Stupell Johnson, RI USA, 1990s, 16½x12" 20.00

Letter holder, tin, Scottie decal, 1940s, 6x4x6", from $30 to 50.00

Pencil box, cardboard/vinyl, blue w/white dog, 1940s, 11x4x2", $20 to 25.00

Pin, gold-tone metal/faux pearl, 1940s, 1", from $10 to....15.00

Planter, ceramic dog at mailbox, 1950s, 4x6x6", from $25 to 35.00

Salt & pepper shakers, ceramic, made in China, 1980s, 2¼", $12 to 15.00

Sherbet, milk glass, red Scotties, 1930s, 3½", from $20 to...25.00

Wall hook, pewter, dog w/shoe string in mouth, 1990s, 3x5", $15 to 25.00

Scouting Collectibles

Founded in England in 1907 by Major General Lord Baden-Powell, scouting remains an important institution in the life of young boys and girls everywhere. Recently scouting-related memorabilia has attracted a following, and values of many items have escalated dramatically in the last few years. Early first edition handbooks often bring prices of $100.00 and more. Vintage uniforms are scarce and highly valued, and one of the rarer medals, the Life Saving Honor Medal, is worth several hundred dollars to collectors.

Rolland J. Sayers is the author of *A Complete Guide to Scouting*

Collectibles; he is listed in the Directory under North Carolina.

Boy Scouts

Ashtray, National Jamboree, souvenir w/logo, 1973 ....**3.00**
Belt buckle, numbered for staff, limited edition, 1989......**45.00**
Belt buckle, 1985 World Jamboree, Max Silber issue of 125 ..**50.00**
Book, Lost Patrol, 1913, EX ..**12.00**

Calendar, Boy Scout with hand raised, oath behind him, Borden's Ice Cream, 1945, 33x16", EX, $45.00.

Cap, Official, red beret w/patch..**3.00**
Cards, Christmas; w/envelopes, 25 in red box, set.................**10.00**
Decal, Full 1st Class, silver, 1930s **3.00**
Figure, Boy Scout stalking, hollow, painted...........................**25.00**
First Aid kit, Johnson & Johnson, tin, sq, flip-lid type **8.00**
Game, Target Ball, marble shooting, 1920......................**125.00**
Kit, woodburning; w/wood & cord **20.00**
Pamphlet, Guide for Good Camping, BSA, 1954 ....**2.00**
Pin, Strengthen the Arms of Liberty, stick-back **3.00**

Postcard, Hero of the Day, scout w/flag, 1920 ....**7.00**
Record, Morse Code Made Easy, 1950, 78 rpm **15.00**
Tie bar, Eagle Scout, sterling, clip-on, logo.............................**5.00**

Girl Scouts

Armband, Senior Service Scout..**20.00**
Badge, Wing Scouting, cloth..**20.00**

Barrette, gold-tone, ca 1950s, 2¼" long, $9.00. (Photo courtesy John Shuman)

Camera, Falcon, 1940 ....**30.00**
Cup, collaspsible; Girl Scout, aluminum, 1950 ....**5.00**
Emblem, Girl Scout Hospital Aide **20.00**
Flags, signal; Official GSA, wooden handles, 1920 ....**15.00**
Handbook, Official Leaders; tan cover, 1920 ....**30.00**
Medal, Life Saving, bronze, 1916, Maltese Cross...............**200.00**
Patch, Treasurers, green twill, 1937 ....**10.00**
Pin, Mariner, 1940................**15.00**
Pin, Wing Scouting, 1941 .....**35.00**
Whistle, Official, cylinder type, 1920s.............................**20.00**

Sewing Items

Sewing notions from the 1800s and early 1900s, such as

whimsical figural tape measures, beaded satin pincushions, blown glass darning eggs, and silver and gold thimbles are pleasant reminders of a bygone era — ladies' sewing circles, quilting bees, and beautifully hand-stitched finery. With the emphasis collectors of today have put on figural ceramic items, the pincushions such as we've listed below are coming on strong. Most were made in Japan; some were modeled after the likenesses of Disney characters.

For more information we recommend *Sewing Tools & Trinkets, Volume I* and *II,* by Helen Lester Thompson (Collector Books).

Needle book, Century of Progress World's Fair, 1933 – 1934, M, $15.00. (Photo courtesy Helen Lester Thompson)

Book, Complete Book of Sewing, C Talbot, w/dust jacket, 1943, EX **15.00**
Booklet, Singer Zigzag Ideas, 1963, 23 pages, EX **7.00**
Box, red leather, hinged, 2 ivory punches, bodkin, ca 1900, 3x4", EX **50.00**
Buttonhook, steel w/bone handle, ca 1910 .... **3.00**

Darner, blown glass, cobalt ball on handle, 7" **165.00**
Darner, glass, hand blown, soft pink, 1920s, USA, 5½"...**55.00**
Darner, wood, maiden form, 1900s, USA, 5½" **60.00**
Darner, wood, mushroom shape, hollow for pins & needles, 1910s, 4½" **25.00**
Hemstitcher, Singer, w/picoting attachment, MIB **25.00**
Needle case, bending; Cambridge Chapel, 3½" **90.00**
Needle case, The Weekend; mountain lake scene, complete..**8.00**
Pin holders, ear of corn, velvet shucks, pearl-head pin kernels, pr **50.00**
Pincushion, bulldog shape, redware pottery, USA, 6" **200.00**
Pincushion, man's shoe, ceramic w/green velvet top, no mark, 5" **50.00**
Pincushion, pig, standing, pot metal, velvet cushion..... **70.00**

Scissors: sterling, USA, marked LSB, plain, 5", $50.00; gilt stork figure, Souvenir of 'Toledo,' enamelwork on beak, 1985 reproduction, $25.00; Sterling, double beading on handle, marked F&B, ca 1915, 4", $40.00. (Photo courtesy Helen Lester Thompson)

Scissors, steel, folding travel type, marked Foreign, open: 4"..**15.00**

Scissors, Woodrow Wilson & Lady Liberty decor, 1922........**50.00**

Tape measure, drum shape, painted flower garden, wood..**28.00**

Tape measure, girl in yellow dress, china, spring action, German..........................**110.00**

Tape measure, pig, pink w/red hair, ca 1920 ....**35.00**

Tape measure, standing flamingo, Florida souvenir, Japan..**28.00**

Tape measure, strawberry, pale red, celluloid, Japan **50.00**

Thimble, basketweave, 3 daisy chain bands, narrow size 9, Webster **31.00**

Thimble, floral band w/decor rim, CR cartouche, 14k gold, Simons, EX...................**100.00**

Thimble holder, Dutch girl, celluloid w/sterling thimble, German...........................**90.00**

Thimble holder, egg shape, turned wood, English, 1880s **40.00**

Thimble holder, perched bird, Black Forest Carvings, German, $90 to **120.00**

Thimble w/holder, Mauchline, red lining, Dove Castle image, 1x1½"...........................**160.00**

Thread winder, bone, concave, USA...............................**18.00**

Thread winder, scalloped edge, mother-of-pearl, England...........**48.00**

Shawnee

The novelty planters, vases, cookie jars, salt and pepper shakers, and 'Corn' dinnerware made by the Shawnee Pottery of Ohio are attractive, fun to collect, and still available at reasonable prices. The company operated from 1937 until 1961, marking their wares with 'Shawnee, U.S.A.,' and a number series, or 'Kenwood.'

Our advisor for this category is Rick Spencer; he is listed in the Directory under Utah. Refer to *Shawnee Pottery, An Identification and Value Guide,* by Jim and Bev Mangus (Collector Books) for more information. See also Cookie Jars. See Clubs and Newsletters for information concerning the Shawnee Pottery Collectors' Club.

Bowl, dessert; Valencia, 6"...**17.00**

Bowl, mixing/open baker; Lobster Ware, #917, 7"...............**45.00**

Butter dish, Lobster Ware, lobster finial, marked Kenwood USA 927 ....**110.00**

Carafe, Valencia...................**50.00**

Casserole, Corn Ware, Queen, marked Shawnee #74, lg..**50.00**

Casserole, French; Lobster Ware, 10-oz **21.00**

Coffeepot, AD; Valencia........**80.00**

Creamer, Laurel Wreath, marked USA **22.00**

Creamer, marked Valencia ..**17.00**

Creamer, Wave, marked USA..**25.00**

Mug, marked Kenwood USA 911, 8-oz **85.00**

Nappy, Valencia, 9½" **20.00**

Pie plate, Valencia, 9¼"........**85.00**

Pitcher, Laurel Wreath, marked USA **24.00**

Pitcher, Stars & Stripes, marked USA **18.00**

Planter, gazelle, turquoise and white, USA #614, $25.00.

Planter, canopy bed, marked
Shawnee 734 .... **65.00**
Planter, globe, gold, marked
Shawnee USA **60.00**
Planter, rocking horse, marked
USA 526 .... **24.00**
Planter, swan & elf, marked
Kenwood 2030 .... **45.00**
Planter, Valencia couple, marked
USA **40.00**
Plate, chop; Valencia, 15" **45.00**

Salt and pepper shakers, Dutch Boy and Girl, large, from $65.00 to $75.00 for the pair.

Salt & pepper shakers, Lobster
Ware, claw, marked USA,
pr **40.00**
Salt & pepper shakers, White
Corn, 3¼", pr **40.00**

Shakers, Dutch boy & girl, blue &
gold, lg, pr **30.00**
Shakers, flower clusters, gold, sm,
pr **65.00**
Shakers, Jack & Jill, gold &
decals, lg, pr **225.00**
Shakers, Jack & Jill, lg, pr .. **60.00**
Shakers, Smiley the Pig, gold
neckerchief, sm, pr **100.00**
Shakers, watering cans, sm,
pr **26.00**
Spoon, Valencia, 9½" **65.00**
Sugar bowl, Corn Ware, King or
Queen, w/lid **36.00**
Teapot, Drape, marked USA, 4-
cup **40.00**
Teapot, Pennsylvania Dutch,
marked USA 27, 27-oz ... **90.00**
Teapot, tulip flower, ribbed collar,
gold, marked USA **65.00**
Tray, relish; Corn Ware, King or
Queen, marked Shawnee #79,
$30 to **40.00**
Vase, flower; Valencia, 8" **28.00**

Sheet Music

The most valuable examples of
sheet music are those related to
early transportation, ethnic
themes, Disney characters, a particularly popular actor, singer, or
composer, or with a cover illustra-
tion done by a well-known artist.
Production of sheet music peaked
during the 'Tin Pan Alley Days,'
from the 1880s until the 1930s.
Covers were made as attractive as
possible to lure potential buyers,
and today's collectors sometimes
frame and hang them as they
would a print. Flea markets are a

good source for sheet music, and prices are usually very reasonable. Most are available for under $5.00. Some of the better examples are listed here. Refer to *The Sheet Music Reference and Price Guide, Second Edition*, by Anna Marie Guiheen and Marie-Reine A. Pafik (Collector Books).

After I'm Gone, Charles Moe & Elise Thompson, 1924 .....**5.00**

Ah But Is It Love?, EY Harberg & Jay Gorney, 1933 ....**5.00**

Amelia Earhart's Last Flight, McEnery, 1939 ....**50.00**

Autumn in New York, Vernon Duke, 1934 ....**2.00**

Ballad for Americans, John Latouche & Earl Robinson, 1918 ....**10.00**

Because of You, RN Doore & Ted Garton, 1918 ....**10.00**

Big Blonde Baby, Alfred Bryan & Fred Fischer, 1912 ....**15.00**

Blue Eyed Violets, Abbie Ford, 1912 ....**5.00**

Bushel & a Peck, Frank Loesser, Musical: Guys & Dolls, 1950 ....**5.00**

Camptown Races, Stephen Foster, 1860 ....**25.00**

Cherries, Marious & Dartmouth, Doris Day photo, 1952 .....**3.00**

Chewin' the Rag, Fred Heltman, Heltman at piano photo cover, 1912 ....**10.00**

Color My World, James Pankow, 1970 ....**3.00**

Cutest Little Red-Headed Doll, Jack Wolf & Carl Sigman, 1947 ....**5.00**

Darn That Dream, Eddie DeLange & Jimmy Van Huesen, 1939 ....**3.00**

Dear Little Boy of Mine, J Keirn Brennan & Earnest R Ball, 1918 ....**15.00**

Echoes From the Woodland, Walter, 1903 ....**5.00**

Empty Saddles, Kiern Brennan & Billy Hill, Bing Crosby photo, 1936 ....**12.00**

Enchanted Sea, Frank Metis & Randy Starr, 1959 ....**5.00**

Extra, Extra, Irving Berlin, Musical: Miss Liberty, 1949 ....**5.00**

Fiddle Dee Dee, Sammy Cahn and Jule Styne, from It's a Great Feeling, Doris Day and Jack Carson cover, 1949, $10.00. (Photo courtesy Guiheen and Pafik)

Five Minutes w/Mr Thornbill, Claude Thornbill, 1942....**5.00**

Fleet's In, Johnny Mercer & Victor Schertzinger, Movie: same, 1942 ....**5.00**

Following in Father's Footsteps, EW Rogers, 1902 ....**10.00**

For the Good Times, Kris Kristofferson, 1968 ....**5.00**

Freedom Ring, James Eaton & Robert Stolz, 1942...........**5.00**

Gangster's Warning, Gene Autry, Curt Poulto photo cover, 1932................................**5.00**

Girl in the Gingham Gown, Manuel Klein, 1913.......**20.00**

Hello Beautiful, Walter Donaldson, Maurice Chevalier photo cover, 1931...........**12.00**

I Believe in Miracles, Barry Mason & Les Reed, 1976.............**3.00**

I Hear You Calling Me, Harold Harford & Charles Marshall, 1908 ....**10.00**

I Love the Way You Say Goodnight, Eddie Pola and George Wyle, from Lullaby of Broadway, Doris Day and Gene Nelson cover, 1951, $10.00. (Photo courtesy Guiheen and Pafik)

Just Walking in the Rain, Johnny Bragg & Robert S Riley, 1953.....................**3.00**

Let's Get Together, Merchant, 1950 ....**3.00**

Little Boy Blue, H Engelmann, 1908 ....**15.00**

Meet Me Neath the Persian Moon, Woolf & Fridland, 1914..**10.00**

Mississippi Moonlight, J Will Callahan & Lee S Roberts, 1919 ....**5.00**

Never Again, Gus Kahn & Ishman Jones, 1924......................**5.00**

Oh! Susanna, Stephen Foster, 1848 ....**35.00**

On the Atchinson, Topeka, and the Santa Fe, J. Mercer and H. Warren, from The Harvey Girls, Judy Garland cover, 1934, $15.00. (Photo courtesy Guiheen and Pafik)

On the Street Where You Live, Lerner & Lowe, Movie: My Fair Lady, 1956................**5.00**

Poor Lizzie, Louis Silver, 1928..**15.00**

Rollin' Stone, Mack Gordon, Perry Como photo cover, 1951...**3.00**

Ruby Tuesday, Mick Jagger & Keith Richards, 1967.......**5.00**

Salute to America, Harry J. Lincoln, 1904..................**10.00**

Silver Bells, Jay Livingston & Ray Evans, 1950.....................**3.00**

Take it Easy, Jimmy McHugh & Dorothy Fields, 1935 ....**5.00**

Voice in My Heart, George M Cohan **10.00**

We're in the Army Now, Tell Taylor, Ole Olsen & Isham Jones, 1917.....................**15.00**

You're Driving Me Crazy, Walter Donaldson, 1930..............**5.00**

You've Made All My Dreams Come True, Jack Darell, 1920...**5.00**

Three Coins in the Fountain, Sammy Cahn and Jule Styne, 1954, $5.00. (Photo coutesy Guiheen and Pafik)

Shot Glasses

Shot glasses, old and new, are whetting the interest of today's collectors, and they're relatively easy to find. Basic values are given for various categories of shot glasses in mint condition. These are general prices only. Glasses that are in less-than-mint condition will obviously be worth less than the price given here. Very rare and unique items will be worth more. Sample glasses and other individual one-of-a-kind oddities are a bit harder to classify and need to be evaluated on an individual basis.

Mark Pickvet is the author of *Shot Glasses: An American Tradition.* He is listed in the Directory under Michigan. See Clubs and Newsletters for information concerning the Shot Glass Club of America.

Barrel shaped, from $5 to.......**7.50**
Black porcelain replica, from $3.50 to......................................**5.00**
Carnival colors, plain or fluted, from $100 to.................**150.00**
Carnival colors, w/patterns, from $125 to.........................**175.00**
Colored glass tourist, from $4 to..**6.00**
Culver 22k gold, from $6 to....**8.00**

Depression, colors, from $10.00 to $12.50. (Photo coutesy Mark Pickvet)

Depression, colors w/patterns or etching, from $17.50 to..**25.00**
Depression, tall, tourist, from $5 to......................................**7.50**
Frosted w/gold designs, from $6 to......................................**8.00**
General, advertising, from $4 to..**6.00**
General, porcelain, from $4 to..**6.00**
General, w/enameled design, from $3 to...............................**4.00**
General, w/frosted designs, from $3.50 to.............................**5.00**
General, w/gold designs, from $6 to......................................**8.00**
General tourist, from $3 to.....**4.00**
Inside eyes, from $5 to............**7.50**
Iridized silver, from $5 to.......**7.50**
Mary Gregory or Anchor Hockng Ships, from $150 to......**200.00**
Nudes, from $25 to **35.00**

Plain, w/ or w/out flutes, from 50¢ to ....**.75**

Pop or soda advertising, from $12.50 to **15.00**

Porcelain tourist, from $3.50 to..**5.00**

Rounded European designs w/gold rims, from $4 to **6.00**

Ruby flashed, from $35 to **50.00**

Sayings & toasts, 1940s-50s, from $5 to **7.50**

Sports, professional teams, from $5 to **7.50**

Square, general, from $6 to....**8.00**

Square, w/etching, from $10 to..**12.50**

Square, w/pewter, from $12.50 to **15.00**

Square, w/2-tone bronze & pewter, from $15 to **17.50**

Standard glass w/pewter, from $12.50 to **15.00**

Steuben crystal, from $150 to..**200.00**

Taiwan tourist, from $2 to **3.00**

Tiffany, Galle or fancy art, from $600 to..........................**800.00**

Turquoise & gold tourist, from $6 to **8.00**

Whiskey or beer advertising, modern, from $5 to **7.50**

Whiskey sample glasses, ea, from $75 to...........................**350.00**

19th-century cut patterns, from $35 to **50.00**

Silhouette Pictures

Silhouettes and reverse paintings on glass were commercially produced in the US from the 1920s through the 1950s. Some were hand painted, but most were silkscreened. Artists and companies used either flat or convex glass. Common subjects include romantic couples, children, horses, dogs, and cats. Many different styles, sizes, colors, and materials were used for frames. Backgrounds also vary from textured paper to foils, colorful lithographs, wildflowers, or butterfly wings. Sometimes the backgrounds were painted on the back of the glass in gold or cream color. These inexpensive pictures were usually sold in pairs, except for the advertising kind, which were given by merchants as gifts.

Our advisor for this category is Shirley Mace, author of *The Encyclopedia of Silhouette Collectibles on Glass* (Shadow Enterprises); she is listed in the Directory under New Mexico.

Art Publishing, girl blowing bubbles while boy watches, flat, 3½x5" **40.00**

Benton, lady admiring boy's catch, $45.00. (Photo courtesy Shirley and Ray Mace)

Benton, boy w/dog going fishing, convex, 8x10"..................**40.00**

Benton, Indian maiden w/mountain scene, convex, 6x8"..**65.00**

Benton, man & woman say fairwell to ship, convex, 4x5".......**40.00**

Benton, man in chair smoking pipe, white, convex, 4x5".........**50.00**

Benton, man plays bugle, convex, 6x8"................................**40.00**

Benton, sailboat, convex, 4x5"..**35.00**

Benton, windmill w/windmill lithographed background, convex, 4x5"..................................**30.00**

Bilderback's, man in tux w/yellow present w/red ribbon, convex, 6" dia..............................**35.00**

Buckbee-Brehm, Happy Bride, friend helps w/dress train, flat, 4x6".........................**40.00**

Buckbee-Brehm, Little Jack Horner w/dog, flat, 4x6"...............**40.00**

Buckbee-Brehm, Touchdown, kids playing football, flat, 4x7"..**35.00**

Deltex Products, lady feeds spotted fawn on silver foil, flat, 4x4"..................................**30.00**

Deltex Products, Scottie dog pulls at lady's dress tie, flat, 8x10"...........................**45.00**

Mary Kerr Fisher, dog & hunter by fence, flat, 3½x3½"...**50.00**

Mary Kerr Fisher, ducks fly over dog & hunter, flat, 17x11".......**45.00**

Mary Kerr Fisher, lady at spinning wheel, flat, 3½x3½"........**40.00**

Newton, boy sits fishing beside water, flat, 6x8".............**35.00**

Newton, boy w/dog going fishing, yellow & blue, flat, 4½x5½"..**35.00**

Ohio Art, horse & sleigh w/cottage background, convex, 4x5"..**35.00**

Peter Watson's Studio, man in tux holding hat & roses, convex, 5" dia..............................**35.00**

Peter Watson's Studio, Mexican sleeping by cactus, convex, 5" dia...................................**30.00**

PF Vollard, Indian chief sits on horse, flat, 9x6½"..........**65.00**

Pickens, boy & girl skating, flat, 5" dia...................................**40.00**

Vernon, boy & dog cross bridge on way to fish, flat, 8x10"...**40.00**

West Coast Pictures, dog on hill w/sun going down, flat, 6x8"..........**30.00**

West Coast Pictures, girl sits on bench watching bird, flat, 12x9"...............................**40.00**

Flowercraft, untitled scene with courting couple, $48.00. (Photo courtesy Shirley and Ray Mace)

Snow Domes

Snow domes are water-filled paperweights. The earliest type was made in two pieces with a glass globe on a separate base. First made in the mid-nineteenth century, they were revived during the 1930s and 1940s. The most common snow domes on today's market are the plastic half-moon shapes made as souvenirs or

Christmas toys, a style that originated in West Germany during the 1950s. Other shapes such as round and square bottles, tall and short rectangles, cubes, and other simple shapes are found as well.

Advertising, Coca-Cola building w/Santa on top of chimney in dome, EX **17.50**
Advertising, Coca-Cola Polar Bear, musical, glass w/resin base, 6", EX **20.00**
Character, Beauty & the Beast, musical, glass w/resin base, M **65.00**
Character, Cinderella, musical, glass w/resin base, 7x4½", NMIB..............................**50.00**
Character, deer (Bambi), plastic dome w/Bakelite base, EX **20.00**
Character, Mickey & Minnie Wedding, glass w/resin base, 9x6", MIB **70.00**
Character, Sleeping Beauty & Her Forest Friends, glass w/resin base, M **40.00**
Character, Sleeping Beauty w/spinning wheel inside dome, NM **25.00**
Character, Winnie the Pooh & Friends, glass dome w/wood base, M **85.00**
Character, Winnie the Pooh Grand Birthday, musical, Michel & Co, MIB **45.00**
Christmas, Santa in flying saucer, lights up, Enesco, 1990, EX......................**45.00**
Christmas, Santa on sled w/tree in background, bell-shaped, EX **10.00**

Christmas, Santa w/globe in belly, hard plastic, Made in Hong Kong, EX **30.00**
Christmas, Snowman w/globe in belly, Made in Hong Kong, 6", VG+................................**25.00**
Christmas, 2 kids build snowman, Santa sits on top, plastic, Hong Kong **25.00**
Figural, cat playing drum w/Santa inside, EX......................**20.00**
Figural, Golf Trophy, Enesco, 1989, 4", EX **17.50**
Halloween/advertising, Starbucks Coffee, house w/bats etc, NM **20.00**

Souvenir, Aloha Hawaii, white base, EX, $15.00. (Photo courtesy Helene Guarnaccia)

Souvenir, Cedar Point, dolphin atop dome on water wave **15.00**
Souvenir, Eiffel Tower, glass w/resin base, 5½" dia, MIB **45.00**
Souvenir, EROS Piccadilly Circus, plastic, calender in base, +EX......................**20.00**
Souvenir, Great Smoky Mountains, bear in woods w/bear stop, EX..............**18.00**
Souvenir, Houston TX, glass w/resin base, 4½" dia, M................**45.00**

Souvenir, New York City, skyline w/Twin Towers/Statue of Liberty etc......................**25.00**

Souvenir, New York World's Fair, 1964-65, NM..................**35.00**

Soda Pop

Now that vintage Coca-Cola items have become rather expensive, interest is expanding to include some of the less widely known flavors of soda — Dr. Pepper, Nehi, and Orange Crush, for instance. For more information refer to *Collectible Soda Pop Memorabilia* by B.J. Summers.

Dr. Pepper

A young pharmacist, Charles C. Alderton, was hired by W.B. Morrison, owner of Morrison's Old Corner Drug Store in Waco, Texas, around 1884. Alderton, an observant sort, noticed that the drugstore's patrons could never quite make up their minds as to which flavor of extract to order. He concocted a formula that combined many flavors, and Dr. Pepper was born. The name was chosen by Morrison in honor of a beautiful young girl with whom he had once been in love. The girl's father, a Virginia doctor by the name of Pepper, had discouraged the relationship due to their youth, but Morrison had never forgotten her. On December 1, 1885, a U.S. patent was issued to the creators of Dr. Pepper.

Beverage set, pitcher, 64-oz, 8 10-oz mugs, West Bend/Thermo-Serv, NM........................**60.00**

Book, Dr Pepper, King of Beverages, Harry Ellis, 268 pages, 1979, EX.............**55.00**

Book, The Enchanted West, John McCarthy, 20 pages, 1944, EX................................**35.00**

Bottle, Saluting 1972 World Champion Dolphins, 16-oz, EX................................**50.00**

Can, red & white, 12-oz, EX.**85.00**

Cards, bridge; lady w/clock behind her on yellow, 1946, EX (VG box)...**85.00**

Charm, miniature bottle, sterling silver, James Avery Craftsman, MIB..............................**155.00**

Clock, bottle cap style, plastic, 11" dia...................................**50.00**

Clock, Drink Dr Pepper w/lion under clock, Hanover Clock, 24x13½x3".....................**60.00**

Clock, plastic w/chrome trim, logo under #s, Pam Clock, 1970s, EX................................**110.00**

Cooler, red letters on green, Progress Refrigerator Co, 16x18x13"....................**215.00**

Crate, bottle; yellow w/red logo, East Lake TX, wooden, 12x18x4", EX.................**35.00**

Doorknob, ceramic w/10, 2, 4 logo in red on white, EX........**50.00**

Family pack, 2 26-oz bottles in cardboard carrier, big DP logo, EX................................**45.00**

Heater, Drink Dr Pepper Hot, 1960s, 8x8", EX.............**50.00**

Light, stained glass-like plastic, 7x8" dia, EX.................**100.00**

Match holder, jadite green colored tin, 1930s, 6⅛".............**95.00**

Mechanical pencil, pearlized body w/red accents, 1940s, 5½" L **60.00**

Mirror, logo, lion & Vim, Vigor & Vitality, oval, 18x26", NM **50.00**

Napkin holder, logo & cap on white, 1950s, metal, 7½x4", EX **35.00**

Paperweight, bottle shape, Dr Pepper Good for Life/logo, brass, 3¾" **70.00**

Paperweight, Perky, kid w/bottle in ea hand, heavy metal, 5¼", EX **135.00**

Perfume bottle, 1963 Tournament of Roses Parade, EXIB ..**35.00**

Picnic cooler, painted metal, white on green, wire bail handle, 18" long, G, $75.00. (Photo courtesy B.J. Summers)

Poster, Have a Picnic at the New York World's Fair, 1964, 12x24", EX......................**35.00**

Safety marker, brass, embossed logo, 3¾" dia....................**40.00**

Sign, clown face w/Dr Pepper, Distinctively Different, 1968, 14½"................................**35.00**

Sign, Drink Dr Pepper, red on white, metal, Stout-Rite Signs, 12x27"..................**70.00**

Sign, Drink Dr Pepper, 10, 2 & 4 in red on white, 10" dia, VG+ **110.00**

Sign, lady holding flowers w/sign, 1940s, 16x25", EX........**165.00**

Sign, lady w/dog in snow scene, cardboard, 1940s, EX................................**260.00**

Sign, The Price Remains the...Same Old Price to You, cardboard, 22x8"...........**70.00**

Telephone, helicopter shape, 10", EX.................................**45.00**

Thermometer, Hot or Cold, Enjoy Dr Pepper, Pam Clock Co, 1961, 12" dia **460.00**

Toy truck, 1955 Diamond T Bottler's Truck, First Gear, 8", MIB................................**55.00**

Tray, Drink Dr Pepper, King of Beverages, 1905, oval, 13⅝x16½"....................**365.00**

Hires

Did you know that Hires Root Beer was first served to fairgoers at the Philadelphia Centennial in 1876? It was developed by Charles E. Hires, a druggist who experimented with roots and herbs to come up with the final recipe. The company originally chose the Hires boy as their logo, and if you'll study his attire, you can sometimes approximate a guess as to when an item he appears on was manufactured. Very early on he appeared in a dress, and from 1906 until 1914 it was a bathrobe. He sported a dinner jacket from 1915 until 1926.

Ad, Why Don't You...Rootbeer?, owl & parrot on branch, 1900s, 3x4", EX..............10.00

Blotter, Real Root Juices Make...Avoid Imitations, 1920, EX........................15.00

Bottle, clear w/embossed Hires, rounded bottom, 1900-1910, EX...................................15.00

Bottle, clear w/orange & black pyro, 8-oz, full, EX.........15.00

Box, held 5-gal of syrup, EX graphics on wood, 15½x10⅜x11", VG+...............................50.00

Box, Hires Root Beer Extract, 1929, 3-oz (makes 5 gal), EXIB............................20.00

Carbonated water bottle, clear w/orange pyro, metal spout, 11¾", EX........................75.00

Clock, Genuine Hires Root Beer on white, plastic, Neon Products, EX...................................55.00

Door push, bottle image w/Hires to You & 2 Glass Size, 1950s, 14x4"..............................215.00

Magazine ad, Got a Minute? Have a Hires, hat box, 1950, 14x5½", EX.....................15.00

Measuring glass, clear w/blue pyro logo, ½-pt, EX.................25.00

Megaphone, heavy wax covered paper, metal rim, 1950s, 10", EX...................................30.00

Menu board, moustached man image, cardboard, 1950s, 27½x14½", VG...............70.00

Mug, baby boy holds mug of root beer, logo, Mettlach, 4¼x4x3", EX...............................175.00

Mug, clear w/red, black & white pyro, miniature, 2½", EX....................................15.00

Menu board, 30x16", EX, $170.00. (Photo courtesy Buffalo Bay)

Mug, clear w/red & white pyro, marked France #25, 5", EX....................................14.00

Pocket mirror, boy pointing w/mug in hand, celluloid, 2¼" dia, EX..........................15.00

Radio, can shape, Draft Style, battery-op, 5x2½" dia, EX..........................25.00

Sign, Drink Hires Root Beer, metal, Press Sign Co, 27½x9½", NM..............170.00

Sign, Enjoy Hires, Healthful Delicious, tin, 1930s, 27½x9½", EX.................50.00

Sign, Hires R-J Root Beer...in Bottles, Ice Cold, 19x27", 1950s, EX......................95.00

Sign, Say! Drink Hires 5¢ It Is Pure, metal, 9½x17", VG....................................85.00

Sign, Victorian boy on bike holding mug, 1897, diecut, 3½x5", EX...................................35.00

Sign, young lady w/goblet of root beer, diecut, 1892, 4⅞x2⅜", EX...................................45.00

Syrup dispenser, front spout, stainless steel w/tin signs, 8½"..............................135.00

Thermometer, blue w/white stripes & bottle at bottom, 27x8", VG **25.00**

Thimble, red & black letters on white, china, 1", EX **13.50**

Toy, root beer barrel, Riedl & Freede, 1960, 11x6" dia, EX (G box) **30.00**

Trade card, Victorian girl w/mug & box of syrup, 5½x3½", EX.................**25.00**

Tray, Drink...Honest Root Beer, 2 girls, Haskell Coffin, 14x10", EX **15.00**

Nehi

Annual Report to Stockholders, 1952, Nehi Corp, 9x6", EX **30.00**

Banner, NE above bottle w/HI below, paper, 1940s, 19x40", VG+...............................**110.00**

Bingo card, Nehi ad, solid wood, vintage, 8x5x½", VG......**10.00**

Bottle, clear w/red & white pyro, 10-oz, EX **12.50**

Bottle, embossed grapes, metal sprinkler head, 9¾", EX.**25.00**

Bottle, Nehi Strawberry, clear w/yellow pyro, 12-oz, NM **13.50**

Bottle, Par-T-Pak Beverages, red & yellow painted label, 12-oz, EX **10.00**

Bottle opener, engraved Drink Nehi, Consolidated Cork Co, EX **15.00**

Bottle opener, marked Nehi Bottling Co, Bellaire OH, metal, 4½", EX...............**60.00**

Matchbook, Royal Crown Nehi Cola, VG+......................**15.00**

Paperweight, pinup-style sailor girl, glass, NM **25.00**

Poster, Drink Nehi Quality Beverages, legs & bottle, 1940s, 21x13", VG..........**40.00**

Sign, Drink Nehi Beverages, painted metal, 18x54", NM...**215.00**

Sign, Drink Nehi Beverages, w/bottle, embossed tin, 11½x29½", EX...............**260.00**

Sign, Drink Nehi...All Popular Flavors, metal, 11x17", EX.................**35.00**

Sign, There's That Look Again...Orange, fiberboard, 1950s, 22x17", EX..........**35.00**

Toy truck, 1951 Ford F-6, First Gear, 1993, MIB **35.00**

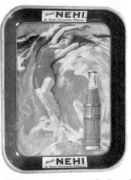

Tray, girl on wave with bottle in foreground, G, $160.00. (Photo courtesy B.J. Summers)

6-pack carton, Take Me Home, Atlanta Paper Co, for 7-oz bottles, EX **35.00**

Nesbitt's

Bottle, clear w/embossed logo & black pyro, 7-oz, EX.........**7.50**

Bottle, clear w/white pyro, 9½" ..**10.00**

Bottle, clear w/yellow pyro, Money-Back Bottle on back, 9½", EX..........................**12.00**

Bottle opener, metal w/embossed Drink Nesbitt's, 3¼", EX..**20.00**

Clock, Drink Nesbitt's Orange, fluorescent tube light, 26x12x4", EX...............**50.00**

Cooler, aluminum w/orange embossed letters, 1950s, 22x13x13", EX.............**185.00**

Glasses, white frost w/blue logo, 12-oz, set of 8, M (EX box)...............................**90.00**

Mug, hot chocolate; brown w/embossed letters, Chefsware USA, 5¼"...........................**15.00**

Shot glass, clear w/orange & white pyro, 2¼", EX................**12.00**

Sign, clown w/2 kids drinking Orange, cardboard, 16x24", EX...................................**25.00**

Sign, Drink Nesbitt's California Orange in Bottles, 7½" dia, EX...................................**35.00**

Thermometer, black, yellow w/red & white letters, 1938, 27x7", EX...................................**195.00**

Thermometer, flying angels drink from bottle w/straw, 17x5", EX...................................**110.00**

Thermometer, metal, message and bottle, yellow and orange on blue, 23x7", G, $160.00. (Photo courtesy B.J. Summers)

Thermometer, Orange Plein de Soleil, oranges below, 1960s, 17x5", EX......................**30.00**

6-pack carrier, Kingdoms of Fun, for 7-oz bottle, EX..........**15.00**

Orange-Crush

Bottle, aqua w/embossed letters, 6-oz, EX.............................**22.50**

Bottle, clear w/embossed letters, ribbed, 24-oz, 1920s, EX..**25.00**

Bottle, clear w/orange & white pyro, Return For Deposit, 10-oz, EX.............................**20.00**

Bottle, dark amber w/orange & white pyro, Fleckenstein, 6-oz, EX...................................**40.00**

Bottle, green w/embossed letters, ribbed, 1920s, 7-oz, 8½", EX.....................**115.00**

Bottle display, 1930s, EX, $350.00. (Photo courtesy Craig Stifter)

Door push, porcelain on metal, 1950s, 9⅜x3½", EX......**930.00**

Menu board, logo & bottle at top, Stout Sign, 1940s-50s, 27x19", EX..................................**95.00**

Postcard, train of oranges & bottle, 1920s, 5½x9", VG+........**25.00**

Scarf, orange w/white flowers, cotton, 21x21", NM.............**17.50**

Sign, bottle cap shape, Stout Sign, tin, 1960s, 19" dia, NM...................................**230.00**

Sign, Drink...Naturally It Taste Better, 1940s, 46½x16½", EX..............................**735.00**

Thermometer, bottle shape, 1950s, 29x7", NM (VG box).....**380.00**

Thermometer, bottle-cap shape, 1950s, 12" dia, EX..........**75.00**

Pepsi-Cola

Pepsi-Cola has been around about as long as Coca-Cola, but since collectors are just now beginning to discover how fascinating this line of advertising memorabilia can be, it's generally much less expensive. You'll be able to determine the approximate date your items were made by the style of logo they carry. The familiar oval was used in the early 1940s, about the time the two 'dots' between the words were changed to one. But the double dots are used nowadays as well, especially on items designed to be reminiscent of the old ones — beware! The bottle cap logo was used from about 1943 until the early to mid-1960s with variations. For more information refer to *Pepsi-Cola Collectibles* by Bill Vehling and Michael Hunt and *Introduction to Pepsi Collecting* by Bob Stoddard.

Bank, gas pump shape w/Pepsi-Cola logo atop, plastic, 20", MIB...............................**35.00**

Bank, vending machine, w/miniature bottles, Louis Marx, EX (G box)...........................**115.00**

Bottle, aqua w/peanut waisted body, 1929-30, 6½-oz, 8⅜", EX **50.00**

Bottle, clear w/embossed Albany...Albany GA, ca 1910, 8⅜", VG+......................**235.00**

Bottle, clear w/embossed Tarpon Springs/Not To Be Sold, ca 1900, EX......................**600.00**

Bottle, Fountain Syrup, clear w/red & white pyro, 12-oz, EX................................**65.00**

Bottle, silver, logo on front, Brazilian label on back, 1970, 8-oz, EX........................**325.00**

Bottle carrier, logo, wooden, holds 6 bottles, EX.................**150.00**

Bottle opener, hook-style end, logo engraved, 1940s-50s, 2½", EX.........................**50.00**

Bottle opener, wall mount, red logo on yellow, 5x2¼", VG **60.00**

Bottle opener/stirring spoon, marked Vaughan Chicago, 1930s, EX **80.00**

Calender, pinup girls, 1945, complete, M...........................**65.00**

Camera, can shape, fixed focus, flash, 35mm, NM **40.00**

Cap, reclosable; EX rubber, 1950s, VG+................................**35.00**

Clock, Drink Pepsi-Cola Ice Cold, bubble-glass front, 1960s, EX **560.00**

Cookie jar, can shape, 2000, 12x7½", MIB **35.00**

Cooler, aluminum w/red logo, 1950s, 22x13", VG+ **55.00**

Cooler, barrel shape, red & white, insulated plastic, 17x14", VG ...**65.00**

Cooler, blue w/white logo, tray/plug/opener, 1950s, 19x19x13", EX..............**175.00**

Door push, Have a Pepsi w/cap on ea side, 1960s, 31½x3½", EX................**70.00**

Doorknob, engraved & painted red on white, ceramic, EX................**65.00**

Glass, Pappy (Warner Bros character), 1970s, EX............**40.00**

License plate, cap w/Winston Salem, aluminum, 5x12", EX.......**35.00**

Lighter, bottle shape, Bakelite, 1950s, 2¾", EX..............**40.00**

Lighter, logo cap on white, musical, 1950s, 2¾x2", VG....**95.00**

Lighter, logo on white, Barlow, NM................**35.00**

Mechanical pencil, white Bakelite w/logo, Eversharp, NM................**38.00**

Menu board, Have a Pepsi, yellow & white stripes, 30x20", EX **90.00**

Menu board, log on top, w/blue plastic letters & numbers, 28x16¾", EX..................**35.00**

Plate, 19th-century girl smelling flower, WE McElree, 1984, 7", NM................**35.00**

Playing cards, Cincinnati Bottling Plant pictured, MIP.......**65.00**

Poster, lady by glass rack, The Light Refreshment, 1950s, 108x228", EX...............**150.00**

Printer's block, 6½x2⅝", EX **40.00**

Salt shaker/pepper mill, bottle shape, wooden, 1973, 8¼", MIB................**35.00**

Service pin, 10 Years, 10k gold, bottle-cap shape, M **85.00**

Sign, bottle w/5¢, 12-oz, celluloid over tin, 1936, 12¼x5¼", EX............**265.00**

Sign, bottle-cap shape, flat metal, tin, 1950s, 15¼x14", EX........**350.00**

Sign, counter display; lady w/hands on hips, tin, oval, 11¾x8", EX....................**70.00**

Sign, embossed tin, 1950s, 4x3½", EX, $100.00. (Photo courtesy B.J. Summers)

Sign, policeman w/5¢ Pepsi-Cola sign, easel back, 7½x6½", EX **145.00**

Sign, Take Home a Carton w/bottle cap, 2-sided, 1960s, 15x15", EX **45.00**

Stickers, pinup girl w/bottle, & cap, ca 1950, 8x5½", set of 4, EX **100.00**

Stocking hanger, snowman, Pepsico Inc, 1997, MIB..**40.00**

Telephone, Everyday Phone, musical, MIB **40.00**

Thermometer, bottle w/Bigger Better, metal, 15¾x6¼", EX........**240.00**

Thermometer, bottle-cap top & bottom, 27x8", EX..........**55.00**

Toy plane, 1932 Stearman Bi-Plane, plated sterling silver, 11", MIB **80.00**

Toy truck, Nylint #5500 Delivery Truck, EX **150.00**

Tray, Bigger & Better, Coast to Coast, bottle on map, 1930s, 1x11", EX **210.00**

Tray, Enjoy Pepsi-Cola, Hits the Spot, 1940s, 14x11", EX...**75.00**

Tray, girl on beach w/Pepsi umbrella, 1993, 13¼x10½", M **35.00**

Tray, pinup girl in yellow bathing suit, 1994, 13x10½", M..**35.00**

Royal Crown Cola

Bottle, red & yellow pyro, 1936, full w/cap, NM+ **20.00**

Bottle opener, raised letters in red on silver, wall mount, Star X, EX **30.00**

Calendar, Ann Blyth w/setter dog, 1951, complete, 24x11½", EX **160.00**

Can, various National League baseball players stats & photos, EX, ea **2.00**

Carrier, red, white & yellow sign, on wire rack, holds 12 bottles, EX **80.00**

Clock, white letters on orange w/white border w/#s, triangular, EX **100.00**

Cooler, red letters on yellow, opener/tray, 1950s, 17x13x9½", EX **115.00**

Crate, bottle; yellow letters on red, wooden, EX....................**30.00**

Hand fan, Shirley Temple w/bottle, cardboard, 12x8¼", EX....**20.00**

Lighter, bottle shape, made by KEM, 1950s, 2", NM+....**20.00**

Lighter, can shape, red logo on white, 1950s, 1½x¾" dia, M................................**25.00**

Poster, surfer w/girl w/bottle on beach, 1960s, 28x11", M .**35.00**

Radio, can shape, marked GE, Hong Kong, EX **20.00**

Sign, Drink..., red & white, lithographed metal, 1950s, 17x34", EX **125.00**

Sign, Drink..., w/bottle, stamped tin, 18x54", EX............**390.00**

Sign, Enjoy..., red, blue & white, 1960s, 12x32", EX........**145.00**

Sign, man & woman having picnic, enameled metal, 12x15½", EX.................**25.00**

Sign, self-framed tin with bottle embossed in center, 36x16", G, $175.00. (Photo courtesy B.J. Summers)

Sign, You'll Flip...ZZZip..., cardboard, w/lady in hat, 11x28", NM+...............................**30.00**

Sign, 2 Free Bottles in Special 8-bottle carton, 1950s, 20x20", NM+...............................**20.00**

Thermometer, Better Taste Calls for RC on bottom, red & white, 21", EX.........................**200.00**

Thermometer, blue RCC w/lg red RC on white, blue border, 12" dia, EX.............................**85.00**

Thermometer, Drink..., white & yellow on red, 1946, 25½x9¾", EX.................................**115.00**

7-Up

Though it was originally touted to have medicinal qualities, by 1930 7-Up had been reformulated and was simply sold as a refreshing drink. The company who first made it was the Howdy Company, who by 1940 had changed its name to 7-Up to correspond with the name of the soft drink. Collectors search for the signs, thermometers, point-of-sale items, etc., that carry the 7-Up slogans.

Bottle, amber w/white & orange pyro, squat, 7-oz, 1920s, 7x2¾", VG+ **35.00**

Bottle, green w/red & white pyro, Hawaii, 12-oz, 12", EX...**25.00**

Bottle opener, Fresh Up With Seven Up, metal, wall mount, EX.....................................**45.00**

Clock, white & green w/red logo, 18x12x5", EX...................**40.00**

Cooler, logo on white w/green bottom & lid, 1950s, 12x21x12", VG+..................................**25.00**

Figure, Fresh Up Freddie, painted rubber, 1959, VG+ **130.00**

Playing cards, green w/logo, no jokers, 1940s, Remembrance, EX (G box)......................**25.00**

Sign, college kids w/We're Seven-Up Steadies, cardboard, 11x20", VG **25.00**

Sign, Fresh Up With 7-Up, Take Some Home Today, metal, 12xx33", EX..................**110.00**

Sign, Instant Fun, 7-Up Floats, 23¾x37", EX..................**60.00**

Sign, We're a Fresh Up Family, cardboard, 1948, 11x21", EX..............................**10.00**

Sign, You Like It, It Likes You, flanged, mounting holes, 12x10", EX......................**40.00**

Telephone, Red Spot figural, 7-Up Co, 1990, EX **18.00**

Thermometer, porcelain, 15", NM, $75.00. (Photo courtesy Dunbar Gallery)

Miscellaneous

Bubble Up, celluloid sign, bubble logo on green background, 9x13", $135.00. (Photo courtesy Gary Metz)

Canadian Club Root Beer, mug, handled, ceramic, 1920s, 5", EX...............................**270.00**

Dad's Root Beer, bottle, Papa's Size, amber w/red & yellow pyro, EX.........................160.00

Dad's Root Beer, chalkboard menu, 1950s-60s, 19½x27½", EX 290.00

Dr Swett's Root Beer, mug, black letters on white, EX.......55.00

Frostie Root Beer, door push, character on ice skates, 1950s, 4x7", EX.........................100.00

Grapette, thermometer, Thirsty or Not, 1930s, 16½x4½", EX 260.00

Kist, clock, Enjoy...Beverages, painted metal behind glass, 15" sq, EX.....................235.00

Mountain Dew, can, green, white & red, 1960s, EX............60.00

Mountain Dew, doll, hillbilly, plush, 1950s-60s, 20", EX.........130.00

Moxie, toy truck, 1952 GMC COE Bottler Truck, First Gear, M (EX box)...........................90.00

Nu Icy, bottle, clear w/embossed letters, pinched waist, 1920s, EX 13.00

NuGrape, match holder, embossed bottle, 1930s-40s, 2½x1½", EX 30.00

NuGrape, thermometer, bottle shape, pressed tin, 16¾x4⅛", EX...............................120.00

Squirt, clock, logo & bottle on white, 1965, 15¼x15¼", EX 190.00

Squirt, cooler, festive scene, 14x11½" dia, EX 55.00

Squirt, sign, red & yellow on blue w/green bottle, 1941, 17½x4", EX................................140.00

Triple AAA Root Beer, bottle, clear w/maroon pyro, 10-oz, M 12.00

Twang Root Beer, can, red, white & blue, cone top, 12-oz, VG+......................460.00

Souvenir Spoons

Originating with the Salem Witch spoons designed by Daniel Low, souvenir spoons are generally reasonably priced, easily displayed, and often show fine artwork and craftsmanship. Spoons are found with a wide range of subject matter including advertising, commemorative, historic sites, American Indians, famed personalities, and more. Souvenir spoons continue to capture the imaginations of thousands of collectors with their timeless appeal. For further information we recommend *Collectible Souvenir Spoons, The Grand Tour, Book I* and *II*, by Wayne Bednersh (Collector Books).

Alaska, transfer print enamel finial, sterling, demitasse, $5 to 15.00

Art Museum Cincinnati in bowl, Mary Warren handle, from $25 to 50.00

Carnegie Library Rockford, IL, bowl, Chantilly handle, Gorham, $30 to 50.00

Chimney Rock on finial, Wisconsin Dells embossed on handle, $10 to 20.00

Cincinnati Bridge engraved in bowl, Paye & Baker, from $50 to 75.00

DAR & temple scene in bowl, Krider, from $50 to........70.00

Echo Hotel Pasadena engraved in bowl, ornate handle, Coddington Bros **75.00**

Flatiron Building, New York, embossed in bowl, various handles, $20 to **75.00**

Flowers form pierced handle, Wallace, from $20 to **40.00**

Furniture Factory, Grand Rapids, MI, engraved in bowl, no mark, $30 to **50.00**

Gerber baby embossed on handle, silver plate, from $5 to ..**10.00**

Harbor Point, MI, lighthouse in bowl, Provence handle, Fessenden......................**50.00**

High Water Mark Gettysburg in bowl, Baronial pattern, Smith, $40 to **75.00**

Mission San Xavier on finial, Tucson, AZ, on handle, Robbins..........................**35.00**

New Casino, Santa Cruz, Cal. Irving pattern, Wallace, from $35.00 to $60.00. (Photo courtesy Wayne Bednersh)

Niagara Falls, embossed handle, waves in bowl, WE Glenn & Sons, $50 to **70.00**

Oregon on handle, engraved web foot in bowl, Mechanic, from $25 to **50.00**

Pine Tree figural handle, Watson, from $75 to **150.00**

Pinocchio enameled figure on handle, plain bowl, stainless steel..............................**10.00**

Presbyterian Church, Hastings, NB, Colfax handle, Gorham, $15 to **30.00**

San Diego Expo, California Building engraved in bowl, Mayer Bros....................**50.00**

State prison, Waupin, WI, engraved in bowl, Puritan pattern, Wallace..................**60.00**

Stork handle, engraved bowl, Lunt, from $30 to..........**60.00**

Sutters Fort, Sacramento, CA, engraved in bowl, Shepard, $25 to **50.00**

Tampa, FL, skyline handle w/pierced bonbon bowl, from $150 to **300.00**

Tipton, IN, courthouse engraved in bowl, simple handle, from $30 to **50.00**

University of OK Normal engraved in bowl, Louvre handle, Wallace....................**35.00**

Waikiki, Hawaii, ornate handle w/long boat scene bowl, from $140 to **200.00**

WC Fields, stainless steel w/red jeweled eyes, from $25 to **50.00**

Sporting Collectibles

When sports cards became so widely collectible several years ago, other types of related memorabilia started to interest sports fans. Now they search for baseball uniforms, autographed baseballs, game-used bats and gloves, and all sorts of ephemera. Although baseball is America's all-time favorite, other sports have their own groups of interested collectors.

Pennant, Indianapolis Speedway, single-sided cloth, 10½x29", VG, $100.00. (Photo courtesy B.J. Summers)

Bank, baseball, Pee Wee Reese/United Cerebral Palsy/Dodgers, glass, EX..**190.00**

Bank, plastic w/10 wooden bats in rack w/team insignias, 6", MIB................................**175.00**

Bank, St Louis Cardinals, white w/red letters, glass, EX...**55.00**

Baseball, Greg Maddox autograph............................**55.00**

Baseball, Johnny Bench autograph **55.00**

Baseball, Roger Maris & Harmon Killibrew autographs...**625.00**

Book of Baseball, Shoeless Joe Jackson image, Colliers, 1911, VG+..............................**325.00**

Card, Babe Ruth, Williard's Chocolates, 1923, 3¼x1⅜", EX **395.00**

Card, Robert (Lefty) Grove, Delong Bubble Gum, VG+..........**80.00**

Decanter, Nebraska Cornhuskers, Mike Wayne Distilleries, 1982, EX......................**240.00**

Face mask, catcher's; Winmore #554, 1930s, VG+.........**155.00**

Figurine, Tom Seaver, Transogram, 1969, MIB......................**220.00**

Football, 2002 Fiesta Bowl National Champions Ohio State, leather, NM.........**30.00**

Game, LA Dodgers Baseball, Ed-U-Cards, 1964, NMIB....**50.00**

Game, Play Ball, chromed metal & wood w/reverse painting, EX **100.00**

Game, World Series Parlor Baseball, United Game Co, 1916, VG.......................**185.00**

Jersey, Marines, gray w/red letters & trim, 1940s, EX **50.00**

Lapel pin, 1956 All Star Game, EX **85.00**

Mirror, Roberto Clemente, Seagrams, 1990, 17x21", EX **225.00**

Ornament, baseball w/anchor, glass, 3x2⅛" dia...........**100.00**

Pennant, Washington Redskins, 1960s, 30" L, EX **120.00**

Photo, 1907 Banzai Tea Team, 7¼x9¼", EX....................**65.00**

Pin-back, Iowa Hawkeye Homecoming, 1966, Ray Negal photo, EX **50.00**

Postcard, Columbia Ball Park, Philadelphia, 1909, EX.................................**75.00**

Postcard, Leroy (Satchel) Paige Hall of Fame plaque, signed, EX **100.00**

Postcard, Ty Cobb at Bat, black & white, HM Taylor, ca 1909, EX **265.00**

Press pass, football; 1951 USC vs Notre Dame, EX.............**30.00**

Press pin, 1961 All Star Game, Boston, red, white & blue enamel, NM..................**215.00**

Program, 1931 Notre Dame Football, 80 pages, 12x9", VG+..............................**115.00**

Program, 1932 World Series, Yankees vs Cubs, 21 pages, VG.................................**310.00**

Program, 1944 Sugar Bowl, EX **160.00**

Program, 1945 All Star Game, Here Comes the Navy, fleet issue, EX........................**55.00**

Program, 1950 Globetrotters vs All Stars, National Tour, photographs and biographies of all players, NM, $175.00.

Program, 1952 Vanderbilt vs Tennessee, VG+ **25.00**

Program, 1959 World Series, Chicago White Sox, EX...**85.00**

Telephone, Miami Dolphin helmet, Riddell Phone Co, EX....**60.00**

Ticket stub, USC vs Notre Dame, 12/1/56, EX....................**25.00**

Yearbook, 1947 Brooklyn Dodgers, 82 pages, by Joe Hasel, EX+ **280.00**

Yearbook, 1951 NY Yankees, photos/biographies, Mantle rookie year, EX.......................**265.00**

Stangl

The Stangl Company of Trenton, New Jersey, produced many striking lines of dinnerware from the 1920s until they closed in the late 1970s. Though white clay was used earlier, the red-clay patterns made from 1942 on are most often encountered and are preferred by collectors. Decorated with both hand painting and sgraffito work (hand carving), Stangl's lines are very distinctive and easily recognized. Virtually all is marked, and most pieces carry the pattern name as well. For more information see *Collector's Encyclopedia of Stangl Artware, Lamps, and Birds* by Robert C. Runge.

Ashtray, Fruit, fluted, 5"......**15.00**

Ashtray, Town & Country, blue, bathtub shape **60.00**

Bowl, cereal; Garden Flower..**25.00**

Bowl, coupe soup; Garland...**30.00**

Bowl, fruit; Blueberry...........**20.00**

Bowl, vegetable; Fruit, 8".....**45.00**

Bowl, vegetable; Town & Country, black or crimson, 8".......**55.00**

Bread tray, Magnolia............**30.00**

Butter dish, Apple Delight...**40.00**

Butter dish, Fruit **65.00**

Butter dish, Fruit & Flowers.**75.00**

Cake stand, Fruit..................**25.00**

Cake stand, Sculptured Fruit, 10"..**20.00**

Casserole, Amber-Glo, skillet shape, 8".........................**25.00**

Casserole, Garden Flower, w/lid, 6"....................................**30.00**

Cigarette box, Mountain Laurel **60.00**

Coaster/ashtray, Amber-Glo..**20.00**

Coffee filter, Orchard Song ..**25.00**

Coffee server, Fruit, casual..**200.00**

Creamer, Blue Crocus **30.00**

Creamer, Festival **25.00**

Cruet, Blueberry, w/stopper ..**50.00**

Cup, Mountain Laurel..........**15.00**

Cup, New Tulip....................**10.00**

Cup, Pink Dogwood, from $10.00 to $12.00. (Photo courtesy Robert C. Runge, Jr.)

Deviled egg plate, Golden Blossom, #5199 ....**40.00**

Dinner plate, Magnolia, 10", $15.00.

Egg cup, Garden Flower.......**25.00**

Egg cup, Golden Grape.........**10.00**

Ginger jar, Town & Country, brown, green, honey or yellow **75.00**

Gravy boat, Amber-Glo.........**15.00**

Gravy boat, Garland, w/underplate **35.00**

Lazy Susan, Orchard Song...**75.00**

Mug, coffee; Tiger Lily..........**30.00**

Mug, stack; Apple Delight....**50.00**

Napkin ring, Cranberry........**25.00**

Pickle dish, Tiger Lily **20.00**

Pie plate, Town & Country, blue, 10½" **65.00**

Pitcher, Bittersweet, 1-pt.....**30.00**

Pitcher, Colonial Rose, 1-pt..**35.00**

Pitcher, Fruit, 1-qt...............**75.00**

Pitcher, Golden Blossom, 1-qt..**35.00**

Plate, Blue Daisy, 7".............**20.00**

Plate, cheese; Caughley, brown or dark green, 12½" **45.00**

Plate, chop; Water Lily, 14½"..**135.00**

Plate, Fruit, 10" **30.00**

Plate, grill; Fruit & Flowers, 11"...............................**60.00**

Plate, picnic; Blueberry, 10"..**12.00**

Plate, Prelude, 9" **20.00**

Platter, Fruit, oval, 11½" ...**140.00**

Salt & pepper shakers, Garden Flower, pr......................**20.00**

Salt and pepper shakers, Orchard, $16.00 for the pair; matching gravy boat, $15.00.

Salt & pepper shakers, Sculptured Fruit, pr..........................**20.00**

Saucer, Apple Delight............**6.00**

Sugar bowl, black or crimson..**30.00**

Sugar bowl, Blue Crocus **35.00**

Tidbit, Bittersweet, 2-tier.....**25.00**

Tidbit tray, 10"......................**15.00**

Tumbler, Magnolia, 12-oz.....**75.00**

Vase, Caughley, triple cylinder, yellow, pink or green **40.00**

Star Wars

Capitalizing on the ever-popular space travel theme, the movie *Star Wars* with its fantastic special effects was a mega box office hit of the late 1970s. A sequel called *Empire Strikes Back* (1980) and a third adventure called *Return of the Jedi* (1983) did just as well, and as a result, licensed merchandise flooded the market, much of it produced by the Kenner company. The last two films were *Star Wars Episode I — The Phantom Menace* and, of course, *Episode II — Attack of the Clones* soon followed. *Episode III* is to be relased in 2005.

Original packaging is very important in assessing a toy's worth. As each movie was released, packaging was updated, making approximate dating relatively simple. A figure on an original Star Wars card is worth more than the same character on an Empire Strikes Back card, etc.; and the same Star Wars figure valued at $50.00 in mint-on-card condition might be worth as little as $5.00 loose. Especially prized are the original 12-back Star Wars cards (meaning twelve figures were shown on the back). Second issue cards showed eight more, and so on. For more information we recommend *Star Wars Super Collector's Wish Book, Second Edition,* by Geoffery T. Carlton;

and *Schroeder's Collectible Toys, Antique to Modern.* Both are published by Collector Books.

Note: Because space was limited, SW was used in our descriptions for Star Wars; ROTJ was used for Return of the Jedi, ESB for Empire Strikes Back, and POTF for Power of the Force.

Bank, C3-PO, Roman Ceramics, M **75.00**
Bank, Yoda, SW, Sigma, M ..**150.00**
Belt, ROTJ, 1983, EX **10.00**
Case, Darth Vader, EX **15.00**
Color 'N Clean Machine, Craftmaster, M **50.00**
Costume, Yoda, Ben Cooper, w/mask, NM **75.00**
Doll, Paploo, Ewok, ROTJ, plush, MIB **135.00**
Figure, Anakin Skywalker, POTF, complete, NM **30.00**
Figure, AT-ST Driver, ROTJ, complete, NM **10.00**

Figure, B-Wing Pilot, Power of the Force, MOC, from $50.00 to $65.00.
(Photo courtesy Martin and Carolyn Berens)

Figure, B-Wing Pilot, ROTJ, MOC..............................**38.00**

Figure, Barada, POTF, complete, NM................................**35.00**

Figure, Ben Obi-Wan-Kenobi, ESB, M (NM card)........**110.00**

Figure, Bespin Security Guard (Black), ESB, M (NM card)...................................**60.00**

Figure, Bib Fortuna, ROTJ, MOC.............................**35.00**

Figure, Boba Fett, ROTJ, desert scene, MOC..................**325.00**

Figure, Bosok, ESB, M (NM card)............................**140.00**

Figure, Captain Tarpuls, Episode 1/Wave 4, MOC..............**15.00**

Figure, Chewbacca, SW, complete, NM..................................**15.00**

Figure, Chief Chirpa, ROTJ, complete, NM........................**12.00**

Figure, Darth Vader, POTF, MOC **130.00**

Figure, Darth Vader, SW, complete, NM........................**30.00**

Figure, Death Star Droid, ESB, MOC **150.00**

Figure, Death Star Gunner, 1995, 4th Series, MOC............**15.00**

Figure, EV-9D9, POTF, complete, NM..................................**45.00**

Figure, General Madine, ROTJ, M (EX card) **35.00**

Figure, Greedo, ESB, M (NM+ card).............................**125.00**

Figure, Hammerhead, SW, M (NM card) (20/21 back) **195.00**

Figure, Han Solo, POTF, Carbonite Chamber, NM.................**100.00**

Figure, Han Solo, ROTJ, trench coat, NM (NM card).......**45.00**

Figure, Imperial Dignitary, POTF, MOC **130.00**

Figure, Imperial Gunner, POTF, complete, NM.................**65.00**

Figure, Jann Tosh, Droids, complete, NM........................**70.00**

Figure, Jar Jar Binks, Episode I/Wave 9, swimming, MOC.............**25.00**

Figure, Jawa, ESB, MOC...**110.00**

Figure, Kyle Katarn, POTF, 1995-present, MOC.................**20.00**

Figure, Lando Carissian, ESB, M (NM card).....................**80.00**

Figure, Lobot, ESB, M (EX+ card)..............................**60.00**

Figure, Luke Skywalker, POTF, battle poncho, NM........**35.00**

Figure, Luke Skywalker, POTF, MOC **480.00**

Figure, Luke Skywalker, POTF, 1995-present, 12", MIB................................**25.00**

Figure, Lumat, ROTJ, MOC..**50.00**

Figure, Paploo, POTF, complete, NM................................**16.00**

Figure, Princess Leia Organa, ESB, crewneck, complete, NM **28.00**

Figure, Pruneface, ROTJ, MOC..**35.00**

Figure, Qui-Gon Jinn, Episode I/Wave 6, MOC **15.00**

Figure, Rancor Keeper, ROTJ, M (EX+ card) **20.00**

Figure, Rebel Commando, ROTJ, complete, M...................**32.00**

Figure, Ree-Yees, ROTJ, M (NM card)..............................**30.00**

Figure, R2 D2, SW, MOC (12-back) **245.00**

Figure, Sand People, ESB, MOC **100.00**

Figure, Sio Bibble, Episode I/Wave 9, MOC **20.00**

Figure, Snaggletooth, ESB, M (NM card)....................**130.00**

Figure, Star Destroyer Commander, ROTJ, MOC **60.00**

Figure, Stormtrooper, ROTJ, M (NM+ card)....................**70.00**

Figure, Teebo, POTF, M (EX+ card)............................**135.00**

Figure, Tuskon Raider, ROTJ, M (G card)..........................**80.00**

Figure, Warok, POTF, complete, NM...............................**26.00**

Figure, Yak Face, POTF, complete, NM......................**160.00**

Hand puppet, Yoda, ESB, MIB **75.00**

Iron-On Transfer Book, Ballantine, 1977, unused, M....................................**20.00**

Mug, Biker Scout, Sigma, ceramic, MIB..................................**30.00**

Pencil tray, C3-Po, Sigma, ceramic, MIB............................**50.00**

Play-Doh Set, ESB, complete, MIB **20.00**

Playmat, SW, Recticel Sutcliffe, UK, NM **125.00**

Playset, Cantina Adventure Set, SW, MIB........................**575.00**

Playset, Droid Factory, SW, MIB **100.00**

Playset, Hoth Ice Planet, M (VG box) **125.00**

Playset, Jabba the Hut, ROTJ, M (EX sealed box) **65.00**

Playset, Turret & Probot, ESB, MIB (sealed).................**175.00**

Sit 'N Spin, Ewoks, MIB **80.00**

Talking Telephone, Ewoks, MIB **50.00**

Vehicle, ATL Interceptor, MIB ..**100.00**

Vehicle, Imperial Cruiser, SB, MIB...............................**150.00**

Vehicle, Jawa Sandcrawler, SW, radio-controlled, MIB ..**665.00**

Vehicle, Imperial Tie Fighter, Star Wars, diecast, MOC, from $75.00 to $85.00.

Vehicle, Landspeeder, SW, MIB...........................**85.00**

Vehicle, Millennium Falcon, ESB, MIB..............................**250.00**

Vehicle, Scout Walker, ESB, MIB **100.00**

Vehicle, Speeder Bike, ROTJ, MIB **45.00**

Vehicle, Y-Wing Fighter, ROTJ, complete, EX **60.00**

Yo-Yo, Darth Vader, sculpted plastic, MOC **5.00**

3-D Poster Art Set, 1978, complete, MIP.....................**30.00**

Strawberry Shortcake Collectibles

Strawberry Shortcake came onto the market around 1980, and immediately captured the imagination of little girls everywhere. A line of related merchandise soon hit the market, including swimsuits, bed linens, blankets, anklets, underclothing, coats, shoes, sleeping bags, dolls and accessories, games, toys, and delightful items to decorate the rooms of Strawberry Shortcake fans. It was short lived, though, lasting only until near the middle of the decade.

Bedspread & sham, print resembling quilt squares, twin size, EX **60.00**

Berry Buggy, Coleco/American Greetings, 1981, NRFB .. **90.00**

Big Berry Trolley, 1982, EX .. **40.00**

Bookcase, American Greetings, 1982, 40x20x9", NM **80.00**

Cookie jar, figural, American Greetings, 10x7", NM .. **475.00**

Covered cake plate, resembles strawberry shortcake w/whipped cream, M **60.00**

Doll, Almond Tea, 6", MIB ... **25.00**

Doll, Almond Tea w/Marza Panda, 6", MIB **65.00**

Doll, Angel Cake, 6", MIB **25.00**

Doll, Apple Dumpling, 6", MIB **25.00**

Doll, Apricot, 15", NM **35.00**

Doll, Baby Apricot, Kenner, 1982, 14", MIB **100.00**

Doll, Baby Needs a Name, 15", NM **35.00**

Doll, Banana Twirl, w/Berrykin (perfume in its pouch), MIB.. **265.00**

Doll, Berry Baby Orange Blossom, 6", MIB **35.00**

Doll, Blueberry Muffin, 6", MIB.. **75.00**

Doll, Butter Cookie, 6", MIB .**25.00**

Doll, Cafe Olé w/Burrito, 6", NRFB **75.00**

Doll, Cafe Olé, 6", MIB **35.00**

Doll, Cherry Cuddler, 6", MIB .. **25.00**

Doll, Crepe Suzette w/Eclair pet, NRFB (NM box) **55.00**

Doll, Lemon Meringue, 14", M **85.00**

Doll, Lime Chiffon, 6", MIB .**25.00**

Doll, Mint Tulip, 6", MIB **25.00**

Doll, Orange Blossom w/Berrykin, Kenner, 1985, MIB **215.00**

Doll, Peach Blush w/Melonie Belle, M **135.00**

Doll, Plum Puddin, 6", M **80.00**

Doll, Purple Pieman w/Berry Bird, NRFB (EX box) **70.00**

Doll, Raspberry Tart, 6", MIB.. **25.00**

Doll, Raspberry Tart Sweet Sleeper, sleep eyes, w/Rhubarb pet, 1984, M **55.00**

Doll, Strawberry Shortcake w/Berrykin & comb, MIB..**220.00**

Doll, Strawberry Shortcake, 12", NRFB **45.00**

Doll, Strawberry Shortcake, 15", NM **35.00**

Doll, Strawberry Shortcake Blow Kiss Baby, NRFB **155.00**

Dollhouse, Berry Happy Home, complete w/furniture, NM.... **600.00**

Dollhouse, Berry Happy Home House, complete, EX.... **165.00**

Dollhouse furniture, attic, 6-pc, rare, M **150.00**

Dollhouse furniture, bathroom, 5-pc, rare, M **65.00**

Dollhouse furniture, bedroom, 7-pc, rare, M **90.00**

Dollhouse furniture, kitchen, 11-pc, rare, M **100.00**

Dollhouse furniture, living room, 6-pc, rare, M **85.00**

Dollhouse furniture, piano, 1983, 4x5", M **110.00**

Figure, Almond Tea w/Marza Panda, PVC, 1", MOC ... **15.00**

Roller skates, EX **35.00**
Sleeping bag, EX...................**25.00**
Storybook Play Case, M **35.00**

Figure, Cherry Cuddler with Gooseberry, Strawberryland Miniatures, MIP, from $15.00 to $20.00. (Photo courtesy Carolyn Berens)

Figure, Grapes w/Dregs, Strawberry Miniatures, MIP, from $15 to **20.00**
Figure, Lemon Meringue w/Frappo, PVC, 1", MOC..................**15.00**
Figure, Lime Chiffon w/balloons, PVC, 1", MOC **15.00**
Figure, Merry Berry Worm, MIB............................**35.00**
Figure, Mint Tulip w/March Mallard, PVC, MOC **15.00**
Figure, Orange Blossom, PVC, MOC **65.00**
Figure, Peach Blush, Strawberry Miniatures, M..............**110.00**
Figure, Purple Pieman w/Berry Bird, poseable, MIB.......**35.00**
Figure, Raspberry Tart w/bowl of cherries, MOC.................**15.00**
Ice skates, EX........................**35.00**
Motorized bicycle, EX...........**95.00**
Mug, Lime Chiffon/Parfait Parrot on white, sq, rare...........**85.00**
Pitcher & tumblers, glass, MXM-LXXX American Greetings Corp, 9-pc set **100.00**

Stroller, Coleco, 1981, large doll size, M, $85.00. (Photo courtesy June Moon)

Telephone, Strawberry Shortcake figure, battery-operated, EX................**85.00**
Vanity & chair, American Greetings, 1981, 39x36x15", EX **65.00**
Wristwatch, Strawberry Shortcake, Bradley, 1980, MIB................................**75.00**

Swanky Swigs

Swanky Swigs are little decorated glass tumblers that once contained Kraft Cheese Spread. The company has used them since the Depression years of the 1930s up to the present time, and all along, because of their small size, they've been happily recycled as drinking glasses for the kids and juice glasses for adults. Their designs range from brightly colored flowers to animals, sailboats, bands, dots, stars, and checkers. There is a combination of 223 verified colors and patterns. In 1933 the original Swanky Swigs came in the Band pattern, and at the present time they can still be found on the grocery shelf, now a clear plain glass with an indented waffle design around the bottom.

They vary in size and fall into one of three groups: the small size sold in Canada, ranging from 3¹⁄₁₆" to 3¼"; the regular size sold in the United States, ranging from 3⅜" to 3⅞"; and the large size also sold in Canada, ranging from 4³⁄₁₆" to 5⅝".

A few of the rare patterns to look for in the three different groups are small group, Band No. 5 (two red and two black bands with the red first); Galleon (two ships on each glass in black, blue, green, red, or yellow); Checkers (in black and red, black and yellow, black and orange or black and white, with black checkers on the top row); and Fleur-de-lis (black with a bright red filigree design).

In the regular group: Dots Forming Diamonds; Lattice and Vine (white lattice with colored flowers); Texas Centennial (cowboy and horse); Special Issues with dates (1936, 1938, and 1942); and Tulip No. 2 (black, blue, green, or red).

Rare glasses in the larger group are Circles and Dots (black, blue, green, or red); Star No. 1 (small stars scattered over the glass in black, blue, green, or red); Cornflower No. 2 (dark blue, light blue, red, or yellow); Provincial Cress (red and burgundy with maple leaves); and Antique No. 2 (assorted antiques on each glass in lime green, deep red, orange, blue, and black).

Band #1, red & black, 1933, 3⅜" .. **3.00**
Band #2, black & red, Canadian, 1933, 4¾" **20.00**
Band #2, black & red, 1933, 3⅜" .. **3.00**
Band #3, white & blue, 1933, 3⅜" **3.00**
Band #4, blue, 1933, 3⅜" **3.00**
Bicentennial Tulip, green, red or yellow, 1975, 3¾", ea **15.00**
Blue Tulips, 1937, 4¼" **20.00**
Carnival, blue, green, red or yellow, 1939, 3½", ea **9.00**
Checkerboard, white w/blue, green or red, 1936, 3½", ea **20.00**
Circles & Dot, any color, 1934, 3½", ea **7.00**
Cornflower #1, light blue & green, Canadian, 1941, 4⅝", ea... **20.00**
Cornflower #1, light blue & green, Canadian, 3¼", ea **8.00**
Crystal Petal, clear & plain w/fluted base, 1951, 3½", ea **2.00**

Ethnic Series, 1974, Canadian, 4⅝": Poppy Red India, Lime Green Calypso, Royal Blue Spanish, Yellow Scottish, $20.00. each. (Photo courtesy Joyce Jackson)

Dots Forming Diamonds, any color, 1935, 3½", ea........**50.00**

Forget-Me-Not, dark blue, light blue, red or yellow, 1948, 3½", ea **4.00**

Galleon, black, blue, green, red or yellow, Canadian, 1936, 3⅛", ea **30.00**

Hostess, clear & plain w/indented groove base, 1960, 3¾", ea ..**1.00**

Jonquil (Posy Pattern), yellow & green, Canadian, 1941, 3¼" **8.00**

Jonquil (Posy Pattern), yellow & green, 1941, 3½", ea **4.00**

Lattice & Vine, white w/blue, green or red, 1936, 3½", ea **100.00**

Petal Star, clear w/indented star base, Canadian, 1978, 3¼", ea...................................**2.00**

Plain, clear, like Tulip #1 w/out design, 1940, 3½", ea.......**4.00**

Provencial Crest, red & burgundy, Canadian, 1974, 4⅝", ea..................................**25.00**

Sailboat #1, blue, 1936, 3½", ea..**12.00**

Sailboat #2, blue, green, light green or red, 1936, 3½", ea **12.00**

Stars #1, black, blue, green or red, 1935, 3½", ea...................**7.00**

Stars #1, yellow, 1935, 3½", ea...**25.00**

Stars #2, clear w/orange stars, Canadian, 1971, 4⅝", ea..**5.00**

Tulip (Posy Pattern), red & green, Canadian, 1941, 3¼", ea..**8.00**

Tulip (Posy Pattern), red & green, 1941, 3½", ea...................**4.00**

Tulip #1, black, blue, green, red or yellow, 1937, 3½", ea **4.00**

Tulip #2, black, blue, green or red, 1938, 3½", ea..................**25.00**

Tulip #3, dark blue, light blue, red or yellow, 1950, 3⅞", ea...**4.00**

Violet (Posy Pattern), blue and green, 1941, Canadian, 4⅝", $20.00; 3½", $4.00; Canadian, 3¼", $8.00.

Teapots

The popularity of teatime and tea-related items continues, and vintage and finer quality teapots have become harder to find. Those from the 1890s through the 1920s reflect their age with three and four digit prices. Examples from the 1700s and 1800s are most often found in museums or large auction houses. Teapots listed here represent examples still available at the flea market level.

Most collectors begin with a general collection of varied teapots until they decide upon the specific category that appeals to them. Collecting categories include miniatures, doll or toy sets, those made by a certain manufacturer, figurals, or a particular style (such as Art Deco or English floral). Some of the latest trends in collecting are Chinese Yixing (pronounced yee-shing; teapots from an unglazed earthenware in forms taken from nature), 1950s pink or black teapots, Cottageware teapots, and figural teapots (those shaped like people, animals, or other objects). While teapots made in Japan have waned in collectibility, collectors have begun to realize many detailed or delicate examples are available. Of special interest are Dragonware teapots or sets where a dragon is molded in relief. Some of these sets have the highly desired lithophane cups — where a Geisha girl is molded in transparent relief in the bottom of the cup. When the cup is held up to the light, the image becomes visible.

For more information we recommend *Teapots, The Collector's Guide* by Tina Carter, listed in the Directory under California. Two quarterly publications are also available; see Clubs and Newsletters for information on *Tea Talk* and *TeaTime Gazette*.

Figural, bear holding candy cane, paw is spout, Fitz & Floyd.............................**75.00**
Figural, birthday cake, candle finial, Lillian Vernon, Taiwan **22.00**
Figural, cat, black & white w/red collar, Cortendorf, Germany **95.00**
Figural, Dutch maid holding jug (spout), Red Wing USA, ca 1940 ....**120.00**
Figural, elf, on knees, Golden Crown, W Germany.......**85.00**

Figural, Jefferson Memorial, Fitz and Floyd, limited edition, 7", from $175.00 to $200.00.

Figural, Nutcracker, Russ, China, 1980s..............................**30.00**
Figural, Santa sits petting dog, Home For the Holidays, China **25.00**
Figural, Snowbear, painted over glaze..............................**18.00**
Figural, Snowman, holds broom & snowball, hat is lid, Fitz & Floyd...............................**75.00**
Miniature, figural, carrot, hand-painted porcelain, Thailand, 2"......................................**18.00**
Miniature, figural pumpkin w/applied leaves & flowers, unmarked, 1"..................**15.00**
Miniature, metal painted white w/Blue Willow design, unmarked, ¾"...................**8.00**
Miniature, white w/blue country heart, ceramic, unmarked, ¾"......................................**5.00**
Miniature, windmill scene, hand-painted, Made in Japan..............................**20.00**
Porcelain, Masons, white w/Eastern Star decal, Enesco, sm **50.00**
Porcelain, white w/poinsettia & ribbon trim, Japan.........**30.00**

Porcelain, Royal Albert, Old English Rose, $125.00.

Porcelain, white w/sunflower decal, Certified International, Thailand..........................**35.00**

Pottery, carousel horse, Heritage Mint, Taiwan **25.00**

Pottery, Father Christmas, hand-painted decor, Sadler, 1930s-40s **150.00**

Pottery, Kansas, green with gold, Hall, six-cup, $225.00. (Photo courtesy Margaret and Kenn Whitmyer)

Pottery, white w/holly leaves, Crawford Pottery, 1950s, sm **20.00**

Pottery, white w/lettuce green band, silver trim, McCormick, 1940s.............................**50.00**

Pottery, white w/Silent Night pattern, Sango, Japan, 1980s..........................**125.00**

Souvenir, Moscow Olympics XXII, white w/red & gold decor, sq **85.00**

Souvenir, Queen Mary's 90th Birthday, white w/transfer, 1990, 2-cup **80.00**

Tiara Exclusives

Collectors are just beginning to take notice of the glassware sold through Tiara in-home parties, their Sandwich line in particular. Several companies were involved in producing the lovely items they've marketed over the years, among them Indiana Glass, Fenton, Dalzell Viking, and L.E. Smith. In the late 1960s Tiara contracted with Indiana to produce their famous line of Sandwich dinnerware (a staple at Indiana Glass since the late 1920s). Their catalogs continue to carry this pattern, and over the years, it has been offered in many colors: ruby, teal, crystal, amber, green, pink, blue, and others in limited amounts. We've listed a few pieces of Tiara's Sandwich below, and though the market is unstable, our values will serve to offer an indication of current values. Unless you're sure of what you're buying, though, don't make the mistake of paying 'old' Sandwich prices for Tiara. To learn more about the two lines, we recommend *Collectible Glassware from the 40s, 50s, and 60s* by Gene Florence (Collector Books). Also refer to *Collecting Tiara Amber Sandwich Glass* by Mandi Birkinbine; she is listed in the Directory under Idaho.

Basket, amber, tall & slender, 10¾x4¾"........................**50.00**

Bowl, amber, 6-sided, 1¼x6¼"..**12.00**

Bowl, salad; amber, slant-sided, 3x8⅜" **20.00**

Butter dish, Bicentennial Blue, from $25 to **35.00**

Cake plate, Chantilly Green, footed, 4x10", from $55 to....**70.00**

Candle holders, Chantilly Green, 8½", pr **45.00**

Canister, amber, 26-oz, 5⅝", from $12 to **20.00**

Canister, amber, 52-oz, 8⅞", from $18 to **26.00**

Clock, amber, wall hanging, 12" dia, from $20 to..............**25.00**

Compote, amber, 8"...............**25.00**

Cup, coffee; amber, 9-oz..........**4.00**

Cup, snack; amber **4.00**

Dish, club, heart, diamond or spade shape, clear, 4", ea **3.00**

Egg tray, Chantilly Green, from $15 to **22.00**

Fairy lamp, Chantilly Green, from $18 to **26.00**

Goblet, table wine; amber, 8½-oz, 5½" **7.50**

Goblet, water; Bicentennial Blue, 8-oz, 5¼", from $8 to......**12.00**

Goblet, water; Spruce Green, 8-oz, 5¼", from $4 to.................**5.50**

Mug, amber, footed, 5½".........**8.00**

Napkin holder, Sandwich, amber, footed fan shape, 4x7½", from $22.00 to $38.00. (Photo courtesy Mandi Birkinbine)

Plate, dinner; amber, 10", from $9.50 to **12.50**

Plate, salad; amber, 8"............**7.00**

Platter, amber, sawtooth rim, 12", from $8.50 to **12.00**

Salt & pepper shakers, amber, 4¾", pr, from $18 to.......**25.00**

Tray, amber, footed, 1¾x12¾"..**35.00**

Tray, divided relish; amber, 4-compartment, 10", from $25 to **30.00**

Tumbler, juice; amber, 8-oz, 4", from $12 to **14.00**

Vase, amber, ruffled, footed, 3¼x6½" **16.00**

Wine set, amber, decanter, tray & 8 goblets **55.00**

Toothbrush Holders

Children's ceramic toothbrush holders represent one of today's popular collecting fields, with some of the character-related examples bringing $150.00 and up. Many were made in Japan before WWII.

For more information we recommend *A Pictorial Guide to Toothbrush Holders* by Marilyn Cooper; she is listed in the Directory under Texas. Plate numbers in the following listings correspond with her book.

Andy Gump & Min, Japan, bisque, plate #221, 4", from $85 to **100.00**

Annie Oakley, Japan, plate #11, 5¾", from $125 to **150.00**

Baby Deer, marked Brush Teeth Daily, Japan, plate #12, 4", $110 to **140.00**

Bear w/scarf & hat, Japan, plate #16, 5½", from $80 to ..**100.00**

Big Bird, Taiwan (RCC), plate #263, 4½", from $85 to ..**95.00**

Boy in top hat, Japan, plate #29, 5½", from $65 to.............**75.00**

Boy w/violin, Japan (Goldcastle), plate #30, 5½", from $80 to.......**90.00**

Bozo w/side tray, Germany, plate #23, 5⅝", from $135 to **150.00**

Calico cat, Japan, plate #37, 5½", from $90 to...................**110.00**

Calico dogs, Japan, from $55 to..**70.00**

Candlestick Maker, Japan (Goldcastle), plate #150, 5", from $70 to **85.00**

Cat on pedestal, Japan (Diamond T), plate #225, 6", from $150 to...................................**175.00**

Circus elephant, Japan, plate #56, from $85 to...................**100.00**

Clown holding mask, Japan, plate #62, 5½", from $110 to..**150.00**

Clown juggling, Japan, plate #60, 5", from $80 to.................**90.00**

Dachshund, Japan, plate #71, 5¼", from $70 to **80.00**

Doctor w/satchel, Japan, plate #206, 5¾".........................**90.00**

Dog w/basket, Japan, plate #72, from $90 to...................**110.00**

Donald Duck, WDE, bisque, plate #83, 5", from $250 to ...**300.00**

Flapper, plate #230, 4¼", from $120 to...........................**140.00**

Indian chief, Japan, plate #115, 4½", from $250 to **300.00**

Little Red Riding Hood, Germany (DRGM), plate #210, 5½", from $200 to.................**250.00**

Mary Poppins, Japan, plate #119, 6", from $100 to **150.00**

Old King Cole, Japan, plate #125, 5¼", from $85 to **100.00**

Old Mother Hubbard, Germany, plate #3, 6", from $350 to...........**425.00**

Pinocchio & Figaro, Shafford, plate #242, 5", from $500 to ...**525.00**

Pluto, Japan, plate #133, 4½", from $300 to.................**350.00**

Skippy, plate #245, jointed arms, 5⅝", from $150 to **200.00**

Soldier, one hole, tray at feet, wall mount, 6¾", $80.00. (Photo courtesy Marilyn Cooper)

Three Bears, w/bowls, Japan (KIM USUI), plate #248, 4", from $90 to............................**125.00**

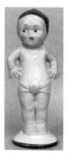

Toddler (leaning against toothbrush holder), body holds tooth powder, shaker holes in cap, Japan, 7½", from $140.00 to $160.00. (Photo courtesy Carol Bess White)

Tom, Tom the Piper's Son, Japan, plate #154, 5¾", from $100 to **150.00**

Traffic cop, Germany, Don't Forget the Teeth, plate #243, 5", from $350 to **375.00**

Toys

Toy collecting remains a very popular hobby, and though some areas of the market may have softened to some extent over the past two years, classic toys remain a good investment. Especially strong are the tin windups made by such renowned companies as Strauss, Marx, Lehmann, Chein, etc., and the battery-operated toys made from the '40s through the '60s in Japan. Because of their complex mechanisms, few survive.

Toys from the 1800s are rarely if ever found in mint condition but should at least be working and have all their original parts. Toys manufactured in the twentieth century are evaluated more critically. Compared to one in mint condition, original box intact, even a slightly worn toy with no box may be worth only about half as much. Character-related toys, space toys, toy trains, and toys from the '60s are very desirable.

Several good books are available, if you want more information: *Collector's Guide to Tootsietoys, Second Edition,* by David E. Richter; *Matchbox Toys, 1947 – 1998, Second Edition,* by Dana Johnson; *Hake's Price Guide to Character Toys, Third Edition,* by Ted Hake; *TV Toys and Memorabilia, Second Edition,* by Greg Davis and Bill Morgan; *Rubber Toy Vehicles* by Dave Leopard; *Collector's Guide to Battery Toys* by Don Hultzman; *Cartoon Toys and Collectibles* by David Longest; *and Schroeder's Collectible Toys, Antique to Modern.* All are available from Collector Books. See also Action Figures; Breyer Horses; Hartland; Character Collectibles; Star Wars; Western Heroes; Clubs and Newsletters.

Battery-Operated

ABC Toyland Express, MT, 1950s, 4 actions, litho tin, 14½", NM **125.00**

Airport Saucer, MT, 1960s, 4 actions, litho tin, 8" dia, NM **140.00**

Alley the Roaring Stalking Alligator, Marx, 1960s, 19", EXIB **350.00**

Animal Train, MIB, from $225 to **300.00**

B-Z Rabbit, MT, 1950s, 4 actions, litho tin, 7" L, NMIB ...**125.00**

Balloon Bunny, rare, MIB..**250.00**

Big Wheel Ice Cream Truck, Taiyo, 1970s, 3 actions, 10", EX .**100.00**

Brave Eagle, TN, 1950s, several actions, litho tin, 11", EX ..**140.00**

Bruno the Walking Bear, rare, MIB, from $300 to **375.00**

Bubble Blowing Dog, M, from $225 to **275.00**

Bulldog Tank, Remco, 1960s, 22", EX (EX box).................**150.00**

Busy Secretary, Linemar, 1950s, several actions, 7½", MIB.....**300.00**

Cannon Truck, Ny-Lint, tin, 23",
EX (G box)....................**140.00**
Chap the Obedient Dog, Rosko,
1960s, 3 actions, MIB, from
$200 to.........................**250.00**
Chee Chee Chihuahua, Mego,
1960s, several actions, 8",
EX...............................**50.00**
Cindy the Meowing Cat,
Tomiyama, 1950s, 4 actions,
12", EX...........................**75.00**
Circus Queen Seal, Playthings,
rare, MIB.....................**375.00**
Climbing Clown, rare, EX ..**1,650.00**
Clown on Unicycle, MT, 1960s, 3
actions, litho tin, 10½", rare,
EX...............................**350.00**
Colonel Hap Hazard, Marx, 1968,
11", EX..........................**700.00**
Comic Choo Choo, Cragstan, 1960s,
3 actions, 10", EX............**65.00**
Cragstan Galloping Cowboy,
litho tin, MIB, from $225
to **275.00**
Cragstan Rolling Honey Bear, rare,
MIB, from $475 to.........**575.00**
Cragstan Yo-Yo Clown, 1960s, 3
actions, 9", NM **250.00**
Dalmatian One-Man Band, Alps,
1950s, plays drums & cym-
bals, 9", NM **125.00**

Dashee the Derby Hat Dachshund, Mego Corp., four actions, 1971, complete with plastic Derby, remote control, MIB, $80.00. (Photo courtesy Don Hultzman)

Desert Patrol Jeep, MT, 1960s,
several actions, litho tin, 11",
NM...............................**125.00**
Doxie the Dog, Linemar, 1950s,
several actions, 9", EX...**50.00**
Drinking Sheriff, NM, from $75
to.................................**100.00**
Drumming Bear, Alps, 1960s,
4 actions, MIB, from $100
to **125.00**
Electro Toy Sand Loader, TN,
1950s, MIB...................**225.00**
FBI Godfather Car, Bandai, 1970s,
3 actions, 10", EX..........**65.00**
Fire Command Car, TN, 1950s,
several actions, litho tin,
EX.............................**260.00**
Firefly Bug, TN, 1950s, 3 actions,
litho tin, EX **100.00**
Flexie the Pocket Monkey,
Alps, 1960s, 3 actions, 12",
EX...............................**115.00**
Flipper the Spouting Dolphin,
Bandai, MIB, from $100
to **125.00**
Fumbling Pussy, MT, 1970s, 3
actions, 10" L, EX **65.00**
Grand-Pa Car, Y, 1950s, 4 actions,
litho tin, 9", EX..............**75.00**
Greyhound Bus, KKK, 1950s, litho
tin, 7", EX.....................**140.00**
Happy Plane, TPS, 1960s, 3 actions,
litho tin, 9" L, EX...........**115.00**
Happy Tractor, Daiya, 1960s, 4
actions, 8", EX...............**65.00**
Hess Fire Truck, Hong Kong, red
plastic, 11", MIB.........**245.00**
Honda Big Ride Motorcycle
#34, litho tin, 10", EX
(worn box)...................**75.00**
Hootin' Hollow Haunted
House, Marx, 1960s, 11",
NM+...............................**750.00**

Howdy Doody World Touring Car, rare, EX, from $700 to ...**800.00**

Hungry Hound Dog, Y, 1950s, several actions, 9½", EX ...**285.00**

Indian Joe, Alps, advances & plays drum, litho tin, NMIB ...**100.00**

Japanese Monster, rare, NM, from $425 to **475.00**

Jolly Santa on Snow, Alps, 1950s, 12", MIB, from $350 to ..**400.00**

King Size Volkswagen, tin, 15", MIB, from $325 to **375.00**

Laffin' Head Indian Squaw, M, from $120 to **150.00**

Lite-It-Up-Ford, Ichiko, 1950s, 7½", EX...........................**170.00**

Little Indian, TN, 1960s, 3 actions, 9", EX.............................**125.00**

Lucky Car, Marusan, rare, NM, from $325 to **375.00**

Magic Action Bulldozer, TN, 1950s, 3 actions, 9½", MIB.......**250.00**

Mary's Little Lamb, Alps, 1950s, 3 actions, 10½", EX.........**150.00**

Mentor Wizard, Hasbro, MIB, from $120 to **150.00**

Mickey Mouse Flying Saucer, MT, MIB, from $200 to **250.00**

Mickey Mouse Trolley, MT, 1960s, 3 actions, litho tin, M ..**175.00**

Mighty Kong, Marx, plush w/shackled hands, 1950s, 11", MIB..............................**700.00**

Mighty Kong, MIB, from $525 to..............................**600.00**

Monkey Mobile, Aoshin, 1967, 12", NMIB...........................**525.00**

Mother Goose, Yonezawa, litho tin, MIB........................**175.00**

Music Hall, Linemar, 1950s, several actions, litho tin, EX **200.00**

Musical Ford, 1955, MIB, from $475 to...........................**535.00**

Musical Monkey Melody Train, MIB, from $225 to **275.00**

Ol' Sleepy Head Rip, Y, 1950s, several actions, 9½", MIB ..**775.00**

Pat the Roaring Elephant, Y, 1950s, 4 actions, litho tin, 9", EX ..**225.00**

Periscope Firing Range, Cragstan, tin, MIB........................**190.00**

Pilot Electro Boat, TN, litho tin, 11", NM (EX box).........**170.00**

Playful Puppy w/Caterpillar, MT, 4 actions, litho tin, 5", EX ..**150.00**

Police Jeep, Rosko, litho tin, 13", MIB, from $500 to **550.00**

Puzzled Puppy, MT, 1950s, several actions, 5", EX..............**150.00**

Radicon Oldsmobile, MT, NMIB, from $600 to.................**700.00**

Roll-Over Rover, Mego, 1970s, 3 actions, 9", EX................**65.00**

Santa on Monorail, rare, MIB, from $600 to.................**650.00**

Shooting Cowboys in Barrel, very rare, EX, from $700 to ..**850.00**

Smokey Bill on Old Fashioned Car, TN, 1960s, 6 actions, 9", MIB ..**250.00**

Smoky (sic) Bear, Marusan, several actions, litho tin & plush, EXIB **225.00**

Smurf Road Race Village Set, Talbot Toys, remote control, 1983, EXIB, $65.00.

Snowman, MIB, from $225 to...**275.00**

Speed King Racer, Y, 1960s, 3 actions, 12½", EX.........**110.00**

Talking Trixie, Alps, 1950s, 4 actions, 6½", EX..............**65.00**

Teddy the Champ Boxer, Y, 1950s, several actions, 9", MIB **435.00**

Thunder Jet Boat, MIB, from $300 to....................................**375.00**

Tumbling Clown, Remco, EX, from $100 to...........................**125.00**

Waddles Family Car, Y, 1960s, MIB, from $135 to **175.00**

Walking (Esso) Tiger, Marx, plush, 1½", MMIB **575.00**

Walking Gorilla, Linemar, MIB **475.00**

Weeping Skeleton, rare, MIB, from $300 to.................**375.00**

Wonderland Locomotive, Bandai, 1960s, 3 actions, 9", EX...**65.00**

Yo-Yo Monkey, YM, 1960s, 12", EX **150.00**

Windups, Frictions, and Other Mechanicals

Amos 'N Andy Fresh Air Taxi, Marx, 1930, G **375.00**

Barney Google on Sparkplug, Nifty, litho tin, 7" L, VG..........**860.00**

Bear in Row Boat, STE, 1950s, 10", NM+IB **275.00**

Big Aerial Acrobats, Marx, 11", EXIB **300.00**

BO Plenty, Marx, 1930s, 8", VG **150.00**

Boob McNutt, Strauss, flat hat version, VG...................**600.00**

Broadway Trolley, Chein, 8", EX **145.00**

Butter & Egg Man, Marx, 1930s, EX **700.00**

Casper Super Ghost Tank, Linemar, litho tin, 4", EXIB **415.00**

Chad Valley Delivery Van, litho tin, 10", MIB **1,760.00**

Charlie McCarthy Benzine Mobile, Marx, 1930s, 7", G+.....**350.00**

Clown Juggler, Schuco, tin w/felt outfit, 5", NMIB..........**470.00**

Clown w/Mouse, Schuco, tin w/felt outfit, 4½", VG.............**250.00**

Clown w/Spinning Umbrella Hat, litho tin, 8", EX............**240.00**

Coney Island Carnival Ride, Technoflix, litho tin, 14x20", NMIB............................**330.00**

Cowboy Juggler, Schuco, tin w/cloth outfit, 5", NM..**725.00**

Curvo 1000 Motorcycle w/Driver, litho tin, 5", NMIB.......**990.00**

Dandy Jim (2 Clowns), Unique Art, litho tin, 9", EX....**400.00**

Dick Tracy Police Car, Marx, battery-op roof light, green, 1950s, NM....................**250.00**

Donald Duck, Schuco, litho tin, long-billed, 6", G+ (original box)............................**1,600.00**

Donald Duck Duet, Marx, 11", EX **450.00**

Dump truck, #352, Wyandotte, MIB, from $140.00 to $175.00. (Photo courtesy Jeff Bub Auctions)

Ferris Wheel, Chein, lithoed base, 1930s, 17", VG **250.00**

Fiat 600 Auto w/Sunroof, Bandai, tin, friction, 7", EX.........**80.00**

Finnegan the Porter, Unique Art, litho tin, 14", EXIB.....**350.00**

Fishing Bear, TPS, litho tin, 7", EXIB.............................**275.00**

Gnome w/Gnome, Schuco, tin w/cloth outfit & leather apron, 4", VG...........................**500.00**

Gorilla, Marx, plush, in shackles & chains, 8", MIB.............**450.00**

Helicoptor on Airfield, Cragstan, litho tin, 10", EXIB......**110.00**

Hessmobile, litho tin, 2 figures, 9", VG.................................**575.00**

Hi-Way Henry, Fischer, litho tin, 10", G.........................**1,100.00**

Honey-Moon Express, Marx, 1930s, 10", VGIB.........**200.00**

Jazzbo Jim, Strauss, EX.....**600.00**

Jiggs Jazz Car, Nifty, 1924, litho tin, 7", EX..................**1,650.00**

Kid Flyer, B&R, litho tin, 8", VG............................**450.00**

Lady w/Fan, painted tin, 7", VG...........................**850.00**

Ludwig Von Drake, Linemar, 1950s, NM, $500.00 at auction (VG, $350.00). (Photo courtesy Jeff Bubb)

Mammy Walker, Lindstrom, litho tin, 8", EX.....................**250.00**

Mary Had a Little Lamb, Wells, plastic, 4½", NMIB......**125.00**

Mickey Mouse Meteor Train, Mar Lines, litho tin, 4-pc, 34", VG......................**575.00**

Military Truck, Tipp, camouflage tin, open bed, 8", VG+...**150.00**

Mirakcar, Schuco, tin, nickel-plated disk wheels, 4½", EXIB................................**110.00**

Monkey Drummer, Schuco, litho tin w/cloth outfit, 4½", EX..**100.00**

Monkey on Motorcycle, Gama, litho tin, 7", EXIB........**575.00**

Mortimer Snerd Walker, Marx, 1939, 9", NMIB............**725.00**

Motorcycle, w/Couple, Tipp, litho tin, 9½", EX...............**1,870.00**

Native on Alligator, Wolverine, litho tin, 15", EX.........**575.00**

Navy Frog Man, Chein, plastic flippers, 12", NMOC....**125.00**

Over & Under Toy, Wolverine, litho tin, 25" L, NMIB...........**165.00**

Peter Rabbit Chick Mobile, Lionel, compo figures, 9", G.....**225.00**

Popeye Express (Wheelbarrow & Parrot), Marx, 9", EX..**750.00**

Radio Car, Schuco #4012, 6", NMIB...........................**400.00**

Renault Coupe, CIJ, painted tin w/rubber tires, 11½", G+..**300.00**

Rudy the Ostrich, Nifty, litho tin, 8½", G...........................**220.00**

Sailor w/Binoculars, Schuco, tin w/cloth outfit, 5", VG...**450.00**

Sam the City Gardener, Marx, 8", VG+...............................**100.00**

Silver Mine Express, Technoflix, litho tin, 22½", NM......**240.00**

Ski Boy, Chein, G..............**150.00**

Tombo Alabama Coon Jigger, Strauss, G **400.00**

Torpedo De Lage, Jep, litho tin, 13", EXIB **2,400.00**

Train Engine, painted tin w/cast-iron spoke wheels, cow catcher, 10" **230.00**

US Army Soldier, Chein, #153, 5", MOC **150.00**

Utility Service Truck & Cable Trailer, Marx, litho tin, 1950s, 19", G+..........................**100.00**

Vebe Tank Truck, painted tin w/composition driver, 14", VG (VG box)........................**850.00**

Wise Pluto, Marx, WDP, 1939, 8", NMIB............................**525.00**

Yell-O-Taxi, Strauss, EX+..**700.00**

Zilotone, Wolverine, litho tin, 7", EX................................**450.00**

Universal

Located in Cambridge, Ohio, Universal Potteries produced various lines of dinnerware from 1934 to the late 1950s, several of which are very attractive, readily available, and therefore quite collectible. See also Cattail.

Baby's Breath, plate, dinner..**19.00**

Ballerina, cake plate.............**25.00**

Ballerina, plate, dinner **6.00**

Ballerina, platter, 12"...........**20.00**

Ballerina (Mist), creamer, from $12 to.............................**15.00**

Ballerina (Mist), plate, cake..**20.00**

Ballerina (Mist), platter, round........................**20.00**

Ballerina Magnolia, cup & saucer...........................**5.00**

Ballerina Rose, sugar bowl, w/lid...**20.00**

Bittersweet, bowl, 10"..........**25.00**

Bittersweet, jar w/lid, 2".......**35.00**

Bittersweet, salt & pepper shakers, 3½", pr.....................**25.00**

Calico Fruit, bowl, oven proof, 8½"...............................**40.00**

Calico Fruit, bowl, 4¼".........**20.00**

Calico Fruit, pitcher, 6¼".....**40.00**

Circus, teapot, white over blue, w/lid...............................**32.00**

Harvest, cup & saucer.........**19.00**

Harvest, plate, sq, 7¼", from $15 to.....................................**20.00**

Fruit salt and pepper shakers, 4", $20.00 for the pair.

Highland, bowl, cereal..........**12.00**

Highland, creamer...............**12.00**

Highland, gravy boat, no under-plate...............................**25.00**

Highland, saucer, from $3 to..**4.00**

Iris, pitcher, cream; 5½x6"...**20.00**

Iris, water server **35.00**

Laurella, bowl, vegetable; coral **19.00**

Rambler Rose, plate, 9".........**6.00**

Woodvine, bowl, vegetable ...**15.00**

Woodvine, gravy boat **20.00**

Woodvine, pitcher, 1-qt, 7"...**27.50**

Woodvine, utility jar, 26-oz ..**20.00**

Van Briggle

The Van Briggle Pottery of Colorado Springs, Colorado, was established in 1901 by Artus Van Briggle upon the completion of his quest to perfect a complete flat matt glaze. His wife, Ann, worked with him and they, along with George Young, were responsible for the modeling of the wares. Known for their flowing Art Nouveau shapes, much of the ware was eventually made from molds with each piece carefully trimmed and refined before the glaze was sprayed on. Their most popular colors were Persian Rose, Ming Blue, and Mustard Yellow.

Van Briggle died in 1904, but the work was continued by his wife. With new facilities built in 1908, tiles, gardenware and commercial lines were added to the earlier artware lines. Reproductions of some early designs continue to be made. The Double AA mark has always been in use, but after 1920 the dates and/or shape numbers were dropped. Mention should be made here as well that the Anna Van Briggle glaze is a later line which was made between 1956 and 1968. For more information see *The Collector's Encyclopedia of Van Briggle Art Pottery* by Richard Sasicki and Josie Fania.

Bowl, embossed acorns & oak leaves, Persian Rose, 3½x5¾"......................**160.00**
Figurine, girl holding shell in lap, white, 8" **100.00**

Dish, Indian lady grinding corn, turquoise, 6½", $125.00.

Figurine, rabbit, deep mulberry, 3½" L **125.00**
Flower frog, duck in pond, turquoise, 2⅞x9¾" frog w/6x14" bowl **160.00**
Lamp, Damsel of Damascus, white, w/original shade **130.00**
Tray, Shell Girl, blue & green, 8½" **150.00**
Vase, butterfly under blue & maroon, post-1930s, 4"..**100.00**
Vase, crescent moon shape, Persian Rose, 7½x7¾".**100.00**
Vase, deer figural, green to blue, signed DM, 9"...............**100.00**
Vase, dragonflies, dark turquoise, 2⅜x8" dia.....................**175.00**
Vase, floral, dark purple on maroon, 1921, 2¾x2¾"................**165.00**
Vase, leaves, cream & white matt, signed FW, 5".................**50.00**
Vase, leaves form body, blue & aqua mottle, post-1930s, 3½"............................**100.00**
Vase, Lorelei, blue shaded to turquoise, AA Van Briggle, ca 1970s, 11".....................**325.00**

Vase, narrow leaves, tall between short, Persian Rose, 1920, squat, 5" **175.00**
Vase, poppies, brown & green, 1920s-30s, 8¼", NM.....**250.00**
Vase, stylized floral, turquoise w/blue overspray, 5¾" ..**125.00**
Vase, twisted design, red w/purple overspray, 7½" **110.00**
Wall plaque, Indian's face, Ming Green, 5½x3½"..............**125.00**

Vernon Kilns

From 1931 until 1958, Vernon Kilns produced hundreds of patterns of fine dinnerware that today's collectors enjoy reassembling. They retained the services of famous artists and designers such as Rockwell Kent and Walt Disney, who designed both dinnerware lines and novelty items. Examples of their work are at a premium. (Nearly all artist-designed lines utilized the Ultra shape. To evaluate the work of Blanding, use 200% of our high range; for Disney lines, 700% to 800%; Kent — Moby Dick and Our America 250%; for Salamina, 500% to 700%.)

For more informtion, we recommend *Collectible Vernon Kilns, Second Edition*, by Maxine Nelson (Collector Books). See Clubs and Newsletters for information concerning *Vernon Views* newsletter. Our values are average. The more elaborate the pattern, the higher the value.

Anytime, bowl, vegetable; divided, 9", from $10 to...............**12.00**
Anytime, coffeepot, w/lid, 8-cup, from $30 to.....................**45.00**
Anytime, mug, 12-oz, from $12 to................................**20.00**
Chatelaine, bowl, chowder; Topaz & Bronze, 6", from $15 to....**25.00**
Chatelaine, creamer, Platinum & Jade, from $40 to...........**45.00**
Chatelaine, plate, salad; Topaz & Bronze, 7½", from $12 to **15.00**
Fantasia, bowl, Winged Nymph, #122, 12" base dia........**300.00**
Fantasia, figurine, Centaur, #31, from $1,100 to...........**1,500.00**
Fantasia, figurine, Donkey Unicorn, #16, from $600 to............**700.00**
Fantasia, vase, Cameo Goddess, #126 ....**700.00**
Lotus, creamer **15.00**
Lotus, plate, offset; 7½"..........**8.00**
Lotus, sugar bowl, w/lid **16.00**
Melinda, bowl, fruit; 5½", from $5 to **8.00**
Melinda, bowl, serving; oval, 10", from $15 to **25.00**
Melinda, egg cup, from $18 ..**30.00**
Melinda, platter, 16", from $35 to **50.00**
Montecito, bowl, mixing; 5", from $15 to..............................**20.00**
Montecito, bowl, salad; 13", from $45 to..............................**75.00**
Montecito, butter pat, individual, 2½", from $15 to.............**25.00**
Montecito, coaster/cup warmer, 4½", from $18 to.............**22.00**
Montecito, pepper mill, wood encased, 4½", from $35 to .**40.00**
Montecito, plate, bread & butter; 6½", from $5 to................**8.00**

Montecito, spoon holder, from $45 to **75.00**

Pan American Lei, ashtray, 5½" **35.00**

Pan American Lei, plate, coupe; 6" **12.00**

San Fernando, bowl, rim soup; 8", from $12 to **20.00**

San Fernando, coffeepot, w/lid, 8-cup, from $35 to **65.00**

San Fernando, plate, dinner; 10½", from $12 to...........**18.00**

San Fernando, sugar bowl, w/lid, from $15 to **20.00**

San Marino, ashtray, 5½", from $15 to **25.00**

San Marino, chop plate, Lei Lani, 14", $125.00; tumbler, $75.00. (Photo courtesy Maxine Nelson)

San Marino, coaster, ridged, 3¾", from $10 to **15.00**

San Marino, custard, 3", from $18 to **22.00**

San Marino, platter, 9½", from $10 to **15.00**

San Marino, teapot, w/lid, 8-cup, 11" W, from $30 to.........**45.00**

Souvenir plate, Fredric Chopin, Music Makers, 8½" **25.00**

Souvenir plate, St. Augustine, maroon transfer, 10½", from $10.00 to $15.00.

Souvenir plate, Tacoma Narrows Bridge, brown.................**35.00**

Souvenir plate, Will Rogers, brown **35.00**

Ultra, bowl, fruit; 5½", from $6 to.................................**12.00**

Ultra, casserole, w/lid, 8" (inside dia), from $75 to.............**95.00**

Ultra, mug, 8-oz, 3½", from $22 to...................................**35.00**

Ultra, plate, chop; 17", from $50 to **80.00**

Ultra, teapot, 6-cup, from $40 to **70.00**

Year 'Round, buffet server, trio; from $35 to **70.00**

Year 'Round, cup & saucer, tea; from $8 to **12.00**

Vietnam War Collectibles

There was conflict in Vietnam for many years before the United States was drawn into it during the Eisenhower years, and fighting raged until well into 1975 when communist forces invaded Saigon and crushed the South Vietnamese government there. Today items from the 1960s and early 1970s are becoming collectible. Pins, booklets, uniforms, patches, and the like reflect these troubled times when anti-war demonstrations raged and unsound political policies cost the lives of many brave young men.

Bayonet, USM8A1 w/self-sharpening scabbard, fits M16 & AR15, EX........................**40.00**

Beret, US Special Forces, w/White Star flash, wool w/plastic liner, EX.......................**265.00**

Book, Vietnam, The Shadow War, soft cover, 8¼x11½", EX..**25.00**

Book, Vietnam Order of Battle, 396 pages, 12x10", EX (w/sleeve).......................**85.00**

Book, 101st Airborne Division, 1968, EX (w/dust jacket)..........**125.00**

Flight suit, US Air Force, EX...**40.00**

Hammock, Jungle green, 1966, EX **25.00**

Knife, Gerber MK1, blued, 6½", w/sharpening steel & sheath, EX **240.00**

Knife, survival; marked Garcia Hackmanm 7" blade, EX (w/sheath)....................**110.00**

License plate, Back Our Boys in Vietnam, red, white & blue, 6x12", EX.......................**40.00**

Life raft, US Navy Mark IV, VG **50.00**

Lighter, Armored Tank emblem, Zippo, VG+ **30.00**

Lighter, MP (Military Police) over crossed dueling pistols, Zippo, EX................................**100.00**

Machette, built-in sharpener in sheath, Ontario Knife Co, EX..............................**50.00**

Mask, US Navy Pilots CO2; MS2201, NM................**195.00**

Medal, Bronze Star, engraved, NM (EX plastic case)............**45.00**

Medic bag, US Army issue, w/contents, dated 1968, EX..**140.00**

Patch, CCN recon RT Alaska, We Kill For Peace, 4" dia, EX **125.00**

Pinback, blue w/white 'OUT', 1⅜" dia, EX........................**170.00**

Poster, Anti-War, LBJ caricature w/The Great Society!?, 29x21", EX................................**25.00**

Poster, This Vacation Visit Beautiful VIETNAM, red and cream, ca 1960, 21x14", M, $35.00.

Survival vest, 11 pockets, Lankford Mfg Co, 1974, VG+ **35.00**

Wristwatch, olive green nylon band, Benrus, military issue, 1975, EX........................**80.00**

Wall Pockets

Here's a collectible that is easily found, relatively inexpensive, and very diversified. They were made in Japan, Czechoslovakia, and by many, many companies in the United States. Those made by companies best known for their art pottery (Weller, Roseville, etc.) are in a class of their own, but the novelty, just-for-fun wall pockets stand on their own merits. Examples with large, colorful birds or those with unusual modeling are usually the more desirable. For more information we recommend *McCoy Pottery Wall Pockets and Decorations* by Craig Nissen; and *Collector's Guide to Made in Japan Ceramics, Vol. III* and *IV,* by Carole Bess White, who is listed in the Directory under Oregon. See also California Pottery, Cleminson; McCoy; Shawnee; other specific manufacturers.

Baby w/swan, marked Bradley Exclusives, Japan **22.00**
Bunting, blue, Morton Pottery, 5" **22.00**
Cherub w/red heart, red stamped Japan, 5" **15.00**
Cup & saucer, Jigsaw Rooster pattern, marked Blue Ridge, 5¾" **10.00**
Dancing lady, blue dress, red-stamped Made in Japan, 8½" **55.00**
Dutch boy, w/goose, black-stamped Made in Japan, 6" **18.00**

Dutch girl w/basket, marked Made in Japan, 6½" **15.00**
Elf in tree, marked SylvaC, made in England **40.00**
Girl on cornucopia, red-stamped Made in Japan, 6½" **15.00**
Girl w/yellow dress & hat, unmarked, 4½" **25.00**
Horseman in top hat, red-stamped Made in Japan, 5¾" **15.00**
Indian chief's head, black-stamped Made in Japan, 6" **20.00**
Lady in white w/green trim on yellow cornucopia, Germany #8922, 7¼" **50.00**
Little Devil, red, stamped Japan in 3-petal flowered wreath, 4¾" **18.00**
Madonna w/Child, holy water font, Italy, 8" **25.00**
Man w/mustache, multicolored, unmarked, 4¼" **25.00**
Parrot on horseshoe, unmarked, 7" L **22.00**
Peacock, flared tail feathers, Morton Pottery, marked USA, 6½" **20.00**
Pears, yellow w/green leaves, sticker, Made in Japan, 4½" ..**12.00**

Radishes, Portugal, 11½", from $28.00 to $40.00. (Photo courtesy Bill and Betty Newbound)

Sailboat, lavender w/gold trim & water, marked Brown China, 5¾".............................**20.00**
Sailors standing on anchor, red-stamped Made in Japan, 5¾"..............................**15.00**
Straw hat, brown w/white wash, Stanford Pottery, 9".......**12.00**
Turkey, black-stamped Made in Japan, 6⅛".....................**20.00**
Violin, white w/gold trim, incised Moyer, 6¾".....................**15.00**

Western Heroes

Interest is very strong right now in western memorabilia — not only that, but the kids that listened so intently to those after-school radio episodes featuring one of the many cowboy stars that sparked the airwaves in the '50s are now some of today's more affluent collectors, able and wanting to search out and buy toys they had in their youth. Put those two factors together, and it's easy to see why these items are so popular. For more information, we recommend *Collector's Guide to TV Toys and Memorabilia, 1960s & 1970s,* by Greg Davis and Bill Morgan; *Roy Rogers and Dale Evans Toys and Memorabilia* by P. Allan Coyle; and *The W.F. Cody Buffalo Bill Collector's Guide* by James W. Wojtowicz. All are published by Collector Books. See also Coloring Books; Comic Books; Games; Puzzles.

Davy Crockett

Davy Crockett had long been a favorite in fact and folklore. Then with the opening of Disney's Frontierland and his continuing adventures on 1950s television came a surge of interest in all sorts of items featuring the likeness of Fess Parker in a coonskin cap. Millions were drawn to the mystic and excitement surrounding the settlement of our great country. Due to demand, there were many types of items produced for eager fans ready to role play their favorite adventures.

Bank, plaster figure, VG....**125.00**
Chalk, Creston Crayon Co, 1950s, EX (EX box)....................**40.00**
Color TV set, WDP, complete w/viewer & 4 rolls of film, NMOC..**175.00**
Dart Gun Target Set, Knickerbocker, 1950s, complete, NRFB **75.00**

Doll, stuffed cloth with hand-painted vinyl chest, name on chest, unmarked, 1950s, 27", EX, $150.00.

Flashlight, litho tin w/red plastic top, 1950s, 3", EX **30.00**

Hobbyhorse, wood w/heavy bouncing springs, 23x33", EX+..................................**200.00**

Night light, head figure, 1950s, EX **50.00**

Penknife, Imperial/WDP, 1950s, 4", NM **35.00**

Ring, from gumball machine, 1960s, M.........................**15.00**

Thunderbird Moccasin Kit, Blaine, 1950s, complete, NM (EX box) **175.00**

Tool kit, Liberty Steel, litho tin chest, 1955, complete, M............**450.00**

Toss-Up Balloon, Oak Rubber/WDP, MOC **135.00**

Wallet, brown vinyl w/faux fur on Davy's hat, 1955, NM, from $75 to............................**100.00**

Gene Autry

First breaking into show business as a recording star with Columbia Records, Gene went on to become one of Hollywood's most famous singing cowboys. From the late 1930s until the mid-1950s, he rode his wonder horse 'Champion' through almost ninety feature films. He did radio and TV as well, and naturally his fame spawned a wealth of memorabilia originally aimed at his young audiences, now grabbed up just as quickly by collectors.

Drum set, 3-pc set w/cardboard figure seated on drum, NMIB **900.00**

Guitar, plastic, 31", EX **150.00**

Official Ranch Outfit, brown suede vest and chaps, red felt trim, Leslie-Henry, 1940s, NM (VG box), $265.00.

Stencil book, Stencil Art, 1950s, unused, NM....................**75.00**

Hopalong Cassidy

One of the most popular western heroes of all time, Hoppy was the epitome of the highly moral, role-model cowboys of radio and the silver screen that many of us grew up with in the 1940s and 1950s. He was portrayed by Bill Boyd who personally endorsed more than 2,200 items targeting Hoppy's loyal followers.

Binoculars, Sport Glass Chicago, metal & plastic w/paper decals, EX....................**165.00**

Bow tie, cloth w/western scenes, 1950s, NMOC.................**75.00**

Chaps, black suede w/image of Hoppy, 1950s, VG..........**85.00**

Coloring Outfit, Transogram, 1950s, complete, NMIB..............**300.00**
Decal sheet, set of 4, 8x3" sheet, M **50.00**
Dinnerware set, 3-pc, EX ...**225.00**
Dominoes, Milton Bradley, 1950, complete, EX (EX box) ..**100.00**

Hold-Up Game, Enterprises of America, 1950, NMIB, $85.00. (Photo courtesy Greg Davis and Bill Morgan)

Mask, Traveling Trading CO, rubber, 8", NM (NM box) ..**225.00**
Picture Gun & Theatre, battery-operated, MIB **350.00**
Sparkler, plastic bust figure w/metal plunger, 1950, 3½", EX **275.00**
Spurs, Olympia, NM...........**200.00**
Switch-A-Buckle Belt, complete, NMOC **225.00**

The Lone Ranger

Recalling 'those thrilling days of yesteryear,' we can't help but remember the adventures of our hero, The Lone Ranger. He's been admired since that first radio show in 1933, and today's collectors seek a wide variety of his memorabilia;

premiums, cereal boxes, and even carnival chalkware prizes are a few examples. See Clubs and Newsletters for information on *The Silver Bullet.*

Action Arcade, 1975, NMIB, from $100 to..........................**125.00**

Atomic Bomb ring, brass with gilt bomb on red plastic fins, 1947, NM, from $125.00 to $145.00.

Crayons, 1953, complete, NM (NM tin box), from $75 to **100.00**
Doll, talker, stuffed cloth, Mego, 1972, 24", MIB **65.00**
First Aid Kit, American White Cross Inc, 1938, complete, EX................................**65.00**
Harmonica, silver plated, 1947, NMIB, from $75 to **125.00**
Horseshoe, rubber, Gardner Games, 1950s, complete, NMIB, from $175 to **195.00**
Magic slate, cardboard w/erasable film sheet, Whitman, 1978, EX................................**65.00**
Movie viewer, Lone Ranger Rides Again, 1940s, lg, NMIB, from $200 to..........................**250.00**
Outfit, TLR Inc, complete w/chaps & vest, 1930s, VG (worn box)...................**250.00**
Pencil box, blue w/embossed gold image & lettering, 1940, NM..................**100.00**

Picture Printing Set, 1938, complete, NMIB, from $200 to........**225.00**

Punch-Out Set, 1947, complete, NMIB, from $175 to **250.00**

Telescope, 1946, NMIB, from $150 to.................................**200.00**

Roy Rogers

Growing up during the Great Depression, Leonard Frank Sly was determined to make his mark in the entertainment industry. In 1938 after landing small roles in films featuring Gene Autry and others, Republic Studios (recognizing his talents) renamed their singing cowboy Roy Rogers and placed him in his first leading role in *Under Western Stars.* By 1943 he had become America's 'King of the Cowboys.' And his beloved wife Dale Evans and his horse Trigger were at the top with him.

Robert W. Phillips is the author of *Silver Screen Cowboys, Hollywood Cowboy Heroes, Roy Rogers, Singing Cowboy Stars,* and *Western Comics;* we recommend them all. Mr. Phillips is listed in the Directory under Oklahoma. See Clubs and Newsletters for information on the Roy Rogers–Dale Evans Collectors Association.

Riding horse, plush Trigger with molded plastic face, Reliable Toy, Canada, 26" long, EX+, $400.00.

Book bag, 1950s brown vinyl w/shoulder strap, image on front, G.**65.00**

Cowboy outfit, chaps & shirt, Plus Brand, 1950s, unused, NMIB **500.00**

Holster set, Roy on Trigger, genuine leather, 2-gun style w/jewels, 1955, NMIB .**425.00**

Ranch lantern, tin litho, 1950s, unused, M (VG box),.....**100.00**

Slippers, leather cowboy-boot style w/image & lettering, EX.**175.00**

Miscellaneous

Annie Oakley, lunch box, on rearing horse, metal, 1955, no thermos, EX **45.00**

Bat Masterson, decanter, figural, McCormick, 1977, miniature, EX **25.00**

Cisco Kid & Diablo (horse), biscuit tin, English, 1950s, 1½x5" dia **50.00**

Daniel Boone, lunch box, fighting Indians, Aladdin, w/thermos, EX **165.00**

Fess Parker as Daniel Boone, lunch box, American-Tradition, 1965, VG+ **35.00**

Gabby Hayes, cannon ring, Quaker Oats premium, EX **160.00**

Gabby Hayes, marbles, The Goucho of the Prairies, EX (original bag).................**15.00**

Rin Tin Tin, Magic Ring, brass, radio show premium, 1954, EX **215.00**

Rin Tin Tin, pen, rifle shape, radio show premium, 6", EX...**30.00**

Sky King, Spy Detector Writer, Peter Pan premium, 1950s, EX **190.00**

Tom Mix, periscope, Ralston premium, 1930s, EX **55.00**

Wild Bill Hickok, badge, black & white photo in center, 1950s, EX **35.00**

Zorro, lunch box, on rearing horse, Aladdin, 1950s, EX **140.00**

Westmoreland

Originally an Ohio company, Westmoreland relocated in Grapesville, Pennsylvania, where by the 1920s they had became known as one of the country's largest manufacturers of carnival glass. They are best known today for the high quality milk glass which accounted for 90% of their production. For further information we recommend contacting the Westmoreland Glass Society, Inc., listed in Clubs and Newsletters. See also Glass Animals and Birds.

Ashtray, English Hobnail, amber or crystal, 4½" sq **7.50**

Basket, Paneled Grape, milk glass w/decor, ruffled, 8".........**70.00**

Bonbon, Wakefield, crystal w/red stain, crimped, metal handle, 6" **35.00**

Bowl, Lotus/#1921, black, round, lg **50.00**

Bowl, nappy, amber or crystal, 4½" sq......................................**7.00**

Bowl, Paneled Grape, milk glass w/decor, bell shape, footed, 9½"................................**110.00**

Bowl, pickle; English Hobnail, amber or crystal, 8" **15.00**

Bowl, Wakefield, crystal w/red stain, crimped, flat, 12"..**75.00**

Box, heart shape, Chocolate..**55.00**

Candle holder, Paneled Grape, milk glass w/decor, colonial handle, 5" **37.50**

Candlestick, English Hobnail, amber or crystal, round base, 9"....................................**25.00**

Celery/spooner, Paneled Grape, milk glass w/decor, 6"....**40.00**

Cheese dish, English Hobnail, amber or crystal, 8¾" **60.00**

Compote, mint; Wakefield, crystal w/red stain, high foot, 5½" **30.00**

Covered animal dish, cat on rectangular lacy base, purple marbled **250.00**

Covered animal dish, chick on pile of eggs, milk glass, no details **35.00**

Covered animal dish, duck on wavy base, purple marbled carnival, Levey, 8", $150.00.

Covered animal dish, fox on diamond base, chocolate ...**200.00**

Covered animal dish, hen on diamond base, purple marbled, 5½"................................**85.00**

Covered animal dish, lion on lacy base, milk glass, 8" **175.00**

Covered animal dish, rabbit w/eggs on diamond base, milk glass, 8" **150.00**

Covered animal dish, rooster on diamond base, chocolate, 7½".............................**175.00**

Creamer, English Hobnail, sq, footed **8.50**

Creamer, Wakefield, crystal, footed **25.00**

Cup, coffee; Paneled Grape, milk glass w/decor, flared **15.00**

Egg cup, English Hobnail, amber or crystal **14.00**

Figurine, butterfly, any Mist color, lg, ea **40.00**

Figurine, cardinal, ruby carnival, solid **30.00**

Figurine, owl on 2 stacked books, milk glass, 3½"...............**20.00**

Figurine, penguin on ice floe, blue.............................**100.00**

Figurine, Porky Pig, cobalt carnival, 3".............................**40.00**

Lamp, candle; Cameo, Crystal Mist w/Roses & Bows, w/shade, mini.................**55.00**

Lamp, fairy; Thousand Eye, crystal, footed........................**20.00**

Lamp, fairy; Thousand Eye, ruby, flat or footed, ea.............**50.00**

Lamp, miniature; dark blue mist with hand-painted Mary Gregory children, #1972, 1970s, $35.00.
(Photo courtesy Frank Grizel)

Mayonnaise, English Hobnail, amber or crystal, 6" **10.00**

Mayonnaise set, Paneled Grape, milk glass w/decor, 3-pc **35.00**

Pin tray, Heart/#1820, Blue Mist **30.00**

Pitcher, English Hobnail, amber or crystal, straight sides, 32-oz...................................**55.00**

Pitcher, Paneled Grape, milk glass w/decor, 16-oz.................**45.00**

Plate, Bicentennial, Paneled Grape/#1881, limited edition, 14½".............................**225.00**

Plate, English Hobnail, amber or crystal, plain rim, 8½".....**8.00**

Plate, English Hobnail, amber or crystal, 12" sq.................**22.00**

Plate, luncheon; Wakefield, crystal w/red stain, 8½".............**22.50**

Plate, Wicket border, milk glass w/Revolutionary War scenes, 9"....................................**60.00**

Punch bowl stand, English Hobnail, amber or crystal..............**70.00**

Relish, Paneled Grape, milk glass w/decor, 3-part, 9"..........**40.00**

Shakers, English Hobnail, amber or crystal, round, footed, pr...**20.00**

Stem, water goblet; English Hobnail, amber or crystal, footed, 8-oz **10.00**

Stem, wine; Wakefield, crystal w/red stain, 2-oz.............**30.00**

Sugar bowl, English Hobnail, amber or crystal, low, flat.............**7.50**

Sweetmeat, Wakefield, crystal w/red stain, crimped......**35.00**

Toothpick holder, Paneled Grape, milk glass w/decor **25.00**

Trinket box, egg, any Mist color, w/white daisy, w/lid.......**25.00**

Tumblers, Della Robbia, #1058: footed iced tea, $30.00; water, $30.00; juice, $35.00 (Photo courtesy Frank Grizel)

Tumbler, juice; English Hobnail, amber or crystal, footed, 7-oz......................................**9.00**
Vase, English Hobnail, amber or crystal, flared top, 8½"..**40.00**

World's Fairs and Expositions

Souvenir items have been issued since the mid-1800s for every world's fair and exposition. Few fairgoers have left the grounds without purchasing at least one. Some of the older items were often manufactured right on the fairgrounds by glass or pottery companies who erected working kilns and furnaces just for the duration of the fair. Of course, the older items are usually more valuable, but even souvenirs from the past fifty years are worth hanging on to.

See Clubs and Newsletters for information concerning the World's Fair Collectors' Society, Inc.

1939 New York

Book, France, #970, 134 pages, 9x12", EX......................**40.00**
Brochure, General Motors Futurama, 20 pages, 7x8", EX **15.00**

Comb, amber plastic, in embossed gold-tone metal case with brass medallion in center, EX, $30.00.

License plate, black on yellow, VG **20.00**
Pennant, Aviation Building, fair scenes on blue, 24", EX...**50.00**
Pin, Trylon & Perisphere, rhinestone & enamel, 2⅛x1⅛", EX **25.00**
Plate, Trylon & Perisphere, tab handled, Cronin China, 10½" **30.00**
Puzzle, jigsaw; Trylon & Perisphere, plywood, EX (EX box) **55.00**
Salt & pepper shakers, Trylon & Perisphere, ceramic, Japan, MIB..............................**60.00**
Tray, fair scenes in aqua & white on red, 17½x13", VG.....**25.00**
Trinket box, Trylon & Perisphere, blue Jasperware, 1½x3½" dia **45.00**

1939 San Francisco

Bandana, multicolored fair scenes, cotton, 29" sq, NM **25.00**

Book, Official Guide Book, Betty Crocker, 116 pages, 5½x8", VG.................................**25.00**

Guide, pictorial, Southern Pacific RR, 12 pages, EX...........**15.00**

Ice pick, San Francisco World's Fair on sides of wooden handle, NM...........................**15.00**

Matches, Playland at the Beach, front strike, unused, NM **10.00**

Scarf, multicolored fair scenes, silk, 18x18", EX **18.00**

Tablecloth, fair scenes, Winne & Sutch, 52" sq, EX...........**40.00**

Window sticker, West Invites You..., Tower of Lights, 3¾"sq, EX **20.00**

1962 Seattle

Bank, Space Needle, red Washington State on base, 5½x3½", EX....................**20.00**

Book, Seymour at the Seattle World's Fair, Barbara Smith, 16 pages, EX **25.00**

Compact, brushed brass, mirror in lid, made by Clarice Jane, MIB, $30.00.

Doll, Miss Seattle World's Fair, black hair, w/banner & stand, 8", EX.............................**20.00**

Fan, battery-operated, log on chrome body, carrying case, EX **35.00**

Flight bag, Space Needle & Century 21 logo, blue & white vinyl, EX.........................**85.00**

Glasses, black & white scene w/color border on frosted glass, set of 8.................**50.00**

Knife, Space Needle, black on yellow, 2-blade, Colonial Prov USA, M......................**27.50**

Model kit, Space Needle, Space Needle Kit Department, EXIB **55.00**

Seat cushion, Space Needle, monorail & logo, Industrial Rubber, 14x13"...........................**20.00**

Spoon, Space Needle finial, sterling, 6", EX.....................**18.00**

Tie tack, Space Needle & logo, sterling, 1", EX...............**20.00**

1964 New York

Bank, dime register, orange & blue scene, ¾x2½x2½", NMOC...........................**30.00**

Bib, child's; kids around logo, white cloth w/vinyl front, EX...............................**22.50**

Book, Persistence of Vision, Disney's involvement, 144 pages, NM **30.00**

Brochure, Monorail, 7 pages, EX **25.00**

Cooler, Pepsi Cola, Disneyland Fun, red, white & blue, w/strap, EX **85.00**

Cowboy hat, white w/black & white band, Arlington, EX **25.00**

Cup, folding; swirled pink plastic, gold logo on lid, EX........**20.00**

Glass set, colored scenes on frosted glass, set of 8, EX **45.00**

Lighter, copper w/raised fair scenes, chrome top, Japan, EX **25.00**

Map, Official Souvenir; NM...**25.00**

Map, WF via New York Subway, folds out to 16x20", EX ...**17.50**

Paperweight, clear cube w/red horse, Swedish Pavillion, 2x1⅜x1¾" **15.00**

Plate, Unisphere w/6 buildings around border, marked USWF, 10", NM **30.00**

Slide set, 64 color scenes, 2" sq, EXIB **40.00**

1982 Knoxville

Coin, commemorative; logo/aerial view, gold-tone, ½" dia ..**10.00**

Creamer, brown glaze w/cream speckled rim, Hull, 4½", EX.........**15.00**

Mirror, bar; Stroh's, Official Beer at the Fair, oval, 14x11", M...**50.00**

Pocketwatch, logo face in red, white & blue, Westclox, M (NM box).......................**50.00**

Wrestling Collectibles

The World Wrestling Federation boasts such popular members as the Iron Sheik, Hulk Hogan, the colorful Sycho Sid, and The Undertaker. Recent tag-team wrestlers include the Legion of Doom and Cactus Jack and Chainsaw Charlie. With these colorful names and (to put it mildly) assertive personalities, one can only imagine the vast

merchandising possiblities. Posters, videos, trade cards, calendars, lighters, and magazines are all popular collectibles, but the variety of items available is limitless.

Belt, Smoking Skull, 40" L, M..**140.00**

Chair, folding; Summer Slam 2001, black & white, NM..........**85.00**

Chair, Raw Is War, red, black & white, 1997, 30", NM...**120.00**

Figure, Adam Bomb, Hasbro, 1994, MOC **65.00**

Figure, Andre the Giant, MOC ..**70.00**

Figure, Bam Bam Bigelow, LJN, MOC, from $35 to **50.00**

Figure, British Bulldog, Hasbro, MOC, from $10 to **12.00**

Figure, Butch Reed, Galoob, 5", M **10.00**

Figure, Haku, Titan, 1989, MOC...........................**65.00**

Figure, Honky Tonk Man, Hasbro, MOC **10.00**

Figure, Honky Tonk Man, LJN, MOC, from $35 to **40.00**

Figure, Hulk Hogan, Hasbro, 4", NM, $25.00. (Photo courtesy June Moon)

Figure, Hulk Hogan, LJN, 16", MIB................................**70.00**

Figure, Hulk Hogan, white shirt, LJN, MOC.....................**30.00**

Figure, Jimmy Hart, LJN, MOC, from $15 to.....................**20.00**

Figure, Killer Bees, LJN, MIB..**95.00**

Figure, Miss Elizabeth, pink skirt, LJN, MOC.....................**80.00**

Figure, Nasty Boys, Hasbro, MOC, from $25 to.....................**35.00**

Figure, Rick Martel, Hasbro, MOC............................**20.00**

Figure, Rick Rude, Hasbro, MOC..........................**25.00**

Figure, Typhoon, Hasbro, MOC **15.00**

Figure, Undertaker, WWE mail-away premium, EX........**75.00**

Figure, Vince McMan, LJN, MOC............................**25.00**

Figure, Warlord, LJN, M......**70.00**

Figure, 123 Kid, Hasbro, M (on green card).....................**85.00**

Sheet set, WWF Superstars, MIP **75.00**

T-shirt, Randy Savage, sunglass image w/Macho Man in black, EX................................**60.00**

WWF Championship Clash Diva's Private Collection Card, Lita, M....................................**65.00**

Directory

The editors and staff take this opportunity to express our sincere gratitude and appreciation to each person who has contributed to the preparation of this guide. We believe the credibility of our book is greatly enhanced through their participation. Check these listings for information concerning their specific areas of expertise.

If you care to correspond with anyone listed here in our Directory, you must send a SASE with your letter.

If you are among those listed, please advise us of any changes in your address, phone number, or e-mail.

Alabama

Cataldo, C.E.
4726 Panorama Dr. SE
Huntsville, 35801
256-536-6893

California

Ales, Beverly L.
4046 Graham St.
Pleasanton, 94566-5619
925-846-5297
Beverlyales@hotmail.com
Specializing in knife rests; editor of *Knife Rests of Yesterday and Today*

Carter, Tina
882 S. Mollison
El Cajon, 92020-6506
619-440-5043
Specializing in teapots, tea-related items, tea tins, children's and toy tea sets, plastic cookie cutters, etc. Book on teapots available. Send $16 (includes postage) or $17 for California residents, Canada: add $5 to above address

Conroy, Barbara J.
P.O. Box 2369
Santa Clara, CA 95055-2369
http://restaurantchina@
attbi.com
Author of *Restaurant China, Restaurant, Airline, Ship & Railroad Dinnerware, Vol I* and *II* (Collector Books)

Elliott, Jacki
9790 Twin Cities Rd.
Galt, 95632
209-745-3860
Specializing in Rooster and Roses

Harrison, Gwynne
P.O. Box 1
Mira Loma, 91752-0001
951-685-5434
morgan99@pe.net
Buys and appraises Autumn Leaf; edits newsletter

Lewis, Kathy and Don
187 N Marcello Ave.
Thousand Oaks, 91360
805-499-8101
chatty@ix.netcom.com
Authors of *Chatty Cathy Dolls, An Identification and Value Guide,* and *Talking Toys of the 20th Century*

Utley, Bill; Editor
Flashlight Collectors of America
P.O. Box 40945
Tustin, 92781
714-730-1252 or fax 714-505-4067
Specializing in flashlights

Colorado

Diehl, Richard
5965 W Colgate Pl.
Denver, 80227
303-985-7481
Specializing in license plates

Connecticut

Sabulis, Cindy
P.O. Box 642
Shelton, 06484
203-926-0176
www.dollsntoys.com
Specializing in dolls from the '60s
– '70s (Liddle Kiddles, Barbie,
Tammy, Tressy, etc.); co-author of
*The Collector's Guide to Tammy,
The Ideal Teen*, and author of
*Collector's Guide to Dolls of the
1960s & 1970s*

Florida

DeLozier, Loretta
101 Grandville Blvd.
Lake Placid 33852
Author of *Collector's Encyclopedia
of Lefton China,
Identification and Values*

Kuritzky, Lewis
4510 NW 17th Pl.
Gainesville, 32605
352-377-3193
Author of *Collector's Guide to
Bookends*

Poe, Bill and Pat
220 Dominica Cir. E
Niceville, 32578-4085
850-897-4163 or fax 850-897-2606
BPoe@cox.net
Buy, sell, trade fast-food collectibles, cartoon character glasses, PEZ, Smurfs, California
Raisins, M&M items

Posner, Judy
PO Box 2194 SC
Englewood, 34295
judyandjef@yahoo.com
Specializing in figural pottery,
cookie jars, salt and pepper shakers, Black memorabilia, and

Disneyana; sale lists available;
fee charged for appraisals

Idaho

Birkinbine, Mandi
P.O. Box 121
Meridian, 83680-0121
tiara@shop4antiques.com
www.shop4antiques.com
Author of *Collecting Tiara Amber
Sandwich Glass*, available from
the author for $18.45 ppd. Please
allow 4 to 6 weeks for delivery.

McVey, Jeff
1810 W State St. #427
Boise, 83702-3955
Author of *Tire Ashtray Collector's
Guide* available from the author

Illinois

Garmon, Lee
1529 Whittier St.
Springfield, 62704
217-789-9574
Specializing in Borden's Elsie,
Reddy Kilowatt, Elvis Presley,
and Marilyn Monroe

Jungnickel, Eric
P.O. Box 4674
Naperville, 60567-4674
630-983-8339
Specializing in Indy 500 memorabilia

Kadet, Jeff
TV Guide Specialists
P.O. Box 20
Macomb, 61455
Buying and selling of *TV Guide*
from 1948 through the 1990s

Klompus, Eugene R.
Just Cuff Links
P.O. Box 5970
Vernon Hills, 60061
847-816-0035

genek@cufflinksrus.com
Specializing in cuff links and
men's accessories

Stifter, Craig'
218 S. Adams St.
Hinsdale 60521
630-789-5780
cocacola@enteract.com
Specializing in soda memorabilia
such as Coca-Cola, Hires, Pepsi,
7-Up, etc.

Indiana
Dilley, David
Indianapolis
317-251-0575
glazebears@aol.com or
bearpots@aol.com
Author of book on Royal Haeger;
available from the author

McGrady, Donna S.
P.O. Box 14, 301 E. Walnut St.
Waynetown, 47990
765-234-2187
Specializing in Gay Fad glass-
ware

McQuillen, Michael and Polly
P.O. Box 50022
Indianapolis, 46250-0022
317-845-1721
michael@politicalparade.com
www.politicalparade.com
Specializing in political memorabilia

Iowa
The Baggage Car
P.O. Box 3735
Urbandale, 50323-0735
Specializing in Hallmark

Devine, Joe
D&D Antique Mall
1411 3rd St.
Council Bluffs, 51503

712-232-5233 or 712-328-7305
Author of *Collector's Guide to
Royal Copley With Royal Winton
and Spaulding, Books I* and *II*

Kentucky
Hornback, Betty
707 Sunrise Ln.
Elizabethtown, 42701
bettysantiques@KVNET.org
Specializing in Kentucky Derby
and horse racing memorabilia; send
for informative booklet, $15 ppd.

Louisiana
Langford, Paris
415 Dodge Ave.
Jefferson, 70121
504-733-0676
Author of *Liddle Kiddles*; specializing in dolls of the 1960s – 1970s

Maryland
Losonsky, Joyce and Terry
7506 Summer Leave Ln.
Columbia, 21046-2455
Authors of *The Illustrated
Collector's Guide to McDonald's®
Happy Meal® Boxes, Premiums,
and Promotions,* ($11 postpaid);
*McDonald's Happy Meal Toys in
the USA* in full color ($27.95 post-
paid); *McDonald's® Happy Meal®
Toys Around the World,* full color,
($27.95 postpaid); and *Illustrated
Collector's Guide to McDonald's®
McCAPS®,* ($6 postpaid); auto-
graphed copies available from the
authors

Welch, Randy
Raven'tiques
27965 Peach Orchard Rd.
Easton, 21601-8203
410-822-5441
Specializing in walking figures,
and tin wind-up toys

Yalom, Libby
The Shoe Lady
3200 NLW Blvd. #615
Silver Spring, 20906
301-598-0290
Specializing in glass and china
shoes and boots. Author of *Shoes of
Glass* (with updated values) available from the author by sending
$15.95 plus $2 to above address

Massachusetts

Wellman, BA
P.O. Box 673
Westminster, 01473-0673
BA@dishinitout.com
Specializing in all areas of
American ceramics; researches
Royal China

White, Larry
108 Central St.
Rowley, 01969-1317
978-948-8187; larrydw@erols.com
Specializing in Cracker Jack;
author of books; has newsletter

Michigan

Nickel, Mike; and Cindy Horvath
P.O. Box 456
Portland, 48875
517-647-7646
mandc@voyager.net
Specializing in Ohio art pottery,
Kay Finch, author of *Kay Finch
Ceramics, Her Enchanted World,*
available from the authors; co-
author of *Collector's Encyclopedia
of Roseville Pottery Revised
Edition, Vol I* and *Vol II*

Pickvet, Mark
5071 Watson Dr.
Flint, 48506
Author of *Shot Glasses: An
American Tradition,* available for
$12.95 plus $2.50 postage and

handling from Antique
Publications, P.O. Box 553,
Marietta, OH 45750

Ross, Michele
P.O. Box 94
Berrien Center, 49102
616-925-1604
peartime1@cs.com
Specializing in Van Briggle and
other American pottery

Missouri

Allen, Col. Bob
P.O. Box 56
St. James, 65559
Author of *A Guide to Collecting
Cookbooks;* specializing in cook-
books, leaflets, and Jell-O memo-
rabilia

Nevada

Hunter, Tim
4301 W Hidden Valley Dr.
Reno, NV 89502
702-856-4357
thunter885@aol.com
Author of *The Bobbing Head
Collector and Price Guide*

New Hampshire

Apkarian-Russel, Pamela
Halloween Queen Antiques
P.O. Box 499
Winchester, 03470
Specializing in Halloween col-
lectibles, postcards of all kinds,
and Joe Camel

Holt, Jane
P.O. Box 115
Derry, 03038
Specializing in Annalee dolls

New Jersey

Litts, Elyce
P.O. Box 394

Morris Plains, 07950
973-361-4087
happy.memories@worldnet.att.net
Specializing in Geisha Girl (author of book); also ladies' compacts

Palmieri, Jo Ann
27 Pepper Rd.
Towaco, 07082-1357
201-334-5829
Specializing in Skookum Indian dolls

Sparacio, George
P.O. Box 791
Malaga, 08328
609-694-4167; fax 609-694-4536
mrvesta@aol.com
Specializing in match safes

Visakay, Stephen
P.O. Box 1517
W Caldwell, 07007-1517
SVisakay@aol.com
Specializing in vintage cocktail shakers (by mail and appointment only); author of *Vintage Bar Ware*

New Mexico
Mace, Shirley
Shadow Enterprises
P.O. Box 1602
Mesilla Park, 88047
505-524-6717; fax 505-523-0940
shadow-ent@zianet.com
www.geocities.com/MadisonAvenu
e/Boardroom/1631
Author of *Encyclopedia of Silhouette Collectibles on Glass* (available from the author)

New York
Beegle, Gary
92 River St.
Montgomery, 12549
914-457-3623
Liberty Blue dinnerware, also most lines of collectible modern

American dinnerware as well as character glasses

Dinner, Craig
Box 4399
Sunnyside, 11104
718-729-3850
ferrouswheel123@aol.com
Specializing in figural cast-iron items (door knockers, lawn sprinklers, doorstops, windmill weights, etc.)

Gerson, Roselyn
P.O. Box 40
Lynbrook, 11563
516-593-8746
Collector specializing in unusual, gadgetry, figural compacts and vanity bags and purses; author of *Ladies' Compacts of the 19th and 20th Centuries* ($36.95 plus $2 postpaid), *Vintage Vanity Bags and Purses,* and *Vintage and Contemporary Purse Accessories;* edits newsletter

Iranpour, Sharon
24 San Rafel Dr.
Rochester, 14618-3702
716-381-9467 or fax 716-383-9248
watcher1@rochester.rr.com
Specializing in advertising and promotional wrist watches; editor of *The Premium Watch Watch*

Watson, James
25 Gilmore St.
Whitehall, 12887
Specializing in Hartland sports figures

Weitman, Stan and Arlene
P.O. Box 1186
Massapequa Park, 11758
scrackled@earthlink.net
www.crackleglass.com

Authors of *Crackle Glass, Identification and Value Guide, Volumes I* and *II* (Collector Books)

North Carolina

Brooks, Ken and Barbara
4121 Gladstone Ln.
Charlotte, 28205
Specializing in Cat-Tail Dinnerware

Finegan, Mary
Marfine Antiques
P.O. Box 3618
Boone, 28607
828-262-3441
Author of book on Johnson Brothers dinnerware; available from the author

Retskin, Bill
P.O. Box 18481
Asheville, 28814
704-254-4487 or fax 704-254-1066
bill@matchcovers.com
www.matchclub@circle.net
Author of *The Matchcover Collector's Price Guide,* and editor of *The Front Striker Bulletin,* the official publication of the American Matchcover Collecting Club (AMCC)

Sayers, Rolland J.
Southwestern Antiques and Appraisals
P.O. Box 629
Brevard, 28712
Researches Pisgah Forest pottery; Author of *Guide to Scouting Collectibles,* available from the author for $32.95 pp.

North Dakota

Farnsworth, Bryce L.
1334 14½ St.
S Fargo, 58103
701-237-3597
Specializing in Rosemeade

Ohio

Bruegman, Bill
137 Casterton Ave.
Akron, 44303
330-836-0668 or fax 330-869-8668
toyscouts@toyscouts.com
www.toyscouts.com
Author of *Toys of the Sixties; Aurora History and Price Guide;* and *Cartoon Friends of the Baby Boom Era.* Write for information about his mail-order catalog.

Young, Mary
P.O. Box 9244
Wright Bros. Branch
937-298-4838
Dayton, 45409
Author of books; specializing in paper dolls

Oklahoma

Ivers, Terri
Terri's Toys and Nostalgia
206 E. Grand
Ponca City, 74601
580-762-8697 or 580-762-5174
toylady@cableone.net
Specializing in character collectibles, lunch boxes, advertising items, Breyer and Hartland figures, etc.

Moore, Shirley and Art
4423 E. 31st St.
Tulsa, 74135
918-747-4164
Specializing in Lu-Ray Pastels and Depression glass

Phillips, Robert W.
Phillips Archives of Western Memorabilia
1703 N Aster Pl.
Broken Arrow, 74012-1308
918-254-8205
rawhidebob@aol.com
One of the most widely published

writers in the field of cowboy memorabila, biographer of the Golden Boots Awards, and author of *Roy Rogers, Singing Cowboy Stars, Silver Screen Cowboys, Hollywood Cowboy Heroes,* and *Western Comics: A Comprehensive Reference*; research consultant for TV documentary *Roy Rogers, King of the Cowboys* (AMC-TV/Republic Pictures/Galen Films)

Oregon

Brown, Marcia
Sparkles
P.O. Box 2314
White City 97503
541-830-8385
Collector Books author specializing in jewelry

Coe, Debbie and Randy
Coes Mercantile
2459 SE TV Hwy. #321
Hillsboro 97123
Specializing in Elegant and Depression glass, art pottery, Cape Cod by Avon, Golden Foliage by Libbey Glass Company, Gurley candles, and Liberty Blue dinnerware

Morris, Tom
Prize Publishers
P.O. Box 8307
Medford, 97504
chalkman@cdsnet.net
Author of *The Carnival Chalk Prize*

White, Carole Bess
PO Box 819
Portland, 97207
Specializing in Japan ceramics; author of books

Pennsylvania

BOJO/Bob Gottuso
P.O. Box 1403

Cranberry Twp., 16066-0403
Phone or fax 724-776-0621
www.bojoonline.com
Specializing in the Beatles and rock 'n roll memorabilia

Greenfield, Jeannie
310 Parker Rd.
Stoneboro, 16153-2810
724-376-2584
Specializing in cake toppers and egg timers

Turner, Art and Judy
Homestead Collectibles
P.O. Box 173
Mill Hall, 17751
570-726-3597
jturner@cub.kcnet.org
Specializing in Jim Beam decanters and Ertl diecast metal banks

South Carolina

Cassity, Brad
2391 Hunter's Trail
Myrtle Beach, 29574
843-236-8697
Specializing in Fisher-Price pull toys and playsets up to 1986 (author of book)

Tennessee

Butler, Elaine
233 S Kingston Ave.
Rockwood, 37854
Author of *Poodle Collectibles of the '50s and '60s* ($21.95 postpaid)

Fields, Linda
158 Bagsby Hill Lane
Dover, 37058
931-232-5099 after 6 pm
Fpiebird@compu.net.
Specializing in pie birds

Grist, Everett
P.O. Box 91375
Chattanooga, 37412-3955

423-510-8052
Author of books on animal dishes, aluminum, advertising playing cards, letter openers, and marbles

Texas
Cooper, Marilyn M.
8408 Lofland Dr.
Houston, 77055-4811
or summer address:
PO Box 755
Douglas, MI 49406
Author of *The Pictorial Guide to Toothbrush Holders* ($22.95 postpaid)

Docks, L.R. 'Les'
Shellac Shack; Discollector
Box 691035
San Antonio, 78269-1035
docks@texas.net
Author of *American Premium Record Guide;* specializing in vintage records

Gibbs, Carl, Jr.
1716 Westheimer Road H
Houston, 77098-1612
713-521-9661
Author of *Collector's Encyclopedia of Metlox Potteries* (Collector Books); specializing in American dinnerware

Jackson, Joyce
900 Jenkins Rd.
Aledo, 76008-2410
817-441-8864
jjpick@firstworld.net
Specializing in Swanky Swigs

Nossaman, Darlene
5419 Lake Charles
Waco, 76710
Specializing in Homer Laughlin China information and Horton Ceramics

Woodard, Dannie
P.O. Box 1346
Weatherford, 76086
371-594-4680
Author of *Hammered Aluminum, Hand Wrought Collectibles*

Utah
Spencer, Rick
Salt Lake City
801-973-0805
Specializing in Shawnee, Roseville, Weller, Van Tellingen, Regal, Bendel, Coors, Rookwood, Watt; also salt and pepper shakers, cookie jars, cut glass, radios, and silver flatware

Virginia
Cranor, Rosalind
P.O. Box 859
Blacksburg, 24063
Author of *Elvis Collectibles* and *Best of Elvis Collectibles* ($21.70 ppd.), available from the author

Henry, Rosemary
9610 Greenview Ln.
Manassas, 20109-3320
703-361-5898; checkers@erols.com
Specializing in cookie cutters, stamps, and molds

Reynolds, Charlie
Reynolds Toys
2836 Monroe St.
Falls Church, 22042-2007
703-533-1322
reynoldstoys@erols.com
Specializing in banks, figural bottle openers, toys, etc.

Windsor, Grant
P.O. Box 72606
Richmond, 23235-8017
Specializing in Griswold

Washington

Morris, Susan and Dave
P.O. Box 158
Manchester 98353
Authors of *Watt Pottery — An Identification and Value Guide,* and *Purinton Pottery — An Identification and Value Guide*

Wisconsin

Semling, Brian
Brian' s Toys
W 730 Hwy 35
P.O. Box 95
Fountain City 54621
608-687-7572; fax 608-687-7573
www.brianstoys.com
Author of book on Star Wars; available from the author

Helley, Phil
Old Kilbourn Antiques
629 Indiana Ave.
Wisconsin Dells, 53965
608-254-8770

Specializing in Cracker Jack items, radio premiums, dexterity games, toys (especially Japanese wind-up toys), banks, and old Dells souvenir items marked Kilbourn

Wanvig, Nancy
Nancy's Collectibles
P.O. Box 12
Thiensville, WI 53092
Author of book; specializing in ashtrays

Watson, James
25 Gilmore St.
Whitehall, NY 12887
Specializing in Hartland sports figures

Clubs and Newsletters

Akro Agate Collectors Club
Clarksburg Crow
Roger Hardy
10 Bailey St.
Clarksburg, WV 26301-2524
304-624-4523
www.akro-agate.com
Annual membership fee: $25

American Bell Assn.
International, Inc.
P.O. Box 19443
Indianapolis, IN 46219
bobbam@bellsouth.net
www.americanbell.org

*Antique and Collector
  Reproduction News*
Mark Chervenka, Editor
P.O. Box 12130
Des Moines, IA 50312-9403
800-227-5531 (subscriptions only)
or 515-274-5886
acrn@repronews.com
Monthly newsletter showing differences between old originals
and new reproductions; subscription: $32 per year

The Antique Trader Weekly
P.O. Box 1050
Dubuque, IA 52004-1050
collect@krause.com
www.collect.com
Subscription: $38 (52 issues) per
year; sample: $1

Autographs of America
Tim Anderson
P.O. Box 461
Provo, UT 84603
801-226-1787 (afternoons, please)
www.AutographsOfAmerica.com
Free sample catalog of hundreds
of autographs for sale

Autumn Leaf
Bill Swanson, Editor
807 Roaring Springs Dr.
Allen, TX 75002-2112
972-727-5527
www.nalc.org

Avon Times
c/o Dwight or Vera Young
P.O. Box 9868, Dept. P.
Kansas City, MO 64134
AvonTimes@aol.com
Send SASE for information

The Baggage Car
P.O.Box 3735
Urbandale, IA 50323-0735
515-270-9080
baggagecar@aol.com
www.baggagecar.com
Includes show and company information along with current
Hallmark listings

Bookend Collector Club
Louis Kuritzky, M.D.
4510 NW 17th Place
Gainsville, FL 32650
352-377-3193
lkuritzky@aol.com
Membership (includes newsletter): $25 per year

Candy Container Collectors of
  America
The Candy Gram Newsletter
Betty McDuff, Membership
2711 De La Rosa St.
The Villages, FL 32162

Cat Collectors Club
Cat Talk Newsletter
Karen Shank
P.O. Box 150784
Nashville, TN 37215-0784

615-297-7403
musiccitykitty@yahoo.com
www.CatCollectors.com

Ceramic Arts Studio Collector's
  Association
PO Box 46
Madison, WI 53701
800-241-9138
Annual membership: $15;
Inventory record and price guide
available

China Specialties, Inc.
Fiesta Collector's Quarterly
P.O. Box 471
Valley City, OH 44280
www.chinaspecialties.com

Collectibles Flea Market Finds
  Magazine
Magazines of America
13400 Madison Ave.
New York, NY 44107
800-528-9648
Subscription: $18.97 for 4 issues
per year

Compact Collector Chronicles
Powder Puff Newsletter
P.O. Box 40
Lynbrook, NY 11563
compactlady@aol.com
Contains information covering all
aspects of compact collecting,
restoration, vintage ads, patents,
history, and articles by members
and prominent guest writers. A
'Seekers and Sellers' column and
dealer listing is offered free to
members.

Cookie Crumbs
Cookie Cutter Collectors Club
Ruth Capper, Secretary/Treasurer
1167 Teal Rd. SW
Dellroy, OH 44620

Subscription: $12 per year,
payable to club

*Cookie Jarrin' With Joyce: The
  Cookie Jar Newsletter*
1501 Maple Ridge
Walterboro, SC 29488

The Copley Courier
1639 N Catalina St.
Burbank, CA 91505

Currier & Ives Dinnerware
  Collector Club
E.R. Aupperle, Treasurer
29470 Saxon Rd.
Toulton, IL 61483
309-896-3331 or fax 309-856-6005

Czechoslovakian Collectors Guild
  International
Alan Bodia, Membership
15006 Meadowlake St.
Odessa, FL 33556-3126
www.czechartglass.com/ccgi
dgdaze@aol.com
The nation's marketplace for
glass, china, and pottery

Doll News Magazine
United Federation of Doll Clubs
P.O. Box 247
Washington, NJ 07882
908-689-7042
fax 908-689-6320
Subscription: $19.95 per year

Doorstop Collectors of America
Jeanie Bertoia
2413 Madison Ave.
Vineland, NJ 08630
609-692-4092
Membership: $20 per year,
includes 2 newsletters and convention; send 2-stamp SASE for
sample

FBOC (Figural Bottle Opener
   Collectors)
Linda Fitzsimmons
9697 Gwynn Park Dr.
Ellicot City, MD 21042
410-465-9296

Fenton Art Glass Collectors of
   America, Inc.
Butterfly Net newsletter
P.O. Box 384
702 W. 5th St.
Williamstown, WV 26187
kkenworthy@foth.com
Membership: $20; Associate member: $5

Fiesta Collector's Quarterly
P.O. Box 471
Valley City, OH 44280
www.chinaspecialties.com/fiesta.html
Subscription: $12 per year

Fisher-Price Collector's Club
Jeanne Kennedy
1442 N Ogden
Mesa, AZ 85205
fpclub@aol.com
www.fpclub.org
Monthly newsletter with information and ads; send SASE for more
information

*Flashlight Collectors of America
   Newsletter*
Bill Utley
P.O. Box 4095
Tustin, CA 92781
714-730-1252
flashlight@worldnet.att.net
*Flashlights, Early Flashlight
Makers of the 1st 100 Years of
Eveready,* full color, 320 pages,
now available; quarterly flash-
light newsletter, $12 per year.

Frankoma Family Collectors
   Association

c/o Nancy Littrell
P.O. Box 32571
Oklahoma City, OK 72123-0771
www.frankoma.org
Membership dues: $25 (includes
quarterly newsletter and annual
convention)

The Front Striker Bulletin
Bill Retskin
P.O. Box 18481
Asheville, NC 28814-0481
704-254-4487 or fax 704-254-1066
bill@matchcovers.com
www.matchcovers.com
Membership: $10 per year

Griswold & Cast Iron Cookware
   Association
Grant Windsor
P.O. Box 12606
Richmond, VA 23235
804-320-0386
Membership: $20 per individual
or $25 per family (2 members per
address) payable to club

Hall China Collectors' Club
   Newsletter
Virginia Lee
P.O. Box 360488
Cleveland, OH 44136

Head Hunters Newsletter
c/o Maddy Gordon
P.O. Box 83 H
Scarsdale, NY 10583
For collectors of head vases; subscription: $24 yearly for 4 quar-
terly issues. Ads free to sub-
scribers

International Nippon Collectors
   Club (INCC)
c/o Gerry Goldsmith
1387 Lance Ct.
Cold Stream, IL 60188

www.nipponcollectorsclub.com
Membership: $30 per year
includes newsletter (published 6
times per year)

International Perfume and Scent
  Bottle Collectors Association
c/o Randall B. Monsen
P.O. Box 529
Vienna, VA 22183
Fax 703-242-1357
www.perfumebottles.org

Just for Openers
John Stanley
P.O. Box 64
Chapel Hill, NC 27514
919-419-1546
www.just-for-openers.org
For collectors of bottle openers;
Membership: $20 per year

*Knife Rests of Yesterday and
  Today*
Beverly L. Ales
4046 Graham St.
Pleasanton, CA 94566-5619
Subscription: $20 per year for 6
issues

The Laughlin Eagle
c/o Richard Racheter
1270 63rd Terrace South
St. Petersburg, FL 33705
813-867-3982
Subscription: $18 per year

Marble Collectors' Society of
  America
P.O. Box 222
Trumbull, CT 06611
BlockMCSA@aol.com
www.blocksite.com

McDonald's ® Collector Club
Membership Director
1001 Sullens Court

Virginia Beach, VA 23455-6902
www.mcdclub.com
Membership: $25 individual per
year; $30 family

National Association of Avon
  Collectors
Department AT
6100 Walnut
Kansas City, MO 64113
Send large SASE for information

National Blue Ridge Newsletter
Norma Lilly
144 Highland Dr.
Bloutville, TN 37617
Subscription: $15 per year (6 issues)

The National Cuff Link Society
Eugene R. Klompus,
  President Emeritus
P.O. 5970
Vernon Hills, IL 60061
847-816-0035
genek@cufflinksrus.com
Membership: $30 per year

National Depression Glass Assoc.
P.O. Box 4008
Marietta, OH 45750
470-374-3345
Membership: $20 per year

National Graniteware Society
P.O. Box 9248
Cedar Rapids, IA 52409-9248
www.graniteware.org
Membership: $20 per year

National Imperial Glass
  Collectors' Society, Inc.
P.O. Box 534
Bellaire, OH 43906
www.imperialglass.org
Membership: $15 per year (+$1
for each associate member), quar-
terly newsletter

National Reamer Association
c/o Debbie Gilham
47 Midline Ct.
Gaithersburg, MD 20878
reamers@erols.com
www.reamers.org

National Society of Lefton
  Collectors
The Lefton Collector Newsletter
Loretta DeLozier
P.O. Box 50201
Knocksville, TN 3795-0201
leftonlady@aol.com

National Valentine Collectors
  Association
Nancy Rosen
P.O. Box 1404
Santa Ana, CA 92702
714-547-1355
Membership: $16

NM (Nelson McCoy) Xpress
Carol Seman, Editor
8934 Brecksville Rd., Suite 406
Brecksville, OH 44141-2318
McCjs@aol.com
www.members.aol.com/nmXpress
Subscription: $26 per year

The Occupied Japan Club
c/o Florence Archambault
29 Freeborn St.
Newport, RI 02840-1821
florence@aiconnect.com
Publishes *The Upside Down
World of an O.J. Collector,* a
bimonthly newsletter.
Information requires SASE.

On the LIGHTER Side
International Lighter Collectors
Judith Sanders, Editor
136 Circle Dr.
Quitman, TX 75783
903-763-2795 or fax 703-763-4953

Annual convention held in different cities in the US; send SASE
when requesting information

Paper Collectors' Marketplace
P.O. Box 128
Scandinavia, WI 54977-0128
715-467-2379 or fax 715-467-2243
(8 am to 8 pm)
pcmpaper@gglbbs.com
www.pcmpaper.com
Subscription: $19.95 for 12 issues
per year

Paper Doll News
Emma Terry
P.O. Box 807
Vivian, LA 71082
Subscription: $13 per year

Paper Pile Quarterly
Ada Fitzsimmons, Editor
P.O. Box 337
San Anselmo, CA 94979-0337
415-454-5552
apaperpile@aol.com
Subscription: $20 per year

Peanut Pals
Judith Walthall, Founder
P.O. Box 4465
Huntsville, AL 35815
205-881-9198
Associated collectors of Planters
Peanuts memorabilia, bimonthly
newsletter *Peanut Papers;* annual
directory sent to members; annual
convention and regional conven-
tions. Dues: $20 per year (+$3 for
each additional household member); membership information:
P.O. Box 652, St. Clairsville, OH,
43950. Sample newsletter: $2

Pez Collector's News
Richard Belyski, Editor
P.O. Box 14956

Surfside Beach, SC 29587
peznews@juno.com
www.pezcollectorsnews.com

Pie Birds Unlimited Newsletter
Patricia Donaldson
PO Box 192
Acworth, GA 30101-0192
pldonaldson@mindspring.com
Subscription: $27 per year

Political Collectors of Indiana
Michael McQuillen
P.O. Box 50022
Indianapolis, IN 46250-0022
317-845-1721
michael@politicalparade.com
www.politicalparade.com
Official APIC (American Political
Items Collectors) Chapter com-
prised of over 100 collectors of presidential and local political items

The Prize Insider Newsletter for
Cracker Jack Collectors
Larry White
108 Central St.
Rowley, MA 01969
978-948-8187
larrydw@erols.com

Rosevilles of the Past Newsletter
Nancy Bomm, Editor
P.O. Box 656
Clarcona, FL 32710-0656
407-294-3980
rosepast@worldnet.att.net
Send $19.95 per year for 6 to 12
newsletters

Roy Rogers - Dale Evans
Collectors Association
Nancy Horsley, Exec. Secretary
P.O. Box 1166
Portsmouth, OH 45662-1166
www.royrogers.commm

Shawnee Pottery Collectors' Club
c/o Pamela Curran
P.O. Box 713
New Smyrna Beach, FL 32170-0713
Send $3 for sample copy

The Shot Glass Club of America
Mark Pickvet, Editor
P.O. Box 90404
Flint, MI 48509

The Silver Bullet
Lone Ranger Fan Club
P.O. Box 1493
Longmont, CO 80502
www.lonerangerfanclub.com
Membership: $30

The Soup Collector Club
David Young, Founder
414 Country Lane Ct.
Wauconda, IL 60084
847-487-4917
soupclub@aol.com
Membership: 6 issues per year for
$22 donation per address

Tea Talk
P.O. Box 860
Sausalito, CA 94966
415-331-1557
teatalk@aol.com

The TeaTime Gazette
P.O. Box 40276
St. Paul, MN 55104
612-227-7415
info@teatimegazette.com

Toy Scouts, Inc.
Bill Bruegman
137 Casterton Ave.
Akron, OH 44303-1552
330-836-0668 or fax 330-869-8668
info@toyscouts.com
www.toyscouts.com

Toy Shop
700 E State St.
Iola, WI 54990-0001
715-445-2214
www.toyshopmag.com
Subscription (3rd class) $33 (US)
for 26 issues

The Trick or Treat Trader
Pamela E. Apkarian-Russell
The Halloween Queen and
C.J. Russel
P.O. Box 499
Winchester, NH 03470
603-239-8875
halloweenqueen@cheshire.net;
subcription: $15 per year for 4
issues or $4 for sample copy

Vernon Views Newsletter for
Vernon Kilns collectors
P.O. Box 24234
Tempe, AZ 85285
Quarterly issue available by send-
ing $10 for a year's subscription

*Vintage Fashion & Costume
Jewelry* Newsletter/Club
P.O. Box 265
Glen Oaks, NY 11004
718-969-2320 or 718-939-3095
www.lizjewels.com/VF
Yearly subscription: $20 (US) for
4 issues; sample copy available by
sending $5

The Wade Watch, Ltd.
8199 Pierson Ct.
Arvada, CO 80005
303-421-9655 or 303-424-4401
Fax 303-421-0317
wadewatch@wadewatch.com
Subscription: $8 per year (4 issues)

Westmoreland Glass Society
Steve Jensen
P.O. Box 2883
Iowa City, IA 52240-2883
www.glassshow.com/clubs/wgsi/w
gsi.html
Membership: $15

The Willow Review
P.O. Box 41312
Nasgville, TN 37204
Send SASE for information

World's Fair Collectors' Society
Fair News newsletter
Michael R. Pender, Editor
P.O. Box 20806
Sarasota, FL 34276-3806
941-923-2590
Dues: $20 per year in US and
Canada, $30 overseas

Index